D1561478

The Economics of
Petroleum Supply

The Economics of Petroleum Supply

Papers by M. A. Adelman
1962–1993

M. A. Adelman

The MIT Press
Cambridge, Massachusetts
London, England

333.8232
A22e

This book was set in Palatino by Asco Trade Typesetting Ltd., Hong Kong and
was printed and bound in the United States of America.

Library of Congress Cataloging-in-Publication Data

Adelman, Morris Albert.
 The economics of petroleum supply : papers, 1962–1993 / by M. A. Adelman.
  p.   cm.
 Includes bibliographical references and index.
 ISBN 0-262-01138-7
 1. Petroleum industry and trade. 2. Petroleum—Reserves—Economic aspects.
3. Petroleum products—Prices. I. Title.
 HD9560.5.A338   1993
 333.8'232—dc20   93-27446
                                                                          CIP

to Mil
Bobi

Larry 1951–1978

Contents

Acknowledgments

These reprinted essays were nearly all written at the MIT Energy Laboratory, headed in turn by David C. White and Jefferson Tester. David O. Wood, up to his untimely death, supplied encouragement and good counsel. James L. Paddock, another recent painful loss, was my coworker in the early stages of estimating cost and supply. Michael C. Lynch has been in turn assistant and consultant. There is no telling how much was gained over years of collaboration with him, Henry D. Jacoby, and Gordon M. Kaufman. Over the years, Paul G. Bradley, Robert Deam, Richard L. Gordon, Jack E. Hartshorn, John C. Lohrenz, Philip K. Verleger, and G. Campbell Watkins contributed more than they might want to admit. Therese Henderson was there to help refit and reassemble, and do endless tasks and details. And my latest undergraduate assistant, Kathleen Lieuw Kie Song, must be named for herself and as standing in for a long line of MIT undergraduates and graduates who gave zest to a life of teaching and research. But none is responsible for errors.

Introduction

This volume of previously published essays on the economics of petroleum supply will be followed by a history of the world oil market since 1970.[1] The primary aim of the essays was to explain how the price of oil has been determined. The first task was to sort out *scarcity*, the effect of competitive supply and demand, from *market control*, or monopoly. In a competitive market, supply and demand bring incremental cost and price together. (Price may be far above average cost and generate large rents.) Under monopoly, they are far apart.

Mineral cost has long been viewed as a bit special, and rightly so. Hence essays on cost and supply shuttle between concepts and data. As might be expected of writings over a period of thirty years, there is change, even conflict, but I think a consistent vision emerged at a fairly early stage.

I

Minerals are inexhaustible and will never be depleted. A stream of investment creates additions to proved *reserves*, a very large in-ground inventory, constantly renewed as it is extracted. Without enough inducement to build new reserves and hold them for years, there would be no investment. The inventory would dwindle and the industry disappear. How much was in the ground at the start and how much will be left at the end are unknown and irrelevant.

Cost, Supply, and Scarcity

Incremental cost, which measures scarcity, is the fresh investment needed at any moment to add another unit to inventory. Starting in the early 1960s, it seemed that even under deliberately extreme assumptions of rapid increase in oil consumption and no new discoveries, the cost would remain low in relation to the then-current price.

The data for monitoring cost have been deteriorating, in quality and quantity. Estimation methods have had to change, and every estimate is a thing of shreds and patches. But the essentials can be pieced together. Cost in the United States was long stable, even as discoveries dwindled, then rose after 1972. Elsewhere, particularly in the Persian Gulf, it rose little if at all.

These results were a bit unexpected. All else being equal, the best mineral prospects are explored first, and the best minerals are used first. Therefore production should go forever from good ore to bad, and from bad to worse. A mineral's cost and price might fluctuate, but it should in the long run rise like a flood tide: the water advances and retreats but always advances more. That has not happened. Mineral prices have if anything declined, because all else is not equal. There has been an endless tug-of-war, increasing knowledge versus diminishing returns. Knowledge has won big—so far.

Allowing for the Future

But there is a paradox. What is not necessarily true of the whole population of deposits is true of any individual deposit at any given time: the more it is developed, all else being equal, the higher the cost of each successive tranche. The value of a unit in ground reflects the cost saved by not going into the next tranche. Thus its value normally exceeds its development cost.

The excess value—variously called user cost, resource rent, maximum economic finding cost, and so forth—is the reward for finding new deposits, or for learning more about the old deposits, thereby lowering the cost of further development. User cost may be large or small. A simple theory suggests that under competitive conditions user cost should be about half of development cost, and in the United States it apparently is. For the large Persian Gulf producers, it is near zero. In an integrated market, so great a difference could not exist. It suggests that the market is somehow split.

Cost and Monopoly

Incremental cost is an indicator of competition or market control. Under competition, each seller must accept the price as given. The seller then expands production to the point where marginal cost equals price. Thus marginal cost tends to equality everywhere. As better sources intrude, lower-cost areas expand at the expense of higher-cost areas.

From 1945 to 1970, prices in the world market declined by nearly 80 percent. Yet world oil output rose sixfold, which signals a massive rightward shift in the supply curve. Later research was an independent confirmation. Lower-cost areas expanded most rapidly. There were elements of monopoly left in the system, but it was certainly evolving on the competitive model.

Then in 1970 a break came with the past. Prices rose, and higher-cost areas expanded, but lower-cost producers slowed or stopped expansion or actually contracted. Since 1970, high-cost producers sell all they can produce, while low-cost producers produce only what they can sell at current prices. One must ask why low-cost producers stand aside for high-cost and give up the rewards of exploiting their enormous deposits, whose estimated size has expanded through time. "Political explanations" for this self-denial make no sense and also conflict with history. Only the simple explanation works: the low-cost producers restrict output to keep up the price. They run a joint monopoly.

Another View of Supply

My view of supply has not been shared by all. The 1973 price explosion was greeted by many economists, and not the least distinguished, as the long-delayed inevitable scarcity. In this view, temporary forces had just happened to keep all mineral prices flat or declining—for a remarkably long time. A great structure of theory and calculation now arose as an upside-down pyramid, resting on one assumption. As a Nobel Laureate wrote: [Hotelling] "applied the calculus of variations to the problem of allocation of a fixed stock over time. All of the recent literature ... is essentially based on Hotelling's paper."[2]

The fixed stock does not exist. We cannot rescue the concept by making it "the economic portion" of the unknown total in-ground. That is circular reasoning. For the economic portion is an implicit unverifiable forecast of all future output, of what will be worth producing through time. That depends on changes in science and technology, which will determine future costs and price, hence future output. One cannot estimate those costs and prices by starting with their assumed result. In fact, ultimate production is unknown. The much larger amount in the ground is unknowable and irrelevant, a nonbinding constraint.

What exists, and can be observed and measured, is not a stock but a flow. The current scarcity of the mineral is measured by the cost and price of a unit of the current flow. The expected scarcity is measured by the value of future output, which governs the value of the mineral asset: reserves in the ground. The ratio of asset price to current price is an implicit price forecast. Both are related to current investment requirements. To monitor the cost and value of the flow is like looking out the window to gauge the weather. To forecast farther ahead requires probabilistic analysis of mineral discovery, a field in which I have not worked.

Hotelling's great contribution, as I see it, was the concept of mineral scarcity as the present value of a unit in the ground. I have suggested that this value should approach the cost of creating a new unit. This concept is used to test, and I think disprove, the assumption of a fixed stock whose value rises forever at the rate of interest, under average conditions.

The concept is an additional test for the existence of monopoly control. If price is expected to rise at the same rate as the discount rate, then in a high-cost deposit the thin margin above cost will rise at more than the discount rate. Then user cost in the deposit is also high, proportional to investment cost. The asset should be held, not produced. Contrariwise, a low-cost deposit benefits least by a price rise, hence its user cost is lowest, and it should be produced quickly. Under competition, low-cost oil would be more quickly and intensively produced in the member countries of OPEC (Organization of the Petroleum Exporting Countries) than in non-OPEC countries. We observe just the contrary, which discredits the idea that OPEC restriction has anything to do with user cost.

Moreover, the same anomaly is seen within OPEC. The lower-cost oil is held back; the higher-cost oil is produced. Again it refutes the thesis that higher prices are due to expected still-higher prices acting via "Hotelling rent." But holding back output by the large low-cost producers fits an old rule in industrial organization, "leader's curse" in a collusive group. The smaller members are freer to cheat on prices and expand production. The larger ones make room, because if they retaliated and expanded output, the cartel would shatter.

No Market Failure

The peculiarity of the mineral industries is the investment in a large inventory and the unusual risk in finding new deposits. But prices of goods and assets in oil are about as good or bad guides to investment and production decisions in hydrocarbons as in other industries. This has long been denied.

Indeed, the earliest essay in this volume deals with the assumption of market failure in oil. The belief is that competition would produce wild swings in investment and prices. Hence the faith that the market must be wisely managed by a concert of multinational companies, or of producing governments, or someone. The belief remains as popular and unfounded as ever.

Of course, markets are interesting only because they work imperfectly. They are, as Winston Churchill might have said, the worst form of economic organization, except by comparison with all the rest. Under competition the path of prices and outputs is deflected by chance and ignorance. Distortions, instability, and waste are inevitable. Monopoly merely increases them, sometimes on a grandiose scale.

Attention has been paid recently to making "sustainable" national product estimates, by allowing for consumption of minerals. Since mineral reserves are renewable, the problem becomes simple and feasible: how to measure the net change in the reserve inventory. Existing data seem to indicate only small changes, and usually positive. But we badly need better statistics on reserves and on unit values.

II

The essays in part II, chapters 14–21, touch on the OPEC nations' control of the oil market. Like any cartel, they try to get all they can. There are alternative pathways: raise prices and then restrict output to satisfy the lesser demand, or cut output to force up the price. Why and how the OPEC nations acted at a particular time belongs to the history in the second volume. But even the simple principle, that they seek higher revenues, makes nonsense of what is still seriously asserted in 1992: the 1973 price explosion came about because the Shah of Iran was encouraged to seek money for arms.[3]

Every cartel has two problems: first, to find and fix the value-maximizing price/output for the group; second, to divide the gains. The optimal price is hidden in the "fog of war," where it can be approached by trial and error—especially error. But dividing the revenues is a zero sum game. Any change, even a favorable change, supplies a fresh contention over revenue sharing. Under competition, market division is automatic: each producer carries output to the point where further expansion would raise the incremental cost above the price. But in a cartel, each producer would profit by higher output. Each cartel member has a reason to cheat and to lower the price a little to sell more.

The two problems must be solved simultaneously. One cannot set the total without somehow dividing it. The group solves both problems by ad hoc expedients, which do not last long. It is not the war of all against all, but it is a welter of collusion and conflict, and a stable price is not likely.

Tolstoy said that happy families were all alike, but each unhappy family was unhappy in its own way. Every cartel is a historical individual. The members of this one are less-developed-countries (LDCs). (Some are now rich, but none have developed.) Sovereign monopolists are more powerful and unrestrained than private ones, but they are also less efficient. Amidst the collapse of socialism, most of the world's oil is produced by national dinosaurs. They are allowed too much money or not enough and are often, though not always, rotted by payoffs, kickbacks, and featherbedding. The sovereign owners have a desire or need for quick gains and short-run payoffs. The conventional wisdom of their "low time preference" (International Energy Agency, *Energy and Oil Outlook to 2005*, 25 April 1991) is the nice contrary of the truth.

The principal reason for the short horizons is that oil revenues make countries more oil dependent. Oil often ruins agriculture and native industry. Towns fill up with hangers-on for whom the state must provide food and other imported necessities at subsidized low prices. Cutting budget and foreign-exchange deficits becomes hard and dangerous. Withdrawal of subsidies threatens revolution. This makes decision making more difficult and less predictable.

The Path of Prices

In 1963, before asking where prices were heading, I tried to see first where they stood. I made, then brought together for mutual confirmation, two independent estimates of the actual arms-length prices for Persian Gulf crude oil. One set was based on a haphazard sample of individual contracts. The other was the "netback" reached by subtracting actual transport cost and refining cost from actual, not posted, refined-product prices. Today, thousands of netbacks are calculated every hour; then, there was some scorn for estimates of such "peripheral," "speculative," and "marginal" market prices.

In 1963, I expected the price to keep decreasing slowly, aside from inflation. First, incremental cost would remain very low; in fact it did. Second, I thought competition would continue pushing price slowly in the direction of cost. I explained how excise taxes were fixed in concert as a price floor. I was quite wrong to think the OPEC members could not raise the floor.

They did it in 1970–1971 and turned the market around. Whether they could have succeeded without the help of the U.S. Government will never be known; one cannot repeat the trial.

They kept raising the tax floor, with a grand upward ratchet in 1973–1974. Formal expropriation of the oil companies was then the epilogue to a thirty-year drama. The French have a wonderfully brief and evocative phrase: *Grande firme, petite nation*. Tiny nations easily overcame the largest firms. Taking the bulk of the revenues, then dramatically increasing them by raising the price, was a great and solid triumph. Formal expropriation of the companies was a moment of bliss, for which they continue to pay.

Once the price leaped ahead, I suggested that it would fluctuate in a wide band between a competitive floor and a monopoly ceiling. The OPEC nations did not "lose power." Their mission was to trade a higher price for a lower market share, to obtain much higher revenues. I think they have reached the limit of the trade-off and will long remain in the "market share trap."

This vision of the oil price was in radical opposition to the consensus that still rules today, but has become more sober: the current price does not differ much from the long-run competitive price (plus or minus an error of estimate), and the price must rise over time because of growing scarcity. I think both propositions are false.

III

The third group of essays, chapters 22–27, is concerned with public policy. The 1967 working paper suggesting what is now called a Strategic Petroleum Reserve was published in French, Italian, and Japanese, but not in the original English. Calling European coal "no longer an industry, only a means of social insurance," gave some offense then but may be acceptable today. As this is written, there is controversy in Britain over the closure of some coal mines and the loss of jobs. Few pretend that the coal is worth producing.

After being forced to recognize, as I said in 1971, that "the genie is out of the bottle," I advanced a view which, had it been accepted, would have simplified policy and lowered the temperature of discussion. There was no energy or oil shortage. "The strait of stringency" was poetry. We could not produce our way or conserve our way out of the nonexistent crisis.

Nor would the problem be solved by "the magic of the market," because there was no problem, only a condition: world oil monopoly. The cartel would let us have all we demanded, at the high unstable price they fixed.

The burden of coping with the price could not be avoided; it could only be minimized, by letting markets adjust. Costly programs to subsidize production or lower consumption were an extra payment, to feed the illusion that we could do something. Nor did it make sense to "conserve resources." We have it on venerable authority (Matthew 25:14) that to keep assets idle in the ground is the mark of an "unprofitable servant," who does not deserve his trust.

But private markets could not, I thought, cope with occasional supply disruptions that were to be expected because price and supply were set by "a clumsy cartel" of governments, some of them unstable, or unruly to neighbors, or both. Hence the need for a strategic reserve, properly used, and for a military defense against any power seizing the Persian Gulf.

This aside, the only sensible options were (and are) either to do nothing or to oppose the cartel. I suggested how to disrupt or weaken the cartel, or divert some of its revenues to consumer-country treasuries. In my view, cooperation with the OPEC nations is not good or bad but merely impossible. They cannot be held to any agreement. Some of the OPEC populations are not unfriendly. Some are bloody-minded, full of hate. It has no effect on oil supply and price. They will in any case try to achieve the value-maximizing price-output combination, as they perceive it and can arrange it.

I had no success in convincing governments. For U.S. natural gas, price ceilings stayed for a quarter century. I urged in 1973 that a selective oil "embargo" would be a sham. But the U.S. Secretary of State bounded all over the Middle East to get the nonexistent "embargo" lifted, and another Cabinet member hinted darkly at using force. Government officials take pride in their "special relationships" and "dialogue" with one or more producing countries. Thereby, after the 1970–71 capitulation to Libya (whose "fanatic anti-Communist" Kaddafi supplied bases for Soviet submarines, and congratulated the anti-Gorbachev coup in 1991) and then to the Persian Gulf producers, "they expected the previously turbulent world oil situation to calm down following the new agreement" (Platt's Oilgram, February 17, 1971). Their successors believed that they persuaded Saudi Arabia to modify oil prices and persuaded Iraq to modify its behavior. Those who have familiar discourse with Excellencies and Majesties and other High-and-Mightinesses find it hard to listen to others.[4]

I suggested that high oil prices would make many bits of barren ground or sea water worth fighting for. Cumulative Persian Gulf 1970–1990 revenues were $2.5 trillion. These revenues have been the means and the motive for two bloody wars, so far. As this is written, there is much concern because Iran is "using its oil wealth to buy weapons systems and sophisticated technologies ... to build nuclear bombs, ballistic missiles, advanced aviation and germ warfare weapons" (Editorial, *New York Times*, November 16, 1992). The market that generates this wealth is worth analysis.

Notes

1. It will condense five working papers done at the MIT Center for Energy and Environmental Policy Research.

2. Kenneth Arrow, "Hotelling," in Eatwell, Milgate, and Newman, *The New Palgrave: a Dictionary of Economics* (London: Macmillan Press, 1987, p. 67)

3. Walter Isaacson, *Kissinger* (New York: Simon & Schuster, 1992), pp. 563–564. In fact, while the Shah talked, others acted. A group of producing nations (excluding "radical" Iraq and "conservative" Iran) cut production, which panicked the market and raised current spot prices. Then all the OPEC nations raised permanent official prices in concert.

4. Things have not changed much in 2000 years. In 81 BC, a group of "literati" urged Lord Grand Secretary of the Chinese Empire to divest the State salt and iron monopolies. But the Lord Grand Secretary said competition would favor "the overbearing and aggressive". The literati were "poverty stricken bumpkins" who "know nothing of the cares of the statecraft." "Now, lovers of disputation, without proper means to support yourselves at home and with no great reputation abroad, poor and inconspicuous that you are, even though you can talk on proper conduct, neither is your weight very great." Esson M. Gale, ed., *Discourses on Salt and Iron: a debate on state control of commerce and industry in ancient China* (Tapei, Ch'eng Wen Publishing Company, 1973), pp. 35, 37, 113.

I

Mineral Scarcity and Depletion: Theory and Measurement

1

Petroleum Production Costs in General

The Production Periods: Exploration, Development, Extraction

It is customary to group oil and gas production costs in three stages: exploration, development and extraction from the earth. We will use "production" as a generic word to cover all three stages. Exploration and development can be said to create reserves, an intermediate product; extraction converts or depletes this asset into a final product. Extraction is like most other economic activities in that current inputs are closely matched by current outputs, so that one can easily compare prices with costs. In the United States, with little recent change, over two-thirds of petroleum production costs are for exploration and development, where current inputs are unrelated to current outputs.[1]

Exploration costs are essentially research—finding out where to drill—and include such items as geological and geophysical work, aerial surveys, core drilling, lease acquisition, etc.; to this is added the cost of drilling one or more exploratory wells to determine whether an oil or gas deposit exists. There is no amount of chronological time which can be said to correspond to the exploration "long run." A given area may be looked at for literally a century before it seems worth drilling. Observations which point to a barren structure, or no structure, may in later years be completely reinterpreted as the result of greater engineering and scientific knowledge, or because of data on similar structures nearby which have yielded petroleum. Many a dry hole is well worth its cost, as is reflected in the oil country institution of "dry hole money"—a sharing of drilling expense by a non-leaseholder in return for information; the money obligation being cancelled if the well turns out to be a producer. In other words, the dry hole drilled in one place, by discouraging further fruitless effort,

Reprinted from *The Supply & Price of Natural Gas* (Oxford: Basil Blackwell, 1962), 1–24.

increases the success ratio generally; or, what comes to the same thing, it lowers the unit cost of reserves found later.

Hence the great bulk of exploration at any given time takes place in the "old" petroleum provinces; and a discovery today may in part be due to expenditures undertaken decades ago, and many miles away, by persons who had no inkling of the ultimate results of their efforts. Yet some part of those earlier apparently unrelated expenditures were part of the total exploration cost of finding this particular deposit; the old and new outlays are joint costs of obtaining the final output of new reserves.

Once something has been found, the question is: how much? The larger the reserve, the lower the unit cost, but only when all else is equal: how long and how costly it will be to extract, because of the ease or difficulty of drilling, the thickness of the productive stratum, the permeability of the formation, or (in the United States for oil, not gas) the permitted output per well per month below the ceiling that good engineering practice would require. The exploratory hole may indicate that the petroleum deposit is too small, or too costly to extract, and that is—for the time being or forever—the end of the matter. But if at existing prices the deposit looks commercial, its horizontal and vertical limits must be established.[2] A pattern of wells is drilled accordingly, progressively outward, and estimates are made of the ultimate recoverable reserves which are "proved" thereby. These newly proved gross reserves increase at a decreasing rate—though, as earlier noted, it may for a time be at an increasing rate if the original well chanced to be at the edge of the field—as the limits of the pool are approached and finally delineated. There is no hard and fast line between "discovery" as the climax of exploration and "development" as its aftermath. For one thing, as the pool's limits are approached, some development wells turn out to be dry holes, and their cost is an exploration expense in the strict sense. For another, a well drilled a few hundred yards from a known producer is, barring a geological discontinuity (a "fault"), obviously a development well; a few thousand yards away, it is a wildcat by one student's standards but not by another's. The AAPG classification system is the most carefully worked out, but it differs substantially from that of the *Oil and Gas Journal*.[3] Hence, reasonable men may differ as to whether a given well opened a new field, or a new pool within an old field, or whether it merely outlined a pool that had already been found.

Reserves as Inter-Temporal Joint Products of Development

At any rate, as stepout exploration takes place, and then development, the initial figures of minimum or "proved" ultimate reserves are constantly revised upward—or downward, as a pool turns out to be smaller than was previously thought.[4] "Revisions" indicate development and more reserves, or a true correction to earlier estimates, on the basis of existing knowledge, or, over a longer term, new knowledge of the field or the reservoir, or, over a still longer term, new technology which permits a reinterpretation of earlier data. The increment to reserves which is proved in any given year may be considered that year's output, and it can be given a market price (for reserves are sold at all stages of development), but it results from earlier expenditures as well as those made in the year just ended.

But there is a great difference of degree between exploration and development. Although we cannot tell how long it will take before a given field is known with tolerable accuracy (and it may never be known), we can at least predict for a given group of fields that the reserves added will increase at a decreasing rate, and finally converge to some limiting value. This group regularity must of course be qualified. In any given field, reserves added per well may increase for a time because the discovery well was far off center. Or reinterpretation of data may cause sharply discontinuous upward or downward revisions of the reserve estimates. Again, some small deposits may be completely developed, and their reserves known as well as they ever will be within a year; such giants as Lacq and Hugoton will take over ten, and even then a boundary will not be fully known.[5]

The method developed by F. H. Lahee is to make no reserve estimates at all for the initial successful exploratory oil or gas well, to wait three years before tentatively putting the deposit in an approximate reserve size category, and then to wait another three years before finally classifying it.[6] Thus, while nothing at all could be said about the exploration time period, one can say in general that it takes some three years to have a good first estimate of a given field, and six years to have a (usually) satisfactory estimate.[7] If we consider, however, that the revisions become less important from year to year, the rule of thumb of four to five years' development may be used as a rough average, both for oil and for gas. Until development is complete, however, one cannot know development costs per unit, because one knows neither the number of units nor the ultimate total costs for the field, though unit development costs for a given well can be accurately determined if we know the percent of reserves-in-place which can actually be extracted.

For economic analysis, price, costs and other variables must be considered in terms of this multi-year period. The outputs of any given year must be related to the inputs of the several preceding years. The increments to proved ultimate reserves added in the year 1960 are strongly related to expenditures of 1959, slightly less to those in 1958, etc., and only negligibly related to development expenditures of earlier than 1954, unless there is secondary recovery or some other substantial change in methods of production. But in 1960 increments are related to the exploration expenditures of so many previous years, and in so unformed and accidental a manner, that we cannot say anything about the time period. We must not, however, make the mistake of thinking a cost does not exist merely because we cannot say anything precise about it.[8]

The final special characteristic of exploration is the unpredictable relation between outlay and receipts in any given effort. As is true of research generally, most exploration and some development are literally wasted effort, a chasing after false leads. There are two implications. First, the cost of a successful effort cannot be ascribed to that effort alone, but rather to the combination of all efforts, and the cost of all efforts, with which it was associated. Or, what comes to the same thing, the cost of the individual successful or unsuccessful project does not exist; it is a joint cost with other efforts of the same or even other companies; as was noted earlier, the experience of Company A in some area, fruitless in itself, may be used by Company B at a later date.

Second, while in any other industry one can make fair to excellent estimates of how much capacity can be secured for any given amount of money investment, in petroleum production this is impossible for any given project, company, area, or even the whole industry. If, instead of $X of exploration expenditures, we spend $2X, everything else remaining equal, we should find more reserves, but we should hardly expect to get about twice as much. The additional reserves found might be negligible, or spectacularly large.

It follows, and it is perhaps the most important single fact about petroleum production economics, that the current additions to producible basic capacity—i.e., to reserves—contain a strong *random* component. Hence there is a great contrast between the growth of supply and of demand. Demand grows in response to total population, *per capita* income, and the needs of household and business consumers. All of these tend to change in relatively slow and continuous fashion, and to offset each other to some extent, so that the total demand tends to be more stable than any of the components. Even so, its rate of growth can fluctuate most embarrassingly. But if we plot total consumption on a chart and then plot new reserves, using a reduced scale to bring the lines together, the reserves-added line will swing up and down past the consumption line. As P. H. Frankel has well said, there is always too much or too little.

This random element has been built into the petroleum-producing industry's reflexes, so that a temporary glut or shortage is not nearly so disturbing to investment and price policy as it is in other industries. This imperturbability is very striking at the present time. But it may have been overdone. The larger the petroleum industry, the less important becomes the random disturbance, relative to current capacity. First, the greater and more widespread the exploratory and development effort, the better the chance of offsetting good and bad luck, and the less the chance of one to six years being exceptionally rich or lean. Second, the importance of the disturbance is inversely proportional to the size of the industry. An East Texas discovery in 1930, when United States output was 900,000 barrels/day, was cataclysmic; even aside from government output control (prorationing), a similar discovery in 1960, with output over 7 million b/d, not to mention foreign sources, would have no such effect. (Readers who disagree with this last statement might ask whether they have in mind the straw which broke the camel's back. If so, they should not blame it all on that last bit added to the load.)

As the size of the market grows, the randomness of discoveries, all else being equal, tends to diminish the relative surpluses or deficits and to stabilize the market. Absolute surpluses or deficits, that is, should over time tend to be a smaller percent of extractive capacity, and weigh less heavily on prices (or act less buoyantly, as the case may be), the larger and more mature the industry. This is not what has happened over the past decade. Why not? In economics, as in geology, an anomaly means something to look into further, and we will do so later.

Price-Supply Relationships

Short-term petroleum price behavior (which involves oil almost exclusively) is subject to conflicting forces. It tends, under competition, to be erratic because both extraction and consumption of petroleum are quite insensitive to price changes. Short-term behavior relates to a well already sunk, whose current expenses are largely overhead, such that either one runs it or not; there is no gradual contraction of output, except (in the United States and Canada) by government restriction. Indeed, even if price were slightly less than operating costs, the well would still continue to operate if there were any hope of a better price in the not-too-distant future; for shutting down and reopening cost something—indeed, they may in extreme cases cost the well, because of sand clogging or water encroachment. Nevertheless, this is at best a minor qualification to a general uncontroversial point, that an operating oil or gas well will not shut down until the price has fallen so low that it is clearly below current extractive operating costs, which may be a large or only a minor fraction of total production costs, including exploration and development, needed to reproduce the capacity—i.e., the reserve. Hence, when demand falls short of current producing capacity, the price must, under competition, fall until it drops below the current cost of many wells, producing a sizeable fraction of output.

However, this instability is moderated both in its range and in its effects. In the very short run, inventories may be accumulated. More important is the fact that output from existing wells is always on the decline, so that there is a built-in cutback mechanism. Certain wells would close this year in any case; given a low price, others will close this year instead of next. It takes a constant development process to overcome this attrition and maintain or increase current extractive capacity. Only if the price change is considered other than temporary will it have an effect on development activities. That is, a price above *short-run* extraction cost may yet cause a reduction of *medium-term* output. For development will not be undertaken unless the expected price will at least cover its cost, which of course includes a normal return on investment and a risk allowance. In turn, an expected price which will only just suffice to maintain all current development plans, i.e., suffice to complete them all, must reduce exploration, which includes a much greater risk allowance.

This three-stage pattern of costs, prices and investment decisions becomes extremely complex in practice, for all three might be moving disparately. A short-term glut could send current prices down; but if this were expected to cease soon, and longer-run prospects were good enough, development might continue routinely and exploration rapidly. To be sure, it would shock many a company's routine to pay for exploration and development out of anything but last year's profits. A serious drop in current income would therefore impose considerable and painful changes in financing patterns. The company which most quickly adjusted to the fact that investment is directed to future output, that profits expected are primary, and finance but a means to the end, and that others will, if they do not, somehow find money for what looks like a profitable venture, would have a competitive advantage. Continued exploration would express the producers' belief that either future demand would increase or else the new extractive capacity secured by the planned development would be less than current capacity. But unless one or both of these expectations were correct, the development effort would be a mere routine reflex—prices have always gone back up, they always will, etc. Such decisions are not always happy.

For the student of industry price-cost-output behavior it is development costs and medium-term prices which dominate the scene, and most repay study, though they may not ultimately be the most important.[9] Exploration is uncertain in its expenditures and its results, and therefore doubly uncertain about the unit cost of the new reserves it will find; short-run extraction is by its very nature a wasting, dwindling activity, with relatively little management discretion. Firms must for their own survival look though current costs and prices to medium-term. They must also look through the medium- to the long-term, but the need is not so urgent. A man was reprieved from a death sentence by the King of France, on condition that within a year he teach the King's favorite horse to speak. 'Don't worry about it,' he told a friend. 'Within a year the King may die, or the horse may die, or I may die—or the horse may speak!' But the indefiniteness of the long-term does not make it any less real; unless expected prices will cover full costs, exploration will not take place. To be sure, no student of industrial economics can overlook the persistence of men in their settled routine. Like the medieval venturer—*navigare necesse est, vivere non est necesse*—many an operator continues in the United States today for no better reason than that he always has.

To sum up: petroleum exploration and development create new reserves. The period between inputs and outputs is indeterminate for exploration and only approximately, and statistically, known for development. The relation between input and output is almost a matter of chance in any division of space or time and can only be defined in a statistical sense over many fields and several years. The inputs and outputs of any one place or short period are not independent of the inputs and outputs of any other place or short period; they are rather joint inputs and joint outputs. The industry is dominated by joint costs, therefore, even if we neglect the joint nature of oil and gas. Before doing this, however, we need to see whether the industry is one of rising or declining real costs.

Petroleum Production as an Increasing-Cost Industry

At any given time, under given conditions of knowledge (which grows slowly), any extractive industry has increasing costs: the less the output the more it can be drawn from lower-cost nearby high-quality sources; while the greater the output the more we must draw upon high-cost distant low-quality sources. But this proposition has been directly contradicted in a reputable source, and also its logical consequences are often denied, implicitly or explicitly. Hence, it is well to rethink the matter. In a United Nations publication, *The Price of Oil in Western Europe*,[10] the industry petroleum is said to be one of decreasing costs, or of increasing returns. Such an industry, "if composed of a large number of autonomous producers, [will] operate at a loss." *The Price of Oil* does not add, but the reader will, that producers cannot keep operating at a loss. Hence, either all but one must disappear, or they must shed their autonomy to join in a single company or a collusive group, which will keep the price high enough to yield a profit. Stated a little differently, a decreasing-cost industry has at all times an inherent surplus, which only a monopolist can keep from driving prices ruinously low. (It follows, in the particular case of petroleum, that to increase capacity by seeking new reserves is foolish, intrinsically a loss operation, unless there is some monopoly or arrangement to keep prices up.)

Hence, a long-established proposition in economic analysis, that competition must break down in an industry of decreasing costs, is often summarized in the phrase "natural monopoly," because in such an industry only monopoly is stable. Now, the name "natural monopoly" may be strongly repudiated by some who as strongly contend that the industry is special because of its allegedly decreasing costs; but this is quite natural, for people often do not wish to see the plain implications of what they say. How indignant must that lady have been who, when she congratulated Samuel Johnson on having left all the obscene words out of his Dictionary, was told, "Madam, I am sorry you looked for them." She had not said it!—only implied it. Similarly, it is not said in *The Price of Oil*, only implied, that petroleum is a natural monopoly.

Public policy is not our present concern, but the idea of petroleum as an industry of decreasing costs is badly mistaken, the direct contrary of the truth. *The Price of Oil* puts forth two reasons, of which one may be quickly dismissed: that in East Texas in 1930 the price of crude oil fell ruinously low. But temporary gluts and surpluses are found in increasing-cost industries, such as agriculture, in all times and places. Furthermore, one must look hard to find a more unrepresentative example: the East Texas field, perhaps the greatest ever discovered in North America; the onset of the Great Depression, the only period when oil consumption actually declined; and above all the rule of capture which for so long has burdened or disgraced petroleum production in the United States. No such unique incident could prove any general rule, or "provide a convincing illustration of the truth of [any] theorem." Actually, it is only an example of the discontinuous or random nature of oil discoveries, discussed earlier.

The second alleged reason is that the ratio of fixed to variable costs is very high in this industry, since most costs must be incurred before extraction even begins. Hence, variable costs are a small part of the total, and "marginal costs will be very low and average costs falling over a very wide range of output." *The Price of Oil* never gets past a very short-run viewpoint—in petroleum, of all industries. Even so, it is notoriously true of many industries, such as farming or retail trade, stock examples of atomistic industry structures, that variable and marginal costs are "very low and average costs falling over a very wide range of output," wider even than in petroleum. The coal industry in Europe and the United States suffers today from excess capacity despite a much lower ratio of fixed to variable costs, so that is not a distinctive reason. Moreover, the production of natural gas is a glaring refutation of any theory of decreasing costs and inherent surplus. With so many anomalies we had better look into the matter more closely, though it is discouraging that one confidently stated error takes pages to analyze.

Figure 1.1 shows the short-run cost structure of an individual reservoir, which we will somewhat loosely call a field; there are normally a number of reservoirs in a field. The great bulk of costs must be incurred before production even begins, so that fixed cost per unit keeps falling to the very physical maximum of output, represented by the vertical dashed line. (This really exaggerates the case, but so much the better.)

There are three independent errors involved, however, in generalizing from figure 1.2 to the petroleum-producing industry; and any one is fatal. First, even for the individual field or well, the picture is almost completely irrelevant. Second, *The Price* has confused economies of *scale* with economies of high-level *output*. Third and most important, it is the fallacy of composition to confuse the individual field with the industry. On the first point: no sane petroleum operator plans otherwise than in terms of the whole period of time over which he will first invest and then recoup his investment in a field. The cost structure of figure 1.1 is only a fragment, or an arbitrary interval. Over the whole life of the deposit, shown in figure 1.2, one must reckon with the need for additional inputs, such as fracturing by explosives or acidizing; workover of the original wells; drilling of additional wells as old ones sand up; water or gas injection; putting the well on the pump.[11] The marginal cost has been drawn to show such additions as nearly discontinuous bumps upward. But even aside from these additional inputs, the lowering of pressure as the field ages either requires more inputs

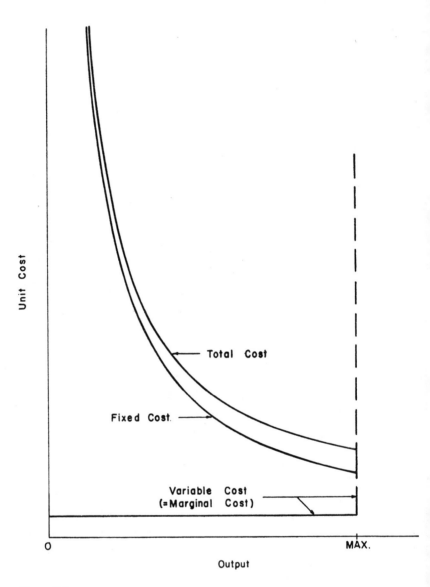

Figure 1.1
Short-run cost structure of an individual deposit

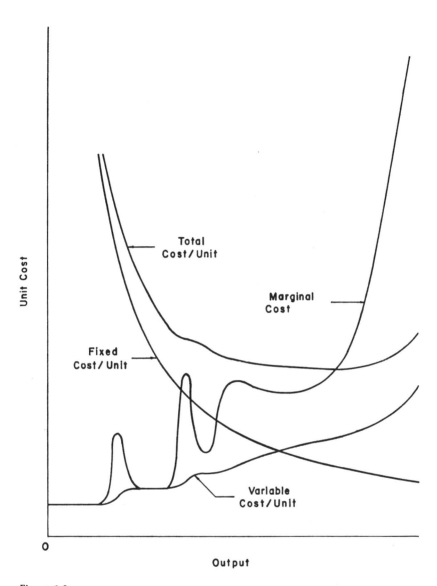

Figure 1.2
Lifetime cost structure of an individual deposit

per unit of output, or gives a lower rate of output per unit of time. Hence the usual warnings against uncritical use of the "life index" to conclude that, e.g., a twelve-year supply means production at current rates for twelve years, after which the rest is silence. Additional output can therefore only be had at rising real costs per unit.

For all these reasons, variable cost per unit rises, the larger is the lifetime output to be obtained from the reservoir. For a long time this increase is overborne by the continued spreading of the fixed costs over more units, but in time cost per unit begins to increase. Marginal cost is unlike variable cost in that it is not a part of total cost, but rather the difference between two adjacent aggregates of cost. Hence, when average total cost per unit is falling, marginal cost must be less than average; when average cost is rising, marginal cost must be greater: and the two coincide where marginal cost is a minimum.

Of course, figure 1.2 gives only the general form of the functions; the particular values are different in every field. But over the lifetime of the well, assuming the best engineering practice, the unit cost of petroleum first decreases with greater output, then increases, and should be thought of as generally U-shaped, though the U may be distorted in an infinite number of ways.

Thus even the individual establishment in petroleum works under increasing costs. It is important that in figure 1.2, unlike figure 1.1, we could not and need not specify any point of maximum physical output. In fact, before that point is ever reached, production stops because marginal cost exceeds price. This is, of course, the regular industry practice; it confirms figure 1.2 and is incompatible with any notion of decreasing costs.

Let us now consider the second error—the confusion of economies of higher-level output with economies of scale. In either figure 1.1 or figure 1.2, output is carried to a maximum, then stops. But this contradicts the notion of an industry of decreasing costs, which is that costs can be lowered *ad lib.*, i.e., there are huge economies of scale to be exploited, by building the productive unit bigger. Since petroleum is found in deposits of limited size, it is physically impossible to go to larger and larger sizes to get lower and lower costs; size has been limited by nature.

This brings us to the most basic error, the fallacy of composition. For even if we neglect all but very short-run costs, the industry is as shown in figure 1.3. Under either rational planning or effective competition, the lower is the demand, the more will output be concentrated in the low-cost fields; contrariwise, the greater the demand, the more it calls out the higher-cost sources of supply, via the fact or expectation of a rising price. In figure

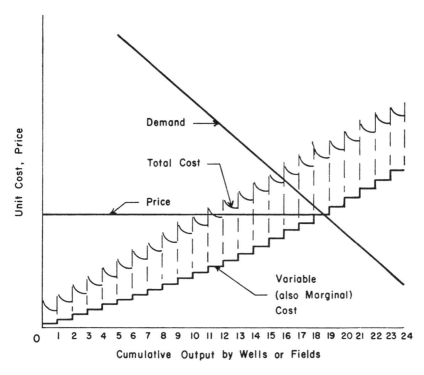

Figure 1.3
Short-run supply schedule of the petroleum industry

1.3 the output of the most efficient nineteen fields sets a price just sufficient to pay the variable (also marginal) cost of the highest-cost field and to provide a return above operating cost for all but the nineteenth.

But figure 1.3 is, like figure 1.1, only a fragment. Figure 1.4 brings together the short- and near-term supply functions. It will be observed that the near-term function does not slope as steeply as does the short-run. This follows from the fact that each near-term cost curve is essentially an average of all the short-run cost curves over the life of the field. A field which is at one point of time very low indeed on the short-run cost function, during the best years of flush production, moves up the function as the years go by; it yields huge profits at first (no. 1), then more modest ones (no. 13), then a return only above bare variable cost (no. 18), then not even that much, and it is closed. Over its whole lifetime, however, it was a profitable field, aggregate receipts exceeding aggregate costs.[12]

But although it is a logical necessity, given the facts of petroleum production, that the slopes be of the relative order shown in figure 1.4, it is

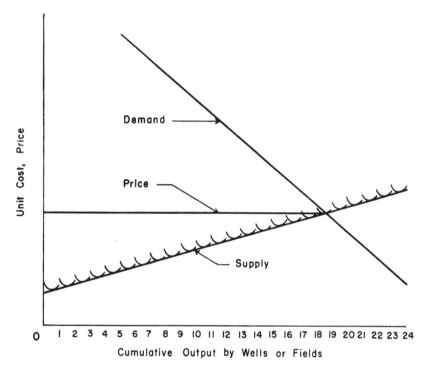

Figure 1.4
Near-term supply schedule of the petroleum industry

by no means necessary that the near-term function intersect the short-run function where the latter intersects with demand to determine price. We have indeed taken a snapshot of the industry at rest—in equilibrium. Let the reader imagine the short-run supply function as moved to intersect with price at a point somewhat to the left, say at no. 16. Then development is out of joint; some wells which would otherwise have continued for some time will need to be shut in sooner than expected; there is a surplus of capacity which must be worked off. Contrariwise, if the short-run supply function sets the price by intersecting with demand to the right of the position in figure 1.4. Then the industry has insufficient capacity, the price is such as to call forth additional development effort and keep operating otherwise uneconomic facilities. In either of these two disequilibria, the system is not at rest, but under tension, which is an accurate but almost indecently cold-blooded way of saying that oilmen will be striving with might and main to do something other than what they have been doing.

Figures 1.3 and 1.4 basically represent what the AAPG system calls "successful wildcats." Like many other technical terms, this is rather misleading. Most discoveries do not pay their full costs, as Lahee's data have long shown. It is well said that the one worse thing than getting a dry hole is getting a deposit which turns out to be so small, or impermeable, or irregular, that it does not even repay the costs of development and extraction—but that is known only in retrospect. Obviously, much of the total volume of petroleum is produced at a loss, even when the whole industry is doing very well. But, of course, the proportion of unprofitable output must be far less than the proportion of unprofitable discoveries; for the most usual reason for unprofitability is small size.

So far, it must be emphasized, we have dealt only with operating expenses in a fully developed field, where the thesis of decreasing costs is most plausible. Even here it fails; but as concerns exploration, it is obvious that the better prospects are explored before poorer or more risky prospects (for risk is a cost). Every concessionaire deciding which blocks to drill and which to turn back is doing an exercise in an increasing-cost activity. The more petroleum we need, the higher a price we must pay for exploration, given the current state of the art and science of petroleum discovery. But although exploration is, in principle, the clearest possible example of an increasing-cost function, it is also the most imprecise because, as we must stress throughout, it is so dominated by random factors; many fields are discovered years after being rejected as bad prospects.

As discoveries are made, they must be developed, and development is as clearly an increasing-cost activity. First, it consists in the delineation or proving of deposits previously found. At any given time, very petroleum producer not only can but urgently must evaluate and rank all available projects in order of their expected unit costs. Let us recall the familiar AAPG findings that only one new-field wildcat in nine ("successful wildcats") finds anything, and only one in thirty or more finds anything worth finding.[13] The discoveries form an array as to the size of the deposit, its location, its permeability, the quality of the petroleum, etc., such that more development can be done only by going more and more into the higher-cost deposits, i.e. those whose reserves will cost more and more per unit to develop and produce. The higher the expected price, the more of them will be developed—the sooner. Furthermore, the individual development project also works under increasing cost. Were we to plot a curve of unit costs of a single development project, it too would fall for a time as initial fixed costs were spread, but then would tend to rise because, as we proceeded to outline the field, the chances would rise of getting pinchouts and dry holes, i.e., very high or infinitely high unit costs for the additional small or zero reserves. Hence, the cost of the additional petroleum reserves *must* rise as more of the field is developed, and the odds against continuing to extend the boundaries of the field must after some point begin to mount.

The nature of increasing costs in field development is well illustrated in a Rocky Mountain field, where, because of the large number of reservoirs, it was possible to make a statistical analysis of the relationship between surface area on the one hand and on the other the average number of delineating dry holes and of ultimate recovery; hence of the expected cost per barrel of additional reserves to be developed. The particular conclusions are only applicable to the particular basin, of course, but the general form of the relationship is our concern. With a past average drilling cost of 92 cents per barrel, the expected average for the next group of wells would be around $1.48, for the next group $1.71, the next at $2.01, and the last at $2.40. But the last three groups were judged uneconomic because the net effective price was around $1.50.[14] It is, of course, rare when data permit such detailed calculations, but the principle is no different at the other end of the spectrum in field size, where a Middle East operator makes a decision between getting more output by fluid injection or by drilling some more development wells, whichever is cheaper. In either case, the cost of the increment is higher than the previous average.

In conclusion: the oft-repeated truism that an oilfield, once discovered, must be produced at capacity, for whatever the market will yield, so long as price at least covers variable or marginal cost, does not imply that, even if the industry is "composed of a large number of autonomous producers," the field will in the long or short run make money, or break even, or lose. It implies nothing whatever. And it compounds the fallacy to say that the petroleum *industry* has at all times a built-in surplus in that more output could at any time be had at decreasing unit costs.

Why should so fallacious an opinion be so firmly held—and not only in *The Price of Oil*? (One must say without irony that a great merit of that work is to be, occasionally, clearly wrong.) The reason is obviously that in the recent past much of the petroleum industry has had to contend with substantial continuing surpluses of producing capacity. It is natural to explain a fact as due to some inherent tendency; yet this is little better than Molière's doctoral candidate who explained that opium put people to sleep because it contained a "dormative power." To assume or assert a basic tendency to surplus is not to explain it. The high ratio of fixed to variable costs is true under certain conditions, and important, but it does not explain; the theory of a decreasing-cost industry is illogical and contrary to fact. To be satisfied with the wrong explanation is to shirk the job of seeking the true one. If there is no inherent physical or cost reason for permanent surplus, and yet a dangerous surplus continues to exist, then we must look to some special set of causes, or at least admit that we don't know.

Increasing Costs and New Supplies

Our theory of increasing costs accords with the common knowledge of the petroleum industry as an interlocking complex of many sources of widely varying average costs, linked together by equality of marginal costs for increments of supply. The student of petroleum economics must take as his guiding motto: *Beware of averages*. Petroleum in one area may on the average be far cheaper than in another, but it does not necessarily or even probably drive it out of existence. As the low-cost area is increasingly exploited, the additional petroleum is increasingly expensive; while the high-cost area must confine itself to its cheapest and best located fields. The market is stable when the cost of *incremental* petroleum settles out in each area to somewhere near equality with the market price and, therefore, with the other. Cheaper sources tend to displace more expensive ones, but this is a question of more and less, not of yes or no.

The price serves as the arbitrating mechanism between Fields A and B, in effect "deciding" how the market is to be divided between them. But if the price is for some reason not permitted to do the task, one or both of the fields will be operating under excess capacity, and the temptation will be very great to produce a little more and sell it, even at a reduced price, to get the large additional profit. But we cannot understand this phenomenon until we understand that it follows from restriction of output. To treat the arrangements of man (however necessary or desirable) as part of the order of nature is a mistake that has been made in all ages, but a mistake none the less.

If any field is not permitted to operate at capacity, unit costs are increased, of course. The U-shaped curve of figure 1.2 is raised at all points, for example. The field itself may now be said to work under "decreasing costs," for the operator could turn out more at a lower unit cost. This would be true of any industry of any cost structure, since it is a fact not of nature but of regulation. Conversely, if the price is held at a higher level than would equate demand with supply, there would be greater output than the market will take, and some mechanism must be found for cutting back production; most usually, by all producing units yielding something.

Under such a condition, all the cost curves in figures 1.1–1.4 would be higher.

So far, however, we have spoken in terms of petroleum cost and supply under any given conditions of knowledge, or under any given conditions of reserves. It remains to show how, in terms of our analysis, new supply makes its appearance on the market.

Were all else to remain equal, the real cost and the price of petroleum would need to increase if new reserves were to be forthcoming even at the same rate per year as before, let alone in larger amounts. But two things have not remained equal. First, exploration has continually spread to new regions, where the best prospects are drilled, in preference to the poorer prospects in the old regions. As Mr. Cram of Continental Oil said of the high success ratio in offshore Louisiana, he and his associates were fighting a 1900 war with 1950 weapons. This applies even more forcibly to more remote regions of the world, where fields have in recent years been discovered by surface geology alone, though surface geology has greatly improved.

The second reason is partly related to the first—the great improvements in the science and art of oil finding and reservoir engineering (particularly secondary recovery, whose greatest triumphs appear to lie ahead), which have frequently and massively lowered the unit costs. Whether this will continue in the future is a problem which is of urgent importance for an old petroleum country like the United States. An "optimistic" view has been presented by Netschert;[15] a "pessimistic" view by Hodges and Steele,[16] the latter seems the more persuasive to us, but the issue is one we need not reach.

Now, we have seen that under the most rigorous competition, petroleum production may in any given place be ruinous *or* vastly profitable, or anything in between. The search for low-cost petroleum is always a rational activity, high-cost petroleum is always a misfortune. But as new low-cost deposits are discovered and developed, they take their place by "bumping" the higher-cost sources. For example, suppose nine fields were found and developed with exactly the same costs as Field 3 in figure 1.4. The result is shown in figure 1.5. Then the cumulative supply curve would have a long, flat stretch through 3–12, the present no. 4 would be no. 13, and in effect the rest of the curve would be skidded over nine places; it would intersect the demand curve at a lower price. Some seven or eight fields (nos. 12–19 in figure 1.2) previously profitable would now be unprofitable. Thus the effect of new discoveries would be higher output,

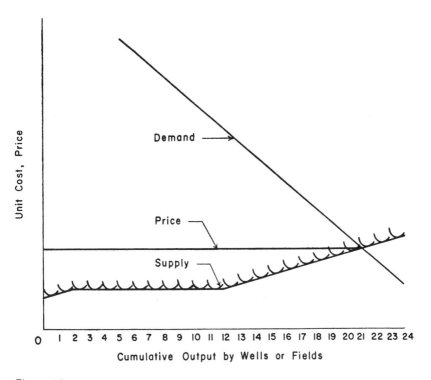

Figure 1.5
Effect of development of very large new low-cost reserves

lower prices, high profits for some but much lower profits or even unforeseen losses for others—*unless* demand kept increasing nicely in step.

But that, as we saw earlier, is just what we cannot expect. The strong
random element is basic to the finding and developing of reserves. One
cannot tell when new deposits will appear, and cause past investment,
intelligently made on the basis of the best possible information, to be
shouldered out of profitable outlets and be run at a loss. The other side of
the coin is that one never knows when a modest amount of exploratory
effort will yield a bonanza, and enable the fortunate operator to reap as
profit the very large difference between his cost and those of the highest-
cost unit, which may be called the industry's marginal cost.

This randomness means that the industry's response to higher or lower
price is inherently awkward and sticky. It operates like an automobile with
a worn and rusted accelerator pedal. The driver may apply a modest additional pressure, with no result; additional pressure, still no more speed; only
a little more pressure and the car shoots forward as though jet-propelled.

The driver releases pressure, but the speed continues just as great; still less pressure, but the same speed; a little less, and suddenly he barely crawls.

The response to randomness is some form of averaging, in time or space, and the industry has brought this to what seems to an academic observer an unparalleled degree. Figure 1.2, as we saw earlier, is really a kind of averaging of successive figures 1.1. But in the short run, the consequences of increased supply without increased demand can be unpleasant. This is what the fact of high overhead costs helps to explain. In most other industries, and in petroleum over a time, the response to lower prices is twofold: curtailed production within most units, and shutting down of marginal establishments. In petroleum, practically the entire burden of adjustment must in the short run come as shutting in of units. The very natural distaste for "a short sharp shock," which may be socially wasteful, too, explains much of the industry's history.

Economies of Scale in Petroleum Production

The "decreasing-cost industry" argument rejected earlier could only have been derived from the notion of economies of scale in petroleum production, throughout the *whole* range of possible output. It would then follow that the larger firm could always drive out the smaller, or at least make it agree on a monopoly price policy. That this argument is mistaken does not imply that there cannot be any important economies of scale. An exploration department must obviously be of some minimum efficient size, though it is difficult to say what that is. Again, a large producer is able to search and drill in many places, and his chances are good of finding enough in some places to pay the cost of both the successful and the unsuccessful searches. A small producer, searching in only a few places, is essentially a small sample of exploration effort, and small samples are notoriously unstable; his chances of either hitting the jackpot or losing his shirt are both much higher than for the large company. The basic mathematical truism is, of course, borne out by common knowledge—no stockholder of any medium or large company can hope to make the kinds of fortunes won by some individual wildcatters, but in return for abandoning this hope they have a good assurance of getting some return, albeit a smaller one; while other wildcatters may lose all. Hence it would seem that the large company would not be wiped out by a run of bad luck in several successive projects, while the small producer could. But this is an economy of scale that can largely (perhaps altogether) be overcome by the small producer participating in several joint ventures. That is, buying into n new-field exploration projects is as good as outright ownership of n projects. In either case, the odds are 1 in 9^n of finding a deposit everywhere, and $(8/9)^n$ of finding a deposit nowhere. It should not be inferred that there cannot be any economies of scale, within *any* range; cost structures are not to be deduced from elementary mathematical theorems. All we need for our purposes is the negative verdict: there is as yet no evidence for the conclusion of production economies of scale reaching into high size ranges.[17]

Notes

1. Production expenditures in the United States (excluding interest and profit) have been calculated to divide as follows (in percent of total):

	1944	1948	1953	1955	1956
Exploration	30	29	30	34	33
Development	40	40	38	38	38
Extraction	30	32	32	28	29

(Independent Petroleum Association of America (IPAA), *April 1960 Report on Cost Study*, p. 6). These figures understate the relative importance of exploration, however, since in the United States there are incentives to put down more development wells than would otherwise pay, and this raises also the operating costs of extraction. One company recently proposed that 87 percent of the *non-marginal* wells in East Texas be shut in without affecting output, yielding large savings to the operators (*Oil and Gas Journal*, August 22nd, 1960, p. 46). Since the plan amounted to setting slightly under 40 acres as maximum spacing, it is obvious that a higher per cent could have been shut in; on the other hand, with more producing days, more capacity would be needed.

2. Exploration is really a spectrum of activities and a range of hopes. The most speculative type, "new-field wildcats" (AAPG system, see p. 5, n. 1 and p. 6, n. 1), are little more than half of all exploratory drilling, and since their success ratio is of course much lower, they account for only about 20 percent of the producers. The other exploratory wells are outposts, new-pool wildcats, deeper-pool tests (which are more akin to new-field wildcats than to outposts), and shallower-pool tests. They all start from a known deposit of oil or gas or both, and are only undertaken if the prospective return from the expanded discovery is sufficient to pay the additional costs. But this is not as neat as it sounds, and the risk may be nearly as great as for a new-field wildcat.

3. In 1958 the AAPG counted 6950 "new-field wildcats," the Journal 9588 "wildcats." Essentially the latter add wells aiming at a new formation, but exclude extensions and shallower- or deeper-pool tests.

4. Of course, if the field is immediately operated, current reservoirs are being depleted as well as increased. The text discussion refers to gross, not net, reserve increases.

5. For Lacq, see *World Oil*, June 1960, p. 167. The Panhandle-Hugoton field was credited with 39–45 trillion cubic feet around 1945, more than twenty years after its discovery; new reserves credited to it since then have amounted to between 25 and 31 trillion. Hassi R'Mel in the Sahara is roughly 50 by 40 miles, and by no means defined; it has only seven wells, and no more are planned for the time being. Oil has been found on two flanks (*Oil and Gas Journal*, February 1, 1960, p. 82).

6. For a full explanation, see the latest June issue of the *Bulletin of the American Association of Petroleum Geologists* (AAPG), article headed "Exploratory Drilling in 19 . . .". B. W. Blanpied and Ben W. Carsey have prepared the articles, succeeding F. H. Lahee, who first applied the method to gas reserves in the AAPG *Bulletin*, September 1958.

7. The late E. DeGolyer put the normal development period of an oil field at four years; that of a gas field "probably considerably longer." (Federal Power Commission, *Natural Gas Investigation*, Docket G-580 (Washington, 1948), p. 50. Hereafter referred to as Smith-Wimberley report.)

8. A comprehensive review of the available cost data, and the theoretical problems of interpretation, is in John E. Hodges and Henry B. Steele, *An Investigation of the Problems of Cost Determination for the Discovery, Development, and Production of Liquid Hydrocarbons and Natural Gas Reserves* (Rice Institute Pamphlet, vol. 46, October 1959). See also R. E. Megill, "The Evaluation of Current Finding Costs," Paper No. 875-14-F, API, Division of Petroleum, April 21st, 1960.

9. Paul W. MacAvoy, "Price Formation in Natural Gas Fields" (unpublished thesis, Yale University, 1959, publication as revised expected 1962), refers throughout to the development period as being the only one amenable to an econometric analysis. The success of this work in explaining the field price structure is a confirmation of the importance of the middle period. In view of the Lahee classification system, of three and of six years, and DeGolyer's opinion, cited above at p. 6, nn. 1 and 2, it might at first seem that MacAvoy's choice of a three-year period for such purposes as measuring concentration was too low, though (because of convergence) six would surely be too high. It seems to make little difference in the results, but a three-year period is probably better because of the threat of drainage to adjoining leases, the expiration of leases or need to pay shut-in royalties (payments due the landowner when petroleum could be extracted but is not) A desire of the royalty owner for quicker returns—unwillingess to wait as long as the producer—seem in most cases to dictate sale of gas reserves by that time. Hence, the average field is sold (its reserve committed) before full development. This is confirumed in numerous Federal Power Commission hearings.

10. Prepared by the Secretariat, Economic Commission for Europe, E/ECE/205 (Geneva, 1955), pp. 16–18.

11. Fluid injection is established practice even in the Middle East; it depends on the unit cost of additional output thus secured at additional cost versus the unit cost of a development elsewhere. See *Oil and Gas International*, March 1961, pp. 29–33, and April 1961, pp. 22–5.

12. *Technical note.* In general, an industry supply curve slopes upward in response to three factors. First, greater output must be squeezed at rising cost within each unit. Second, increasingly inefficient units are brought into operation. Third, the industry becomes so large a part of the market for some components or services that it bids up the price, and hence its total costs. Figure 1.4 practically neglects the first factor for simplicity's sake; and we are simply agnostic on the third. A supply curve which would satisfy the (properly) purist reader would therefore differ, but not appreciably, from the simple envelope curve in Figure 1.4. In the longer run, certain interactions would develop which would tend to make industry costs fall with size: chiefly greater knowledge, and the development of specialized services at lower costs. In this sense only can we speak of petroleum as an industry of decreasing costs. But the simplest and best way to introduce this factor is by decreasing the slope of the supply curve over time (rotating it clockwise).

13. A new tabulation by the AAPG appears to show a steady decline from 1945–47 through 1951–53 in the percentage of all oil discoveries that were evaluated as profitable after six years of production history—from about 30 per cent to about 23 per cent. But the corresponding *gas* percentage has been steady between 45 per cent and 50 per cent. B. W. Blanpied, in AAPG *Bulletin*, vol. 44 (June 1960), p. 678.

14. J. J. Arps and T. G. Roberts, "Economics of Drilling for Cretaceous Oil on the East Flank of the Denver-Julesburg Basin," AAPG *Bulletin*, vol. 42 (November 1958), pp. 2549–66.

15. Bruce C. Netschert, *The Future Supply of Oil and Gas* (Baltimore, 1958).

16. Hodges and Steele, op. cit.

17. Cf. James W. McKie, "Market Structures and Uncertainty in Oil and Gas Exploration," *Quarterly Journal of Economics*, 74 (1960), pp. 543–71. Some economies of scale may exist for special and possibly transitory reasons. Contrast the one concessionaire in Saudi Arabia in the 1930s with the twenty in Libya in the 1950s.

2

Efficiency of Resource Use in Crude Petroleum

The current crisis in world petroleum is due to restraints, largely by governments, upon the workings of market forces. The reasons and justifications for these restraints, however good or bad, need not detain us. The reader must decide for himself whether he really wants competition in the world oil trade. A competitive price would be much lower than the current price, with very dangerous political results. The present disequilibrium is also dangerous. Our business, however, is only to find out what has happened. Since efficiency of resource use is an adjustment to what nature and knowledge give any generation, we must first explore the basic cost and supply conditions in petroleum before turning to what has been done in the United States and abroad.

I The Production and Supply Functions

The array, from lowest to highest cost, of the many possible sources of petroleum defines the supply curve of an industry of increasing costs (1, SPNG, NRID). Over time, with greater knowledge of the earth's crust and of better finding and producing methods, the upward-sloping function shifts to the right. Increasing costs do *not* mean that because of a finite earth there must eventually be scarcity, or that the big fields have all been found, or that real costs must increase over time—propositions of doubtful truth or relevance. It does mean that during any pre-defined period, however short or long, the greater the amount to be produced, the higher is the minimum attainable cost per unit. Under either effective competition or rational monopoly, great effort is expended to draw any given amount of output from the cheapest sources. Given the present complex market structures, which are neither fully monopolistic nor competitive, this tendency

Reprinted from *Southern Economic Journal* 31 (October 1964): 101–116.

to minimize costs generates a set of very strong dammed-up pressures. The individual producer, forced by regulation or fear of spoiling the market to restrict output, has excess capacity and therefore decreasing costs in his own operation. It is this opposition, between inherent tendency and the blocks built against it, which we must investigate. But we must first get rid of deep-rooted error that looks like truth. "The accidental proscriptions of authority, when time has procured them veneration, are often confounded with the laws of nature, and those rules are supposed coeval with reason, the first rise of which cannot be discovered" built against it which we must investigate.

The influential theories of high fixed-to-variable cost ratios, decreasing costs, inherent surplus, etc., are one and all either wrong in themselves, or irrelevant, or simply never explained (28, 1). If industry incremental cost were compelled by nature to be always or usually below average cost, then price would be under corresponding competitive pressure to fall below average cost also, and inflict losses on the industry; this is "natural monopoly." But, restriction aside, the petroleum industry is inherently stable because industry incremental cost always exceeds industry average cost.

But there are some occasional destabilizers. First, the array from lowest to highest is always being jarred by the addition of new sources. When large, new, low-cost fields come in, some high-cost, barely marginal sources find themselves disemployed. Now, the intrusion of these new sources is an unforeseeable event. Even for the world industry as a whole, though admittedly not always for every part of it, it is impossible to predict whether a given expenditure to find new reserves will find little or much. Anyone who doubts this might reflect on the Middle East or North Holland. Hence, one cannot tell when, where, and how many high-cost producers will get knocked out, although we will see later that the process is much less brutal than it sounds at first.

The second destabilizer is apparent when we look to the cost curve of the individual deposit. Were there no discounting, there would be no problem in choosing a development plan: each pool would most cheaply be drained by a single well. The longer it was in operation, the greater would be total output and the lower the unit investment cost. But output must be at a progressively decreasing rate per unit of time, while operating costs are fairly constant. Therefore, operating costs per unit of output must increase as a function of output and usually, though not necessarily, until they overbear decreasing investment cost to make total unit cost touch a minimum, then rise, the greater is total cumulative output. In any case, when output falls to the "abandonment rate," where operating cost has risen to equal price, the well closes.

Time, and the need to discount, radically steepen the upward slope. Nearly always it pays to drill additional wells, thereby trading off higher investment and operating costs per unit against lower unit deferment cost. Looking now at a development plan *ex ante*, incremental development cost is always on the increase and unit total cost nearly always touches a minimum at some point defined essentially by three parameters: the indivisible start-up costs, the production decline curve, and the appropriate discount rate. But minimum costs are not maximum profits. By drilling more wells, the rate of output can be profitably increased past the rate which minimizes cost, to the point where the incremental cost, rising by reason of more wells to the given pool, equals the price; this type of calculation has been greatly refined since World War II. The higher the discount rate chosen, the lower is the optimum inground inventory, i.e., crude reserves, and the greater the supply available for development at any given price; but the higher also is its development cost. Under stable expectations, rising incremental costs are a fairly gentle brake on higher output; more wells can be drilled, old wells can be kept going a little longer.

The industry rate of discount, or necessary rate of return, summing up the varying time preferences of individuals, may be considered imperfect or objectionable on some broader welfare calculus, and if so we ought to act as if the discount rate were equal to some other "true" rate of time preference (27). But any discount rate is ill-defined and subject to change without notice. Greater hopes or fears of the future make people more or less willing to wait, on their own or on others' behalf. Higher discounting rates generate large excess inventories to drill up and sell off, hence a large addition to current product flow, and downward pressure upon prices (or vice versa). The multiplier effect generated by discounting changes can be a true source of temporary industry instability, and has in fact been one.

Depending on the relation of the stock to expected output and prices, a barrel of undeveloped oil may have negligible or zero present value: that is, no future gain is lost by developing it immediately. Then its replacement cost is irrelevant, but the competitive floor to price is *not* short-run operating cost alone—another myth which makes the oil industry too jittery. For, outside the topsy-turvy world of United States regulation, the relevant variable cost is development-plus-operating cost. Indeed, short-period price determination hardly exists. The cost of stopping a continuous flow of liquid is so great that contracts for less than a year are the footnote rather than the text. But, most important, given the production decline rate, and in addition a growth in demand, capacity must be increased by something like 10 to 15 percent annually. It is not rational behavior to be investing—drilling and equipping wells—while you are selling off oil below its investment cost. Hence, in the oil industry the only relevant fixed costs in the price-determining period are finding costs, which for the great bulk of the world's reserves are a minor fraction of variable costs. (14, p. 89) Moreover, incremental industry development cost always exceeds average because greater output requires not only increasingly costly infill drilling in any given field (intensive margin) but also more costly fields to be operated (extensive margin). The influential myth of industry incremental cost below average cost is in truly striking contradiction to the facts, and would be so even if development costs were fixed and only operating costs variable. For operating costs are an increasing function of current output rate, and can go very high as this presses upon capacity; and a price just equal to the operating cost of the highest-cost fields may give a good return over the cost of the more productive wells. But it is much more useful to think in terms of *ex ante* calculation for a given project; the higher is total planned output, and the sooner it is taken out of the ground, the higher is unit development-plus-operating cost, while inequality of costs makes this *a fortiori* true for the industry.

Even under pure competition, a petroleum price equal to industry incremental cost must be above average cost for all but the highest-cost operators, who are the only ones failing to draw rents. Note that the impact of the new lower-cost sources is softened precisely because operating costs are usually so low. A field is pushed out only gradually, because it pays to keep producing from it, though not to develop further, if price "exceeds" operating cost. Hence, those owning and working the field do get notice before being displaced.

Subject, then, to our two occasional irregular destabilizers, the industry is inherently self-adjusting. The current "imbalance" simply registers the pressure of its inherent equilibrating forces pushing against the restraints. We now apply these principles to the United States, and to the rest of the world, hoping to learn both from differences and from similarities.

II   The United States

The history of the domestic oil industry records a contradiction between many property holdings and the oil and gas pools which disregard them (1, NRID, 72–75). A well on one property would drain every adjoining lot;

hence, you must drain your neighbor before he drains you. It is precisely like giving every retailer in a crowded commercial district the keys to every other retailer's stock. The rate of discount is thereby pushed up to 100 percent or more per annum so that everybody must grab all he can and try to sell at any price in excess of bare operating cost. How much solemn ink has been shed over this as the normal case of competition, and of private *versus* social discount rates! Thirty-five years ago there were, broadly speaking, two ways to handle the problem. One was compulsory unitization of every pool, letting competition and the industry's upward-sloping cost function decide who would produce how much, and at what price, to match output with market demand. There is good reason to think that this might have come about in the 1930s, but it was not to be; the Great Depression and the East Texas field presented an acute emergency of massive physical waste—oil running into creeks, etc. The States chose in haste what seemed like a reasonable halfway house: market-demand pro-rationing, having a government body assess demand at the current price, to divide it "fairly" among the various sources. One might allocate among pools on the basis of reserves, or past production, or some other more or less arbitrary criterion. But his too was rejected in favor of prorating a fixed total output to every individual well. The result of "fair shares for all" is, of course, unnecessary wells drilled to get more allowables. Growth of demand, and the Second World War, for a time masked the basic vicious circle—higher overdrilling raising costs, Commission restriction then supporting higher prices, which encouraged more drilling, and so on. In the prorated states, especially Texas, current producing capacity is today far enough above demand that the short-run floor to price is no longer development cost, but the low operating cost of semi-idleness. Were there no source of supply outside the United States, this would not matter; as costs went up because of overdrilling, prices would again be raised with perfect "justification." But prices cannot be raised further, the industry is in trouble, and some attempts are being made to curb overdrilling—not by letting some competition into the system, but by improving regulatory standards. Much has been done, and some of the State commission members have shown an admirable responsibility and courage in the face of vilification; hence, it is an ungrateful task to report that this has not helped much, since excess capacity has at best levelled off; nor will it help much in the future.

The prorationing system differs from the usual type of fair-shares cartel (with freedom of entry) in three important respects. First, there is system-atic bias in the State laws in favor of drilling more wells than necessary; the more wells drilled in any pool, the greater the allowables for the pool. The more economically one develops a reservoir, the more he is penalized. Secondly, the deeper the well drilled, hence the more expensive to drill it, the higher the allowables.

But the most striking waste is in the so-called stripper or marginal wells (terminology is far from consistent). They are exempted from regulation because otherwise most, though not all, would be shut down and their reserves lost; the goal is maximum ultimate recovery. Now, in the oil country there is only one thing worse than a dry hole, and that is finding a deposit which looks commercial but which the operator finds out the hard way is not—after he has spent his money developing it. In other words, he and society would have been better off had the reserve never been found. So to the argument that letting uneconomic strippers close would be to lose their reserves, the only answer is: by all means, go get lost! In Texas alone it would be worth paying about $1.3 billion to get rid of this public nuisance, a liability masquerading as an asset; nationally the saving would be over twice as great (see appendix 2.2). Worse yet, something like half the new wells drilled annually are probably strippers even at the beginning, the expenditures on them being largely though not wholly waste. The Russians classify a well producing less than twenty barrels daily as "inactive," and get rid of it as soon as possible; we cherish and fertilize these weeds at the expense of the flowers.

The annual charge of this whole system of organized waste, *including* the import controls needed to insulate it from foreign competition, has been rather conservatively estimated by an interdepartmental government committee at $3.6 billion. A better estimate, in my opinion, is just over $4 billion (see appendix 2.1). The rationale is, in brief, that foreign oil is available today at over one dollar less than the domestic price. If the price were permitted to fall by a dollar per barrel, much of the domestic industry would disappear and much would survive, leaner and more efficient, freed of the wasteful regulation which is now forced upon it by the States. Confident predictions of how much would survive are easily made; I have heard 10 percent and 90 percent, and others in between, but with no facts to support them.[1] *Many of the more efficient producers would be much better off*. This becomes clear when we investigate a narrower concept of waste (see appendix 2.2), the amount that could be saved at *current* levels of domestic output, if stripper wells were jettisoned, and if, by unitizing, the clearly avoidable expense were saved. We estimate in the appendix that it would be in the neighborhood of $2 to $2.5 billion, or about 80 cents to a dollar per barrel of domestic crude, at current output.

Our estimates of waste, or avoidable expense in the developing and producing of crude oil (see appendix 2.2), are deplorably rough, and tend to be too low, because we must perforce use very crude methods to segregate better from poorer wells. Moreover, we have been able to make only the roughest kind of allowance for the production of natural gas, which is not subject to market-demand prorationing, and whose price would be competitively determined if there were not a regulatory scheme (whose efficacy I do not know) to hold the price down (20). Despite the profusion of oil industry statistics, there is nothing on the distribution of well capacities, the array from best to worst. It is no accident that this is a closed subject. If all wells have a pre-emptive right to share in the market, it is mischievous and dangerous to ask how much more efficient some are than others, since this inevitably suggests that some might be chosen over others; this is "selective buying" and "discrimination"—the most damning of epithets. And with all the voluminous discussion of the costs of finding-developing-producing oil, it is the greatest of rarities to see a cost distribution mentioned, even in theory. If this paper serves to irritate the powers-that-be into providing the statistics which they will soon need even more badly than they do now, it will have accomplished something.

Be this as it may, if prices were permitted to fall by about a dollar per barrel, and the States unitized output to cut out unnecessary drilling, the domestic industry would be about as well off as it is today, and the threat from imports and oil shale would be much reduced; many superfluous producers would have disappeared.

But there is nothing precise or sure about such an estimate, and here we touch on national defense, which as Adam Smith emphasized is more important than "opulence." In my opinion, the national security, quite aside from nuclear war, requires a substantial domestic oil-producing industry and, if need be, import restriction to preserve it. If this criterion is sound, the prorationing system is not a failure but a menace.

First, when the national Administration declared that the national interest required increased output during the Suez crisis, the State Commissions would not permit it until a month after they had forced up the price by forcing a shortage. The oil lift to Europe was a failure; targets were not met. We can take no credit for the mild winter and the quick reopening of the canal, which first eased and then ended the crisis. But it would in any case deserve to be called a failure on this fact alone; that with plenty of unused capacity at the Gulf Coast, tankers had to be sent halfway around the world, to the Middle East, to pick up cargoes. Efficiency and competition and the national interest required more oil to be produced near tide-water where it was demanded. But "fairness" and abhorrence of "selective buy-ing" determined that there could be none until West Texas inventories were down. The Commissions are not primarily to blame. They did not misinterpret or abuse their mandate, under State law. They were never directly asked by Washington for higher output until the crisis was over.

"Those who ignore the past are condemned to repeat it." The House and Senate reports on the Suez crisis debated whether the big oil companies were heroes or villains or both; or whether the price rise was "justified," and other irrelevancies. But they never inquired or wondered about control of supply (21, 24). There is a world where market forces are banished, where nobody asks about control of supply because everybody knows, to use fashionably pompous language, that Concentrated Corporate Power is wielded through Administered Prices. (2) So long as we think words instead of things, our policy will be blundering and impotent.

Second, despite the high price, the statistics show decreasing discovery effort. Wildcat wells, even including natural gas, are down by 38 percent since 1956 and successful oil wildcats 54 percent (35). New reserves found per year are declining; in particular, such imperfect statistics as we have show newly *discovered* crude oil, even after allowing for later extensions and revisions, to be steeply declining. This is the fruit of "fair shares." Why risk money—and despite all the exaggeration, oil finding is risky—to find new oil which, after a brief grace period, must be produced at a fraction of well capacity? The solicitude for strippers and other high-cost sources is killing the domestic oil-finding industry, and indeed, were it not for tax advantages and natural gas, one may wonder how much would still exist. If other things were equal, a higher price would mean greater inputs into exploration and development, but in the United States the higher price is secured only by greater restriction of output, which is a disincentive to higher inputs. Regulation has generated, in the place of a normal supply curve, a very complex profit function with a maximum, and the industry has been led well past it (8).

The system survives when even the industry as a whole is being hurt, simply to keep the inefficient in business. This is glimpsed in the inter-agency Committee's hurried remark that lower prices or production would create distress and unemployment. In 1960 the Texas Railroad Commission rejected a scheme to reduce operating costs—and jobs—by shutting in a useless seven-eighths of the East Texas non-marginal wells (though leaving untouched the even more wasteful but politically impregnable marginal wells) (1, NRID, 55–58). The prorationing system is, in short, work re-lief—it has become a boondoggle costing $4 billion per year, and it is harmful to national security. The beneficiaries are the smaller domestic producers, the States and localities which get tax revenues, the royalty owners, and the local supply population.

How long will the system last? In general, the more costly a featherbedding scheme, the more people it benefits, and the politically stronger it is. But because a badly overbuilt industry is vulnerable to even small amounts of uncontrolled capacity, prorationing can be abolished any time the President wishes. Suspension of the ban on interstate shipment of oil produced in violation of State regulations, plus an increase in import quotas, plus the freeing of offshore production on Federal lands from State allowables, would bring the whole system down in a few weeks or months. The Kennedy-Johnson Administration has never contemplated any such action —quite the contrary, as will soon appear. But in some future crisis some president may have to live up to the American tradition that the executive or the courts do the necessary, difficult jobs. The system may end with a bang, not a whimper.

An abrupt end is not necessary, nor efficient, nor pleasant. The industry has plenty of unused brains and public spirit to find some gradual ways out. But little constructive is to be heard from it today. The ridiculous natural gas price freeze is a real grievance which has the noxious side effect of making oilmen dwell on their wrongs instead of recognizing that while natural gas, natural gas liquids, and—least of all—imports, have slowed the growth of demand for oil, it is market-demand prorationing which prevents any normal competitive adjustment to this demand deceleration, and has made the domestic industry incurably sick. If in time or by lucky chance output gets back up to higher levels, even short of capacity, or when costs are appreciably lowered by technical progress, operators will start putting down even more unnecessary wells than today, just as farmers producing surpluses buy more fertilizer, and airlines with half-empty planes buy more for the profitable runs. Cutting down imports even more, or giving one or another State the "fair share" it claims, or "buy American," or a world crisis, etc., can give no more than a temporary respite until capacity quickly moves up. The States must each begin to plan how to bring about compulsory utilization and phase out marginal wells, as soon and as smoothly as possible.

The most hopeful factor today is that the States are gradually being pushed in the direction of reform because some competition exists among them for exploration and development dollars. Relative attractiveness is determined largely by the uncontrolled facts of nature, but partly also by regulatory policy. The more severely a State restrains output, the more it raises unit costs of operation within its borders. Hence, Louisiana's increased market share is, in part, because Louisiana is more permissive and lower-cost. Resentment is voiced in Texas, and indeed a recent report to the governor cannot mention its neighbor without snarling (26). Texas could permit greater production and get more of the market, but the greater production would wreck prices. This is the classic dilemma of the largest producer in a cartel, who holds the umbrella for those nibbling away at its market share. Texas could cut costs and improve its share without hurting prices, by doing away with the marginal wells, but this is today politically impossible. Hence, they prefer to pressure the big integrated, politically vulnerable companies: by questionnaires on how much non-Texas crude they are buying, etc.

Just as it is easier to talk "administered prices" than to work at analyzing markets, it is easier to accuse the large integrated companies of favoring production out of State, rather than buying from Texas independents, than to ask why they do it. Of course, the companies or anyone else will buy or produce more cheaply every chance they can. Size and integration may at most have helped, but have not caused, inter-State competition to begin to undermine the State control structure. And one would feel more hopeful if the United States Department of Justice had not issued a dire warning against the process. (32) It is not waste, or control of supply, that concerns them, but "availability of shares of that total to individual competitors" for to them that "determines the shape and strength of competition" (p. 4). The independent producer is said to suffer more, proportionately, from cutbacks in output than do companies operating in several States (pp. 19, 23–24) and this "leads to concentration of existing production resources" (p. 24). In fact, the independent producer in the non-market-demand State is better off than the large company in several States. The shift to non-market demand areas in also a "threat to adequate development of new production capacity, since the independent traditionally has been the industry mainstay in exploratory drilling" (ibid.). This confuses development with exploration. It also repeats the usual story that independents do most of the exploratory drilling, without asking whether an independent drilling on a farm-out from a major company is exploring or is merely working for the explorer. It also ignores the connection between price-cost relations and investment in exploring or developing: the "traditional" way of life explains things. On the same page comes the venerable fallacy that a customer buying from a competitor is at a competitive disadvantage.

The Justice Department is worried about integrated companies' "evasion" of State controls, and the "major companies" getting the production limitations they like. The truth is neatly to the contrary: the major companies tend on the whole to own less of the marginal facilities and hence to be dis-favored. However, the Department is correct in fearing that "even moderate liberalization of controls in one area might swamp stabilization efforts in others . . . and wipe out precisely those independent elements . . . which are so important to competition" (p. 26). In short, the breakdown of the present control system is to them a clear and present danger. Not for the first nor the one-hundredth time, solicitude for the small producers is the bulwark of a stagnating monoply. As the States slowly try to slough off the worst of the present featherbedding, the Department of Justice tries to keep them where they are in order to keep superfluous producers in business. For an orderly transition from the present mess, it is far from sufficient but it may be necessary for the Federal Government, or at least the Department of Justice, to keep out.

But the chief obstacle to remedial action is in the mental habits of the producers, royalty owners, local suppliers, and other beneficiaries, not to mention the State treasuries. Their state of mind is far more dangerous to them than the state of their finances. We see it well revealed in a valuable document released last December, and already referred to, a report to the Governor of Texas on the 1963 World Petroleum Congress (26). There is alarm over the constant talk of efficiency, "which has almost reached fetish proportions in some quarters" (p. 5) and on the failure to recognize the danger of a "monopoly problem"—as the Attorney-General's report, just mentioned, sees "monopoly." Despite allegiance to free enterprise [sic], there is a demand for government action, and it is cause for complaint that the world industry paid no attention to a search for better methods of restricting supply (pp. 5–6). Something must be done by government to control output or the whole world industry will topple—this is considered the fundamental issue (pp. 8–9). The Department of Justice report is repeatedly and favorably cited, of course (pp. 10, 31, 32, 35). The authors' major worry, and quite correctly, is that "the marginal and stripper wells in the United States . . . could be rendered uneconomic by being forced into open competition with the more prolific wells and fields *here* and abroad" (p. 9, emphasis added); and that ". . . and effort is being made to give wider latitude to favored high potential fields, at the expense of the marginal and stripper category. This is an indirect assault upon the whole concept of across-the-board proration" (p. 35), and of course it is.

There is a legend, repeated by many who ought to know better, that the big companies run the oil industry, and the oil industry runs Texas. It is the contrary of the truth. One can only hope, for the sake of national security,

that those in control realize in time that to survive they must indeed let
competition get rid of marginal and stripper wells in favor of "high potential fields." They must acquire a willingness to look at truth and leave off
the mind-destroying habit, by no means peculiar to them, of asking which
side is who on (major *or* independents, producers *or* consumers, etc.) rather
than what are the facts. The greatest menace to the future of the Texas and
other producers is their obsession that the world owes them a living. It is
this loss of touch with reality that seems to mark a group as being ripe
for destruction: "The Lord shall smite thee with madness, and blindness,
and astonishment of heart; and thou shalt grope at noonday, as the blind
gropeth in darkness, and thou shalt not prosper in thy ways."

III Outside the United States

The same economic principles apply in a different setting outside North
America. Most obviously, and peace be to the anti-trust lawyers, the world
oil industry is far more competitive. We have at home thousands of firms,
but only about five production decision-making units, i.e., State Commissions, with quite a high concentration even among them, and no anti-trust
inhibitions. Abroad one finds a big eight producers (or nine if we include
the Soviet Union) who have not been collaborating (the World Oil Cartel
is a fiction), plus a steadily growing fringe of independents (1, NRID
79–80). Economies of scale are no longer large relative to the market—
the Japanese entered with only ten million dollars—and the number of
sellers is increasing. The rapid growth of the oil market has drawn in new
sellers and buyers and has offered rewards for aggression and penalties for
conservatism—i.e., has greatly increased competition.

For a decade after the war the normal viscosity of prices set by a small
group was thickened by a combination of accidents —Korea, Iran, Suez—
and government policies. But Arabian crude which in 1957 was posted, and
was really selling, at $2.08 per barrel, today is posted at $1.80 and realizes
something around $1.40, and sometimes less (1, OPLR). The time is ripe for
some entrepreneurs (who will also be called other names) to offer supply
contracts at just enough below today's "abnormally low" prices to induce
buyers to sign. In years to come these enterprisers will fulfill the contracts
at a handsome profit. Short selling is the way to make money on a falling
market.

To be sure, open-market crude oil sales at discount prices represent
only a small fraction of total output, but end-product prices have come
down even more. The implication is plain: apparently profitless refining-

marketing operations merely reflect discounts on crude, even though companies for various private reasons may continue to "sell" crude from their right to their left hand at higher prices than really exist. Tanker rates are far down, because the tanker market is also competitive, outside the United States, and lower costs are transmitted in lower prices.

Whether or not competition abroad should be considered "workable," I cannot say, but since there is so much more of it than at home, the wastes of monopoly are much less. Peaceful co-existence of production centers with varying average costs is no disproof; under competition, nothing is more commonplace. Supply sources like Venezuela, with higher average cost, do not stay in operation because of industrial "statesmanship" or "fair shares." Since the oil industry works under increasing costs, competition tends to an equating of *incremental, not average*, costs in various supply centers. A great deal of Venezuelan and North African oil can be produced and delivered to the United States or Northwest Europe at a lower total laid-down cost than Middle East oil; but the limits—where incremental cost would rise—are reached far earlier than in the Middle East.

There is not even a small fraction abroad of the wasteful United States practice of deliberately holding back cheaper supplies to make room for the dearer, to say nothing of pre-empting a share for the very highest cost. But it does not follow that the current pattern is necessarily the one that would minimize total crude oil production plus transport plus refining costs. Some, though by no means all, of the cross-hauling between Eastern and Western Hemispheres is waste. To an increasing extent, production may be governed by access to markets rather than by comparative costs. Some new areas are uneconomic but are being developed as insurance, which is a genuine cost, to be sure. That the price, though much reduced, is still far above finding-developing-operating costs is evidenced by the strenuous efforts to find and develop one's own crude rather than buy someone else's. From the other end, as every producer tries to realize the implicit crude profits by carrying through to sell at the final stage, the result will undoubtedly be a surplus of refining capacity. But that has not yet come about, and if crude prices keep declining, perhaps it never will. New refineries are rising in every developing country, needed or not, for a local refinery which a local government can use to force down the landed price of crude is a paying proposition to the locals even if, on a world view, a waste of resources. Of course, some of these refineries will never pay anybody in anything but prestige.

Opinions differ widely, and I have none to offer, as to how much of world producing capacity is getting close to an untenably low producing profit after royalties and taxes, and therefore toward a clash with the host governments on profit sharing. Companies and governments at least agree that royalty and tax payments are a cost; in fact, they are a sharing of profits, which competition is today gradually eroding away. A strong dislike of confrontations between companies and governments makes me wonder whether, on purely political grounds, competition is not too strong, but this is obviously not relevant to my subject of efficiency.

Opinion seems unanimous that whatever the future, there is a huge present surplus of oil supply, and surpluses are usually considered a symptom of wasted resources. Yet current producing capacity is only 10 to 15 percent in excess of current output (4). Considering an annual growth rate of over 10 percent, the inevitably uneven rates of development of a worldwide system, and the need for insurance (to consider which as surplus would be double counting), this hardly seems appreciable; the price response seems disproportionate to the stimulus. I submit that the notion of surplus is correct, but it is a surplus not of current capacity but of available reserves. These can be turned quickly into capacity by a relatively small development investment, and this is the relevant incremental cost.

The world oil industry's condition clashes with mental habits formed in the past: for some time to come, finding cost is no part of long-run supply price. In general, the cost of committing a reserve to development is the *lower* of (a) the cost of finding a new barrel to replace the old, or (b) sacrificing the present value of the barrel. As matters stand today, given the reserves in known deposits, available at the cost of development with a few exploratory fringes (we leave to one side the fruitless guessing about resource base and undiscovered deposits), the expected rates of consumption over the next fifteen-odd years, and a realistic discount rate, the present value of a known but undeveloped barrel in a big Middle East or Venezuelan reserve is zero, and these reserves can supply the world for well over a decade ahead. More oil produced today does not mean less available tomorrow, but only less to be left in the ground for the landlord —the host government—to take over when the lease is up. To be sure, the search for new deposits goes on at a high rate outside the United States, and will continue, for several reasons. Refiners with crude deficits, consuming corporations, and even companies with more oil than they expect ever to use, keep exploring because new discoveries may yet have lower discovery-development-production-transport costs than the old deposits have development-production-transport costs—Libya is the outstanding example—or to seek diversification of supply and a better bargaining position against their host governments, or because they would rather have a new concession themselves than let newcomers have it, even at the expense of unneeded development (22).

The scramble of companies and governments to get into oil discovery reflects the universal belief that the total cost of newfound oil will be less than the current price—and it is not for me to say they are wrong.

Must the oversupply of oil reserves be considered as a waste? A very tentative answer would be no, though I confess to some trouble even formulating the question. First, given the tremendously skewed size distribution of oil deposits, much or nearly all the oversupply was really due to chance, not overinvestment. Second, one hesitates to classify as waste the new reserves which transformed our ideas of oil availability and made it clear that oil was now like coal, and that there was enough low-cost liquid fuel available to let costlier and less convenient fuels go by. It is no answer to the question, but does help to give us perspective, to recall that exploration expenditures are quite a small part of total investment on production—again, outside the United States. Even, therefore, if we did regard over-investment in exploration as waste, it could not be large. And as indicated earlier, there has not been any considerable over-investment in development as a whole, although there has almost surely been some in mal-distributed development.

As for the effects on income distribution, the present system certainly gives the operators and the host governments, taken together, much more than they would get in the fully competitive case, though even in that case there would be some very large rents. But whether it makes income distribution more or less unequal is hard to say, if only because the producing countries are so unlike—the per capita income of Kuwait exceeds that of the United States. But not only do we not know the effect on income distribution; we do not know to what use the money is being put, even though it is now the major fraction of profits, and is at the rate of over $2 billion annually, and increasing—a far bigger chunk of foreign aid than what they quarrel about today in the developed world.

The final aspect of efficiency is in the impact on competing fuels, a process brought into sharpest focus today in Western Europe. At current prices, unquestionably there is a social loss in using costlier coal instead of cheaper oil. But Europe does not yet believe in the permanence of current prices. Putting aside the perennial popular notions that the big bad companies or the big bad Soviets are sharpshooting to put nice people out of business, there are some respectable official and unofficial studies contending that oil prices are going to rise through 1970–1975 (5, 14, 31, 34 and incorporating others, less easily available, by reference). My own estimate, that oil prices will not only not rise but even go lower (1, OPLR) must be treated so far as heresy. But the analytical disagreement only concerns what fraction of European coal can in fact exist without subsidy or protection, and the policy debate is over how much ought to be kept for security: how much uneconomic coal capacity is on the way out, how soon. To many Europeans the progress here is maddeningly slow or dangerously fast. But either way, to an American it is cause for envy that the problem is in the open: how best to close out high-cost facilities and transfer people from disguised work relief to productive employment. Considering the inherent difficulties of estimation, the costs of transfer, and finally a security problem even more pressing than in the United States, European fuel policy is far ahead of our own.

Finally, there is nuclear energy for electric power. The wheels are already in motion and for better or worse a large construction program is under way all over the world. According to the Atomic Energy Commission, nuclear plants can compete with coal and oil (see table 2.1) (10).

There have been repeated past disappointments over nuclear power and it is doubtful that anybody knows what it really costs because of the foggy nature of plutonium "by-product" credits. As weapons production is cut back, the price of enriched uranium is expected to rise, thus raising nuclear fuel costs (10). But taking AEC figures as solid, power from oil would now and for long continue to be cheaper. In Boston, an area of high fuel costs, fuel oil could at current prices and tanker rates be landed from Venezuela at under $1.75 per barrel if it were not for restrictions on residual fuel oil imports, even putting aside crude oil quotas. Residual fuel oil quotas have no slightest basis in national security; they are political muscle (33). It is a bit anomalous to calculate that nuclear energy is economic because conventional fuel costs are high in certain areas when it is merely another arm of the government which is keeping them high. And indeed what is the use of protecting the high-cost portion of the coal industry with import quotas if they are to lose the market anyway to nuclear power?

Table 2.1

Nuclear plant			Competitive with fossil fuels costing		
Size (MW)	Starting	Operating	Cents/million BTU	$ per barrel (fuel oil)	$ per short ton (coal)
500	1967	1972	36.2–43.2	2.21–2.64	9.50–11.15
500	1972	1977	27.2–35.1	1.66–2.14	7.10– 9.20
1,000	1980	1985	21.1–26.1	1.29–1.59	5.53– 6.81

It is possible, however, that nuclear power costs are considerably lower than the AEC figures just quoted. Early in 1964 the news exploded in the trade of a private, non-subsidized nuclear plant to be installed by Jersey Central Power & Light, with equipment from General Electric. According to the Jersey Central calculations (18), cost equates with coal or fuel oil at 20 cents per million BTU, i.e., $5.24 per short ton, and $1.22 per barrel, respectively, far below prevailing prices. There are reasons to consider this a special promotional price, offered by General Electric to keep its nuclear engineering force and manufacturing facilities in being. First, the technology of the boiling-water reactor is well known and no striking innovations were either expected or announced. Second, General Electric has announced that future prices would be higher: comparable plants would eventually get as low as 23 cents per million BTU (= $6.02 per short ton, $1.40 per barrel), but only after the third nuclear fuel load was in. Initial costs were to be just under 28 cents (= $7.35 per short ton, $1.72 per barrel). If we assume a 10 percent discount rate, five years at 28 cents, five at 25.5, and five at 23 cents, the weighted average cost is 26.2 cents over the first fifteen years.[2] But even this more realistic figure is very low. Apparently basic reactor technology has not advanced, but important innovations have been made in fabrication, which have brought costs down considerably, though not as far as the Jersey Central costs.

Time will tell where in the present range of 24–28 cents the costs will settle. Moreover, the costs expected by Jersey Central assume a 20 percent excess of actual capacity above the guaranteed capacity of 515 megawatts. At the lower figure, it is clear, the nuclear plant has little advantage even for Jersey Central. For smaller capacities, the nuclear plant becomes rapidly and substantially more expensive. In some parts of the United States, distance plus high loads will make nuclear power competitive even at current technology and prices.

The Jersey Central report is at least as important for its current information as for its cost predictions. The company's current coal prices are around 29.5 cents per million BTU ($7.73 per short ton for coal, $1.80 per barrel for fuel oil). This is well below the prices ruling even as late as 1962. When considering the new plant, Jersey Central received firm offers of a long-term contract for coal at 26 cents ($6.80, equated to $1.59). Moreover, in accordance with informed opinion now (10), they expect coal prices at the mine to drop through 1980 because of new machinery and increasing concentration of coal output in the more mechanized and more productive mines. Moreover, although large savings in rail freight have already been realized by running trains of conventional hopper cars as units, an additional 15 percent reduction, or more, is expected when the new 100-ton special hopper cars come into operation, with some operating novelties which their use permits.

The reduced nuclear reactor prices may be much more important for Western Europe and Japan than for this country. Even at the more conservative estimate of 28 cents per million BTU, it is evident that the ceiling for heavy fuel oil in Western Europe cannot much exceed $1.74 per barrel, which is about what it now fetches in open-market sales, both at the North Sea ports and in the interior, thanks to the new crude pipelines leading to inland refineries. It is yet another nail in the coffin of most European coal.

If, therefore, we have to appraise the role of nuclear power up to now, then even if we supposed that no nuclear plant was worth building today, the investment in nuclear development has probably already paid off. For it was the railroads' and coal operators' fear of nuclear power that jolted them out of a self-pitying routine not unlike the independent oil operators', and led to the present delivered coal prices, which are expected to go even lower. Both coal and railroads were suffering a profit squeeze; they "deserved" and needed higher prices and profits in order to generate the funds needed to modernize and reduce costs to serve the national welfare and security . . . and so on. But the threat of losing markets coerced them into cutting costs to improve profits; and where there was money to be made, money was found. A great deal of United States coal, much more than one would have guessed only two years ago (up to the winter of 1962–63), is going to survive in the fuel market. I suspect the best judgment will in retrospect be that of the President of Rochester & Pittsburgh Coal Company who said that unless breeder reactors appeared, with coal at 25 cents per million BTU, coal would keep most of the increase in electric power output, while at 22 cents no nuclear plant would pay (25).

If oil prices continue indefinitely at present levels, and coal merely keeps pace, then in Boston the equality between fossil and nuclear plants is getting close. But if we consider the competitive supply price (including of course a development profit and substantial rents) at which oil could today be landed in Boston, nuclear plants would not be competitive even in 1980. (Even this, it must be stressed, is earlier than I expected late last year.) But looking that far ahead is not too rewarding. The market price, though I expect it to decline, will probably continue to be held above competitive supply price. And if I am mistaken, if governments of producing and of most consuming countries *do* succeed in maintaining present oil prices indefinitely (the oil companies can do even less to maintain prices in the future than in the recent past), then to be sure, a large-scale campaign aiming at plants in service even before 1975 is sensible, even though it is an economic waste. It will probably be undertaken in any case.

There is a second source of possible error in my estimate. Long-run incremental development cost is an increasing function of output in relation to reserves. I think the supply of oil in known deposits, available at the cost of development, is adequate to any likely demand over the next fifteen-odd years. But the longer the time period over which a forecast is made, the greater the probable error. I may well be wrong in assessing the complex supply-demand mechanism. This ought to be, but is not yet, the happy hunting ground of the econometricians.

Sometime after 1975, though in my opinion surely not before, the rate of discovery *may* fall so far behind production that replacement cost will again be positive, development costs will rise, and total supply price mount. *Nobody knows when or whether this will happen.* There should be respect and support for those who are trying seriously to understand the process of finding petroleum reserves, and to estimate future availabilities, but their gusses are not yet knowledge. Faced, therefore, with uncertainty about the future amount, and therefore the future unit cost, of petroleum, we might well wish to take out insurance and act as if sometime after 1975, though not before, the cost of fossil fuels will start going high enough to make nuclear plants widely competitive (see 29). If it is prudent to assume, though it is wrong to predict, a true scarcity, rising real costs, developing past 1975, then current nuclear developments of known technology ought to be de-emphasized in favor of intensive research on the new fast-breeder reactor techniques which promise much lower costs, but are much further from commercial operation. This would be insurance against the scarcity which may possibly come, not waste of resources adding to the plenty which is here today. But the actual prospect is for more duplication and hence increasing over-supply in the world energy market, especially the world oil market, with substantial economic wastes, and with a constant and politically dangerous struggle, among companies and governments over markets and between companies and governments over the division of profits. The time of trouble may be, not prevented, but perhaps mitigated. The world oil problem is political before it is economic, but the economist's contribution is not therefore contemptible, any more than the meteorologists advising the commanding general of what he can or cannot do, without presuming to say what he should or should not.

Notes

This paper is a revision of one given at the 1963 meetings of the American Economic Association, and appears here by permission of the President, George J. Stigler, and the Secretary, Harold F. Williamson. It is part of a project of research on the world petroleum market since World War II, supported by Resources for the Future, Inc. I have benefited by many suggestions and criticisms received from various individuals; but the usual disclaimer must be made with unusual emphasis —none of them necessarily agrees with any opinion expressed here, and the one thing they have in common is my gratitude: Leslie Cookenboo, Jr., P. M. Davidson, J. H. Ellender, R. J. Gonzalez, R. B. Heflebower, O. C. Herfindahl, R. J. Kruizenga, S. M. Livingston, P. W. MacAvoy, R. P. Manes, J. W. McKie, H. B. Steele, and, not least, the participants in a conference on economic aspects of conservation regulation, convened at Southern Methodist University on April 23–25, 1964, by Paul T. Homan and Wallace F. Lovejoy, whose forthcoming work deserves the most careful attention. They cannot all be named; I should like to mention just one of the participants, Robert E. Hardwicke of the Texas bar, to whom my indebtedness dates from correspondence many years back. Having contributed so much to current regulation, he might be pardoned for seeing only good in it, yet he has worked tirelessly for its improvement. He would agree with very little said here.

1. In an interesting paper appearing after this essay went to press, ("The Economics and Politics of United States Oil Imports," mimeographed), Mr. John H. Lichtblau estimates the possible displacement by foreign crude. Unfortunately, he calculates using either posted prices and AFRA (Average Freight Rate Assessment) tanker rates, which nobody today pays, or else small unexplained discounts and unexplained "typical spot rates." His prediction of higher freight rates with rising imports would at most hold only for the short time needed to build more tankers, and would never happen if imports rose gradually—e.g. by a million daily barrels a year. He thinks foreign crude prices would rise if the United States were open to imports. Experience in Europe and Japan has proved the contrary; competition resulting from greater sales opportunities has brought price down, not up.

Mr. Lichtblau argues against the procedure of multiplying the per-barrel premium, on exchanges of crude versus domestic oil, by total consumption (see appendix) because only about half the oil coming in is thus exchanged. This is irrelevant. The price at which a few shares of a stock sell today determines the value of every share. The amount buyers are willing to pay for the ticket to bring in a barrel of foreign crude applies to every barrel, even when they are lucky enough to get the ticket free of charge.

We agree on the need to exclude residual fuel oil imports, and to allow for pipelining costs of crude shipped inland (Appendix table 2A.2); also on a decline in domestic crude prices serving to limit imports.

2. A better estimate is 27 cents. See the excellent testimony of Philip Spern before the Joint Committee on Atomic Energy, 17 July 1964.

References

1. M. A. Adelman, *The Supply and Price of Natural Gas* (Oxford: Blackwell, 1962), cited as SPNG; "The World Oil Outlook," in Marion Clawson, ed., *Natural Resources and International Development* (Johns Hopkins University Press, 1964), cited

as NRID; "Oil Prices in the Long Run," *Journal of Business of the University of Chicago*, April, 1964 (translated with permission from *Revue de l'Institut Français du Pétrole*, December 1963), cited as OPLR.

2. *Administered Prices: A Compendium on Public Policy*, 88th Congress, 1st Session, Subcommittee on Antitrust and Monopoly of the Committee on the Judiciary, U. S. Senate, 1963. There are of course a few dissenters.

3. American Petroleum Institute, et al., *Joint Association Survey*, Part 1, *Industry Drilling Costs, 1961*; Part 2, *Estimated Expenditures and Receipts of the United States Oil and Gas Producing Industry, 1961* (1963).

4. Sir Maurice Bridgman, board chairman of British Petroleum, in addressing the American Petroleum Institute in November, 1963, estimated non-Communist non-United States excess producing capacity at 1.8 million barrels daily, which is 13 percent of mid-1963 output. It is only fair to indicate a disagreement; it is not this surplus which bears on the price, in my opinion, but the ability to expand it "enormously," as he puts it, in 12 to 18 months.

5. Comité de los Nueve, Alianza para el Progreso, *Evaluación del Plan de la Nación, 1963–1966, de Venezuela*, Septiembre de 1963, 100–104, actually expects 1960 prices, or possibly even higher.

6. Leslie Cookenboo, Jr., *Crude Oil Pipelines and Competition* (Cambridge: Harvard University Press, 1957).

7. Cf. Paul M. Davidson, "Policy Problems of the Domestic Oil Industry," 53 *American Economic Review* (1963). I world confine "user cost" to the finding stage. It is not logically wrong to apply it to development, but in my opinion it adds too little.

8. Warren B. Davis, "A Study of the Future of Productive Capacity and Probable Reserves of the United States," *Oil and Gas Journal*, February 24, 1958, p. 114, commits, I believe, the error of taking the supply of new crude oil as always a positive function of the price; this is unfounded, except under competition. [1, SPNG, 38–40]

9. *Electrical World*, 161 (May 4, 1964), p. 55.

10. Federal Power Commission, *National Power Survey*, Advisory Committee Reports No. 15, Table 1(b), and No. 21. Assumptions: 26.2 million BTU/short ton of bituminous coal, 40.7 million BTU/long ton of "residual" or heavy fuel oil, 6.65 barrels/long ton; f.o.b. Venezuela $1.55/barrel, transport cost 18 cents (Intrascale less 48 percent), which is higher than the current long-term rate because East Coast ports are not deep enough for large tankers. See also Philip Mullenbach, *Civilian Nuclear Power* (New York: Twentieth Century Fund, 1962), and my review in *Economica*, February, 1964, cited respectively as NPS and CNP.

11. Thomas C. Frick, ed., *Petroleum Production Handbook* (New York: McGraw-Hill, 1962), vol. 2, ch. 38, written by J. J. Arps.

12. Robert E. Hardwicke, *Antitrust Laws et al. v. Unit Operation of Oil and Gas Pools* (New York: A.I.M.M. & P.E., 1961, rev.).

13. ———— and M. K. Woodward, "Fair Shares and the Small Tract in Texas," *Texas Law Review*, 41 (1962), 75–102.

14. Haute Autorité de la Communauté Européene du Charbon et de l'Acier, et al., *Etude sur les Perspectives Energétiques à Long Terme de la Communauté Européene* (Luxembourg, 1962).

15. Paul T. Homan and Wallace F. Lovejoy, *Petroleum Conservation Regulation* (in preparation).

16. Interstate Oil Compact Commission, *National Stripper Well Survey* (annual, reprinted in various places, including [17].

17. Interstate Oil Compact Commission, *Compact Bulletin*, 20 (June, 1961), p. 81.

18. Jersey Central Power and Light Company, *Report on Economic Analysis of Oyster Creek*, 1964, especially Tables 1–3.

19. Wallace F. Lovejoy and I. James Pikl, eds., *Essays on Petroleum Conservation Regulation* (Dallas: Southern Methodist University, 1960).

20. Paul W. MacAvoy, *Price Formation in Natural Gas Fields* (New Haven: Yale University Press, 1962).

21. *Petroleum, the Antitrust Laws and Government Policy*, Report of the Committee on the Judiciary, U. S. Senate, 85th Congress, 1st Session (1957).

22. *Petroleum Press Service*, December, 1963, p. 445.

23. Petroleum Study Committee, *Conclusions and Recommendations*, submitted September 4, 1962, made public June 29, 1963, and reprinted in various places, including *Platt's Daily News Service, The Oil Daily, Petroleum Intelligence Weekly*, etc. The Committee professes itself unable to say whether the price reduction would be permanent, because (if I understand them properly) letting some competition into the system would eliminate all but a very few producers. The chances of this are small; but even if the whole industry were eliminated, it remains to be proved why the price would then go above the world price, unless the world industry can contrive discrimination against the United States. In fact, and regardless of whether it is politically desirable, freedom to import into this country would probably bring the world price down, not up. See (1, OPLR, 160). Or perhaps the Committee thinks than refining is unprofitable and can only exist at current prices through subsidies from production; if so, I must again disagree. But the hint is too brief for long discussion.

24. *Petroleum Survey*, Preliminary Report of the Committee on Interstate and Foreign Commerce, H. R. Report No. 314, 85th Congress, 1st session (1957).

25. Potter, Charles V., Pres. Rochester & Pittsburgh Coal Co: Informal talk before Washington Coal Club, digest in Coal Chronicle, May 1964.

26. State of Texas, Sixth World Petroleum Congress Committee, *Report to Hon. John B. Connally, Governor* (Austin, Dec. 27, 1963).

27. United Nations, E.C.A.F.E., *Formulating Industrial Development Programs*, 1961, Section 3.

28. ———, E.C.E. *The Price of Oil in Western Europe* (1955). M. G. DeChazeau and Alfred E. Kahn, *Integration and Competition in the Petroleum Industry* (Yale University Press, 1959), pp. 66–69, 375.

29. Sam H. Schurr, "Some Observations on the Economics of Atomic Power," (Kennecott Lectures, University of Arizona, 1963), which reads as well after as before Oyster Creek.

30. U. S. Department of the Interior, Bureau of Mines. *Annual Petroleum Statement*.

31. *Id.*, Office of Coal Research, *The Foreign Market Poetential for U. S. Coal*, 1963, Appendix C.

32. U. S. Department of Justice, *Report of the Attorney General* ... [on] *Interstate Compact to Conserve Oil and Gas*, 1963.

33. U. S. Office of Emergency Planning, *Memorandum for the President* [on residual fuel oil import], February 13, 1963.

34. *Untersuchung uber die Entwicklung der gegenwartigen und zukunftigen Struktur von Angebot und Nachfrage in der Energiewirtschaft der Bundesrepublik unter besonderer Berucksichtigung des Steinkohlenbergbaus* (Berlin, 1962), a report to the German Government, usually and mercifully referred to as either *Energie-Gutachten 1961* or the *Friedensburg-Bade Report*.

35. *World Oil*, February 15, 1964, p. 132, 134.

Appendixes: Some Rough Estimates of Waste in the United States Petroleum Economy

Appendix 1: Cost of Excluding Crude Oil Imports

The theory of this calculation is that foreign crude oil is available at United States East Coast ports at about $1.25 less than equivalent domestic crude; hence, if it were freely available, the price of both domestic and foreign crudes, and of their refined products, would tend to fall by about that much. Since imported residual fuel oil is not made from either domestic or imported crude, however, it must be excluded. It could be made available more cheaply by dropping the import restrictions on residual fuel oil, but that is a separate subject, briefly discussed in part III of the text. The imports of cheaper crude would displace much domestic crude, though—for reasons stated in the next appendix—not nearly as much as is usually supposed. If foreign crudes were to penetrate 450 miles inland, that would enable them to cover states accounting for over half of total consumption; this pipelining cost would in part offset the saving on cheaper foreign crude.

Table 2A.1
Cost of excluding crude oil imports

1	Total domestic consumption, million b/d	10.4
2	Less: residual imports, million b/d	1.0
3	Equals total domestic and foreign crude oil and natural gas liquids consumed, million b/d	9.4
4	Value of import "ticket," per barrel	$1.25
5	Crude pipelining cost, per barrel per 100 miles	.02
6	Maximum penetration of foreign crude needed to take half of domestic market (in miles)	450
7	Pipelining cost absorbed, per barrel	.09
8	Net premium on foreign crude, $1.25 less .09	$1.16
9	Total daily consumption from domestic and foreign crude (line 3 × 365 × $1.16)	$4.0 billion

Sources: Lines 1, 2, 6 from Bureau of Mines, *Annual Petroleum Statement*; Line 4 from (1 − NRID), line 5 [6], pp. 26–29.

Some variants on this approach are worth following up, though we lack the space to do so here. The premium on foreign crude is only about 90 cents at the Gulf Coast, since it costs about 35 cents to ship oil to the East Coast. (This charge, we may note in passing, is well above the competitive cost of moving oil, and is largely due to the restriction of United States coastal traffic to United States flag shipping which is far more expensive to build and operate. The result of this price support for shipping is two large-diameter pipelines built from the Gulf to the East Coast. This is another obvious waste, since tankers would be cheaper; but to oil companies it is the second-best.) There is little doubt that, if the Gulf Coast price fell by 90 cents and the more prolific fields were unitized and permitted to operate freely, none of them would need to shut down; but a great many small pools probably would.

Appendix 2: Avoidable Expense in United States Crude Oil Production, 1961

Marginal and Stripper Wells, Particularly Texas   In Texas there were on the average 92.5 stripper wells in 1961 producing 175 million barrels that year, 480 thousand b/d, 5.2 barrels per well per day.[1] Assuming that it is administratively impossible to regulate these wells,[2] we consider them en bloc, and assume that each produces at the 5.2 average. Assuming a wellhead value of $2.75/barrel, and daily operating costs of $5 (see below), the abandonment output, where operating cost just equals price, is 1.8 b/d. At

Table 2A.2
Hypothetical distribution of new district III oil wells, 1954–1961

Percent of wells		Number of wells (thousands)		Percent of capacity		Amount of capacity (thousands of barrels)	Capacity per well
Class	Cum	Class	Cum	Class	Cum		
17.0	17.0	18.3	18.3	47.0	47.0	1,888	103
14.1	31.1	15.2	33.4	24.9	71.9	1,000	66
11.7	42.8	12.6	46.0	13.2	85.1	530	42
[57.2	100.0	61.5	107.4	14.9	100.0	599*	10]
⌈ 9.7	52.5	10.4	56.4	7.0	92.1	281	27 ⌉
8.1	60.6	8.6	65.0	3.7	95.8	149	17
6.7	67.3	7.2	72.2	2.0	97.8	79	11
5.6	72.8	6.0	78.1	1.0	98.8	42	7
4.6	77.4	4.9	83.1	0.6	99.4	22	4
3.8	81.3	4.1	87.2	0.3	99.6	12	3
⌊18.8	100.0	20.1	107.4	0.2	100.0	—	— ⌋
[57.2	100.0	61.5	107.4	14.9	100.0	598*	10]

* Actual sum, 584; result of rounding.

an 8 percent decline rate per annum, time to abandonment is 14 years, cumulative output of the wells is 1,494 million barrels. This affords us an independent check on our calculations, since primary reserves, available at zero development cost—secondary reserves will cost money to develop —are publicly estimated at 1,672 million (16).

Initial year revenues at the same $2.75 barrel from the 175 million of production were $480 million per year. Assuming the same 8 percent decline rate, discounting at a safe interest rate of 5 percent per year, and 14 years, the present gross value of these reserves is $2.88 billion.

As against this, we must consider operating costs. There are some 400,000 strippers in the nation, but many of them are in Appalachia, producing less than half a barrel daily, which means that operating costs are around $2.35 per well daily (assuming $4.71 per barrel wellhead value) (28). This gives us some idea of the lower edge of the range. For wells generally, a national average is around $6.72 (table 2A.4), but this is of course distorted downward by the many strippers; a modal value for non-strippers seems to be around $10 daily, with much concentration around it; for shallow wells in the 2–4 thousand range, with no unusual problems, the variation seems to be between $3 and $7, so we may take $5 (11, p. 23). Hence, operating costs in 1961 for the Texas strippers were about $169

Table 2A.3
Calculation of development expenditures, 1961

1.	Development costs (2 *JAS*, p. 4)	2,070	$ million
2.	Producing costs, excl. taxes (ibid.)	1,455	"
3.	Overhead (ibid.), producing and development combined	457	"
4.	Overhead allocated to development (1 ÷ (1 + 2) × 3)	268	"
5.	Oil well drilling expense (1 *JAS*, 36)	1,087	"
6.	Total dry hole footage (ibid.)	73	million feet
7.	Total dry hole expense (ibid.)	774	$ million
8.	Dry wildcat footage (*World Oil*, February 15, 1964, p. 132)	37	million feet
9.	Development dry hole expense (7 − [8 ÷ 6) × 7])	386	$ million
10.	Oil plus gas development footage (ibid.)	113	million feet
11.	Oil development footage (ibid.)	83	"
12.	Oil development dry hole expense [(11 ÷ 10) × 9]	281	$ million
13.	Oil wells drilled (1 *JAS* 36)	21	thousand
14.	Oil plus gas wells drilled (ibid.)	27	"
15.	Equipping leases, oil plus gas (2 *JAS*, 4)	446	$ million
16.	Oil lease equipment expense [(13 ÷ 14) × 15]	346	"
17.	Oil overhead [4 × (13 ÷ 14)]	209	"
18.	*Total oil development expense* (5 + 12 + 16 + 17)	1,923	"
19.	Cost per new oil well (21,204, per *World Oil*)	91,450	"

Sources: *JAS, Joint Association Survey*: vol. I, *Industry Drilling costs*, 1961; vol. II, *Estimated Expenditures and Receipts of the U.S. Oil and Gas Producing Industry*, 1961 (A.P.I., I.P.A.A., M.O. & G.A., 1963).

million. Over 14 years, optimistically assuming no additional costs of workovers, nor increasing salt-water disposal, etc., again using a safe discount rate of 5 percent, and a 3 percent abandonment rate, present value of the expenditures to which these wells commit us is $1.39 billion. (The abandonment rate is of course much lower than the decline rate, which is to say that operating costs per barrel climb steadily as one approaches abandonment.)

The net present value of the Texas stripper reserves is then about $2.88 less $1.39 or $1.49 billion, and applying the usual 75 percent factor (11, p. 9), this comes to $1.12 billion net market value. Another check is possible here, in that this is 76 cents per barrel in the ground for stripper production facilities as a whole. This, I believe, is optimistic. Those interested in discrediting it as pessimistic should by all means sponsor a research project showing actual transaction prices, and methods of extending them to make estimates for all strippers. It is in their own interest to realize that

Table 2A.4
Calculation of oil producing costs per well, 1961

1.	Producing costs, oil plus gas, all wells	1,644	$ million
2.	Operating oil wells, total	594	thousand
3.	Operating gas wells, total	97	"
4.	Appalachian oil wells (Pennsylvania, New York, Ohio, West Virginia)	111	"
5.	Annual producing cost of Appalachian oil wells (Line 4 × $2.35 × 365)	96	$ million
6.	Operating oil wells (non-Appalachian)	483	thousand
7.	Annual producing cost, excl. Appalachian oil wells (Line 1−Line 5)	1,548	$ million
8.	Operating non-Appalachian oil wells as percent of all operating non-Appalachian wells [6 ÷ (2 + 3)]	83	percent
9.	Annual operating cost, non-Appalachian oil wells (Line 8 × Line 7)	1,281	$ million
10.	Cost per oil well per year (Line 9 ÷ Line 6)	2,655	"
11.	Cost per well per day	7.27	dollars

Sources: Line 1, *1961 Joint Association Survey*, part 2; Line 5, see text; all others from *Petroleum Facts and Figures*, 1963 edition.

statements that "they know otherwise from personal experience" carry not the slightest conviction to any disinterested observer.

If the additional $480 million of additional revenues were taken from the strippers and assigned instead to the other Texas wells, they would involve no additional development cost, and only a negligible increment to operating cost, because of excess capacity among nonmarginal wells. For stripper production in Texas was 19.9 percent of the total. Since the excess capacity in the Southwest (P. A. D. District III, using I. P. A. A. data) was about one-half of production and since it was by definition confined to non-strippers, the latter could have expanded output by 62 percent. For Texas, indeed, this is a substantial underestimate, since excess capacity is worse there (probably exceeding actual output) than for the whole of District III.

Therefore, the net gain to the non-strippers in the initial year would be $480 million clear, but the present value would be greater to them than to the strippers. For the non-strippers, who averaged about 21 barrels daily in 1961, are much further from their economic limit, or abandonment rate, than the strippers. Since they produce about four times as much on the average, and cost about twice as much, it would take them not 14 but 21.5 years to get to na abandonment rate twice as high. Hence, additional

Table 2A.5
Estimated expenditures for finding, developing and producing oil and gas in the United States, 1961 (in millions of dollars)

	Costs		Rents or profits
	Oil	Gas	
Exploration:			
Dry holes	388		
Lease acquisition			428
Geological and geophysical	280		
Land leasing, scouting	115		
Lease rentals			189
Other	65		
TOTAL, excl. ovhd.	848		617
TOTAL, incl. ovhd.	1,067		
Development:			
Producing wells drilled	1,087	537	
Development dry holes	281	105	
Equipping leases	346	100	
Overhead	209	59	
TOTALS	1,923	861	
TOTAL, oil plus gas	2,724		
Production:			
Producing costs	1,210	245	
Production taxes			346
Ad valorem taxes			195
TOTALS			541
TOTALS, oil plus gas	1,644		
Industry totals	5,435		1,158

Source: See tables 2A.2 and 2A.3.

revenues of $480 million annually, compounded as before at an 8 percent decline rate and 5 percent safe interest rate over 24 years, amount to $3.22 billion, and again applying the 75 percent factor, present value is $2.41 billion. Thus, if output were transferred, there would be a clear gain to the non-strippers of $2.41 billion, versus a loss to the strippers of $1.12 billion, a net gain of $1.29 billion for Texas.

Since Texas strippers account for 30 percent of national stripper production, it might at first sight appear that we ought to multiply this saving by 3.33 to approximate the national saving. This would, I believe, exaggerate because in some areas the non-marginal capacity is really not available to take up the marginal slack. Texas stripper production is about half of stripper production in District III; hence, a rough guess might be that the possible national saving was upwards of twice the Texas saving, or say 2.5 times $1.5 billion, roughly $3.75 billion of present value.

In other words, the State of Texas could levy a tax on the oil industry to pay off the strippers once and for all, and the industry would be money ahead. So could the other states, but one cannot put it as precisely.

However, this loss is only a minor part of the total cost of permitting stripper wells, since it is confined strictly to those already in existence. A much heavier cost results from everyone's knowing that a well producing 10 barrels daily or less is exempt and can produce to capacity. Hence, it is worth while to drill still more useless stripper or near-stripper wells. If we figure a well-head price of $2.75, a 10-barrel well brings in $27.50 in daily revenues; reckoning 25 cents for production taxes and perhaps trucking, if without pipeline connection, etc., and at the same $5 operating costs, 8 percent decline rate, 5 percent safe discount rate, and a 75 percent risk factor over the 21 years needed to reach the 1.8-barrel economic limit, the present value comes to $36 thousand. In Texas in 1961, there were approximately 4.139 wells, out of a total of 7,556 drilled, which cost that much or less to drill. (Our method of estimate is such that it yields a result biased downward.)[3] Hence, upward of 54.8 percent of all new oil wells in Texas could have been stripper wells.

Let us try to use another independent set of statistical fragments. In District III, during 1954–1962 (January 1), the net increase in capacity was 1,921 thousand barrels daily (MBD), according to the IPAA.[4] Cumulative District III output during those years was 11,945 million barrels;[5] hence, at an 8 percent decline rate the capacity lost was 2,095 MBD, and gross new capacity installed was (2,095 + 1,921) or 4,016 MBD. The total number of new productive oil wells completed in District III during 1954–1961, inclusive, was 107,357.[6] Thus, the average newly completed oil well had a capacity of 37.5 barrels daily. For the average to be so low, most wells had to be around 10 barrels daily. A rough check may be had by looking at Texas, where in March, 1961, the wells on discovery allowables, exempt from market-demand proration, were allowed 80 b/d (17). This was not capacity, nor most economic production rate, but only their basic allowable under the so-called Yardstick formula. Their capacity was really higher. True, the new District III wells drilled in 1954–1961 were not for the most part new-pool wells, which might to a mild degree bias their average capacity downward, though this is not necessarily true, especially since new pools in Texas tended to be so small.

At any rate, if 60 percent of the new District III wells averaged 10 barrels daily (and since few could have been below the average flow, few were above it), the other 40 percent had to average 85 barrels—not an implausibly high figure at all, in view of the Texas figures. On the other hand, if as few as 50 percent of the new wells averaged 10 barrels daily, then the other 50 percent averaged only 70 barrels daily capacity, which seems too low. I do not see any escape from an order of magnitude of over half the new wells being in the neighborhood of 10 barrels daily.

Let us try a different test with other Texas data. In mid-march there were 109 thousand wells in the "marginal" and "all other exempt" classes combined, producing 1,094 MBD. Subtracting the 92 thousand strippers and their production of 479 MBD, the exempt wells not classified as strippers numbered 19,000, their output was 515 MBD, or 27.8 barrels daily per well, on the average. Thus, 17 percent of all the exempted wells accounted for 47 percent of the output.

If the population of all new District III wells was no less skewed than the exempted Texas wells, and we would expect it to be more skewed since the exempted wells are such because the top of the distribution is cut off, and if we suppose this distribution held throughout all of the newly drilled wells, it would look as shown in table 2A.2.

It is clear upon inspection that the true distribution must begin to flatten off radically as the wells become smaller, and that few can have gone far below 10 barrels daily, for reasons just discussed. Hence, the true distribution must be closer to the lower classes lumped together in the bracketed line, the lower 57 percent of the wells averaging only 10 barrels daily. If we suppose that the flattening-off effect comes sooner rather than abruptly after the forty-barrel class, we may say that three rough but independent tests indicate that between 50 and 60 percent of the District III wells must have been in the neighborhood of 10 barrels daily initial capacity.

Superfluous Development in P.A.D. District III   Let us now get some idea of how much superfluous development drilling went on in P.A.D. District III (Alabama, Arkansas, Louisiana, Mississippi, New Mexico, Texas) during this period. As noted earlier, new capacity installed was 4,016 MBD. Since 1962 production was 4,450, and we assume 15 percent spare capacity needed, total capacity needed beginning 1962 was 5,115 MBD. Since District III started with 4,952 MBD capacity, the amount needed to be installed over these eight years was 2,252 (2,000 replacement plus 162 new). Subtracting this from the 4,016 actually installed leaves 1,764 MBD as superfluous capacity, or 43.8 percent.

But the proportion of superfluous wells must have been much higher than 44 percent, because of this same dispersion of well capacities. Again, let us use the dispersion among the exempt Texas wells: if the best 31 percent of all wells accounted for 72 percent of the capacity, interpolating back we can say that 22 percent of the new wells could have sufficed to produce the 56 percent of new capacity actually needed to satisfy demand. In short, about 78 percent of all new wells were superfluous.

It is difficult to say whether much less than 78 percent of all development expenditures were unnecessary. Presumably it must have been somewhat less, but even that is hard to tell. For, while many superfluous wells were small and relatively cheap, others were relatively expensive, possibly adding little or nothing to total capacity but still worth drilling because the incremental payout was sufficient. Moreover, the cost of a well is not at all proportional to its productivity. Perhaps the best we can do at this point is to speak only in terms of major fractions, and say that something like three-fourths of all new oil wells were superfluous, but that these may have accounted for no more than two-thirds of all development expenditures.

The appended table 2A.3 estimates that total United States development expenditures in 1961, for oil wells apart from gas—which undoubtedly introduces much inaccuracy—were around $1,911 million. This includes development dry holes, which are usually but in my view incorrectly included with exploration. Two-thirds of this amount would be $1,310 million; a similar proportion of oil producing expenditures would be $800 million, or a total of $2,110 million per year. During 1955–61, so far as we can tell from the *Joint Association Survey*, the expense totals changed relatively little in total and composition. Since there was a good deal of creeping improvement in the *JAS* reports, we are perhaps beter off, therefore, in taking the 1961 figures and multiplying by eight. Then the total waste of resources in those eight years was around $16 billion, assuming the level of output to have stayed where it actually was. If we look at development expenditures alone, it is apparent that when Mr. Halbouty said that well over half the new oil wells drilled in Texas were unnecessary, and had cost several billion dollars (1, NRID, 56), he knew what he was talking about.

An end to over-drilling, therefore, would bring annual savings of around $1,310 million in developing cost and $800 million in producing cost. These estimates tend to be biased downward. First, we have used a distribution of well capacities which is probably too flat, more equal than the true distribution, because ours was in effect topped off, the more productive wells removed because they were more productive. We have calculated the savings made possible by leaving the unnecessary wells undrilled and unproducing, but not the savings by drilling only the best possible ones, and producing only from them. Second, when too many wells are drilled, the economic limit, or abandonment rate per pool is correspondingly higher. Thus, if one well were drilled into a pool and it cost $10 daily to operate, it would last until daily output was worth no more than that amount; but two wells would need $20, and four wells would need $40. Oil which would still be worth producing with one well becomes too expensive to produce with more; and hence, overdrilling causes reserves to be abandoned sooner than necessary—obvious physical waste. Finally, if the cutback were made not by administrative fiat but by unitizing oil pools and then letting price do the job, many small wells would continue because they really were more economic than larger, more expensive ones. Price is simply a more precise and delicate selective mechanism than administration.

Summing up: the demonstrable savings are around $2.15 billion a year, but since the estimate is biased downward, we are not too far from the truth in saying in round unmbers that at these levels of output there are $2.5 billion a year; since crude oil output has in recent years been around 2.6 billion barrels annually, there are roughly no less than 85 cents to a dollar per barrel which could be saved by ceasing the present wasteful practices forced on the industry. The difference between two and a half billion dollars and four billion is essentially the additional saving on getting genuinely cheaper oil from abroad than can be produced non-wastefully at home. This is where the security problem enters.

Notes

1. According to (16) there were 90,893 Texas strippers the first of January, 1961, and 94,031 a year later.

2. This is not altogether justified; see (13), pp. 90–92.

3. (3) *Joint Association Survey*, Part 1, Table 32, interpolating linearly between the means of the fourth and fifth depth class, so that we include 194 of the wells in the 3,751–5,000 foot depth bracket.

4. IPAA, *Report of the Productive Capacity Committee*, respective years.

5. U. S. Bureau of Mines, *op. cit.*

6. *World Oil*, February 15, respective years.

3   Crude Oil Production Costs

The potential over-supply that has tended to depress crude oil prices for almost a decade is likely to persist for another 15 years. This is the minority view of an American who has devoted a good deal of time and thought to the economics of the oil business. He is Professor M. A. Adelman, professor of economics at the Massachusetts Institute of Technology, who presented his latest findings in a paper to the annual meeting of the American Institute of Mining Engineers on March 1 [1966].

Professor Adelman emphasizes the wide gap between crude oil prices, even the most heavily discounted, and production costs—which for the main Middle East producers he estimates may be of the order of 12 to 20 cents a barrel over the next 15 years. Oil men would comment that the gap seems wide because virtually the entire profit from world-wide integrated operations is imputed to the production stage of the business. Indeed, it is not uncommon for imputed profits from production (based on posted prices) to exceed total earnings, implying that downstream operations are conducted at a loss. It is scarcely necessary to point out that this peculiar and in many ways unsatisfactory cost-price structure is attributable to constant pressure by host governments for a larger share of the profits of the oil business.

Even though host governments take an ever-increasing share, the crude oil cost-price gap means that "it will pay, as it does now, not to buy from the abundant available supply, but instead to spend large amounts on exploration and development in the not unreasonable hope of recouping the investment and making a profit after even a few years of operation at current, or even much lower, prices." Looking ahead, Prof. Adelman accordingly envisages "a long price decline," though he himself describes this as a minority view. Those who do not agree with him might well argue

Reprinted from *Petroleum Press Service* (now *Petroleum Economist*) 33 (May 1966): 177–179.

that he underestimates OPEC's success during the past few years in under-pinning the structure of posted prices in the Middle East and that he takes insufficient account of the increasing pressure likely to be brought to bear on oil companies there (as in Venezuela) to reduce their discounts—i.e. to raise their selling prices. This pressure may prove very difficult to resist.

Cost Comparisons

This somewhat controversial view of the future course of the oil mar-kets emerges from a lengthy and valuable analysis of producing costs in four main areas—the United States, Venezuela, the Middle East and Africa. (The author's definitions are given in the accompanying panel and should be carefully noted.) It will not, of course, be news to the knowledgeable reader that the cheapest of these sources is the Middle East and the dearest the United States; the broad cost relationship is common knowledge. But Prof. Adelman's estimates serve to bring some rather vague notions of cheap-ness and dearness into sharper focus. Though he does not pretend that they are more than approximations, these estimates of comparative costs are worth examining in some detail.

They are made up of two elements—operating costs and capital, or development, costs. The author's estimates under the first heading [see author's definitions in Notes] are derived from U.S. experience and he thinks that they may err on the high side. As the following table shows, the average operating cost is put at 17 cents a barrel for the United States, 6.5 cents for Venezuela, 2.2–3.9 cents for the new African fields and 1.0–1.8 cents for the main Persian Gulf producers.

Much larger are the capital charges, or development costs. According to this author, the investment required to develop one barrel-per-day of capacity varies all the way from $3,250 in Texas (with a very large number of low-yielding wells) to just over $860 in Venezuela and to under $70 in Iraq. Translated into cost per barrel of oil produced, the capital charges vary between 138 cents a barrel in Texas and a mere 3 cents a barrel in Iraq. And when he adds the two elements together, Prof. Adelman arrives at total cost figures which range from 151 cents a barrel in the United States to 62 cents in Venezuela and right down to 4 to 10 cents in the Middle East.

These comparisons do not, however, tell the whole story. To complete the tale one needs to take account also of proximity to main markets, and of the freight advantage or disadvantage thus entailed. The value placed on proximity to market obviously depends on the level of freight rates as-

Table 3.1

	Operating cost (cents per barrel)	Development investment per initial daily barrel (dollars)	Development cost (cents per barrel)	Total cost (cents per barrel)
Area and Year(s)				
United States, 1961–62				
Texas	18	3,250	138	156
Louisiana	10	2,542	108	118
Total	17	3,155	134	151
Venezuela, 1962–64	6.5	863	55	62
Africa				
Libya, 1963–64	2.2	149	13[a]	15
Algeria, 1962–64	3.9	656	42[b]	46
Nigeria, 1964	2.7	590	28	31
Persian Gulf, 1962–64				
Iran	1.0	130	6	7
Iraq	1.2	69	3[c]	4
Kuwait	1.8	167	8	10
Saudi Arabia	1.5	160	8	10

a. Including 6 cents pipeline cost.
b. Including 10.7 cents pipeline cost.
c. No pipeline allowance since Kirkuk field has net transport advantages in pipeline outlet to East Mediterranean, and cost comparison is on Persian Gulf basis.

sumed, and Prof. Adelman assumes Intascale less 60 percent. This may seem rather low in relation to the current AFRA figure of Inta. less 41.8 percent for large tankers, but it accords fairly closely with what many observers would regard as the likely long-term norm for crude oil transport by mammoth tankers.

On this basis, U.S. and Venezuelan crudes enjoy a freight advantage over Persian Gulf crudes in western hemisphere markets of about 45 cents a barrel. On the same basis, the freight advantage over Persian Gulf shipments in West European markets amounts to 34 cents a barrel for Algerian crude, 30 cents for Libyan and 20 cents for Nigerian.

Taking this factor into acount, the author concludes that Libyan oil has the lowest average cost in the world and that Algeria is more or less on a par with the Persian Gulf. He adds the warning that "Nigerian production costs appear higher than Middle East plus freight advantage, but this is a statistical mirage since the spectacular 1963–65 discoveries are not yet reflected in the production statistics." And again: "Taking account of freight advantage, much Venezuelan output seems uneconomic, but the bulk of production there is as cheap as Middle East, or cheaper."

Costs in the Future

A question which concerns oil companies, consumers and governments alike is whether and to what extent costs are likely to rise over, say, the next 15 years. To fix an upper limit for such an increase Prof. Adelman makes "extremely optimistic" assumptions about the growth of oil consumption, though the summary of his paper does not reveal the growth rate assumed; he further assumes zero discoveries in order not to confuse development costs with discovery costs. In this situation the maximum strain would be imposed on existing fields. It would reduce the free world reserves-to-production ratio from today's figure of about 35 : 1 to something like 20 : 1 by 1980, and it would considerably increase total costs per barrel. (For this purpose no allowance is made for improved technology.)

The effect of intensive development of existing fields would not, however, be uniform. In the producing countries of the Persian Gulf the intensive development envisaged might raise costs per barrel as follows: in Iran from 7 to 10 cents; in Iraq from 4 to 6 cents; in Kuwait from 10 to 14 cents; and in Saudi Arabia from 10 to 13 cents. The increase would be much greater in the new African fields because known reserves there are very much smaller than in the Middle East.

Estimates of the cost increases likely to result from intensive development of existing fields help to determine what it is worth spending (from the narrow economic standpoint) on the search for new reserves. Prof. Adelman uses the term "maximum economic finding costs" to express the amount which it is worth spending to offset exactly the otherwise inevitable increase in development and operating costs as reserves in known fields become depleted. And he adds that "this concept of finding costs is a sufficient explanation for the paradox of crude-rich companies continuing to explore." (It does not follow, of course, that this is the sole explanation.)

The maximum finding cost for the rest of the world is set by long-run costs in the Persian Gulf, the cheapest source, plus freight advantage—assuming, of course, that trade is free. Including the economic finding cost, the author reckons that the long-term supply price—identical with long-term cost—for Persian Gulf crudes[1] is 15 to 20 cents a barrel. Adding on the freight advantage, the corresponding figures for the other countries considered are: 60 to 65 cents for the United States and Venezuela; 49 to

54 cents for Algeria; 45 to 50 cents for Libya and 35 to 40 cents for Nigeria. The fact that these figures are above current production costs in the Persian Gulf, in Africa and in much or most of Venezuela, concludes the author, "ensures the continuance of a strong exploration effort outside the United States, where it has been declining for 10 years."

The cost estimates in Prof. Adelman's paper may be open to detailed criticism from oil company sources: the producers are, after all, in possession of information not accessible to outside investigators. Since presenting his paper the author has himself become aware of certain slips in his calculations: e.g., of the fact that his figures for Iran do not include pipeline costs; equivalent to perhaps 2 cents a barrel. These are of little importance. He does not believe that if better cost data were provided they would invalidate his broad conclusions. And in this he is almost certainly right.

Notes

M. A. Adelman, "Oil Production Costs in Four Areas." The author has sent us a summary of his paper, which will be published in full by the American Institute of Mining Engineers later this month [May 1966].

Author's definitions: The estimates of costs are based on operating conditions and technology of the early 1960s; payments to governments are excluded. Cost is identical with the economist's "supply price."

Operating cost—Estimates were made of the producing capacity of non-marginal wells in the United States and operating expenditures were divided by capacity. Estimates were then derived for the rest of the world by assuming that operating cost per well increases as the square root of capacity. Rough tests suggest that the estimates may be high but the absolute amounts, outside the United States, are small.

Development cost—Development cost, or break-even price, is the necessary return on development investment, or cost of capital per unit. Rate of return is that available on the best alternative investment, allowance made for risk. Development cost per unit is the development investment divided by the number of present-barrel-equivalents to be obtained.

1. He assumes an average growth rate of demand for Persian Gulf crudes of 13.4 percent annually in 1965–75 and of 4.2 percent annually in 1975–80.

4

Economics of Exploration for Petroleum and Other Minerals

The little we know about the economics of mineral exploration is important. Exploration is only one of the several methods of increasing supply, which all compete for scarce capital funds. This substitution makes a mineral industry stable. Steady supply does not depend on a few lucky throws of the dice, but rather on a continuing game played incessantly for small stakes and occasionally for large. The odds have so far been pretty consistently in favor of the human race.

Today as ever, we hear cries of alarm (or murmurs of delight) about impending mineral scarcity. We need not take them all seriously. When the British National Coal Board predict a shortage of fossil fuels in the year 2000, arguing that one should therefore continue to use high-cost British coal and save lower-cost fuel available elsewhere, they are trying to convince themselves and the public that they are earning their keep in a useful occupation. In fact they are pensioners, wards of the state. But even recent sober and disinterested warnings of "affluence in jeopardy" (Park, 1967) are vague on the effects.[1] The problem was posed very well 17 years ago in the United Sates, by the Paley Commission: "exhaustion is not waking up to find the cupboard is bare, but the need to devote constantly increasing efforts to acquiring each pound of materials from natural resources which are dwindling both in quality and quantity.... The essence of the materials problem is costs."

The Paley Commission noted the tendency for mineral prices to decline, but: "... this downward trend in real costs may be stopped or reversed tomorrow—if indeed this has not already occurred" (Anonymous, 1952, pp. 13–14).

In fact, far from this reversal having already been under way in 1950, real prices—i.e., adjusted for changes in the general price level—have

Reprinted from *Geoexploration* 8 (1970): 131–150.

generally continued to fall since 1950 (Potter and Christy, 1962; Barnett and Morse, 1963; and see below). The sharpest price drop has been in the mineral whose current visible reserves are the smallest in relation to current output. At the Persian Gulf, the greatest crude oil supply source, the real price is down by roughly 80 percent since World War II (Adelman, 1970).

This is the basic paradox of mineral economics. At any given moment, man is running down his limited stock of minerals, and running up the cost of their extraction. Yet as time passes real costs and prices fall more often than they rise. Scarcity threatens but recedes, because the threat leads men not to moan but to act. Conscience makes no cowards of us all, but rather inspires to "enterprises of great pith and moment," not of great variety.

Depletion of Mineral Stocks

The economic theory of mineral deposits has been that of a non-renewable inventory.[2] The problem, whether for an individual firm or for anyone concerned with public policy, becomes: the best time profile of use. This depends on the price and extraction cost expected to rule at each moment of time in the future, and on the rate of interest or discount which equates a future value to a present value. The stock should be used at such a rate over time as to maximize its present value.

This theory is logically sound, but it appears less useful the more we learn the nature of the inventory. The distinction between renewable and non-renewable resources is tenuous and perhaps in the last analysis untenable. Timber is called renewable and coal exhaustible. But look at the ancient Mediterranean. The hills overlooking the sea were stripped of trees by goats and men seeking food, fuel, and building material. Farm and pasture land dwindled as the topsoil washed off the hills into rivers and bays, the harbors silted up, and towns were destroyed as the sea moved away. The timber and all that went with it were not renewable. As for coal: in the United States and for the world at large, there seems not the slightest chance that we will ever run through what we now have. Two examples do not prove or disprove a theory, but they do suggest that we had better look more carefully at the economic process of mineral exploitation.

The Phases of Mineral Exploitation

Extraction   Extraction is the application of facilities in place to a designated in-ground stock. This is the short run, where variable costs are very low in relation to the price. It takes a strong price rise or fall to raise or cut output, especially because operators are reluctant to stop production and then start it up again. (Lead is an exception: see Heineke, 1969.) Moreover, short-run demand is also unresponsive to price. Most metals and fuels are only a small part of the total production cost of the products in which they are embodied. Even motor gasoline directly consumed by individuals is only a small part of the total cost of automobile transport. Moreover, metallic minerals are embodied in durable goods, which are often subject to severe fluctuations in demand and output. The result is a pattern of strong short-run price fluctuations. Hence producers and users alike have found it expedient to contract for much output in advance, at a known price, in the well-founded expectation that the swings will cancel the roundabouts.

Extraction with given facilities is therefore dominated by the problem of managing a given in-ground inventory. But extraction is by nature a decreasing flow, hence a disappearing problem. As soon as we consider investment, new variables dominate.

Development   What counts for the future of any mineral industry is whether expected prices will justify new investment to develop further the deposits now being worked. Development cost per unit is that amount which if paid for each unit as produced would pay operating cost and generate a barely sufficient rate of return on the investment, i.e., would pay the cost of capital. Expected extraction outlays should be reduced to a present value, and then treated as an investment cost (Adelman, 1970).

If the cost of development-plus-extraction were expected to be constant, and the price afforded some surplus over cost, one would be best advised to develop the mineral as fast as possible, and not defer the receipt of income. Owners would vie with each other in investing and increasing output, until overproduction brought the price down with a resounding crash and many of them had to stop producing. This does not generally happen. Let me say emphatically of crude oil that it does not happen except where (in the United States) a very peculiar legal system makes it happen. What does happen is: costs rise as more and more of the deposit is exhausted. As the cost rises to equal price at the margin, there is a cutoff to a additional development. This cut-off serves to stabilize the industry.

In the particular case of a petroleum reservoir, the damping effect of rising costs is somewhat stronger because when more wells are drilled into a pool, well "interference" decreases the output of the pre-existing wells.

Rising costs *within* any given deposit are reinforced by a more important effect. At any given moment, and with any given stock of knowledge concerning deposits and methods of extraction, it is rational economic conduct to exhaust the lower cost sources before the higher cost ones. Hence additional development investment is slowed by the friction of rising cost.

Rising cost for higher output from more investment not only stabilizes expectations and prevents overproduction, but also gives an incentive to learn of new deposits. A new deposit available at a *total* cost, of finding-plus-development, which is less than the incremental development cost of an existing deposit, is a net saving. The increase in development-extraction cost can therefore be called the Maximum Economic Finding Cost (M.E.F.C.). It measures the incentive for knowing more, which equals the penalty for not learning more.

But the search for new deposits is only a special case of the search for greater knowledge, including better productive methods. The French have a feeling for words, and when they use *recherche* to mean both research and exploration, they are conveying a truth we cannot afford to overlook. Greater knowledge of the earth's crust and greater knowledge of the science and technology of extraction are only two exercises of the human spirit, two alternatives for investment.

Relation of Output, Reserves, and Mineral-in-Place

This brings us to the nature and measurement of the mineral stock itself, as known at any given moment. Out knowledge is painfully imprecise, but it does suffice to serve as a check on our theory (Blondel and Lasky, 1956). The basic fact is that only a small percentage of the mineral-in-place, usually called "reserves," is actually committed or known to be worth committing. We cannot tell precisely how large is the total mineral-in-place, because the knowledge costs money which is not worth spending until additional committed reserves are needed. And as the reserves are depleted, the choice is forever present: invest to develop reserves further out of the known deposits, or seek new ones.

Crude oil   In the United States, annual crude oil production is about three billion barrels, "proved recoverable reserves" about 30 billion, oil-in-place about 300 billion barrels.[3] I cannot emphasize too strongly that the 300 billion represents conventional crude oil deposits *now* known and now or previously exploited. It has nothing to do with deposits "to be discovered," nor with oil shales. Untold confusion has resulted from not understanding the difference between reserves, the fruit of past development expenditures, and total oil-in-place, most of which is never impounded into reserves. One often reads of new reserves being "discovered," or that "we need to discover" some given amount of reserves in some given time. In fact, reserves are never found, only oil-in-place; reserves are only developed. How many of the undeveloped 270 billion barrels of U.S. crude oil will some day become reserves depends on expected prices and costs.

The oil industry is forever making many decisions whether to drill within the limits of a given reservoir, or extend it, or venture modestly into the unknown by looking for new horizons in an old pool; or seek new pools in the same field: or risk more and perhaps profit more by looking for a new field.

This choice is illustrated dramatically in the American statistics. Of the new reserves developed during 1946–1950, 80 percent were from newly-discovered oil-in-place. By 1961–1965, the percentages were reversed; only one-fifth of the new reserves from discoveries, the rest taken from previously known fields. Many small scrubby fields continue to be found —a burden not an asset to my country—but few of respectable size, and the annual additions to oil-in-place have dwindled since about 1950. Yet real prices have not risen, nor costs (at least not through 1963) (Adelman, 1967). The cost calculations are not precise, but they are confirmed by the evidence on new techniques[3] (National Petroleum Council, 1967).

Outside the United States one should not expect oil-in-place to be ten times proved reserves, since fewer fields have been abandoned as uneconomic. In Canada the relation seems on the order of five to one, in the Persian Gulf perhaps four to one (Torrey et al., 1963). Since Persian Gulf proved reserves are about 65 times annual output, indicated oil-in-place there is roughly 250 times annual output—I would guess at something a little lower (Adelman, 1970, ch. 1).

Iron ore   Since World War II there have been some large new discoveries in Canada, Venezuela, and of course Australia. But ore bodies known long before have probably furnished the larger part of the new known ore-in-place and new reserves. When my country was girding up its loins for the effort of World War II, it was feared that the stepped-up wartime consumption would lead us very close to exhaustion. Real iron ore prices (allowing for general price level changes) rose in the U.S. through the mid-1950s; since then they have declined and are at pre-World War II levels (Mancke, 1969). Outside the United States, production has tripled since 1946, but delivered prices to Europe are down since 1957 from 35 to 65 percent among the three biggest suppliers to the Common Market (Annual Reports E.C.S.C.). The principal reason was a great though non-measurable increase in reserves, partly out of new discoveries and partly from existing deposits which improved upon acquaintance. By 1963, world "reserves" (meaning largely ore-in-place) were estimated at $3 \cdot 10^{11}$ tons, enough for 300 years (U.N. Economic Commission for Europe, 1966, p. 5). They are much larger today, thanks partly to Australian finds. Of course this lumped together ore of widely differing qualities, just as do oil-in-place and even proved reserves: ore rich enough to be directly usable in blast furnaces or needing beneficiation; ore near the surface or needing underground mining; ore easily accessible near the coast or in distant hard-to-reach locations, etc.

Unfortunately, mineral reserves tend to be classified in two dimensions only loosely related to each other: (a) degree of precision, as when the U.S. Geological Survey classifies iron ore reserves as "measured," "indicated," and "inferred," and (b) cost of development, which is the relevant economic variable.

Iron-ore reserves are also estimated more narrowly in some American States for tax purposes; properties blocked out through drilling and other development work are assessed at a higher figure, which is type (b). This does not result in "understating" reserves.[4] On the contrary, it offers a meaningful definition: ore bodies which have been prepared for extraction by investment in facilities. It thus corresponds loosely to proved recoverable reserves of oil. Separate study would be needed to judge the precise meaning and quality of these data. But we must avoid the common error of calling ore reserves "conservative" or "understated." The in-ground inventory prepared by investment in facilities can only be a minor fraction of mineral-in-place.

The U.N. Economic Commission for Africa distinguishes reserves: (1) recognized and in production; (2) recognized deposits for which production plans have been or are being drawn up; and (3) no extraction envisaged at present and not necessarily of economic interest (U.N. Economic Commission for Europe, 1966, p. 89). Thus (1) would correspond to proved reserves of oil, or to taxable reserves in Minnesota, (2) to what might be called probable reserves and (3) to the remaining mineral-in-place in known deposits, ruling out future discoveries. In the Soviet Union, what are classified as "industrial reserves" (denoted $A + B + C_1$) are "used as basis for financing the construction of new mines and the expansion of existing mines." Perhaps they correspond to the two first classes of the U.N.E.C.A.[5] It is interesting that in 1941 the Soviet Union had only 5 billion tons estimated industrial reserves, and 100 billion in the mid-1960s, despite the interim consumption. Beyond "industrial reserves" is about an equal amount of "promising" reserves and beyond them about twice as much in respect of classes "marginal" and "estimated" (U.N. Economic Commission for Europe, 1966, p. 229).

Australia provides a classic example. In 1939 an embargo was imposed on iron-ore exports, in order to prevent the early exhaustion of about 450 million tons, probably none of it worth extracting because it was in the interior and needed costly rail transport. In 1960 export of up to 50 percent of newly found ore was permitted. By 1965 resources were guessed at about 10 billion tons (today doubtless much more) and they will be mined and used and sold to the benefit of all concerned (U.N. Economic Commission for Europe, 1966, p. 98).

Outside Australia, a very large part of what are now "reserves" exposed and planned for production owe their economic though not their physical existence to great improvements in beneficiation developed since World War II. In the United States, the increase in reserves has been particularly linked to new processes which made it possible to use some of the taconite ore which had tantalized the industry for a century.

Other Minerals: The "Dollar Threshold"

In any given solid mineral deposit, the cumulative content seems to increase geometrically as the richness decreases. If there is a fair degree of uniformity among deposits, one may perhaps generalize such a relation to the whole resource-in-place in deposits now known. In copper, the relation approximates $C = Ke^{-ar}$, where C is cumulative content, K a limiting value of about 10^9 tons, r is percent metal content at the margin, and a is a constant equal to about 0.8 (Anonymous, 1952; Brooks, 1967). (This relates to the metallic content of known deposits, not "future discoveries.") Thus about one-fifth of the total stock is in deposits of over 2 percent metal; about 45 percent in deposits of over 1 percent: two-thirds in deposits of over .5 percent. The precison of these estimates is in my opinion only apparent, but the relation is basic. In consequence, a technical advance tends to unlock a very large increment to the resource-in-place which can be developed into reserves at current development costs. In addition to taconite and copper (Herfindahl, 1959, pp. 207–227) a less important example is mercury (Rohlfs, 1969).

In the United States, coal reserves have sometimes been directly though very loosely classified by development cost characteristics. Reserves exploitable at 1960 prices were estimated at 20 billion tons (40 years' production), with another 15 billion available at roughly a 6 percent higher price (elasticity roughly 12.0). Over twenty times as much was available in lower grades (S. G. Lasky in N.F.E.S.G., 1962).[6] Uranium resources have been estimated similarly. The International Atomic Energy Authority reckons that there are about 750,000 tons "reasonably assured" as minable at $10 per pound or less. Another 600,000 tons are "conservatively estimated" minable at under $10; 900,000 tons are available at $10 through $15, and much larger amounts at lower grades (Spinrad, 1969). For the United States, the recent increase seems rather astonishing. At the start of 1969, reserves were estimated as 160,000 tons minable at no more than $8 per pound. By the end of the year this figure was 200,000 tons and the A.E.C. estimated that an additional 40,000 to 50,000 would be added because "drilling has produced a backlog of unevaluated information." Although the A.E.C. speaks of "actual reserves" they are obviously referring to indicated deposits or to probable reserves, which would mean probably to be developed. For they reckon an increase of over 50 percent in the under-$8 class in the one year. But there has been no such increase in productive capacity, as the A.E.C. itself stresses. A few years ago, "potential resources" were reckoned at 350,000, now about 600,000, again a much larger amount than what are called reserves, which in turn appear like an aggregation of cumulative expected output (Faulkner, 1969).

It would be very desirable if the method used for estimating coal and uranium reserves could be applied to other types of minerals, since the prospective development cost is the key to how much and what part of the resource-in-place we may expect to see used in the near future. But of course a rational method or approach does not in itself give us good statistics, for the range of error in the estimates is very wide and the unknowns too great to make the reserve figures anything but rough approximations (Anonymous, 1965).

Transport

Whether a deposit is worth developing at a given price depends not only on development-extraction cost, but also transport cost. Most minerals are found a long way from where it is most economic to process or use them: transport costs may swamp development costs. Here too we have had dramatic change. On the morrow of World War II the rate allowed by the British Ministry of Transport gives a rough indication of the supply price of oil tanker transport. From the Persian Gulf to Melbourne it was about U.S. $7.15 per long ton. For the past two years long-term ship hire contracts for 250,000-ton ships, which are far from being the largest, and seem destined to be the workhorses of the tanker fleet, are being written at rates which allow the voyage to be made for no more than $2.50 per long ton (Adelman, 1970). I do not refer to single-voyage rates nor the so-called AFRA rate nor any meaningless jumble of old with new charters and single-voyage rates with long-term rates, but rather to the availability at any given time of long-term contract service. Since the general price level has approximately doubled, the real price of oil transport has declined by about 80 percent in the past 25 years. Other minerals transport is now rapidly moving from general cargo to bulk carrier vessels: the tons of iron ore, bauxite, and coal they carried increased by respective factors of 5, 5, and 16 during 1960–1968. Bulk carriers now transport 81 percent of iron ore, 67 percent of the coal, 60 percent of the bauxite (Manners, 1967; Fearnley and Egers, 1969). The size composition of the fleet is shifting rapidly upward. Bulk carriers are not as large as oil tankers and cannot therefore go as cheaply, all things being equal. A 75,000-ton bulk carrier costs about twice as much to operate per ton mile of cargo as a 225,000 tanker. But other things are not necessarily equal. The combined ore-oil or ore-bulk-oil carriers allow backhauls and triangular or quadrangular voyages at lower costs. This amounts to a substantial rearrangement of mineral deposits favoring those of lower cost but much farther away and bodes well for Australia. (The British Iron and Steel Federation could only learn their economics the hard way. Never is resistance to reason more strong than when dressed up with computers, linear programming, and statistical simulation (Wilsher, 1965).) Moreover, loading and unloading of both oil and ore is to some extent already by-passing harbors to take place in the sea, favoring even larger ships and cheaper transport. But the extent of this change remains to be seen.

To sum up: the production of minerals is not the exploitation of a fixed stock which must be husbanded by balancing present against future needs, and replenished for fear of exhaustion. We deplete the small economic portion, a quantity approximately estimated, of a very much larger resource, of which our knowledge trails off rapidly. The rising cost of depleting the known proved and probable reserves generates more knowledge both of the occurrence of new deposits and of better ways to exploit and transport them. We see the visible part of an iceberg. It can and sometimes does roll over to expose another topmost portion.

Seen as an economic activity, exploration is only one member of a large family, one method among many toward cheaper mineral production. Small advances in knowledge occur all the time, bringing small dividends in cost reduction: large advances in knowledge, including knowledge of new deposits, come occasionally.

Search for New Mineral Stocks

It follows from what has just been said: exploration is *never* for minerals as such, *always* for cheaper minerals. To speak of need without mentioning price is to say nothing.

Most calculations of huge wealth in the ground are therefore irrelevant. In the United States, there are trillions of barrels of oil locked up in the shale deposits of the Rocky Mountains. A conservative estimate of oil content, multiplied by a conservative estimate of price, equals many billions of dollars. But given 1970 technology U.S. shale oil deposits are worth what they were with 1920 technology: less than nothing. The cost of extracting the oil exceeds the price, which is to say the cost (including return on investment) of using up resources to procure it from another source. The same drab story is told in Scotland, France, and South Africa.

In the United Nations, there is today much earnest debate over the exploitation of the seabed and its untold riches. Ownership and jurisdiction over exploitation will be eloquently argued for many a year. We might recall, however, that sea water can be processed by anyone with access to the oceans anywhere, and that there is enough gold dissolved in sea water to make any nation rich and solve the world's balance-of-payment problems. But so costly is extraction that nobody is trying to monetize the oceans' gold.

Offshore oil exploration and development is cheaper, per unit of what is found and developed, than onshore. The industry is being drawn not pushed into the sea (Weeks, 1969). But as for other mineral resources on or underneath the ocean floor, the old proverb warns against selling the bearskin before shooting the bear.

Investment in Exploration and Development

Exploration is a search not for disappearing minerals, but for cheaper minerals: an investment, where outlays today need to be weighed against future and therefore uncertain returns.

Unfortunately, data on past exploration investment are very scanty, and estimates of "required" future expenditures are not to be taken seriously. In the United States for iron ore, copper, lead and zinc, and gold and silver we have only expenditures on exploration and development combined, and that only for the years 1954, 1958, 1963, and 1967 (Preston, 1960).[7] From another source, it would appear that in the United States, 98 percent of all exploration expenditure if for crude oil and gas; 96 percent of land acquisition outlays; 92 percent of developments costs. If we use American companies operating outside their country as a sample of world-wide activities—we have no other statistics—the corresponding percentages are 99, 98, and 90.[8] Geophysical exploration expenditures are 95 percent petroleum outside the United States (excluding the Communist blocks) and 97 percent inside (Tucker, 1968; Hood and Kellog, 1968). World exploration and development spending are overwhelmingly in petroleum.

For the United States it is possible to reckon exploration expenditures on oil and gas combined over the past ten years, though not before (Adelman, 1967).[9] Outside the Communist blocs and North America, petroleum exploration-plus-development expenditures were about U.S. $2,550 million annually in 1967 (Annual of the Chase Manhattan Bank). What is designated by C.M.B. as "exploration expense" is too low because it excludes exploratory drilling and too high because it includes lease rentals. In fact, the global figure of exploration-plus-development is too high because it includes payments for the right to explore and drill in any given place. To the oil company, lease bonus and lease rental payments are an after-the-fact expense, like an income tax; but they are a transfer payment not a cost; not a tribute paid to nature but a sharing of profits. Lease bonuses or lease rentals are a sharing of hoped-for profits, income tax a sharing of past profits. We will consider them a little later.

In a few countries, it is possible to calculate oil development investment, per unit of new capacity added. In the principal producing concessions of the Persian Gulf it costs up to $125, mostly less, to develop a daily barrel of additional production in a known reservoir. It is not possible to calculate oil exploration outlays. Australia is a welcome exception in publishing both types of outlays, but data are lacking to convert them to unit cost or to investment per unit of new added capacity.[10] Expenditures on geophysical work have only recently begun to be estimated very approximately, depending in part on rather coarse estimating factors. Thus a crewmonth is assigned a given cost, whether on land or sea; and expenses of playback and interpretation are calculated as a global percentage of field expenses. We have no right to complain of what some people are giving us as a labor of love, but better information would seem worth paying for. At any rate, geophysical expenditures outside North America were $420 million in 1967 (Tucker, 1968, p. 88), but we have no way of estimating the cost of exploratory drilling, except in certain areas (Adelman, 1970).

Outside the United States, we lack information not only of inputs (exploration expenditures) but also of outputs (newly found oil-in-place). For the United States we have good estimates made available in recent years (see note 9). One can draw a limited but important conclusion: in contrast to development cost, real finding costs in the United States must have risen very quickly since the early 1950s, even allowing for the complication of joint supply of oil and gas. As indirect evidence, we have the econometric study of my colleague Fisher (1964). He showed that in 1946–1956, all else being equal, the fewer the exploratory wells drilled, the larger the average reserves (a proxy for oil-in-place) of new discoveries. The number of wells declined after 1956, but the average size decreased substantially. I would interpret this as meaning that "all else" had changed very much, in that the stock of good prospects had dwindled.

One reason for our confidence in the accuracy of the U.S. data derives from the law of large numbers. The new oil-in-place is in many very small fields. But in general, when a very large accumulation is found, there is great difficulty in estimating its extent, and the likelihood of finding more pools on or near the same geological structure. This appears to be true of minerals generally. The contents of a given discovery may not be known until after many years of development. Only then can we tell what the mineral body was "worth" over and above what it cost to develop and produce it. In 1944, the oil reserves to be developed in the four principal Persian Gulf countries were estimated by a highly competent authority at 16 to 21 billion barrels; by 1968, those fields had already produced 26 billion, with many times that amount in 1968 reserves (Adelman, 1970).

The Idea of Finding Cost

So far, we have spoken of exploration inputs (expenditures) and outputs (discoveries), but only skirted the central idea. Exploration is a probing of the unknown in various places. The cost in any one place has only limited economic meaning, since the search would never have been undertaken against long odds had there not been a universe of other places also being explored. Many individual mineral bodies have been found at practically zero cost. But this tells us nothing about the finding cost of the whole mineral in the world market as it compares with the incremental development cost of known deposits, with M.E.F.C., and therefore nothing of how it affects investment and prices at any given time. Only expected finding costs have any economic significance. Once the mineral is found, bygones are bygones, and only development cost matters. What we need to know are the chances of finding something equally good by the expenditure of a given amount of money.

The popular idea of "replacement cost" is therefore an irelevance. Investment in developing a given mineral deposit is or is not worth while regardless of its bygone finding costs. An exploratory venture is or is not worth making regardless of whether one is depleting a mineral deposit elsewhere.

Discovery of minerals is a game of chance. Most exploration is chasing after false clues, which must all or mostly be followed up, or else there are no discoveries. Two implications follow. First, the higher the expected price, the more it pays to chase slight or farfetched leads, and the higher the discovery cost per unit. Higher prices induce higher costs as well as vice versa.

Second, the few good ones pay for many bad only when there is active competition among the various hunting grounds. Investment in any one place must be directly or indirectly in rivalry and subject to comparison with investment and prospective return in every other. But the links are broken whenever an area becomes a separate enclave, with special exploration incentives by way of tax or price concessions or import controls, etc. Then experience in one place is altogether irrelevant to experience in another, and the long odds against finding cheap minerals in some places are no part of discovery cost anywhere else. In the United States, during the ten years ending in 1968, about 65,000 wells were drilled in search of new oil fields. Eventually only 7 to 10 billion barrels of proved reserves will be developed from them—if prices and costs do not change too much (Dix and Van Dyke, 1969). If this dismal record had even a remote bearing on prospects in any other area, that area would be a good place to stay away from. The few good ones found outside the United States are in no way helped by the many dry holes and bad ones found inside, under various forms of government subsidy.

But if exploration investment is a matter of playing the odds on future finds, we must admit that we have no body of knowledge on the incidence of mineral deposits which can be translated into economic terms. The Allais hypothesis is that the chemical reaction generating mineral deposits makes them follow a Poisson distribution as to their occurrence within a given area, and a logarithmic-normal distribution as to their content. The hypothesis has been applied to several areas, most work being on oil and gas. An excellent summary and application is in the forthcoming paper by Bradley (1970). Oil and gas differ from solid minerals in one important respect. Between the generation of the fluid mineral and its final incidence is the process of migration and entrapment, which may be more important than its original occurrence. Perhaps this is why a test of the Province of Alberta, Canada, shows more clustering, i.e., more areas where a given minimum number of reservoirs appear, than the Poisson function would predict. Perhaps good conditions to receive and entrap fluid hydrocarbons tend to draw in more than would be concentrated if there were no migration.

The prediction of pools and fields to be found in a given new area starts with the projection of average results from similar areas, and must be gradually supplanted by the projection of results from the area itself. In other words, just as the operator of a pool refigures the contents in the course of development, so must the operators in a given area constantly redo their sums in guessing at what the area still has to offer.

A logarithmic-normal or similar distribution means that one finds a great many small fields, and a very few large ones. In the United States, where exploration has been most intensive, about 200 large fields out of 10,000 account for rather more than half of the reserves.

The research on probability analysis is the true knowledge frontier of mineral economics. The resources devoted to it thus far have been negligible.

Investment, Profit, and Forecasting

We have repeatedly called mineral exploration a form of investment: it is time to consider its reward.

Rates of Return on Investment

Our vision of investment in developing minerals and in improving methods of extraction has knowledge of new mineral deposits as a special case. Somehow the process works, since people do explore and find enough so that long-term price movements are relatively continuous, and stable or downward. There is no other way of judging what is "enough." But I know of only one satisfactory study of the rate of return on mineral investment (Frankel, 1967). It does not consider exploration separately, but only the total return to gold mining exploration and development together. For the industry as a whole, there is nothing to support the idea that more money has been sunk into mines than taken out of them, which would mean the investment was a waste. Over very long periods of time taken as a whole, gold mining investment has shown a modest premium over equity investment elsewhere. The international capital market has worked well, drawing funds into the industry on terms which afforded a modest but unmistakable excess over returns for securities of somewhat lower risk. However, since

World War II, investors in gold mining "... have foregone higher rates of return in investment opportunities elsewhere ... If and when the gold price is raised, the long-run investor will perhaps again be seen to have obtained a return on his investment, which will have been more in line with returns from investment in other directions (including a positive payment for uncertainty bearing)."

Investors in gold mines, mistakenly it would now seem, expected governments to make them rich. In what other mineral industries may they be making the same mistake?

A similar study of crude oil in the Middle East (Mikdashi, 1967) is hampered by two unavoidable limitations of the data. First, the profits depend on a crude oil price which is extremely hard to approximate. Secondly, a crucially important fact for any such calculation is the value of the asset held at the end of the period, i.e., the right to continue production. The gold mining study had a valid if imprecise measure: the stock exchange value of the companies' securities. Nothing of the kind was available for the companies operating in the Middle East, which were all subsidiaries of international integrated concerns, with many other activities to affect the value of their shares.

There have been some estimates that crude-oil exploration-development-refining investment in the Eastern Hemisphere draws no more than the average for manufacturing in the U.S. or Great Britain (roughly 10 percent after tax on net worth), or even less. Such estimates cannot be checked or even understood because the basic data are not revealed; nor can they be reconciled with the fact of continued heavy investment by old and new companies.

Rents and Landlord-Tenant Relations

These few indications, direct and indirect, that the development process including exploration is on the average mildly more profitable than less risky investment, in no way conflicts with the radically skewed distribution of the size and richness of mineral deposits, and a consequently skewed distribution of profits. A small or negligible outlay may uncover a huge store of wealth and serve as a windfall or "rent" to the particular persons finding it. A rent is a payment which can be decreased without any supply response. In mineral production, what is cost and what is rent depends on the time horizon. To insure continued production requires new development investment, on which the return is no rent. A development profit more than sufficient to maintain production is a rent.

The great uncertainties of finding lead to some predictable relationships among landowners and producers, when landowners are governments. In the beginning is a piece of completely unexplored land. A mineral company is not willing to pay much for the right to explore and produce. Since the few good discoveries must pay for the many failures, they are only willing to offer a sort of average value as bonus payment and royalties. If the landowner wants more than what the company thinks is the maximum value of exploration rights, the company goes elsewhere. If the landowner accepts and then learns others would have paid more, he is sorry he let the tract go so cheaply. Contrariwise, if the nearest alternative offer was much lower than the price accepted, the landowner is glad and the mining company sad. But these are bygones. Once the tract is explored, uncertainty is greatly reduced, and replaced by some real knowledge. If there is no mineral body worth developing, the company's money has been wasted. But if there will be large profits on the development investment, the landowner wishes he had held out for much more. With foreknowledge, the producer would willingly have paid much more.

This is the great divide of the mining industry: *a rich discovery means a dissatisfied landlord*. He knows that the tenant's development profit is greater than is necessary to keep him investing. The landlord wants some of the surplus above the bare minimum necessary rate of return. If he gets some, he wants more.

If mineral operators are deprived of the hope of making occasional big profits, then the expected return from good and bad discoveries taken together is lower. Less capital and enterprise will be available, ultimately reducing supply. But what is true for the industry as a whole may safely be neglected in any one instance. A landlord could confiscate all the rent being gained on his property without any perceptible effect on the industry or on the supply and price of the mineral.

Where the landlord is bound by laws and contracts, he cannot follow self-interest and demand the whole producer's rent, up to that rather shadowy point where the operator will receive just enough to keep him investing. But where a landlord is a government, and is not compelled to observe a contract, it can force the operator to hand over the rent or else be expelled and succeeded by someone willing to accept a lower return. Expropriation of a concessionnaire is only the unfortunate accident, the unlooked-for breakdown in "renegotiation." The endless palaver about fairness, justice, ancestral wrongs, etc., is not to be despised, for it serves an important purpose. It slows down both the landlord-government and the concessionnaire, giving each some protection against being carried away by his own eloquence and moving too precipitately for his own good. In addition, governments may intervene in price determination. They have done this with great success in the international oil industry. What are in effect excise taxes, in money amounts per unit of production, have served as a floor to the price, which at the Persian Gulf is 6–10 times cost including a 20 percent return on development investment. I do not think this restraint on competitive price evolution will work indefinitely (Adelman, 1969). But with the control of oil prices as an example, governments are trying to do the same in iron ore[11] and have formed an organization in copper (Herfindahl, 1969). Recently, their assurance that they were not trying to raise prices was greeted with some disbelief.[12] Obviously companies and governments have a common interest in higher prices, but agreement on production control is difficult, and without the cooperation of consuming-country governments, impossible.

The threat of host governments to raise prices and confiscate some or all of the rents or above-minimum profits—and expropriation or expulsion is merely the ultimate in confiscation—stimulates exploration elsewhere, both for security and in the hope of profiting from the higher price. The end result is obviously a larger supply and an even lower price. This factor must be taken into account by anyone trying to make long-run predictions about any particular mineral industry.

Forecasting: Technology, Competition

Because the minerals industries deal with long-lived assets, they must and do live in the future and calculate with expected not current variables. But predictions more than a decade ahead lose interest rapidly. Those past 25 years are probably more misleading than helpful. The search for useful knowledge, including exploration, is a high-risk occupation because the chances of making a mistake are high. It follows that when we look past the horizon of known reserves projected from known conditions of cost, the chance of error increases considerably and longer-term predictions must be discounted at a higher rate. The most important variable in the long run is the least predictable: technical progress both in supply and in utilization (of which we have said nothing in this paper).

The value of a forecast is in pointing to one decision in preference to another. Suppose we believe that a given action will save us a dollar ten years hence. Even at a 10 percent discount rate, the present value of that dollar is less than 40 cents, and if the saving must wait until 1990 it is only

15 cents. At a more realistic discount rate of 15 percent, the respective savings are 25 cents and 6 cents. To spend half a dollar today in the hope of saving the dollar in 1985 is extravangance, not thrift. Long-term projections must be discounted intellectually as well as financially, whether done by public or private parties. For no matter who does the calculation, the basic question is still the same: the best alternative use of resources in an equally risky activity. A company which holds on to developed reserves or to minerals-in-place[13] or a government which subsidizes exploration for fear of scarcity in 1980 or 1990, is helping insure itself into poverty.

Perhaps the very concept of exhaustible resources ought to be discarded as wrong or irrelevant. Not much of the resources we know today will ever be used because better ones will be found. Or the need itself may disappear before the resource, as is most likely with fossil fuels and possibly even uranium (if nuclear fusion ever develops). Or if real scarcities develop, higher prices will ration end uses, promoting substitution and (for metals) scrap collection. Somehow this unthinkably complex set of possibilities needs to be reduced to a set of present values by which people can be guided in making commitments to the future.

The investment of mineral producers in development and exploration is guided partly indirectly, by expected prices over the life-time of their investment; partly directly by the term contracts they are willing to sign, the prices upon which they are willing to commit to deliver. Current prices embody producers' and customers' estimates of future prices and costs, including development cost and hoped-for improvements in it, perhaps by discoveries. These estimates are affected by all we have at present: exact science, technical art, economics, guesswork, hunches. Prices are a distant-early-warning system of impending glut or scarcity. A market system is a uniquely valuable piece of social machinery because it gathers and sifts data, and generates information. We are therefore better off bearing with its frictions and insufficiencies (Kravis and Lipsey, 1966), many of which only express attempts at distorting the data.

A recent warning by the U.S. Atomic Energy Commission is that although uranium is no longer in a seller's market, yet "a high level of (uranium) exploration will be needed for an indefinite period" (Faulkner, 1969, p. 7). The industry is "unduly pessimistic." It may be so; but perhaps the A.E.C. is unduly optimistic. Who is right depends on many rates of learning. For example: (1) the sooner breeder reactors develop, the less uranium will be demanded, and the lower should prices be *today*; and, vice versa, (2) the competitive frontier between nuclear and fossil fuels is not clear. Atomic energy plants of the American type (light-water reactors) are being built in Europe to be barely competitive with fuel oil selling at 40 cents per million B.T.U. (Bechtel, 1967). It is almost a decade since free-market fuel oil prices in Europe were anywhere near this figure, and seldom has a more costly error been more stubbornly maintained. During 1969, with tankers still scarce, heavy fuel oil prices ranged between 23 and 26 cents at the North Sea ports. In Great Britain, heavy investments are made in a nuclear power method so expensive that it gets only brief and contemptuous dismissal even from those with a strong motive to favor it over the American alternative.[14]

The true cost of air and water pollution, once measured and assigned, may tilt the balance of advantage either way. But as knowledge replaces ignorance in this area, it will generate bidding for one resource in preference to another, and thereby affect prices.

In order to receive and digest new data, the mineral industries are particularly in need of prices set by competition, as information to help guide investment decisions. Nor is there anything inconsistent between competition and the large firms often necessary for mineral development or exploration. What matters is whether the total market can accommodate enough firms able to achieve the threshold of economies of scale to make their cooperation difficult or unimportant. No swarm of small competitors is needed to bring the market price close enough to the competitive level so that a forecast can treat it as a minor qualification or disturbance (Herfindahl, 1969). Even small groups of mutually sympathetic firms find it difficult to stay together over the long run (Brubaker, 1967; Herfindahl, 1969; Mancke, 1969; Adelman, 1970). It is often said that the relation of price to short-run variable cost makes competition unstable; but as seen above, this is not true even in the short run, still less when investment is in question.

Anyone who considers investment in mineral exploration, development, transport, or use, must make a forecast of costs and prices, and a forecast of a mineral price must include competition as an explicit variable. A competitive market generates a price which accurately reflects long-term investment values in mineral exploration, under present conditions of knowledge. A non-competitive market generates a higher price. A non-competitive price has nothing to do with huge corporations, nor with fairness, justice, moderation, or wisdom. It means a price substantially above the minimum cost of expanding output by new development investment. Such a price generates a market tension by offering a particularly strong inducement to some interloper, or to a faithless member of the combination. Whether the tension is great enough to bend or break the price structure is a question to be asked by anyone forecasting. The answer will vary among products. A non-competitive price of crude oil is in the process of a long decline. A non-competitive price for mercury seems much more stable (Rohlfs, 1969); nickel is more doubtful, while the price of copper is simply hard to discern (Herfindahl, 1969).

If market control deteriorates and the prospect is for more competition, those who bet on lower prices will do better. Many today who wager on higher prices for oil, coal, nickel, iron ore, copper, etc, will be greatly disappointed in the next two decades. What happens after that does not much matter today because a better outcome then, as compared with a worse, has a negligible present value. At any rate, since nobody knows what will happen, nobody ought to pretend to know.

Acknowledgments

This paper has benefitted from the comments of Professors Paul G. Bradley and Richard L. Gordon.

Notes

1. See also the Meeting of the American Association for the Advancement of Science, Boston. Papers summarized in *New York Times*, January 4, 1970. And: National Academy of Sciences National Research Council, Division of Earth Sciences, Committee on Resources and Man; *Resources and Man: A Study and Recommendations*, Freeman, San Francisco, 1969.

2. The works upon which this discussion relies are Mason (1958), Barnett and Morse (1963), Gordon (1967), Herfindahl (1967) and Scott (1967). Obviously there is no necessary agreement among all these writers, nor with me, but they have defined the issues as I understand them.

3. In the United States, prices do not correspond to costs because competition is severely distorted by government regulation (Lovejoy and Homan, 1968).

4. See the report of the Federal Trade Commission on the Control of Iron Ore for the Antitrust Subcommittee of the Committee on the Judiciary (Washington, 1952, p. 82).

5. Soviet reserve concepts and measurements may have evolved considerably in the past decade. Cf. Brod and Frolov (1957, pp. 6, 13–14), where the stress is rather on degree of precision than on cost.

6. *Report of the National Fuels and Energy Study Group* (U.S. Senate Committee on Interior and Insular Affairs, Washington, 1962, pp. 81–83).

7. See also U.S. Department of Commerce, Bureau of the Census: *Census of Mineral Industries*, various years. See for 1963, Vol. I, pp. 10B1, 10C1 et seq.

8. See the U.S. Treasury Department, Office of the Secretary: *Depletion Survey 1958–60* (Washington, 1963). The totals given in this source are substantially less, the differences ranging between 10 and 20 percent, than the corresponding totals in the *Joint Association Survey*, Part II. Since the Treasury survey covered only 350 corporations, accounting for about 85 percent of the total universe, this is to be expected. But the Treasury amounts for acquisition outlays are substantially greater, a discrepancy not explained.

9. See also American Petroleum Institute, Independent Petroleum Association of America, Mid-Continent Oil and Gas Association: *Joint Association Survey, Estimated Expenditures and Receipts of U.S. Oil and Gas Producing Industry*. Various years until 1959, annual since.

10. See Government of Australia, Bureau of Mineral Resources, Geology and Geophysics: *Petroleum Newsletter*.

11. See Annual Reports of the Ministry of Mines and Hydrocarbons, 1967, 1968, Republic of Venezuela.

12. Cf. *New York Times*, Dec. 11 and 14, 1969.

13. Except in a tacit understanding with other large holders: not to sell reserves or resources to newcomers in order to keep down the number of competitors.

14. See Commission Consultative pour la Production d'Electricité d'Origine Nucléaire: *Les Perspectives de Développement des Centrales Nucléaires en France*. Avril, 1968.

References

Adelman, M. A., 1967. Trends in finding and developing. In: S. Gardner and S. Hanke (Editors), *Essays in Petroleum Economics*. Univ. of Colorado Press, Denver, Colo., pp. 54–91.

Adelman, M. A., 1969. A long-term oil price forecast. *J. Petrol. Technol.*, 1969: 1515–1520.

Adelman, M. A., 1970. *The World Petroleum Market*. (In preparation.)

Anonymous, 1952. Report of the President's Material Policy Commission. *Resources for Freedom*, 1: 13–14.

Anonymous, 1965. *The Outlook for Uranium*. Stoller Ass., New York.

Barnet, H. J. and Morse, C., 1963. *Scarcity and growth*. Resources for the Future, Washington, D.C., 288 pp.

Blondel, F. and Lasky, S. G., 1956. Mineral reserves and mineral resources. *Econ. Geol.*, 51: 686–697.

Bradley, P. G., 1970. Economic models of petroleum exploration. In: M. A. Adelman, P. G. Bradley and C. A. Norman (Editors), *Economics of North Slope Oil*. Praeger, New York, N.Y., 140 pp.

Brod, I. O. and Frolov, E. F., 1957. *Finding and Development of Oil and Gas Deposits*, Nauka, Moscow, 233 pp. (In Russian.)

Brooks, D. B., 1967. The lead-zinc anomaly. *Trans. Soc. Mining Engrs.*, 1967: 1–8.

Brubaker, S., 1967. *Trends in the world aluminum industry*. Resources for the Future, Washington, D.C., 260 pp.

Dix Jr., F. A. and Van Dyke, L. H., 1969. North American drilling activity in 1968. *Bull. Am. Assoc. Petrol. Geologists*, 53: 1151–1180.

Faulkner, R. F., 1969. Uranium supply and demand. *Uranium Comm., Am. Mining Congr.*, October 19, 1969, 16 pp.

Fisher, F. M., 1964. *Supply and costs in the U.S. petroleum industry*. Resources for the Future, Washington, D.C., 177 pp.

Frankel, S. H., 1967. *Investment and the Return to Equity Capital in the South African Gold Mining Industry, 1887–1965*. Harvard Univ. Press, Cambridge, Mass., 131 pp.

Gordon, R. L., 1967. A reinterpretation of the pure theory of exhaustion. *J Political Econ.* 75: 274–286.

Heineke, J. M., 1969. Demand for refined lead. *Rec. Econ. Statistics*, pp. 374–378.

Herfindahl, O. C., 1959. *Copper cost and prices*. Resources for the Future, Washington, D.C., 260 pp.

Herfindahl, O. C., 1967. Depletion and economic theory. In: M. C. Gaffney (Editor). *Extractive Resources and Taxation*. Univ. of Wisconsin Press, Madison, Wis., pp. 63–90.

Herfindahl, O. C., 1969. The long range outlook for copper and nickel. *Ann. Meeting AIME, Minnesota Sect., January 14, 1969*, 24 pp.

Hood, P. J. and Kellog, W. C., 1968. Geophysical activity in 1967 applied to mining exploration. *Geophysics*, 33: 903–910.

Kravis, I. B. and Lipsey, R. E., 1966. Comparative prices of non-ferrous metals in international trade. *Natl. Bur. Econ. Res., Occasional Papers*, 98: 56 pp.

Lovejoy, W. F. and Homan, P. T., 1967. *Economic aspects of oil conservation regulation*. Resources for the Future, Washington, D.C., 295 pp.

Mancke, R. B., 1969. *The American Iron Ore and Steel Industries*. Thesis, Massachusetts Institute of Technology, Cambridge, Mass., 225 pp.

Manners, G., 1967. Transport costs, freight rates and the changing economic geography of iron ore. *Geography*, 52: 260–269.

Mason, E. S., 1958. The political economy of resource use. In: H. Jarrett, (Editor), *Perspective on Conservation*. Resources for the Future, Washington, D.C., 432 pp.

Mikdashi, Z., 1967. *A Financial Analysis of Middle Eastern Oil Concessions, 1901–1965*. Praeger, New York, N.Y., 340 pp.

National Petroleum Council, 1967. *Impact of New Technology on the U.S. Petroleum Industry, 1946–1965*. Government Printing Office, Washington, D.C., 257 pp.

Park Jr., C. F., 1968. *Affluence in Jeopardy.* Freeman, San Francisco, Calif., 368 pp.

Potter, N. and Christy Jr., F. T., 1962. *Trends in natural resource commodities.* Resources for the Future, Washington, D.C., 568 pp.

Preston, L. E., 1960. *Exploration for non-ferrous metals.* Resources for the Future, Washington, D.C., 198 pp.

Rohlfs, J., 1969. *Economic Analysis of the Mercury Industry.* Thesis, Massachusetts Institute of Technology, Cambridge, Mass., 250 pp.

Scott, A. C., 1967. The theory of the mine under conditions of certainty. In M. C. Gaffney (Editor), *Extractive Resources and Taxation.* Univ. of Wisconsin Press, Madison, Wisc., pp. 25–62.

Spinrad, B. I., 1969. The role of nuclear energy in the world's future energy production. *Seminar Organ. Petrol. Exporting Countries, July, 1969,* 27 pp.

Torrey, P. D., Moore, C. L. and Weber, G. H., 1963. World oil resources. *Proc. World Petrol. Congr., 6th, 1963,* pp. 83–114.

Tucker, R. L., 1968. Geophysical activity in 1967 applied to petroleum exploration. *Geophysics,* 33: 885–902.

U. N. Economic Commission for Europe, 1966. *Economic Aspects of Iron-Ore Preparation.* Geneva, 278 pp.

Weeks, L. G., 1969. Offshore petroleum development and resources. *J. Petrol. Technol.,* 1969: 377–385.

Wilsher, P., 1965. Ports and ore carriers. *Steel Rev.,* April 1965.

5

Population Growth
and Oil Resources

I

In looking to the possible limiting effect of oil resources on population growth, we need to understand the dramatic 1970–1973 events in the world oil market, where turbulence will continue for years. For any product a stable competitive equilibrium is in the neighborhood of long-run marginal cost; a stable monopoly equilibrium is where a price rise would so restrict demand as to reduce profits. The demand for oil is highly inelastic. Therefore, the distance between the two equilibria is enormous, and depending on whether competitive forces are stronger or weaker, the price will rise or fall between these two extremes, the higher being some fifty times the lower.

Since before World War I the problem for the international oil industry has been to keep at bay a huge potential surplus that would drive the price toward the competitive level. Between the wars, a cartel functioned fairly well, though it could not keep the price from deteriorating. The cartel was never revived after World War II, but a small group of producing companies managed to keep the decline rather slow, although between 1945 and 1960 the price was down in real terms by over 50 percent. The decline alarmed the producing countries who by 1960 were the principal beneficiaries, and in that year they revised the tax system to put a firm floor under the price. This kept the price decline during 1960–1970 within close bounds. But the dramatic events of 1970–1971 opened an altogether new chapter in economic history, that of a cartel or shared monopoly of a group of sovereign states. Such a monopoly is not subject to any kind of national or international control. Private corporations are subject to sanctions by the states in which they operate. The monopoly of the OPEC

Reprinted from *Quarterly Journal of Economics* 89 (May 1975): 271–275.

nations (but not OPEC itself) is by far the greatest in world history, and the least restrained.

The potential surplus will now grow apace. The world price is now around $8 to $9 at the Persian Gulf, while the long-run marginal cost (assuming a 20 percent return on investment and an improbably fast shrinkage of reserves) approaches a limit of 20 cents. In such relatively high cost regions as Algeria or the North Sea, a big field produces at $1 to $1.50. Again, this is a very small proportion of the price.

How fast the potential capacity will grow we cannot say nor—more important—how fast will be the translation of potential into actual producing capacity? My own guess is that a chronic surplus will appear by 1976. The cartel may be broken up or may even reduce its price. A respectable argument can be made, that present value of the monopolist's holdings are maximized at a considerably lower price than the current one. We need not discuss these issues. The basic fact is clear, that the recent dramatic increase in price has nothing to do with real scarcity, and is explained simply by the change from a slowly retreating monopoly into a rapidly advancing one.

II

We can now look at the long-run problem. Assuming that population grows at about 2 percent over the next fifty years, and per capita income also by about 2 percent (as seems to have been the case in the United States between 1929 and 1973) total world income will grow by a factor of seven in fifty years. There is no "need" or compulsion for oil consumption to grow even this rapidly. If the price rises high enough, even transportation (which outside the United States accounts for less than one-fourth of the barrel) can be far less oil-intensive than it is today, while coal and uranium can be substituted in direct heat production. Short of an elaborate and purely hypothetical simulation, the best we can do to pose the question is to assume the worst case, that consumption, and hence production, grows by a factor of seven.

1972 oil production was about 19 billion barrels, out of a ready inventory or "proved reserves" of 673 billion barrels, or 2.87 percent. This inventory could support a much larger volume of output, at a small increase in real cost. It is a commonly accepted rule of thumb in the industry that one can do with no more than fifteen years' production (7.5 percent depletion rate) as proved reserves, and in the United States the ratio is only about eight; undoubtedly, however, raising costs thereby.

If we assume a somewhat more rational world order fifty years hence, but not fully rational, it is reasonable to take twenty years' production, or a depletion rate and decline rate of 5 percent as acceptable, rather than the 7.5 percent rule of thumb. If so, then it is a conservative estimate that to support an output level seven times as great as the current one, it will take about four times as much "proved reserves." Hence reserves must grow, net of production, at 2.82 percent per year over the next fifty years.

To get some perspective, we can go back to 1938, the earliest year available. Over the next thirty-four years, world proved reserves grew by a factor of twenty, or by 9.2 percent per year. This hardly proves it will happen again; but there is nothing strange about an increase one-third as great.

Looking to natural gas, world proved reserves were about 313 billion barrels oil-equivalent at the end of 1972, and were being depleted somewhat more slowly than oil, at 243 percent per year. But only about half of those reserves, in the United States, Canada, and the Soviet Union, were the results of a deliberate search. Elsewhere, natural gas deposits were the accidental result, or by-product, of the search for oil. Hence there is a larger stock of untried gas prospects than oil prospects.

What are the chances of expanding oil and gas reserves by a factor of 4, over and above production, in the next half century? This depends on the cost, and on how much mankind is willing to pay. "Is there enough oil and gas in the world" is a nonsense question and has yielded many a foolish answer. In fact, *we shall never know* our endowment in fluid hydrocarbons. It is trivial that they are limited because the earth itself is limited. Long before we get to the end of these resources, we shall have ceased to use them, either because the cost has become so impossibly high or because a better and cheaper source of heat has been found. the relevant question, therefore, is what will happen to the long-run marginal cost of finding and developing inventories, i.e., reserves. Obviously the cost at any given time must include "user cost," an allowance for the future values of the resource used up now. But its future value depends in turn on the future development cost, which in turn also depends on how much is *then* being held out for future use, and so on ad infinitum. But the relevance of future cost dies away at any reasonable rate of discount. For the period ending in 1984, I have taken a "worst case" of zero Persian Gulf discoveries, which puts marginal cost up from 12 to 20 cents. Nordhaus's "worst" is an elaborate simulation of the year 2000; he has arrived at a present value of future scarcity rents of about $1.20.[1] These results are compatible, but the Nordhaus figure seems improbably high in view of the fact that the

Persian Gulf price before the dramatic turnabout had for the better part of a decade been in the range $1.15–$1.40.

Mineral industries have faced the problem from time immemorial. In practice, they have taken the poet's advice not to heed the rumble of a distant drum, and they have been justified in treating user cost as though it were essentially zero. For there has been no tendency for costs to rise in the long run.[2]

A functioning market provides a distant (thought not infinitely distant) early warning signal of scarcity ahead. For if the owners of mineral deposits expect higher prices to rule in the future, they will set aside or truly "reserve" some properties for future exploitation, rather than developing them into the ready shelf inventory that we call "proved reserves." By narrowing the base and decreasing the amount of known mineral that is available for exploitation, they force upon the remainder of the deposits a more intensive rate of exploitation. The existing inventory is more rapidly depleted when owners are reluctant to commit underdeveloped mineral deposits, hoping for larger profits from later exploitation. As the rate of development is speeded up, investment requirements and long-run marginal costs must also increase. Hence a rise in development cost summarizes a mass of facts, hunches, hopes and fears, in registering a general expectation of approaching exhaustion. (Oil investment requirements outside the United States fell by about half in the 1960s—hardly a symptom of scarcity.)

The current oil prices, extravagantly or recklessly high as they are in relation to real costs, may yet be serving some purpose. Dr. Pangloss would maintain that the OPEC nations have collapsed time, and are confronting us with a price level that reflects not the plenty of the day but the scarcity which—who knows?—will be waiting for us decades hence. The reaction throughout the developed world has been to conserve energy and go for substitute energy sources: the extraction of petroleum fluids from coal, shale, and tar sands, and the large-scale production of electricity from nuclear reactors. The odds are that this is mostly a huge waste of resources, and that the great pools of low-cost and relatively clean energy now known to exist around the Persian Gulf will be used late or never. It probably cannot be helped, and the best we can hope for is to minimize the waste and get some valuable knowledge. In any case, the substitute resources just mentioned are much larger than any conceivable volume of use over the next fifty years. Primary energy has cost about 4 percent of the GNP, even a rise to 10 percent of a larger per capita income seems like no important barrier to progress in the developed countries. The impact on the LDCs will be devastating.

Economic growth will not be constrained by lack of oil. Growth may be constrained by air or water pollution; by the need to move such prodigious quantities of dirt for the sake of energy or other minerals that mankind will have good reason to curb growth. The heating up of the atmosphere may be as dangerous as some now suspect. All these and other problems deserve more study than they have yet received. We shall have more time for this if we stop worrying about limits imposed by oil scarcity.

Notes

This paper draws on my book, *The World Petroleum Market* (Baltimore: Johns Hopkins University Press, 1972); an article, "Is the Oil Shortage Real: Oil Companies as Tax Collectors," *Foreign Policy*, (Winter 1972), 69–107; and unpublished work done in collaboration with Dr. Martin L. Baughman of the Energy Laboratory at M.I.T. The best recent summary of energy resource is by the National Petroleum Council, *U. S. Energy Outlook 1971–1985* (1972).

This note was written in January 1974. The world price is now (February 1975) around $10–$10.50. The surplus predicted for 1976 arrived by the middle of 1974, largely because of the world-wide recession not foreseen by the author.

1. William D Nordhaus, "The Allocation of Energy Resources," *Brookings Papers on Economic Activity*, No. 3 (1973), 529–70.

2. Richard L. Gordon, "A Reconsideration of the Pure Theory of Exhaustion," *Journal of Political Economy*, LXXV (June 1967), pp. 274–86.

6 Worldwide Production Costs for Oil and Gas

with Geoffrey L. Ward

I Introduction

This chapter has two objectives. First, we wish to calculate the investment required in various countries to maintain and increase crude oil production, differentiating onshore and offshore areas. Since the factors affecting these requirements tend to change slowly, requirements calculated from recent data will probably apply at least in the near future.

The second purpose is to develop a method of calculating those requirements in any area, down to the individual reservoir, where we have one or two simple parameters: drilling time per well onshore, drilling time and depth of water per well offshore. These data are always known though rarely made public. If the method is correct, and works within tolerable degrees of error, then it can serve as a vehicle for doing disaggregated analysis of development cost, and for constructing disaggregated models of the development process.

Disaggregated development cost estimates also serve to aid analysis of exploration. The distribution of reservoirs to be found in some given new area must be assumed to resemble the distribution of reservoirs already found in the area, or found in some analogous area which the new area most resembles. Whatever the proper analogy, once it is determined, we have means of estimating, to a first approximation, development costs in the new area.

Calculating development costs in an area before exploration may sound like walking backwards into the future. Yet it is the only rational conduct. Exploration is the tribute paid to nature, just as lease bonus or rental is the tribute paid to a landlord, for the privilege of profitable development. If the prospect of profit looks too small because development investment, in

Reprinted from *Advances in the Economics of Energy & Resources* 3 (1980): 1–29.

terms of dollars per barrel, is greater than the expected price then the privilege is worthless and there should be no exploration. If the prospective profit is high, then the gamble on exploration is worthwhile.

To build a supply model it is necessary to estimate, for any given producing area, the two interrelated variables: average and marginal costs of producing oil (or gas), and the capital requirements to bring up an additional daily barrel.

Published information is extremely limited. Infrequently published reports never explain sources, methods, or comparability with any other time or place. An outstanding exception is the North Sea, where a combination of an open capital market and close governmental supervision has yielded a rich harvest of data. Even here it is incomplete as to number of wells and performance; and the North Sea is so unusual a place that one can apply its cost factors in only a few other places.

The only published estimates of capital requirements and costs per barrel (Adelman, 1972) were based on pre-1970 data. The method used there is no longer applicable because of the growth of offshore development, and because the basic investment component was capital expenditures in various regions. Reported capital expenditures are now a blend of oil and gas production and gas-gathering outlays, even when gas-processing plants are netted out of the totals.

II   Theoretical Background

For various oil-producing regions we propose to estimate drilling costs, the principal component of oil- and gas-development costs, according to the amount of drilling time spent. This is not the first attempt to relate costs to some observable physical dimension. Drilling cost was related to depth of well in a classic paper (Fisher, 1964).

Although well depths are known with fair precision for every large producing field in the world it is not possible to estimate costs from them because drilling costs per foot vary so much from one place to another, due to some formations being more difficult to drill. It has long been realized that a well of given depth costs more in one part of the United States than in another; moreover, since costs probably increase more than proportionally with depth, any variations are magnified the deeper the well.

Nonlinearity in the depth-cost relation at a given place can be explained by nonlinearity with time. As well depth increases actual drilling (rotating) time increases, at least proportionally (although the use of more powerful rigs with increased depth may lead to smaller increases or even decreases in drilling time over some depth ranges, see this section following). When bits wear out drilling stops, and the whole pipe must be pulled out of the well to replace the bit and related tools (Bottom Hole Assembly, or BHA) while the rig stays in place. If a substantial quantity of the drilling fluid ("mud") starts escaping into the formation the "lost circulation" stops work. In either case if *non*drilling rig time required to remedy a given interruption increases with depth and the frequency of the interruptions increases with depth then nondrilling rig time arising from these delays increases more than proportionally with depth.

Further interruptions occur when the pipe breaks or gets stuck in the formation, and the pipe and BHA must be "fished" out. It is "often cheaper to cover the fish with cement and sidetrack and redrill the hole past it."[1] The chances of this happening when drilling another foot deeper increase as total well depth increases. This and the above tend, on average, to make *total* (rotating and nonrotating) drilling time increase more than proportionally with depth.

The preceding suggests that if cost were related to drilling time rather than depth a simpler and more accurate relation might be obtained, because the ease or difficulty of drilling a given depth had been captured. Other arguments can be advanced in favor of this alternative cost predictor. It is generally accepted that rig time has grown increasingly efficient over time, as shown by the increasing number of feet drilled per rig day. A cost estimate based on well depth is thus likely to become increasingly biased upwards. Furthermore, drilling efficiency varies greatly over different parts of the world.

A standard figure in any field history in a trade or technical journal plots rig *rotating* hours against well depth. Rig time increases nonlinearly, thus incidentally giving additional weight to the argument of a nonlinear depth-cost relation, but also the whole curve tends to shift over as the hours needed to drill successive wells of a given depth in the field decline. The decline is often substantial. Rig time thus captures increased efficiency due to experience accumulated over a sequence of drillings within a short time period as well as from longer-run technological advances.

As mentioned earlier, variations in geological conditions cause variations in the costs of wells of given depth. We intend to estimate costs per well in various parts of the world, with great dispersion in both local geology and drilling efficiency. Possible inaccuracies on either account, when estimating costs from depth are evidently great when either differs from the sample area. Rig time is suited to account for such differences.

Quick and dirty evidence of the time-cost relation is provided by a haphazard sample.[2] Define C as the cost, in thousands of 1971 dollars, incurred in drilling a series of wells in a field.[3] Let W equal the number of wells that were 'drilled in the field and let RY equal the total rig years required to drill the wells. Then for a 1971 cross section of onshore wells, and assuming linearity for simplicity and as a reasonable first approximation, one obtains:

$$C/W = 55.2 + 3066.0\,RY/W \qquad R^2 = .87 \qquad SER = 127$$
$$\quad\ (2.18)\quad(14.26) \qquad\qquad n = 32$$

where the numbers in parentheses are t-statistics under the null hypothesis that the coefficient is zero, SER is the standard error of the regression, and n is the sample size.

For a cross section of offshore wells using observations from Texas and Louisiana in 1970 and 1971[4] one obtains:

$$C/W = 91.9 + 5909.4\,RY/W \qquad R^2 = .73 \qquad SER = 180$$
$$\quad\ (1.14)\quad(6.21) \qquad\qquad n = 16$$

The results seem satisfactory. Drilling an offshore well incurs a higher fixed cost and higher costs per rig year than drilling an onshore well. The above numbers are of little use today, nine-ten years after the sample period, but do give an indication of what could be obtained if more data on individual wells were available.

Table 6.1 gives an approximate classification of costs of drilling and completing wells, as compiled by the Independent Petroleum Association

Table 6.1
Drilling and equipping costs as percentages of total

Depth Dependent	38.8	Time Dependent	47.6
Drilling mud, additives	6.9	Payments to drilling contractors	36.6
Cementing	3.7	Transportation	3.9
Logs, wireline evaluations	3.2	Special tool rentals	3.1
Casing and tubing	17.5	Supervision and overhead	2.1
Formation treating	3.0	Well site logging and/or monitoring	1.2
Drill bits and reamers	1.6	Other physical tests	0.7
Fuel	1.1	Not Classified	13.6
Casing hardware	0.7	Road and site preparation	4.1
Directional drilling services	0.6	Other equipment and supplies	2.0
Plugging	0.5	Wellhead equipment	1.8
		Perforating	1.1
		All other expenditures	4.6

Source: Independent Petroleum Association of America, Report of the Cost Study Committee, October 1978.

of America (IPAA), whose cost indices have long been recognized as reliable industry standards. Changes in the relative weights of the listed costs have been very small over the past fifteen years, as may be seen by an examination of the reports of the IPAA Cost Study Committees, thus it may safely be concluded that the table gives a good indication of what the composition of drilling costs will be as well as what it was. The items which are primarily time-related comprise less than 50 percent, the depth-related items less than 40 percent. The rest can be related to neither time nor depth. Note that in a case such as when lost drilling fluid stops the work, but costs continue to be incurred, that the increased expenditures on drilling mud which we have classified as depth-dependent will be more time-dependent.

Of course table 6.1 does not prove that time is a better predictor of cost. Time and depth are clearly related, as detailed previously. Since increased rig time per well generally implies increased well depth, the possibility arises that total expenditures increase more than proportionally with drilling time. The deeper the well the larger and more powerful the rig needed. A rig designed to go to 5,000 feet will need about a 750-horsepower engine, one going from 15,000 to 20,000 feet will need a 4,000-horsepower engine. Thus a well going twice as deep needs a rig plus ancillary equipment costing more than twice as much. If these costs increase faster with depth than does rig time (or slower), then a cost-rig time nonlinearity is introduced.

A second reason costs may rise more than proportionally with rig time is the presence of substitution possibilities. In exceptionally hard formations special tungsten carbide or diamond bits may be used instead of the ordinary rock bits. They are more expensive but save time. Furthermore, there is much overlapping between the capabilities of larger and smaller rigs, and in the overlapping zones tradeoffs are possible. A heavier, more expensive rig may save time. In every case of this substitution an observation is generated that lies above the simple straight line that otherwise relates rig time per well to cost per well.

III   Data

The geographic area of the sample is the continental United States. The observation points were individual states in individual years, except that Louisiana and Texas were subdivided into the usual (Texas Railroad Commission and Louisiana North/South/Offshore, respectively) producing districts. Onshore and offshore regions were segregated in the data analysis as both prior intuition and preliminary results suggested that the fundamental differences between the two types of operation were not adequately represented, e.g., by a regression dummy variable. Additional comments on offshore rig-time factors are made below.

Total drilling and equipping costs incurred, number of wells drilled, and the number of dry holes encountered were taken from the annual *Joint Association Survey, Section 1: Drilling Costs*,[5] 1967 to 1976 editions. The index used to transform all expenditures into constant dollars was obtained from the IPAA Cost Study Committee reports of May 1979, June 1975, and April 1969[6] (see following paragraph on work in progress adjustment). Rig-time figures were obtained from Hughes Tool Company in greater detail than usually published. To make clear the form of the data: Joint Association Survey data gave the number of wells drilled, dry holes encountered, and drilling and equipping costs incurred in a given region during a given year. The Hughes Tool reports gave the rig years used in drilling wells in that region during the year.

Slight problems arise due to the fact that expenditures for a given well are contracted over several months. With inflation one ideally would have a monthly cost index to transform each month's expenditures into constant dollars and thus obtain the true real expenditures for the well. A second best alternative would be to account for the overlap between years, e.g., for a well completed in 1976 but with costs dating from 1975, the 1975 portion of expenditures could be converted to 1976 dollars with the IPAA index, giving an approximation to the total cost of the well in 1976 dollars. Owing to the manner in which work in progress numbers are reported in the U.S. Census Bureau's *Annual Survey of Oil and Gas*[7] exact computations using this later method are also impossible; however, approximate calculations are possible and they indicate that for the United States as a whole, total costs for 1974, 1975, and 1976 are understated by 2 to 3 percent. The bias is apparently not large. Cost figures below do not account for this but it can easily be incorporated.

IV Onshore Drilling Costs

Cross-sectional regressions on the onshore regions for each year 1967 to 1976 showed that the real cost of a rig year of drilling was quite stable from 1967 to 1972, less stable thereafter. Since the most recent years' costs more closely reflect current costs we pooled the 1973 through 1976 observations of 29 producing areas in a time series cross-section regression. The included areas were chosen on the basis of having had at least ten rig years of drilling done in 1976. The result, where costs are now in thousands of 1974 dollars, was:

costs/wells = −1.15 + 3094.8 rig years/wells − 45.0 percent dry
          (−.07)   (23.2)   (−1.55)
    $R^2 = .83$ $n = 116$ SER = 52.5

where figures in parentheses are t-statistics under the null hypothesis that the coefficient is zero, and percent dry is the ratio of dry holes found to well completions (during the year for that region).

The rig year coefficient estimate translates to $8,480 per rig day. This is an estimate not of rig hire, which as table 6.1 indicated was 37 percent of the total, but rather of the total costs of operation per day the rig is active. The 95 percent confidence interval for this estimate is (7793, 9197) in dollars per rig day. This is lower than the figure of $11,067/rig day, translated into 1974 dollars, from the onshore field sample regression shown earlier. Some cost-reducing technological progress undoubtedly occurred in the intervening years, but some of the discrepancy can probably be ascribed to the much greater degree of aggregation in this latter sample. The extent that the use of aggregated samples has changed our results remains unclear throughout this paper.

The standard error of prediction $52.5 thousand per well compares favorably with the simple standard deviation of costs/wells over the same sample of $125 thousand. The sign of the percent dry variable reflects the fact that one saves development costs if a well is dry. Dry exploratory wells are often very expensive, but the expense is captured in the rig time.

As indicated earlier, one might expect a nonlinear relation between expenditures per rig day and the number of rig days. This was not observed. When the residuals of the above equation were plotted no systematic bias depending on rig time was discernible as their distribution about zero appeared random. When the rig time variable was allowed to have an exponent of other than unity the least squares estimate of the exponent was nevertheless almost exactly unity. It is quite possible that nonlinearities present in the drilling of an individual well would be invisible when many wells are aggregated into a single observation.

The average absolute value of the forecast error did increase greatly when rig years/wells exceeded about 0.1. The principal outliers with the largest errors were Utah, Alabama, south Louisiana, and Texas Railroad Commission District 5 (northeastern Texas). The average magnitude of the prediction error for those observations with more than 0.1 rig years per well was $98,600 versus $25,200 for those with less than 0.1 rig years per well. It appears that factors that theoretically cause nonlinearities in the cost function may instead add greater variance to its random component.

V Offshore Drilling Costs

Relations are very different in offshore drilling. An exploratory well drilled from a drill ship or a semisubmersible rig may not have a large fixed component relative to the cost of hiring and operating the craft and the rig. However, our business is primarily with development. A development well, which is ordinarily drilled from a fixed platform, will have a very high fixed component of costs relative to the variable rig time costs. For the four years 1966–1969 *Joint Association Survey, Section I* reported platform costs, in 1964 dollars, of about $200,000 per offshore well. Total well costs were in the range of $800–900,000. Probably the publisher considered these data unsatisfactory, since their publication was discontinued. In general, the deeper the water and the worse the weather the higher the fixed platform cost factor in proportion to the variable rig time cost will be, for a rig can be removed, albeit at high cost, when the alternative is to leave it on the platform during the period when the weather prevents its being manned.

Additionally, there are offshore wells drilled off only four states,[8] Louisiana, Texas, California, and Alaska, under very diverse conditions. The kind of time series cross-section regressions used to estimate onshore costs are therefore not advisable. Table 6.2 shows the simple means and standard deviations, in thousands of 1974 dollars, of per well costs for the four areas.

Since the Louisiana offshore is the most extensively developed, the number of wells being much larger than the rest of the country combined,

Table 6.2
Offshore well costs in the United States

Offshore region	Sample period	Average of costs/wells over sample period in thousands of '74 dollars	Standard deviation
Louisiana	1967–76	798.3	84.8
Texas	1967–76	835.9	206.3
California	1967–75	423.6	142.7
California	1967–76	553.0	271.0
Alaska	1967–76	2045.1	699.3

Source: Total costs and wells drilled are from *Joint Association Survey, Section 1*, and the cost index is from the IPAA, as given in the text, Section III.

we first did a time series regression on that region over the sample period 1967 to 1976. The result, with costs here and in subsequent regressions in this section being in thousands of 1974 dollars, was:

$$\text{costs/wells} = 211 + 6130 \text{ rig years/wells} \qquad R^2 = .46 \qquad SER = 63.4$$
$$\phantom{\text{costs/wells} = } (.89) \quad (2.61) \qquad\qquad\qquad DW = 1.4 \qquad n = 10$$

DW is the Durbin-Watson statistic. The percent dry variable varied little from year to year in any one region and therefore was omitted from the time series regressions.

If we compare the standard error of this regression with the standard error around the simple mean given in table 6.2, both refering to the same sample, it can be seen that having a rig years figure for an area on average decreased the standard error of the forecast by 25 percent.

One test of the results from the Louisiana time series regression is to use them as a predictive device for Texas offshore. Since this area is immediately adjacent to Louisiana, is similar geologically and climatically, and is served from the same supply bases, it should have similar characteristics. Table 6.2 shows the difference in mean cost per well to be small. The regression results for Texas offshore over the sample period 1967 to 1976 were:

$$\text{costs/wells} = 433.2 + 4211.4 \text{ rig years/wells} \qquad R^2 = .33 \qquad SER = 175$$
$$\phantom{\text{costs/wells} = } (1.74) \quad (1.97) \qquad\qquad\qquad DW = 1.34 \qquad n = 10$$

The fixed factor is higher and the variable factor is lower than the respective Louisiana offshore factors. This could have been due to the small sample sizes. As another test the errors from forecasting offshore Texas per well costs using the coefficient estimates from the Louisiana offshore regression were plotted. They were almost randomly distributed around zero, albeit not tightly. Finally, the appropriate F test failed to reject the hypothesis of identical coefficients for the two regions. Thus indications of underlying similarity are present.

California drilling has always involved a very small number of rigs relative to Louisiana. For reasons we cannot explain the California 1976 average cost per well was three times the 1967–1975 average for that area, even though rig time per well was comparable to previous years. We have taken the liberty of treating the 1976 observation as an outlier and have excluded it from the following regression. The results for California offshore over the 1967 to 1975 sample period were:

$$\text{costs/wells} = 121.8 + 4674.5 \text{ rig years/wells} \qquad R^2 = .73 \qquad SER = 78.9$$
$$\phantom{\text{costs/wells} = } (1.65) \quad (4.38) \qquad\qquad\qquad DW = 1.6 \qquad n = 9$$

The specification applied to California over the 1967–1975 period appears to have substantial explanatory power, judging by the standard error of the regression, since it is not much over half of the simple standard deviation. The fixed cost element for California offshore appears to be lower than that of Louisiana offshore, although this may be the fortuitous result of many shallow-water wells and a few deep-water wells, despite the Continental Shelf's sloping more sharply off California. Of course since both intercept estimates have high sample variances any observed differences may be illusory.

The California variable cost element also seems lower. We did a test of the hypothesis that the slope parameters, dollars per rig year per well, are the same for offshore Louisiana and offshore California, while the intercepts are not similarly constrained. The test did not come close to rejecting the hypothesis, which must be retained as provisionally valid. We leave it for possible future use. For the time being, we leave as our estimate for Louisiana: $6.13 million per rig year in 1974 dollars, or $9.44 million in 1978 dollars, for drilling offshore.

For the sake of completeness the results when the previous specification was tried on Alaska are presented. When applied to the sample period 1967 to 1976 they were:

$$\text{costs/wells} = 2208.7 - 663.6 \text{ rig years/wells} \quad R^2 = 0.2 \quad SER = 734$$
$$\quad (4.65) \quad\quad (-.41) \quad\quad\quad DW = 1.34 \quad n = 10$$

It is clear that the consideration of additional factors will be necessary to obtain a reasonable model for predicting costs in Alaska, or in similar areas.

The regression estimates of platform costs per well are not reliable. Since the platform component is often larger than the rig time component this is a serious gap. We try to close this gap using two sets of data.

The first set is from the *Joint Association Survey, Section I.*[9] Our assumption is that drilling conditions are essentially the same in south Louisiana and offshore Louisiana. We have drilling cost statistics for both by depth classes. Here we propose the equation, where OFF is a variable equaling 1 if the well is an offshore well, 0 otherwise:

$$\text{cost} = a + b \text{ OFF} + (c + d \text{ OFF}) \text{ depth}^r$$

where cost and depth pertain to a single well here.

The constant b, indicating the additional offshore fixed costs, should capture the cost of the platform. The depth factor should capture variable costs, i.e., those incurred drilling and equipping the wells. While the depth coefficient would apply only to the sample area, platform costs in the Gulf of Mexico apply with some reliability to other areas in the world (see following). It is expected that variable costs of drilling to a given depth will be less for an onshore versus an offshore well. Delay time, for example, is generally greater per foot drilled for offshore wells. As argued previously, one expects the exponent r to be greater than unity.

As a check we used a slightly different functional form, with the same economic assumptions:

$$\text{cost} = a + b\ \text{OFF} + (c + d\ \text{OFF})(e^{r\,\text{depth}} - 1).$$

The sample consisted of 76 observations from south and offshore Louisiana in the 1974–1977 period. Sample data was in the same form as described previously, except that the further breakdown given in the *Joint Association Surveys* of each region into depth classes was used. We also have the new variable measuring depth. An observation on depth is the average well depth of the wells drilled to a depth within given bounds in a region during a year. Costs, e.g., are now total costs incurred in drilling wells whose depth lay within the bounds, as opposed to all wells, in the region for the year. OFF indicates whether the region was onshore or offshore.

As the equations above have depth entering nonlinearly, it is not quite correct to simply substitute in the observed average depth of several wells to obtain an empirical counterpart to the equations for estimation purposes. As our many approximations are rough anyway, this should lead to no additional reservations.

Results, as usual in thousands of 1974 dollars, were:

$$\text{costs/wells} = 109.5 + 514.2\ \text{OFF}$$
$$\quad\quad (5.64)\quad\ (15.9)$$
$$\quad\quad\quad\quad R^2 = .964$$

$$\quad + (1.28 \times 10^{-12} + 4.99 \times 10^{-13}\ \text{OFF})\ \text{depth}^{3.55},$$
$$\quad\quad (28.4)\quad\quad\quad\quad\quad (5.0)$$
$$\quad\quad n = 76$$

$$\text{costs/wells} = 36.6 + 447.0\ \text{OFF} + (46.7 + 21.9\ \text{OFF})(e^{2 \times 10^{-4}\,\text{depth}} - 1).$$
$$\quad\quad (1.68)\ \ (11.6)\quad\quad (27.6)\quad\quad\quad\quad (5.6)$$
$$\quad\quad\quad R^2 = .962\quad n = 76$$

In appendix A we give details on the year-to-year stability of the results, and discuss estimation methodologies and other econometric issues pertaining to the above equations.

In 1978 dollars, the platform cost per well is $792,000 according to the first equation and $688,000 according to the second. The first specification seems somewhat preferable for its simplicity, but the choice is a close one.

The onshore intercepts (the coefficient "a"), especially in the first specification estimates, are positive and significant, unlike the 38 region onshore regression shown earlier. This may be due to some specification error reflected in the difference in right-hand side variables; or again it may be due to the different degrees of aggregation in the respective samples. Focusing on one area and further breaking down the sample enables one to isolate the fixed factor that was lost in the noise in the aggregated regional sample. The discussion in appendix A offers further insights. Since rig years will be the independent variable used and since onshore fixed costs are relatively small and vary much more than platform costs over regions, onshore fixed costs are ignored in subsequent cost estimates.

The second body of data yields a result fairly close to the above results. A 1978 survey by Brown and Root was summarized in *Offshore*.[10] For a single well in 60 feet of water or less, the cost of a caisson to protect the pipe ranged from $75,000 to $100,000. A well protector platform, which must still be connected to a production platform, costs from $500,000 to $1.2 million for "several wells." Maximum water depth is about 200 feet. A production platform costs from $4 million to $8 million. These are somewhat shallow depths, and the lack of any well information precludes their use for any cost estimates.

In the same survey, Brown and Root report, "The minimum self-contained drilling and production platform is the most common unit in the Gulf of Mexico for reasons of reservoir size, low initial investment, mild environmental conditions, and relatively shallow water." The platform can operate in a maximum water depth of 400 feet.

The API self-contained drilling and production platform can take twice as many wells, 12 to 24, as the minimum platform, and allows production to start while drilling is still going on. Hence its higher initial cost may be offset by the larger number of wells (an economy of scale); and the quicker receipt of income is then a net gain. Costs of the two platform types are compared in table 6.3.

Oil and Gas Journal, April 30, 1979, p. 4, estimates that the Cognac platform, in 1000 feet of water, cost $265 million for 60 wells, or $4.4 million per well. A cost 6.66 times as great ($6.66 = 4.4/.661$, see table 6.3) in water 2.5 times as deep (1000 vs. 400 feet) suggests a depth-platform cost exponent of 2.1 ($2.5^{2.069} = 6.66$). This is the net effect of much higher costs partly offset by scale economies.

Table 6.3
Comparison of minimum and API self-contained platforms

	Minimum	API
Number of wells	6 to 12	12 to 24
Total cost ($m.)	4.85 to 6.151	10.20 to 11.25
$m/well	.808 to .513	.850 to .469
avg. $m/well	.661	.660

Source: *Offshore*, vol. 38, no. 13, December 1978, pp. 46–56.

Table 6.4
Sample comparison of calculated versus actual platform costs

Well slots per platform	Water depth (feet)	Cost per well $ thousands	
		Calculated	Actual
12	320	548	583
24	325	558	458

Source: *Oil and Gas Journal*, Aug. 20, 1979, p. 54; *Oil and Gas Journal*, Aug. 27, 1979, p. 43.

We proceed as follows. Outside the United States, if we know that depth is below 60 feet we will assign $87,500 platform cost per well (87,500 = 1/2 (75,000 + 100,000), see above); where depth is unknown we will use $700,000, in 1978 dollars. Where depth (D) is known and exceeds 400 feet, we will use the factor $700,000 \times (D/400)^{2.0}$. Where depth is known and lies between 60 and 400 feet we will use the factor $87,500 \times (D/60)^{1.1}$, as $(700/87.5) = (400/60)^{1.1}$. The latter rule can be tested by two recent examples off Louisiana. The comparison is given in table 6.4. The fit is reasonably good, but we do not capture economies of scale.

In effect, we treat the regression results as a strong confirmation of the Brown and Root estimates. They include various water depths, hence must differ from Brown and Root, except by chance.

We will add the rig time factor derived from the Louisiana time series regression to the platform costs per well to get total investment per well. This is not completely logical and tends to overstate U.S. costs, but it is the best we can do, particularly because it allows us to control for the effect of depth of water in areas outside the United States.

In equal circumstances offshore drilling costs do not vary much around the world. Labor is cheaper in Southeast Asia and some Mediterranean areas, but material costs are "universally the same ..., except in remote areas ..."[11] North Sea platforms are of course far more expensive, and

Southeast Asia platforms somewhat cheaper because lesser wave action permits lighter structures. "Platform costs everywhere else are virtually the same as the [U.S.] Gulf of Mexico and contractor charges today are comparable for the same structure. But there is plenty of variability inside each area, and no two platforms are ever the same."[11]

VI Nondrilling Well Expenditures

Until now the focus has been on explaining the drilling and equipping expenses of a well, as a function of some of the characteristics of the well. However, there are other well-related expenses such as lease equipment and overhead which also must be included to obtain a true marginal cost of drilling. In applying the previously developed cost factors to other parts of the world we will have as data total rig years for a given region. We would prefer to have exploratory and development rig years separately, but usually only have a total.

Given development rig years for an onshore region, or development rig years and the number of development wells for an offshore region, the previously derived cost factors can be applied to give total drilling and equipping (D & E) expenses for development wells. Other development well-related expenses to be accounted for are (1) lease equipment, (2) improved recovery programs (by water or gas injection), and (3) general and direct overhead. From 1966 to 1975, for the United States as a whole, the ratio of D & E expenses to D & E plus the other three expenses was stable.[12] The average ratio was .604, with no one year having a ratio of less than .587 or greater than .625. Thus a simple and apparently reliable way to obtain total development well-related expenses from development D & E expenses is to divide the latter by .604. The relationships between total well-related development expenses and the component expenses is summarized in table 6.5.

Well-related expenses in addition to D & E expenses incurred during exploratory drilling are (1) contributions towards test wells, and (2) direct and general overhead. Their relations to total exploratory well related expenses are summarized in table 6.6.

Where we do not know how many well completions are exploratory and how many are development we will use the expedient of considering them all development, dividing drilling and equipping outlays by .604. Obviously this will overstate costs, but there is no practical alternative. The proportions of developments and of exploratory wells to total wells in the United States are not the same as in another country, except by chance.

Table 6.5
Development well-related expenses in the United States

Development well expense	Average ratio of the expense to total development well expenses, 1966–75	Range of the ratio, 1966–75
Drilling and equipping	.604	.587 to .625
Lease equipment	.165	.145 to .189
Improved recovery programs	.095	.075 to .121
Other including direct overhead	.063	.048 to .078
General and administrative overhead (allocated to development)	.074	.061 to .083

Source: *Joint Association Survey of the U.S. Oil and Gas Producing Industry, Section II: Expenditures for Exploration, Development, and Production,* 1969, 1974, and 1975 editions, issued by the statistics department of the American Petroleum Institute.

Table 6.6
Exploration well-related expenses in the United States

Exploration well expense	Average ratio of the expense to total development well expenses, 1966–75	Range of the ratio, 1966–75
Drilling and equipping	.705	.666 to .755
Contributions towards test wells	.022	.013 to .026
Other including direct overhead	.109	.094 to .124
General and administrative overhead (allocated to exploration)	.163	.132 to .191

Source: *Joint Association Survey of the U.S. Oil and Gas Producing Industry, Section II: Expenditures for Exploration, Development, and Production,* 1969, 1974, and 1975 editions, issued by the statistics department of the American Petroleum Institute.

Hence a blended or average U.S. factor would in general not be correct. When and if we acquire more knowledge of exploratory and development wells separately we can quickly reduce the estimate by substituting in the new numbers, with no need to recalculate the factor for nondrilling and equipping expenditures.

VII   Investment Coefficients

The costs of drilling and equipping a development well are now applied to calculate the dollar requirements per initial daily barrel ($/idb) in the principal oil producing areas of the world. The costs per initial daily barrel include nothing about the expected length of life of the wells; however, see the section following on operating costs. The basic calculation using historical data, for a country c and year t, is:

$$(\$/idb)_{ct} = \frac{(\text{rig years})_{ct} \times (\$/\text{rig year})}{\text{new oil-well capacity})_{ct}} \times \frac{\text{development well expenses}}{\text{total D \& E expenses}}$$

$$\times\ 365$$

for the onshore section, and

$$(\$/idb)_{ct} = \frac{[(\text{rig years})_{ct} \times (\$/\text{rig year})] + [(\text{oil-well completions})_{ct} \times (\$/\text{platform})]}{(\text{new oil-well capacity})_{ct}}$$

$$\times\ \frac{\text{development well expenses}}{\text{total D \& E expenses}} \times 365$$

for the offshore area.

The factors ($/rig year), ($/platform), and (development well expenses/ total D & E expenses) are constants, whose derivation has been the subject of this paper heretofore. To summarize, the values used, in 1978 dollars, were: rig year onshore, $4.766 million ($3.094m in '74 dollars); rig year offshore, $9.44 million ($6.13m in '74 dollars); well platform, $700,000, except for Venezuela, where $87,500 was used; development well expenses/ total D & E expenses, 1.65(= 1/.604). Flow from new oil wells was unavailable, therefore it was approximated by: (new oil-well capacity)$_{ct}$ = (oil-well completions)$_{ct}$ × (weighted average flow rate)$_{ct}$. Data sources and methods are now explained.

Data

Rig Years   Rig years were obtained from the Hughes Tool international rig count reports. Data were in the form average number of rigs running during the year, over all months. When all months were not reported the average of the reported rigs running during the available months was used. Hughes Tool differentiates onshore and offshore rig operations.

New Oil-Well Capacity   *World Oil* magazine reports each year in its August 15 issue the number of oil-well completions for each country during the previous year. To find, where necessary, how many of these completions were offshore several sources were used. Usually *Offshore* magazine's June 20 issues gave satisfactory numbers for total offshore oil-well completions. For some countries in some years only total offshore well (oil, gas, and dry hole) completions were given. In this case it was assumed that both onshore and offshore well completions that year had the same proportion of oil wells to total wells as did the whole country, as reported in *World Oil*.

When *Offshore* offered no information or the information appeared incomplete, well completions were tabulated from the lists in the October issues of the *AAPG Bulletin*. Finally in two cases, Venezuela 1976 and Nigeria 1977, the change in the offshore operating oil-well stock, from 1975 to 1976 and 1976 to 1977, respectively, as reported in the *Oil and Gas Journal (OGJ)* "World Wide Oil" reports, in the final issues of the respective years, was used as the only available proxy. In every case breaking out development oil-well completions from the total was impossible, so all completions were assumed to be development wells. As all rig years likewise had to be assumed to be development rig years the resulting biases were mutually offsetting to a large degree.

For a country in a given year the weighted average flow rate per well was calculated as $\Sigma_i(Q_i/Q_m)(Q_i/W_i)$, where Q_i = production in major field i, $Q_m = \Sigma Q_i$ = total production of all major fields, W_i = total producing wells in major field i. "Major" fields are those listed in *International Petroleum Encyclopedia (IPE)*. All figures were obtained from listings in *IPE* or, if those data were suspect or unavailable, from *OGJ*'s "World Wide Oil" report, last issue of every year. Here Q_i/Q_m is used as the weighting factor, $\Sigma(Q_i/Q_m) = 1$, with the intention that the flow rates per well of fields whose production comprises a greater proportion of the country's total production will get greater weight in the estimate of the typical flow rate of a new oil well for that country, in that year. An example is given in table 6.7. As the larger fields have the greater flow rates the weighted average flow rate is greater than the simple unweighted average.

Table 6.7
Flow rate example

Field	Q_i	Q_i/Q_m	W_i	Q_i/W_i	$(Q_i/Q_m) \times (Q_i/W_i)$
A	10	1/6	5	2	1/3
B	20	1/3	4	5	5/3
C	30	1/2	5	6	3
	$Q_m = 60$			13	6

Note: unweighted average flow rate = 13/3 = 4.33; weighted average flow rate = 6.

North Sea   As capital expenditures were directly available for the North
Sea, and the per rig year and per well costs developed before do not apply
in extreme conditions such as are present in the North Sea, there was no
need to take the indirect route to estimate them. Expenditures were taken
from Wood, Mackenzie, October 27, 1977, *Section 2 of the North Sea Service,
Revision of Parts A, B and C.*

Calculated Coefficients

The calculated coefficients presented in table 6.8 were computed as given
in the formulas (7.1) or (7.2) except that instead of using data from a single
year, total rig years and wells completed from 1974 to 1977 were used in
the numerator, and $\Sigma_{t=1974}^{t=1977}$(well completions)$_{ct}$ × (weighted average flow
rate)$_{ct}$ in the denominator. Coefficients for individual North Sea fields are
presented in appendix B.

Some of the coefficients are small sample absurdities, and are left as
examples of the consequences of applying the methodology with insufficient data. The outstanding example is Australia where an average of four
and a quarter rigs ran during 1976, on both exploratory and development
work, while only one oil producer, producing only 112 barrels daily, was
brought in. Similar sample characteristics make Kuwait much too high; and
Brazil and Mexico too are improbably high, the latter because of a surge in
drilling and the delayed production response.

Uses and Limitations of the Coefficients

The coefficients in table 6.8 are national averages. They will not, therefore,
apply to any given field. But with a relatively small amount of information
for a specific field we can calculate investment requirements and per barrel
costs there. Hence the methods developed in this paper serve as a bridge
from the highly aggregated measures of table 6.8 to an individual reservoir.

To some extent, however, the figures in table 6.8 can be used for disaggregated analysis. For example, Nigeria is trying to encourage investment in exploration. The kinds of reservoirs to be found will most likely
resemble those already found. We can take the average investment per
onshore well, from the worksheets to table 6.8, as constant. Offshore well
cost can be varied with water depth by the use of the platform costs, and
the pipeline costs described in appendix C. Then we can, to a first approximation, treat the cost per barrel in each field as the average investment
divided by the field flow rate, and calculate a frequency distribution of

Table 6.8
Investment requirements per initial daily barrel of capacity, 1974–1977, in 1978 dollars

Africa			Central and South America		
Algeria	onshore	3,310.3	Argentina	onshore	15,805.4
Egypt	onshore	5,078.4	Brazil	onshore	9,211.7
	offshore	2,188.7		offshore	23,962.8
Libya	onshore	604.2	Mexico-total	onshore	31,718.8
Nigeria	onshore	534.6	Mexico-Reforma	onshore	NA
	offshore*	1,667.6		offshore	NA
Rest of North	onshore*	3,702.0	Venezuela	onshore	643.6
Africa	offshore*	1,846.0		offshore^c	5,482.4
Rest of Central	onshore	2,390.1	Rest of Central	onshore	1,560.9
& So. Africa	offshore	4,838.9	& So. America	offshore	4,296.9
Europe			Middle East		
North Sea		6,088.0^a	Bahrain	onshore	7,290.0
(1976–77)		8,908.3^b	Iran	onshore	206.9
Rest of Europe	onshore	2,709.9		offshore	961.2
	offshore	57,791.1	Iraq	onshore	400.2
Central and East Asia			Saudi Arabia &	onshore	106.1
Malaysia/Brunei	offshore	2,817.1	Neutral Zone	offshore	418.1
Rest of Central	onshore	4,121.9	U.A.E.	onshore	200.7
& East Asia				offshore	1,925.7
			Far East/Oceania		
			Australia	onshore*	298,548.6
				offshore	2,672.5
			Indonesia	onshore	807.0
				offshore	1,785.3
			Rest of Far	onshore*	90,117.8
			East/Oceania		

*One or more years omitted in calculation due to too few reported rig years or well completions those years.
a. Excludes costs of transportation to shore.
b. Includes costs of transportation to shore.
c. Lake Maracaibo

investment per unit of initial output, and cost per barrel of each current Nigerian field onshore and offshore.

If the new fields were drawn out of the same universe as the old, then our best estimate of costs in the fields to be discovered would be the mean costs in the old fields; we could specify probabilities of how much above or below the mean would be the investment required for the development of the to-be-discovered fields. But it is more likely that the new fields will be smaller and less prolific than the old. The extent of an upward cost shift is the subject of research now under way; see Eckbo, Jacoby and Smith, (1978), e.g., on predicting the sizes of future reservoir discoveries in an area based on the area's history.

The limitations of our estimates are several, technical problems aside. We have on two occasions made an arbitrary choice: the combination of higher rig time cost and higher platform cost estimates for offshore areas, and the treating of all oil wells as if they were development wells. In both cases we have taken the higher cost option and have avoided attempting an offsetting adjustment, because it will permit easier substitution when better numbers become available.

There are also factors of understatement. The most important is the omission of transport costs, where they are properly part of development expenditures. These include the gathering system, the offshore or onshore pipeline to a loading terminal, and the terminal itself. In the case of the North Sea, transportation costs comprise about 50 percent of total investment, and are absolutely high; elsewhere they are a smaller percent of the total, and in absolute dollar terms very much less. Initial estimates of some pipeline cost determinants are presented in appendix C.

Some omissions or understatements are desirable. The cost of new facilities in the Persian Gulf and other booming areas is often inflated by port congestion, demurrage, special transport charges, and by the general inefficiency and corruption that accompanies such conditions. These are not costs, although the case of congestion may warrant closer consideration, but transfer payments, which should be netted out of total costs.

Another inaccuracy may work either way. We have used the average U.S. factor for improved recovery programs, i.e., fluid injection, in going from drilling and equipping expenses to total well-related expenses. For many places this average overstates costs, in some cases it very much understates them. The most important case is for Saudi Arabia, where the great Ghawar field is being expanded by massive water injection at a cost much higher than for drilling and equipping alone. We show in appendix D that a widely quoted figure released by the U.S. Senate Foreign Relations

Committee on the cost of capacity expansion in Saudi Arabia is too high by factor of 4 to 8. A sufficient demonstration of this is that if one expected undeveloped onshore fields in Saudi Arabia to be even ten times as expensive as the old, but with no need for fluid injection, then the Ghawar project would be uneconomic. Hence the project cannot cost more than a small fraction of what it is alleged to cost.

The cumulative effects of the various understatements and overstatements may be discerned to some extent from the comparison of our expenditure estimates with some reported investment figures, presented in appendix E.

VIII   Operating Costs

Operating costs, unlike capital costs, vary little with well depth. A set of estimates by the Bureau of Mines, continued by the Department of Energy, shows that for onshore wells in six important U.S. areas, a sixfold increase in depth barely doubles operating costs, i.e., costs increase approximately as the 0.4 power of depth.[13] We take as the representative U.S. figure: $11.7 thousand per well. It corresponds to a south Louisiana 8,000-foot well. California is the most expensive and western Texas the cheapest, respectively, about 120 and 75 percent of south Louisiana, area in terms of operating costs for a similar well. For any given area we can make a depth adjustment according to the average depth of well by using the 0.4 rule, and keeping in mind that for any depth the cost may easily deviate 25 percent upwards or downwards.

The D.O.E.-E.I.A. estimates are for a well producing 100 barrels daily by some form of artificial lift. A flowing well would be cheaper. Some minor economies of scale are incorporated by assuming a 10-well producing unit.

Additional equipment needed for secondary recovery (e.g., fluid injection) was slightly more expensive than needed for primary recovery. Thus our procedure of spreading all improved recovery expenditures over all wells somewhat overstates investment in primary recovery. More importantly, the greatest part of the total investment in all secondary recovery operations, from two thirds to three fourths, consists of the cost of drilling injection wells, which we capture in total drilling time.

In addition, the total annual operating cost for secondary recovery is about twice as high as for primary recovery, while secondary recovery produces about three times as much output. Our neglect of secondary recovery in making estimates for foreign production costs thus imparts a mild upward bias to the estimates.

Offshore, direct operating costs are so little dependent on well depth that no attempt has been made to estimate them, all calculations being for 10,500 true vertical feet (eliminating the effect of directional drilling). Greater economies of scale are allowed for in using 12 to 18 slot platforms. Every slot was assumed to drain one oil and one gas zone, and to produce 917 barrels of oil and 3.3 mmcf of gas per day. In adapting these data to non-American operations gas production will be ignored, except in special cases. This again overstates operating costs per oil well.

Offshore operating costs are rather insensitive to depth of water as well. Moreover, the estimates include transportation of personnel and other distance-related expenditures, so that the depth-distance association is explicitly included. Thus for an 18-slot platform, a sixfold increase in water depth (from 100 to 600 feet) increased annual operating costs by only 21 percent, i.e., to a power of .106. As a representitive figure we choose $146,000 per well per year on a 12-slot platform in 300 feet of water.

A well on an 18-slot platform would cost only $113,000 per year. Obviously, economies of scale are still substantial in the range between 12 and 18 slots per platform. Of course some North Sea platforms contain 42 slots but only deeper water and much more severe operating conditions maintain economies of scale over so wide a range.

If these estimates are to be used elsewhere in the world a severe problem is to allow for greater output per well than 100 and 917 barrels daily for onshore and offshore wells, respectively. If the basic operation of production is that of putting fluid through a cylinder, then material costs expand proportionally to the square root of production increases. Operating costs would not proportionally increase as much, but this square root rule will be used until contrary evidence is found.

Much of the discussion in this section is summed up in table 6.9. All else equal, an offshore barrel abroad should cost about three times as much as an onshore barrel.

With a discount rate ρ, a decline rate α, and a well lifetime T we may multiply the operating expense by $(1 - e^{-(\alpha+\rho)T})/(\alpha + \rho), = \int_0^T e^{-(\alpha+\rho)t}dt$, to obtain a present value equivalent to be added to the investment per daily barrel.[14] For example, with a discount rate of .15, a decline rate of .05, and a well life of ten years the equivalent investment per daily barrel for the onshore United States would be $631, = [(1 - e^{-2})/.2] \times \$.40 \times 365$; for the onshore foreign well it would be only $205. These are small but not negligible additions to total investment.

We hope that those of our readers with special knowledge and data will communicate them to us. Especially useful would be data on individual

Table 6.9
Current operating expenses

		Output in barrels/day/well	Cost in $/day/well	$/barrel	Source
Onshore:	U.S.	100	40	.40	DOE-EIA
	Foreign	1000	126	.13	Hypothetical
Offshore:	U.S.	917	389	.42	DOE-EIA
	Foreign	5000	908	.18	Hypothetical

Source: DOE-EIA numbers from U.S. Department of Energy—Energy Information Administration, *Cost and Indices for Domestic Oil Field Equipment and Production Operations, 1978* (1979), DOE-EIA-0185, p. 8, Table 3.

fields for calibration. The cost of drilling and equipping is much more variable for the expensive wells, as noted above. Outside the United States, we expect, those costs generally run higher. Of course, as pointed out in the beginning, to the extent that lesser efficiency in any particular country consists of more rig time per well, our method captures it.

Appendix A: Platform Cost Regressions

The nature of the sample used in the regressions was time series cross-section, as detailed in section V. One expects that in a given observation cell, i.e., a given depth category in one of the two regions (south or offshore Louisiana) in a given year, the average observed costs are more likely to reflect "true" costs when the number of wells is large, since outliers have less chance to have significant effects. The offshore Louisiana sample cells often had very few wells and frequently the average cost per well for such a cell looked suspicious, usually too low. Such observations were omitted in estimating the regressions. In keeping with the policy of giving cells with a larger number of wells more weight the observations in the sample were weighted by the square root of the number of wells in computing the regression parameters, i.e., each side of the equation to be estimated was multiplied by the square root of the number of wells in the observation cell before the least squares parameters were found. This is equivalent to a heteroskedasticity correction where the variance of the random term is inversely proportional to the number of wells making up the observation.

A problem whose significance is hard to assess arises from possible correlation between depth and the (assumed) additive random error terms on the equations' right-hand sides; indeed similar problems may occur in all of the other regressions in this paper as well. If it is noticed that the random term is going to be negative, for example the drilling seems to be going exceptionally easily, then the well might be drilled deeper than otherwise, either on the chance of tapping a deeper marginally attractive horizon (development), or on the chance of making a hit (exploratory). Looking at it another way, for deep wells to be profitable they perhaps need to have small or negative random terms. This type of dependence leads to upwardly biased intercept estimates and downwardly biased slope terms. As the parameter of principle interest, the coefficient b in the equations, is the difference between the onshore and offshore intercepts the resulting bias there may be small.

Similar reasoning indicates that a bias might arise due to dependence between the well count per cell and the random term. Again, the resulting bias of the measured difference in intercepts may be small. In either case, however, even if the bias of some coefficient estimates is negligible the bias of the t-statistics and the R^2 may be significant.

In both equations the depth factor r enters nonlinearly. As the available nonlinear regression packages diverged in the estimation attempts, grid search methods were used. Fixing r, one minimizes the sum of squared errors to get the other parameter estimates that enter linearly, and obtains the resulting sum of squared errors. Searching over possible values of r, the r that results in the smallest sum of squares is chosen as the estimate, along with the corresponding other estimates. The t-statistics shown in the text were computed with r fixed at its chosen value and thus do not reflect any uncertainty in that choice.

In table 6.10 the year-to-year weighted least squares estimates of the two equations are presented, and the results from the combined sample are repeated from section V. The year-to-year stability of some coefficient estimates is less than ideal though, arguably, never alarming. It appears that (real) costs associated with offshore drilling may have increased in the 1976–1977 period, in which case assuming that the same coefficients hold throughout is wrong. For our purposes the values of b from the full sample are reasonable approximate estimates.

Appendix B: North Sea Fields

Data available on the North Sea enable us to calculate investment coefficients directly, without taking the rig time/well number route. These are given in table 6.11 in the form of total capital expenditures per daily barrel of peak production. Peak production, or expected peak production in some

Table 6.10
Platform cost equation stability

cost = $a + b$ OFF + $(c + d$ OFF$)$ depth$^{3.55}$			
Sample period	a	b	c	d
1974–77	109.5	514.2	1.28×10^{-12}	4.99×10^{-13}
1974	111.2	456.1	1.12×10^{-12}	2.66×10^{-13}
1975	104.2	486.2	1.32×10^{-12}	2.88×10^{-13}
1976	92.3	513.8	1.33×10^{-12}	6.22×10^{-13}
1977	135.4	574.3	1.32×10^{-12}	7.27×10^{-13}

cost = $a + b$ OFF + $(c + d$ OFF$)(e^{2 \times 10^{-4} \text{depth}} - 1)$			
Sample period	a	b	c	d
1974–77	36.6	447.0	46.7	21.9
1974	46.8	411.9	41.4	12.2
1975	24.0	438.4	48.6	13.4
1976	18.8	431.4	48.0	27.4
1977	62.7	488.7	47.9	30.9

cases, is given in the reports on individual fields. Capital costs are given in current dollars, where expected future capital costs "take future inflation rates into account," although this is not explained. The most reasonable transformation we could come up with was to use the IPAA index to transform past expenditures to 1978 dollars (lacking a better index for the area) and to assume expected future expenditures are in 1978 dollars. Capital expenditures are also given in the individual field reports. Note that the costs and outputs are a combination of ex ante anticipations and ex post realizations, and that peak production is sustained longer in some fields than others.

Appendix C: Pipeline Costs

Pipeline costs frequently are an important component of the capital costs of expanding offshore, and sometimes onshore, production. Initial results on the determinants of the costs of pipeline construction, taken from a recent sample, are presented herein. Data points consist of 69 pipeline construction contracts listed in *Offshore* magazine, July 1979, pp. 51–60.

The critical dimensions of a pipeline to be constructed are its diameter and length. Presumably material and assembly (fitting and welding, e.g.) costs are proportional to the product of the two. These costs may differ for oil and gas pipelines due to their possibly different specific requirements. In

Table 6.11
Investment requirements per daily barrel of peak production in the North Sea in 1978 dollars

Field	$/daily barrel	Peak production (tbd)	Peak year
Argyll	2,955	22	1976
Auk	2,032	48	1980
Beatrice	7,500	80	1981
Beryl	7,156	70	1979
Brent-oil	8,727	550	1982
Buchan	5,840	50	1980
Claymore	3,567	150	1980
Cormorant	9,467	60	1981
Dunlin	6,160	150	1982
Ekofisk area	4,174	765	1981
Forties	3,188	500	1980
Fulmar	5,939	165	1982
Heather	9,180	50	1979
Montrose	5,300	40	1980
Murchison	8,185	120	1983
Ninian	11,868	250	1980
Piper	3,090	300	1978
Statfjord	9,198	400	1984/85
Tartan-oil + LPG	8,390	77	1981
Thistle	5,790	200	1978
Valhall	8,200	95	1983

mean = $6470/daily barrel of peak production
standard deviation = $2642/daily barrel of peak production
weighted mean using peak daily production as weights = $6266/daily barrel
Source: Wood, Mackenzie and Co., *North Sea Report*, November 23, 1978, and October 26, 1977.

addition, there may be a fixed component of costs and a cost associated with the laying down of the pipeline that is proportional to its length but does not depend on the pipeline's diameter or on whether the line is for gas instead of oil. A cost function resulting from this theory would look like:

$$\text{cost} = a + [(b + c\,\text{GAS}) \times \text{diameter} \times \text{length}] + d\,\text{length},$$

where GAS = 1 if the pipeline is for gas, 0 otherwise.

An alternative specification is:

$$\text{cost} = a\,e^{b\text{GAS}}\,\text{diameter}^c\,\text{length}^d,$$

a functional form that has little theory behind it in this case, but has a long history in empirical applications. Taking logs of both sides one obtains:

log(cost) = log(a) + b GAS + c log(diameter) + d log(length).

The estimation results, where cost is in millions of current dollars, length is in miles, diameter is in inches, and the figures in parentheses are t-statistics under the null hypothesis that the coefficient is zero, were:

cost = 1.06 + [(.015 + .012 GAS) × diameter × length] − .000075 length
$\quad$ (7.14) (9.15)$\quad$ (5.53)$\qquad\qquad\qquad\qquad$ (−.001)
R^2 = .869$\qquad\qquad\qquad\qquad$ $n = 69$

log(cost) = − 1.3 + .5 GAS + .45 log(diameter) + .52 log (length)
$\qquad$ (−3.0) (3.32)$\quad$ (2.59)$\qquad\qquad$ (8.62)
$\qquad$ R^2 = .668$\qquad\qquad$ $n = 69$

The results from applying the first specification suggest that the only important variable costs are those proportional to material costs, and that there is a modest fixed component in pipeline construction costs. The results from applying the second suggest that cost is approximately proportional to the square root of material requirements. The first result seems more reasonable intuitively.

A criterion for deciding which specification is preferable is to see which one gives results that better predict costs once one is outside the sample ranges of the right-hand side variables. The vast majority of the pipelines in the sample here were 10 miles long or less, with diameters of 6 to 16 inches. Now the predicted cost of a hypothetical oil pipeline 50 miles long and 20 inches in diameter is $16.1 million according to the first specification and $8.04 million according to the second. While it is hard to say with no further information which is a better estimate, it seems fairly clear from looking at the few sample points outside the cluster defined above that the latter is probably a large underprediction while the former may not be unreasonable. In any case it is reasonable that economies of scale in construction indicated by the square root rule may not extend to very long pipelines. Further investigation will be necessary before any definitive results can be found.

Appendix D: Capital Costs in Saudi Arabia

Reference: "The Future of Saudi Arabia Oil Production," A Staff Report to the Subcommittee on International Policy of the Committee on Foreign Relations, U.S. Senate, April 1979, 96th Congress, first session.

On page 33: "As of 1977, the Aramco facility capacity of 11.1 mmbd had been built and maintained at an investment cost of $5 billion or $455 per B/D of oil capacity." For the whole Middle East, total cumulative expenditures since 1946 amounted to about $11.8 billion according to Chase Manhattan Bank's *Capital Investments of the World Petroleum Industry* reports of the past 15 years. Dividing this by approximately 28 million barrels of daily capacity in 1977 gives $421 per daily barrel. But much of the Chase Manhattan Bank "production" investment is for exploratory drilling, lease rentals, and gas-gathering outlays which are not related to oil production. Moreover, a substantial part of "Mid East" investment has taken place in such areas as Syria, Turkey, and Israel, which have swallowed substantial funds but produced little oil. Since $455 exceeds by a fair margin $421 *less* some allowance for these factors of overstatement, the report implies that Aramco unit capacity costs have been substantially higher than the average in the Middle East. This is implausible, to put it mildly. The alleged past investment outlay of $5 billion must therefore be rejected.

An approximate comparison of historical Aramco unit capacity costs verus those of the entire Middle East may be obtained by noting that over the years 1959 through 1970 plus 1973 through 1977, Saudi Arabian rig time (exploration and development) comprised less than one tenth of total Middle East rig time, while at the beginning of 1978 they had more than 40 percent of the total Middle East capacity. Indications are thus that Aramco capacity costs were as little as one quarter of the average Middle East capacity costs, i.e., as little as on the order of $105 ($=$421/4$) per daily barrel.

There is another independent error in the estimate of $455 per daily barrel for past investment. Any figure of cumulated costs has a significant bias. Aramco proved reserves are today around 110 billion barrels. Cumulative production through 1977 was about 31 billion barrels. Hence total past expenditures went to develop reserves that were about 1.28 $[(110 + 31)/110]$ times current proved reserves. Reserves and production capacity are closely linked, and we can therefore make an approximate correction for past capacity used up and replaced by dividing the figure of cumulative expenditures by 1.28, which brings the estimated development requirements down accordingly. Thus if $455 per daily barrel of current capacity had really been spent in the past for oil development, and nothing was expected to change, then the best estimate we would make is $355 $=$ $455/1.28, for an additional daily barrel of capacity. By past standards— which may not govern any more—$355 is probably too high.

On page 32: "... anticipated cost of expanding facility capacity from 11 mmbd to 16 mmbd was projected to be approximately $11.4 billion in current dollars, or $2,280 per barrel of daily capacity." It appears that this may be an overstatement by a factor of 4 to 8. Around $10 billion of the $11.4 billion is to be used on projects other than increases in crude oil output.

The water flood project in the Ghawar and Abqaiq fields is to increase capacity from the current 5 mmbd to 7 mmbd at a cost of $1 billion, with possibilities of expansion to 10 mmbd later.[15] Thus if at a cost of $1 billion output can be expanded by 2 mmbd, the cost per daily barrel of new capacity is $500. If the full scheme is implemented, possibly at a cost of $1.4 billion ($11.4 billion less $10 billion), output would be expanded by 5 mmbd, or at a cost of $280/daily barrel.

An independent upwardly biased estimate may be obtained. The reference, p. 33, gives cost of water injection facilities at $280 per daily barrel, and cost of desalting equipment of $165/daily barrel. If these costs are added to the Saudi Arabian investment coefficient in table 6.8 of $106 per daily barrel the resulting sum is $551/daily barrel. This estimate involves some double counting because part of the $106/daily barrel includes cost of drilling and equipping water injection wells which usually constitute the bulk of the investment (see section VII). In any case, $2,280/daily barrel is evidently far outside plausible limits.

The implication of another statement in the report will now be considered (p. 32): "The absolute cost of maintaining and expanding capacity must be evaluated in relation to the alternative uses of these capital funds to the Saudi government. In this context, petroleum revenues today must be used and invested for the day when oil revenues decline. The alternative investment to new capacity is investment in other productive assets which would maintain the Saudi Arabian government revenues after the oil has been depleted."

Assume that oil is sold at $14 per barrel, and that operating costs are 25 cents per barrel. Then net cash flow for the year will be around $5,020 per daily barrel of utilized capacity. This is a rate of return on $2,280 or more than 200 percent. It would be interesting to know of any "other productive assets" that yield as much as one tenth of 200 percent.

Appendix E: Comparison of Expenditure Estimates

While no analogs to the investment coefficients in table 6.8 are known to the authors, some rough checks for accuracy are possible. Chase Manhattan

Table 6.12
Estimated investment expenditures vs. Chase Manhattan Bank reported investment expenditures, millions of current dollars[a]

	1974	1975	1976	1977
Africa	750	825	1,000	950
	(758)	(1,005)	(1,243)	(1,586)
Far East	1,075	1,500	1,175	1,300
	(1,052)	(1,353)	(1,250)	(1,317)
Middle East	975	1,000	1,375	1,925
	(684)	(962)	(1,168)	(1,315)
Venezuela	290	240	250	375
	(291)	(193)	(196)	(236)
Western Europe	2,375	3,600	4,200	5,275
	(NA)	(5,697)[b]	(5,845)[b]	(5,217)[b]

Source: Chase Manhattan Bank, *Capital Investment in the World Petroleum Industry*, 1974–77 editions.
a. Our estimates were converted to current dollars via the IPAA index used elsewhere in this paper. In table Chase Manhattan figures are given with our corresponding estimate underneath in parentheses.
b. Calculated by adding estimated Rest of Europe expenditures, computed the usual way, and capital expenditures in the North Sea reported by Wood, Mackenzie.

Bank in its annual report, mentioned in the previous appendix, on capital investment in the world petroleum industry gives a figure on total expenditures on oil and gas "production" for various aggregate regions. These figures can be compared with our expenditures estimated from rig years and well completions. As Chase Manhattan Bank includes in its figures outlays on gas-gathering systems,[16] terminals, and lease rentals (a transfer payment within the industry), these numbers should exceed ours. Both series include some exploratory drilling, as we include all rig years in estimating expenditures. The comparison is presented in table 6.12.

Our estimates for Africa exceed Chase Manhattan's numbers, and by 1977 the difference has grown quite large. The reverse is true for Venezuela. We are unable to account for these discrepancies, although in the latter case it is possible we underestimate the cost of offshore wells in Lake Maracaibo. In the Far East we are close and a little over in 1976–1977, probably because drilling conditions there tend to be easy. The Chase Manhattan Bank's Middle East numbers are considered larger than ours, as expected, largely because of the huge gas-gathering systems being built there. Finally, Chase Manhattan's Western Europe figures are usually higher than ours, perhaps because of a difference in accounting systems between Wood, Mackenzie and Chase Manhattan.

The Chase Manhattan Bank numbers indicate, in a rough way, the limits of probable errors in our calculations of capital expenditures. In Africa the true figure may be as much as a third below ours; in the Middle East, the true figure should not be more than half again as high as ours.

Acknowledgments

Respectively, professor and doctoral candidate, Department of Economics, M.I.T. This work was supported by the National Science Foundation under Grant No. SIA75-00739, and is part of a larger project to develop analytical models of the world oil market. The authors would like to thank other members of the project and others for their comments, criticisms, suggestions, and corrections, and the Hughes Tool Company for allowing us access to unpublished rig time data.

Notes

1. Hobson and Pose (1973), pp. 120–121. This condition is so common that the instructions in the Joint Association Survey take notice of it. When giving depth of a well the respondent is told to "exclude bypass footage resulting from remedial side track drilling operation."

2. From *Oil and Gas Journal*, "Journal Survey of Active Fields," Sept. 21, 1970, and Sept. 20, 1971, pp. 106–103 and 144–156.

3. Wells include flowing wells, pumping wells, and dry holes.

4. 1970 dollars were converted to 1971 dollars using an IPAA cost index; see Section 3 and footnote 6.

5. Issued annually by the statistics department of the American Petroleum Institute (API).

6.

1967	60.7	1971	75.9	1975	116.4
1968	62.8	1972	80.3	1976	127.4
1969	65.0	1973	83.5	1977	138.3
1970	68.9	1974	100	1978	154.0 (preliminary)

7. U.S. Bureau of the Census, *Current Industrial Reports, Series MA-13K* (76)–1 (Washington, D.C.: Government Printing Office).

8. Except for to date small scale exploration and production operations off New Jersey, Florida, and Georgia, among others.

9. See Section 3.

10. *Offshore*, vol. 38, no. 13, December 1978, pp. 46–56. We requested the source study unsuccessfully.

11. *Offshore*, vol. 38, no. 10, September 1978, pp. 86–88.

12. Data used were aggregated (total) U.S. figures obtained from the *Joint Association Survey of the U.S. Oil and Gas Producing Industry, Section II: Expenditures for Exploration, Development, and Production*, issued by the statistics department of the American Petroleum Institute, 1969, 1974, and 1975 editions.

13. U.S. Department of Energy—Energy Information Administration, *Cost and Indices for Domestic Oil Field Equipment and Production Operations*, 1978 (1979), DOE/EIA-0185, p. 8, Table 3.

14. The average well does not of course have a production profile wherein the peak production is achieved immediately and a constant decline rate over the life of the well follows. In the more general case where P(t) is the production of the well as a function of time, and the initial capacity of the well is R barrels daily [P(O) = R], then we may multiply operating expense by $\int_0^T e^{-\rho t} P(t)/R \, dt$ to obtain a present value equivalent per daily barrel, for that particular well, to be added to investment per daily barrel.

15. David Mansfield, "Saudi Arabia: Uncertainty Hits Forward Planning," *Petroleum Economist*, August 1978, p. 333.

16. See *Oil and Gas Journal*, July 9, 1979, p. 65. Saudi Arabia associated gas to be gathered and processed under facilities already complete or under way: 1.46 trillion cubic feet/year, or 7.3 percent of total U.S. production. This is counted by Chase Manhattan into "production."

Also see *Lloyd's List*. June 15, 1979. Aramco gas-gathering scheme started in 1974 with scheduled completion in the early 1980's will have an ultimate cost greater than $20 billion.

References

Adelman, M. A., *The World Petroleum Market*, Baltimore: Johns Hopkins University Press, 1972.

Eckbo, P. L., H. D. Jacoby, and J. L. Smith, "Oil Supply Forecasting: A Disaggregated Process Approach," *Bell Journal of Economics*, Vol. 9, No. 1, Spring 1978.

Fisher, F. M., *Supply and Costs in the U.S. Petroleum Industry, Two Econometric Studies*, Washington, D.C.: Resources for the Future, 1964.

Hobson, G.D., and W. Pose, *Modern Petroleum Technology*, London: Applied Sciences Publishers, 1973.

7

The Growth of Proved Reserves in the United States and The Relation of Probable Reserves to Proved Reserves

The process by which proved reserves are increased at one end while being depleted at the other is the movement of inventory from the poorly lit warehouse of probable reserves onto the well-lit shelves of proved reserves, from where it is sold and disappears.

Type of Wells

Reserves are added by drilling, and wells have for years been classified by the Lahee system, devised by the geologist Frederic H. Lahee (figure 7.1). The 1978 statistics, with the percentage of dry holes an indicator of increasing risk, are as follows[1]:

Type of well	Percentage dry holes
Development	22.7
Exploratory:	
Shallower pool	19.2
Outposts	58.3
Deeper pool tests	65.0
New-pool wildcats	61.8
New-field wildcata (approximate 1966–1970 average)	98.3

Each type of well, if successful, adds to proved reserves. Development wells may enlarge the area of a known reservoir, and additional reserves thus credited are the "extensions" of tables 7.1 and 7.2. As reservoirs become better known through operating experience, changes up or down in their

Reprinted from *Energy Resources in an Uncertain Future; Coal, Gas, Oil, and Uranium Supply Forecasting,* Cambridge, MA: Ballinger Publishing Co., 1983.

OBJECTIVE OF DRILLING	INITIAL CLASSIFICATION φ WHEN DRILLING IS STARTED	FINAL CLASSIFICATION AFTER COMPLETION OR ABANDONMENT	
		SUCCESSFUL ● ○ ■	UNSUCCESSFUL ⊕
Drilling for a new field on a structure or in an environment never before productive	1. NEW-FIELD WILDCAT	NEW FIELD DISCOVERY WILDCAT	DRY NEW-FIELD WILDCAT
Drilling for a new pool on a structure or in a geological environment already productive — NEW POOL TESTS — Drilling outside limits of proved area of pool	2. NEW-POOL (PAY) WILDCAT	NEW-POOL DISCOVERY WILDCAT — New-Pool Discovery Wildcat (*Sometimes an extension well*)	DRY NEW-POOL WILDCAT
Drilling inside limits of proved area of pool — For a new pool below deepest proven pool	3. DEEPER POOL (PAY) TEST	NEW-POOL DISCOVERY WELLS (*Sometimes extension wells*) — Deeper Pool Discovery Well	DRY NEW-POOL TESTS — DRY DEEPER POOL TEST
For a new pool above deepest proven pool	4. SHALLOWER POOL (PAY) TEST	Shallower Pool Discovery Well	DRY SHALLOWER POOL TEST
Drilling for long extension of a partly developed pool	5. OUTPOST or EXTENSION TEST	EXTENSION WELL (*Sometimes a new-pool discovery well*)	DRY OUTPOST OR DRY EXTENSION TEST
Drilling to exploit or develop a hydrocarbon accumulation discovered by previous drilling	6. DEVELOPMENT WELL	DEVELOPMENT WELL	DRY DEVELOPMENT WELL

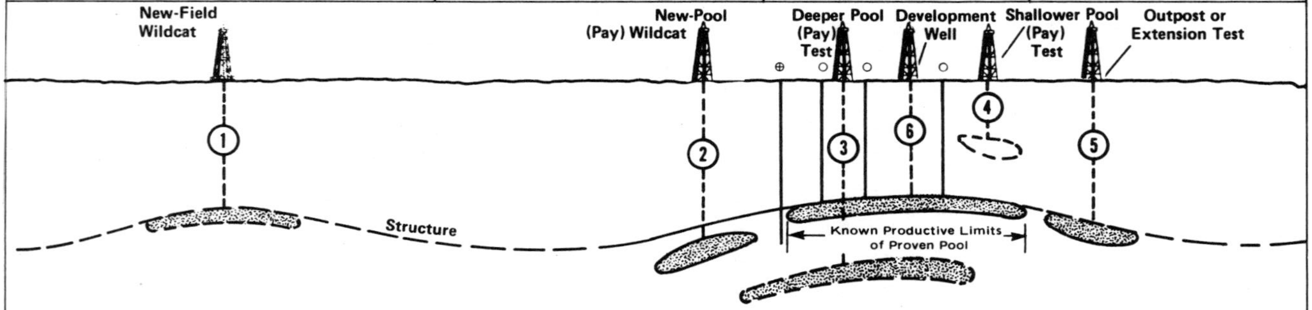

Diagram labels:

New-Field Wildcat ① · New-Pool (Pay) Wildcat ② · Deeper Pool (Pay) Test ③ · Development Well ⑥ · Shallower Pool (Pay) Test ④ · Outpost or Extension Test ⑤ · Known Productive Limits of Proven Pool · Structure

LAHEE CLASSIFICATION OF WELLS, AS APPLIED BY CSD

Figure 7.1
AAPG and API classification of wells. Source: The American Association of Petroleum Geologists, "North American Drilling Activity," AAPG Bulletin (Annual Drilling Issue) 63, no. 8 (1979) Figure 8, titled "AAPG and API Classification of Wells," p. 1202. © American Association of Petroleum Geologists, Tulsa, Oklahoma. Reprinted with permission.

Table 7.1
Crude oil reserves in the United States,[a] by new and old fields, 1946–1975

Period	(1) New field "discoveries"	(2) Exploratory wells (000s) Total	(3) NFW[b]	(4) Recovery (1976 evaluation) from fields discovered in period	(5) Gross additions to proved reserves	(6) New oil from old fields (5)−(4)	(7) Ratios of columns (1)/(4)	(8) (4)/(3)	(9) (6)/(5)
1946–1950	1.8	42.7	20.6	12.7	14.8	2.1	.142	.616	.142
1951–1955	1.4	65.5	35.3	8.8	16.2	7.4	.161	.246	.457
1956–1960	0.9	69.0	31.0	7.1	14.1	7.0	.130	.222	.496
1961–1965	0.7	52.7	33.1	4.3	12.8	8.5	.163	.130	.664
1966–1970	0.6	45.5	27.8	3.6	13.8	10.4	.176	.122	.754
1971–1975	0.7	39.7	26.4	2.1	8.3	6.2	.467	.057	.747
Total	6.1	315.1	174.2	38.6	80.0	41.6	.163	.215	.520

a. Excluding Alaska.
b. New-field wildcats.
Sources: Cols. (1), (4), (5) from API-AGA-CPA, Reserves of Crude Oil, Natural Gas Liquids, and Natural Gas in the United States as of December 31, 1978, (Washington, D.C.: API-AGA, 1976), Tables II and III. Columns (2), (3) from AAPG Bulletin "North American Drilling" issue (various years).

Table 7.2
Natural gas reserves in the United States,[a] by new and old fields, 1946–1975, trillion cubic feet

Period	(1) "Discoveries"[b]	(2) Exploratory wells (000s) Total	(3) NFW	(4) Recovery (1978 evaluation) from fields discovered in period	(5) Gross additions to proved reserves	(6) New gas from old fields (5)–(4)	(7) Ratios of columns (1)/(4)	(8) (4)/(3)	(9) (6)/(5)
1946–1950	18.4	42.7	20.6	67.8	81.8	14.0	.27	3.3	.17
1951–1955	26.0	65.5	35.5	66.9	82.1	15.2	.39	1.9	.18
1956–1960	32.5	69.0	41.0	74.2	98.1	23.9	.44	2.4	.24
1961–1965	32.2	52.7	33.1	50.0	96.4	46.4	.64	1.5	.48
1966–1970	23.5 (11.0)[c]	45.5	27.8	27.8	70.3	42.5	.84 (.40)[d]	1.0	.60
1971–1975	21.5 (9.3)	39.7	26.4	30.2	45.4	15.2	.71 (.31)	1.1	.33
Total	154.1 (129.4)	315.1	174.2	316.9	474.1	157.2	.49 (.41)	1.8	.33

a. Excluding Alaska.
b. Numbers represent "total discoveries," that is, new-field discoveries plus new pools in discovered fields.
c. Numbers in parentheses represent new fields alone.
d. Numbers in parentheses represent calculations using the new-field values from column (1).
Sources: Columns (1), (4), (5) from API-AGA-CPA, *Reserves*, 1978 issue, Tables II and III. Columns (2), (3) from *AAPG Bulletin* "North American Drilling Statistics," issue (various years).

reserves are the "revisions." Upward and downward revisions in estimates of oil were and perhaps still are approximately equal in number, but upward revisions are almost invariably larger because "individual upward revisions are more concentrated among the larger reservoirs which experience has begun to show often turn out to be better with respect to reserves and of longer life than they were judged to be in their earlier years."[2] New reservoirs may be found in old fields shallower, deeper, or removed horizontally. Finally, there are wells drilled to find new fields.

Reported "Discoveries"

Discoveries is a much abused term. One often reads of new reserves "discovered" that are in fact recent additions to proved reserves in known pools. Much more misleading is the implication that petroleum producers need to *discover* some amount to maintain or expand output. They need new reserves, but nobody ever found a reserve. Oilmen find reservoirs, the contents of which they gradually develop into reserves.

Another error is in treating the reserves-added in any given year by API-AGA "discoveries" as though they were an approximation, or at least an indication of, what has in fact been discovered. Year-to-year fluctuations in recorded "discoveries" are largely independent of the year-to-year variation in what has actually been newly found. In fact, oil and gas operators drill development wells into an asssortment of reservoirs, depending on convenience and cost. New reservoirs are typically overrepresented, of course, because they tend to be flush production at lower cost. But as column (5) of table 7.1 shows, from 1946 to 1975 approximately 80 billion barrels were added to proved reserves of oil (excluding Alaska), of which about 39 billion barrels represented newly found oil fields. But the aggregate of annual oil "discoveries," in column (1), over the period amounted to only 6 billion. (Corresponding natural gas numbers were 474, 317, and 157 trillion cubic feet.[3]) The reserves contained in the new fields discovered unfolded by development in subsequent years were first published in the 1961 National Petroleum Council Report,[4] and since 1966 have appeared in the annual API-AGA-CPA *Reserves* volumes. It is surprising that after 1961 there was any econometric work utilizing the series "discoveries" of oil and gas. In fact, there was much.

Table 7.1 summarizes the respective contributions of new and old fields to American crude oil supply over thirty years. Discoveries in column (1) is a misleadingly low total, as explained. Except for 1971–1975, the total is never as much as one-fifth of what is actually discovered in a given year, and probably 1971–1975 only confirms the rule of thumb that it takes six years to evaluate an oil or gas field. It must be said, however, that with the average size of new fields decreasing, the time lag should become much shorter.

Column (4) records the reserves from fields discovered in those years, as estimated in 1978, with the benefit of operating experience, development drilling, exploration in and around the original reservoirs, and improvement in recovery methods. Column (4) is the real *discovery* record. Newly discovered oil has been diminishing since at least 1950, despite increased effort, shown in columns (2) and (3). The payoff to exploratory effort, column (8), dropped by 60 percent from 1946–1950 to 1951–1955, declining more gradually thereafter.

Sources of New Reserves in Old Fields

By subtracting the newly discovered oil, column (4), from the gross additions to reserves in each period, column (5), an indicator of the contribution of new oil from old fields can be derived. The resulting figure in column (6) is imprecise, however, because some of the new oil from 1946–1950 discoveries, for example, was not impounded into reserves until many years later. It is as though column (5) represented cumulative transfers of cash into an account for outpayment while column (4) represented a mixture of cash and short-term securities received by the corporation. With this qualification, column (6) is an estimate of how much new oil was made available from old fields. A sharp turnabout is visible around 1950. As it was becoming increasingly costly to find new oil in new fields, more effort was devoted to obtaining oil from old fields. The absolute amount tripled from the first to the second period, and continued to increase through 1970, when it in turn confronted sharply rising marginal costs. By 1970 new oil from old fields was providing over four-fifths of new proved reserves, column (9).

Table 7.2 shows a similar but less dramatic change for natural gas. The contribution of new gas from old fields rose from less than 20 percent before 1955 to over 50 percent in 1960–1970, falling sharply again in 1971–1975. For reasons to be stated later, new gas from old fields is not as important as new oil from old fields.

In both tables, column (8), the amount of new hydrocarbon per new-field wildcat well, is of ordinal significance only. That is, it is not known how many such wells ought to be considered as aimed at gas or at oil. The best that can be done is to divide discoveries of each hydrocarbon by the total of all such wells. There are sharply decreasing returns to exploration during thirty years. In oil, the decline in discoveries is continuous and very steep; in gas, not nearly as much.

New Oil or Gas: After Discovery

The API report on definitions for estimation of oil reserves[5] outlines some typical sequences in the discovery and development process. A new reservoir has been found. If the porosity (liquid per cubic foot of sands) and permeability (rate of fluid flow through the sands) are low and interrupted, 10–20 acres around the well is assumed as the area for reserves calculation. Given better conditions of thickness, the area is assumed to be 20–40 acres. A thicker but steeply plunging section is allotted the same 20–40 acres, whereas if the dip is gentle the discovery is allotted 60–100 acres. Such judgments will be made on the spot.

Another case is one with a dry hole followed by a success, which between them furnish enough information for an estimate of a proved drilled area of 40 acres or of a proved undrilled area of 170 acres. But doubt exists as to the cross section. A fault seals one end of the reservoir and water seals the other, but between the low of the proved oil and the high of the proved water there is a gap; then the intervening space is "prospective," not proved.

Still another case has three successful wells in sequence, which expand the "proved drilled" area from 40 to 100 acres; the "proved undrilled" area rises from 50 to 425 acres. An additional well hits salt water, outlining the pool, but it also finds a new pool, which is assigned 15–20 acres. This oversimplified sequence, moreover, gives no hint of what is being discovered or about the driving mechanism for the oil—gas, water, or gravity—which may strongly affect the estimates of both oil-in-place and of the fraction that can be recovered. This process of development cum fringe exploration accounts for the great bulk of oil production investment and additions to reserves.

THE RELATION OF PROBABLE RESERVES TO PROVED RESERVES

Thus far the topic has been oil reservoirs (or pools). A *reservoir* can be rigorously defined as a closed hydrodynamic system with precise limits in which fluid pressure (gas, oil, water) is balanced by the strength of the containment materials. Changes in pressure at any one place produce changes in pressure everywhere else. By contrast, *field* is a loose term meaning an assemblage of adjacent or overlapping reservoirs that are inside the ill-defined boundaries of a geological structure. Adjacent fields have some geological event or cataclysm in common, and may be called a *trend*. Two or more trends may make up a *basin*. The oil or gas *play* is an investment in gathering knowledge about the limits of the first reservoir, the presence of neighboring reservoirs, and their aggregation into fields, basins, and trends.

Table 7.3 shows that surrounding the proved reserves are probable reserves, which consist of estimates of what may be produced from the undrilled portions of known reservoirs, from the new horizons in those reservoirs, and from adjacent pools. Most of these pools exist in *structures*, deformations of the rock strata in areas about which a great deal is known. The number of pools and the likelihood and amount of hydrocarbon content are estimated by analogy and extrapolation.

The ratio of these probable reserves to proved reserves must be fairly high. In the United States, for example, during 1946–1965 the production/reserve ratio stayed, within narrow limits, around 8 percent. In 1978 it was up to 13.7 percent.[6] Thus an operator planning to maintain constant output despite a 14 percent decline rate must plan ahead ten years with 1.745 times the amount of the proved reserves.[7] Small wonder that two reasonable persons would differ 75 percent when estimating the operator's "reserves." the evaluation of known structures and pools, their contents known not with reasonable certainty but only with reasonable probability, would well repay immediate systematic estimation.

Some efforts are being made to fill the gap between estimates of proved and probable. The Canadian Petroleum Association defines *probable reserves* as follows: "Probable reserves are a realistic assessment of the reserves that will be recovered from known oil or gas fields based on the estimated ultimate size and reservoir characteristics of such fields."[8] The term will be used here to denote amounts in known fields not now in proved reserves; the term "proved plus probable" $(P + P')$ is their sum.

Table 7.4 shows that Canadian probable crude oil reserves have diminished since 1963, the first year estimated, absolutely and even more relatively; natural gas liquids have increased absolutely but not relatively; probable and proved natural gas reserves have doubled.

In the United States, the American Gas Association devolved the estimate of nonproved reserves to a Potential Gas Committee, whose work it supports, monitored by the Potential Gas Agency, a group at the Colorado School of Mines. They define probable reserves as "resulting from the growth of existing fields" trough extensions and new pools. Table 7.5

shows that probable reserves in the lower forty-eight states diminished by over one-third, from 300 trillion cubic feet (TCF) in 1966 to 192 TCF in 1976. Probable reserves drained into proved reserves (the exact coincidence of 108 TCF, is of course, accidental). The drainage was not offset by exploration and development. The years 1973–1976 inclusive was a time of relatively low, though rapidly increasing, exploratory drilling. The effect of higher drilling rates remains to be seen.

Probable reserves in Alaska diminished by much more than might be expected in a new area. Much reserves seemed likely, but further evaluation was very disappointing.

Probable Reserves as the Stretch Factor on Proved Reserves

It is evident that the flow from probable reserves into proved reserves is of the first importance. Because of the long decline in American discovery efforts, the pressure to stretch has been greatest in this country. Hence, experience in the United States anticipates what will happen elsewhere.

Tables 7.6 and 7.7 show two samples of the process of transition from probable reserves (not estimated nor tabulated) into proved reserves. If PR = proved reserves, PBR = probable reserves, UR = ultimate recovery, O = original year, and T = final year, then $PBR_O = UR_T - (UR_O + PR_O)$, and the stretch factor for reserves is S.

$$S = \frac{PR_O + (UR_T - UR_O)}{PR_O} = \frac{PR_O + UR_O((UR_T/UR_O) - 1)}{PR_O}. \tag{7.1}$$

If an experienced observer in 1945 anticipated that ultimate recovery in 1977 (UR_T) from those fields known in 1945 would be about 98 BB, then 1945 probable reserves were 30 BB ($= 98 - 48 - 20$), and the stretch factor on proved reserves in the base year 1945 would be equal to

$$\frac{20 + 48(98/45(-1))}{20} = 3.8.$$

Similarly, in 1972, with proved reserves at 28 billion barrels, another 5.4 billion were due to be added in the next five years in fields known in 1972. The importance of unestimated probable reserves in oil supply is also seen by a comparison in table 7.6 of sixty-six large oil fields over twenty years. The list was obtained by comparing the 1977 100 largest, minus Alaskan fields, with any of the same name that could be found in the *Oil and Gas Journal* listing of large fields twenty years earlier. Some fields are missing from the earlier tabulation simply because no data were available; some few

Table 7.3
Classification of petroleum reserves

Energy source	Degree of proof	Development status	Producing status
Primary Reserves These reserves recoverable commercially at current prices and costs by conventional methods and equipment as a result of natural energy inherent in the reservoir	*Proved* Primary reserves that have been proved to a high degree of probability by production from the reservoir at a commercial rate of flow or in certain cases by successful testing in conjunction with favorable complete core-analysis data or reliable quantitative interpretation of log data	*Developed* Proved reserves recoverable through existing wells	*Producing* Developed reserves to be produced by existing wells from completion lateral(s) open to production *Nonproducing* Developed reserves behind the casing or in certain cases at minor depths below the producing zones which will be produced by existing wells
		Undeveloped Proved reserves from undeveloped spacing units in a given reservoir that are so close and so related to the developed units that there is every reasonable probability that they will produce when drilled	
	Probable Primary reserves that have not been proved by production at a commercial rate of flow, but being based on limited evidence of commercially producible oil or gas within the geological limits of a reservoir above a known or inferred water table are susceptible to being proved by additional drilling and testing		
	Possible Primary reserves that may exist but where available data will not support a higher classification		

Secondary Reserves
Those reserves recoverable commercially at current prices and costs, in addition to the primary reserves as a result of supplementing by artificial means the natural energy inherent in the reservoir, sometimes accompanied by a significant change in the physical characteristics of reservoir fluids

Proved
Secondary reserves that have been proved to a high degree of probability by a successful pilot operation or by satisfactory performance of full-scale secondary operations in the same reservoir or in certain cases a similar nearby reservoir producing from the same formation

Probable
Secondary reserves that are thought to exist in a reservoir by virtue of past production performance or core, log, or reservoir data, but where the reservoir itself has not been subjected to successful secondary operations

Possible
Secondary reserves from reservoirs that appear to be suited for secondary operations but where available data will not support high classification

Developed
Proved reserves recoverable through existing wells from a reservoir where successful secondary operations are in progress

Undeveloped
Proved reserves that will be produced upon the installation and operations of a secondary recovery project and or by drilling of additional wells

Producing
Developed reserves to be produced by existing wells in that portion of a reservoir subjected to full-scale secondary operation

Nonproducing
Developed reserves to be produced by existing wells upon enlargement of the existing secondary operations

Source: Jan J. Arps, "Estimation of Primary Oil and Gas Reserves," in *Petroleum Production Handbook*, eds. T. C. Frick and R. W. Taylor, © McGraw-Hill Book Company. New York, 1962. Reprinted with permission.

Table 7.4
Canada: Proved and probable hydrocarbon reserves

	1963	1976
Crude oil, BB		
Proved	4.48	6.65
Probable	2.21	1.18
$P + P'$	6.69	7.83
Natural gas liquids, BB		
Proved	0.70	1.59
Probable	0.12	0.16
$P + P'$	0.82	1.75
Natural gas, TCF, 1964		
Proved	21.2	57.0
Probable	6.2	13.5
$P + P'$	37.4	71.5

Source: American Petroleum Institute-American Gas Association-Canadian Petroleum Association, *Reserves of Crude Oil, Natural Gas Liquids, and Natural Gas in the United States as of December 31, 1978* (Washington, D.C.: API-AGA, 1964, 1978), CPA Section, Tables I and II. Reprinted with permission.

Table 7.5
United States: Probable reserves of natural gas, end of 1976, trillion cubic feet

Year	Lower 48 states			Alaska
	Probable reserves	Increment	Gross increments to proved reserves	Probable reserves
1966	300	—	—	n.a.
1968	238	−62	+35	22
1970	218	−20	+20	39
1972	212	− 6	+19	54
1976	192	−20	+34	23
		−108	+108	

Sources: Potential Gas Committee, *Potential Supply of Natural Gas in the United States*, School of Mines, Golden, Colo., 1976, p. 16; gross increments to proved reserves, from API-AGA-CPA, *Reserves*, various years. Reprinted with permission.

Table 7.6
Proved reserves, ultimate recovery, and intervening production and reserve additions in
large fields, 1957–1977, million barrels

End of 1957	Already produced.	15,364	Ultimate recovery,
	Remaining reserves.	9,900	25,264
1958–1977	less production,	− 16,686	
	plus reserves added.	+ 16,638	
End of 1977	equals remaining reserves.	9,852	Ultimate recovery,
	Already produced.	32,050	41,902

Sources: For 1977, API-AGA-CPI, *Reserves*, 1978, Table VIII. For 1957, *Oil and Gas Journal*
(January 27, 1958): 163–68. Proved reserves for those two years for the total United States
were 30.4 billion and 19.7 billion.

because they originally were not large enough to be counted and have
subsequently grown. Hence the sample is one of large mature fields, which
in 1957 and 1977 amounted to about one-third and one-half of all U.S.
reserves, excluding Alaska.[9] Using formula (7.1), the stretch is estimated to
be 2.68, as compared with a thirty-year stretch of 3.5 for all fields in
1945–1977.

All these estimates exclude the North Slope of Alaska. There and in the
lower forty-eight states one of the things we would most wish to know is
the volume of probable reserves in known fields that can be added into
proved reserves in the near future. There is nothing automatic about the
process. The amount depends on what is in the ground, on the cost of
developing it, and on expected prices: The price-reserve increment curve is
the heart of the problem.

A little can be gleaned by a careful examination of tables 7.7 and 7.8. As
might be expected, the early years after discovery are usually the most
rewarding, since there is most to be learned then. This aside, fields discovered before 1920 are most consistent in stretching. The 1931–1940
group outdoes them before the middle 1960s, then slumps.

The poor showing in 1972–1977, after the price explosion, is to some
extent explained by price ceilings. Although this regulation undoubtedly
distorted the reserve-adding effort, it can hardly be said to have offset the
large 1972–1977 increase in development wells and new-pool wells that
furnish the new reserves in old fields. Putting this alongside the generally
poorer showing as one goes from older to newer fields (pre-1920 to 1960–
1970) it is hard to avoid the conclusion that diminishing returns do finally
overcome the stretch factor. If we think of every barrel of proved reserves
as carrying a complement of probable reserves equal to the difference

Table 7.7
Increased ultimate recovery of oil in old fields, United States,[a] billion barrels, and growth in percent per year

Year of estimate: Proved reserves, BB:	1945 19.9	Growth to 1960, %	1960 20.5	Growth to 1967, %	1967 31.4	Growth to 1972, %	1972 28.2	Growth to 1977, %	1977 22.0	Growth to Total, %
Period of discovery										
Pre-1920	14.6	1.22	17.4	2.72	21.1	2.43	23.8	2.31	26.7	1.89
1920–1930	17.9	2.36	25.5	1.80	28.9	0.61	29.8	0.00	29.3	1.53
1931–1940	15.9	2.82	24.1	1.90	27.5	1.28	29.3	0.10	30.8	2.09
1941–1950			18.5	1.55	20.6	0.68	21.3	1.02	22.4	1.13
(1951–1954)			(5.9)	(2.26)	(6.9)	(1.02)	(7.3)	(0.08)	(7.3)	(1.25)
1951–1960					13.7	1.97	15.1	0.97	15.9	1.47
(1961–1967)							(4.4)	(1.54)	(4.7)	(1.54)
1961–1970							6.1	−1.35	5.7	−1.35
Total	48.5		91.37		111.8		125.38		130.68	

a. Excluding Alaska.
b. Numbers in parentheses are excluded from totals to avoid double counting.
Sources: 1945 and 1960 data from National Petroleum Council, *Report of the National Petroleum Council—Committee on Proved Petroleum and Natural Gas Reserves and Availability* (Washington, D.C.: NPC, 1961). Other years, API-AGA-CPA, *Reserves*.
Note: Both sources are drawn from the same basic data, which were published regularly in 1966–78.

Table 7.8
Increased ultimate recovery of natural gas in old fields, United States,[a] trillion cubic feet, and growth in percent per year

Year of estimate:	1960	Growth to 1967, %	1967	Growth to 1972, %	1972	Growth to 1977, %	1977	Growth to Total, %
Period of discovery								
Pre-1920	75.7	1.74	85.4	0.58	89.9	0.76	91.3	1.11
1920–1930	88.1	1.05	94.8	2.38	95.4	1.46	102.6	0.90
1931–1940	110.1	2.30	129.1	0.28	130.8	−0.59	127.1	0.85
1941–1950	94.9	3.22	118.5	0.47	121.3	1.03	127.7	1.76
(1951–1954)	(50.1)	(0.45)	(52.7)	(0.97)	(54.2)	(0.80)	(56.4)	(0.70)
1951–1960			135.9	1.08	143.5	−1.41	140.6	0.34
(1961–1967)					(67.1)	−1.28	(62.8)	(−1.28)
1961–1970							78.7	
Total	419.1	—	563.7	—	646.1	—	668.0	—

a. Excluding Alaska.
b. Numbers in parentheses are excluded from totals to avoid double counting.
Sources: 1945 and 1960 data from National Petroleum Council, *Report*. Other years, API-AGA-CPA, *Reserves*.
Note: Both sources refer to the same basic data, which were published regularly in 1966–78.

Table 7.9
Contributions of improved recovery factor (RF) and of new oil in place (OIP) to increased ultimate recovery (UR), 1967−1972, billion barrels

Year of estimate:	RF, %		OIP, BB		UR, BB		Contribution of:	
	1967	1972	1967	1972	1967	1972	RF	OIP
Period of discovery								
Pre-1920	24.9	25.7	84.7	92.4	21.1	23.8	.68	1.92
1920−1930	34.0	34.7	84.9	86.0	28.9	29.8	.59	.37
1931−1940	34.3	36.6	80.2	80.0	27.5	29.3	1.84	−.07
1941−1950	29.1	29.7	70.9	71.7	20.6	21.3	.43	.23
1951−1960	28.4	28.4	48.2	53.2	13.7	15.1	0	1.40
Total	30.3	31.1	368.9	383.3	111.8	119.3	2.95	4.36

Source: API-AGA-CPA, *Reserves*, Table III, various years. Reprinted with permission.

Table 7.10
Contributions of improved recovery factor (RF) and of new oil in place (OIP) to increased ultimate recovery (UR), 1972−1977, billion barrels

Year of estimate:	RF, %		OIP		UR		Contribution of:	
	1972	1977	1972	1977	1972	1977	RF	OIP
Period of discovery								
Pre-1920	25.7	27.1	92.4	98.3	23.8	26.7	1.30	1.50
1920−1930	34.7	36.0	86.0	81.2	29.8	29.3	1.10	−1.66
1931−1940	36.6	37.5	80.0	82.2	29.3	30.8	.72	.80
1941−1950	29.7	30.4	71.7	73.6	21.3	22.4	.50	.56
1951−1960	28.4	29.0	53.2	54.8	15.1	15.9	.32	.45
1961−1965	28.0	28.5	11.5	12.2	3.21	3.5	.06	.20
Total	31.0	32.0	394.8	402.3	122.5	128.5	4.0	1.85

Source: API-AGA-CPA, *Reserves*, Table III, various years. Reprinted with permission.

between present and future ultimate recovery, that complement, if we could estimate it, would be shrinking.

For the period 1967−1977, the stretch factor for crude oil can be divided into two parts: new oil added in the old fields and a higher recovery percentage of the oil already included. Tables 7.9 and 7.10 show that new oil in place furnished 4.4 billion barrels in 1967−1972 but only 1.85 billion barrels in 1972−1977, despite the slightly larger base.

However, the growth of oil in place is understated. New pools discovered in old fields are not credited to the discovery year of the old field if the new pools "are themselves geologically significant and were dis-

Table 7.11
Additional reserves, billion barrels

Oil price	National petroleum council	Mathematica, Inc.	
(1976 $/barrel)	U.S.	3 States	3 States
5	2	2	7
10	7	7	28
15	13	12	37
20	20.5	18	—
25	24	19	—

Source: National Petroleum Council, *Enhanced Oil Recovery* (Washington, D.C.: NPC, December 1976), pp. 57–61 and Appendix G.

covered through application of a new exploration concept." For such new pools, "the assigned discovery years are the ones in which they were actually discovered," following "gelogical and exploratory judgments best developed by the experts in the local Subcommittees."[10] This procedure is biased because it understates the contribution of new knowledge in an old area. In any case, newfound oil in old fields provided most of the additional reserves in 1967–1972, but improved recovery was more important in the next five years, first 3.0, then 4.0 billion barrels. These large amounts constitute only a tiny fraction of oil in place, but the apparent decline in spending on "improved recovery programs" and in service wells drilled may not bode well for contributions here.

The future lies with unconventional or, as they are usually known, "enhanced oil recovery" methods. Estimates of available reserves vary widely, as might be expected. Two studies had access to a very large data base of 245 individual reservoirs in Texas, Louisiana, and California, and used very similar methods, but results differed considerably (see table 7.11).

The National Petroleum Council (NPC) task force estimated lower efficiencies and higher unit costs in the new processes, thereby ruling out many reservoirs included by the Mathematica group. Perhaps the NPC estimates are a better estimate of what can actually be done now,and the Mathematica numbers are a proxy for what later technology might do. The analysis of small areas for probable reserves should have been done years ago, to discover how much stretch there is in existing reserves. It still remains to be done.

Natural gas (table 7.8) requires little comment. "Stretch" consists almost entirely of new gas, since the recovery factor is high (modal value around

75 percent) and is rarely amenable to pressure maintenance or fluid injection. A brief comparison may be made between the factors suggested by table 7.8 with those of the Potential Gas Committee (table 7.5). For example, ultimate recovery in fields known in 1967 was stretched by 1977 from 564 to 589 TCF (668.0 less 78.7 equals 589.3). Anyone able to estimate this in 1967 from existing data would have seen that the 300 TCF probable reserve was much too high.

Notes and References

1. "North American Drilling Activity in 1978," *AAPG Bulletin* 63, no. 8 (August 1979): Tables 1, 3, 16, 17. Note that only a minor fraction of the "successful" new-field wildcats find commercial fields, but this evaluation takes years to make. Hence, statistics are only published with a six-year lag; e.g. for 1970 in the volume covering 1976 developments.

2. Morris Muskat, "The Proved Crude Oil Reserves of the United States," *Journal of Petroleum Technology* (September 1963): 919.

3. In this case, discoveries include "total discoveries".

4. National Petroleum Council, *Report of the National Petroleum Council Committee on Proved Petroleum and Natural Gas Reserves and Availability*, Washington, D.C., NPC, 15 May 1961.

5. American Petroleum Institute, *Organization and Definitions for the Estimation of Reserves and Productive Capacity of Crude Oil*, Technical Report No. 2, Washington, D.C.: 1970), pp. 38–42.

6. AGI-AGA-CPA, *Reserves*, Table II, dividing production by average reserves for the year.

7. That is, over ten years the cumulative output will be (.137 × 5.44) = .745 of the existing reserves, and new reserves must be provided to replace them.

8. API-AGA-CPA, *Reserves*, 1978, p. 263

9. The source for 1977 is API-AGA-CPA, *Reserves*, 1978, Table VIII. For 1957 *Oil and Gas Journal* (January 27, 1958): 163–68. Proved reserves for those two years for the total United States were 30.4 billion and 19.7 billion barrels.

10. API-AGA-CPA, *Reserves*, 1978, p. 18.

8

Scarcity and World Oil Prices

Statement of the Problem

Many public and private investment decisions, affecting a significant fraction of world income, depend on the expected price of crude oil. Since the price explosion of 1973, and especially since the second explosion of 1979, there has been a wide consensus: Oil has become, and will continue to be, in increasingly short supply for the rest of the century. Further price increases are necessary and inevitable.

We need cite only a fraction of even the post-1978 predictions of rising oil prices, which were and are used as a basis for private and public investment, and taxation. (U.S. CIA, 1979, p. iii; Fesharaki, 1980; U.S. Senate, 1982; OGJ, 1982, pp. 118, 210; OGJ, 1984a, p. 32; Canada, 1980, 1981a, 1981b.)

The price decline since 1980–81 has not weakened the consensus, but has lowered the rate of expected increase. Prices are expected to be weak or stable for a few years, then begin the inexorable increase. (EMF 6, 1982; US. GAO, 1983; World Bank, 1983, p. 28; and 1985, pp. 37–38; New York Times, 1984; DOE, 1985; Erickson, 1985; Saunders, 1984.) The oil-company acquisitions of 1983–84 were obviously based on the consensus view. An expert panel convened by the CIA in April 1985, like one convened by the California Energy Commission, expected that prices would rise, at an increasing rate, starting around 1990. (*Wall Street Journal*, 1985; California, 1985.) The International Energy Workshop of the International Institute of Applied Systems Analysts compiled a consensus forecast in December 1981, July 1983, and July 1985 (see figure 8.1). The first consensus was that the price would nearly equal $60 in 1990; the most recent has in approaching that number only by 2010. A twenty-year postpone-

Reprinted from *Review of Economics & Statistics* 68 (August 1986): 387–397.

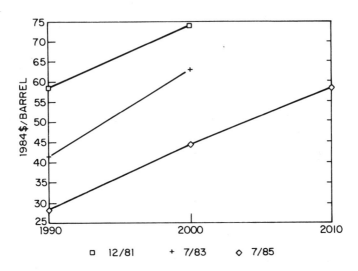

Figure 8.1
IEW world oil price forecasts
Source: Mann and Nordhaus (1985)

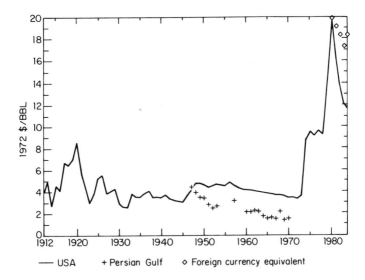

Figure 8.2
Crude oil prices, 1912–83
Sources: Oil prices: before 1949, from API (1959), p. 374: afterward from [US, DOE: EIA: AR], using only the uncontrolled series. Persian Gulf prices from Adelman (1972), pp. 134, 141–144, 158n, 183, 190. Deflation was by the GNP Implicit Price Deflator starting in 1929, from [US, CEA]. For earlier years, it was from [US, DOC] p. 201.

ment is no small change, of course. But in each case, the consensus was that the current price of oil was approximately equal to, or mildly above, the scarcity-determined price. In the long run, it would have to rise above the current level (Manne and Nordhaus, 1985; it should not be assumed that they themselves share he consensus, or that they do not).

The Economic Theory of the Consensus

In general, absent monopoly restriction of output, a rising price registers increasing scarcity as consumption puts increasing strain upon productive resources. Some formal oil price models are explicitly competitive. (Mead, 1979, 1985; Cremer and Salehi-Isfahani, 1980; MacAvoy, 1982; Roumasset et al., 1983).

More often, competition is an implicit major premise. Prices are said to reflect not monopoly but "market forces" or "deeper forces." Or it is said that if the cartel of producing nations (not the unimportant organization OPEC) disappeared, oil prices would not be strikingly different from what they are. Or that discoveries had been shrinking, and demand increasing up to 1973, hence prices had to rise, so at most the cartel pushed them up a bit faster. Other models are "non-committal," but implicitly competitive, in that they have price driven by total consumption pressing against reserves.

Figure 8.2 does not, of course, disprove this proposition but it does suggest that if scarcity pushed up prices, scarcity must have been very sudden and strong.

There have also been attempts to model the oil market as a monopoly, in the generic sense: a few sellers restraining output and raising prices. (For an excellent survey, see Gately (1984).) But these models are also based on rising scarcity. They aim to show the difference between the competitive response and the monopoly response.

Perhaps, given the increasing scarcity inherent in an "exhaustible natural resource ... there is a very limited scope for the monopolist ...; indeed, under the natural 'first approximation' of constant elasticity demand schedules, with zero extraction costs, monopoly prices and competitive equilibrium prices will in fact be identical" (Stiglitz 1976).

Gately points out that the monopoly models have done badly, but this might be because the assumptions either of monopoly or of increasing scarcity were incorrect—not to mention possible errors of data or model construction. He also notes that a wide range of models uncommitted as to monopoly generate a price for 2000 AD between the 1980 value and 100 percent above it (Gately, 1984, p. 1105).

Gately's own view is that rising scarcity explains much or most but not all of the price increases: "[I]n the light of plausible estimates for the demand elasticities and the costs of oil and of alternative energy sources, ... pre-1973 oil prices were too low to be sustained much beyond the mid-1970s. Similarly, pre-1979 prices were too low to be sustained beyond the mid-to-late 1980s" (p. 1113).

The passage shows how explaining the past and predicting the future run into each other. In brief: the cost of oil approached or exceeded the price in 1973, and has continued to increase, necessitating a price at least higher than existed in 1978. Gately may or may not share the consensus, that in time the price will be driven by increasing scarcity to advance from its *current* level (Summer, 1985). If this is correct, the current level must be approximately at the level set by scarcity under competitive conditions.

This chapter's thesis is that greater scarcity explains little if any of the price changes since 1973. We measure scarcity of oil by its marginal cost, consisting largely of investment in drilling and related to drilling.

(The babel of tongues about how much remains to be produced from old and new fields are at best a help and more usually a beclouding of the real issue: current and expected marginal cost.)

First, we show that the level and dispersion of marginal costs cannot be reconciled with a price determined by scarcity. Second, we assume that a depletable resource has a non-negligible cost (often known as "user cost" or "Hotelling rent") over and above marginal development cost. Here data are almost completely absent, but it can be shown that an allowance for this cost only strengthens the case.

Approach Through Marginal Cost

Theory: Level and Dispersion of Marginal Cost

We start with the proposition that scarcity of any commodity is measured by its marginal cost, which registers the pressure of demand upon supply. Marginal cost does not determine price, nor vice versa; the two gravitate toward equality in competitive equilibrium.

Marginal cost of oil, or supply price, is the sum of (1) marginal operating cost, which is rarely available, fortunately small, and mostly correlated with (2) marginal capital cost, the amount per unit which would provide an acceptable rate of return on the necessary investment in maintaining or expanding production.

Our second postulate is that in any mineral industry under steady state competitive conditions, there will be great variation in *average* production cost among producing areas because of variation in size and accessibility of the deposits. Hence there will be great variation in profitability. But there should be only relatively small chance variation in *marginal* costs. For if each producer takes the market price as a datum and adapts to it, he will, to maximize his profits, set production as close as possible to the point where marginal cost is in the neighborhood of the price.

Actual Level and Dispersion of Marginal Cost

But in fact, the capital investment required to expand or maintain a unit of production varies enormously among areas. Disregarding the small-sample freaks, the highest is 90 times the lowest (Adelman and Ward, 1980, table 8). A regression analysis shows that these estimates are systematically related to the intensity of development, the percentage of reserves removed per year. This depends on an investment decision, which is at the discretion of the owners (Smith and Paddock, 1984).

These are marginal, not average, investments (hence costs) per unit of output, and the extreme dispersion seems incompatible with anything approaching competitive equilibrium.

Moreover, one can make a quick *over*-estimate of the unit operating-plus-development cost by dividing the investment per initial daily barrel by 1000. This assumes a decline rate of 7 percent, operating costs of 7 percent, and a lush rate of return of 22.5 percent, total 36.5 percent. (For an explanation of the method, see Adelman (1972), ch. 2.) Then an investment of $1000 per daily barrel would be barely profitable with annual receipts of $365, or $1 per barrel, every day.

In 1978 the great bulk of reserves were in fields whose incremental investment coefficients were below $3000 per daily barrel, hence incremental development costs around $3, only a small fraction of the 1978 price, let alone later higher prices. This hardly looks like pressure on resources even in 1978.

A Comparison: Saudi Arabia and United States

Let us look more closely at the largest reserve-holder, Saudi Arabia, and the largest competitive producer, the United States.

Table 8.1 shows that in 1978, before the second price explosion, the investment needed to develop an incremental daily barrel in the United

Table 8.1
Investment requirements per initial daily barrel, and total cost per barrel, United States and
Saudi Arabia, 1978

Item		
(1)	Saudi Arabia: development oil wells drilled	37
(2)	Do., average wells	145
(3)	Do., average depth	5,555 feet
(4)	USA: drilling cost per well depth interval 5–7,000 ft (avg 6,100)	256 $ thousands
(5)	USA: adjustment for nondrilling costs	1,60842
(6)	Saudi investment in new oil production capacity [5 * 4 * 2]	59,651 $ thousands
(7)	Average daily output per well	10,099 thousand barrels
(8)	New Saudi capacity [7 * 1]	374 thousand barrels daily
(9)	(a) Incremental investment per initial daily barrel [6/8]	160 dollars
	(b) Capital cost per barrel (3% decline, 20% return)	0.101 $
	(c) Operating cost per barrel	0.031 $
	(d) Total cost per barrel	0.131
(10)	USA: oil development investment	6,002 $ millions
(11)	USA: reserves-added: total	1,444 million barrels
(12)	USA: investment per incremental barrel of reserves [10/11]	4.16 $
(13)	(a) USA: investment per initial daily barrel of capacity (depletion 13.9%)	10,915 $
	(b) Capital cost per barrel (13.9% decline, 10% return)	7.15 $
	(c) Operating cost per barrel	0.91 $

Sources by line:
(1), (2): *World Oil*, August 15, 1979, pp. 63, 206.
(3), (7): *Oil & Gas Journal*, December 25, 1978, p. 141 (including fields with 0.85733 of producing oil wells)
(4): *Joint Association Survey 1978*, table 2
(5), (10): Bureau of the Census. *Annual Survey of Oil & Gas 1978*, MA-13K(78)-1, tables E, 2, 3. Since oil wells accounted for 44.2% of oil-plus-gas drilling expenditures, we take that percentage of all development outlays as attributable to oil. The adjustment of (1/.811) is for adjustment to gross from net company basis. Hence $11,012 * .442/.811 = $6,002.
(9), (13): For method of cost calculation, see Adelman (1972), chapter 2.
(11): API-AGA. Reserves report 1978, pp. 24, 123. Includes associated-dissolved natural gas liquids, but no allowance for oil equivalent of associated-dissolved gas.
(12): Ibid., p. 24, gives production-reserves ratio, excluding Alaska, as 0.139. If the decline rate is approximately equal to the depletion rate, then initial output per year is 0.139 barrel, and initial daily output is 0.139/365. The ($4.16/.139) * 365 = $10,915 per initial daily barrel.
(13c): Calculated from ASOG, allocating between oil and gas on the basis of number of respective wells, from *World Oil*. February 15 issues. The weighted average output per well is 6.1 times the unweighted, an average cost is considered to be the square root of the reciprocal. For the rationale of this calculation, see Adelman (1972), p. 47.

States was about 69 times the corresponding cost in Saudi Arabia.[1] The 1978 estimates are not biased upward by the frenzied drilling boom of the next few years. Furthermore, the Saudi cost is overstated because it includes some exploration, and gas wells drilled to supply local consumption. It does assume U.S. price levels. Real additional cost in an old-established operation like that in Saudi Arabia cannot be substantial; though local inefficiences might double or treble money cost.

Capital costs in 1978 averaged about 10 cents per barrel in Saudi Arabia, and about $7.15 in the United States. As a check for the United States, we add estimated average operating costs, which are higher than marginal because older wells become increasingly high cost, while marginal operating costs refer to newly drilled and started wells.[2]

The total is $8.06 per barrel. We have not made any allowance for exploration cost or equivalent, to be considered below. But there is no reason to suppose investment was restrained short of the competitive level where marginal cost would equal price.

But there was obviously massive restraint in Saudi Arabia. The sum of marginal capital and operating cost (the latter assumed at the industry rule of thumb of 7 percent of capital cost) was about 1 percent of the price of $12.70.

Table 8.2 shows drilling costs per newly-developed barrel of reserves in 27 geographical units in the United States. Recall that total development costs are drilling costs multiplied by a factor for non-drilling outlays. Hence the relative though not absolute dispersion is the same as the total development costs. The standard deviation of the logarithms is 0.5740. The logarithm of 1/69 is over 7 standard deviations from the logarithmic mean. This would indicate only a negligible chance that the long-run marginal cost in Saudi Arabia would be drawn from the same universe as in the United States. Perhaps this is pedantic overkill; it is hard to think of anyone disputing the conclusion.

To be sure, there must always be much variation in drilling investment. Data are imprecise. A small area may be dominated by a large project, for which we know average, not marginal, cost (average cost at the margin is of course marginal cost when the margin becomes slim). Perhaps more important, the process of equating marginal costs among deposits and areas takes time. Newly developed reservoirs may *look* deceptively expensive at first, since the investment comes before reserves and production. In fact, they are typically cheap to develop. They are gradually drilled up, at rising costs, to the point where an additional barrel is no cheaper to develop than in other previously known pools.

Table 8.2
Frequency distribution of U.S. oil drilling costs, 1978

	Drilling cost ($M)	Reserves added (M brls)	Dollars/ barrel	Natlog of $/barrel
Alaska: total	119	79	1.51	0.4113
Arkansas	29	27	1.07	0.0680
California: total	284	187	1.52	0.4201
Florida	15	8	1.89	0.6387
Illinois	33	11	3.13	1.1400
Indiana	13	6	2.29	0.8292
Kansas	106	46	2.29	0.8305
Kentucky	11	2	5.03	1.6147
Louisiana: north	37	24	1.54	0.4330
Louisiana: south (inc. offshore)	617	215	2.87	1.0559
Michigan	38	92	0.42	−0.8721
Mississippi	44	23	1.94	0.6650
Montana	56	19	2.98	1.0912
Nebraska	12	4	3.23	1.1713
New Mexico: total	113	73	1.54	0.4335
North Dakota	103	36	2.86	1,0506
Oklahoma	450	87	5.15	1,6398
Texas: District 1	66	13	5.11	1.6315
Texas: District 5	11	4	2.88	1.0579
Texas: District 6	29	11	2.64	0.9716
Texas: District 7B	72	17	4.30	1.4576
Texas: District 7C	105	21	5.02	1.6129
Texas: District 8	251	81	3.12	1.1370
Texas: District 8A	194	118	1.64	0.4960
Texas: District 10	63	13	4.80	1.5676
Wyoming	222	120	1.85	0.6178
Appalachian[a]	121	19	6.38	1.8527
Other USA[b]	15	5	3.26	1.1832
Total USA (sum of sample)	3,229	1,358	2.38	0.9359
Total USA (JAS, API)	3,700	1,347	2.75	1.0105
Standard Deviation	—	—	1.46	0.5740

Sources: Drilling Cost, Joint Association Survey, 1978. Nondrilling costs not known by states. Reserves added. API-AGA Annual Report 1978. Natural gas liquids not included. Includes positive and negative revisions.
Note: Deviation from log mean [ln(2.75/69) − .9359] = −4,1585
    Number of standard deviations = −7.245]
a. New York, Ohio, Pennsylvania, West Virginia.
b. Arizona, Missouri, Nevada, Virginia.

In fact, the variation in the United States must in part be due to this lag. This makes Saudi Arabia even more of an outlier than at first appears. It also suggests another test.

Investment Rates and Marginal Cost Dispersion

In a market governed by scarcity not monopoly, and by long lags, low-cost production should gradually displace high-cost. This would be reflected in a much higher growth rate of output and investment in Saudi Arabia and other low-cost areas than in the United States and other high-cost areas. This was the case for many years before 1973, despite the barriers against imports into the United States.

But since 1973 there has been a complete reversal. The highest-cost areas, chiefly the United States, have expanded investment most, and have maintained or even increased output, at sharply rising cost. In ten years the United States extracted and replaced approximately as much oil as existed in 1973 reserves (ex-Alaska) (API/AGA; US.DOE.EIA.R). In contrast, reserves in the lowest-cost areas, chiefly those around the Persian Gulf, have been little depleted and have even increased.

In 1985 following a shakeout, the United States will drill four times as many oil wells as in 1973; Saudi Arabia, less than one-third of the 1973 number.[3] Yet the real price of crude oil rose by a factor of 5.9 in Saudi Arabia, and of only 3.3 in the United States.[4] In fact, the price to which the U.S. producer responds has risen even less than the real price unmodified, because of the loss of tax advantages.

Real costs have increased greatly in the United States. As appendix B shows, there was no perceptible cost increase in Saudi Arabia. Furthermore, even in 1978, when the price of oil was much lower than today, the discrepancy between price and marginal cost was gross, to be stated in hundreds of percent.

If we assume the oil market has been ruled by competitive scarcity, then since 1973 water has been running uphill. And the restriction of investment in the best areas makes nonsense of the argument that reserves have not increased "sufficiently."

A Missing Cost Element?

However, the cost data cited thus far include only development, the investment needed to transform a resource into a reserve ready for production. We have not yet considered the value of the resource used up in development-production, which should be added to marginal development cost.

Like any other asset, the value of the resource is the lesser of: (a) the present value of what it will earn in the future, or (b) the present value of what it would cost to replace it in the future. These two values converge, and are equal in long-run equilibrium. When (a) exceeds (b), it gives the signal for investment in exploration.

It is widely believed, and we will assume it for the sake of the argument, that because mineral resources are "limited and finite," minerals must grow increasingly scarce and valuable, their price rising at a rate related to the interest rate. A good recent statement is by Miller and Upton (1985, p. 24): "No viable alternative paradigm exists" to the "Hotelling Principle or 'r-percent rule'." We assume, therefore, that for any given deposit, the margin over development cost will be larger in the future.

If the resource cost is to explain any substantial part of the price increase, then it must be *inversely* related to development-operating cost. For only then could it offset or neutralize the discrepancies in marginal development cost. The remaining variations might then be small enough to be explained by chance. Indeed, for the total development-cum-resource cost to be in the neighborhood of the market price, the resource cost in the better areas would need to be many times the development cost.

To decide this question, we must put it in terms of the choices open at every moment to a mineral operator, particularly in oil or gas: (1) develop existing deposits more intensively; or (2) develop previously known but unexploited deposits, thereby *ceteris paribus* raising development costs; or (3) search for new cheaper deposits; or (4) postpone expansion along any or all of the previous three paths because later investment is more profitable than earlier.

Each of the four strategies is a substitute for the others. Hence their costs must vary directly not inversely.

The higher are costs of intensive development (option 1) or extensive development (option 2), the more attractive is exploration (option 3). Similarly, if we expect the price of a mineral to rise, then the more the operator needs to invest for development and finding today (options 1–3), the greater the gain by postponing the investment. Suppose the price is 100, and is expected to be 105 next year. If the cost is zero, the royalty (margin over cost) is 100, and will increase by 5 percent in a year. If the cost is 99, the royalty is 1, and next year it will be 6, an increase of 500 percent.

Thus if output were being restrained because of the belief in yet-higher prices in the future, the restraint would be strongest in the United States

Table 8.3
Calculation of U.S., Saudi oil finding cost and value 1978

A. United States: Cost

Exploration expenditures ($ M)	Oil exploration ($ M)	Discoveries (M brls)	Finding cost ($/brl)	Present barrel factor $(1 + (i/a))$	Cost per barrel above ground ($/brl)
7381	2155	562	3.83	1.769	6.78

B. United States, Saudi Arabia: Values

	Prices ($/brl)	Operating cost ($/brl)	Development cost ($/brl)	Value development cost ($/brl)	Net of finding cost ($/brl)
United States					
"Lower tier"	5.46	0.91	7.15	−2.60	−9.38
"Upper tier"	12.15	0.91	7.15	4.09	−2.69
Saudi Arabia	12.70	0.03	0.10	12.57	12.51

Sources for panel A: Expenditures from Census. Annual Survey of Oil & Gas 1978, oil allocated by proportion of oil to gas drilling outlays on successful wells. Discoveries from AAPG (American Association of Petroleum Geologists) Bulletin, vol. 63/8. "North American Drilling Activity in 1978." N.B. Transfer payments excluded.
Sources for panel B: Prices, from DOE/EIA. Operating and development costs from table 1. For Saudi finding cost, see text.

and non-existent in Saudi Arabia—just the contrary of what has happened. (No difference in discount rates could explain such gross differences in behavior. But we will show elsewhere that oil-producing governments have shorter horizons and higher discount rates than private oil companies.)

If the price of oil were ruled by expected future scarcity, duly discounted, there would have been no glut at any time, and no attempt to sell more than the market would absorb. Owners would be content to hold the asset and wait. They have in fact been very discontented.

Table 8.3 shows a test using the third option—discovery. We calculate that in the United States in 1978 about $2.2 billions were spent on finding new oil deposits, as distinct from developing known deposits; and 562 million barrels were found. The cost of $3.83 per barrel found is not, however, comparable with price. It must be multiplied by a factor to cover the cost of holding an underground asset, as was done with development. (See appendix A.) Adjusted finding cost was $6.78. It is net of all transfer payments to landowners, including the U.S. Government.

The lower panel of table 3 compares the prices (from US.DOE.EIA, 1983, p. 127) of "lower tier" and "upper tier" oil, less the operating and development costs calculated earlier. An existing average producing oil well classified as "lower tier" was worth operating, since the price was much above operating cost. Under the same average conditions, a new well was not worth drilling to get a "lower tier" price. But it was worth drilling in a known deposit which was entitled to get an "upper tier" price. However, it was not worth spending money to find such a deposit, since it would yield less than the sum of finding and development cost.

Hence one would predict that the year's production would not be fully restored by new proved reserves added; and that the oil impounded into those new proved reserves would not be fully offset by new additions to probable reserves. (Proved reserve changes and production are from API/AGA 1978, tables II and III, respectively. New discoveries, which will only be developed into proved reserves in the future, stated in table III.) In other words, our estimates of finding cost and of operating-development cost, however rough, are at least consistent with each other and with the data on reserve increment.

In Saudi Arabia, the 1978 surplus over development cost was $12.45 per barrel. No discounted finding cost, nor discounted future value nor increase in development cost, could have been anything but a negligible fraction of that amount. But there happens also to be an authoritative estimate of resource value. The 1976 buyout agreement with the Aramco companies allowed them 6 cents per barrel of oil they would find (at their own expense) in what *Petroleum Intelligence Weekly* called "the many potential oil structures known to exist in the Aramco concession area" (PIW, 1975, 1976). The agreement escalates the finding fee with the industrial price index of the International Monetary Fund: in 1985 prices it is about 10 cents per barrel.

The Saudi Discovery Allowance as Cost and as Value

We cannot tell how much the Saudis expected to have discovered for them at the offered fee. Six cents per barrel represents only the height of the point where the unobserved finding supply function crosses the unknown value function. Supply: the more the Saudis offered, the more new oil they would receive. Value: the faster they expected their development costs to rise as they extracted more from known deposits, the greater the value to them of the additional discovered oil. Alternatively, the faster they expected the price to rise—assuming for the sake of argument that they were price-takers—the greater the value of the additional oil.

Thus the 6 cent fee was an informal guesstimated equalization of the two alternative measures discussed above: (a) the present discounted value of a barrel to be developed and produced and sold in the future with (b) discovery cost. The fee was approximately one-half of 1 percent of the current margin over operating-development cost. So low a present value to additional supply is inconceivable to a price-taker. It makes good enough sense if the seller is an informed monopolist, looking to the effect of additional sales on price, and also aware that the value of an additional barrel must be heavily discounted because it would need to be held a very long time before sale.

We often hear that Saudi Arabia does something, or refrains from doing something else, because their reserves will last into the next century, etc. This only shows the power of repetition. *Why* do they extract so little of their underground asset that it will last so long? (Of 47 listed oil fields, only 15 are operated (AAPG, 1981, p. 2142).) Monopoly is a sufficient reason. There may be others. (See Griffin and Teece (1982), especially chapters 1–3.)

Conclusion

It is often said that "low-price oil is gone forever," and this may be perfectly true—but only so long as the low-cost oil remains dammed up. If the dam breaks, so will the price.

The current world oil price, and changes since 1973, cannot possibly be explained by scarcity, or by changes in scarcity. Cost outside North America was trending down not up before 1973[5] Even if cost had increased since then by several times, which did not happen, it would be vastly profitable to expand output by several times in the great bulk of world oil reserves.

To add replacement-postponement cost to development cost only increases the contrast. Replacement cost is considerable in the high-cost areas, where there has been massive investment to replace reserves; it is negligible in the low-cost areas, where investment is at a very low ebb.

We have not explained this massive restraint. To do so, we must refer more extensively to the economic theory of mineral depletion, and of non-competitive markets.

Nor have we estimated what a competitive price would be today. A lower than current price would mean higher consumption and production. More intensive development in the low-cost areas would *ceteris paribus* increase costs. With price roughly 100 times cost in early 1985, there was plenty of room for higher output to make cost rise and price to fall, the two meeting somewhere between.

But the rising costs of more intensive development would themselves set off an explosion of exploration in these areas, with unknowable results. One example must suffice. In Kuwait, several wells were drilled recently in a search for natural gas for local electrical power generation. The trade press reported that they found "only" [sic] an oil field with reserves now estimated at between 25 and 35 billion barrels, and with development costs so low that the new field will replace some of current production. (World Oil, 1980–84; OGJ 1984b, p. 49.) If that was found inadvertently in a tiny country, one may guess what they would find if they really tried, and over a larger area.

But there will be no discovery effort in the most remunerative areas, unless the price breaks sharply, and the owners of the large low-cost reserves try to save something from the wreck by drastically increasing investment and output. These perverse effects are a measure of the basic instability of the market, whereby a price increase or decrease becomes cumulative and self-reinforcing.

Moreover, the sovereign owners of most of the oil reserves are politically unstable and unruly to each other. The Iranian Revolution, and then the Iran-Iraq war, have at least temporarily destroyed or immobilized a large fraction of Persian Gulf capacity. An outbreak of peace would be devastating to prices. Strenuous violent efforts will be made to maintain the current restrictions, though I cannot tell who will attack/invade/occupy whom.

Hence we attempt no price forecast, thereby doubtless disappointing some readers. But there is an obvious moral for forecasters: somehow they must capture the process of restriction, or else they are correct only by chance.

Appendix A

Relation of Cost Per Unit in Ground and Cost or Price Above Ground as Sold

Essentially, we need to convert a cost per barrel held in the ground to a cost per barrel as sold above ground, years later. We define: R = reserves; Q = initial output in barrels per year; a = the constant percentage decline rate, percent per year; i = risk-adjusted discount rate, percent per year;

P = price. Then

$$R = Q \int_0^T e^{-at}\,dt = (Q/a)(1 - e^{-at})$$

The undiscounted total of above ground receipts:

$PR = (PQ/a)(1 - e^{-at})$.

The discounted present value of the stream of receipts:

$PV(PR) = (PQ/(a + i))(1 - e^{-(a+i)t})$.

Then the ratio of undiscounted above-ground to discounted below-ground:

$$\frac{PV(PR)}{PR} + \frac{PQ(a + i)(1 - e^{-aT})}{PQ(a)(1 - e^{(a+i)T})}.$$

Usually, but not always, given realistic values for T and/or a and i, the expression approaches the limit:

$$\frac{PV(PR)}{PR} = (a + i)/a = 1 + (i/a).$$

Intuitively, this is plausible. The higher is i, the higher the cost of holding the asset. The higher is a, the shorter is the holding time, and the lower the cost. (But a higher decline/depletion rate requires a larger investment.) The expression $(1 + (1/a))$ has surprisingly many applications.

Appendix B

Saudi Arabia Development Cost 1963–83

Figure 8.A1 gives two indicators of productivity in oil production in Saudi Arabia since 1963: output per well per day, and the number of wells drilled per rig-year (one drilling rig operating for one year). Output per well is a determinant not only of operating cost per unit, but also of capital cost. The higher it is, the greater the additional capacity secured by drilling a well.

During 1963–74, output grew five-fold. It then dipped in 1975, grew strongly again through 1977, decreased in 1978, then rebounded in 1979, held steady for two more years, then plunged downward. These fluctuations affected both indicators. Output per well rose pretty steadily, except for relapses during years when production dropped. The number of oil

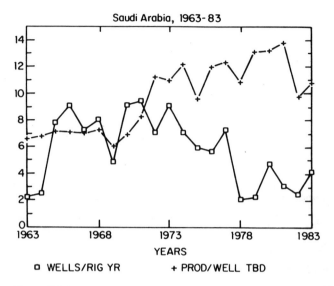

Figure 8.A1
Productivity indicators

wells drilled per rig-year was fairly steady through 1972, but then turned downward. What may be the strongest downward force is not a fluctuation, nor a distortion—the drilling of many service wells for water injection into the great Ghawar field. This is not inefficiency, but rather higher necessary factor inputs.

Figure 8.A2 combines both indexes by multiplying the number of wells completed by the average output per well. This gives an overstatement of new capacity, since by no means all wells are productive oil wells; but the trend is probably well indicated. Clearly there is a relationship between the change in output in any year and the apparent addition to capacity. Relapses in output both lower the average per well and distort the rate of construction to put facilities in place. An ordinary least squares regression of increased "capacity" per rig year upon the year's change in output, and time as a residual, gives the following results (t-statistics in parentheses):

"Capacity" (thousands of barrels daily added per rig-year)

$$= 48.2 + .013 \text{ (year's output change)}$$
$$(4.6) \quad (2.9)$$

$$+ .592 \text{ (year less 1963)}$$
$$(.69)$$

adj. $R^2 = .26$; F-statistic $= 4.3$; D.W. $= 1.51$; $N = 20$.

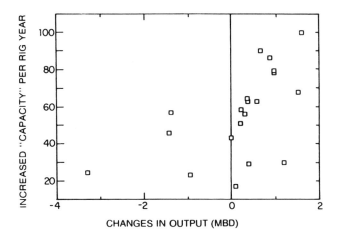

Figure 8.A2
Added "capacity" per rig year as a function of output changes

The apparent improvement over time does not differ significantly from zero; it merely suggests that any change in cost has been too weak a signal to read through the noise. Since the amount and quality of data have declined, there is probably little hope of doing anything more precise.

The year 1978, which we used for table 8.1, marks an all-time low in "productivity" per rig-year, hence a high in cost in absolute terms, of course, any cost changes were trifling

Notes

The research for this paper has been supported by the National Science Foundation, grant SES-8412971, and by the Center for Energy Policy Research of the M.I.T. Energy Laboratory, I am obliged to Michael C. Lynch for valuable assistance. For many helpful comments and criticisms. I am indebted to Paul G. Bradley, Harry G. Broadman, Richard L. Gordon, William W. Hogan, Gordon M. Kaufman, Stephen Martin, James W. McKie, Joe Roeber, James L. Smith, G. Campbell Watkins, and to two anonymous referees. But any opinions, findings, conclusions or recommendations expressed herein are those of the author, and do not necessarily reflect the views of the NSF or any other person or group.

1. The method of table 8.1 differs from that in the Adelman-Ward paper, which regressed U.S. expenditures upon rig-years, deriving factors applied to other areas. It was necessary to derive capacity increments from all wells drilled, rather than from development wells alone. Moreover, the factors could not be applied to the United States because of the extreme dispersion and skewness of output rates per well in this country. We are able to avoid these two sources of error in table 8.1, although the econometric method is, in general, superior. For Saudi Arabia, we

exclude the costs of the huge gas-gathering system, not to mention the highly expensive plants for stripping liquids from gas. They are excluded from U.S. costs See U.S. Census, ASOG, 1982, appendix A, line 47. Both are unnecessary for producing oil, and are the consequence of high oil revenues.

2. We calculated with a weighted average output of 60 barrels daily per well. This is obtained by weighting average output per well, in each producing state, by the production in the state. It may be too low.

The base cases used in (US.DOE.EIA, 1979), p. 8, table 3, are 100 barrels daily onshore and 917 offshore. Operating costs are 40¢ and 42¢, respectively. By the square-root rule (see reference below), a 100 barrel onshore well should cost $(60/100)2 * 91 = 70$ cents. Our estimate is not nearly as overstated as would first appear, since our calculation averages in wells of all ages, many very high-cost; while the DOE base case is a newly drilled well before decline has set in. In effect, the higher cost used in our table approaches the present value of future expenditures, divided by the present-barrel-equivalent of future output. To convert barrels in the ground to barrels produced, or vice versa, we use the conversion factor $(a + i)/a$, where a is the depletion/decline rate, and i is the relevant discount rate. See Adelman (1972), ch. 2 for a fuller explanation; and appendix A.

3. For the United States, see U.S. EIA.MER, May 1985 (published August 1985), p. 65: 10.25 and 42.2 thousand, respectively. For the first six months, the decrease from 1984 to 1985 is 6.8%, indicating an increase by a factor of 3.8 from 1973 to 1985. For Saudi Arabia, see *World Oil*, August 15, 1985, p. 29. There were 62 oil wells drilled in 1984. The 1985 total was forecast to be approximately 48, as against 177 in 1973.

4. For the United States, see U.S. EIA.AER 1983, p. 139, and MER since. For Saudi Arabia, see US. EIA.IEA, and, more recently, PE 1985. The respective prices of U.S. domestic oil and Saudi oil were $3.89 and $2.41 in 1973; $25.87 and $29 in 1984. The U.S. GNP implicit price deflator was 105.8 and 215.6 in the two years.

5. Adelman (1972), chapter 2 and appendices. The estimating methods used there are no longer possible, because of the shrinking data base, and the "pollution" of the capital expenditure totals by large outlays on gas production and processing. Hence we do only a trend calculation in appendix B.

References

Adelman, M. A., *The World Petroleum Market* (Baltimore: Johns Hopkins University Press for Resources for the Future, 1972).

Adelman, M. A., and Geoffrey L. Ward, "Worldwide Production Costs," *Advances in the Economics of Energy and Resources* 3 (1980), table 8, p. 17.

American Association of Petroleum Geologists (AAPG). *Bulletin* 65 (Oct. 1981).

American Petroleum Institute, *Petroleum Facts and Figures* (API.PFF), annual (ceased publication).

American Petroleum Institute, American Gas Association, Canadian Petroleum Association (API/AGA), *Reserves of Crude Oil, Natural Gas Liquids, and Natural Gas in the United States and Canada* (ceased publication).

California Energy Commission, *Results of the 1985 CEC Star Delphi Survey on Future Oil Prices* (prepared for August 27, 1985 Hearing of the 1985 Biennial Fuels Report. Docket 85-BFR-1).

Canada, *National Energy Program 1980*.

————, *Memorandum of Agreement between the Government of Canada and the Government of Alberta Relating to Energy Pricing and Taxation*, 1 September 1981(a).

————, Department of Energy, Mines & Resources, *Background Information on Alberta-Canada Energy Agreement*, 14 September 1981(b).

Cremer, J., and D. Salehi-Isfahani, "Competitive Pricing in the Oil Market: How Important Is OPEC?" working paper, University of Pennsylvania, 1980.

Energy Modeling Forum (EMF 6), *World Oil: Summary Report* (Stanford: Stanford University, 1982).

Erickson, Edward C., "Prospects for a Tighter World Oil Market," *The Energy Journal* 6 (Jan. 1985).

Fesharaki, Fereidun, "Global Petroleum Supplies in the 1980s Prospects and Problems," *OPEC Review* (Summer 1980).

Gately, Dermot, "A Ten-Year Retrospective: OPEC and World Oil Market," *Journal of Economic Literature* 22 (Sept 1984), 1100–1114.

Griffin, James M., and David J. Teece (eds.), *OPEC Behavior and World Oil Prices* (London: George Allen & Unwin, 1982).

MacAvoy, Paul W., *Crude Oil Prices: As Determined by OPEC and Market Fundamentals* (Cambridge, MA: Ballinger, 1982).

Manne, Alan, and William Nordhaus, "Using Soviet Gas to Keep OPEC Reeling," *New York Times*, September 22, 1985, section E, 3.

Mead, Walter J., "An Economic Analysis of Crude Oil Price Behavior in the 1970s," *Journal of Energy and Development* 4 (Spring 1979), 212–228.

————, "An Economic Analysis of OPEC as a Cartel," in Mark Baier (ed.), *Energy and Economy: Global Interdependencies* (Bonn: International Association of Energy Economists/Gesellschaft fur Energiewissenschaft und Energiepolitik, 1985), 13–34.

Miller, Merton H., and Charles W. Upton, "A Test of the Hotelling Valuation Principle," *Journal of Political Economy* 93 (Feb. 1985), 24.

New York Times, October 7, 1984, Sec. 3, 8–9: Philip Shabecoff, "The Quest for Offshore Oil."

Oil and Gas Journal (OGJ), weekly (Sept. 27, 1982), 118, 210.

————, (July 16, 1984a), 32.

————, (October 8, 1984b), 49.

Petroleum Economist (PE), monthly (Aug. 1978).

————, monthly (1985).

Petroleum Intelligence Weekly (PIW), (July 14, 1975).

————, (Mar. 29, 1976).

————, monthly reports of capacity (1978). (The CIA capacity estimates are not used because they are inadequately explained, and also appear to confuse capacity, an external fact, with the decision to use a given percentage of it.)

Roumasset, J., D. Isaak, and F. Fesharaki, "Oil Prices without OPEC: A Walk on the Supply Side," *Energy Economics* 5 (July 1983), 164–170.

Salomon Brothers, *Oil Service Monthly* (Jan. 1985), 24.

Saunders, Harry T., "On the Inevitable Return of Higher Oil Prices," *Energy Policy* 12 (Sept. 1984), 310–320.

Smith, James L., and James L. Paddock, "Regional Modelling of Oil Discovery and Production," *Energy Economics* (Jan. 1984), 5–13.

Stiglitz, Joseph E., "Monopoly and the Rate of Extraction of Exhaustible Resources," *American Economic Review* 66 (Sept. 1976), 655–661.

U.S. Census, *Annual Survey of Oil and Gas* 1982 MA-3K(82)-1, annual (discontinued).

U.S. Central Intelligence Agency (US.CIA), *The World Oil Market in the Years Ahead* (Aug. 1979), iii.

U.S. Council of Economic Advisers (US.CEA), *Economic Report of the President* (1986).

U.S. Department of Commerce (US.DOC), Bureau of the Census, *Long-term Economic Growth* (Oct. 1966).

U.S. Department of Energy, Energy Information Administration (US.DOE.EIA.AER), *Annual Energy Review 1983*, DOE/EIA-0384(83).

————, *Annual Energy Outlook 1984*, DOE/EIA-0383(84).

————, AR, *Annual Report to Congress*, DOE/EIA-0173.

————, *Costs and Indices for Domestic Oil Field Equipment and Production Operations 1978* (1979), DOE/EIA-0185.

————, R, *U.S. Crude Oil, Natural Gas, and Natural Gas Liquid Reserves*, DOE/EIA-0216(84), annual.

————, MER, *Monthly Energy Review*.

————, IEA, *International Energy Annual*, DOE/EIA-0219(83).

U.S. General Accounting Office (US.GAO), *An Analysis of Natural Gas Pricing Policy Alternatives* (1983).

U.S. Senate, Senate Report No. 96-394 (1982).

Wall Street Journal, April 23, 1985.

World Bank, *World Development Report 1983* (New York: Published for World Bank by Oxford University Press, 1983), 28.

————, *World Development Report 1985* (New York: Published for World Bank by Oxford University Press, 1985).

World Oil, monthly, annual "International" issue, Aug. 15.

9 The Competitive Floor to World Oil Prices

Years ago, I suggested that there was no current or impending oil shortage. Growing consumption, static U.S. production, and other reasons offered then and now did not imply that prices would rise. That conclusion only made sense if the pressure on reserves was increasing, a situation that would be signaled by rising costs of maintaining and expanding output. There was and is no sign of this.

But oil-exporting nations had tasted the fruits of collusion on a modest scale in 1970 and 1971. The genie was out of the bottle, and they would try harder to get more from him.

The cartel was a great success, but it overreached. Lower consumer demand and rising noncartel output cut their exports drastically. In theory, the members could have agreed—can still agree—on sharing the smaller pie, to leave them all better off. In practice, they have not been able to agree.

The burden of output cutbacks was shoved onto the biggest member, as is usual in coalitions. (The role of the United States in NATO and Asian defense is another example of this phenomenon.) When Saudi exports fell to near zero last summer, they had to make good on their repeated threats. They began to sell under netback contracts, which set no bottom at all to prices.

The Saudis may be able, by judicious infliction of pain,[1] to rally the troops to get the price back up to the neighbourhood of $20. If so, then, barring military action by producing nations to remove productive capacity by force, the underlying surplus will be maintained indefinitely as consumption stagnates and noncartel output creeps up. The cartel will bump from crisis to crisis.

Reprinted from *The Energy Journal* 7 (October 1986): 9–32.

At some point, conceivably, the price may fall to the competitive floor. It is worth trying to locate, however approximately, the short- and long-term competitive price level.

We look at the two ends of the spectrum of producing areas. Our results in brief: at the high-cost end, it would take a price as low as $4 to produce an immediate shutdown of nearly half of capacity in the United States, and as low as $2 to do the same in the North Sea. A price of $10 would stop development investment for the bulk of U.S. oil and over a third of North Sea oil. Capacity would therefore decline.

At the low-cost end (assuming competition and completely independent decisionmaking) a price of $5 would make it profitable for the OPEC nations to expand their output to over 60 million barrels daily. That price would be sustainable past 1995 at the least.

Shutdown Costs for North Sea and United States

We take only strictly economic costs into account, disregarding taxes, royalties, and other charges, which vary from country to country. They can and will be changed by governments in response to bad news. Those quicker to adapt will be penalized less than the more stubborn.

Operating Costs

As table 9.1 shows, during 1983–1984 operating costs in the British North Sea averaged a little over $2 per barrel. From what is known about the distribution of those costs (OGJ, 1986a), approximately 60 percent of North Sea oil is produced at or below average cost, and 80 percent is produced at or below twice the average. Hence it would take a price as low as $4 to reduce North Sea output by 20 percent.

In the United States, as table 9.2 shows, 1982 average operating costs were $4.84, which we have reduced to just under $4.00 to take into account a decline since then (DOE/EIA, 1986, table E1). Since these costs include some allocation of overhead, they overstate true variable costs. In the 1960s, the distribution of well costs in the United States seemed to have a longer, thinner tail than in the North Sea. About 65 percent of production was at or below average cost, and another 30 percent was at or below twice the average (Adelman, 1972). This may still be true.[2] If so, a price of $8 would have little effect, but a price of $4 would suppress more than one-third of U.S. production, practically overnight.

Table 9.1
Development and operating cost, offshore United Kingdom

		1982	1983	1984
1	Output mty	100.1	110.5	120.8
2	Output mbd	2.029	2.240	2.449
3	Reserves (mmbrls)	7237	6845	5920
4	Annual depletion/decline	0.102	0.119	0.151
5	Lost capacity mbd	—	0.248	0.331
6	Gross gain mbd	—	0.459	0.540
7	Development investment, $mm	—	2727	2862
8	Do., $/idb	—	5937	5300
9	Development cost, $/brl	—	4.57	4.43
10	Producing outlays ($/mm)	—	1863	2135
11	Operating cost ($/brl)	—	2.28	2.39
12	Developing plus operating cost ($/brl)	—	6.85	6.82

Note: Lost output is equal to current year output multiplied by average ratio production/reserves, given year and preceding year. Gross gain is sum of lost output and net increase.

Discount rate is taken as 16 percent nominal on development projects. It assumes investor has access to U.S. capital markets. Rate is sum of 8.0 percent riskless end-1985 and 8.0 percent risk premium on oil and gas operations. The riskless rate will probably decrease because of lowered inflation expectations, and the risk premium may increase because of the perceived greater uncertainty of oil prices.
Sterling is converted at $1.50
The discount rate is calculated at 17 percent nominal.
Tonne = 7.4 barrels.
Source: U.K. Department of Energy. *Development of the Oil and Gas Resources of the United Kingdom, 1985, 1984* (HMSO 1985, 1984). Output: Appendix 8, p. 68. Capital expenditures: Appendix 14, p. 77. Operating expenditures: Appendix 14, p. 78.

Thus even a very low price would not quickly shut down oil production, even in the highest-cost areas. But to the extent that it was no longer profitable to invest in additional capacity, there would no longer be any offset to the natural decline rate in all reservoirs, which would reduce production. In general, the fraction of known reservoirs that would continue to be developed would vary with the price. We would like to know the price that would at least maintain development.

There is, however, a qualification. Suppose the price falls to $8, and an operator expects that it will revive to $29 by 1995 (API, 1986). For an average developed barrel costing $4 to produce, and perhaps another 20 percent of the price consisting of royalties and state and local taxes, the gross return would then be as follows:

Year	Price	Cost	Taxes and Royalties	Net
1986	$8	$4	$1.60	$2.40
1995	$29	$4	$5.80	$19.20

Whether an eightfold return in nine years (26 percent per year) is good enough depends of course on the risk attached to it. Or to state the problem a little differently: considering production in 1995 as an option, how much would the option be worth in the market?

Asking these questions is more important than finding specific answers. Discussion of the oil market has long been plagued with confusion about such things as the alleged wide gap between full and marginal costs; if full cost means average cost, then marginal cost may be much more or much less. One false assumption that gets in the way of clear thinking is that the price floor is the out-of-pocket cost of the last barrels, because investment is a sunk cost. If this were true, nearly every single industry would show wild price fluctuations at all times because investment would have no effect on price. But in the oil industry as elsewhere, the statement is untrue.

Table 9.2
Development of operating cost, United States, 1984

1984					
Development outlays ($mm)	Gross reserves added (mm brls)	Development cost per barrel in ground ($)	Depletion/ decline rate	Ratio above-to in-ground value	Development cost as produced ($)
14174	3748	3.78	0.115	2.39	9.04

1982					1984
Operating outlays ($mm)	Oil fraction	Oil operating outlays ($mm)	Production mm bbl	Operating cost/bbl ($)	Estimate
17453	0.674	11762	2432	4.84	3.87

Sources:

Development: Outlays, Census, Annual Survey of Oil and Gas 1982 adjusted to 1984 by Joint Association Survey. Gross reserves added. DOE/EIA. Depletion/decline rate, ratio of production to average annual proved reserves, per DOE/EIA. Depletion/decline rate, ratio of production to average annual proved reserves, per DOE/EIA. Ratio = $(1 + (i/a))$, where i = discount rate, taken at 16 percent, and a = depletion/decline rate.

Operating: U.S. Bureau of the Census. Annual Survey of Oil and Gas 1984 Production and expenditures are for the sample of companies. Oil fraction calculated by taking the ratio of oil wells to wells and assuming gas wells cost one-third more. They are reduced by 20 percent to reflect lower costs. (See Independent Petroleum Association of America. Report of Study Committee (May), showing much larger decline for drilling expenditures.)

Oil development consists of spending large sums of money to build a shelf inventory, proved reserves. No manufacturer or shopkeeper will give away his wares because his stock-in-trade is a sunk cost. What he sells he must replace. Even if he is going out of business, others will buy his inventory for their cost of replacement.

For oil, too, the true price floor includes replacement cost. The problem in the world oil market is the excess of price over operating-plus-replacement cost for the great bulk of the world's reserves.

Development Cost

Table 9.1 shows that oil development investment in the British North Sea was about $5.5 billion in 1983–1984 (converting the pound sterling at $1.50). Since output was equal to capacity, the increase from 2.029 to 2.449 million barrels daily represented a net capacity gain of 420,000 barrels per day over two years. But since there was a continuing decline in old reservoirs, the capacity lost and replaced during those two years must be added back. This can be approximated by assuming that the ratio of production to reserves is about equal to the rate of decline, as it would be under conditions of constant exponential decline for an unlimited period.[3] There is reason to think that this exaggerates the decline rate for 1984, but if so, the error will be offset by an error in the opposite direction. This will be demonstrated in the next paragraph.

The North Sea development outlay of about $5600 per initial daily barrel is for a diminishing flow. The amount per barrel that would make production just barely worthwhile is found by multiplying the investment by the sum of the depletion/decline rate and the minimum acceptable rate of return.[4] In the U.S. capital market in early 1986, the riskless rate of return on U.S. treasury bonds was about 8 percent. It has declined because of lower inflation, and may decline further. Adding the risk premium on oil operations—which according to various researchers historically seems to be about 8 percent-yields a total of 16 percent. Added to the apparent 13.5 percent decline rate (which constitutes the offset), a total return of 29.5 percent is necessary: initial year cash flow as percent of up-from investment.[5]

In the United States, development expenditures were calculated by using the 1984 *Joint Association Survey* to update the 1982-unfortunately, the last —issue of the U.S. Census *Annual Survey of Oil and Gas*. Division of total development expenditures between oil and gas was made in proportion to the respective drilling development expenditures. An estimate of the increment to capacity would be a much less reliable number than the gross addition to reserves, which in 1984 was 3748 million barrels, or $3.78 per barrel in the ground.[6] We are forced to exclude natural gas liquids (from associated-dissolved gas production), since this number is no longer compiled by DOE/EIA (1984). This results in a small cost overstatement.

The in-ground cost per barrel is converted into a wellhead-cost per barrel by a method that is mathematically equivalent to the one used for the North Sea (Adelman, 1986, appendix A). The cost of holding the reserve barrel until produced and sold off varies directly with the cost of capital and inversely with the depletion/decline rate; the quicker it is produced, the cheaper it is to hold. In the United States, where i = the discount rate and a = the depletion/decline rate, the multiplier $(1 + (i/a))$ = $(1 + (0.16/0.115))$ = 2.39. Hence the average development cost at the wellhead is reckoned at $9.04.

If the real, not the nominal, discount rate is used, the multiplier is $(1 + (0.10/0.115))$ = 1.87, and the wellhead-cost is $7.07. This would be relevant if and when one thought the price of oil had really gone to some equilibrium level and would henceforth fluctuate with the general price level, modified by its own supply and demand.

Summary: United Kingdom and United States

In the North Sea, the sum of average operating plus development costs is a bit less than $7 per barrel. Therefore a $7 price, net of all taxes, would support continued development of about half the U.K. fields. AT $14, or twice the average, nearly all fields would still be worth further development. In the United States, average development-plus-operating cost is about $13, so a $14 price would stop development in fields accounting for nearly half the total. A price of $10 per barrel would stop development investment for the bulk of U.S. oil and over a third of North Sea oil.[7] (For effects on exploration, see below.) Lower costs will lower these thresholds.

At this point, we must digress to deal with a widely cited estimate that cannot be reconciled with the real world.

The Myth of $70,000 Per Daily Barrel in Non-OPEC-Producing Nations

A little mental arithmetic shows this is impossible. It is twelve times the 1983–1984 average for the British North Sea, and would therefore require a price of over $85, after taxes, to break even. (That is, ($70,000/ $5300)·($4.43 + $2.12) = $86.51). In the United States, the break-even price would be even higher. Not long ago most oilmen believed such a price was coming—some day. But to suppose they spent billions up front at this rate, for years on end, without losing their jobs or their companies to takeovers or stockholder's suits is not credible. Even in 1982, when reputable consulting firms were predicting prices of $200 per barrel, a North Sea development project was canceled because it would have cost $4 billion to develop about 300 million barrels (*New York Times*, 1982), very roughly $44,000 per daily barrel.[8] Thus even around the height of the delusion, an investment of only 63 percent of the supposed average cost was ruled out.

Finding Cost (Resource Value)

We have assumed up to now that the decline rate would stay constant. That is not true. Without newly found reservoirs to freshen up the mix, increasingly intensive development is bound to increase the percent of reserves depleted, and the rate of production decline, every year. That is what happened in the United States after about 1965.

A price double the average development cost supplies an incentive to find low-cost fields. There is some indirect evidence bearing on this question: the per-barrel value of a reserve sold in the ground.

In late 1985 the price of a barrel of oil in a developed reserve was $6, give or take $1 (OGJ, 1985). However, an allowance for the tax benefits of drilling would raise the pretax cost to about $7. If our estimate in table 9.2 is correct, this divides neatly in half, and the value of undeveloped oil in the ground would have been $3.50 per barrel. With the collapse of oil prices after late 1985, this value today must be much lower. Except where expected finding cost (excluding development) can be brought this low, or lower, it does not pay to explore.

Unfortunately, we cannot compare the value of an undeveloped barrel in the ground with the cost of finding it. There are no data from which to estimate finding costs per unit. There are data on exploration expenditures—the most recent from 1982—but there are no data on the amount of newly found oil aside from the usual meaningless finding that lumps together development and discovery.

The published Energy Information Administration (EIA) statistics on "discoveries" are fragments masquerading as data. This is because the initial-year estimates are only a small fraction of what will ultimately be credited to a new field or pool. Through 1979 the American Petroleum Institute and American Gas Association published a valuable series of back-dated oil and gas discovery estimates, but this (and much else) was lost when their series ceased publication, a casuality of mindless hostility to the oil and gas industry (cf. National Academy of Sciences, 1985).

Hence we have no information on finding costs per unit. Estimates published under that heading are meaningless. However, it seems plausible that not enough can be found even at $3.50 to maintain the reservoirs. In fact, for many years most of the additions to reserves have come from old fields, both by improved recovery and by adding to the known oil in place.

To sum up: in the United States and the North Sea, a $20 price (at which the windfall profits tax becomes irrelevant) would make the continued development of known prospects, except for extremely high-cost wells, profitable. It would also supply an incentive for exploration of good prospects, that is, those whose combined costs would not exceed $20. But many leases would not be worth further investment, and production would slowly decline unless costs were sharply reduced.

Costs have, of course, come far down, and reduction in deep-water off-shore drilling have been dramatic. Hence the currently reported cutbacks (June 1986) in oil-production capital spending do not mean an equally great cutback in real effort and investment. Moreover, efficiency is rising steeply, both because of better use of equipment, and because the poorer prospects are cut first. The decrease in drilling has not been matched by the decreased number of wells and of feet drilled. There were 45 percent fewer rigs operating in the first six months of 1986 than in the same months of 1985 (MER, 1986), but numbers for well-completions and footage were only 25 percent lower (OGJ, 1986d). Moreover, many of the cutbacks in spending and drilling have been precautionary steps taken until the dust settles. In the North Sea and elsewhere, lower taxes will restore profitability to some projects currently uneconomical.

Other Noncartel Areas

Some of these resemble the United States and United Kingdom because they are competitive, and production is carried out to the point where incremental cost is equal to price. Here lower prices would force cutbacks.

But many, and probably most, noncartel countries have been explored and developed below their potential. In such countries reserves and production will increase because government and public opinion are, with agonizing slowness, shedding the illusion of oil and gas as appreciating assets that are worth keeping in the ground. This illusion is powerfully reinforced by the notions—so vague as to defy analysis and common sense—that oil is strategic, whatever that means, and that oil deposits are family heirlooms, not vulgar commodities to be managed for maximum return. These countries will begin to negotiate and to tax on the basis of real prices.

For example, the world price decline after 1981 caused Canada to abandon its National Energy Program and to promote investment and exports. The Dutch stopped cutting back exports and began actively seeking customers. The price collapse of early 1986 led Norway to accept a price for the Troll and Sleipner gas fields (OGJ, 1986c) that was half (or less) of what they had previously demanded. This development is the direct result of lower prices. The probability of revising government policy in order to minimize the loss of revenue is what makes pretax calculations relevant.

Taking the noncartel areas as a group, if the price is again raised to $20, there is no basis for supposing that these countries will have lower reserves and production in 1995 than they do today. But a price in the $4–$8 range would indeed shrink the oil industry in those nations. An intermediate price is much harder to read.

We turn therefore to the low-cost areas to see what, under competitive conditions, would be available at such a range of prices.

The Supply Function in the OPEC Areas

The Competitive Floor Price

In 1970 the Persian Gulf price was $1.20 (which at present-day drilling cost levels would be about $3). Supply was ample, and the price was stable, tending to decline very slowly. How different would things be in the 1980s and 1990s?

With no cartel, each producing nation would become a pricetaker. To maximize returns, they would increase output to where the incremental cost of more production approached the market price. They might yearn for the good old days of the cartel, but that would not matter so long as they could do no more than yearn.

As with the North Sea and United States, we need to know how much money must be spent to obtain a barrel of oil at daily capacity, to be translated into cost per barrel.

Table 9.3 shows the calculations underlying figure 9.1. We have the estimated curve for the year 1995, allowing ten years for some of the OPEC nations to build their capacity up to 5 percent of their proved reserves. The industry rule of thumb is one-fifteenth annual depletion, or

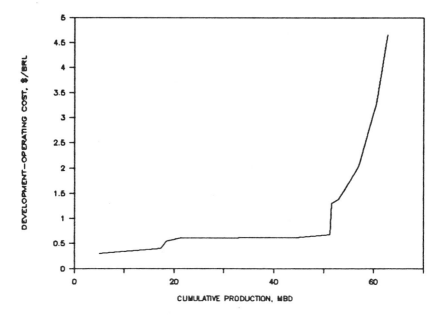

Figure 9.1
Supply curve: OPEC 1995 (1985 cost levels, producing 6 percent reserves)

6.7 percent. In the United States and the United Kingdom, depletion rates are above 10 percent. (Cf). tables 9.1 and 9.2).

Our reference year is 1978, the last year before data were radically distorted by the second price explosion and the output cutbacks. Line 1 shows the number of wells of all types completed that year, line 2 the average depth of well. Line 3a shows the average cost of an onshore well in the United States at that depth. For Iran and Nigeria, however, we choose not the average value but the maximum, to allow for exceptionally difficult drilling conditions. For countries that produce both onshore and offshore, we multiply by the ratio, calculated from the *Joint Association Survey*, of well-costs for all wells to well-costs of onshore alone, yielding the adjusted average well-cost in line 3b.

In addition to drilling and equipping wells, there are also the outlays for lease equipment, improved recovery systems, overhead, and other expenses comprising total development cost. These have historically averaged 66 percent of drilling costs, with little variation. Well-cost must be scaled up by that percentage.

Multiplying (a) the number of wells drilled by (b) the drilling plus non-drilling cost for each well yields total drilling-related expenditures, shown

Table 9.3
Development-operating costs in OPEC nations (1978 conditions, adjusted to 1985 drilling costs)

	Iraq	(1980)[a] Kuwait	Qatar	Saudi Arabia	Indo-nesia	Libya	Iran	Algeria	Abu Dhabi	Vene-zuela	Nigeria
1 Wells drilled	42	36	32	145	499	175	112	177	61	807	68
2 Approximate average depth (Tft)	9.238	2.156	7.046	5.661	5.301	6.698	9.800	8.853	8.849	5.353	9.667
3a 1985 Average cost/well ($mm)	0.571	0.069	0.337	0.238	0.212	0.312	0.637	0.527	0.526	0.216	0.621
3b Do., adjusted	0.571	0.069	0.367	0.251	0.224	0.312	1.033	0.527	0.577	0.228	1.008
3c Adjustment class			a	a	a		a,b		a	a	a,b
4 Investment ($mm)	40	4	19	60	186	91	192	155	58	305	114
5 Output, tbd	2593	1894	484	8066	1630	1983	5149	1164	1446	2166	1905
6 Operating wells	197	545	102	700	3042	1113	445	1057	257	11333	1404
7a Average, tbd/well	13.162	3.475	4.745	11.523	0.536	1.782	11.571	1.101	5.626	0.191	1.357
7b Weighted average tbd/well[c]	19.093[b]	3.889[b]	9.679	11.168	1.092	3.515	16.853	1.736	6.487[b]	0.330	1.725
8 Oil wells drilled	36	24	12	46	334	134	49	105	17	598	33
9a New capacity, tbd	474	83	57	530	179	239	567	116	96	114	45
9b Adjacent new capacity, tbd	687	93	116	514	635	471	826	182	110	197	57

Table 9.3 (continued)

	Iraq	(1980)[a] Kuwait	Qatar	Saudi Arabia	Indo-nesia	Libya	Iran	Algeria	Abu Dhabi	Vene-zuela	Nigeria
10a Investment/bd (t$) = cost per barrel ($)	0.084	0.049	0.342	0.114	1.037	0.380	0.339	1.339	0.611	2.673	2.540
10b Adjacent investment/bd (t$) = cost per barrel ($)	0.058	0.044	0.168	0.118	0.292	0.192	0.233	0.849	0.530	1.548	1.998
11 Supply price ($/brl)	0.145	0.110	0.419	0.294	0.731	0.481	0.581	2.124	1.325	3.870	4.995
12 1978 capacity, mbd	4	3	0.65	12	1.8	2.5	7	1.2	2.1	2.4	2.5
13 1978 reserves, bbl	32.1	66.2	4	165.7	10.2	24.3	59	6.3	30	18	18.2
14 1985 reserves, bbl	44.1	89.8	3.3	168.8	8.5	21.3	47.9	8.8	31	25.6	16.6
15 1995 potential (5%), mbd	6.0	12.3	0.5	23.1	1.2	2.9	6.6	1.2	4	3.5	2.3
16 Cumulative potential, mb	6	18	19	42	43	46	53	54	58	62	64
17 1995 investment/bd (t$) = cost per barrel ($)	0.159	0.334	0.353	0.556	0.567	0.641	0.671	1.527	2.592	3.976	4.982

Notes: The 2.5 adjustment (line 11) assumes a highly skewed distribution of well efficiencies and costs, as is true of an area with a very large number of very small wells. It is a substantial overstatement for other parts of the world.

It is assumed that the cost per unit is proportional to the depletion rate. This is usually, though not always, an overstatement. Reservoir development should aim to stop well short of the point where costs go nonlinear.

a. No wells were drilled in Kuwait in 1978–1979.

b. Adjustment for partial offshore production market a; adjustment for unusually difficult drilling conditions marked b.

c. In the calculation of the weighted average daily output per well, data on individual field's productions are taken from the first six months of 1978. For any country, whose total number of oil fields is less than 15, we calculate the weighted average daily output for all at nation's wells. Otherwise we only use the number of wells from its major oil fields in our calculation.

Sources: Wells drilled: "World Oil," annual International Outlook issue, August 15, 1979, Nigeria and Abu Dhabi suspended wells estimated at world-wide percentage. Well depth: same source; total footage divided by completions. Daily output: same source. Operating wells: same source; included flowing and artificial lift wells. Drilling cost: DOE/EIA, *Indexes and Estimates of Domestic well Drilling Costs 1984 and 1985* (DOE/EIA–0347(84-85)). These are exclusively onshore wells. Adjustment (a) is average ratio of total U.S. to onshore U.S. cost for given well depth, from 1984 Joint Association Survey. Adjustment (b) is ratio of maximum to average composite drilling cost for given depth, from DOE/EIA, op. cit. Adjustment for nondrilling costs: Bureau of the Census, *Annual Survey of Oil and Gas* (discontinued after 1982). Output of newly drilled wells assumed equal to average flow of existing wells. Capacity from *Petroleum Intelligence Weekly*, April 9, 1979. Year-end reserves from *Oil and Gas Journal*, issues of December 1978 and 1985. Weighted average output per well using data from *Oil and Gas Journal*, December 25, 1978, and from *International Petroleum Encyclopedia*, 1976, 1978, and 1979. Potential defined as a 5 percent depletion rate of reserves as estimated by *Oil and Gas Journal*. Industry rule of thumb is one-fifteenth, or 6.67 percent. Decline assumed as percent production is of reserves. Subtracting it from gross new capacity installed (above line 9) implies a net capacity increase of 5.6 percent for 1978.

Table 9.3a
Development-operating costs of oil fields in Comalcalco and in Gulf of Campeche, Mexico (1984 conditions and drilling costs)

		Comalcalco	Gulf of Campeche
1	Wells drilled	45	35
2	Approximate average depth (Tft)	17.286	12.622
3a	1984 average cost/well ($mm)	3.697	4.291
3b	Do., adjusted	3.697	4.291
3c	Adjustment class		
4	Investment ($mm)	276	249
5	Output, tbd	721	1738
6	Operating wells[a]	357	100
7a	Average, tbd/well	2.020	17.380
7b	Weighted average, tbd/well[b]	5.765	18.333
8	Oil wells drilled	30	27
9a	New capacity, tbd	61	469
9b	Adjusted new capacity, tbd	173	495
10a	Investment/bd (t$) = cost per barrel ($)	4.558	0.531
10b	Adjusted investment/bd (t$) = cost per barrel ($)	1.597	0.504
11	Supply price ($/bbl)	3.992	1.259
12	1984 capacity, tbd	721	1738
13	1984 year-end reserves, bbl	9.3	31.8
14	1995 potential (5%), mbd	1.28	4.36
15	Cumulative potential, mb	1.28	5.64
16	1995 investment/bd (t$) = cost per barrel ($)	7.071	3.158

a. Data on the numbers of operating wells are as of July 1, 1984. There are 249 flowing and 108 artificial lift wells in Comalcalco area, and 100 flowing and zero artificial lift wells in Campeche area.

b. In the calculation of the weighted average daily production per well, data on individual field's daily productions are taken from the first six months of 1984.

Sources: Wells drilled: "*Memoria de Labores, 1984*," (Instituto Mexicanos del Petroleos, 1985). Well depths: same source, total footage divided by completions. Daily output: same source. 1984 year-end reserves: same source, included 5 bb condensate in both areas. Drilling cost: 1984 *Joint Association Survey*. Since wells in each region are either all onshore or all offshore, no adjustment is necessary. We use the data on average drilling cost in the United States for given depth in the calculations. Operating wells: *Oil and Gas Journal*, December 31, 1984 issue, annual report on worldwide production. Weighted average output per well was calculated using data from the same source. Capacity assumed equal to production.

in line 4. This includes gas wells and equipment and exploratory drilling (but not geological-geophysical work, which ought to be excluded). Nonetheless, the total is considered oil-development expenditure.

Operations outside the United States, where there is no infrastructure of people and service industries and supples in place, tend to be more expensive. But the countries we are considering are all mature producers. Furthermore, we disregard local peculiarities, public or private, that increase expense but are not necessary.

New capacity is calculated by taking the adjusted average production per well per day (line 7b), assuming that the average new well produces as much as the average old well. This average is multiplied not by total wells drilled, but only by new successful oil wells, to yield gross new capacity added, country by country (line 9b). There is a factor of overstatement here because some successful oil wells are exploratory holes that do not add to capacity. Exploration, however, was at a low level in these countries, a fact to be discussed more fully below.

Dividing total investment (line 4) by the new capacity added by drilling (line 9b) yields investment per additional daily barrel (line 10b). We must now translate this into cost per barrel by the same method as was applied to the North Sea.

We assume the production decline to be equal to the 1995 production/reserve percent, in this case 5 percent, as would be true of exponential decline over an infinite period. Operating expenses are assumed to be 7 percent of investment. The total gross rate of return is 36.5 percent, which makes arithmetic easy. (For example, if the investment per daily barrel is $1000, then unit cost = $1000 \cdot (0.05 + 0.07 + 0.245)/365 = $1.) However, this is fortuitous. We assume a cost of capital, in nominal terms, at 24.5 percent. This is half again as high as what it would be for private oil and gas operators in the United States or similar developed countries.[9]

The limitations on these estimates are several. First, like those for the United States but unlike those for the North Sea, they are strictly wellhead costs, with no allowance for transport. Second, they are costs per average well. This involves some opposing biases.

On the one side, the cost per barrel from the average well may, and usually does, overstate the cost per barrel from all wells. This happens when (as in the United States) there is a long thin tail of small wells. This can be adjusted for by calculating a weighted average flow rate, weighting the average flow rate for each field by the production of the field (Adelman and Paddock, 1980). A weighted average for all wells would be preferable but is impossible. The weighted average flow rate is shown in line 7b. It is usually higher, but sometimes lower, than the unweighted average in line 7a.

But, on the other side, even an adjusted average cost curve is not a supply curve. As pointed out earlier in discussing the United States and the United Kingdom, a substantial fraction, but less than half, of the oil is produced at costs above average. Hence, for each country one must make an allowance for the more expensive output. Our procedure is to multiply the average cost, line 10b, by 2.5, yielding the supply curve segment of line 11. This adjustment in effect yields a 50 percent or greater rate of return for more than half the existing capacity, which serves as an incentive to discovery of new fields. Hence, we have a substantial implicit allowance for exploration costs.

It need not be said that every item has a wide margin for error. Indeed, among the lowest-cost suppliers, the order tells more about our adjustment rules than about true relative costs. For example, Saudi expenditures were unusually high in 1978 because of a large water-injection project, and oil well expenditures were relatively low; Libya, on the other hand, was completing an unusually large number of oil wells that year.

For some of these countries, going to 5 percent depletion involves a very large buildup. In 1978, for example, Saudi Arabia produced only 2.6 percent of its proved reserves. I assume that investment per unit is proportional to the depletion rate. Hence, the Saudi investment is increased in the proportion 5.0/2.6, or by 92 percent. This represents a considerable overstatement because reserves would be increasing along with capacity. The assumption is kept, however, to be consistent with a later treatment. (See below, the "zero reserves-added model.")

The supply cost for the group as a whole is that for the highest-cost members. Venezuela and Nigeria. The 1978 cost (at 1985 factor prices) in Nigeria was $2. With much of its output known to be at higher costs, we multiply the average by 2.5, for a result of $5. Producing at 5 percent of 1985 proved reserves would be a slightly higher percent of reserves than in 1978, although the absolute amount would be lower. Hence, the supply price increases only slightly.

Venezuela and Nigeria are the only countries where estimating errors make any difference. For the others, even large relative errors would be negligible in absolute terms. That is, if the true cost is twice our calculated cost, and the latter is 50 cents, the error is only 50 cents. There is no way of changing the conclusion: in these countries oil ranges from cheap to dirt cheap.

Declining oil prices have lowered costs greatly, both by lower factor prices and by greater efficiency. Costs will undoubtedly decline from 1985 levels, but we cannot tell by how much.

How Long Can a Competitive Price Be Sustained?

We have assumed that it takes a decade to reach equilibrium. We need to estimate rates of reserve buildup and drawdown before we can start to answer the ultimate question: still assuming competition, how long can this price level be sustained?

World non-Communist consumption in 1985 was 45.5 million barrels daily (DOE/EIA/ICID. March 1986, p. 10), of which 39 million barrels per day was supplied by crude oil (OGJ, March 10, 1986, p. 80) and the rest by natural gas liquids, Communist-block exports, and inventory drawdown. We focus on crude oil supply and demand.

At much lower prices consumption would increase. We assume average annual economic growth at 3 percent, and an oil: GNP annual growth of 2 percent, for an oil consumption growth rate of 5 percent.[10]

Table 9.4 shows that this consumption turnaround could have been supplied entirely from the stock of proved reserves at end-1985. Noncartel oil production is assumed to decline steadily at about 8 percent per year, which is almost surely excessive, while output of cartel oil (OPEC plus Mexico) would increase by a factor of three. Most of the growth in cartel output would merely reactivate capacity already in existence in 1985.

Table 9.4 is a model not merely of zero discoveries but of *zero reserve additions from known fields*. In any given time period these are always the great bulk of all reserve additions. Nevertheless, there is no problem of supply at the competitive floor price for a decade. It is during this time that

Table 9.4
Zero discovery and reserve—additions model, 1985–1995 (billions of barrels)

Year	Production (mbd)		Cumulative production		Proved reserves	
	Cartel	Noncartel	Cartel	Noncartel	Cartel	Noncartel
1985	18	21	—	—	525	94
1995	54	9	138	50	387	44
1995 production/reserves					0.051	0.075

Note: Cartel includes OPEC nations plus Mexico. Noncartel includes all others outside the Communist bloc. For explanation of 1995 values, see text.
Source: *Oil and Gas Journal*, "World Wide Oil," (1985). For 1995, see text.

reserves would in fact be added, at the cost per barrel shown in table 9.3, to support consumption after 1995.

Sustainability after 1995

It is conservative to assume that enough additional reserves will be created during 10 years, at the costs shown in table 9.3, to supply the world past 1995 for a few years, at least. But we consider it a mistake to estimate the rate of reserve additions as if they were some kind of exogenous fact. Reserves are ready inventory. The rate of reserve-building results from profit-maximizing investment decisions, which are radically different under competitive and monopoly systems.

Any monopoly must restrict output in order to maintain price. Hence, there is underinvestment. With a reversion to competition, the rules governing investment would again be turned upside down to be right side up.

In a competitive market low-cost sources of supply grow faster than do high-cost sources. This was true before the 1973 price explosion. It was evident in the bitter twenty-year fight in the United States over restricting imports. Since 1973 water has been running uphill. Drilling in the United States increased by a factor of four through 1985. In Saudi Arabia drilling dropped by two-thirds because only sharply lower production would maintain the price.

If the monopoly disappeared and every producer acted independently, competition would first induce them to use all of their existing capacity and would then set them off on an investment boom. They would hate it, of course, and some of them would have real financial problems in raising the relatively small amounts needed. But the only way to save something from the wreck of the cartel would be to explore, develop, and produce to the maximum.

The difference between oil and uranium is instructive. After 1974 the price of uranium soared almost as spectacularly as oil, but there was no cartel to restrict investment. Accordingly, there was a massive increase in supply. Less than five years after the first surge, uranium prices began to drop, and went to the lowest level since they were first recorded (Neff, 1984). The Neff paradigm will hold also for oil if the monopoly disappears; the question is how far down the price will go.

We look first at development of known fields, which provide the great bulk of new reserves added in any time period.

In 1944 a team of distinguished geologists calculated Persian Gulf oil reserves at 16 billion proved, with another 5 billion probable. Excluding later discoveries, this has already been surpassed by a factor of roughly 30. These geologists were neither foolish nor conservative; as good scientists, they interpreted from the data known then. As more is known, reserve estimates grow.

For Saudi Arabia to produce 20 million barrels daily requires them only to dust off the 1973 plans for 1980. Of the 50 commercial oil fields discovered in that country, only 15 have been developed. If the price collapses, we will find out how much is in the other 35.

No OPEC country is as intensively drilled today as was the United States in 1945. Excluding those in Alaska, practically all the big fields had been found before that year. Proved reserves in 1945 were 20 billion barrels. But in the next 40 years the lower 48 produced not 20 billion but 100 billion barrels, and they still have nearly 20 billion on the shelf.

Those additional 100 billion barrels plus were no gift of nature. Through heavy investment, many small fields were found, and the old fields were greatly expanded. Yet from 1945 until at least through 1972, there was no increase in finding-developing cost. (Great turbulence, and disappearance of some statistics, make it difficult to say just what happened afterward, but there is reason to think the cost may have doubled in 1972–1984).

In Venezuela reserves stagnated until costs began to creep up. Reserves amounted to 18 billion barrels at end-1978. In the next seven years, another 13 billion were added, without major discoveries. A nationalized industry does not have the difficult problem of skimming the operator's rents without taking so high a percentage as to reduce the total take. In Nigeria, Indonesia, Malaysia, Egypt, and other places, better terms will be granted to local operating companies because it will minimize the revenue losses.

Turning now to exploration: it is prudent to assume that the oil industry will find smaller oil and gas fields than in the past.[11] It does not, however, follow that newly discovered oil will decrease. That depends on the slope of the size-decline curve (Smith and Paddock, 1984) and on the amount of investment in exploration.

The most promising areas of the world are the least explored. In Kuwait, an oil field of about 30 billion barrels was discovered as the inadvertent result of drilling for gas for local power generation in 1983. This oil is so cheap to produce that it will replace part of current production. Kuwait is a tiny country. Saudi Arabia is as large as Texas and Louisiana combined. In 1985 those states operated an average of 963 rigs. Saudi Arabia averaged ten. Yet Saudi Arabia is a far better hunting ground. We will find out how much better when and if the cartel disappears—not before.

In a kind of twilight between exploration and development are large resources of heavy oils, especially in Canada and Venezuela. Much is profitable at a price below $10. Indeed, just as high prices and low demand put the Orinoco belt on hold, low prices and high demand would make it a major producer.

In short, the evidence points to a replacement of 1985–1995 consumption at the cost levels of table 9.3, which is ample to accommodate consumption through A.D. 2000. There is too little basis for going farther, nor is there any need to. The change in marginal cost is an unknown with which buyers and sellers must somehow cope. The only meaningful question is: what would be the effect upon the supply price of oil in 1986–1990 of the unknown chance of sharply rising marginal cost after A.D. 2000?

Long-run Cost and Price Changes

The belief that oil prices must somehow rise in the long term is grounded in the fact of diminishing returns. We need assume nothing about exhaustible resources. The amount of a mineral in the earth is unknown and irrelevant. The limit to growth is cost at the margin.

In any mineral industry, ceteris paribus, the biggest deposits are more likely to be found first, even by chance, because they are biggest. The best ones are exploited first. (Failure to do so, as we saw earlier, implies monopoly control.) Life is one long slide from good to bad and bad to worse. Hence, marginal cost must keep rising over time, and the price with it. As the cost and price rise, consumption and production dwindles.

Yet for nearly 30 years it has been clear that there is no persistent widespread upward price drift; most minerals prices actually decline in the long run. Diminishing returns are opposed by increasing knowledge, both of the earth's crust and of methods of extraction and use. *The price of oil, like that of any mineral, is the uncertain fluctuating result of the conflict.*

Thus the value of a mineral body is subject to the kind of uncertainty found in every industry. Every mineral or nonmineral firm must reckon as a current cost the depletion of assets. That cost is the less of (a) the present value of the asset's future revenues or (b) the present value of reproduction cost. Either of these values is very uncertain, but there is no escape from the pain of choice for an investment decision. In fact, (a)/(b) is as familiar to economists as Tobin's Q. Mineral economics is merely an important special case.

In long-run equilibrium, the fraction (a)/(b) approaches unity. We have an interesting example of a firm working out the problem at its leisure.

In 1976, when Aramco was expropriated, the operating companies were allowed 6 cents (about 10 cents in 1985 prices) for every barrel discovered.

This gives us a fix on Saudi marginal finding costs (equal to user cost) and marginal revenues. The low value should not be surprising. Given proved reserves of 166 billion barrels (and probable reserves perhaps half again as great) and current annual output of 3 billion, the present discounted value of an incremental Aramco barrel was tiny almost without regard for the future price. Were Aramco producing at the levels hypothesized in table 9.3, development cost and also resource value (user cost) would be much higher.

In 1976, in the United States, an undeveloped barrel in the ground would sell for several dollars. The future net revenue, that is, the difference between price and operating-development cost, was only a small fraction of the margin in Saudi Arabia. But the present value of the smaller margin was many times as great because it would be realized within a few years— not decades or centuries—if at all.

If current information indicates higher prices in the future, then it pays to refrain from investing in reserves that would be profitably depleted today to save them for even more profitable future use. The higher the cost, the lower the current profit, and the greater the gain from postponement.[12] Or, what comes to the same thing: the lower the cost of creating the reserves (development cost), the lower the opportunity cost (user cost) of producing now rather than deferring production.

Thus the notion that the cartel nations were reserving their oil in the ground for later, more profitable, use is proved false by the fact that owners of higher-cost oil were striving to get it out more quickly, while the owners of lower-cost oil lagged far behind. This upside-down behavior is characteristic of a noncompetitive industry with a competitive fringe.

Moreover, the increased cost of developing known reserves puts a limit on what is worth finding; some years ago, I called it the Maximum Economic Finding Cost (Adelman, 1972; and see Devarajan and Fisher, 1982). Hence, an estimated increase in development cost is an implicit allowance for exploration cost.

Our only sensing device for future shortages is a competitive market price. Estimates and models of resources and reserves are inputs into price formation. Assumptions about conditions past A.D. 2000 will be discounted so heavily by rational actors that their influence is minor or imperceptible. The price reflects all the information, models, guesses, hypotheses, hunches, and mistakes. The fog surrounding any future price is like Napoleon's "fog of war." But the estimate of that future price is subject to constant correction.

The probability of marginal costs rising strongly after A.D. 2000, whatever it may be, will have little near-term effect, but it will have a substantial effect 10 years hence.

It is not unreasonable (even if unproved) to expect the competitive price of oil to increase over the long run from the current competitive shadow price. What will amaze the historian is that when the price of oil was raised far above that competitive level, and was therefore subject to an additional downward risk, it was confidently expected that it would keep increasing. The International Energy Workshop provides what is about the most moderate and cautious (as it is one of the most recent) of innumerable analyses and forecasts of prices higher than 1981 or 1985.

Price Forecasts

But even if the price reaches (as it approached in 1970) a level that expresses long-run supply and demand, it will probably not stay there. The cartel members need not wait for A.D. 2000 or even 1987. Lower sales have not directly forced down cartel prices. It is rather that lower revenues have made them resist the need to share burdens. But if they can make, and, more important, keep an agreement to cut production, they can quickly raise prices again.

The cartel is basically unstable because a movement in either direction becomes self-reinforcing and cumulative. "The better the financial condition of the sellers ... the less pressure on them to cheat and undersell each other in order to pay their bills ... Once the price begins to slip, the OPEC nations will be under great pressure to produce more in order to acquire more revenue, and the more they produce, the further the price falls" (Adelman, 1982 [chapter 20, this book]).

Most likely, the price will fluctuate between the monopoly ceiling and the competitive floor. The ceiling seems first to have been envisaged around $28, but more recently OPEC spokesmen have spoken of $20. The floor as we perceive it here is about $8 in the short run, below which there will be large cutbacks in U.S. production, and $5 in the longer run, which would suffice to maintain a flow of investment in new reserves and capacity in the noncartel area and elsewhere.

Concerted output cuts by the revived cartel would, as in the past, be a clumsy way of raising the price, resulting in the kind of overshoot that occurred in 1979–1981.

What should be done to cope with this instability is another question. Pent-up forces often behave violently. The world oil monopoly is both the largest of all time, and is also the greatest in the divergence of price from long-run marginal cost. The accumulated tension between actual and competitive market conditions is therefore unprecedented.

Notes

1. It is hard to imagine any greater encouragement than to hear from the vice president of the United States how much pain they are inflicting. One is reminded of how an undersecretary of state was dispatched to the Persian Gulf in January 1971 to inform the producers there how much damage they would inflict by an embargo.

2. For example, the Kern River field in 1985 had 6254 wells producing 139 tbd (*Oil and Gas Journal*, January 27, 1986, p. 104). Average output was thus 22 bd per well. In early 1986, 1500 wells that had produced 17 tbd, an average of 11 bd per well, were closed (*Wall Street Journal*, March 12, 1986, p. 5). Thus the highest-cost 12 percent of output was produced at a cost about twice average for the field.

3. Thus if initial output $= Q$, and the annual decline rate $= a$, output in any year $t = Q_t = Q e^{-at}$, and proved reserves $R = Q e^{-at} dt = Q/a$ or $a = Q/R$.

4. That is,

$$NPV = PQ \int_0^x e^{-(a+i)t} dt - K = 0$$

Then

$PQ/(a + i) = K$

and

$P = (KQ)(a + i) =$ supply price

5. The risk premium on oil operations is a thorny question, of course. Recent price declines might be a reason for increasing it. Yet, since 1973, oil prices have been, if anything, negatively correlated with changes in incomes and asset values generally. Hence the covariance with the general asset market may not be much more than that of other kinds of company share ownership.

If we could assume that oil prices will henceforth move approximately with the general price level, we would use the real, not the nominal, cost of capital—not 16 percent but 10 percent. Then the total required return would be 23.5 percent. The same is true for the United States and other areas, as set forth below.

6. Another fortuitous resemblance: 3.78 is not 3748 scaled down.

7. The distribution of development costs probably does not have as long a tail as that of operating costs because development costs are a larger portion of the total. Hence a price double the average of development cost would preclude a somewhat higher portion of the total than a price double the average of operating cost.

8. Let $K =$ investment, $Q =$ initial daily output, $R =$ reserves, and $a =$ the decline rate. Then as shown earlier, $Q = Ra/365$. Then K/Q is equal to $(365/a) \cdot (K/R)$. If a

is taken as approximately 11 percent, then $K/Q = (365/0.11)(\$4 \cdot 10^9/300 \cdot 10^6) = 44.231$.

9. In a forthcoming paper [chapter 22, this book] it will be explained why the discount rate for an oil-producing country whose oil income is a large part of its revenues must be considerably higher than for a private operator.

10. I think the reaction would be slow because of (1) improved technology in combustion and building; (2) the developed countries have been approaching the North American level of automobile saturation: (3) excise taxation of oil products by consuming-country governments: and (4) the retrofitting asymmetry. Part of the reaction to higher prices was the alteration of existing structures, but the alteration will not be undone because of lower prices. Insulation will not be ripped out of buildings.

11. Prudence is not necessarily truth. It involves extrapolating the model of diminishing returns from a given field or play to a whole country or continent or world. The extrapolation, as Kaufman has put it, "breaks the model's legs in several ways."

12. Suppose this year's price for some product is $1, the relevant discount rate is 10 percent, and the best estimate of next year's price is $1.05. If the marginal cost (bare operating cost for facilities in place, development-plus-operating cost for facilities proposed) is 50 cents, production should be postponed to next year. That is, the net return would be 55 cents next year, which is 10 percent above this year. Or, what comes to the same thing, user cost is 5 cents, which added to marginal cost makes production this year unprofitable. But lower cost operations should not be postponed. In general, marginal cost is correlated with user cost; the higher the marginal cost the greater the gain to postponement.

Option theory adds another dimension. Suppose we have no estimate of next year's price, but we do have some estimate of the future variability of price. The greater its variability, the better the chance that some time in the future the price will be sufficiently higher than now to make production so much more profitable as to be worth waiting for. Thus an operation with zero or negative current profits may have a positive present value. If there is a market in values, the individual needs no discount rate to make a decision. (But waiting may have costs over and above mere postponement. At the limit, it may be impossible to resume operation once it is halted.)

The important point for us is: The lower the current earnings, the greater the value of variable expectations. An operation out of the money is the best candidate for waiting; one deep in the money is the poorest. This is perfectly consistent with the maxim that we use the lowest-cost mineral resources first and also with our thesis that user cost is positively correlated with development-operating cost.

References

Adelman, M. A. (1966). "Oil Production Costs in Four Areas." *Proceedings of the Council of Economics of the American Institute of Mining, Metallurgical, and Petroleum Engineers.*

Adelman, M. A. (1972). *The World Petroleum Market*. Baltimore: Johns Hopkins Press for Resources For the Future.

Adelman, M. A. (1982). "OPEC as a Cartel." In Griffin and Teece, eds., *OPEC Behavior and World Oil Prices*. London: George Allen & Unwin, p. 55.

Adelman, M. A., and J. L. Paddock (1980). *An Aggregate Model of Petroleum Production Capacity and Supply Forecasting*. WP79-005. M.I.T. Energy Laboratory.

Adelman, M. A. (1986). "Scarcity and World Oil Prices." *Review of Economics and Statistics* 68: 25–35.

American Petroleum Institute et al. (1984). *Joint Association Survey.*

American Petroleum Institute (1986). Public Affairs Group. *Response.* R-348, April 1.

Devarajan, S., and Fisher, A. C. (1982). "Exploration and Scarcity." *Journal of Political Economy* 90: 1279–1290.

Energy Information Administration (EIA) (1984). "U.S. Crude Oil, Natural Gas, and Natural Gas Liquids Reserves, 1984." DOE/EIA–. Washington, D.C.: U.S. Department of Energy.

Energy Information Administration (EIA) (1986). "Indexes and Estimates of Domestic Well Drilling Costs, 1984 and 1985." DOE/EIA–. Washington, D.C.: U.S. Department of Energy.

Energy Information Administration (EIA), International and Contigency Information Division (ICID) (1986). "International Petroleum Statistics Report." March 20: 10.

DOE/EIA/ICID–. Washington, D.C.: U.S. Department of Energy.

Gately, D. (1984). "A Ten-Year Retrospective: OPEC and the World Oil Market." *Journal of Economic Literature* 22 (3): 1100–1114.

Griffin, J. M., and Teece, D. eds. *OPEC Behavior and World Oil Prices*. (London: George Allen & Unwin), p. 55.

Manne, Alan S., and Schrattenholzer, L. eds. (1986). *International Energy Workshop: Overview of Poll Responses* (Stanford, Calif.: International Energy Workshop).

U.S. Bureau of the Census (1982). *Annual Survey of Oil and Gas.*

National Academy of Sciences, Panel on Statistics on Natural Gas (1985). *National Gas Data Needs in a Changing Environment* (National Academy of Sciences: National Academy Press, 1985), ch. 4.

Neff, T. (1984). *The International Uranium Market*. Cambridge, Mass.: Ballinger Publishing Company. Especially Chapter 2 and a private communication from the author updating the price series.

New York Times, May 5, 1982, p. D-3.

Oil & Gas Journal, November 25, 1985, p. 48.

Oil & Gas Journal, February 17, 1986, p. 25.

Oil & Gas Journal, March 10, 1986, p. 80.

Oil & Gas Journal, June 9, 1986, p. 19.

Smith, J. L. and J. L. Paddock (1984). "Regional Modeling of Oil Discovery and Production." *Energy Economics* 6(1): 5–13.

Oil Development-Operating Cost Estimates, 1955–1985

with Manoj Shahi

This paper introduces estimates[1] of the supply price of oil for all non-Communist and non-OECD countries for each year 1955–85 inclusive (estimates for the United States and the United Kingdom are in reference [2]). The underlying theory has been set forth in various published papers listed at the end. Here we explain the construction and rationale of the estimates.

The first step is to estimate investment factors by depth of well, offshore and onshore, from publicly available data for the United States. These factors are applied to all other countries to estimate development investment, the expenditure needed to install one daily barrel of capacity. By making certain stated assumptions about the rate of return required, and the relation of operating cost to development investment, one can calculate a unit cost.

Clearly ours is a very broad and summary procedure. It is set out in detail to permit a modular treatment. Anyone with access to better information on any item can substitute it for ours, and reach a better estimate. Some of our results, especially for small countries, are impossible, the result of small-sample instability and the mismatching of inputs and outputs. Typically, drilling in a new area is slow and wasteful, and with few productive completions. Once the startup phase is over, we can glimpse the steady-state investment relations.

After presenting the details of estimation, we summarize the results. It is obvious that up to 1973 there was no abiding tendency for constant-dollar cost to rise, even after we set improvements in technology to zero. The boom in upstream investment after 1973 raised factor prices and degraded efficiency. We can allow for the first, but not the second. Whether there

Reprinted from *Energy Economics* 11 (January 1989): 2–10, and is reproduced here with the permission of Butterworth-Heinemann, Oxford, UK.

was any long-deferred depletion effect after 1973 cannot be discerned from
the data without further analysis.

Details of Estimation

In this section we define our terms and set out a sample table,[2] to which we
will refer from time to time.

Wells Drilled

Wells drilled in row[3] 1 refers to all types of wells (oil, gas, dry, exploratory,
development) drilled in a given year. These are revised numbers obtained
from the 15 August "International outlook" issues of *World Oil*, published
two years after the year in question. In the few cases where revised numbers were not available, we used unrevised numbers from the issue published one year later.

Average Depth

The approximate average depth of the wells drilled in row 2 was calculated
by dividing the total footage drilled by the total number of wells drilled.
Except in a few instances, the numbers for total footage drilled are revised
figures.

Average Costs per Well

The figures for average costs reflect the cost of drilling an onshore well of
a given depth in the United States in 1985. It is assumed that drilling costs
are the same across all nations and are equivalent to the U.S. drilling costs
since no country-specific drilling costs are available.

The first step is to calculate, for each depth class, the cost in row 3a of
drilling an onshore well in 1985. For this we use the figures published by
the Department of Energy in reference (9). For Iran and Nigeria, where
costs are very high due to exceptionally difficult drilling conditions, we use
maximum values rather than average values for drilling costs.

However, we need to distinguish between onshore and offshore drilling.
If a country is engaged in only onshore drilling then the cost per well
calculated in row 3a is the correct number. But where drilling is mixed (that
is both onshore and offshore) or entirely offshore, we multiply the cost in

Table 10.1
Tabulation of development-operating costs for oil (1984 conditions, adjusted to 1985 drilling costs)

		Source or formula where applicable
1	Wells drilled	International Outlook Issue, *World Oil*, 15 August 1986
2	Approximate average depth (ft × 10³)	(Total footage drilled/wells drilled); total footage drilled from International Outlook Issue, *World Oil*, 15 August 1986
3a	1985 average cost/well ($ × 10⁶)	Calculated from costs given in "Indexes and estimates of domestic well drilling costs 1984 and 1985," DOE/EIA-0347(84–85) and average well depth given in Row 2
3b	Ditto, adjusted	Row 3a multiplied by the ratio as indicated by the adjustment class
3c	Adjustment class[a]	See note below
3c.1	Adjustment (a): total USA	Total US drilling cost from 1984 Joint Association Survey on drilling costs
3c.2	(JAS) onshore	Total onshore US drilling cost from 1984 Joint Association Survey on drilling costs
3c.3	Adjustment (aa): offshore	Total offshore US drilling cost from 1984 Joint Association Survey on drilling costs
3c.4	(JAS) onshore	Total onshore US drilling cost from 1984 Joint Association Survey on drilling costs
4	Investment ($ × 10⁶)	Adjusted average cost × wells drilled = (Row 3b × Row 1)
5	Average output, bbl × 10³/day	International Outlook Issue, *World Oil*, 15 August 1986
6	Operating wells (year-end)	International Outlook Issue, *World Oil*, 15 August 1986
7a	Average, bbl × 10³/day per well	Average daily output/number of operating wells = (Row 5/Row 6)
7b	Weighted average bbl × 10³/day	From weighted average table for 1984, derivation explained in text

Table 10.1 (continued)

		Source or formula where applicable
8	Oil wells drilled	International Outlook Issue, *World Oil*, 15 August 1985
9a	New capacity, bbl × 10³/day	Unadjusted average production per well × number of oil wells drilled = (Row 7a × Row 8)
9b	Adjusted new capacity, bbl × 10³/day	Weighted average production per well × number of oil wells drilled = (Row 7b × Row 8)
10a	Investment/bbl/day ($ × 10³) = cost per barrel ($)	Total annual investment/unadjusted new capacity = (Row 4/Row 9a)
10b	Adjusted investment/bbl/day ($ × 10³) = cost per barrel ($)	Total annual investment/adjusted new capacity = (Row 4/Row 9b)
11	1984-end reserves, bbl	*Oil and Gas Journal*, December 1984 (or *International Petroleum Encyclopedia*, 1985)

a. Adjustment class: (a) = Row 3c.1/Row 3c.2 (correction for mixed drilling ventures)

(aa) = Row 3c.3/Row 3c.4 (correction for entirely offshore drilling)

(b) = maximum cost/Row 3a. Maximum costs calculated from DOE/EIA and onshore cost from JAS. Used only for Iran and Nigeria.

b. In the calculation of the weighted average daily output per well, data on individual field's productions are taken from the first six months of 1984. We use, in our calculations, only those fields whose average daily production is equal to at least 3% of the average daily national output. Sources for other years (except 1956) follow identical patterns. For 1956 we used *World Oil*, 15 August 1957 rather than 1958 for Rows 1, 2, 5, and 6.

row 3a by the appropriate weights calculated from the current *Joint Associa-tion Survey on Drilling Costs* (JAS). For countries engaged in both offshore and onshore drilling, the weight used is the ratio of total drilling expendi-tures per well to onshore drilling expenditures per well for a given depth class. For entirely offshore drilling countries, the weight used is the ratio of offshore drilling expenditures per well to onshore drilling expenditures per well.

For example, consider a well drilled to 9,750 feet in 1982, estimated for 1985 conditions. Reference (9) gives the costs of drilling a 7,500 foot and a 10,000 foot onshore well in United States as $338,000 and $638,000 respectively. Given these cost figures, we interpolate linearly to find the cost of drilling an onshore well to 9,750 feet. This comes out to be:

$$((9{,}750 - 7{,}500)/(10{,}000 - 7{,}500)) \times (638{,}000 - 338{,}000) + 338{,}000$$

$$= \$608{,}000$$

This is the estimate if the country is investing entirely in onshore drilling ventures. But if the country is engaged in both onshore and offshore drill-ing, we go to reference (8) and interpolate from the figures listed there the average cost and onshore cost of drilling a well in 1982 to 9,750 feet: $1,289,000 and $1,104,000 respectively. To get the desired cost, we multi-ply $608,000 by the ratio (1,289/1,104) to get $710,000. This is the aver-age cost of drilling a 9,750 foot deep well in the United States at 1985 prices and technology.

These adjusted costs are given in row 3b. They are strictly drilling costs. But there are important non-drilling outlays: for lease equipment, improved recovery, and overhead expenses. These expenses have historically been equal to about 66 percent of the drilling costs (7). Hence we raise the cost by this percentage to estimate total development cost per well. Our hypo-thetical well cost is therefore (1 + 0.66) × $710,000 or $1.179 million.

Total Country Investment

The total drilling and non-drilling investment in row 4 is calculated by multiplying the average expenditure per well by the number of all wells drilled for that given year. However, this includes not only oil wells but also gas, dry and exploratory oil wells, which should all be excluded since our objective at this point is development cost alone. Thus the estimated oil-related investment is upward biased.

Output, Operating Wells and Average Output per Well

Output in row 5 is the average total number of barrels of oil produced per day. Operating wells in row 6 are the total number of wells producing naturally or artificially at year end. They are revised figures from the 15 August "International outlook" issues of *World Oil* published two years after the year in question.

Average output per well in row 7a is simply total output divided by the number of operating oil wells at the end of the year. But, for certain countries that have many very small oil fields, and where most of the production is by the more productive wells in the large field, the simple average (production divided by total wells) is an underestimate. To deal with this, we have weighted the output of each field by the number of wells in that field. We need to weight the average output of each field by its share of national output, obtaining the adjusted output per well in row 7b.

Example of Adjustment

Table 10.2 lists all the fields producing oil in Tunisia in 1984. The table is an extract from "World-wide productions" in reference (10), December 1984. The table includes data on the number of wells (naturally flowing, artificially flowing and shut ins), average daily production and cumulative production for each individual field.

The data from only those fields which are producing at least 3 percent of Tunisia's total average daily output, are entered in the format shown in table 10.3 below. Let Q be the output and W be the number of operating wells in any one of the N fields. Then "$\text{Sum}(Q^2/W)/\text{Sum}(Q)$" is the average adjusted field output per well. This is given in column seven of table 10.3.

In most instances, the weighted average output per well exceeds the unweighted average output per well. In some countries, only total national data or data on groups of fields were available rather than data on individual fields. In such instances, we were forced to treat each group of fields as a single field, thereby understating output per well.

New Capacity

Newly added capacity is simply the product of the average output per well and the number of oil wells drilled. But since the numbers for oil wells drilled are not revised[4] as in the case of total wells drilled which were used to calculate investments, new capacity could be understated or overstated

Table 10.2
Production by field: Tunisia

	Names of field, discovery data	Number of wells, depth (ft)	Flow	Artificial lift	Shut-in	Bbl/day average, first 6 months 1984	Cumulative barrels to 1 July 1984
Elf[a]	Ashtart	10,500	6	7	2	24,809	140,333,390
Aquitaine	Douleb/Semmama	1500–2,500	—	14	1	1,025	16,505,280
Tunisie	Tamesmida	2,500	—	3	—	332	1,701,900
CFP	Sidi El Itayem, 1971	7500–7,800	—	11	1	2,739	17,985,261
	Other	—	—	—	—	—	655,000
Petrofina	Laarich, 1979	8,031	1	—	1	168	116,300
	Makhrouga, 1980	7,893	3	—	—	1,506	640,000
	Debbech, 1980	8,202	1	—	—	244	90,200
Shell/Agip/Etap[a]	Tazerka	4111–4,232	4	—	—	9,026	7,305,915
Agip-Tunisia (Sitep)	El Borma, 1964	8250–8,900	53	27	17	73,448	403,958,547
	Chouech es Saida, 1971	12,600	1	—	—	442	1,940,355
	Total		69	62	22	113,739	591,232,148

Note: The table is reproduced from "Worldwide production" section of the *International Petroleum Handbook* published in January 1985 by *Oil and Gas Journal*.
a. Implies an offshore field.

Table 10.3
Weighted average of output per well: Tunisia (1984)

Field	Production Q(bbl × 10³)	Q²	Wells (W)	Q²W	Summ all Σ(Q²/W)	Weighted average Σ(Q²/W)/Q_{tot}	Unweighted average Q/W
A	24.809	615.486	13	47.345			1.908
B	9.026	81.469	4	20.367			2.257
C	73.448	5394.609	80	67.433			0.918
Totals	107.283		97		135.145	1.260	1.106

Source: Table 10.2, "Production by field: Tunisia."

depending on whether the "true" number of oil wells drilled was greater or less than the numbers we used. Moreover, some of the oil wells drilled are exploratory wells that do not add to capacity. Hence there could be an overstatement of new capacity. Two types of additional capacities are calculated from the data, one from the unadjusted output per well, and one from the adjusted.

Investment per Daily Barrel of Oil

The total oil development expenditure (investment) divided by new capacity (barrels/daily) yields the investment (in thousand dollars) that went into installing capacity of an additional barrel of oil daily. Because we have two different numbers for new capacities, we have two different costs per barrel of oil: unadjusted in row 10a and adjusted in row 10b.[5] The adjusted costs in most cases are lower than the unadjusted.

Rows 10a and 10b equate *investment per daily barrel* of new capacity created to *cost per barrel*, by some broad-brush assumptions. We assume:

(i)   operating costs of 5 percent of the investment,

(ii) a depletion/decline rate of 10 percent and

(iii) a discount rate of 21.5 percent per year.

Then for every $1,000 investment per daily barrel, the cost per barrel is $1. That is:

$$\$1,000 \times ((0.05 + 0.1 + 0.215)/365) = \$1/bbl$$

This is only a quick view, of course. The operating cost percent is actually an industry rule of thumb. For any given country, the depletion/decline rate may be approximated by dividing annual average output by reserves; and using any discount rate that seems appropriate to the reader. Reference (3) explains why the discount rates imputed to oil producing countries, especially those in OPEC, should be much higher than those of private companies.

These rows also afford a quick check on the estimates. Where they exceed the price, they are obviously overestimated. These costs are strictly well-head costs, exclusive of transport to the loading point.

Finding Cost (User Cost)

One element of cost has not yet been discussed. It is known in theory as *user cost*, which is essentially the present value sacrificed by developing the

Table 10.4
Unadjusted development-operating costs: 1955–1985, $ × 10³/daily barrel capacity = $/barrel cost

	Middle-East OPEC								Other OPEC and Mexico							
	Abu Dhabi	Dubai	Iran	Iraq	Kuwait	Neutral zone	Qatar	Saudi Arabia	Algeria	Ecuador	Gabon	Indonesia	Libya	Mexico	Nigeria	Venezuela
1955			0.032	0.045	0.040	0.272	0.165	0.187	67.872	11.482		0.803		3.487		2.325
1956			0.065	0.182	0.062	0.211	0.873	0.065	71.105	16.801		1.401		3.815		3.037
1957			0.226	0.231	0.053	0.175	0.184	0.158	95.273	30.312		(ii)		6.367		1.782
1958			0.202	0.235	0.135	0.227	0.111	0.107	39.650	25.872		0.873		6.043	14.713	2.767
1959			0.257	0.127	0.055	0.194	(i)	0.081	1.641	50.025	3.105	1.018		6.667	8.304	3.936
1960			0.323	0.109	0.056	0.198	0.348	0.120	1.529	34.822	3.133	0.651		5.897	8.947	3.101
1961			0.279	0.194	0.201	0.300	0.195	0.191	0.695	18.040	3.348	1.002	1.339	6.984	2.685	2.272
1962	0.561		0.196	0.055	0.099	0.205	0.338	0.093	0.978	34.782	3.910	1.166	0.643	8.703	1.234	1.693
1963	0.571		0.145	0.008	0.149	0.554	0.109	0.124	1.134	22.078	(i)	0.758	0.534	11.354	2.096	1.727
1964	0.177		0.136	0.011	0.097	0.297	0.145	0.093	0.802	19.917	0.862	1.383	0.289	13.270	1.580	0.931
1965	0.281		0.159	0.007	0.204	0.861	0.116	0.093	0.798	21.985	1.707	0.740	0.323	13.713	1.259	1.112
1966	0.175		0.283	0.030	0.112	0.470	0.121	0.093	0.780	25.918	1.312	0.693	0.489	16.534	1.547	1.114
1967	0.209		0.143	(i)	0.032	0.895	0.312	0.149	1.090	35.102	0.971	0.458	0.453	13.857	0.316	2.582
1968	1.115		(ii)	0.060	0.174	(ii)	(ii)	0.368	(ii)	(ii)	0.812	(ii)	(ii)	12.515	(ii)	2.343
1969	0.519		0.181	(i)	0.226	0.497	(ii)	0.509	1.059	86.464	1.526	0.521	0.333	10.862	1.404	1.949

	Middle-East OPEC								Other OPEC and Mexico							
	Abu Dhabi	Dubai	Iran	Iraq	Kuwait	Neutral zone	Qatar	Saudi Arabia	Algeria	Ecuador	Gabon	Indonesia	Libya	Mexico	Nigeria	Venezuela
1970	0.456		0.301	0.018	0.147	0.547	(ii)	0.345	1.278	93.233	1.408	1.203	0.290	11.977	0.786	1.754
1971	0.145	0.553	0.171	0.032	0.106	0.435	0.532	0.131	1.289	163.534	0.979	0.862	0.835	9.177	0.795	1.849
1972	0.324	0.819	0.152	0.816	(i)	0.211	0.520	0.107	1.350	7.263	1.307	0.850	0.844	17.340	1.204	2.426
1973	0.256	0.820	0.251	0.063	(i)	1.216	0.276	0.089	0.992	4.560	0.651	0.880	0.312	10.717	1.011	3.348
1974	0.542	1.773	0.193	0.060	(i)	0.411	(i)	0.098	1.258	4.208	2.275	0.934	0.345	9.154	2.205	2.812
1975	0.583	1.121	0.178	0.066	(i)	0.582	1.020	0.128	0.942	6.454	4.985	0.827	0.742	8.711	2.493	2.636
1976	0.504	1.541	0.167	0.090	0.191	0.671	0.652	0.088	1.274	4.462	3.237	0.730	0.649	10.512	0.803	2.369
1977	0.509	1.007	0.187	0.088	1.427	0.847	1.144	0.082	1.305	6.052	5.202	0.861	0.318	8.494	2.211	2.577
1978	1.439	0.805	0.339	0.072	(i)	(i)	0.357	0.105	1.859	6.386	4.949	0.499	0.342	7.108	6.081	2.334
1979	0.816	2.275	(ii)	0.089	(i)	0.288	0.537	0.078	1.913	3.804	6.170	0.835	0.584	5.539	3.106	2.275
1980	0.629	1.589	(ii)	0.193	0.048	0.635	0.280	0.061	2.383	23.651	4.928	1.459	0.551	3.670	5.055	2.674
1981	0.721	1.152	(ii)	(ii)	1.248	1.448	0.316	0.065	1.065	2.689	4.346	1.536	0.875	3.733	1.116	3.691
1982	1.683	1.804	(ii)	(ii)	0.296	1.708	0.606	0.200	1.917	2.561	4.242	5.443	0.705	2.933	2.945	2.774
1983	1.624	3.564	(ii)	(ii)	0.202	1.262	0.560	0.082	(ii)	2.005	5.654	1.622	(ii)	2.098	2.182	2.374
1984	0.927	5.102	(ii)	(ii)	0.755	(i)	0.349	0.190	(ii)	2.123	6.065	1.590	2.203	3.878	1.928	1.405
1985	1.234	4.609	(ii)	(ii)	0.621	0.454	0.454	0.148	1.580	2.076	4.333	1.876	6.795	4.536	2.254	1.508

Table 10.4 (continued)

	Western Hemisphere							Africa					
	Trinidad/Tobago	Argentina	Bolivia	Brazil	Chile	Colombia	Peru	Angola/Cabinda	Cameroon	Congo	Egypt	Tunisia	Zaire
1955	10.820	14.698	1.408	13.296	6.478	7.866	19.026				0.642		
1956	9.298	13.976	2.281	11.773	9.226	8.407	16.526				3.761		
1957	7.903	2.033	(ii)	2.684	9.668	8.581	15.963				2.694		
1958	9.030	12.172	4.557	1.520	8.207	7.331	13.839	16.116			2.419		
1959	9.689	12.305	7.856	3.124	9.627	8.575	15.580	20.456			1.121		
1960	7.362	10.469	7.705	3.751	6.876	11.970	14.309	168.856			1.317		
1961	8.220	7.919	13.308	3.165	4.898	13.102	13.647	3.202			2.076		
1962	8.844	8.322	11.211	2.172	7.911	11.061	10.750	1.514			2.142		
1963	8.801	12.297	9.754	2.564	6.068	9.483	11.876	(i)			2.097		
1964	9.454	12.011	13.985	1.706	7.484	11.517	14.108	(i)			1.551		
1965	7.558	13.855	7.985	2.364	12.050	9.046	14.456	(i)			1.145		
1966	5.839	11.229	9.564	2.209	40.749	8.862	16.400	2.164			3.695	1.563	
1967	5.638	12.856	5.156	3.801	10.522	14.826	13.474	1.257			0.890	0.374	
1968	7.039	(ii)	4.005	3.446	9.469	26.333	(ii)	(ii)			(ii)	(ii)	
1969	10.901	13.149	5.708	5.110	14.236	(ii)	(ii)	1.003			1.429	0.833	

	Western Hemisphere							Africa					
	Trinidad/Tobago	Argentina	Bolivia	Brazil	Chile	Colombia	Peru	Angola/Cabinda	Cameroon	Congo	Egypt	Tunisia	Zaire
1970	8.294	11.031	3.872	4.325	11.120	(ii)	(ii)	1.762			0.853	(i)	
1971	6.791	9.176	8.333	6.059	12.588	5.637	19.177	1.717			1.196	1.275	
1972	5.836	10.136	10.541	5.527	15.817	10.712	20.442	1.653		6.716	1.612	2.408	
1973	5.307	10.787	4.426	10.748	26.034	8.870	23.514	1.195		0.877	2.029	0.267	
1974	4.507	11.296	8.046	9.334	35.290	26.574	25.525	0.775		5.515	1.821	1.439	
1975	3.794	9.507	8.853	6.715	29.620	11.533	25.752	0.733		3.092	3.696	0.624	
1976	4.972	8.724	4.051	5.638	23.434	8.836	19.501	0.418		2.939	4.455	13.177	5.462
1977	3.964	7.384	4.879	8.818	75.565	8.718	15.564	0.523	0.849	5.323	3.420	2.322	9.633
1978	4.059	8.930	19.727	10.130	34.578	13.920	11.822	2.001	0.151	6.369	1.366	1.993	14.649
1979	4.149	8.137	14.215	10.003	14.471	12.892	3.284	2.598	0.770	5.593	1.979	2.332	9.633
1980	3.695	8.563	65.950	7.928	7.325	18.158	3.837	1.164	1.746	4.958	1.765	5.785	3.521
1981	4.260	8.493	46.579	4.990	19.183	11.051	11.523	1.633	1.687	5.137	1.212	9.172	0.468
1982	7.493	8.716	31.365	4.689	11.690	9.478	4.701	2.443	0.761	5.842	1.834	5.026	1.012
1983	3.583	11.350	9.918	3.856	9.155	8.726	10.515	0.983	0.955	8.794	1.874	5.067	3.638
1984	3.494	12.853	34.806	2.831	9.457	7.186	10.452	1.042	0.392	5.712	1.161	9.289	2.745
1985	4.242	11.262	34.238	2.749	8.926	10.459	7.807	1.869	0.212	13.931	1.080	6.991	7.020

Table 10.4 (continued)

	Bahrain	Oman	Syria	Turkey	Burma	India	Pakistan	Thailand	Australia	Malaysia/ Brunei	Brunei	Malaysia
1955	0.715			1.489						1.637		
1956	0.489			2.460						1.948		
1957	0.507			7.064						2.475		
1958	0.464			6.101	4.055	103.094	96.083			1.558		
1959	(i)			5.991	11.041	86.932	140.330			2.215		
1960	0.476			0.718	9.395	57.192	127.630			3.177		
1961	0.955			7.831	14.297	36.690	135.173			5.446		
1962	0.637			6.809	10.977	18.327	36.153			(i)		
1963	0.565			4.151	(i)	13.017	(i)			3.234		
1964	0.524			4.238	(i)	7.809	32.482		17.757	7.525		
1965	0.822			4.152	15.695	11.140	39.467	62.708	7.923	6.874		
1966	0.715			3.058	13.214	7.117	28.151	15.719	12.534	3.166		
1967	0.608	0.068		0.384	13.214	4.176	2.699	58.925	2.704	4.062		
1968	(ii)	0.020		2.377	(ii)	0.799	21.612	(ii)	4.799	(ii)		
1969	(ii)	0.036		4.049	(ii)	17.538	(i)	(ii)	5.757	2.187		

	Bahrain	Oman	Syria	Turkey	Burma	India	Pakistan	Thailand	Australia	Malaysia/ Brunei	Brunei	Malaysia
1970	(ii)	0.076		4.960	(ii)	5.232	14.538	(ii)	3.182	1.425		
1971	0.506	0.121		0.370	0.797	7.919	5.563	(i)	4.278	1.345		
1972	0.846	0.124		1.950	19.171	41.353	(i)	(i)	27.928	4.272		
1973	0.822	0.242	1.311	3.445	15.990	14.674	13.082	(i)	1.546		5.035	3.178
1974	1.040	0.351	2.034	4.888	157.489	7.025	12.160	1316.928	2.709		26.700	7.616
1975	1.306	0.225	1.468	7.340	22.153	6.367	(i)	(i)	13.343		9.445	4.418
1976	1.195	0.339	1.732	6.778	8.923	6.522	(i)	(i)	21.854		11.802	1.684
1977	0.589	0.284	0.601	4.970	9.408	7.613	14.534	123.441	13.164		8.848	2.611
1978	1.056	0.465	1.804	4.939	14.651	8.831	7.371	(i)	10.057		11.110	2.551
1979	1.206	0.262	2.210	3.018	20.565	16.108	5.268	(i)	1.134		6.703	4.408
1980	1.047	0.307	7.736	5.905	22.874	7.586	18.267	(i)	2.360		12.188	3.348
1981	0.726	0.339	(ii)	8.488	26.327	8.803	10.301	(ii)	3.448		5.596	4.520
1982	1.029	0.433	(ii)	7.808	28.157	5.990	4.541	30.900	3.675		11.338	4.379
1983	3.581	0.494	3.263	7.740	14.677	5.044	8.970	31.946	2.269		19.931	13.697
1984	5.497	0.749	(ii)	11.265	6.586	5.085	4.431	6.963	2.351		9.218	0.737
1985	4.071	0.455	(ii)	12.364	12.475	5.180	3.095	5.502	2.026		26.535	3.724

Notes: See text for explanation on how these costs were estimated and for sources of underlying data.
(i) Unable to calculate unadjusted development-operating cost because no new oil wells were drilled.
(ii) Unable to calculate unadjusted development-operating cost because of missing data.

Table 10.5
Adjusted development-operating costs: 1955–1985, $ × 10³/daily barrel capacity = $/barrel cost OPEC countries and Mexico

	Middle-East OPEC								Other OPEC							
	Abu Dhabi	Dubai	Iran	Iraq	Kuwait	Neutral zone	Qatar	Saudi Arabia	Algeria	Ecuador	Gabon	Indonesia	Libya	Mexico	Nigeria	Venezuela
1955			0.016	0.049	0.037	0.175	0.158	0.155	88.487	12.706		0.355		0.814		0.854
1956			0.039	0.244	0.055	0.173	0.870	0.071	85.647	15.038		0.410		0.617		0.897
1957			0.164	0.088	0.048	0.078	0.132	0.146	278.198	26.606		(ii)		(ii)		0.751
1958			0.105	0.082	0.127	0.099	0.096	0.086	7.706	23.722		0.173		2.048	9.028	0.866
1959			0.160	0.065	0.051	0.103	(i)	0.062	1.308	48.635	2.652	0.277		2.656	7.853	2.354
1960			0.223	0.078	0.053	0.114	0.235	0.103	0.436	31.272	2.932	0.120		3.398	3.343	(ii)
1961			0.145	0.072	0.196	0.150	0.143	0.155	0.298	31.043	3.017	0.256	33.846	4.293	3.676	1.591
1962	0.293		0.082	0.026	0.094	0.233	0.346	0.075	0.444	34.888	2.803	0.244	0.226	4.954	0.859	(ii)
1963	0.260		0.084	0.005	0.132	0.205	0.105	0.105	0.469	11.554	(i)	0.208	0.278	5.456	1.214	0.619
1964	0.212		0.078	0.009	0.093	0.083	0.156	0.082	0.393	18.657	1.003	0.330	0.137	7.108	1.098	(ii)
1965	0.341		0.089	0.005	0.194	0.860	0.109	0.078	0.386	18.886	0.850	0.109	0.128	6.698	0.748	0.394
1966	0.161		0.122	0.013	0.115	0.141	0.110	0.079	0.261	20.178	0.793	0.097	0.199	7.981	1.105	0.372
1967	0.172		0.069	(i)	0.032	0.243	0.320	0.132	0.491	0.494	0.607	0.058	0.300	6.485	1.479	1.068
1968	0.840		(ii)	0.040	0.186	(ii)	(ii)	0.157	(ii)	(ii)	0.395	(ii)	(ii)	6.356	0.827	0.925
1969	0.369		0.104	(i)	0.264	0.310	(ii)	0.244	0.116	89.915	0.722	0.041	0.143	5.999	1.219	0.788

	Middle-East OPEC								Other OPEC							
	Abu Dhabi	Dubai	Iran	Iraq	Kuwait	Neutral zone	Qatar	Saudi Arabia	Algeria	Ecuador	Gabon	Indonesia	Libya	Mexico	Nigeria	Venezuela
1970	0.310		0.173	0.011	0.201	0.217	(ii)	0.169	0.131	101.810	0.642	0.112	0.127	3.767	0.603	0.670
1971	0.107	0.524	0.093	0.020	0.105	0.188	0.332	0.065	0.581	187.720	0.467	0.100	0.340	4.307	0.600	0.939
1972	0.267	0.622	0.088	0.126	(i)	0.182	0.408	0.106	0.657	0.641	0.647	0.131	0.341	9.590	0.642	1.158
1973	0.194	0.697	0.143	0.043	(i)	0.359	0.201	0.078	0.461	0.499	0.639	0.158	0.160	7.616	0.580	1.565
1974	0.219	1.475	0.118	0.052	(i)	0.211	(i)	0.093	0.690	0.485	2.631	0.180	0.145	1.074	1.258	1.334
1975	0.500	1.031	0.101	0.050	(i)	0.329	0.429	0.116	0.486	0.865	2.584	0.207	0.435	0.541	1.992	1.887
1976	0.312	1.502	0.100	0.105	0.177	0.468	0.284	0.080	0.636	0.289	1.867	0.181	0.249	0.386	0.579	0.528
1977	0.391	0.972	0.133	0.100	1.402	0.527	0.562	0.071	0.773	0.768	3.191	0.218	0.110	0.454	1.577	1.285
1978	1.196	0.718	0.219	0.098	(i)	(i)	0.172	0.104	1.216	0.972	5.306	0.136	0.173	0.380	4.332	1.335
1979	0.649	1.984	(ii)	0.104	(i)	0.126	0.209	0.075	1.597	0.398	5.612	0.198	0.304	6.068	2.121	1.245
1980	1.014	1.304	(ii)	0.122	0.045	0.241	0.164	0.053	2.232	3.596	5.523	0.239	0.308	0.186	3.636	0.732
1981	0.499	0.924	(ii)	(ii)	1.435	0.728	0.208	0.064	1.077	0.370	3.898	0.566	0.403	0.131	1.032	1.376
1982	0.932	1.749	(ii)	(ii)	0.512	0.987	0.199	0.143	(ii)	0.347	4.795	1.085	0.470	0.122	3.052	1.835
1983	0.615	3.182	(ii)	(ii)	0.289	0.746	0.475	(ii)	(ii)	0.533	4.170	0.396	(ii)	0.072	1.891	0.922
1984	0.634	3.515	(ii)	(ii)	0.843	(i)	0.193	(ii)	(ii)	0.630	5.581	0.299	1.079	0.196	1.272	0.698
1985	1.045	3.483	(ii)	(ii)	0.962	0.231	0.412	(ii)	(ii)	0.442	4.370	0.411	3.276	0.285	1.446	0.891

Table 10.5 (continued)

	Western Hemisphere							Africa					
	Trinidad/Tobago	Argentina	Bolivia	Brazil	Chile	Colombia	Peru	Angola/Cabinda	Cameroon	Congo	Egypt	Tunisia	Zaire
1955	10.619	7.580	0.851	9.564	4.188	6.424	17.304				0.499		
1956	5.027	23.453	1.533	8.123	15.243	2.608	13.597				2.104		
1957	7.931	18.312	(ii)	1.034	6.431	2.357	10.558				1.353		
1958	8.752	17.879	2.539	0.848	5.656	2.301	10.367	6.211			0.613		
1959	9.517	8.380	8.051	1.225	10.275	2.358	11.843	18.144			0.586		
1960	7.315	8.271	3.291	1.520	4.830	1.695	12.621	207.945			0.885		
1961	8.135	4.590	7.397	1.503	4.581	2.506	9.937	3.964			1.301		
1962	8.980	10.714	7.809	1.813	5.613	2.808	8.352	1.004			1.121		
1963	9.084	9.284	9.370	2.598	4.148	2.426	8.701	(i)			0.957		
1964	9.421	9.063	13.336	1.821	4.894	1.838	13.375	(i)			0.342		
1965	7.514	7.326	4.737	1.341	7.777	1.111	12.376	(i)			0.246		
1966	6.484	5.577	6.705	1.229	28.879	0.673	13.102	1.085			1.055		
1967	2.209	6.551	2.039	1.797	7.732	1.684	7.986	0.417			0.300	0.503	
1968	1.054	(ii)	1.555	1.883	6.572	2.981	(ii)	(ii)			(ii)	(ii)	
1969	1.208	3.597	2.686	2.681	9.890	(ii)	(ii)	0.622			0.259	0.762	

	Western Hemisphere							Africa					
	Trinidad/Tobago	Argentina	Bolivia	Brazil	Chile	Colombia	Peru	Angola/Cabinda	Cameroon	Congo	Egypt	Tunisia	Zaire
						(ii)	(ii)					(i)	
1970	2.074	3.761	1.216	2.768	6.165			0.443			0.234		
1971	1.808	1.565	4.353	3.970	9.025	0.777	5.950	0.619			0.358	1.104	
1972	0.673	3.815	7.423	3.240	13.017	1.473	8.446	1.012		5.408	0.525	1.773	
1973	0.249	0.357	2.845	6.453	26.882	1.420	5.920	0.682		0.455	0.619	0.199	
1974	0.323	0.304	3.160	5.522	28.111	4.350	6.301	0.413		4.346	0.737	1.445	
1975	0.204	0.262	4.735	2.495	31.171	2.123	4.863	0.564		1.796	0.416	0.348	
1976	0.261	3.815	2.126	2.302	25.256	1.737	3.792	1.775		3.022	0.660	5.444	3.712
1977	0.212	2.211	2.641	3.966	93.795	2.010	1.959	0.267		5.664	0.568	0.862	0.682
1978	0.235	6.323	11.494	5.147	40.422	1.568	0.430	1.614	0.485	7.989	0.245	0.685	4.299
1979	0.319	6.422	6.926	2.265	6.119	3.229	0.121	1.245	0.804	3.577	0.314	0.837	2.617
1980	0.309	7.301	31.174	0.966	2.614	17.108	0.131	0.662	1.340	3.907	0.382	2.595	1.901
1981	0.462	7.176	24.929	0.405	6.991	14.833	0.359	0.836	1.321	3.950	0.293	5.241	0.250
1982	0.705	8.108	8.587	0.406	3.468	17.367	0.195	1.451	0.675	4.067	0.551	2.903	0.472
1983	0.371	8.875	3.210	(i)	3.780	7.556	0.593	0.610	1.191	8.285	0.590	3.448	1.788
1984	0.446	10.767	9.685	0.083	4.681	4.895	0.966	0.591	0.645	5.105	0.441	7.306	0.541
1985	0.425	10.791	17.081	0.097	4.708	2.063	0.617	0.870	0.370	10.835	0.409	5.993	0.991

Table 10.5 (continued)

	Bahrain	Oman	Syria	Turkey	Burma	India	Pakistan	Thailand	Australia	Malaysia/Brunei	Brunei	Malaysia
1955	0.704			0.882						1.028		
1956	0.442			1.404						1.332		
1957	0.496			4.697						1.641		
1958	0.474			4.968	4.135	107.467	18.418			0.991		
1959	(i)			5.640	8.538	96.021	23.051			1.376		
1960	0.463			12.842	11.065	1.539	35.846			2.004		
1961	0.925			7.973	16.079	1.371	16.393			3.589		
1962	0.661			6.294	10.673	13.879	4.242			(i)		
1963	0.542			3.559	(i)	4.984	(i)			2.185		
1964	0.532			3.694	(i)	3.171	3.673		11.682	4.497		
1965	0.853			1.732	15.345	5.193	12.647	77.339	8.621	2.572		
1966	0.719			0.975	0.903	2.535	4.171	7.932	8.505	0.526		
1967	0.600	0.228		0.115	0.895	1.598	2.732	51.560	1.170	1.175		
1968	(ii)	0.022		0.417	(ii)	1.355	8.026	(ii)	3.850	(ii)		
1969	(ii)	0.036		0.670	(ii)	36.314	(i)	(ii)	5.301	0.666		

	Bahrain	Oman	Syria	Turkey	Burma	India	Pakistan	Thailand	Australia	Malaysia/Brunei	Brunei	Malaysia
1970	(ii)	0.046		0.994	(ii)	9.918	7.608	(ii)	0.811	0.526		
1971	0.536	0.083		1.271	0.530	17.212	2.334	(i)	0.532	0.248		
1972	0.892	0.101	0.577	0.478	4.731	55.591	(i)	(i)	5.859	1.799		
1973	0.870	0.167	0.824	0.710	3.761	14.674	8.368	(i)	0.312		1.705	2.667
1974	1.051	0.301	1.555	1.440	43.503	8.808	9.793	802.313	0.348		10.176	4.449
1975	1.199	0.198	1.701	2.606	6.321	7.700	(i)	(i)	1.516		3.971	3.930
1976	1.258	0.262	0.459	2.676	4.670	7.461	(i)	(i)	3.433		5.846	1.230
1977	0.607	0.221	1.586	2.027	4.514	(ii)	10.517	115.212	2.061		4.344	1.881
1978	1.041	0.378	2.186	1.705	7.970	11.459	2.509	(i)	2.197		5.983	1.904
1979	1.147	0.182	6.401	1.411	17.234	16.327	1.613	(i)	0.213		3.211	3.326
1980	1.023	0.240	(ii)	2.447	19.073	7.418	4.502	(i)	0.479		6.316	2.321
1981	0.708	0.331	(ii)	4.414	17.652	7.991	3.873	(ii)	0.618		3.450	3.249
1982	0.972	0.285	(ii)	3.204	19.073	(ii)	1.579	70.400	0.530		6.448	3.091
1983	3.306	0.369	(ii)	4.706	8.338	(ii)	3.771	46.067	0.357		12.038	7.867
1984	5.277	0.508	(ii)	4.729	4.260	(ii)	2.252	16.796	0.289		4.557	1.691
1985	4.003	0.303	(ii)	5.042	4.556	5.118	0.811	10.641	0.221		23.386	3.658

Notes: See text for explanation on how these costs were estimated and for sources of underlying data.
(i) Unable to calculate adjusted development-operating cost because no new oil wells were drilled.
(ii) Unable to calculate adjusted development-operating cost because of missing data.

barrel today rather than at some later date. It is over and above the development expenditures needed to develop the resource into a reserve.

User cost may be estimated or approximated in a number of ways. One is to find or estimate the market value of the developed reserve, and subtract out the development cost. This has been done for the United States for 1955 to 1985 (5), but there are no data for other countries.

Another approach is to calculate a proxy for user cost: discovery cost, the amount needed to find another unit below ground. If a barrel can be found to replace the barrel used up by development, then the cost of finding sets a limit or cap to the value. This requires dividing the exploration expenditures in a given area in a given year by the amount newly found in that area in that year. The task is nearly always impossible, for lack of any measure of the quantity found.

The U.S. Department of Energy series labelled "discoveries" is irrelevant, a fragment masquerading as data. It represents only the tip of the iceberg: the amount of oil that has been developed into reserves during the current year from fields and pools newly found during the year. The average age of discovery is about six months. But the overwhelming bulk of what has been found will not be known for years or even decades. What are called "finding costs" in the business press are an illogical mixture of discovery with development, oil with gas, which applies to none of the activities.

Yet another approach is to calculate the *upper limit to user cost*: the loss of present value incurred by moving a barrel within a reserve from future to present production. In some cases, increased output would damage the reservoir, and is ruled out. The upper limit is infinity, a trivial result. In others, increased depletion is feasible at rising cost. As is demonstrated in Reference (4) the unit capital cost is equal to:

$$c = K(a + i)/Q \tag{1}$$

where K = development expenditures, Q = initial annual output, i = discount rate, and a = intensiveness of development or depletion/decline rate and is equal to Q/R where R is reserves to be developed.

Development expenditures K are the result of three factors: the amount of new capacity Q, the intensiveness of development a, and a factor k, representing better or poorer cost conditions. Hence:

$$K = kaQ = kQ^2/R \tag{2}$$

Substituting equation (2) into equation (1), we have:

$$c = (kaQ/Q)(a + i) = ka(a + i) \tag{3}$$

The additional investment per unit of additional output is:

$$dK/dQ = 2kQ/R = 2ka \tag{4}$$

and the cost of accelerating the expansion of output from a constant reserve is:

$$c' = (dK/dQ)(a + i) = 2ka(a + i) \tag{5}$$

Comparing equations (3) and (5): acceleration doubles the marginal development cost, i.e., user cost is equal to development cost. The limiting assumption is that development creates no additional reserves, which is rarely true.

Suppose now that the price of oil is expected to rise, then the higher the cost in a given reservoir, the lower the margin over cost, and the more is to be gained by postponement. (For a formal proof, see (4), pp 29.) Thus *user cost is proportional to development cost*. Whether we consider cost or price (and *a fortiori* when we consider both together), the higher is the development/operating cost, the higher is the user cost. Perhaps this is only a roundabout way of stating the axiom: lower-cost oil should be developed earlier, higher-cost oil later. The oil most penalized by early production is high-cost oil.

It is nearly always the case that additional investment in known fields will increase reserves. This has been borne out in the widely disparate regions of the Persian Gulf and the USA, where the increase in cost was rather small. Here user cost was modest relative to development cost (5).

The value of an incremental barrel, divided by the cheapest replacement cost, is a special case of the fraction familiar to economists as "Tobin's Q."

Comments on the Results

We have already commented on user cost, or discovery cost, which is proportional to development cost. Hence the lower the cost given in table 10.5, the lower is user cost.

A serious omission is infrastructure (e.g., access roads). Outside the United States it may equal or exceed drilling and equipping outlays. Another important distortion, or omission, is the lack of allowance for depth of water offshore. It seriously understates results for recent years in Brazil. It can be remedied by using factors calculated elsewhere (7).

Because of the use of 1985 factors the estimates are in constant dollars. This procedure has also removed the effects of changes in technology over a 30-year period. The earlier the year, the greater the overstatement of true cost as of that year. The trend line of our estimates has been tipped upward, either falling less or rising more than the "true" line did. (Complicating matters is the deterioration in efficiency during the wild drilling boom after 1973 and especially after 1979.) Our purpose has been to isolate, as far as possible, the effect upon cost of the continuing depletion and renewal of inventories (proved reserves) which is the investment-production process in crude oil.

Usually development costs are quite low as compared with prices, even in low-priced years, which raises the question why output has not expanded much more. In the OPEC countries and Mexico, the answer is obvious: output is restrained to increase or maintain prices.

In the non-cartel countries, development costs are usually higher, hence also user costs. But the explanation lies mostly in the factors omitted from our calculation: taxes to local governments, and such burdens as non-tax payments, goldplating, feather-bedding, and requirements for packaging of uneconomic with economic projects. These tax and non-tax burdens would matter less if they were well designed to skim off rents, but in fact they add to costs as the operator must reckon them. Finally, the expropriations of the 1970s have greatly devalued contracts and increased the degree of risk.

All these non-cost burdens rose along with prices, and have been reduced since the turnaround of 1981. That explains why, outside the USA, non-cartel output has actually expanded since then. Continued decline in prices has promoted sobriety, improved contract terms, and lowered perceived risk. Never has the theoretical distinction between costs and non-cost outlays been of greater practical importance than today.

Notes

At the time of writing, Manoj Shahi was an undergraduate in the Department of Economics at MIT.

The research for this paper has been supported by the National Science Foundation, grant #SES-8412791, and by the Center for Energy Policy Research of the MIT Energy Laboratory. We are grateful for the help of Betty Bolivar, Elise Erler, Kevin Lam and Michael C. Lynch, but any opinions, findings, conclusions or recommendations expressed herein are those of the authors, and do not necessarily reflect the views of the NSF or any other person or group.

1. The basic data and complete calculation are recorded in the Tables in Appendices A and B in Reference (6). Lotus 1–2–3 spreadsheets on IBM-compatible diskettes are at the Center for Energy Policy Research at the MIT Energy Laboratory.

2. Table 10.1 is the Lotus format we used to estimate the development-operating costs from 1955–85. Here we list the sources that we used to get the numbers to estimate the development-operating costs for 1984. The sources for other years follow identical patterns.

3. Henceforth, reference to rows are to the rows of table 10.1.

4. No revised series was available.

5. See table 10.4 and 10.5 for the unadjusted and adjusted development-operating costs by countries for the period 1955–85. Note that the adjusted development-operating costs in table 10.5 are almost always lower than the unadjusted costs in table 10.4. This is due to the average weighted output per well that we calculated in row 7b, which resulted in higher new capacity.

References

1. M. A. Adelman, *Oil Production Costs in Four Areas*, Proceedings, Council of Economics of AIME (American Institute of Mining, Metallurgical and Petroleum Engineers) 1966, summarized in Petroleum Press Service 1966.

2. M. A. Adelman, "The competitive floor to world oil prices," *The Energy Journal*, Vol. 7, No 4, October 1986.

3. M. A. Adelman, "Discount rates for oil producer nations," *Resources and Energy*, Vol. 8, December 1986, pp 309–329.

4. M. A. Adelman, *Mineral Depletion with Special Reference to Petroleum*, MIT Energy Laboratory Working Paper No. MIT-EL 88-002WP, January 1988.

5. M. A. Adelman, *Finding and Developing Costs in the USA 1981–1986*, MIT Energy Laboratory Working Paper No MIT-EL 86-008WP, forthcoming in John R. Moroney, ed, *Advances in the Economics of Energy and Resources*, Vol. 11, JAI Press, 1988.

6. M. A. Adelman and Manoj Shahi, *Oil Development-Operating Cost Estimates: 1955–1985*, MIT Energy Laboratory Working Paper No. MIT EL 88-008WP, May 1988.

7. M. A. Adelman and Geoffrey L. Ward, "Worldwide production costs for oil and gas," *Advances in the Economics of Energy and Resources*, Vol. 3, JAI Press, 1980, pp 1–29.

8. American Petroleum Institute et al, *Joint Association Survey on Drilling Costs*, annual.

9. Energy Information Administration (EIA), *Indexes and Estimates of Domestic Well Drilling Costs, 1984 and 1985*, DOE/EIA-0347(84-85), U.S. Department of Energy, Washington, DC.

10. *Oil & Gas Journal*, annual *World Wide Oil*, last issue in December.

11. World Oil, annual *International Outlook*, 15 August 1956–87.

11

Mineral Depletion,
with Special Reference
to Petroleum

The Problem Stated

The vision of mineral and particularly oil prices forever rising has many and distinguished adherents: "The price of oil should increase through time, growing at the rate of interest" (Starrett, 1987). "No viable alternative paradigm exists" (Miller and Upton, 1985a, p. 24). The successive issues of the International Energy Workshop (1981–1988) have repeated the rising-price consensus. (See also Hogan and Leiby (1985).) Price increases confirm the law; decreases are transient.

The 1973 oil price has been considered untenably low. The 1978 price, several times as high, would in turn soon have become untenably low (Gately, 1984, p. 113; Samuelson, 1986, pp. 896–897). Some suggest that even the peak 1981 price was artificially low, held down by Saudi Arabia. The mineral holdings (chiefly petroleum) of the United States Government were valued at $860 billion, on the assumption that 1981 oil prices would rise at 3 percent real per year, the revenue flow discounted at a riskless 2 percent (Boskin et al., 1985). (Present value is about $42 billion if we multiply the estimate by 13/52 to allow for the actual 1988 price, and apply the conventional oil industry 10 percent discount.) On their assumptions, 1981 Mexican oil reserves were worth nearly $2,000 billion, and it was ultra-conservative to borrow only $60 billion against them.

These statements and many more are based on what is loosely called "the Hotelling theory": one renowned paper (Hotelling, 1931) and a voluminous body of subsequent work. I propose not to review or criticize the literature, but only to discard one assumption of fact and draw the consequences.

Reprinted from *Review of Economics & Statistics* 72 (February 1990): 1–10.

Inexhaustible Resources, Rising Costs

The assumption dropped is that there exists "an exhaustible natural resource ... a fixed stock of oil to divide between two [or more] periods"
(Stiglitz, 1976). There is no such thing. The total mineral in the earth is
an irrelevant non-binding constraint. If expected finding-development
costs exceed the expected net revenues, investment dries up, and the
industry disappears. Whatever is left in the ground is unknown, probably
unknowable, but surely unimportant: a geological fact of no economic
interest.

    We cannot save the principle of a fixed stock by defining it as the
economic portion, estimated under uncertainty about quality and cost.
(Pindyck, 1980; Devarajan and Fisher, 1982). If ultimate production is determined by future costs and prices, the estimated resource cannot be the
starting point for estimating costs and prices.

    What actually exist are flows from unknown resources into a reserve
inventory. Now, there are good reasons to expect reserve replenishment to
show diminishing returns over time. Ceteris paribus, the larger deposits
would be found earlier even by chance. Once found, the better mineral
would be developed first. Thus marginal costs and prices would rise, even
if ultimate depletion were infinitely distant. The fixed-stock assumption is
both wrong and superfluous.

Failure of the Rising-Price Paradigm

Yet in the long run, practically all minerals prices have declined (Manthy,
1978; World Bank, 1984). In oil, before 1970 there was no sign of any
upward price trend.[1] According to Smith (1978), prices may not have
declined; one cannot reject the null hypothesis. Non-rejection is not acceptance. But accepting it for the sake of argument; the null hypothesis would
refute the paradigm of prices generally rising. Smith's data ended with
1973. Many believe there was "a marked upward drift in the prices of oil
and most other industrial materials which began in the early 1970s and
accelerated further at the close of the decade" (Miller and Upton, 1985a,
p. 2). In fact, during 1970–86, the real prices of nonfuel minerals declined
nearly 40 percent (IMF, 1987).

    Slade (1982) estimated a quadratic function with minerals prices bot-
toming out by 1970, then rising. Actual prices in 1985 were in all cases
lower than predicted by the Slade estimating equations; on average, one-
third lower (appendix, table 11.1). The price of uranium ore soared in the

1970s and then fell until by 1984 it reached (and has stayed at) an all-time low for the 39 years during which any price existed (Neff, 1984, p. 16).

A Road Map

We aim to study the endless tug-of-war between diminishing returns and increasing knowledge.[2] The struggle is registered in the investment needed to add an incremental unit: of in-ground inventory, or of capacity. (See note 11 for a fairly simple conversion.) The many kinds of investment are all substitutes for each other, and the marginal cost of reserves added by one method should approach equality with the marginal cost of the others. Changes in the observed may be used as proxies for changes in the unobserved. Oil development investment per unit, which can be measured annually for decades back, therefore represents cost changes incurred in using all other investment types. It serves as a current indicator of scarcity.

A unit of inventory is an asset. The relation between its value and its replacement cost is the familiar "Tobin's Q." Value and replacement cost need not be equal in the short run, but are strongly related. Data on oil values exist for some decades. Oil value less development cost is discovery value, or resource rent.

Because development is central, and measurable, we form a simple model to show how the optimal investment and depletion rate of a reservoir are determined by price, cost, and the rate of interest. This permits some corollaries on taxation and expropriation, relevant to recent experience. Our perspective is in decades not centuries.[3]

Development Cost, In-ground Value, and Finding Cost

Economists have sometimes estimated in-ground ore value by fitting data to a production function, with marginal cost and resource value as mathematical derivatives.[4] Our method is to take current investment outlay per unit of current reserves-added, or of capacity added, as a direct measure of marginal investment cost; and to use independent data on value. We first show the general relation among the estimated variables.

The Marginal Equalities of Hydrocarbon Investment

Additional oil or gas reserves can be obtained by (1) more development drilling in known reservoirs; or (2) finding new reservoirs for development. The boundaries overlap, of course, but there is a basic difference between locating a new pool, and installing wells and lease equipment in a known pool. Most money is spent in development, and it is a widespread unfortunate error to lump it in with exploration (Adelman et al., 1983).

In thousands of projects, there are comparisons between the market value and the cost of reserve-additions in reservoirs exploited; known but unexploited; incompletely known; suspected; hoped-for . . . and so on. Marginal cost in each is constantly driven towards equality with cost everywhere else. Therefore, change in any type of cost is a proxy for change in every other. We look first at the development of known reservoirs, where most money is spent.

Equalizing Marginal Costs across Deposits under Diminishing Returns

It is widely believed that "the better quality deposit will be mined first until it is exhausted, and the lower quality deposit will be mined subsequently. This is precisely what considerations of efficiency dictate" (Dasgupta and Heal, 1979, p. 173).

This half-truth ignores rising marginal cost within the deposit. At any given moment, many deposits are being expanded. The market serves as a sensing-selective mechanism, scanning all deposits to take the cheapest increment or tranche into production (Lee and Aronofsky, 1958). Over time, newer lower-cost fields expand more rapidly than older higher-cost fields. Therefore, when high cost areas expand and low-cost areas contract —a glaring anomaly in oil since 1973—it is a sure sign of a noncompetitive market.

Development Creates Reserves and Capacity

Persian Gulf reserves in 1944 were reckoned by a special expert mission at 16 billion barrels proved, 5 billion probable[5] (Oil and Gas Journal, 1944). By 1975, those same fields, excluding later discoveries, had already produced 42 billion barrels, with 74 billion "remaining" (International Petroleum Encyclopedia, 1976). (The numbers are much larger today, but not published.) The 1944 team estimated correctly from data known then. Development investment changed the data. Zarrug and Bois (1983) estimated 1981 Middle East "undiscovered reserves" at 208 billion barrels. But reserve accretions in 1981–1988 were 316 billion, despite almost no discovery. (Oil and Gas Journal. World Wide Oil issue, 1981–88, and a later Saudi release).

Oil discovery in the United States (excluding Alaska) peaked before 1930, and most oil is in fields discovered by then. Yet annual reserves-added increased and then were fairly steady until 1974, the start of a frantic wasteful drilling boom. Proved reserves in 1930 were 13 billion; in 1988, about 20. In the interim, 120 billion were added and used. Many smaller fields were found; more important was the continuing expansion of oil fields (Adelman, 1990). During 1966–77, oil reserve additions (excluding Alaska) totaled just under 19 billion, of which more than 17 billion were from old fields (AHKZ, 1983, p. 58). Data are lacking for earlier or later periods.

The new reserves in old fields were no gift of nature, but the payoff to development investment. Their unit cost will be examined below. But models which postulate a phase of "exploration," and a temporary price drop, followed by the final irreversible price rise (Dasgupta and Heal, 1979, and many others) ignore the principal source of reserve-additions, which is development of known fields. In oil, as in uranium, and in copper and iron ore (Trocki, 1986), a discovery initiates a long sequence of reserve additions.

In-ground Values and Development Costs

An autonomous increase of in-ground values (e.g., by higher prices expected) induces more development and finding effort, raising incremental costs. Similarly, if newer fields are becoming smaller, deeper, more faulted, etc., then more development investment is needed to book an incremental reserve barrel. This increases the value of a known reserve barrel.

More specifically, the expected cost of securing an additional barrel through further development sets a limit to the amount worth spending to find a new barrel, and to the value of a developed barrel.[6] I first applied this principle in 1966. "Maximum economic finding cost" (MEFC) of Persian Gulf oil was estimated by assuming zero new-field discoveries over the next 15 years, and very fast production growth. The resulting massive depletion of existing Persian Gulf fields would greatly increase development costs relatively, but by very little absolutely (Adelman, 1972, pp. 5–6 and 66–75). The 1976 Aramco buyout agreement set a discovery fee which was a uniquely well-informed estimate of Saudi Arabia finding cost and value undeveloped: six cents per barrel produced.

Finding Costs

(a) *Offsets to diminishing returns* Diminishing field size holds only for a given basin or "play" containing a population of reservoirs sampled by exploration. To extrapolate into an unknown area "breaks the model's legs in several different ways" (Kaufman in AHKZ, 1983, p. 294). The whole world is not one great play, with diminishing size throughout.[7]

But even within a given basin, decreasing average size of new fields does not necessarily imply increasing exploration cost per unit found, because the prior finding-development process provides two external benefits: a physical infrastructure, and greater knowledge of the local geology.[8] Average newly-found reservoir size shrinks, but so do the resources expended to find and develop it. The net result may go either way.[9]

(b) *The great unknown*   Finding cost per unit cannot usually be reckoned at all, because as mentioned earlier the amount found will not be known for years afterward, if ever.[10] Changes in finding cost can only be traced out by changes in development cost, or in resource rent (user cost). We now turn to some detailed results.

Development Costs and In-ground Values in the United States

Some recent research (Adelman, 1990) can be briefly summarized. An ordinal measure of total finding-developing-operating cost drops sharply during the period of large discoveries ending around 1930, and is followed by a long period with no pronounced tendency, then a surge during the post-1973 boom.

Marginal oil development cost, defined as annual deflated oil development expenditures divided by annual reserves-added, was stable in 1955–1972, then approximately doubled. I have not been able to separate out the depletion effect—if any—from the general waste and inefficiency of the boom, which sagged after 1981 and collapsed in 1986 (Adelman, 1990).

The in-ground (undeflated) value of oil reserves was essentially flat between 1947 and 1973. Inground value, less development cost, is resource rent or user cost. At a riskless rate of 2 percent, it should have risen by 43 percent real in 1955–73. In fact, it was stable in nominal terms, i.e., declining in real terms (Adelman, DeSilva, and Koehn, 1989). The value surge after 1973 set off the drilling boom and pulled costs up with it.

Worldwide Development Investment

Figure 11.1 shows investment per daily barrel of added capacity (reserve additions are far too unreliable) for all oil producing nations excluding North America, Europe, and the Communist blocs, over a 30-year period.

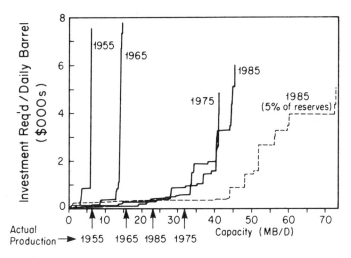

Figure 11.1
NCW supply curve (excluding North America and Western Europe)

(Data are from Adelman and Shahi (1989).) Both factor prices and technology are as of 1985, in order to isolate as far as possible the effect of resource depletion. The horizontal shows current capacity, defined as highest past output. The strong rightward shift ended when output ceased to grow.

In the low-cost regions, the 1985 costs are over-stated. Average output per well was depressed because wells could not be shut in as fast as production declined. The increment to capacity (output per well times new oil wells completed), was thereby understated, inflating the investment per unit added.

The dotted line sets an upper bound to resource rent in the low-cost regions. It shows 1985 investment requirements if producers would expand capacity to 5 percent of 1985 reserves. Actual investment requirements are multiplied by $.05/n$, where n is the much lower actual depletion rate. For example, estimated Saudi cost was multiplied by 2.4 and Kuwait by 4.5. This represents the penalty for transferring barrels from future to present production, when reserves are fixed and output can only be increased by investing in higher depletion intensity. Of course the assumption is far fetched. If we used 1988 reserves, the production line would extend rightward, far off the scale.

The low and stable development investment per unit shows that resource rent continues to be negligible in all the great OPEC producers. But it need not remain so. Under competition, output would be much higher, and if reserves could not expand at the same rate, development cost and hence resource rent would be much higher. This would be an inducement to invest in both finding and developing, with unpredictable results.

Discount Rate, Depletion Rate, Postponement

Having shown the central role of development investment, we turn now to its determination. Many respected names can be cited in support of the proposition that the higher the interest rate, the faster is optimal depletion. (See references in Adelman, 1986, p. 324).) The implicit major premise is zero investment. Current value is the discounted value of "future alternative use." Higher interest rates lower that value, hence lower the opportunity cost of near-term depletion. But since development investment absorbs many billion dollars every year, its determinants merit study.

Development Model for a Reservoir or Tranche

Let

R = reserves = cumulative project output

Q = initial output, barrels per year

a = depletion/decline rate, percentage per year

V = net present in-ground value per barrel

P = constant expected price, net of operating cost

K = project capital expenditures = kaQ

k = investment factor, reflecting better or worse reservoir conditions[11]

i = discount rate, percentage per year.

Exponential decline is conventional among reservoir engineers. Given the usual values of a and i, an infinite time period T makes little difference even quantitatively.
Then

$$R = Q \int_{t=0}^{T} e^{-at} dt \underset{T \to \infty}{=} Q/a,$$

or

$$Q = Ra.$$

Net present value $= VR$

$$= PQ \int_{t=0}^{T} e^{-(i+a)t}\, dt - kaQ$$

$VR \underset{T\to\infty}{=} PQ/(a+i) - kaQ.$ (2)

To make all projects comparable, we divide through equation (2) by PR, price multiplied by reserves. PR is the deposit's limiting value, if it could all be brought up instantaneously.

$VR/PR = (PQ/PR)/(a+i) - kaQ/PR.$

Substituting from (1) and canceling, we have:

$VR/PR = V/P = a/(a+i) - ka^2/P.$ (3)

The Valuation of Developed Reserves

To test whether $a/(a+i)$ is useful, consider a fully developed deposit, with investment zero: $V/P = a(a+i)$. The so-called "Hotelling valuation principle" is that value must equal spot price (Miller and Upton, 1985a) but they could not replicate their results with other data. (Miller and Upton, 1985b). But this is the impossible case of instantaneous production. The depletion/decline rate a rarely exceeds 20 percent per year.

The data points in figure 11.2 (from appendix, table 11.2) refer to lease sales in the late 1950s. At that time a consensus rate of return was 9 percent (Adelman, 1972, pp. 53–55). Hence the curve is the expected ratio $a/(a + .09)$. There is a systematic discrepancy. I suggest that the buyer is paying for an option: more intensive development of the known pool, or exploration elsewhere on the acreage acquired, or both. The narrowing of the gap with increasing a seems to confirm this. Another test: since World War II, a has been approximately equal to i. Then $V = P/2$. This explains why the in-ground value per barrel has long fluctuated around a mean near one-half of the net price (one-third of gross wellhead price), in conformity with an industry rule of thumb (Adelman, DeSilva, and Koehn, 1989; *Petroleum Engineering Handbook*, 1987, ch. 41, p. 7). (Appendix table 11.3 has a rough test for coal.)

Looking now at the investment term of equation (3): the quadratic captures rising costs. However, the true curve is often much flatter, up to the point, or the neighborhood, of some maximum tolerable rate, after which it rises steeply.

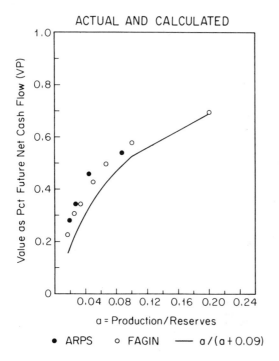

Figure 11.2
Reserve values
Source: *Petroleum Engineering Handbook* (1987), ch. 41, p. 5

Given depletion intensity a, average cost of the incremental tranche is marginal cost of the deposit. To maximize present value, we need the optimal depletion rate a^*, where there is no gain in moving production between present and future. Differentiating equation (3):

$$\frac{dV}{da} = \frac{Pi}{(a + i)^2} - 2ka = 0$$

$$a^* = \sqrt{Pi/2ka} - i. \tag{4}$$

Equation (4) is a form of the cubic:[12]

$$2ka^3 + 4ka^2 i + 2kai^2 - Pi = 0. \tag{5}$$

The discount rate works both ways. The higher the rate, the greater the premium on near-term revenues, *but* the greater the opportunity cost of investment. It can be shown that the depletion rate is at a maximum when $P/k = 4a(a + i)$. Higher or lower discount rates reduce depletion.

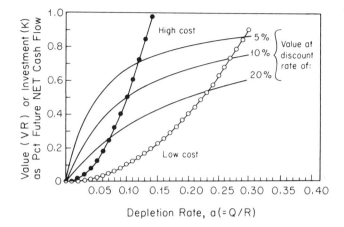

Figure 11.3
Value as function of depletion and discount rates

The axes of figure 11.3 are the same as figure 11.2. On the horizontal is the depletion rate a ($= Q/R$), on the vertical are the two right-hand terms of equation (3): gross present value and capital expenditures, each as a percentage of PR. In the "high cost" reservoir, the investment factor k is 5 times that in the "low cost" pool. Here 14 percent depletion, even if technically feasible, would cost more than the total undiscounted value of the reserve.

For both reservoirs, present value is optimized where the slopes are equal. Within the range of commercial discount rates, 5 percent to 20 percent, the changed discount rate does not greatly affect optimal depletion. Higher discount rates, far from speeding up production, force a shutdown. But at any given discount rate, optimal depletion dwindles quickly as cost rises.

Reserves as Options

The owner of an undeveloped deposit has an option on a developed reserve, exercised by paying development cost. At 25 percent discount, the high-cost reservoir would have zero present value. But the probability of a future higher price, lower cost, or lower discount rate, would give it some positive value, not to develop but to hold (Paddock, Siegel and Smith, 1988). This value is a more refined estimate of resource rent. The better the deposit, the less important the option value. Where deposits are not marginal, "we simply develop the property immediately." Thus the higher is production cost, the greater the penalty for producing not holding, i.e., the higher is user cost. Again, the better deposit or tranche is exploited earlier.[13]

Two Corollaries in Taxation and Nationalization

(1) Mineral production is commonly taxed by a royalty or excise, the sovereign taking a given percentage of the output, or of its market value. A very high percentage has major effects on depletion. For example, if the sovereign takes 80 percent of the price, the low-cost reservoir in figure 11.3 equates to the high-cost. Even in the United States, where rates are much lower, the effect is not negligible (Lohrenz et al., 1981). Given even a mild increase in risk, and in the discount rate, even the low-cost project is not worth investing in. Contrariwise: a reduction of the royalty and/or risk increases the optimal depletion rate.

This resolves a paradox. Since the price of oil began to decline in 1981, and crashed in 1986, non-cartel production outside the United States has actually increased, because of reduced tax rates and better assurance of contract observance.

(2) The price explosions of the 1970s have been explained as a competitive response to a drastic fall in discount rates. Private corporations rightly expected confiscation. Their high implicit discount rates made earlier production more attractive relative to later. Hence production was higher, and price lower, than the long-run competitive level. But the expropriating nations had no such fear, used properly low rates, therefore depleted more slowly. Hence, lower production and higher prices were not a cartel result; they were actually closer to the long-run competitive norm (Mead, 1979; Samuelson, 1986).

Anyone familiar with Persian Gulf depletion rates must be astonished at the suggestion of too-rapid depletion, since rates there were the lowest in the world, one-sixth or less of the industry's rule-of-thumb normal. For many years, host governments had persistently demanded *higher* output from resident companies (at the expense of other governments). Moreover, these governments have shorter time horizons and higher implicit discount rates, because their wealth portfolios are undiversified, concentrated in the more volatile sector of a single industry (Adelman, 1986). It would be tempting to take this as proof that governments must deplete faster. But as just seen, discount rate changes do not seem important.

What was important: expropriation abolished the excise tax wedge. The investor now received all of the net price, not a minor fraction. In terms of figure 11.3, expropriation rotated the investment line clockwise, from "high cost" to "low cost." Under competitive conditions, expropriation and the removal of the excise tax would have greatly *increased* the optimum depletion rate.

Assumption of an Expected Price Change

We now assume an exogenous price increase of g percent per annum. In equations (1) to (5) above, we substitute $(i - g)$ for i. For a developed reservoir:

$$P/V = a/(a + i - g)$$

$$g = i + a(1 - (P/V)). \tag{6}$$

The chief weakness of the measure is the need for a precisely measured interest rate. Some rough estimates, using 10 percent real, are in Adelman (1990). The estimated g stayed mostly in the range ± 2 percent, with a high of 5 percent and a low of -7 percent.

The Gain or Loss to Postponement

To restate net present value as a function of time, we drop the a^* designation, and treat the depletion rate as predetermined. The net present value of the project initiated in any later year t is

$$VR(t) = [(PQe^{gt}/(a + i - g)) - kaQ]e^{-it}$$

$$= [PQ/(a + i - g)]e^{(g-i)t} - kaQe^{-it} \tag{7}[14]$$

In a fully developed deposit, or in a very low-cost pool, with almost no investment, the negative term approaches zero. Then aside from the unlikely case of the price increase g exceeding the interest rate i, the higher is t, the less is VR. Postponement is unprofitable.

At the other extreme is a project which would barely repay the cost of capital, i.e., $PQ/(a + i - g) = kaQ$, and $VR(0) = 0$.

$$VR(t) = PQ/(a + i - g)[e^{-(g-i)t} - e^{-it}]. \tag{8}$$

For any positive value of t, the bracketed expression of equation (8) is positive, $VR(t)$ exceeds zero, and it pays to postpone. Waiting raises the expected revenues, but not the needed investment. Therefore a "dog" of a project is always worth postponing, and has only option value. (For a good example, see Paddock, Siegel, and Smith (1988).) A good project should usually not be postponed. An expected lower cost (a lower k-factor) acts like an expected higher price, and will cause a marginal project to be postponed.

The penalty for investing to produce sooner rather than later is less (negative) for the low-cost project, greater for the high-cost. It has been a consistent result: resource rent (user cost) changes in the same direction as development cost. The result holds for the determinate or the probabilistic case (option value), and whether prices are expected to remain stable or to rise.

Conclusions

1. There is no mineral "fixed stock ... to divide between two [or more] periods." Its allocation over time to do justice as between us and our posterity is like the number of angels who can dance on the point of a pin: a difficult non-problem.
2. A rising price is not needed to prevent arbitrage, i.e., to induce the owner to keep the mineral in the ground instead of selling it off forthwith. Depletion has a built-in brake, rising cost at the margin (Houthakker, 1980).
3. In-ground value approaches the avoided cost of (a) more intensive development of existing deposits or (b) discovery-cum-development of new deposits. Investment is guided by comparing value with thousands of (a) and (b), making the system stable. Because they are alternatives, change in development cost is an indicator of changes in discovery cost and in resource rent.
4. Replacement cost (discovery and development) and value are the uncertain fluctuating resultants of two opposing forces: decreasing returns versus increasing knowledge. Mineral assets are risky.
5. A higher discount rate makes quick depletion more desirable but less accessible. Since it works both ways, the net effect of a changed discount rate on the depletion rate can go either way and cannot be very great.
6. Private markets do not systematically under-value in-ground assets, as compared with other assets. They may often be beautifully wrong as to both. A market in mineral reserve values is a market in good and bad ideas about future scarcity.
7. Under the assumption of a fixed mineral stock, the time-pattern of depletion and rising prices under competition is similar to, and may even be identical with, the pattern under monopoly. Monopoly price is higher at first, but rises less. But the assumption is wrong, and there is no family

resemblance. In non-monopolized uranium, the low-cost areas boomed at the expense of the high-cost, and brought down the price (Neff, 1984). In contrast, oil wells drilled in the United States in 1987 were 60 percent more than in 1973, in Saudi Arabia 95 percent less.

8. The expropriation of Persian Gulf oil reserves during the 1970s was equivalent to a reduction of roughly 80 percent in investment require-ments. It would have led to much faster depletion, hence lower prices, had each nation-owner operated in independent pursuit of maximum present value. Lower depletion was the result of collusion to maintain prices.

9. A current indicator of crude oil resource scarcity is development invest-ment per unit of reserves added, or per unit of capacity added. Reserve value is a leading indicator. In the United States, neither indicator increased before the 1970s.

10. Elsewhere in the world there has been no increase in development cost since 1955. Even assuming a very fast increase in consumption, the supply price will remain far below the current market price (roughly $15 since mid-1986). Resource rent remains negligible. But if and when the cartel loses control, prices drop sharply, and output grows, cost (and rent) may increase greatly. We can track it, if we wish to, at modest cost.

Appendix

Table 11.1
Calculated and actual price changes: nonfuel minerals 1970–1985, 1985 price as percentage of 1970

Mineral	Calculated	Actual	A/C	Average annual error
Aluminum	1.25	1.01	0.81	−0.014
Copper	1.20	0.41	0.34	−0.069
Iron*	1.24	0.99	0.80	−0.014
Lead	1.06	0.44	0.41	−0.058
Nickel	1.42	0.61	0.43	−0.055
Silver	1.54	1.24	0.81	−0.014
Tin	1.21	1.22	1.01	0.001
Mean	1.25	0.86	0.69	−0.029

Source: Calculated, Margaret Slade, "Trends in Natural-Resource Commodity Price," Journal of Environmental Economics and Management, vol. 9, 122–137 (1982). Actual, Statistical Abstract of the U.S. (Washington, 1987), pp. 678, 690, 692, 693. Deflated by Producer Price Index, All Commodities.
*Calculated: finished iron; actual, iron ore 1970–84.

Table 11.2
Effect of deferment on market value

Reserves/ production $(R/Q = 1/a)$ (1)	Value as percentage of undiscounted net cash flow at present prices		Regression estimate (4)	Theoretical $a/(a + i)$ (5)
	ARPS (2)	FAGIN (3)		
5	—	0.695	0.756	0.714
10	—	0.577	0.556	0.556
11.5	0.540	—	0.572	0.521
15	—	0.497	0.464	0.455
20	—	0.428	0.408	0.385
22.5	0.458	—	0.425	0.357
30	—	0.343	0.341	0.294
37.5	0.345	—	0.338	0.250
40	—	0.308	0.300	0.238
52.5	0.281	—	0.291	0.192
60	—	0.227	0.251	0.172

Source: J. J. Arps, "Valuation of Oil & Gas Reserves," ch. 38 in Frick, ed., *Petroleum Production Handbook* (1962), p. 38–9. (Included also in *Petroleum Engineering Handbook* (1987).
Regression estimate: $\ln(\text{ValPct}) = .436 - (.44\ln(R/Q)) + .09$ dum, Arps = 1, Fagin = 0
$R^2 = .96$, t-stats 4.9, 15.6, 2.1
"Theoretical": $a = Q/R$, $i = .08$

Table 11.3
Relation of in-ground value to net price bituminous coal 1980–82

A. Relation of net to gross receipt, 1982

1	Value of Shipments	28261
2	Value Added	18455
3	Payrolls	6736
4	Net receipts (inc. taxes, royalties)	11719
5	Net/gross, unadjusted	0.415
6	Less taxes, royalties	0.100
7	Net/gross, adjusted	0.315

B. Relation of values to net prices

	Year	Average gross price ($/short ton)	Average in-ground value	Relation: value to adjusted net price
8	1980	24.51	0.82	0.106
9	1981	26.30	0.56	0.68
10	1982	27.12	0.21	0.025

Sources: Lines 1–3, *Statistical Abstract* 1987, p. 673; Line 4 = (2) − (3); Line 5 = (4)/(1);
Line 6, rough allowance; Lines 8–10: prices, *Statistical Abstract* 1987, p. 675
In-ground sales values, unpublished tabulation by Martin B. Zimmerman
Relation, value divided by 31.5 percent of sales

Notes

This paper is a condensed rewritten version of MIT Energy Lab Working Paper No. MITEL 88-002WP revised May 1988. The research was supported by he National Science Foundation. Grant #SES-8412971, and by the MIT Center for Energy Policy Research of the MIT Energy Laboratory. I am grateful for the help of John C. Lohrenz, Michael C. Lynch, Thomas L. Neff, James L. Paddock, James L. Smith, Geoffrey L. Ward, and two anonymous referees. My debt to Paul G. Bradley and Richard L. Gordon is long standing. Any opinion, tindings, conclusions or recommendations expressed herein are those of the author, and do not necessarily reflect the views of the NSF or of any other person or group.

1. Boskin et al. (1985), p. 926 make the highly misleading statement that "the average annual rise in real oil prices received by U.S. producers was 3.5 over the period 1950–82." The price declined consistently for the twenty years 1950–1972, rose for the next nine years, then declined by 16 percent in their terminal year 1982.

2. Harris and Skinner (1982) emphasize discontinuities in certain metals. Exploitation below some threshold requires an "abrupt change" in technology. Similarly, offshore oil is produced, oil shale is not.

3. Gordon et al. (1987) build a model of rising copper costs and prices for the next 180 years. Output expands five-fold in 100 years but then declines. By the time one must learn to process common rock, very little copper is being extracted (pp. 56, 114). Their vision of increasing scarcity may prove true for copper, and for fuels. The question remains: within what confidence limits may we expect a given increase in a given year? Jevons in 1865 correctly saw the coal problem as rising cost not exhaustion. He used available knowledge of depth and other cost-determining characteristics of British coal to project an increase that went increasingly wrong.

4. Stollery (1983) fitted a Hotelling model governed by rising costs to the International Nickel Company. Calculated resource rent during 1952–72 stayed close to one-sixth of the (rising) price. Halvorsen and Smith (1984) estimated the "shadow price of the ore in situ" for Canadian metal mining, by "estimating its reproducible cost function and then differentiating ... with respect to [the output volume] ..." (p. 958). Real shadow price of unextracted ore declined in 1956–1974 by 80 percent; price of final output (with a very large component of non-mining value-added) was practically unchanged. Farrow (1985) found "the Hotelling model" inconsistent with the data on prices, extraction rates, and "stock remaining in the mine" in a hard-rock mining operation. Mining more low-grade (higher cost) ore during periods of higher prices, and less high-grade, implied a negative discount rate. In my opinion, the practice related only to the short term, with capacity fixed, and does not discredit "the Hotelling model"—which is in any case much wider than his variant.

5. For a discussion of proved, probable, and possible (potential) reserves, see AHKZ (1983), ch. 2.

6. Devarajan and Fisher (1982) state that resource rent cannot exceed marginal "discovery" cost: they do not distinguish development.

7. In uranium, in the United States, extraction was always from ever-lower grades and deeper and more costly sources. Outside the United States, many rich new deposits continue to be found (Neff, 1984).

8. Cf. the practice of "dry hole money": Operator A promises to share the cost of drilling a wildcat well on Operator B's lease, if the well turns out to be dry, in return for getting the well drilling records.

9. Harris and Skinner (1982) say of nonfuel minerals: "Exploration effectiveness is declining and exploration costs are rising" (323). An exhaustive recent study does not bear this out. See Tilton. Eggert, and Landsberg (eds.) (1988), p. 12.

10. The financial press has occasional estimates of "finding cost per barrel of oil equivalent." This is defined as (a) exploration plus development expenditures divided by (b) oil reserves-added plus gas reserves-added (converted to an "oil equivalent"). Both (a) and (b) are incorrect aggregation. There is no fixed or natural oil: gas ratio, either as to price nor as to any species of cost. The result is meaningless.

11. Marginal investment requirements per unit are alternatively $K/Q = ka$, or $K/R = ka^2$. Thus k is given by nature and knowledge, a is the decision variable.

12. Gordon M. Kaufman has demonstrated that one root of (5) is real, two imaginary.

13. The greater the expected price variance, the greater the option value, because the better chance of a very high price is worth something, while a lower price cannot make the reservoir be worth less than zero.

14. The general equation for optimal t is available from the author.

References

Adelman, M. A., *The World Petroleum Market* (Baltimore: Johns Hopkins University Press, 1972).

————, "Discount Rates for Oil Producer Nations," *Resources & Energy* 8, (Dec. 1986), 309–329.

————, "Mineral Depletion, with Special Reference to Petroleum," MIT Energy Lab Working Paper MITEL 88-002WP, May 1988.

————, "Finding and Developing Costs in the USA 1918–1986," MIT Energy Lab Working paper No. MITEL-86-008WP, forthcoming in John R. Moroney (ed.), *Advances in the Economics of Energy & Resources*, vol. 11 (Greenwich, CT: JAI Press, 1990).

Adelman, M. A., Harindra De Silva, and Michael F. Koehn, "The Valuation of Oil Reserves," SPE 18906 (Society of Petroleum Engineers) (Mar. 1989).

Adelman, M. A., and Manoj Shahi, "Development Cost Estimates for Oil Producing Countries, 1958–1986," *Energy Economics* 11 (Jan. 1989), 2–10 (Condensed and revised from MIT Energy Lab Working Paper No. MITEL-008WP, cited as Adelman and Shahi (1988), with contains the complete estimates from which figure 1 was calculated.)

Adelman, M. A., John C. Houghton, Gordon M. Kaufman, and Martin B. Zimmerman (AHKZ), *Energy Resources in an Uncertain Future* (Cambridge, Mass.: Ballinger, 1983).

Boskin, Michael J., Marc S. Robinson, Terrance O'Reilly, and Praveen Kumar, "New Estimates of the Value of Federal Mineral Rights and Land," *American Economic Review* 75 (Dec. 1985), 923–936.

Dasgupta, Partha, and Geoffrey M. Heal, *Economic Theory and Exhaustible Resource* (Cambridge: Cambridge University Press, 1979).

Devarajan, Shantayanan, and Anthony C. Fisher, "Exploration and Scarcity," *Journal of Political Economy* 90 (Dec. 1982), 1280–1290.

Farrow, Scott, "Testing the Efficiency of Extraction from a Stock Resource," *Journal of Political Economy* 93 (1985), 452–487.

Gately, Dermot, "A Ten-Year Retrospective: OPEC and the World Oil Market," *Journal of Economic Literature* 22 (Sept. 1984), 1100–1114.

Gordon, Robert B., Tjalling C. Koopmans, William D. Nordhaus, and Brian J. Skinner, *Toward a New Iron Age?* (Cambridge: Harvard University Press, 1987).

Halvorsen, Robert, and Tim R. Smith, "On Measuring Natural Resource Scarcity," *Journal of Political Economy* 92 (Oct. 1984), 954–964.

Harris, DeVerle P., and Brian J. Skinner, "Assessment of Long-Term Supplies of Minerals," in V. Kerry Smith and John V. Krutilla (eds.), *Explorations in Natural Resource Economics* (Baltimore: Johns Hopkins University Press for Resources for the Future, 1982), 245–326.

Hogan, William W., and Paul N. Leiby, "Risk Analysis with Energy Security Models," Kennedy School of Government. Harvard University, 1985.

Hotelling, Harold, "The Economics of Exhaustible Resources," *Journal of Political Economy* 39 (1931), 137–175.

Houthakker, Hendrik S., "The Use and Management of North Sea Oil," in Richard E. Caves and Lawrence B. Krause (eds.), *Britain's Economic Performance* (Washington, D.C.: The Brookings Institution, 1980), p. 331 and appendix A.

Manne, Alan S., and Leo Schrattenholzer, *International Energy Workshop: Overview of Poll Responses* (Jan. 1988).

International Monetary Fund, *Primary Commodities: Market Developments and Outlook* (Washington, D.C.: May 1987).

International Petroleum Encyclopedia 1976.

Lee, A. S., and J. S. Aronofsky, "A Linear Programming Model for Scheduling Crude Oil Production," *Petroleum Transactions AIME*, vol. 213, pp. 389–392.

Lohrenz, John C., Bernard H. Burzlaff, and Elmer D. Dougherty, "How Policies Affect Rates of Recovery from Mineral Sources," *Society of Petroleum Engineers Journal* 271 (Dec. 1981), 645–657.

Manthy, Robert S., *Natural Resource Commodities—A Century of Statistics* (Washington, D.C.: Resources for the Future, 1978).

Mead, Walter J., "An Economic Analysis of Crude Oil Price Behavior in the 1970s," *The Journal of Energy and Development* 9 (Spring 1979), 1–25.

Miller, Merton H., and Charles W. Upton, "A Test of the Hotelling Valuation Principle," *Journal of Poltical Economy* 93 (Feb. 1985), 1–25.

————, "The Pricing of Oil and Gas: Some Further Considerations," *Journal of Finance* 40 (3) (1985b), 1009–1020.

Neff, Thomas, *The International Uranium Market* (Cambridge, MA: Ballinger, 1984).

Oil and Gas Journal (March 23, 1944), 45.

Oil and Gas Journal, World Wide Oil issue (last of year).

Paddock, James L., Daniel R. Siegel, and James L. Smith, "Option Valuation of Claims on Real Assets: The Case of Offshore Petroleum Leases," *Quarterly Journal of Economics* 98 (3) (Aug. 1988), 479–508.

Petroleum Engineering Handbook, Howard B. Bradley (ed.) (Richardson, Texas: Society of Petroleum Engineers, 1987).

Pindyck, Robert S., "Uncertainty and Exhaustible Resource Markets," *Journal of Political Economy* 99 (Dec. 1980), 681–721.

Salant, Stephen W., *Imperfect Competition in the International Energy Market: A Computerized Nash-Cournot Model* (Lexington, Mass.: Lexington Books, 1982).

Samuelson, Paul A., *The Collected Scientific Papers of Paul A. Samuelson*. Kate Crowley (ed.), vol. V (Cambridge, Mass.: MIT Press, 1986) 896–897.

Slade, Margaret, "Trends in Natural-Resource Commodity Prices," *Journal of Environmental Economics and Management* 9 (1982), 122–137.

Smith, V., Kerry, "Measuring Natural Resource Scarcity: Theory and Practice," *Journal of Environmental Economics and Management*, 5 (1978), 150–171.

Starrett, David A., "*Production and Capital*: Kenneth Arrow's Contributions in Perspective—A Review Article," *Journal of Economic Literature* 25 (Mar. 1987), 92–102.

Stiglitz, Joseph E., "Monopoly and the Rate of Extraction of Exhaustible Resources," *American Economic Review* 66 (Sept. 1976), 655–661.

Stollery, Kenneth R., "Mineral Depletion with Cost as the Extraction Limit: A Model Applied to the Behavior of Prices in the Nickel Industry," *Journal of Environmental Economics & Management* 10 (June 1983), 151.

Tilton, John E., Roderick G. Eggert, Hans H. Hansberg (eds.). *World Mineral Exploration: Trends and Economic Issues* (Washington, D.C.: Resources for the Future, 1988).

Trocki, Linda Katherine. *An Analysts of the Role of Exploration in the Opening of New Iron and Copper Mines*, unpublished Ph.D. thesis, Pennsylvania State University, 1986.

World Bank, *The Outlook for Primary Commodities, 1984 to 1955* (Washington, D.C.: World Bank, 1984).

Zarrug, A. Y., and C. Bois, "Potential Oil Reserves in the Middle East and North Africa," *Proceedings of the World Petroleum Congress 1983*, PD11(4) (1983), 261–275.

12

User Cost in Oil Production

with Harindar De Silva and Michael F. Koehn

1 Introduction

To reckon the income generated in mineral production, whether in a single unit or a whole nation, one must subtract out the value of the ore used up. In estimating this value, commonly called user cost (or resource rent), an initial fixed "non-renewable" mineral stock is usually assumed. In equilibrium the value must rise at the appropriate discount rate, or else it pays to arbitrage.[1] Prices (net of extraction cost) must rise at that rate. The higher the discount rate, the less the present value of the asset, and the faster the optimal depletion rate (Hotelling, 1931; Dasgupta and Heal, 1979). Hence the emphasis many writers place on the importance of the 'social' discount rate, which allegedly is much lower than the market rate, in determining a nation's optimal depletion rate.

However, the assumption of an initial fixed stock is superfluous, and wrong. Only a fraction of the mineral in the earth's crust, or in any given field, will ever be used. The size of the fraction will depend on costs and prices, including those of substitutes. To define the initial fixed stock as "the economic portion" of what is in the earth, and then derive a price-output profile from it, is circular reasoning. Prices need not rise over time. In fact, decreases are usual, increases rare (Adelman, 1990).

What we observe in the real world are not one-time stocks immaculately created to be consumed, but inventories of "proved reserves," constantly renewed by investment in finding and development. Over time, the investment needed per unit-added is forced up by diminishing returns, and forced down by increasing knowledge. So far, knowledge has prevailed. It need not always do so. There is no general law. The observed price trend varies among minerals, in the short and long run.

Reprinted from *Resources & Energy* 13 (December 1991): 217–240.

Removing a wrong assumption does not make the Hotelling theory wrong. It makes it useful by focusing on the true measure of mineral scarcity: the present value of a mineral reserve to be extracted. To estimate reserve values concentrates the minds of scientists, engineers, and investors. Economists need to observe the market in asset values, which is a market in ideas, good and bad.

An Opposing View

Nordhaus (1973, pp. 530–538) gives a very good statement of the case that resource prices and values are not valid indicators of real mineral scarcity.

[A] full set of futures and insurance markets is not available.... In the cosmic framework of the ultimate exhaustion of fossil fuels ... [sales of in-ground reserves] cover a very short span. (pp. 534–535)

[Consequently, private discount rates are too high, and resources undervalued.] Too high an interest rate casts a long shadow over the future ... resources are consumed too quickly. [Decisions are myopic, planning horizons too short.] (p. 535)

[Therefore private markets are] an unreliable means of pricing and allocating exhaustible appropriable natural resources. (p. 537)

However, if we drop the assumption of a fixed stock, none of these strictures apply. A high interest rate may speed up *or* slow down the depletion rate, and the effect will not be strong because the force works both ways (Adelman, 1990). If mineral reserves are a type of inventory, in which investment is governed by the usual incentives and errors, they are no worse valued than any other asset. And both buyers and sellers have a strong inducement to use the recommended "carefully constructed econometric and engineering model of the economy." (p. 537)

Purpose

This note is confined to crude oil. We first suggest how the in-ground value and the user cost are related to development investment. We test these concepts with a data set for the United States, then apply them briefly elsewhere.

2   Investment Requirements and In-ground Values

Investment in oil production consists of two activities: *discovery* of new pools, and their *development* by drilling and equipping wells. The investment creates the inventory of developed barrels of "proved reserves," which are essentially a forecast of cumulative production through existing installations. At any given moment, if there is a market in reserves, we can write (Bradley, 1989):

$$VR - K(R) = UR, \tag{1}$$

i.e., in-ground value of a developed reserve, less development investment incurred, equals user cost. This permits us to calculate past user cost from past market values and development cost, and we do so below. But it does not explain any of the variables, nor enable us to predict.

The cost of creating reserves by various methods should approach equality at the margin. The cost of creating new reserves through more intensive or extensive development of known pools can be called marginal development cost and should in equilibrium equal marginal finding cost, which should equal marginal user cost, which should equal the market price net of development cost. Discovery, development, and purchase are all competing investment outlets, alternative methods of acquiring reserves. If the operator chooses to develop a known pool more intensively, increased development cost is the penalty for using not holding. He should not incur a penalty greater than the value of an undeveloped barrel, i.e., user cost.

To develop a reservoir, or a tranche thereof:

Q = initial new production, barrels per year,

a = exponential decline rate of Q, percent per year,

R = current reserves = $Q \int_0^T e^{-at} \, dt = Q/a, \quad t \to \inf$,

$$a = Q/R, \tag{2}$$

K = capital expenditures = kaQ,

k = an empirical constant per barrel, reflecting better or poorer geology.

The value of an undeveloped barrel, in infinite time

$$VR = PQ/(a + i) - kaQ, \tag{3a}$$

$$V = Pa/(a + i) - ka^2. \tag{3b}$$

The decision variable is Q, hence a. All others are exogenous. It can be proved (Adelman, 1990) that value is maximized when

$$2ka^3 + 4ka^2i + 2kai^2 - Pi = 0. \tag{4}$$

To calculate the development cost of higher production rates, we make two extreme opposing assumptions, which bracket all possible cases:

(1) *No Resource Limitation*   Assume that the long-run supply curve is horizontal. Production and reserves increase in the same proportion. That is, $dR/R = dQ/Q$, and $dR/dQ = R/Q$. Then a remains constant, because from (2),

$$da/dQ = \frac{R - Q(dR/dQ)}{R^2} = \frac{R - Q(R/Q)}{R^2} = 0.$$

Investment per additional annual barrel:

$$dK/dQ = ka + kQ\,da/dQ = ka = K/Q. \tag{5}$$

Investment per additional barrel in ground: $dK/dR = K/R = ka^2$.

(2) *The Reserve in Inventory R is Fixed*   Assume that additional investment can only accelerate output, not increase the total. Then a must increase proportionately with Q:

If $dR/dQ = 0$,

$$da/dQ = [R - Q(dR/dQ)]/R^2 = 1/R = a/Q, \tag{6}$$

$$dK/dQ = d(kaQ)/dQ = ka + kQ(a/Q) = 2ka.$$

Therefore in the limiting case of zero reserve additions from new investment, the investment per additional unit of capacity is twice what it would be in the opposed limiting case of new reserve creation. At the limit, the user cost, of shifting output from future to present, is equal to, and, additive to, the cost of creating the new capacity. This follows from the exponential decline curve, obviously oversimplified but not untrue.

If the reserve is fixed, the cost of creating a new barrel in the ground is by assumption infinite. We treat the cost of creating an increment of capacity as a surrogate for the cost of obtaining the same result from creating a new barrel of reserves.

If the ratio of user cost per barrel to development cost per barrel fluctuates between zero and unity, then by equation (1) the ratio of total in-ground value to development cost fluctuates between unity and 2. We turn now to the data.

3   Reserve Values: Analysis of Sales of Properties

The market value MV of an oil/gas property is a function of the amount of oil reserve O, unit value b, and of the amount of gas G and unit value c:

$$MV = bO + cG + e. \tag{7}$$

Table 12.1 shows regression estimates for recent years. There are some obvious problems. The samples are small. They cover only voluntary disclosures. The independent variables are measured with error. Non-reserve assets and liabilities and other special factors may greatly influence the value of a transaction. The sizes of the properties sold vary enormously. A regression showing heteroscedasticity (asterisk) was replaced by a weighted regression (Kmenta, 1984, p. 287). Since a large property is likely to contain much of both oil and gas, the two might seem to be collinear. We think this is only one aspect of heteroscedasticity.

We also computed all "pure oil" or "pure gas" cases, considering everything above 90 percent as "pure." For example, in 1979, the average wellhead oil price was \$12.64, and average wellhead gas price (a defective figure due to price regulations, but all we have) was \$1.178 (Monthly

Table 12.1
Regression estimates of oil and gas reserve values, 1979–1988.[a]

Year	1979	1980	1981	1982	1983	1984	1985	1986	1987	1988
Sample	7*	10	5	5	12*	20*	15	26	46*	37*
Oil value										
\$/brl	7.62	14.34	5.02	5.83	4.42	5.95	6.85	5.72	4.35	5.32
t-stat	8.0	22.0	8.3	20.5	1.6	10.8	19.3	6.5	3.8	5.8
"Pure oil"										
Number	2	2	1	1	1	3	3	3	12	8
Avg. val.	8.32	7.07	5.34	8.10	3.39	5.64	6.60	6.30	5.06	6.06
Gas value										
\$/MCF	0.26	1.96	1.53	0.89	0.68	0.99	0.32	0.81	0.81	0.74
t-stat	1.6	8.6	1.7	9.6	1.1	6.9	2.9	20.3	10.0	9.4
"Pure gas"										
Number	—	2	—	—	4	2	2	9	11	7
Avg. val.	—	0.57	—	—	1.19	0.88	1.5	0.65	0.79	0.69

a. Asterisk* indicates heteroscedasticity, in which case we use the corrected (weighted) regression results. "Pure oil" and "pure gas" explained in text.
Source: Scotia-OGJ Data Base, using "adjusted price." Method: ordinary least squares regressions.

Energy Review). Shell Oil Co. bought the South Belridge field, credited with 364 BCF of gas and 365 MMB of oil. The current value of the oil was therefore 92 percent of total current value, and the oil consideration was then estimated as $3.36 billion (92 percent of $3.65 billion), which came to $9.20 per barrel. This looks extremely high, but there is balm in hindsight. During 1979–1989 inclusive, cumulative production from the field was 494 million barrels, or 35 percent more then the total estimated reserve bought. It produced in 1989 four times as much as in 1978, and at the end of the year its current reserves were figured at 357 million (*Oil & Gas Journal*, 1-29-79, p. 133, and 1-29-90, p. 74), which is probably too low. Obviously Shell won big when it bet on improved technology.

Turning to table 12.1: the 1980 oil and gas values are hardly credible, 2–3 times as high as the two "pure" cases. The 1985 gas value is hard to credit. In the next three years, however, the samples are larger and the results more stable. The 1986 decline was relatively mild, but continued even stronger into 1987, as old purchase/sale commitments ran out and the industry faced the new price levels. The 1988 revival reflected the price recovery of late 1986 and 1987.

Following a procedure similar to our earlier paper (Adelman et al., 1989), the Scotia group have classified acquisitions as predominantly oil or predominantly gas. We use them below to calculate a market estimate of expected price changes, to be compared with actual change.

One piece of information is missing: current production in the properties sold. Papers published by J. J. Arps and by K. M. Fegin over 30 years ago (Frick, 1962, and Bradley, 1987) showed that the higher the ratio of production to reserves (Q/R), the higher the ratio of values to wellhead price (V/P). A glance at equation (3b) shows that for a developed reserve, with development cost zero by definition, reserve value and wellhead price are connected by the formula

$$V/P = a/(a + i), \tag{8}$$

where V is the per-barrel value, P is the price net of current costs and taxes, $a = Q/R$, and i is the discount rate. There is a good fit (Adelman, 1990), but a bias: buyers consistently pay more than they "should." We suggest that in return they are getting an option on more intensive development. The Shell purchase was a strong example.

These results have an important implication for the theory of mineral depletion. Given the fixed-stock assumption, the value of a unit in-ground should equal the spot price net of extraction cost (Dasgupta and Heal, 1979, p. 158; Miller and Upton, 1985). If this assumption held, then the price would appreciate at the appropriate interest rate, and the waiting time to production (i.e., the inverse of the depletion rate) would not affect the value of the reserve. But in fact, as these results show, there is a strong effect. And where oil in the ground is worth roughly one-half of its net wellhead price, coal reserves are usually less than one percent (For some recent examples, see appendix A). This cannot be reconciled with a "tilt (upward) in the competitive price path which is an inescapable feature of an exhaustible resource" (Dasgupta and Heal, 1979, p. 159).

In appendix B we show that the better the project, the less the optimal postponement, and for very good projects it may be a high negative number. Therefore, when we observe low-cost OPEC members cutting back more radically than high-cost, the logic of user cost shows this to be incompatible with any assumption of independent competitive behavior. But under group monopoly, the larger producers bear more of the burden of curtailment.

4 Inter-temporal Changes in Values and Costs

User cost is the penalty for developing more intensively at any given time instead of waiting for a later data and expected higher prices. But if development cost, or discovery cost, or both, are expected to increase in the future, the present value of an existing barrel will also increase. This increases user cost and with it the incentive for additional investment in discovery.

For long-term perspective, we have tabulated the oil reserve valuations issued by the John S. Herold Company beginning 1946. They calculate the present value of the proved reserves of a large number of companies, as they are expected to be depleted over time, and discounted at what the estimators consider an appropriate rate.

We make only a limited use of these data. The Herold reserve estimate and valuation for a specific company are not substitutes for estimates made by a professional team who expose their data and reasoning, and sign their names. A market transaction is based on these professional appraisals, and incorporates a "peer review," because the final number has been accepted by both sides who are wagering money on the accuracy of the work.

We use no specific Herold numbers, but we do calculate annual averages to measure time trend. This is defensible because, first, the Herold valuations are themselves subject to a market process; the nearer they come to what investors consider reasonable, i.e., would pay or demand, the more successful they are. the survival of the company for this long a period

Table 12.2
Wellhead price, cost, and reserve values, U.S.A., 1946–1987 (current dollars per barrel)[a]

Year	Wellhead price		Avg. res. value	Standard deviation	Sample size	Development cost		User cost (value less post-tax cost)	Value as ratio to			
											Development cost	
	Gross	Net				Pre-tax	Post-tax		Gross price	Net price	Pre-tax	Post-tax
1946	1.41	0.91	0.30	0.04	16				0.21	0.33		
1947	1.93	1.24	0.43	0.06	7				0.22	0.35		
1948	2.60	1.67	0.75	0.19	25				0.29	0.45		
1949	2.54	1.64	0.73	0.09	19				0.29	0.45		
1950	2.51	1.62	0.70	0.05	21				0.28	0.43		
1951	2.53	1.63	0.73	0.14	16				0.29	0.45		
1952	2.53	1.63	0.68	0.07	23				0.27	0.42		
1953	2.68	1.73	0.75	0.19	41				0.28	0.43		
1954	2.78	1.79	0.69	0.07	38				0.25	0.39		
1955	2.77	1.78	0.89	0.22	88	0.80	0.71	0.18	0.32	0.50	1.11	1.25
1956	2.79	1.80	0.95	0.25	103	0.80	0.71	0.24	0.34	0.53	1.18	1.33
1957	3.09	1.99	0.94	0.18	118				0.30	0.47		
1958	3.01	1.94	0.91	0.18	117				0.30	0.47		
1959	2.90	1.87	0.88	0.21	124	0.50	0.45	0.44	0.30	0.47	1.77	1.98
1960	2.88	1.85	0.83	0.22	110	0.66	0.59	0.24	0.29	0.45	1.25	1.41
1961	2.89	1.86	0.83	0.19	110	0.58	0.52	0.31	0.29	0.46	1.43	1.61
1962	2.90	1.87	0.87	0.20	131	0.77	0.69	0.19	0.30	0.47	1.13	1.27
1963	2.89	1.86	0.83	0.20	79	0.74	0.66	0.17	0.29	0.45	1.12	1.26

Year	Wellhead price		Avg. res. value	Standard deviation	Sample size	Development cost		User cost (value less post-tax cost)	Value as ratio to			
	Gross	Net				Pre-tax	Post-tax		Gross price	Net price	Development cost	
											Pre-tax	Post-tax
1964	2.88	1.85	0.87	0.20	117	0.61	0.54	0.33	0.30	0.47	1.43	1.60
1965	2.85	1.84	0.83	0.21	103	0.53	0.48	0.35	0.29	0.45	1.55	1.75
1966	2.88	1.85	0.84	0.29	119	0.54	0.48	0.36	0.29	0.45	1.55	1.74
1967	2.92	1.88	0.82	0.22	111	0.56	0.50	0.32	0.28	0.44	1.46	1.64
1968	2.94	1.89	0.83	0.23	113	0.71	0.63	0.20	0.28	0.44	1.17	1.31
1969	3.09	1.99	0.85	0.23	123	0.85	0.75	0.10	0.28	0.43	1.00	1.13
1970	3.18	2.05	0.81	0.24	125	0.63	0.56	0.25	0.26	0.40	1.29	1.45
1971	3.39	2.18	0.90	0.36	96	0.68	0.61	0.29	0.27	0.41	1.32	1.48
1972	3.39	2.18	0.99	0.56	112	1.10	0.98	0.01	0.29	0.45	0.90	1.01
1973	3.89	2.51	1.41	0.59	119	0.89	0.79	0.62	0.36	0.56	1.58	1.78
1974	6.74	4.34	2.28	0.83	121	1.46	1.30	0.98	0.34	0.53	1.56	1.75
1975	7.56	4.87	2.39	0.84	130	2.99	2.66	−0.28	0.32	0.49	0.80	0.90
1976	8.19	5.27	2.74	0.03	126	4.17	3.71	−0.97	0.33	0.52	0.66	0.74
1977	8.57	5.52	3.03	1.71	137	3.85	3.43	−0.40	0.35	0.55	0.79	0.88
1978	9.00	5.80	3.39	1.29	145	2.76	2.45	0.94	0.38	0.58	1.23	1.38
1979	12.64	8.14	4.62	2.11	143	3.35	2.98	1.64	0.37	0.57	1.38	1.55
1980	21.59	13.9	7.91	3.58	131	3.48	3.10	4.81	0.37	0.57	2.27	2.55
1981	31.77	17.51	9.72	3.90	132	6.42	5.71	4.01	0.31	0.56	1.51	1.70
1982	28.52	16.28	8.31	2.94	129	11.29	10.05	−1.74	0.29	0.51	0.74	0.83

Table 12.2 (continued)

Year	Wellhead price		Avg. res. value	Standard deviation	Sample size	Development cost		User cost (value less post-tax cost)	Value as ratio to			
	Gross	Net				Pre-tax	Post-tax		Gross price	Net price	Development cost	
											Pre-tax	Post-tax
1983	26.19	15.43	8.62	4.49	126	4.00	3.56	4.96	0.33	0.55	2.13	2.39
1984	25.88	16.67	8.80	2.58	130	3.60	3.20	5.60	0.34	0.53	2.45	2.75
1985	24.09	13.80	8.19	2.64	122	4.08	3.63	4.56	0.34	0.59	2.01	2.26
1986	12.68	8.15	5.88	2.16	129	4.96	4.42	1.46	0.46	0.72	1.19	1.33

a. Average values; 1959—one outlier omitted: $4.73/barrel; 1961—two outliers omitted: $90, $331/barrel; 1970—one outlier omitted: $959/barrel; 1971—two outliers omitted: $7.02, $7.75/barrel; 1972—one outlier omitted: $193/barrel; 1975—one outlier omitted: $59/barrel.

Explanation: Post tax costs

The reduction in cost aims to capture the net advantage of drilling for oil instead of buying. This is the result of the tax advantage of charging off intangible drilling expenses.

Intangible drilling costs are "between 60 and 70 percent of the entire well cost" (*Petroleum Production Handbook* 1962, p. 22–38, repeated at p. 11–44 of *Petroleum Engineering Handbook*, 1987). However, a special API tabulation released in 1985 showed intangibles as 34 percent in 1984. This discrepancy is due to the fact that drilling and completion account for only about 60 percent of total development cost including lease equipment, pressure maintenance programs, etc. For the whole period, therefore, development outlay post tax is reckoned at 83 percent of pretax, by the formula; $X = 1 - (0.34)(1 - 0.5) = 0.83$. The net present value is 63 percent of the gross saving. This is calculated by assuming that cost would otherwise be uniformly charged off over 25 years, and discounting at 10 percent. This would be worth 0.367 of an immediate payment, i.e. $1 - 0.367 = 0.633$. Then $0.17(0.63) = 0.11$, and development cost is reduced by 11 percent.

We have not made any adjustments to cost to allow for the effects of percentage depletion. That would be double counting, since the present value of percentage depletion is already reflected in the value of the developed reserve.

Source: Price, DOE/EIA, *Annual Energy Review 1986*, tab. 60. For 1946–1948, DeGolyer and McNaughton, *Twentieth Century Petroleum Statistics 1986*, page 99 (ultimate source DOE). Net price is gross less operating costs, royalties, and taxes excluding Federal income taxes but including Windfall Profits Tax after 1979: from Adelman (1991). Average ratio of net to gross during 1955–1980 was 0.644, standard deviation 0.016. The ratio of net to gross was considerably less, and fluctuated, in later years, so individual years' values are used. Data cease to be available after 1984. For 1985, we have used the 1981–1984 average. For 1986–1987, we have used the previous average. The difference is almost entirely in the Windfall Profits Tax, which

indicates that they have been useful, and used. Herold valuations are frequently quoted in the financial press, a more demanding use than ours.

Second we can test the reasonableness of the Herold annual averages by comparing them with our regression results, with an industry rule of thumb, and with altogether independent estimates of oil development cost. The details are in table 12.2.

In table 12.2, column (1) shows the average gross wellhead price of crude oil. Column (2) is an estimate of the price net of operating expenses, royalties, State severance taxes and the Windfall Profits Tax, which was an excise per barrel, not a profits tax. For 1955–1982, there are actual data on these deductions. Since the dispersion about the period mean is quite small, it seems safe to extend it forward and back.

Columns (3) and (4) show, respectively, the annual average and standard deviation of the Herold reserve valuations for the individual companies. We will use their relation to oil prices, and to oil development costs, to demonstrate user costs following equations (1)–(6).

5   Oil Reserve Values and Oil Prices

The One-third Rule   For many years, the industry has had a rule of thumb of in-ground value as one-third of the wellhead price, i.e., about one-half of the net price (ex-operating costs, royalties, and non-income taxes). Recall equation (8) above: if $a = Q/R$) and i are roughly equal, as has been true since World War II, then V should be approximately half of net P and one-third of gross P.

The one-third rule seems to agree well with our estimates. Column (3) is generally mildly lower than one third of column (1) before 1973, mildly higher afterward.

Reserve Asset Value as Predictor   In general, a long-lived asset rises in price when the market expects an increase in the prices of the goods in which the asset will be embedded through future production. Hence asset price changes are a leading indicator of product price changes.

As columns (9) and (10) show, reserve values in 1946–1972 failed to reflect higher prices to come. There is a clear shift in 1973. Higher percentages beginning that year were correct at least as to sign in predicting higher prices, through 1980.

The gradual weakening of prices in 1985, and collapse in 1986, are only partially reflected in value changes, and therefore columns (9) and (10) go to record heights. This reflects the expectation of a large price rise: false after 1985, true after 1986.

For a little more precision, we can re-write equation (8) above to allow for an expected price increase at some constant annual rate g:

$$V/P = a/(a + i - g),\tag{9}$$

$$g = i + a(1 - (P/V))\tag{10}$$

This measure is a residual, sensitive to errors in the discount rate, as well as in the estimated value. However, it seems to be of some help in interpreting fluctuations in recent years.[2]

Table 12.3 presents estimates of expected changes in wellhead price (net of extraction costs and taxes), in recent years, in percent per year. We have used the 12 percent discount which is conventional in the investment community. (Since expected inflation varied over those years, the time discount rate must have varied.) The implied forcasts were surprisingly good for oil. Prices were expected to decline during 1982–1985. The low prices of 1986 were not expected to last, and the anticipation of rising prices was borne out in 1987, when pessimism again took over and was justified the next year.

But for gas, the price forecasts were all too optimistic. Gas prices were expected to rise soon because a temporary surplus would disappear. Instead, the "gas bubble" become the "gas sausage." There is no sign of increasing gas prices, yet reserves have stabilized. This suggests that current prices induce enough investment to maintain reserves.

6 Reserve Values and Oil Development Costs

Returning to table 12.2, we now compare oil reserve values with development cost per barrel of newly-booked reserves. Since values are ex-tax, they should be compared with the post-tax development cost, column (7) of table 12.2. The sum of development drilling and non-drilling expenditures are divided by gross reserve-additions to give unit development cost.

To estimate finding cost per unit, corresponding to development cost per unit, would require knowledge of separate oil and gas finding expenditures. That is impossible because much or most finding cost is joint. Econometric analysis might give us marginal relations, but only with data on the amounts of oil and gas found year by year (not merely what has been developed into new proved reserves). No such numbers exist. The financial press frequently quotes "finding costs per barrel of oil-equivalent." This equals the sum of exploration plus development expenditures, oil and gas together, divided by increments to proved reserves, oil plus gas equiva-

Table 12.3
Oil and gas prices and reserve values, 1982–1990

Year	Net price	In-ground value	Ratio	$Q/R = a$	Discount rate	Implicit price forecast (change/yr)
Oil values ($/brl)						
1982	16.28	8.50	0.52	0.106	0.12	0.022
1983	15.43	7.10	0.46	0.109	0.12	−0.008
1984	16.67	6.80	0.41	0.106	0.12	−0.032
1985	13.80	7.50	0.54	0.108	0.12	0.028
1986	8.15	6.50	0.80	0.111	0.12	0.092
1987	9.927	5.10	0.51	0.105	0.12	0.019
1988	8.10	5.50	0.68	0.105	0.12	0.070
1989	10.21	5.10	0.50	0.105	0.12	0.015
1990 :1Q	11.44	3.80	0.33	0.105	0.12	−0.090
Gas values (c/mcf)						
1982	NA	1.20	NA	0.099	0.12	NA
1983	NA	1.30	NA	0.090	0.12	NA
1984	NA	1.10	NA	0.099	0.12	NA
1985	1.62	1.20	0.72	0.095	0.12	0.083
1986	1.11	0.90	0.81	0.088	0.12	0.099
1987	0.97	0.75	0.78	0.092	0.12	0.094
1988	1.13	0.80	0.71	0.092	0.12	0.082
1989	1.16	0.80	0.69	0.092	0.12	0.079
1990 :1Q	1.23	0.65	0.53	0.092	0.12	0.038

Sources: Oil prices, *Monthly Energy Review*. Gas prices are spot, from *National Gas Clearing House*, reprinted montly in *Oil & Gas Journal*; annual average. Reserve values are from *Scotia/OGJ Data Base*, classified as predominantly oil or predominantly gas, value rounded to nearest 10 cents. Q/R ratios, from *Basic Petroleum Data Book*. Discount rate assumed (usual published assumption in financial press).

Current $/brl

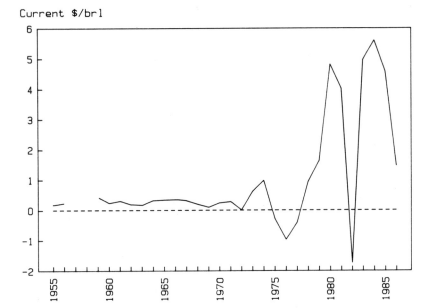

Figure 12.1
User cost (developed value less development cost), U.S. crude oil

lents. But not only does it omit newly-found undeveloped reserves, there
is no stable or necessary relation of oil to gas in respect of price, value,
or cost. "Finding cost per barrel of oil equivalent" amounts to adding
apples to oranges, then dividing by pineapples plus bananas. It deserves no
attention.

Following equation (1), figure. 12.1, from column 8 of table 12.2, shows
oil user cost. It is a surrogate for finding cost. In long-run equilibrium, they
should be equal.

The market value averaged 1.47 times development cost during 1955–
1973, and all observations were in the predicted range between 1.0 and 2.0.
During 1974–1986, the mean was 1.62 but the dispersion much greater.
This suggests that user cost/finding cost has been about one-half of development cost.

Before 1973, there was no upward trend in gross or net values, nor in
development cost as measured here (and also in an independent ordinal
measure (Adelman, 1991)). It may seem surprising that there was no increase in scarcity, nor in finding cost, in view of the well-known decrease
in average size of new fields found. But just as average size of new fields
discovered is a decreasing function of cumulative effort, knowledge is an
increasing function. The more wells drilled, the more physical infrastruc-

Tobin's Q

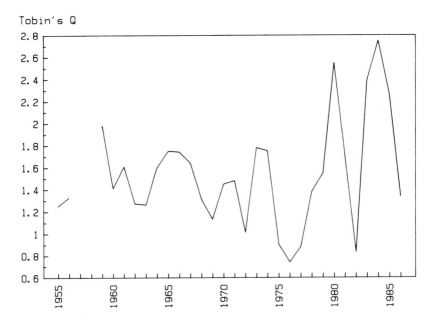

Figure 12.2
Value relative to development cost: crude oil, United States 1955–1986

ture, the better the technology, and the more is known about the geology of the proved and unproved areas, hence the more efficient the search process. It is a perpetual tug-of-war. An important qualification: development cost and market value stayed approximately constant because the strain on the system increased only very slowly. When the effort was stepped up, efficiency suffered greatly, both because poorer prospects were drilled, and because of the general waste of a frantic boom. (This separate analysis of movement along the curve and movement of the whole curve is pursued in Adelman, 1991.)

The recent report (AAPG, 1989) on reserves which might be developed under various price levels is in effect a forecast that the future will resemble the past. The process of wringing more oil out of old fields, which has dominated the industry since discoveries began dwindling in 1930, still has a long way to go.

7   An Application: 1976 User Cost in Saudi Arabia

For Saudi Arabia, 1973 development investment per daily barrel is given in one place at $147 (World Oil, 1973a), in another at $197 (PIW, 2-4-74:5, for capital expenditures; PIW, 5-14-73:6, for the increased capacity, which may be too low: see PIW, 4-22-74:12). Over the next three years, drilling factor prices rose by 58 percent (IPAA), so for 1976 we estimate $312 per daily barrel, or $0.854 per annual barrel. Production was 2 percent of proved reserves (*Oil & Gas Journal*, 1977). By equation (2), the investment to develop one additional barrel of reserves is $K/R = (K/Q)a = $0.854 \times 0.02 = 0.0170. Assuming fixed reserves, then by equation (6) the marginal development investment would be another 1.7 cents per barrel, and this is the maximum estimate of user cost.

We adjusted to the year 1976 because for that year the estimate can be compared with an independent observation: a market value for an undeveloped barrel, i.e. user cost. The 1976 buy-out agreement, between Arabian-American Oil Co. (Aramco) and the Saudi government, set a discovery fee for newly discovered (i.e. undeveloped) oil of 6 cents per barrel, as produced. We assume zero development time: upon discovery, depletion starts immediately, at the current Saudi 2 percent per year. Let U' be the value of the undeveloped barrel, and i the discount rate. Then the present value of the stream of fee payments of 6 cents per barrel would be:

$$U'R = (\$0.06)\,Q\int_0^T e^{-(a+i)t}\,dt = (\$0.06)Q/(a+i).$$

Substituting Q/a for R,

$$U' = (\$0.06)a/(a+i). \tag{11}$$

Assuming the discount rate alternatively at 5 and 20 percent:

$U' = 6(0.02)/0.07 = 1.71$ cents per barrel,

$U' = 6(0.02)/0.22 = 0.54$ cents per barrel.

Summing up: the estimated 1976 user cost, based on development cost, and on an actual transaction, are both in the neighborhood of one cent per barrel. The range of estimates is large relatively but tiny absolutely. No allowance for error can have an important effect on the result.

It should be no surprise that the fee was only 6 cents, and in-ground value no more than 2 cents, at a time when the world market price was over $12; market·price and in-ground value in the United States were respectively $8.19 (*Monthly Energy Review*) and $2.74. When marginal cost is very low, so is the optimal marginal revenue of a monopolist. Saudi reserves were superabundant. Beyond the very low production/reserve ratio in the 15 developed fields, there were 22 other commercial fields identified in 1976, but not operating (AAPG:B, 1977). In 1988, with 52 fields now identified, only the same 15 produced (Saudi Arabian Oil Company, 1989). Despite oil prices many times as high, Saudi oil well completions fell 96 percent from 1973 to 1988 (World Oil, 1974, 1989). Since Saudi Arabia was the only buyer, its marginal revenue set the value of new reserves. A higher discovery fee would have brought them more new-found oil, but for them it was not worth finding. (See also the discussion of Saudi Arabia below.)

This extraordinary gap in asset values is a symptom of the unbalanced world oil market, where low-cost reserves are kept out of production to maintain the price. Were the world oil monopoly to disappear, prices would fall to a fraction of their present levels. In-ground values and user cost in high-cost countries would decline sharply, and investment with them. But in low-cost areas there would be a burst of investment as the owners tried to save something from the wreck, and compensate for low prices by higher production. Reserves would expand, but production would expand much more, as the reserves/production ratio would rise toward the optimal, the industry rule of thumb being about 15. Development cost would rise, and so would the present value of a barrel in-ground. This would stimulate discovery, also at increasing cost.

At some point, rising values in the low-cost countries and falling values in the high-cost countries would come together, until a barrel in any country was worth the same as a barrel in any other. That would signal the end of the monopoly. It is not in view.

8   National Accounting

In recent years, work has been directed to estimating national income adjustments because of mineral production. On the usual assumptions, the question is well posed as: what accumulation of reproducible capital would just offset current production, which depletes some of the initial non-reproducible fixed stock? (Solow, 1986, p. 144).

El Serafy (in Ahmad et al., 1989) has devised a measure of user cost which is a special case of our equation (3). Consider a fully developed reservoir, with no production decline. Output Q and sales receipts PQ are constant over a finite time T, then shut off. The value of the reserve is the present value of the flow. The interest rate measures time preference of consumption, since there is no investment in the system and no risk. Now define the true income Y^* as a perpetual stream with the same present value.

$$Y^* \int_0^\infty e^{-it}\, dt = Y^*\Big/ i = PQ \int_0^T e^{-it}\, dt = PQ(1 - e^{-iT})\Big/ i,$$

$$Y^*/PQ = (1 - e^{iT}). \tag{12}$$

The fraction Y^*/PQ is the ratio of true income to apparent income. The user cost component or 'capital component' of the nominal stream PQ is

$$(1 - (Y^*/PQ)) = e^{-iT}. \tag{13}$$

"The unit of the total resource is the same as the current price."

Disregarding this (cf. above section 3), and some other untenable theses,[3] we apply his concept (using the lower 5 percent of his two suggested discount rates) to the large Persian Gulf oil producers for 1989. Obviously Y^* comes so close to PQ that the user cost component is negligible. (See table 12.4.)

Askari and Weitzman (Askari, 1990, including appendix I, by Martin L. Weitzman) also apply Solow's principle. They modify equation (10) by allowing P to increase by g percent per year, as in equation (8) above. Then we have

$$Y^* = iPQ[1 - e^{(i-g)T}]/(i - g). \tag{14}$$

As with El Serafy, there is no consideration of the decline rate a, nor of any investment cost factor k.

The Askari-Weitzman "base case" is where $g = i$, which is said to be "not a bad assumption empirically." It is very bad assumption empirically, but it is the standard Hotelling assumption. Let us apply it to equation (4):

Table 12.4
User cost component of sales receipts

Country	Reserves production ratio	User cost as percent of sales receipts discounted at[a]	
		5 percent	10 percent
Abu Dhabi	200	0	0
Iran	83	1.6	0
Iraq	100	0.7	0
Kuwait	167	0	0
Saudi Arabia	143	0	0

a. Percentages rounded to nearest tenth of one percent.
Sources: Reserve: production ratios from Oil & Gas Journal, December 25, 1989. User cost factors from El Serafy (in Ahmad et al. (1989, table 3-2, p. 15)).

$$2ka^3 + 4ka^2(i - g) + 2ka(i - g)^2 - P(i - g) = 0 \qquad (4')$$

If $i = g$, the optimal depletion rate $a = 0$. This is entirely logical. If the value of the asset grows at the same rate as the return on future receipts gained from investing today, there is no reason to invest.

Returning to equation (14), where $g = i$, Y^* is indeterminate, 0/0. Weitzman avoids this by using L'Hôpital's rule, taking the first derivative with respect to g of the numerator and the first derivative of the denominator. At the limit $(i = g)$,

$$Y^* = iPQT, \quad \text{or} \quad Y^*/PQ = iT = iR/Q. \qquad (15)$$

Table 12.5 applies Weitzman's formula to recent years. For example, in 1989 conditions, if the real rate of return is 3 percent (as against El Serafy's 5 percent), the true or permanent income is actually four times as large as conventional income.

In general, if $i(R/Q)$ (the discount rate times the reserve/production ratio) exceeds unity, the conventional national product understates the theoretically correct value. For example, with $i = 0.03$, the critical value is $R/Q = 33$.

Askari (1990, p. 16, ch. IV, p. 182) and Weitzman (in Askari, 1990, p. 198) argue that a higher rate than 1 percent is a better choice. At a modest 3 percent, which they themselves use, their thesis is overturned. For in every large OPEC country the reserve/production ratio exceeds 33, and true NNP necessarily exceeds conventional NNP. Applying equation (12), Saudi 1989 user cost is a large negative: $1 - (Y^*/P) = 1 - 1(1/0.24) = -3.2$, or negative \$3.20 for every dollar of conventional income.

Table 12.5
Saudi Arabia: Ratio of conventional to true national product[a]

Year	Reserves/ production	Assumed real rate of return (pct/year)	
		1%	3%
1981	46	2.17	0.72
1982	71	1.41	0.47
1983	102	0.98	0.33
1984	113	0.88	0.29
1989	143	0.71	0.24

a. Reserves and production, *Oil & Gas Journal*, last issue of year. Estimation formula, Weitzman in Askari (1990, App. I, eq. (16)).

This odd result should not be taken too seriously, since it derives from the particular assumption that $g = i$. The important point is that the ratio Y^*/PQ and the user cost $(1 - Y^*/PQ)$ may be positive or negative, much or little, depending on the parameters.

El Serafy, Askari, and Weitzman disregard investment in oil, a procedure which follows logically from the original premise of a fixed stock, which is "running out."[4] But even on that premise, one might ask: why do these asset holders keep such excessive in-ground inventory that it has, at the margin, no present value, and makes the national product less than it could be? Far from having long horizons and low rates of time preference: all but Kuwait have for years overspent their incomes, which was one reason for the Iraqi aggression in 1980 and 1990.

Be that as it may, the large OPEC producers have negligible (or negative) user cost. The massive gap between price and operating-cum-development cost remains unexplained. The calculations of El Serafy and Askari and Weitzman support the hypothesis that these producers are holding production off the market in order to maintain the price; i.e., are acting as a cartel.[5]

Indonesia

The valuation by Repetto et al. (1989) of 1984 Indonesian oil reserves at $24 per barrel in-ground is the market price, net of operating cost, undiscounted. They must assume, with El Serafy that: "The unit value of the total resource is the same as the current price."

We now attempt a measure for 1989. Up to this point, we have only considered private values of reserves. In the United States, because oil profits are relatively lightly taxed, this does not involve any serious distortion. Elsewhere, it does. Table 12.6 makes the adjustment.

We take as average values $8 for oil and 75 cents for gas, halfway between the new lightly taxed hydrocarbon and the old heavily taxed and higher-cost. Then we can calculate the total or social addition or subtraction during the year 1989 (see table 12.7).

Indonesia gained, on balance, $2.5 billions in 1989. Almost everywhere in the world outside North America, proved reserves have increased; hence true NNP exceeds conventional NNP (see table 12.8).

Producer Country Policies

If we discard the fixed-stock assumption, we can see how overestimation of in-ground values and user costs has been costly to many countries. They

Table 12.6
Indonesia: 1990 public and private values

	New oil		Old oil	
	Wellhead price	In-ground value	Wellhead price	In-ground value
A. Oil: $/barrel				
Private share	10	5	5	1
Public share	8	4[a]	13	6[a]
Total	18	9	18	7
B. Natural gas: $/mcf				
	New gas		Old gas	
	Wellhead price	In-ground value	Wellhead price	In-ground value
Private share	0.94	0	1.23	0.09
Public share	0.76	0.37[a]	1.23	0.56[a]
Total	1.7	0.84	1.7	0.65

a. Inferred: assumes same ratio of value to price on public as on private new (low-cost) oil.
Sources: *Panel A*—Johnston (1990). *Panel B*—Prices from *World Gas Intelligence*, 6-90-13. Rest of table assumes same tax treatment as oil, in panel A.

Table 12.7
Indonesia: Change in values of oil and gas reserves, 1989

	Increment to reserves	Unit value	Change in value (in million $)
Oil	− 50 million barrels	$8.00	−$400
Gas	+ 3.43 trillion cu ft	$0.75	+$2,916
Total	—	—	+$2,515

Source: *Oil & Gas Journal*, end-of-year issues for 1988 and 1989.

Table 12.8
Net change in oil reserves and values, end-year 1988 to end-year 1989

Area	Increment (MB)	Unit value ($)	Value ($B)
U.S.A.	−640	6.25	−4.0
Canada	−653	5.00	−3.3
Other market economies, ex OPEC	+11,021	4.00	+44.1

Sources: Reserves changes from *International Oil and Gas Exploration and Development Activities*, fourth quarter 1989 (Department of Energy, 1990). Unit values from First Boston Corporation, *Oil and Gas Exploration and Production*, OL 0675, March 21, 1990. N.B. These values are private; complete or social values are larger, as calculated in the Indonesian example above.

demanded too much for oil exploration/development rights, hence lost revenue they might have received. Moreover, by supposing a fixed stock of mineral wealth, they were careless of contract obligations because they overlooked the role of investment in creating new wealth.

The higher the discount rate, the lower the present value of an existing barrel. I have suggested (Adelman, 1986) that in oil investment small less-developed countries (LDCs) have much higher discount rates than do private multinational companies (cf. Vaish, 1990). If so, a given oil development is more valuable to a private company than to an LDC, and we would expect to see a drift toward allowing companies some oil development rights in countries which had previously nationalized their oil. The movement is now perceptible in nearly all OPEC countries (as well as the Soviet Union and China) (PIW 7–16–90; Special Supplement). It is going very slowly, and may not make much difference soon, but is worth study.

9   Conclusions

(1) There is no fixed mineral stock, only an uncertain flow into mineral inventories, "proved reserves."
(2) Mineral reserves are risky assets, like all other reproducible wealth. Capital markets do as good or bad a job of valuing them as they do other assets.
(3) User cost or resource rent, the market value of an undeveloped reserve unit in-ground, is a valid measure of mineral scarcity.
(4) This value is rarely observed directly. But it equals the market value of a developed reserve less the development investment, *or* the present value of changes in investment required per unit of reserves. At the margin the two are equal.
(5) Adjustments to Net National Product, to allow for the depletion of mineral assets, are like any other adjustments for inventory change. They may in theory be large or small, positive or negative. Oil inventory changes appear to be relatively small, and mostly positive. A fortiori, this is true for coal; and probably for most minerals.
(6) User cost explains none of the price-development cost gap for Persian Gulf crude oils. Monopoly is the only tenable explanation offered thus far.

Appendix A: Recent Coal Reserve Sales

A   Payment of $715 million, for 55 percent of the assets of Peabody Coal Co., reported as producing 9 percent of coal produced in the United States, with reserves at about 100 years at current rates (*Wall Street Journal*, 3-30-90; A10). Using 1989 coal production from MER (January 1990, p. 69) and 1988 minemouth prices from DOE (1988, p. 191), one may calculate as follows:

$$\text{Value per ton in-ground} = \frac{\$715\ m}{975 \times 0.09 \times 100 \times 0.55} = \$0.148/\text{ton}.$$

Value/minemouth price = $0.148/$22 = 0.0067.

B Payment of $115 million for "more than 390 million tons of saleable coal reserves." Revenes in 1989 were $380 million on sales of 14.1 million tons. (New York Times, 5-26-90; 31). Then value per ton in ground was $0.295, value/price was 0.011, and reserves were 27.7 times annual output.

These data are unfortunately subject to rather gross errors. But no allowance for them could increase the ratios by 30 times to be near equality with the ratios for oil.

Appendix B: Gain or Loss to Postponement

Restating equation (3) as a quadratic:

$$a = \sqrt{Pi/2ka} - i. \tag{A.1}$$

To restate net present value as a function of time, we take the depletion rate as predetermined. The net present value of the project initiated in any later year t is

$$VR(t) = [(PQ\,e^{gt}/(a + i - g)) - kaQ]e^{it}$$

$$= [(PQ/(a + i - g)]e^{(g-i)t} - kaQ\,e^{-it}. \tag{A.2}$$

In a fully developed deposit, or in a very low-cost pool, with almost no investment, the negative term approaches zero. Then aside from the unlikely case of the price increase g exceeding the interest rate i, the higher is t, the less is VR. Postponement is unprofitable.

At the other extreme is a project which would barely repay the cost of capital, i.e., $PQ/(a + i - g) = kaQ$, and $VR(0) = 0$:

$$VR(t) = PQ/(a + i - g)[e^{(g-i)t} - e^{-it}]. \tag{A.3}$$

For any positive value of t, the bracketed expression is positive, $VR(t)$ exceeds zero, and it pays to postpone. Waiting raises the expected revenues, but not the needed investment. Therefore a "dog" of a project is always worth postponing, and has only option value.

To find the optimal time to postponement, we rewrite (A.2) and differentiate with respect to t:

$$VR(t) = [PO/(a + i - g)e^{gt} - kaQ]e^{-it}$$

$$= PQ/(a + i - g)e^{(g-i)t} - kaQ\,e^{-it},$$

$$d(VR(t))/dt = [PQ/(a + i - g)](g - i)e^{(g-i)t} + kaQ(i\,e^{-it}) = 0.$$

Divide by $-Q(i - g)e^{-it}$.

$$-P/(a + i - g)\frac{(g - i)}{(i - g)}e^{(g-i)t}/e^{-it} = kai\,e^{-it}/i - g(e^{-it}).$$

Cancelling $P/(a + i - g)e^{gt} = kai/i - g,$

$$e^{gt} = \frac{k\,ai(a + i - g)}{P\quad i - g},$$

$$t = [(\ln k - \ln P) + \ln a + \ln i + \ln(a + i - g) - \ln(i - g)]/g. \qquad (A.4)$$

The lower is the cost factor k, the less the postponement. Good projects should not wait. Negative t means project should have commenced before year 0. Saudi t runs to negative decades.

As for the derivative, only the last two terms in (A.4) are terms in g. Hence:

$$dt/dg = \left[\frac{g1(-1)}{(a + i - g)} - \ln(a + i - g)(1)\right]\Big/g^2$$

$$- \left[\frac{g1(-1)}{(i - g)} - \ln(i - g)(1)\right]\Big/g^2,$$

$$dt/dg = \left[\frac{g}{(i - g)} - \frac{g}{(a + i - g)} + \ln(i - g) - \ln(a + i - g)\right]\Big/g^2.$$

Note that $g(i - g)$ must always exceed $g(a + i - g)$, while $\ln(i - g)$ must always exceed $\ln(a + i - g)$, and since both are negative the algebraic sum must be negative. Hence the first two terms sum to a positive, the second pair to a negative. But as g increases, the positive terms increase, the negative terms decrease in absolute values, so all terms increase algebraically. Hence while dt/dg may possibly be negative at small values of g, it must be positive as g increases.

The equation works empirically: if we take any likely values, and calculate values from (A.4), t varies directly with g, and first differences are always positive.

Notes

This is a revised version of the authors' "The Valuation of Oil Reserves," Society of Petroleum Engineers' Paper 18906. The research has been supported by the National Science Foundation, grant no. SES-8412971, and by the Center for Energy Policy Research of the M.I.T. Energy Laboratory. The help of John C. Lohrenz, Michael C. Lynch, Rachel E. Obstler, G. Campbell Watkins, and Martin L. Weitzman is gratefully acknowledged. But any opinions, findings, conclusions or recommendations expressed herein are those of the authors, and do not necessarily reflect the views of the NSF or of any other person or group.

1. If the expected rate of price increase exceeds (is less than) the discount rate, it pays owners to hold ore off the market (offer more ore), until the current price rises (declines) to where the two rates are equal.

2. Verleger (1990) has analyzed a royalty trust issued by British Petroleum Company. Its current market value contains an implicit forecast of the future price of crude oil, given assumptions about inflation and interest rates. He concludes (p. 12) that "investors do not expect increases in oil prices to exceed the rate of inflation in the near future." The price spike of July–August 1990 was due to an unexpected restraint on supply.

3. (1) "[T]he oil market had long been an oligopsonistic market, dominated by powerful multinational conglomerates" (12). This implies prices below some long-run competitive level. But the multinational companies were *sellers* not buyers, whose interest was in higher not lower prices, both to increase profits, and to decrease domestic political threats from European coal miners and USA oil producers.

(2) OPEC allegedly did not restrict competition, because they had no formal market allocation until 1982. (Actually, there was one in 1980.) Thus the private oligopolists could affect prices without formal market division, but the sovereign oligopolists, even more concentrated than the private, cannot. He does not explain this double standard.

(3) "... [M]any analysts in the 1970s appeared to think that if free competition were to prevail, competitive equilibrium would indicate a price equal to the marginal cost of *extraction* ..." (page 12, emphasis in original). He cites none of the "many," and it is doubtful that he can find even one.

4. Both El Serafy and Askari err in supposing that production can proceed at a constant rate then abruptly cease. The decline rate stands at the center of every reservoir engineering calculation. Moreover, the rate of extraction is limited by sharply rising marginal costs (Adelman 1990). However, this correction would not basically change the problem.

5. Like El Serafy, Askari believes (p. 28) that before 1970 "the majors [multinational oil companies] kept oil prices at what may be considered artificially low levels." He does not explain why they should act against their own interests. Askari's policy prescription of a high savings rate makes good sense, if we disregard the "depletable nature of oil" as an un-fact, and instead accept that monopoly prices are inherently unstable and may drop sharply.

References

(Periodicals cited by name, month-day-year: page)

Adelman, M. A., 1986, Discount rates for oil producing nations, Resources and Energy 8, 309–329.

Adelman, M. A., 1990, Mineral depletion, with special reference to petroleum, Review of Economics and Statistics 72, Feb., 1–10.

Adelman, M. A., 1991, Finding and development costs in the USA, 1945–86, in: John R. Moroney, Advances in the economics of energy and resources (JAI Press, Greenwich, CT), forthcoming.

Adelman, M. A., H. De Silva and M. F. Koehn, 1989, The valuation of oil reserves, Paper 18906 (Society of Petroleum Engineers, Richardson, TX).

Ahmad, Yusuf J., Salah El Serafy, Ernst Lutz, 1989, Environmental accounting for sustainable development, a UNEP-World Bank Symposium (World Bank, Washington, DC).

American Association of Petroleum Geologists, Bulletin (AAPG: B) 1977, Vol. 61, monthly 1798.

American Association of Petroleum Geologists (AAPG), 1989, Report of the Committee on the Resource Base (AAPG, Tulsa, OK).

Askari, Hossein, 1990, Saudi Arabia's economy: Oil and the search for economic development, including Appendix I, Net national product for an exhaustible resource economy, by Martin L. Weitzman (JAI Press, Greenwich, CT).

Bradley, Howard B., ed., 1987, Petroleum engineering handbook (Society of Petroleum Engineers, Richardson, TX).

Bradley, Paul G., 1989, Remarks to the national energy board workshop on benefit-cost analysis and export impact assessment, Calgary, 27 Nov.

Dasgupta, Partha and G.M. Heal, 1979, Economic theory and exhaustible resources, Cambridge Economic Handbooks (Cambridge University Press, Cambridge).

Department of Energy, DOE, various years, Annual energy review (Department of Energy, Washington, DC).

Department of Energy, DOE, various years, Monthly Energy Review (MER) (Department of Energy, Washington, DC).

Frick, Thomas, ed., 1962, Petroleum production handbook (McGraw-Hill Books, New York).

Griffin, James M., 1985, OPEC behavior: A test of alternative hypotheses, American Economic Review 80, 954–963.

Hotelling, Harold, 1931, The economics of exhaustible resources, Journal of Political Economy 39, 137–175.

Independent Petroleum Association of America (IPAA), various years, Report of the Cost Study Committee, twice yearly.

Johnston, Daniel, 1990, How Indonesian production sharing contracts work, Offshore, July, 42–44.

Kmenta, J., 1984, Elements of econometrics (Macmillan, New York).

Miller, Merton H. and Charles W. Upton, 1985, A test of the Hotelling valuation principle, Journal of Political Economy 93, Feb., 1–25.

Nordhaus, William D., 1973, The allocation of energy resources, Brookings Papers on Economic Activity, no. 3.

Oil and Gas Journal, various years, weekly, annual supplement World Wide Oil, last issue of year.

Petroleum Intelligence Weekly (PIW), various years, various issues.

Repetto, Robert, William Magrath, Michael Wells, Christine Beer, Fabrizio Rossini, 1989, Wasting assets: Natural resources in the national income accounts (World Resources Institute, Washington, DC).

Saudi Arabian Oil Company, 1989, Annual report 1988, 5.

Solow, Robert M., 1986, On the intergenerational allocation of natural resources, Scandinavian Journal of Economics 88, no. 1, 141–149.

Vaish, Pankaj, 1990, Appropriate discount rates for crude oil cashflows of the OPEC members: Saudi Arabia, Kuwait and Venezuela, Unpublished M.S. thesis (Sloan School of Management, MIT, Cambridge, MA).

Verleger, Philip K., Jr., 1990, Reading the tea leaves in a tempestuous tea pot, in: CRA Petroleum Economics Monthly 7, no. 5, May.

World Bank, 1988, World development report (World Bank, Washington, DC).

World Oil, 1973a, Monthly, April, p. 15.

World Oil, 1973b, International Oil, August issue.

13   Modelling World Oil Supply

Introduction

Modelling supply in the world oil market presents two special problems. First, oil is a mineral. Analysis and data-gathering have been distorted by the myth of "limited resources": the quest for non-existent fixed stocks and the neglect of flows.

Second, supply is unlike demand. The amount of oil demanded results from the independent choices of millions of households and firms. A higher price means less is demanded, a lower price means more. But a few governments make the most important supply decisions. The higher the price, the less the OPEC nations produce. Even non-OPEC countries do not respond in any simple positive way to price changes. Moreover, cartel control makes the system *unstable*. Small changes may bring large results; movements are often cumulative and self-reinforcing.

The Current Consensus and Its Implicit Major Premise

Price changes are caused by the pressure of demand upon "limited supply." Prices rose when the market became "tight," then fell because of a "glut" which must in time disappear. Indeed some models are explicitly cyclical: too low a price once caused deficient investment and output, hence higher prices, which drew in too much investment to bring down prices to the current "low" level, and so on (World Bank 1989) (Hogan 1989). The market will again tighten in the 1990s, as the pressure of rising consumption presses against reserves dwindling everywhere but the Persian Gulf.

Competition or monopoly make only a minor difference. Long-term, the price must rise in any case because oil is a "nonrenewable resource."

Reprinted from *The Energy Journal* (special issue in memory of David O. Wood) 14 (1993)

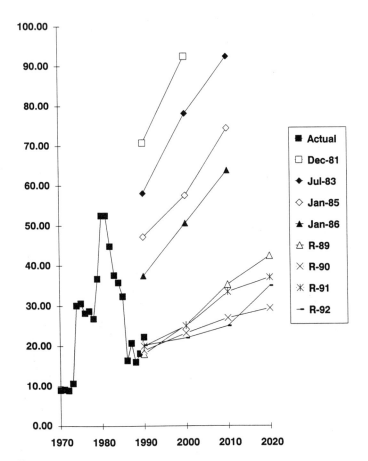

Figure 13.1
Crude oil prices (1990 $/barrel) actual and successive IEM polls

The monopoly price is at first higher than the competitive, but it rises more slowly, and in the long-run it is little different (Heal and Dasgupta, chap. 6). Indeed on some plausible assumptions there is no difference at any time.

Figure 13.1 embodies the consensus. Each forecast starts from the current price, and rises. Year after year, as the current price itself declined, the whole profile was displaced downward. But the forecast remained forever upward.

There are two basic assumptions: (1) The current price is the long-run competitive price, plus an error of estimate. A drop in the current price merely shows that the starting level was too high, an error now corrected.

(2) The long-run competitive price must rise because of inherent growing scarcity. Both assumptions are wrong.

A Contrary View

The price has no relation to scarcity, present or future. Long-term marginal cost, even with an excessive allowance for resource rent or user cost, remains a small fraction of the price. To support that price, the excess supply is restricted by a cartel. This creates constant tension, hence the volatility since 1970.

Oil Supply in Theory

The Essential Difference

In manufacturing, the inventory of input materials is on the average about six weeks' production. In oil, the rough rule-of-thumb optimum for proved reserves is 15 years. The industry spends billions of dollars every year to replenish the inventory. Replacement cost is the measure of scarcity.

There are not fixed stocks of resources, only flows of reserve-additions. If the cost of locating and extracting mineral for inventory exceeds the expected market price, investment dries up and the industry disappears. What's left in the ground is unknown, an economic zero. There is no such thing as "limited resources." The amount of any mineral in the earth is an irrelevant non-binding constraint.

We cannot rescue the concept of a fixed mineral stock by making it "the economic portion" of the unknown total in the ground. That is circular reasoning. For the "economic portion" depends on future costs and prices. One cannot estimate costs and prices by starting with their result. The "economic portion" is a forecast, an implicit unverifiable prediction of how much inventory will be worth creating and using. Estimates of "ultimate production" are useful only to expose varying assumptions on incidence and cost.

Over the years, estimates grow with knowledge. In 1944, Middle East proved reserves were estimated at 15 billion barrels; in 1984, at 398 billion (OGJ-WWO 1984, p. 5). The U.S. Geological Survey (USGS 1987) estimated a 5 percent probability that total resources were as much as 620 billion barrels, i.e., another 222 billion barrels remaining to be discovered and developed. By end-1989, 23 billion barrels had been produced since 1984, and proved reserves were 654 billion barrels, or 279 billion added in

all. The event with near zero probability over many years had been surpassed in five.[1] In the United States, the maximum ultimate recovery of the
largest fields was actually surpassed in 15 years (Nehring 1981, OGJ-RF
1991).

Prices "Should Rise," and Do Not

The assumption of an initial fixed mineral stock is not only wrong but
superfluous. All else being equal, the replacement cost of any mineral
should constantly increase over time, and the price with it. First, the average size of new-found deposits should constantly decrease. The biggest
would be found first even by chance, let alone by design. Second, the
better, i.e., lower cost mineral should be used up first.

Yet prices of minerals have not risen. Practically all have been flat or
actually declining in the long-run.[2] The argument among econometricians
is whether we must reject or accept a long-term downward trend for
minerals prices. Long-term increase is not even in question. All else has not
been equal. Mineral depletion is in fact an endless tug-of-war: diminishing
returns versus increasing knowledge. So far, the human race has won big.
This need not continue. We need to look at each mineral separately, and
monitor the amount and cost of the flow of reserve additions.

Worldwide Investment Requirements per Daily Barrel

Supply consists of the cost of maintaining and expanding inventory: the
investment per additional reserve barrel or per additional unit of producing
capacity. Basic data, never plentiful, are getting more scarce.[3] In 1966, my
original paper was carefully examined and its findings accepted by company experts (PPS vol. 43, pp. 177–179). That would be impossible today,
now that the companies have left the main producing areas.

The investment coefficient has recently been about $13,000 per daily
barrel in the U.K. North Sea and $11,000 in the United States. (An appen-
dix with complete data is available from the author.) Table 13.1, whatever
the inevitable errors of estimation, shows that the OPEC nations are in a
different world. The investment usually pays out in weeks. Only in Indonesia, where it is clearly overstated, does it take more than six months.[4]

There have been some estimates of OPEC investment requirements over
$12,000 per daily barrel. They should simply be laughed out of court. That
they have not been tells us much about the level of discussion. The U.S.
Department of Energy has contributed also.

Table 13.1
Investment per additional daily barrel of capacity ($): Ten OPEC nations, 1985–1990

Country	1985	1986	1987	1988	1989/90
Abu Dhabi	2912	2110	2229	2850	2033
Algeria	4570	4648	4401	6641	3533
Indonesia	5908	5391	2739	2966	5637
Iran	NA	NA	271	2362	1433
Iraq	NA	NA	NA	231	145
Kuwait	1455	151	533	1785	895
Libya	24199	13969	9528	NA	NA
Nigeria	3179	5097	6794	NA	2611
Qatar	1331	1131	0	1556	1408
Saudi Arabia	692	357	596	492	373

The dispersion among marginal investment factors shows that the world industry cannot be competitive. Under competition, marginal rates of return tend to equality. Each producer expands up to the point where further expansion would not pay. That is how long-term incremental cost approaches the price.

There must be some powerful restraint on the expansion of the lower-cost producers.[5]

Comparisons over time show the same block. Before 1973, for example, drilling expanded rapidly in Saudi Arabia and contracted in the United States. The lower-cost source was gradually displacing the higher cost. Then, in response to higher prices, wells drilled in the United States tripled, while in Saudi Arabia they fell by as much as 95 percent. Among the OPEC nations, the lowest-cost producers have cut back the most, an additional symptom of cartel control.

Hotelling: Paradigm, Rule, Valuation Principle

The grip of the rising-price paradigm is remarkable. The 1973 price explosion was forthwith greeted by economists, and not the least distinguished, as the long-delayed inevitable surge. Market control was a surface phenomenon. Temporary deflecting forces had just happened to keep all mineral prices flat or declining. Oil is growing more scarce, and the price must continue to rise.

For some (e.g., World Bank 1988), the sudden price increase proved that the multinational oil companies had been holding the price down artificially low. Hegemon America controlled the market until the Third World expelled it. In fact, the U.S. government supported higher prices; there was a slow reluctant retreat by the oil companies, for whom lower prices meant smaller profits and greater political dangers from domestic oil and coal producers.

A great structure of theory, and calculation forms an upside-down pyramid, resting on a single point. Arrow (1987, p. 670) notes that Hotelling "applied the calculus of variations to the problem of allocation of a fixed stock over time. All of the recent literature ... is essentially based on Hotelling's paper" (Hotelling 1931). The initial fixed stock was simply assumed.

Heal and Dasgupta (1979, p. 158) stated the "Hotelling Rule" as: $g = i$, where 'g' = the annual growth rate of the "net price" (net of cost) and 'i' = the interest rate. Several econometric studies sought to prove that there was some such relation, for some metals. Miller and Upton (1985a) showed that the studies' data and econometrics were inadequate for any conclusion. Accordingly they restated the Rule as the "Hotelling Valuation Principle." In-ground unit value V had to equal the net price P:

$$V(0) = P(t)e^{-it} = P(0)e^{-(i-g)t} = P(0) \tag{1}$$

This elegant formula was verified, they thought, by their study of oil company market values, with non-reserve assets backed out. But their second data set yielded estimates of V/P closer to 0.5 (Miller and Upton 1985b).[6]

We state the relation by first recognizing an oil or gas reserve as cumulated production, decreasing at an annual rate 'a':

$$R = Q \int_0^T e^{-at}\, dt = \frac{Q}{a} \tag{2}$$

The reserve value is subject to a compound discount factor:

$$RV = PQ \int_0^T e^{-(a+i-g)t}\, dt = \frac{PQ}{(a+i+g)} \tag{3}$$

Substituting from (3), multiplying both sides by a/Q, and rearranging:

$$g = i + a[1 - (P/V)] \tag{4}$$

The Hotelling Valuation Principle (1) is a special testable case of (4). If in fact, $V = P$, then 'a' vanishes, and $g = i$. The evidence is all to the contrary.

First, it is generally accepted in the engineering literature that the higher the value of 'a', the higher is V/P, which, however, never approaches unity (Bradley 1987). This makes the $g = i$ equality doubtful at best.

A closer test of the HVP: For many years, an industry rule of thumb has been that in-ground value of a developed reserve is one-third of wellhead price, or about one-half of price (net of operating costs, royalties, and taxes). This is confirmed by a series from 1947 through 1986, where V/P fluctuates around a value of 0.5, but never approaches unity. In addition, if a and i are approximately equal, as they were for a long time, then $g = 0$, which would have been a good forecast for that time. Regression analysis of actual sales of reserves during the 1980s confirms values around $0.5P$ (Adelman et al. 1991, p. 10). A study of Canadian reserve sales in 1989–91 shows that $(V/P = 1)$ is several standard deviations away from actual (Watkins 1992). A regression of those Canadian reserve sales (Adelman and Watkins 1992), and in several countries in 1988–89 shows V as ranging from less than half to about three-fourths of P. Moreover, the calculated price change expected is flat for oil and positive for gas. This accords with contemporaneous opinion.

The Hotelling Rule and Hotelling Valuation Principle are thoroughly discredited. A valid theory was joined to a wrong premise, the fixed stock. It gave results contrary to fact.

The Hotelling Contribution: "Scarcity" A Measurable Present Value

Once we discard the false assumption of a limited stock, we can see Hotelling's great contribution: to reduce the vague notion of "resource scarcity" to an observable economic fact: the present value of a unit of inventory, subject to the same errors as any other asset values. When over a long period there is no up-creep in the market values there is no increase in scarcity.[7]

Asset value can be defined as the smallest penalty which the oil operator must pay to use up a unit today instead of holding it for the future. The various penalties are all substitutes. Change in one is a proxy for change in another.

The penalty is defined by the basic fact of the oil or gas production decline curve, usually caused by declining pressure, but possibly also by water intrusion into edge wells or lower-horizon wells as production depletes the lighter oil or gas on top. A given reserve yields a decreasing flow. If nothing were done, in time production would cease.

In a given reservoir, let $V =$ the unit in-ground value, $D =$ its development investment, and $U =$ its user cost (or resource rent, etc.). Then $V = D + U$. Let us make the extreme assumption that additional reserves and capacity could be provided by additional investment, at the same per-unit amount as the last increment. The value of the asset oil-in-ground could not exceed the development investment per unit, since another unit could always be provided at that cost. If so, $V = D$, and $U = 0$.

At the other extreme, assume it is impossible to add reserves. The operator can invest only to accelerate production. Then as proved in the appendix, note 1 (available from the author), development cost will be approximately doubled. Then $V = D + U = 2D$, and $D = U$. User cost would just equal development cost *if* there were no alternative way of expanding capacity.

But, of course, there are many more alternatives along the spectrum: create more reserves in a partly developed reservoir; develop a previously known but undeveloped reservoir; search for new reservoirs in old fields; for new fields in old "plays," new "plays" in old basins, and finally in new basins. Most of the effort will be in adjacent deposits or strata, and bring an externality of more knowledge. The industry is a giant scanner, to provide new reserves and capacity from the cheapest available source.

An alternative to any of these investment types is simply to purchase reserves. Thus the market value of an existing reserve barrel serves as a standard for the any and all type of investment to create reserves.

Equality at the Margins

User Cost, Development Cost Increase, Discovery, Purchase

Finding cost, user cost, and the increase in development cost, are all penalties for developing, not holding. They are proxies for each other. An increase in any of them is an upward tug on the others. Higher value makes profitable more development and exploration, driving up the respective marginal costs until they equate with values. Since this takes time, leads and lags are always present to distort. *The early-warning signal of scarcity is a persistent rise in development cost and in the in-ground value of oil reserves.* Appendix, note 3 (available from the author) gives development cost calculation in sometimes tedious detail. And oil reserve values are as uncertain as other market signals.[8]

"Backstop Technology"

Another marginal equality is with the supply price of an assumed "backstop technology," i.e., a higher-cost alternative in unlimited supply. It is necessary to estimate prices, demand relations, and consumption, to calculate the time when the rising cost of the superior resource will finally exceed the backstop supply price. That price, discounted to the present, is the present value of a unit of the current stock. It is another marginal equality, like the three sketched earlier. But it is highly unreliable. Nearly all the parameters must be invented out of thin air. Estimates are very sensitive to time factors and discount rates.

The United States as a Test of Marginal Equivalence

The United States is the oldest, largest, and most intensively exploited area, with good proved reserve numbers. The oil *discovery* peak was just before 1930, and as of 1988, half of "lower 48" oil is in fields discovered before 1945 (DOE/EIA 1990). Yet the amount of annual reserves-added first rose, then was fairly steady for over 43 years after the discovery peak, and only became ragged after 1973—the start of a frantic wasteful drilling boom.

Proved reserves in 1930 were 13 billion barrels; in 1990, 20 billion (ex-Alaska). But in the meantime, 124 billion had been added and used; the inventory has turned over nine times thus far. Large field discoveries dwindled but many small ones continued to be found; more important was the continuing expansion of old fields. Discovery is like R & D—the French call both *recherche*. Once something is found, development investment provides reserves. Unit development cost per barrel of reserves-added was stable for 1955–73, then fluctuated and is today about three times 1973.

A different approach is by way of:

$$P = e^{aR} - 1 \quad \text{or} \quad a = \ln(P + 1)/R \tag{5}$$

where P is the current price, in a competitive industry equal to the supply price; R the year's addition to reserves; and 'a' the coefficient of the exponential supply curve. A persistent increase over time in the coefficient 'a' would show a leftward shift of the supply curve. In fact there is stability 1947–73, and the same increase afterward. There is as yet no way of telling how much of the increase was due to the boom, and how much to mineral depletion.

United States: Test of the Relation of Reserve Value to Development Cost

In theory, the value of the oil in a developed reserve is the sum of development cost plus user cost, i.e., $V = D + U$, and the value of U is between

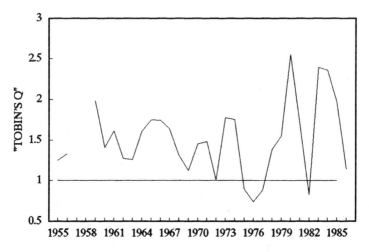

Figure 13.2
Value relative to development cost crude oil, United States 1955–1986

zero and D; the value of V is from D to $2D$. With many projects under way, the average value should fluctuate around $1.5D$. This has been the actual case.

The relation of market value of a reserve barrel to development cost is a special case of "Tobin's q." It fluctuates around a mean not of unity but of about 1.5, since replacement cost is limited to development cost. On average, that is, in the United States over a long period, user cost has been fairly stable at about one-half of development cost.

The in-ground value of a barrel was about 75 cents in 1948. In the next 22 years, the GNP deflator increased by a factor of 1.78. Had the value increased at real 3% per year, it would have been $2.56 in 1970, i.e., $.75 × 1.78 × 1.92. In fact, it was $.81 (Adelman 1992a).

Finding Cost Unknown

There are good estimates of exploration expenditures, but oil and gas are combined; and there is nothing on the amount found in any given year. "Discoveries" is a rank misnomer; it consists of what has been developed out of new fields and pools during the year. It takes years to learn the contents of a new-found pool or field, and the learning curve is highly variable as to level, slope, and terminal. Hence it is usually impossible to know the unit cost of newly-found oil or gas[9] (NRC 1985). User cost, as calculated above, is a surrogate for finding cost. To lump together gas/oil

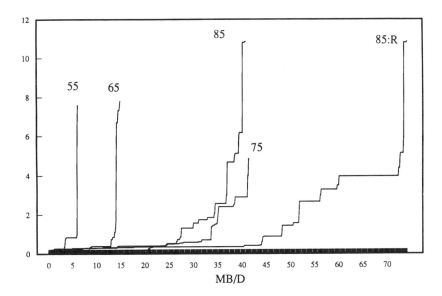

Figure 13.3
NCW supply curve
1955, 1965: Actual production—all countries, excluding North America and North Sea
1975, 1985: Non-OPEC—actual productions; OPEC—capacity
1985: R: Non-OPEC—actual 1985 production; OPEC—5% of 1985 year-end reserves

exploration expenditures with development expenditures for a given year (e.g., Cleveland 1991) makes the results doubly meaningless.[10]

Outside the United States

Outside the United States, the scarce data tell the same story of field growth. In 1944, as noted earlier, a special expert mission estimated Persian Gulf reserves at 15 billion barrels proved, 6 billion probable. As of 1975, those same fields (excluding later discoveries) had already produced 42 billion and had 75 billion "remaining." Both numbers must be much larger today, but are not publicly available. Again, development made the difference.

For the world outside the United States, reserve-added figures are un-reliable. But we can estimate investment per daily barrel of capacity, at 1985 price levels and 1985 technology, in each country.[11] This is a crude approximation of the supply curve. In figure 13.3, it is cumulated by coun-tries, from lowest to highest, for 1955, 1965, 1975, and 1985. During 1955–75, the rightward shift is dramatic, matching the output increase. By

1985, much OPEC capacity had been lost, but the effect of neglect is not clear, because there was so much unused capacity.

The dotted line showing "1985: potential" is based on the assumptions (1) that reserves are fixed at the 1985 level, and cannot be expanded; (2) that each OPEC country expands capacity and production to 5 percent. The cost per unit increases proportionately, often by a factor exceeding five.[12] At the extreme left, the difference between actual and potential 1985 cost is a rough estimate of maximum user cost, the value sacrificed by increased output. It assumes fixed un-expandable reserves. But in fact, from end-1985 to end-1990, the Persian Gulf producers increased their reserves by 65 percent. If we used end-1990 reserves for the "potential" line, it would ride well off the chart.

Oil Price "Too Low," "Too High" ... [?]

One often hears that the price of oil was once "too low." This means—if it means anything—that it was too low to pay out an acceptable return on investment. At its lowest, in 1970, the Persian Gulf price was $1.21. In Saudi Arabia (and its neighbors were not too different), lifting cost was about five cents. The return to investment to produce one barrel daily was then $442 per year (($1.21 − .05) × 365), for years to come. The value of such a revenue stream must be several thousand dollars. To obtain it took roughly $100 in development investment. Thus the "low" price was far above the competitive level, including even a lush allowance for user cost.

Persian Gulf User Cost, Development Cost, and Reserve Changes

Table 13.2a shows the kind of assumptions needed in estimating user cost. In the 27 years since 1963, 44 percent of the original reserves were depleted. But the reserves added were nearly five times as great. Discovery effort was very modest; the great bulk of the expansion was, as in the United States, by the growth of existing fields. The intensity of production, i.e., its ratio to proved reserves, has scarcely changed.

Table 13.2b shows a simulation I made in 1966 with 1962–64 data. The numbers have all been restated to 1990 drilling-equipping cost levels. The experiment was to assume that consumption would grow more rapidly than in the past; that the growth would come altogether from the Persian Gulf, where there would be zero new-field discoveries, but continued expansion of old fields, by a factor less than had been experienced in the United States.

Table 13.2A
Persian Gulf "Big Four:" 1963, 1989 reserves depleted and added (in billions of barrels)

	1963 Reserves		1960–1990		1990 Reserves	
	Amount	% Prod. in year	Cumul. output	Reserves added	Amount	% Prod. in year
Iran	37	1.5	24	80	92	1.2
Iraq	26	1.6	12	86	100	1.0
Kuwait	64	1.1	14	44	95	0.6
Saudi Arabia	60	1.0	33	231	255	0.7

Source: Oil & Gas Journal, annual "World Wide Oil" issue.

Table 13.2B
Persian Gulf "Big Four:" 1963, 1990 costs, (dollars, 1990 cost levels)

	1963 Actual		1980 Hypothetical	1985–1990 Actual
	Investment/DB	Operating + devel. cost	O + D Cost	Investment/DB
Iran	634	0.34	0.49	1355
Iraq	336	0.20	0.29	188
Kuwait	814	0.49	0.68	964
Saudi Arabia	780	0.49	0.63	502

Source: (Adelman 1966). Table XXXI. Adjusted to 1990 cost level by the (IPAA) drilling cost index. The 1990 level is 5.31 times the 1963 level.

The object was not to forecast but to see the consequences of putting much greater pressure on existing fields than was likely to happen. The greater strain on those fields would ceteris paribus increase the required investment, and the capital and operating costs. By 1980, the anticipation of yet-higher costs would give rise to an expected supply price well above developing-operating cost. The increment I aimed at was "maximum economic finding cost," a variant of user cost.

As the far-right column shows, the allowance for user cost, designed to be generous, turned out to be prodigal. Real 1985/90 costs are little different from what they were in 1963, despite some intervening cataclysms and long-continued neglect of human and material capital. Iran is twice as high, a moderate penalty considering the reckless destruction of the 1978 engineering teams. Kuwait is about the same, while Iraq and Saudi Arabia are lower.

The 1976 Value of a Persian Gulf Barrel

The 1976 buyout agreement between Saudi Arabia and Aramco named a discovery fee of six cents per barrel, as produced. Assuming the Saudi production rate for that year (2 percent of reserves), and indefinite decline, the present value of a barrel produced at that rate is about one cent if discounted at 10 percent, two cents discounted at 5 percent.[13] That gives us a fix on what an additional undeveloped barrel was worth to the Saudis, and also on what it might cost to find one. At that time, the price was over $12. The discrepancy of 100 : 1 or 200 : 1 looks amazing but merely reflects the discrepancy between price and a monopolist's marginal revenue, which ought to be in the neighborhood of zero. Two other measures of user cost, somehow not applied by their authors (Askari 1990; World Bank 1988), both show user cost as either near-zero or actually negative for the Persian Gulf producers (Adelman et al., 1991).

In the Persian Gulf area, inventories (reserves) are so large, and their average time of production so far off, that present value is zero, and production cost is so low that doubling it as a rough allowance for user cost would still leave it a tiny fraction of the price. Of course, if the production rate increased radically, so would development investment per barrel, the value of an already-developed barrel, and of an undeveloped barrel because its production would be much nearer in time.

Concluding Remarks on World Oil Supply in General

In a functioning competitive market, scarcity is measured by price, which equals incremental cost, including an allowance for the sacrifice of better ore used now and lost for the future. This "user cost" is captured by changes in the development cost per unit of newly added reserves or per unit of new capacity, and by the value of reserves already developed.

The price increases since 1970 have no connection with increased scarcity, and must therefore be due to market control. Sellers' behavior confirms this. The higher-cost producers sell all they can produce; the low-cost producers produce only what they can sell at current prices, and cut back production to match demand. The sharp investment cutbacks in the lower-cost areas, and expansion in the higher-cost, fit the same picture, of output restricted to maintain prices.

The OPEC member nations are the lowest-cost producers but the suppliers of last resort: price makers where the others are price-takers. To model the restricting group, emphasis must be on their investment behavior, which determines capacity. Treating capacity as an exogenous variable ignores what is most important.

The Monopoly of Sovereigns

The conventional cartel model is as follows: a group of sellers trying to fix prices and outputs in concert, in order to maximize wealth. They do so by trial and error, especially error.

Governments Seek Maximum Revenues

Some models have governments making oil production decisions for non-economic reasons. This confuses means with ends, and getting with spending. A state seeks first to survive; then, to cultivate its garden, or spread the true faith, or bash its neighbors, or anything else. But whatever the objectives, the more wealth the better. A state that deliberately avoids wealth-maximizing is a special story, which had better be a good one. There are no authentic examples.

The price target informally set in 1973, then more explicitly by the long-term price policy committee of OPEC in 1978–80, was the cost of synthetic liquid fuels. That is a clear example of monopoly profit maximizing. For only when oil no longer competes with oil can its market price approach the supply price of the nearest alternatives.

But those in high office in the consuming countries want to believe in non-economic objectives in the producing countries. If producing governments produce less oil than would clear the market, the allocation takes place by these governments' grace and favor. "Special relationships" will help obtain "access" to oil, and security of supply. Masterly diplomacy, firm yet conciliatory, assures "access." And of course the public wants to believe they have some say in deciding the sauce in which they are to be eaten.

The statesman is "dressed in a little brief authority, most ignorant of what he's most assured." The U.S. government helped Kaddafi in 1970. The State Department considered him "a fanatic anti-Communist"—who in 1991 hailed the "magnificent" anti-Gorbachev coup (*Economist* 11-23-91:51). Washington claimed credit for the 1971 Tehran agreements to raise oil prices, because "the previously turbulent world oil situation would now quiet down." Secretary Kissinger bounced all over the Middle East in 1973–74, and others in President Nixon's cabinet hinted darkly at force— to end an "embargo" against the United States which had not happened and could not. The market precluded it. (I had pointed this out beforehand (*Economist*, 7-7-73: Survey: 12).)

The Carter Administration expected the wells to start drying up in the 1980s, and kept jawboning Saudi Arabia and congratulating themselves on the Saudis' "moderation" in raising the price from $12 to only $34. In 1986, Mr. George Bush urged the Saudis to cut back output to support prices; in 1990 his Administration said it wanted "a rapprochement" with Persian Gulf countries "to ensure that the oil will continue to flow" (PE 2-90) and his ambassador encouraged Saddam Hussein to force others to cut back production to support prices. (See below, "From Enforcer to Hijacker.") And in May 1991, the White House thought they had "special communication" with Saudi Arabia (Press release 5-3-91). To study the workings of a cartel of sovereigns we must ignore these fantasies.

Peculiarities of the OPEC Cartel

OPEC members are (1) all Less-Developed-Countries (LDCs). (See below, "Growth Without Development.") (2) No matter what their revenues, nearly all run chronic deficits.

The Unleashed Cartel

In no industrial country would sellers dare to join to raise the price of oil by a factor of 20, inflation-adjusted, as did the OPEC nations from 1970 to 1980. They would injure groups far more numerous and powerful than themselves. Every country has its own way of disciplining them. In the United States they would go to jail for anti-trust violation.

But in a small exporting LDC there is no such conflict. The burden of higher prices is wholly on foreigners; the benefit is all to the domestic economy. The sellers are sovereign, and bound in by no law.

OPEC Investment: The False and the Real Capital Crunch

One often hears today that additional OPEC capacity will require $60 or more billion. Even if it were true, it is a minor fraction of a single year's revenues. Moreover, nowhere is oil development investment even one tenth of annual revenues. The problem of insufficient funds for oil investment is *state ownership*.

Private investment is created by expected profit. If there is money to be made, money will be found, if not by one company then by another. But in a government, one must build a political coalition to get a share of expenditures. Oil revenues are a cash stream, into which all groups try to dip. Oil investment must get in line along with all other claimants. Each one tries to be a free rider, getting the benefit of oil investment while others cut back their demands. Oil earnings are urgently "needed" for current expenditures, to cover the budget deficit, supply foreign exchange, etc. It is all too easy to under-invest or under-maintain; or invest too much, and badly, to create jobs or reward friends. Much OPEC history is summed up in a recent news item: "Algeria's revenue was used to keep the new privileged class comfortable. Investments in schools, housing, medical care, agriculture, and even the vital oil industry have stopped" (Yussuf Ibrahim, in NYT 1-19-92:E3).

Even more important is the lack of technical and management expertise. Individuals and corporations were expelled from Iran and Iraq. In Kuwait, advanced know-how seemed superfluous, with vast low-cost oil fields in steady operation. Saudi Arabia kept the companies as hired hands, and its good sense has paid off.

Nearly every OPEC country is now trying to get foreign oil companies back, particularly to work over old oil fields and expand them. This promises much. As we saw above, it was the great achievement of American oilmen after 1930. But very little has been accomplished. In early 1990, Iran expected to be at 4-mbd-capacity within a year "via foreign contracts" (PIW 3-26-90:1). They may do it by 1993, [PIW 10-19-92:1].

In March 1990, Iraq sent teams to various countries to persuade investors to finance the development of some existing fields. It was inherently a low-risk operation. But they met "a chilly reception" in Tokyo (PIW 4-9-90:7). Investment is not attractive in a country where companies were once expropriated with derisory compensation, and are hated by much or most of the population. Risk is further increased because the company must abide by OPEC production limitations. When a company requires something resembling an equity interest, and the chance of a high return, negotiations stall.[14] But even when no equity participation is needed, Kuwait, supposedly the most businesslike, moves on feet of lead.[15]

OPEC Governments Have Short Time Horizons, High Discount Rates

The budget and current account balances of Saudi Arabia show OPEC governments have short time horizons and high discount rates. The official Washington gospel was that the Saudis and other "low absorbers" really didn't want more money. They preferred to keep oil in the ground, and only produced it because of solidarity with the West, and because of our "special relation" with them. In fact: their imports of goods and services soon surpassed their revenues. Their 1974 surpluses turned into deficit in four years. The surplus of 1980–81 was even bigger and turned into deficit in only two years. They have been in deficit ever since. In 1981, Saudi Arabia had about $160 billion in foreign assets. Roughly $14 billion was left at end-1989, before the Persian Gulf war.

Growth Without Development

The OPEC nations have grown but not developed. They remain largely monocultures. They draw no income from spending on infrastructure, a bloated public sector, money-losing industries, weapons, subsidies, etc. Dependence on oil is no less. "Non-oil" industries like retailing or construction simply support the oil industry and its beneficiaries.

The risk on any income stream is directly proportional to (1) its fluctuations, and (2) the degree with which those fluctuations are correlated with the holder's other assets, or other income. As to (1), the OPEC nations' income is especially risky. They are the swing producers, who must cut back output to maintain price, while others maintain output. As to (2), the oil income is not only a high percent of national income, it drives the non-oil sector. Hence the risk on oil income is greater than that of private companies operating the same oil fields (Adelman 1986a).

Moreover, these governments are nearly all despotic. Opposition works only by violence and conspiracy. They are unruly to each other: Sunni against Shia, Arab against Persian, religious against secular. The Middle East is a dangerous neighborhood.[16] (I wrote in the original EMF paper, in September 1989: "With peace restored, and enough Kurds massacred to keep the northern provinces quiet, Iraq may now make another attempt to seize Kuwait." That was no forecast, merely a recognition of what might happen. The U.S. government knew better, as it always does.)

"The Future Leaves Them Cold. They Want Money Now."

Back in 1935, an oilman so reported to his company on Mideast governments. It is still true. Because of the high rates at which they discount revenues, short-term gains outweigh long-term losses. The present-value weighted elasticity of demand is much lower for them than for private companies. Hence, they raise prices faster and farther than even an unrestrained private monopoly. "Take the money and run" is simply a rational response to difficult conditions.

The Long-Term Strategy Committee mentioned earlier had wisely recommended that price increases should be at the OECD rate of growth.

That would have been only a small percent per year, and zero in some years. The OPEC nations could not hold to their own sound doctrine in 1979–80, and they made prices jump by abruptly cutting output and giving no assurance they would restore it.

Because of their high rate of time discount, the cartel not only is likely to go beyond the profit-maximizing price, but also to be an unstable and clumsy instrument in other respects. More of that later.

Supply II: Permanent Excess Capacity in OPEC

The cartel oscillates between two models: (1) The largest firm sets output, and all others produce *ad lib*. (2) All firms participate in setting an output total, and dividing it (Adelman 1978). Variant (1) is easier to manage, (2) is more rewarding. Both are unstable: in (1), the dominant firm will try to make others share the burden; in (2), cheating may force the dominant firm willy-nilly into (1).

Since the first price explosion in 1973, the cartel has lived with a surplus of not only potential but current capacity. Coping with it has been the chief topic at nearly every meeting. (While the consuming nations have been and still are obsessed with fear of insufficient OPEC capacity, "not enough for our needs".) There was no excess for about a year after the August 1990 Iraqi invasion. But the OPEC nations' wrangling over production shares in late 1991 and early 1992 proved that excess capacity was back, even with Kuwait at a fraction of its capacity and Iraq shut down. Shakespeare had it right: "A little more than a little is by much too much." *The excess will never disappear so long as the cartel remains.*

With no excess capacity a member gets no respect. Its bargaining power depends upon its ability to create a nuisance or danger if it is not treated "right." Therefore every member desires some surplus capacity. There is no escaping the principle: a joint monopoly embodies collusion *and* conflict, each member protecting himself by doing what is bad for the group. OPEC will keep expanding, but some members will be quicker to set aside funds and, more important, find a management team to invest it.

Non-Cartel Supply

United States

Proved reserves-added are a forecast of future production, and since 1985 they have been stable around 2.3 billion barrels per year, or 6.5 million barrels per day, a little less than current production. But costs appear to be rising. In my opinion, discoveries will not freshen the mix enough to keep the level of reserve-additions at the current level, and U.S. production will decline slowly.

Other Non-OPEC

In the United States, wells drilled fell from 90,000 in 1981 to 27,000 in 1991. The rest of the non-Communist world showed practically no change, at 5,000 in both years. The consensus, that non-OPEC producing countries will soon use up most of their reserves, is correct. They did so in the 1960s, again in the 1970s, and again in the 1980s. More than half of the non-OPEC reserves at the start of each decade were depleted during the decade, but reserves at the end were larger than at the start.

At current oil prices, reserves and productive capacity will continue to grow, probably more rapidly than in the past. Current "low" price levels are still high in relation to the cost of creating new reserves. But that is a necessary not sufficient condition.

The Under-Achievers

Non-OPEC countries produce less oil and gas than would be profitable. Some have national oil companies, mostly inefficient and underfunded, often rotted by payoffs, kickbacks, and featherbedding which buy local support. Private, especially foreign, oil companies are overtaxed, and produce less than would profit both parties (Kemp 1987).

Matters were worse through 1981. Rising oil prices were extrapolated, and governments demanded the earth of oil companies. The economic mistake was reinforced by xenophobia. "The oil is ours," the family jewels, not a vulgar asset. The fear of being called a dupe of foreign capitalists, and the delusion that the price of oil will rise and the oilmen return later to offer more, makes governments overreach and get nothing. Even in North America and the North Sea, taxation is inefficient and aborts production which is profitable pre-tax, sometimes to a startling degree (Kemp, Reading, and Macdonald 1992; Lund 1992).

A recent paper (OGJ 1990) gives typical capital and operating expenditures, decline rates, and project lives, for three fields, of respectively 15, 50, and 350 million barrels. At the author's hypothetical price of $18, even the smallest highest-cost field would earn 40 percent before taxes. A large number of known contracts are reduced to 20 types. Only four of the 20 provide 15 percent return after tax for developing the small field. In only seven of the 20 countries is it worth developing even the intermediate field, which earns 60 percent before tax. The large field is always worth developing.

The result in a typical country is that *none* of these fields will ever be found. Exploratory effort typically finds many more small than large fields. A small field, if taxed on its profits, would provide the company with funds and a stable beachhead for more exploration. But if it is known in advance that nothing small is worth while, the chances of complete loss are unacceptably high. Large fields will not be found because small fields are overtaxed.[17]

Common Sense Infiltrates Slowly

Yet people do learn. Outside the United States, in the 1980s, as prices *fell*, production and reserves *rose*. Public and government opinion slowly awoke from dreams of ever-rising prices. In many countries, taxation has been revised, and public ownership is shrinking. International oil companies are now spoiled for choice; countries which once threw them out now want them back. That explains the bafflement of an OPEC spokesman: "I just cannot understand how this low price can sustain investments in high cost oil areas.... Somebody, somewhere, must be losing his shirt" (Ali Jaidah 1988, p. 3).

Ex-Soviet Prospects

The biggest under-achievers are the ex-Soviet republics. A BP executive (Harding 1991) thinks there is more oil to be found in the Soviet areas than at the Persian Gulf; but that will take time.

Long-run prospects are good. American experience shows the expansion potential of old fields. An oil and gas industry can function efficiently in an otherwise inefficient economy. Moreover, there is a strong incentive to maintain the primary supplier of foreign exchange. But the republics must learn to let prices be set in markets, to tax rationally, control parochial interests, and not to play beggar-my-neighbor. It will not be easy or quick.

The end of the Soviet Union is having an effect already. Like the United States after 1970, ex-Soviet oil is breaking out of a separate enclave, and is blending into the world market. Inter-republic trade has become exporting, at world prices. Some exporting is already private, both refineries and production units selling abroad to gain the higher prices there. As market boundaries expand, the OPEC share declines—even if Soviet production declines. The shape of things to come was seen as early as Summer 1992: "Deliveries [by C.I.S. republics] have risen ... to 2.4 million b/d despite falling production levels, *leading OPEC to complain of market disruption*" (OGJ 8-17-92: NL3, emphasis added).

What one cannot safely say of any individual non-OPEC country is a good bet for all of them taken together. Non-OPEC output will continue rising, small decreases in the United States more than offset by growth elsewhere.

Natural gas is a sleeping giant slowly beginning to stir. For decades, Canada was ruled by a fetish: require 25 years of reserves before permitting exports. It worked: with no export market, there was less investment and reserve-additions. This "proved" they were running out of gas, which strengthened the refusal to export. In 1980 the Canadian government barred exports at $5 per thousand cubic feet (mcf). The great god Consensus knew the price was going up to glory. Today the border price is around $2, a capital loss of about 75 percent on those aborted sales. Canada has learned the lesson, discarded the fetish, and gas exports are climbing.

In Europe, huge amounts of low-cost natural gas would permit a very large expansion (Adelman and Lynch 1986). Low prices have induced the Netherlands to increase their exports. Before 1986, Algeria had skillfully used the fears of a shortage to raise prices above even an inflated market. The French and Italians paid Algeria an additional premium for political credit, or influence, or something. Some get a thrill from *grandeur*, which is more addictive than cocaine. But the high is nearly gone. Contracts calling for a $7 delivered price have now been partly reinstated at about $2.50–$3.00 per mcf (WSJ 8-18-88:35; OGJ 8-15-88:27). Once $7 was none too much for gas from "high-cost Troll" off Norway. Around 1984, Norway vainly came down to $4. The price will probably not exceed $2.50. Strenuous attempts are being made to lever the European price structure back up. Whatever the degree of success, it will be in the teeth of increasing plenty.

Caution on Non-OPEC Supply

A paper which argues that non-OPEC production will decrease beyond this century actually shows the contrary. Curcio (1989) predicts that non-OPEC output from fields operated in 1986 will fall by 9.4 percent per year, or 75 percent between 1986 and 2000. The nearest thing to a laboratory test is experience in the United States, where large fields producing in 1945 decreased by about 3.5 percent per year through 1988. (Some production rates dropped to almost nothing, some were steady, some actually rose.) Apply a 3.5 percent decrease to 1986 fields instead of 9.4 percent, and Mr. Curcio's estimates of total non-OPEC production, including also new fields, would show not a decline but a net increase of some 3.6 million barrels daily (Lynch 1990). In fact, non-OPEC production outside North America and the CPEs rose by 1.1 mbd, or 4.6 percent, through 1991.

Non-OPEC supply will keep increasing as the under-achievers learn and improve. Development costs are low enough to induce much higher output. Samuel Johnson's friend wanted to be a philosopher, but cheerfulness kept breaking through. Common sense and the national interest have been breaking through here and there, to move the aggregate non-OPEC supply curve to the right. But there is nothing inevitable about the process, and others may read the political tea leaves differently. In any case, a competitive fringe will always be there, disrupting the cartel's market allocations, and starting squabbles which like cracks in metal can propagate far from the original break.

A 10-year Prospect

In early 1986, I suggested that the cartel would hold together, and the price of Arabian Light would fluctuate around $15. That was halfway between a monopoly ceiling around $25, and a floor of about $5, my estimate of the long-run competitive equilibrium price, including a generous allowance for user cost. To avoid misunderstanding: $15 is not an equilibrium price, but rather the brute average of higher and lower. I expect this to continue into the next century.

OPEC could of course raise the price at any time, just as they have repeatedly done in the past: cut production and leave buyers guessing as to how soon the cut will be restored. As in the past, buyers will do the rest: a wave of *precautionary* demand, for hoarding not use, will sand up prices; whereupon a wave of *speculative* demand will send them up even more. But once the temporary stimulus is spent (and the reversion begins), output must be reduced permanently.

OPEC in a Market Share Trap

We anticipate a little by assuming the ex-Soviet oil industry fully integrated into the world market. In 1991, OPEC exports were about 21 million barrels daily out of world consumption (ex-OPEC) of about

62 mbd.[18] With one third of the market, price elasticity of demand is three times that for crude oil generally. In order to cut any given fraction of the world supply, OPEC must cut its own production three times as hard.

For the year 2000, assume with IEA that growth will be about 11 mbd. If it all goes to OPEC, a 44 percent market share (32/73), makes it uncertain whether they can increase revenues by raising prices. That was their market share in 1981. But if, as we expect, non-OPEC output expands, the price cannot be raised.

Plenty of Oil Causes "Shortages," Upheavals

This sounds reassuring: plenty of oil, *therefore* no price upheavals. But if our analysis is anywhere near correct, the conclusion is just the reverse. There has never been any worldwide shortage. On the contrary: with too much cheap oil potential, the competitive price would be much lower. Strenuous resistance to competition keeps the price volatile and the market in turmoil. The events of 1990 are only the most recent example.

The 30 Years' Wait

In 1961, Iraq claimed Kuwait and mobilized its army on the border. The British flew in a brigade, about 5,000 men, which ended the threat. Thirty years later it took a force one hundred times as great and far more heavily armed to expel the Iraqis from Kuwait, with terrible devastation on both sides. The difference between 1960 and 1990 was $2.5 trillion (at 1990 prices) which had poured into the Middle East.

High Oil Revenues: Means and Motive for War

Oil revenues gave Saddam Hussein the means and motive for war. His 1980 attack on Iran looked easy and promised much: most Iranian oil production is less than 200 miles from Basra. The venture failed, despite a million dead, many more wounded, refugees, etc. The next Iraqi venture grew out of the 1990 low price and over-quota production.

The 1990 Crisis of Overproduction

In mid-June 1990, the Persian Gulf price was down to $12, with most members producing over quota, and discounting. As the Oil Minister of Kuwait said: "Those who could cheat, did. Those who couldn't, complained." The Kuwaitis were blunt, or perhaps only nervous. In March 1989, Saudi Arabia had isolated Kuwait by signing a nonaggression pact with Iraq, without the consent of the Gulf Cooperation Council. Kuwait asked Iraq for such a pact soon afterward. It was brusquely refused.

From Enforcer to Hijacker

Iraq turned the market around in mid-July 1990, when it threatened violence to the overproducers. Saddam Hussein was like the late Jimmy Hoffa keeping the truckers in line. The Saudi government warned that its "protection would not be extended to Kuwait in the face of Iraqi anger" (NYT 7-18-90:D1). Oil experts called the cooperation of Saudi Arabia and Iran with Iraq the most important event since 1979, and one "coined the phrase 'Saddam factor' to explain the new realities in OPEC" (WSJ 7-24-90:A3).

When Kuwait and the UAE capitulated, and promised to stay within quota, an expert called this "a historic turning point"; another called it "a landmark in the history of OPEC" (NYT 7-26-90:A1), or "a whole new ballgame," for which he thanked Saudi Arabia and Iraq (WSJ 7-27-90:A2). Another summed up: "Discipline is guaranteed by a principal player which carries a loaded gun" (NYT 7-28-90:A1). Bloated inventories and stagnant consumption were overborne because "Iraq as the enforcer has become the key" (WSJ 7-30-90:A4). "The Saudis purred. They pretended not to see the gun Iraq was pointing at Kuwait's head" (*Economist* 8-4-90).

Threats of armed force to keep price cutters in line were supported by the United States. A week before the invasion, the American Ambassador told Saddam Hussein that the United States sympathized with his "need" for more money, never mind for what; that some in the United States wanted an even higher oil price than the $25 Iraq demanded; and the United States had no opinion on Iraq's border demands on Kuwait.[19] The Ambassador was only shocked when Iraq occupied *all* of Kuwait (NYT 9-19-90:A29). Even then, Professor Brzezinski thought Iraq had "financial and territorial claims (not all of which were unfounded)" (NYT 10-7-90 OpEd); the president of the Council on Foreign Relations urged "concessions to Iraq regarding oil pricing and production, territory and debt" (NYT 11-30-90 OpEd).

The Lessons of 1990

The oil crisis of 1990–91 was much milder than 10 years earlier. (1) The Saudis acted differently. After a month's profitable silence, letting the price rise, they increased output and let it be known they would keep it high. That was a far cry from 1979–80, when their prolonged refusal to assure continued high output kept driving up the price for over a year. (2) There were no price controls in consuming countries, hence no incentive to hoard crude oil or products for the forthcoming higher prices, hence no additional kick to speculative demand. Consumer demand was cut back more quickly, in response to the quicker price stimulus. (3) I think the use of futures markets also helped, although this is harder to prove. (4) Strategic petroleum reserves in the United States, Japan, and Germany, although unused, were like a wartime fleet over the horizon. The reserves bought time to take diplomatic or military action, without a gun pointed at our head. The reserves would have been used, better late than never, as a seller of last resort. Thereby they moderated though they could not preclude a suddenly swollen precautionary/speculative demand. It was like an *ad hoc* consortium to tide financial markets over panics, before the Federal Reserve System was set up.

But prices will remain volatile and supply insecure. OPEC is a clumsy cartel, which cannot fine-tune the market with the coarse instruments of production quotas and fixed prices, without timely data on consumption and inventories, or sometimes even production. The cartel is flying blind, with several hands grabbing at the controls.

Because oil supply will remain plentiful, and prices under pressure, violent action is always likely, to suppress the plenty and keep up the price. The local powers will always be tempted to aggression, both for immediate wealth and for greater power over oil prices. If OPEC were unified at the Gulf, or could expand its membership, the monopoly price could hold at much higher than the prices I have guessed at here.

Lower prices may goad them into such action. Trillions of petrodollars have changed the Middle East from a local hot spot to a world problem.

Conclusion

I said in 1971 that "the genie is out of the bottle." He still is. The rewards of controlling the world oil industry have been so great that the nations cannot give up the effort. If the cartel collapses, it will be put back together again, with a partly different membership. If a cat has nine lives, a cartel of sovereign states may have more. The cycle will continue: meetings—quotas—firm prices—cheating—price declines—threats and promises—meetings . . . with here and there some drastic political-military moves.

Modelling a supply system must include worldwide development investment/operating costs, but also the unbound unstable cartel, and the underachieving non-cartelists. Models which disregard these problems, and instead address "geological assessments," have no tie to reality, and will give us no insights, let alone numbers.

Appendix

The full 15-page appendix to this paper may be secured by writing to the Energy and Environmental Policy Research Center, E40-479, MIT, Cambridge, MA, 02139, USA. The summary is as follows:

1. Investment per daily barrel of oil production:
UK: (1990) $12,901; (1991) $17,749; (1992–98) $14,378.
USA: (1989) $10,694; (1990) $12,021.
Venezuela: (1988) $1,602; (1989) $1,180 (1990) $1,830.

2. Ten other OPEC nations: investment per daily barrel of production 1989–90, median $1,433, payback in 89 days, oil investment two-thirds of one percent of total annual revenues.

3. As a check, estimated total oil and gas expenditures for the Middle East and Africa are estimated by the method we use for the OPEC nations. They are totalled for 1985–87, and compared with the last estimated expenditures for these regions compiled by Chase Manhattan Bank. The latter are 24 percent above our estimates. The true discrepancy, if any, is less, because our coverage is more narrow, and we can make no allowance for non-cost outlays: local overspending and corruption.

4. Part of the estimating procedure involves an allowance for higher expenditures outside the United States, because of economies of scale in supply and services. The estimating regression is shown in full.

5. There are several examples of "production costs in Never-Never Land," which have received wide publicity.

6. There are two demonstrations: user cost as limiting value to development cost; and correction of decline rate when the ratio of initial output to reserves developed is high. This is important for calculation of the U.S. and U.K. estimates.

7. It is suggested we should disregard "finding costs per barrel of oil equivalent," which has become popular in the financial press. It is meaningless.

8. Some details are given on estimation of Saudi Arabian foreign holdings in 1983 and 1990.

Notes

This paper summarizes research, reported in various places, on a project supported by the National Science Foundation and by the MIT Center for Energy and Environment Policy Research. But any opinions, findings, conclusions or recommendations expressed herein are those of the author, and do not necessarily reflect the views of NSF or of any other person or group.

David Wood and I had many conversations on this subject, and he encouraged me to prepare a paper for a September 1989 session of the Energy Modelling Forum. It has been enlarged and rewritten, to incorporate working and published papers completed since then, thanks in no small measure to David Wood's friendship and support.

1. The mean of the distribution was 552 billion. In a normal distribution, 5 percent probability is reached at 1.96 standard deviations. Hence the standard deviation was $(620 - 552)/1.96 = 34$ billion. The actual total was $(687 - 552)/34 = 3.97$ standard deviations from the mean, which has a probability of one in ten thousand.

2. "For commodity producers, 1991 was another dismal year ... [Prices ended at] the lowest level in real terms since this newspaper began calculating an all-item commodity-price index in 1845." "Incommodious commodities." *London Economist*, January 11, 1992, p. 66.

3. The annual capital investment compilations by the Chase Manhattan Bank have ceased, and so have the annual development reports of the American Association of Petroleum Geologists. The trade journals no longer have data on individual fields' production, and have long ceased to publish estimated field reserves. In the USA, the change from private to public coverage in 1979 meant the loss of valuable data on reserves, especially concerning discovery (NRC 1985).

4. Moreover, the financial drain is negligible, a very small percent of revenues as the bottom line shows. How, then, explain the widespread complaints of insufficient finance? We do so below.

5. Hartwick (1991, p. 137) ascribes to me "the assumption that average and marginal unit costs are the same." He should read *Review of Economics & Statistics*, vol. 68 (1986), especially page 389: "Under steady state competitive conditions, there will be great variation in *average* production cost among producing areas ... but there would be only relatively small chance variation in *marginal* costs." Emphasis in original.

6. Both studies are invalidated by large scale measurement errors in dependent and independent variables. Prices and values are given for "oil equivalents", gas converted to oil at 5.8 mcf per barrel. But the oil: gas ratios, both prices and values, have generally been much higher, and have fluctuated considerably.

7. One may, of course, maintain that even the "correct" market value cannot measure the real social value of the inventory because market discount rates are not true social discount rates, at least not for minerals. For example, there is controversy in the U.S. today over opening the Alaskan National Wildlife Refuge

(ANWR) to oil exploration. The in-ground value of a barrel is today very roughly $4, development cost $2.50, and finding cost $1, leaving $.50 for net benefit. This is based on the conventional oil industry discount rate of about 10 percent, or perhaps somewhat more. But if the true social discount rate is a riskless 3 percent, then the in-ground value is $13.33, and the guessed-at net benefit is over $10, or 20 times as much as at 10 percent.

8. Rising development cost induces rising user cost, and vice versa. One reads too often that a mineral price has remained stable, or is declining, because rising user cost has been offset by declining other costs. The statement is self-contradictory. Technology may lower the cost of doing a given operation, but if it is applied to an ever-leaner and more refractory resource, the cost of providing another barrel for the reserve may increase. If so, the value of a barrel already developed rises, the increase in user cost keeping pace with the increase in development cost.

9. A developing industry consensus seems to be that because of improved technology "it costs far less now to find a barrel of oil than it did a few years ago". [NYT 5-25-92:35] In fact, nobody has any idea of whether oil *finding* cost has changed in any direction. Oil *development* cost has come down since 1981, but largely or wholly because the rents and inefficiencies of the boom have been largely squeezed out. Since 1984, development cost in the USA has moved persistently up for oil, and down for natural gas. Outside this country, data are not good enough to confirm any change.

10. Cleveland (1991) also writes (p. 183) that I "claim that decreasing field size does not lead to increasing exploration cost per barrel found." What I actually said was: (1) exploration cost cannot be observed, but good proxies, because of substitution, are (a) the value of existing reserves and (b) the capital cost of development: and that (2) despite decreasing average field size, neither (a) nor (b) increased for many years before 1973, and both increased afterward.

11. The absolute numbers should all be doubled, but this does not affect the year-to-year comparison.

12. Investment is considered a quadratic function of newly installed capacity, hence unit cost a linear function (Adelman 1990).

13. If V is the value of the barrel, 'F' the discovery fee per barrel, 'a' the percent of the barrel produced per year, and 'i' the discount rate, then in infinite time $V = Fa/(a + i)$.

14. OPEC governments (and others) need a form of contract which gives companies an ownership interest in oil production in fact but not in appearance. The doctor of laws in Mozart's *Marriage of Figaro* said he could fix things with a synonym here and an equivocation there. "*Qualche garbuglio si trovera*": some tangle of confusion could be found to make a zig look like a zag. Calling Dr. Bartolo!

15. "A reconfiguration of the Kuwaiti oil fields currently under way could return output to two million barrels a day by the end of 1993. But attaining that goal will depend to some extent on how quickly they can obtain an agreement with BP.

Because Kuwait oil wells flowed prolifically with little mechanical prompting before the damage by the Iraqis, the oil men there say they haven't the sophistication needed to do the best job of reconfiguring the fields. Negotiations have been dragging on for almost six months, with the oil company asking unusually high fees for its services, the Kuwaitis say. The British oil company is an especially good candidate to help rework Kuwait's oil fields. BP was very active there before the nationalization of the oil industry, and it has retained much of the geological data" (WSJ 2-24-92:B3C). Some of the difficulties may have been composed (PIW 3-23-92:7).

16. The most notorious Middle East conflict, between Israel and the Arabs, has had no effect on oil prices. Of the four ratchet operations which forced up prices in 1970–71, 1973–4, 1978–9, and 1990–91, the Arab-Israel conflict was invoked only in the second one. Even there, it was unimportant. Prices had been raised for years by raising taxes, at an accelerating rate. The 1971 Tehran "agreements" had been repeatedly violated and the decision to repudiate had been made two months before the war broke out. The production cut was made allegedly in support of demands for Palestinian rights. It ended after only two months, without any demands being met. In 1982, the Israeli invasion of Lebanon provoked outrage, not least in Israel (The Arab nations were silent). "In fact, there was little popular indignation in any Arab country." James E. Akins, "The New Arabia," *Foreign Affairs*, vol. 70, Summer 1991, p. 42.

17. In a similar study (OGJ 9-17-90:29), P. J. Hoenmans, of Mobil Oil E & P, took a sample of 25 countries under 1989 published terms. In a hypothetical 50 mb field, government take ranged from 35 percent to 90 percent. Only in six countries was profit after tax acceptable. In four countries, even a 200 mbd field was unprofitable.

18. OPEC local consumption is a local benefit which is unaffected by prices, has no effect on prices, and brings in no revenue. We subtract it throughout.

19. The Ambassador later said this report, published in the press (e.g., (NYT 9-23-90:19)), was "fabrication. It is disinformation" (NYT 3-21-91:A1, A15). But: (1) No specific errors in the report are cited. (2) There has been no authenticated version. (3) "An unidentified senior State Department official was quoted in the New York Times as having said it (the news report) was 'essentially correct'" ((NYT 3-22-91:A1)). (4) To the same effect, see also Elaine Sciolino. *The Outlaw State: Saddam Hussein's Quest for Power and the Gulf Crisis* (New York: John Wiley & Sons, 1991), pp. 179, 271. (5) Senators who finally secured access to the original documents were indignant over the Ambassador's evasive and inaccurate version of them (NYT 7-13-91:A1).

References

Note: periodicals have been cited by month-day-year: page

(Adelman 1966) M. A. Adelman, "Oil Production Costs in Four Areas," *Proceedings of the Council on Economics of the AIME 1966* [American Institute of Mining Metallurgical and Petroleum Engineers]

(Adelman 1978) ———, "Constraints on the World Oil Monopoly Price," *Resources and Energy*, vol. 1, pp. 3–19

(Adelman 1986a) ———, "Oil Producing Countries' Discount Rates," *Resources & Energy*, vol. 8, pp. 309–329

(Adelman 1986b) ———, "The Competitive Floor to World Oil Prices," *The Energy Journal*, vol. 7, pp. 9–35

(Adelman 1989) ———, "Offshore Norwegian Development Cost Calculated From Project Data," *Energy Exploration & Exploitation*, vol. 7, no. 1, pp 53–62

(Adelman 1990) ———, "Mineral Depletion, With Special Reference to Petroleum," *Review of Economics & Statistics*, vol. 72, pp. 1–10

(Adelman 1992a) ———, "Finding and Developing Costs in the United States 1945–1986," *Advances in the Economics of Energy and Resources*, vol. 7, pp. 11–58 (Greenwich, Conn.: JAI Press)

(Adelman, 1992b) ———, "OPEC at High Noon," MIT Center for Energy and Environmental Policy Research, MIT CEEPR 92-003WP

(Adelman & Lynch 1986) ———, and Michael C. Lynch, "Natural Gas Trade in Western Europe: the Permanent Surplus," in M. I. T. Center for Energy Policy Research, *Western Europe Natural Gas Trade* (December 1986)

(Adelman & Ward 1980) ———, and Geoffrey Ward, "Worldwide Production Costs for Oil and Gas," *Advances in the Economics of Energy and Resources*, J. R. Moroney, ed., vol. 3 (Greenwich, Conn.: JAI Press)

(Arrow 1987) Kenneth Arrow, "Hotelling", In John Eatwell, Murray Milgate, and Peter Newman, *The New Palgrave: a Dictionary of Economics* (London: Macmillan Press)

(Adelman & Watkins 1992) ———, and G. Campbell Watkins, "Reserve Asset Values and the 'Hotelling Valuation Principle'," Working Paper No. MIT-CEEPR-92-004WP

(API et al. 1990) American Petroleum Institute et al., *Joint Association Survey on Drilling Costs*, Table 4

(Askari 1991) Hossein Askari, *Saudi Arabia's Economy: Oil and the Search for Economic Development* (Greenwich, Conn.: JAI Press)

(Cleveland 1991) Cutler J. Cleveland, "Physical and Economic Aspects of Resource Quality: the cost of oil supply in the lower 48 United Stated 1936–1988," *Resources & Energy*, vol. 13 (1991) 163–188

(Bradley 1987) Howard B. Bradley, editor-in-chief, *Petroleum Engineering Handbook* (Richardson, Texas: Society of Petroleum Engineers)

(Curcio 1989) Edgardo Curcio, AGIP, "Oil Supply Prospects in 1990s from Non-OPEC Producing Countries," *Energy Supply in the 1990s and Beyond: Proceedings of the Eleventh Annual International Conference* (International Association for Energy Economics: Caracas, June 26, 1989) pp. 101–110

(Ebinger 1982) Charles K. Ebinger et al, *Energy and National Security in the 1980s*, with an introduction by Henry A. Kissinger (Cambridge, Mass.: Ballinger)

(Economist) *The Economist*, weekly

(DOE/EIA 1989) Energy Information Administration, *International Energy Outlook 1989: Projections to 2000* (Washington 1989)

(DOE/EIA 1990) ———, *U.S. Oil and Gas Reserves by Year of Field Discovery* (Washington 1990)

(GER 1992) *Global Energy Report*, issued quarterly by Center for Global Energy Studies (London)

(Harding 1991) D.C. Harding, talk to Institute of Petroleum, London, April 1991

(Hartwick 1991) John M. Hartwick, "The non-renewable resource exploring-extracting firm and the r% rule," *Resources & Energy*, vol. 13 (1991) pp. 129–143

(Heal & Dasgupta 1979) Geoffrey M. Heal and Partha Dasgupta, *Economic Theory and Exhaustible Resources* (Cambridge University Press)

(Hogan 1989) William W. Hogan, *World Oil Price Projections: A Sensitivity Analysis* (Cambridge, Mass.: Harvard Energy and Environmental Policy Center, 1989)

(Hotelling 1931) Harold Hotelling, "The Economics of Exhaustible Resources," *Journal of Political Economy*, vol. 39, pp. 137–175

(IPAA) Independent Petroleum Association of America, twice-yearly *Reports of the Cost Study Committee* (Washington: IPAA, 1963-date)

(Jaidah 1988) Ali Jaidah, "Oil Pricing: a Role in Search of an Actor," paper at Oxford Energy Seminar, reprinted as Special Supplement to PIW 9-12-88

(Kemp 1987) Alexander Kemp (with postscript by Campbell Watkins), *Petroleum Rent Collection Around the World* (Halifax, Nova Scotia: The Institute for Research on Public Policy)

(Kemp, Reading, & Macdonald 1992) Alexander G. Kemp, David Reading and Bruce Macdonald, *The Effecs of the Fiscal Terms Applied to Offshore Petroleum Exploitation of New Fields: a Comparative Study of [Ten Countries]* North Sea Study Occasional Paper No. 37. Department of Economics, University of Aberdeen, April 1992

(Lund 1992) Diderik Lund, "Petroleum taxation under uncertainty: contingent claims analysis with an application to Norway", *Energy Economics*, vol. 14, No. 1, January, pp. 23–31

(Lynch 1990) Michael C. Lynch, "An Omitted Variable in OECD Oil Supply Forecasting," *Proceedings of the Twelfth Annual North American Conference of the International Association for Energy Economics* (Toronto, October 1990), pp. 206–214

(Mattione 1985) Richard P. Mattione, *OPEC's Investment & the International Financial System* (Washington: Brookings, 1985)

(Miller & Upton 1985a) M. H. Miller and C. W. Upton, "A Test of the Hotelling Valuation Principle," *Journal of Political Economy*, 93(1)

(Miller & Upton 1985b) ———, and C. W. Upton, "The Pricing of Oil and Gas: Some Further Results," *Journal of Finance*, 40(3)

(Nehring 1981) Richard Nehring, *The Discovery of Significant Oil and Gas Fields in the United States* (Santa Monica: The Rand Corporation)

(NRC 1985) National Research Council, Panel on Statistics on Natural Gas, *Natural Gas Data Needs in a Changing Regulatory Environment* (Washington: National Academy Press 1985)

(NYT) *New York Times*

(OGJ-RF) *Oil & Gas Journal*, "Review & Forecast," annual issue

(OGJ-WWO) *Oil & Gas Journal*, "World Wide Oil," annual issue

(OGJ 1990) David A. Wood (of International Petroleum Corp.) "Appraisal of economic performance of global exploration contracts," *Oil & Gas Journal*, 10-29-90:48

(PE) *Petroleum Economist*, monthly, previously named *Petroleum Press Service*

(PIW) *Petroleum Intelligence Weekly*

(PPS) See *PE*, above

(Storting 1989) Kingdom of Norway, Ministry of Finance. *Report No. 4 to the Storting: Norwegian Long-Term Program 1990–1993* (Oslo, 1989)

(USGS 1987) US Geological Survey, "World Resources of Crude Oil ...," paper at World Petroleum Congress 1987

(Watkins 1992) Watkins, G. C. "The Hotelling Principle: Autobahn or Cul de Sac?," *The Energy Journal*, 13(1): 1–24

(Wood 1989) David O. Wood, "Can We Model World Oil Markets?," paper at Workshop of the Center of Applied Research and the Central Bureau of Statistics of Norway, given June 8, 1989

(World Bank 1988) World Bank, *World Development Report* (Washington: 1988)

(World Bank 1989) *World Petroleum Markets: a Framework for Reliable Projections* by The Petroleum Finance Company Ltd. World Bank Technical Paper No. 92. Washington, D.C.: The World Bank, 1988

(WSJ) *Wall Street Journal*

II

Market Control in World Oil

Oil Prices in the Long Run, 1963–1975

Every attempt to predict oil prices is certain to result in mistakes. But if we can analyze the elements of the problem one by one before fitting them together, we can learn much. Moreover, the degree of ignorance is not the same in every part of the analysis. Even if we are incapable of correctly foreseeing the whole picture, we can at least establish some partial truths which could in turn help government officials, business management, etc. Application of economic theory to issues in petroleum pricing that involve short-run and long-run marginal cost should contribute to better understanding of both concepts and issues. And many of the questions require dialogue and even co-operation between economists and engineers. The most urgent task is to bring to light the chief influences that bear on oil prices today and tomorrow in order that experts can utilize these materials for reflection and research. This chapter is intended to stimulate such debate.

L'Étude sur les perspectives énergétiques de la Communauté européenne, published at Luxembourg in December, 1962, by the intercommunity working party, has defined the problem: the prices at which oil can be supplied from the present to 1975. Despite any doubts of their conclusions, one must be deeply grateful to the authors of this study, for they have been able to pose the problem as a consistent, coherent whole; it is hardly too much to say that they have demystified it.

We propose to study the problem in four stages: (1) the structure of real, not posted, prices today; we need to ask if such a structure even exists.[1] (2) Setting aside, for the moment, the price of crude oil, can this structure maintain itself over the long run, or does it contain distortions or inconsistencies which will make it change in the near future? (3) What developments are expected to influence the costs (aside from the price of crude) and

Reprinted from *Journal of Business* 37 (1964): 143–161. © 1964 The University of Chicago.

Table 14.1
Receipts and refinery margins, Northwest Europe

			April 1962		April 1963	
Product	Percent (1)	Gallons per barrel (2)	Price cents per gallon (3)	Receipts in dollars per barrel (4)	Price in cents per gallon (5)	Receipts in dollars per barrel (6)
Gasoline	19.8	8.32	8.2	0.681	7.7	0.640
Kerosene	4.3	1.81	10.0	.181	10.4	.188
Gas oil	21.8	9.16	7.8	.715	8.0	.731
Fuel oil	36.4	15.30	4.5	.689	4.7	.719
Other	10.9	4.59	.4	.375	8.8	.394
Losses, waste and refinery fuel	6.7	2.82	0.0	0.0	0.0	0.0
Total	100.0	42.00	—	2.641	—	2.672

Note: (1) Because a simple refining process is envisaged, without cracking, account is taken only of regular gasoline, around 90 octane. (2) "Other" products include LPG, bitumen, etc., and are calculated at the average value of gasoline, kerosene, and gas oil. (3) Fuel oil calculated at 6.7 barrels per long ton, price C.P.I. $12.60 in April, 1962; $13.10 in April, 1963.
Source: Col. (1), *World Petroleum Statistics*, 1961; Cols. (3) and (5), Platt's Channel Port Index. (Publication of the "high" ceased at the end of 1962.)

hence the prices of refined products? (4) What forces bear on the price of crude oil, up or down, and how can we evaluate them?

We take no account of general price movements or of political influences (except in Part IV), or of great technical innovations, either in the use of energy or in supply. Whatever may be the influence of this type of change on the basic facts, we aim to provide a framework into which the changes can be fitted.

Tables 14.1 and 14.2 show the structure of prices, limited to northern Europe and the Middle East. Sources and methods are indicated in detail. The general principle of table 14.2 is the following: The structure of prices contains five elements—price f.o.b., price of transport, price c.i.f., price of refining, and prices of products. These five elements are not independent, however. Hence it is possible to verify and check, and to compare a computed or theoretical price with an actual observation.

Apparently there does exist a consistent price structure, although we could not say that it is precise. On the contrary, each element is within a wide enough range. Besides, the Channel Port Index prices are based on a false theory, namely, that prices are determined by Caribbean f.o.b. plus

Table 14.2
Structure of real prices, Middle East–Northwest Europe

		Per barrel	Per metric ton
1.	Receipts for refined products	$2.67	$19.76
2.	Refining margin	0.68	5.00
3.	Crude oil 43°, c.i.f.	1.99	14.76
4.	Present freight rates, term characters (Scale less 45 percent)	0.61	4.49
5.	Crude oil 34°, f.o.b.	1.38	10.27
6.	Discount implied	0.41	3.04
7.	Check: five contracts Arabian crudes, July, 1962–February, 1963, range of discounts	0.34–0.44	2.50–3.27
8.	Check: four sales contracts North African crude, October, 1962–March, 1963, discounts	0.49–0.52	3.60–3.85
9.	Check: Venezuelan crudes f.o.b. $1.78, c.i.f. $2.11, discrepancy 11 cents per barrel, 82 cents per ton		

Note: Detail does not always add, because of rounding.
Sources: Row 1, see Table 1; 7.51 barrels per long ton, 7.40 barrels per metric ton; row 2, see *L'Étude sur les perspectives*, p. 92. We use the lower value of the range ($5–$6) because a refinery no less than 40,000 barrels daily (two million tons annually) is envisaged; row 4, Intrascale flat Ras Tanura to Rotterdam, $6.71/long ton at 55 per cent $3.69 plus $0.875 Suez Canal fee; rows 7, 8, and 9, see "The World Oil Outlook," now in press. Crudes are adjusted to 34°. N.B. In the range of 30°–40° A.P.I., Venezuelan crudes should normally command a premium of $0.05–$0.10 because of low sulfur and hydrogen sulfide content.

spot freights, even though these prices are acceptable simply as observations and because Caribbean prices are themselves reflections of European.

We can safely say that, given the real prices which prevail today at the Persian Gulf and with which there is a mutual accommodation by Venezuelan and North African prices, the products being supplied today by northern European refineries are available at the approximate indicated prices, without practical limits.

Of course, prices actually charged to customers may be much higher because of tariffs, special taxes, etc., or because of price structures on refined products, which may be slowly collapsing, as seems to be the case in Britain. On the other hand, the prices given in table 14.1 are higher than the prices quoted by the AFM (Assenhandelsverband für Mineralöl), and perhaps are a sort of average. In any event, the tables indicate the availability of these products at these or lower prices.

Some larger refineries (higher than 40,000 barrels per day) may have lower costs than those shown in table 14.2. They draw a rent like that of the owner of a very good oil field. Or perhaps a refinery may produce a smaller range of products, worth less than the average (say, no LPG (liquefied petroleum gas) or bitumin, products which are profitable in Europe). If so, both the receipts and refining costs, as well as the cost of crude charged, are lower, but supply is little affected. We do not wish to wave aside these individual cases but, on the contrary, to emphasize the complexity of present-day refining patterns.

As for present-day freight rates, they should correspond, as the *Étude sur les perspectives* well puts it, to a dependable flow (*un acheminement régulier*) from origin to destination, and should, therefore, rest on term charters. True, individual cargoes are available at lower prices, which correspond to a succession of single-voyage ("spot") charters, but then one must take account of costs of making contracts, costs of waiting for a given ship to be ready where and when needed, costs of stockpiling to avoid expensive interruptions in the flow of crude to refineries or fuel oil toward the power plant, etc., or the insurance premium against an unexpected sharp increase in rates. During the rigorous winter of 1962–63, for example, spot freights doubled and then collapsed to even less than their old levels, while term charters hardly budged.

We must not exaggerate the disparity between spot and term freights. For a number of years it was quite stable at around ten points of Scale, that is, about $0.90 per ton; today it is perhaps half again as large, or $1.35. The least one can say is that present and recent prices are, in fact, based on the cost of a dependable flow and not on the cost of isolated shipments. These two species of freight, which embody alternative methods of furnishing the transport service, are not necessarily very different. But in any case, for five or six years, term contracts have been made around $4.49 per metric ton from the Persian Gulf to the Channel. (It is interesting that the recent restrictive legislation by the German parliament is aimed precisely at term contracts, limiting them to twenty-four months without special authorization.) In a word, the present structure does not depend on the happenstance of temporarily low freight rates, which will disappear some day, but on term commitments (unless Intertanko succeeds in getting them up again, which I do not believe will happen).

We have no reliable publicly known figure for delivery price of crude oil into northern Europe. Some readers know whether our estimates are too far from the truth. On the other hand, the f.o.b. crude oil prices correspond well enough to discounts publicly known and recognized, account taken of differences in specific gravity. For example, since January 1, 1963, Japanese buyers have been getting Persian Gulf crude at $1.26 per barrel f.o.b., indicating a discount of $0.16 from the posted price of $1.42. But the latter is itself a discounted price. In other words, a price of $1.26 plus $0.14 (or less) in respect of 7° gravity A.P.I. indicates a price of $1.40 (or less) for 34° crude, a discount of $0.40 a barrel, roughly $3.00 per ton, or even more. We can be sure that higher discounts exist, because the real value of 1° gravity A.P.I. is less than $0.02. The formula of $0.02 per degree is only a rule of thumb. Sulfur or wax content can be more important than the lower viscosity indicated by higher A.P.I. degree number. Besides, we have recently seen bids to buy at $1.00 per barrel and even less for the Khafji crude but these offers were refused, and such discounts are probably exceptional at present. If they were important, either the prices of refined products would be below their present level or else refiners would be realizing an abnormally high profit per unit by passing up additional markets, which seems unlikely.

Finally, the discounts sketched here do not seem too far from the truth because they are consistent with the other elements of the price structure. Certainly these figures will (or so we hope) undergo many corrections in detail, and the object of this essay is precisely to arouse the attention of those able to furnish more precise facts. However, we think a global rejection is improbable.

One objection comes immediately to mind: that this structure represents only a small percentage of the flow of oil which passes through the open market, when everybody knows that by far the larger portion stays within one or another of the integrated companies. But in fact the "prices" at which these companies "buy" and "sell" are not prices at all but accounting figures. They are certainly necessary and proper in order to render an accounting of income, particularly to governments (who are the ones to judge), but they cannot be used for an inquiry like ours into supply and markets. Besides, it is the competition of this small part of the market which has made the price structure what it is,[2] a result natural or paradoxical or both, but in any case a known fact whose existence we cannot ignore.

Can this structure persist over the long run, even if the real costs of transport and of refining are assumed not to change?

A given price may at any given time be temporarily below the level necessary to evoke a permanent supply of the product at the current level. In the long run, if the price does not rise, costs can no longer be covered (including the minimum necessary profit on the investment); supply shrinks and price rises. In other words, a higher price is a necessary condition for maintaining the current level of output. It would, of course, be pointless to let the market act in this clumsy way, eliminating productive facilities in order to bring them back later. But in fact (and in theory) the market does not act this way if the suppliers can foresee the price rise; they reduce their offers but do not leave the market so long as prices stay above current variable costs; they keep their capacities, and are not ready to sell off their assets at any price as the start of their exit.

Can we find, in the structure of real prices, an element which must increase if the supply is not to be inevitably reduced in the future? With respect to refining, the answer seems to be "No." *Étude sur les perspectives* gives no indication that the margin is insufficient. The rapid rate of increase in western European refining capacity, including those independent refiners who cover a substantial part of their needs for crude oil by purchasing it, reinforces this opinion. It is difficult, if not impossible, to reconcile an annual refinery-expansion rate of around 10 percent with the idea that refining does not pay its way. Of course, there are and will be refineries producing a range of products more varied and valuable, whose outlays and receipts are both greater, whose costs and prices are above the mean; and there will be others which are below.

Heavy fuel oil is worth special attention. In 1962, its price was around $12.50 a metric ton, today around $13.10.[3] Without going into details, there seems no doubt of some improvement over the last eighteen months. At the same time gasoline prices have fallen, with excess production making sillier than ever the clichés about "main products" and "by-products," slogans which for too long have hindered sober reflection on petroleum price structures.

Now, if these two opposing movements came about at the same time, it was not by chance; actually the one is the cause or the necessary condition for the other.

Petroleum products are joint products, and it is altogether useless to seek or to pretend to have found the costs of the individual products, which do not exist. One sometimes hears that heavy fuel oil "ought to make a fair and equitable contribution to amortizing the investment," etc., an idea which is nothing but a barrier to serious discussion, and of which *Étude sur les perspectives* is happily free. It is a waste of time to try to impute this or that part of refining costs to this or that product. Refining a ton of crude oil is profitable and will be done if the receipts cover the total costs of the operation, including the necessary profit; while no *individual* product will be forthcoming if the market price is above its incremental cost.

But this idea of "incremental cost" can be misunderstood. The notion, too widespread, that incremental cost is necessarily below average cost, or below the price, must be completely rejected. When and if a refinery is working at less than optimum percentage of capacity, an additional barrel can be produced at a rather low cost, below the average cost; then the price of the refined products is under downward pressure. On the other hand, when a refinery is being pushed toward maximum output, the cost of the additional barrel becomes higher and higher because of product deterioration, lack of normal down time for maintenance, cleaning and repair, etc. In general, incremental cost rising with higher output expresses the resistance of output to expansion and gives the signal that production is pressing against the limits of capacity. When this situation is expected, or when it arrives unexpectedly, it is time to plan for expanding capacity. Thus the reckoning of short-term incremental cost, that of making the best choice given the present capacity, is replaced by considering long-run incremental cost, that of adding the best type and amount of incremental capacity, either in a new refinery, or in building an addition to one already on stream. In general, when a branch of the economy is rapidly expanding, its incremental cost is a mixture of short and long term and is high in comparison with a permanent level of output no greater, which these facilities will produce later on.

In the United States, despite a slow growth of demand, the availability of natural gas liquids and of visbreaking (viscosity breaking) has reduced the need for distillation; hence refinery capacity has been practically static for several years. Hence there is much well-founded complaint about that famous or infamous "incremental barrel," which must always be denounced at every trade meeting and in every trade magazine, and the very mention of which is considered a dirty word by some refiners.

But in western Europe the problem is different. Aside from some small and localized surpluses, the incremental cost of the petroleum products taken together is not below the average cost, the incremental barrel is not cheaper, and prices are therefore not under any pressure from that source—from others, to be sure, but not from that one. It is too bad that this way of thinking and speaking about the incremental barrel as ultra-cheap, justified today by the facts in the United States, should be mechanically transferred to Europe where it corresponds to nothing. Perhaps excess refining capacity will come later, as producers of crude oil try to realize their profits at the product level, but it does not yet exist.

But if there is no pressure on the price of the whole output, there can surely be a surplus of any particular product available at a very low incremental cost when the others are produced at high incremental costs and sold at high prices. For when products are joint in variable proportions, between certain limits the incremental cost of a single joint product does exist, even if its average cost does not. This type of incremental cost is perhaps too complex for precise statement except in mathematical terms because two phenomena must be taken into account: outlays which vary with the refinery structure to produce more of one and less of another product, and also the loss of revenue from the products being sacrificed. In the United States, for example, the incremental cost of heavy fuel is low because of the high prices of gasoline and other products into which it can be cracked (which more than compensate the high costs of cracking), while the price of fuel oil is also low because of the competition of coal and gas. In Europe the incremental cost and the price of fuel are higher. In fact (and on this everyone seems agreed) it is the growing demand for heavy fuel and more recently for gas oil which has occasioned an overabundance of gasoline and a fall in its price. Consequently the incremental cost of fuel oil has been and remains (in early 1963) *higher* than two years ago. Hence it is an error to say that the incremental cost of heavy fuel is today abnormally low for temporary reasons. In fact, it has been on the increase for several years. Naturally, the oil industry has taken some measures to curtail surplus gasoline, particularly by developing heavier crude oils which give a higher fuel-oil yield and less gasoline. There is also a continuing search for new outlets in gas manufacturing or petrochemicals; for lack of anything better, the reinjection of naphtha (raw gasoline, in effect) into the ground— literally a subproduct.

For simplicity, we have spoken only of heavy fuel and of gasoline as though these were the only refinery products. But taking account of gas oil ("middle distillates," as they are aptly known in the United States) and other products changes nothing essential. To the extent that the prices and outputs of other products increase, there is a downward pressure on the price of any given product. The very active demand now registered by middle distillates exerts a downward pressure on the prices both of gasoline and of heavy fuel.

Let us now pose the problem in relation to the construction of new refineries up to about 1970. A refinery will not be built if it is not profitable (unless it is really a disguised price cut on crude oil, which we will examine later). If one aims at a higher fuel-oil percentage, there must be a higher profit margin on each product in order to offset the loss of receipts on the products selling at higher prices. But one must also consider the savings made through buying heavier, and therefore cheaper, crude, of using simpler and cheaper refinery processes, and of the better prices obtained for gasoline as its output is reduced relative to demand. These counterforces are not negligible. For example, a 31° Kuwait crude yields 47 percent heavy fuel, which implies a loss of 19.3 cents per barrel by comparison with table 14.1,[4] but this crude is cheaper by 21 cents (at posted prices) than the crude assumed there, so that the refiner is actually money ahead on the change. The real price difference, as we saw earlier when discussing Khafji crude, is less; but even so, there is hardly any loss to be compensated by an increase in price. Indeed, the very reason for existence of the gravity structure of crude oils is to compensate just these differences in receipts on refined products.

But now let us suppose that heavier crudes are not available, and that the growth of European output thereby brings about an inevitable fall in gasoline prices. Let us go to the limit and suppose that the price of gasoline falls to crude-oil value, $14.60 per ton, $1.72 per barrel, $0.041 per gallon. At this point, the conversion of naphtha into gasoline would not be worthwhile, and the absence of any reforming or cracking in the new refineries would lower their refining process costs. Let us disregard this fact also and calculate that there is a loss of $0.30 per barrel of crude charged, which must be compensated for by an increase in the revenues from other products, from $2.026 to $2.326, or by 12.5 percent. Since the elasticity of demand for middle distillates (gas oil) and other products is less than that of fuel oil, their prices ought to rise by more, and fuel oil by less, but let us disregard that too. An increase of 12.5 percent from the present $13.10 would bring the heavy fuel oil price to $14.80. If, with a heavier crude, the gasoline yield fell from 20 to 15 percent, for example, each non-gasoline product increasing proportionately, the same reckoning would give a fuel oil price of $14.01 per ton. To get higher prices, one must invent circumstances improbable or even impossible.

Therefore, so far as concerns the new refineries, if the tendency continues toward a higher fuel yield and a lower gasoline price, the difference between the price of crude oil and the price of heavy fuel can decline only mildly from the present-day $1.50 per ton. On the other hand, it is even possible that the price of heavy fuel oil is abnormally high today, and if we knew that the price of gasoline plus middle distillates were on the increase, we would have to conclude that the price of heavy fuel oil would decline even more in relation to crude oil. But it seems profitless to speculate; the subject well deserves discussion among refining specialists.

Another way of stating the problem is more elegant. One part of the refinery's output, heavy fuel oil, is a simple combustible, which is worth no more than any other source of heat, if allowance is made for special handling costs which are a little lower than for coal. On the other hand, all other products have special possibilities not shared by heavy fuel oil, coal, or even, for the most part, by natural gas. Therefore the price of heavy fuel oil cannot go appreciably above the price of crude oil, or else consumers would burn the crude entire. (The technical problems, particularly of flash point, are sloved cheaply enough, as Japanese experiments have just shown.) The prices of the other products cannot go below the price of crude, or else the refiners would not pay the expenses of refining; and in any case the products would have at least fuel value. The basic rule is, therefore, that to the extent that the prices of other products go above the price of crude oil, the price of heavy fuel oil is below it; on the other side, when the prices of other products tend toword their lower limit, the price of crude oil, the price of heavy fuel tends toward its upper limit, which is also the price of crude oil. At this limit, there is no longer any refining.

Hence, while the price of fuel oil can get closer and closer to the price of crude oil, it cannot exceed it, except for such special and temporary reasons as a crude whose naphtha fraction is so light, with so low a flash point, that it must be topped before being burned. Therefore the topped crude is worth more than the original.

No matter what refining center or refining and crude oil sale we look at, even setting aside those where the fuel oil fraction is below 35 percent, it is rare to see a heavy fuel oil price above crude, except for those very heavy crudes which are, in effect, fuel oils. It must be admitted that price comparisons, even of real, not posted, prices at Venezuela and the Persian Gulf are not too convincing because the refiners there are also producers; and the profitability of refining depends not on the incremental cost of fuel (compared with its price) but rather on the incremental cost of crude. An additional barrel of crude charged into the refinery does not sacrifice a barrel which could be sold as crude; hence the price of crude does not exist as an opportunity cost of refining the barrel. Sales of crude are limited anyway. This argument has considerable force for the Caribbean and Middle East, but little for California (1948–54) or for western Europe today, where the price of heavy fuel is below that of even heavy crudes. This price relation exists for basic economic reasons and not because of the wisdom or the good or ill will of any individuals or companies.

We can deal only briefly with an interesting problem. The companies which today are reinjecting naphtha into the formation do so despite its fetching "quite a respectable realization" above the price of crude oil.[5] But the marginal revenue for the producer who is also a refiner with a large part of the ultimate market can even be negative, because to sell more gasoline could depress prices and even total profits. Hence a sale of gasoline which would be good business for a refiner with a small part of the final market could be a loss for one with a major part. Hence the companies which are reinjecting naphtha are letting a part of the growing European and other markets go to the smaller refiner-producers—as the statistics on new European refinery projects seem to show. In any case, reinjection slows the tendency toward continued drop in gasoline prices, hence also toward a rise in fuel-oil prices.

Thus we may conclude that the present relation seems stable enough and that the real price of heavy fuel oil will stay below the real price of crude oil—perhaps a little higher than it is today, perhaps a little lower, But if, as is possible but cannot be evaluated today, the demand for fuel is lowered by the availability of large amounts of natural gas or of imported coal, the amount of crude run to stills will be less, the prices of other products will be somewhat higher, and the price of heavy fuel will be lower.

Let us now look at transport costs. At the outset, we must drop all notions of a surplus of ships. There is none. Two years ago, to be sure, it was still difficult to make predictions because one could not yet tell whether freights then current, of Scale less 45 percent, were self-sustaining in the long run or whether they only reflected a temporary surplus of ships. But in mid-1961, several shipowners ordered new ships built to charter at the level. This implies that for large new ships, Scale less 45 percent was profitable enough to pay out a large investment. The impression is widely current that the oil company lent the owners the money, but this is incorrect, although it is true that a shipowner with a twenty-year contract in hand can easily find credit to build the ship. If neither prices nor operating costs were to rise, freight rates could not go higher.

By late summer, 1961, it was becoming clear that the so-called surplus was no more than the normal stock of high-cost ships not worth using except during seasonal peaks.[6] By the middle of 1962, the surplus was entirely gone, and even ships formerly in the grain trade were returning; yet term charters showed no tendency to rise.

Since the end of January, 1963, we have seen a wave of new orders, the greatest since 1957, at ship prices quite low by comparison with the preceding year.[7] During 1958–62, the price of a modern tanker of 50,000 or more tons was around $135–$145 per ton, but there were few orders. Current prices are around $95–$100 per ton, even less for some simpler ships designed for the North African–southern European run ($80 per ton). Since the cost of the ship is about half of the total (including the minimum return on investment), one would expect a new large tanker to be profitable and worth building at roughly 10–12 percent less, and hence the price of freight service ought to go down to about Scale less 50 percent. In trying to verify this hypothesis, we can see that the term-charter market, on re-awakening in 1963, has established a level of around Scale less 50 percent for new ships now being ordered. And these contracts are predominantly for three to five years rather than twenty. As long as this condition lasts, long-term freight costs cannot exceed this amount because no oil company will pay more if it can itself get the same service by building its own ships. Moreover, a producing-refining company can always get its bunkers cheaper than an independent buyer.

But the analysis is not yet complete because it is not certain that tankers will always be available at $95–$100 per ton. It is possible that these prices only reflect a temporary situation arising from excess capacity of shipyards, and that price will rise again once this surplus has disappeared because, to maintain the supply of ships, prices cannot stay at their present levels. This is surely possible, but we ought to be careful about predicting it. The very low prices have been a great shock to the shipbuilding industry, as well as to allied trades, and the natural reaction is to call it a temporary condition and expect the normal state of affairs to return. But it is better to stay a bit skeptical; too often the wish is father to the thought. Swedish and Japanese shipyards have no lack of orders and no more excess capacity, which indicates that their incremental costs are probably not abnormally low. Indeed, three Japanese shipyards have recently announced plans for expansion. The new Japanese and Swedish shipyards certainly build faster and at lower cost. But the problem is difficult to resolve, and, everything else being equal, it is at least possible that the prices of ships will reach a level such that the minimum freight needed to keep them being built will be around Scale less 47 or 48 percent. Hence Scale less 45 percent ought to be regarded as an upper limit.

Conclusion: Products

The present price structure contains no internal distortions to exert any great pressure upward. The price of fuel oil may move up a little toward the price of crude oil, but the most probable development is between a mild increase and a mild decrease, both of freight and of the price of fuel oil in relation to crude oil (which will happen if the prices of other products strengthen). The most likely forecast seems to be the continuance of the present structure.

However, all that has been said takes no account of the influence of technical progress on costs or of changes in the price of crude. We consider now the first possibility.

We can say little that is positive about refining costs. In general, one expects a mild decrease because of technical progress. But what interests us most is the change, if any, in the respective incremental costs of the various products. And at this point we must criticize our own table 14.1, which represents a state of affairs that is visibly disappearing. First, the statistics of refined products leave much to be desired. The separation of heavier gas oils from heavy fuel oil is neither consistent from one country to another nor very well done in any place. This makes it difficult to verify any hypothesis. For example, if refiners are aiming at the maximum fuel-oil output, and if $31°$ crude gives 47 percent, then taking account of even heavier crudes coming from the Middle East and Venezuela, how can we arrive at an average yield which corresponds to a $34°$ crude? Possibly because refineries no longer are trying to maximize fuel oil but gas oils, but possibly also because the statistics are faulty. Besides, the class "other products" takes in too many varieties from the point of view of market values. But the error, or the inadequacy, which will become the worst is the identification of naphtha with gasoline. It is time to recognize the separation. Naphtha, the light end of the distillation process, today is not worth much over its fuel value—sometimes less. But with additional processing, particularly reforming, naphtha can be upgraded into various grades of gasoline or jet fuel. Hence it is a matter of comparing the additional costs with the additional revenues. And perhaps a careful study of this question would show that the prices of gasolines will be so low that the incremental cost of fuel oil will be correspondingly high. But we cannot stop here because of the recent introduction of a process to convert naphtha cheaply into town gas. At first, the distributors of gas will regard this innovation as welcome but of only modest importance. Later they will come to see—as did their opposite numbers in the United States—that an investment to permit all their networks to carry high-calorific-value gas would in effect double their capacity and permit them to add to it at about half the previous cost, and would pay very well if the consumer found it attractive to use gas outside the kitchen—above all, for space heating. Hence there is an inexpressibly complex play of forces, involving the price and supply (incremental cost schedule) of naphtha, of town gas faced by the competition of electricity and therefore indirectly of coal and heavy fuel oil, of natural gas as it will become available from North Africa and the North Sea region (in quantities unknown today), and of middle distillates. Gas oil will compete with gas as domestic fuel, and as a fuel for diesel engines with railroad electrification and hence, again, with coal and heavy fuel oil. Refiners will seriously study what would have been madness recently, how to use catalysts to minimize liquid yields and maximize gas yields, because the value of gas will equal the value of naphtha plus the cost of conversion into gas. In truth, the complexity of relations among incremental costs of refined products reflects faithfully the complexity of technical relationships and the wide spread of possibilities of marginal transformations in the long run, not to say the interplay with demand functions. Like Lord Cornwallis surrendering to General Washington, we will be asking the band to play a tune called "The World Turned Upside Down." This is why electronic calculators, having speedily conquered the operations of individual refineries, now are in the process of also taking over the operations of whole groups.[8]

One must candidly admit the limits and shortcomings of his own methods. We can refute logical errors by verbal reasoning and perhaps sketch general relationships. But quantitative relations among supplies and demands and prices of refined products can only be expressed by mathematical (usually called linear) programming, taking into account the demands for various kinds of energy, long-term incremental costs of crude oil and products, and the kinds of constraints stated earlier. The sooner this kind of work gets under way the better.

The situation is different with maritime freight rates; there is no doubt that they will diminish. If the "normalized" level is perhaps around Scale less 45 rather than Scale less 50 percent, we can predict that technical progress will overcome this regressive tendency, even without taking account of innovations unknown today. First, even if the prices of ships go back to somewhere between today's $95 and yesterday's $135, the new ships will be more automated with a smaller wages bill. Moreover, because of increasing volume of shipments there will be increasing room for economies of scale which are limited by the size of the local market; hence more and more ports and discharging facilities will be adapted to larger ships. Also, modern ships will be replacing older ones. Hence the marginal ship which fixes the price of shipping service, that is, the least efficient ship, will itself become a more recent and efficient ship, as well as a larger one. To sum up: Even if one takes account of a certain upward normalization of ship prices and technical innovations already in operation, the best estimates of freight costs seem to be around Scale less 50 percent, say about $4.20 per ton, from the Middle East to northern Europe, $3.00–$3.55 to Mediterranean ports.

Conclusion: Delivered Prices

Toward 1970–75, taking account of any internal stresses in the current price structure and also of technical change, if the price of crude oil remains at about the present level, the price of a barrel of refined products as a whole, and of heavy fuel oil in particular, will not be very different from what it is today. A mild decline seems likely.

It is time now to look at the price of crude oil, which is the most important element in the price structure and the hardest to analyze or predict, and for which one's forecasts must have the greatest margin for error because one must take account of political influences upon the market. We must admit to having no special knowledge in this field; but we can ask what political influence can accomplish given the economics.

The general expectation, if there is one, is that the royalties (used here as a general term to include also income taxes and all other types of payments) will increase in the future, bringing about an increase in price. This implies that these royalties are a kind of cost, but in fact they are a sharing of profits. Of course, royalties and prices move in the same direction usually—but have not done so recently—but to suppose that the increase of royalties is a cause of higher prices is to put the cart before the horse. Worse than a logical error, it is an evasion of the real problem.

Can the supply of crude oil, and therefore the price, be controlled or not? To be sure, the royalties can form part of a price-maintenance mechanism, as we will see in a moment, but that is all.

The present crisis exists because one can easily drill enough wells to install a producing capacity much larger at a cost not much higher, if at all, than the present one, and in any case well below present prices; the situation will not change through 1975, despite the great increase foreseen in consumption.[9] Furthermore, this capacity is divided among eight independent countries: Kuwait, Saudi Arabia, Iraq, Iran, Libya, Algeria, the Soviet Union, and Venezuela, not to mention some Persian Gulf sheikdoms. (Because of their location, we need not include the United States and Indonesian output has been relatively static, though undeveloped reserves are very large.)

Every nation and every producing country has the power, and claims the right, to produce much more than it produces and sells today.[10] The individual interest of every country and of every producer is always to produce and sell much more, but the group interest of the sellers is to limit output in order to keep prices from dropping.

The problem of reconciling the two interests can only be avoided by a detailed, lasting agreement. (The 1928–39 cartel, a looser one, was never more than half-successful and became decreasingly so.) This necessity or necessary condition has not always existed. Up to about 1950, there was hardly any crude-oil market at all. The integrated companies produced for their own needs in refined products and hardly sold or bought, aside from a few exchanges and some long-term contracts. But after 1950, a market gradually came into existence and grew more rapidly after the Suez crisis because the number of sellers (including Soviet Russia) and buyers increased greatly.

The famous World Oil Cartel by all evidence has not existed since 1939. As a Shell official wrote with equal wit and truth, "Competition in this industry is massive rather than hysterical," meaning that it works slowly but does work in the long run. This competition, and not the will or the tactic of any group, has, since 1957, been responsible for the fall in crude- and refined-product prices. Accusations against the companies, or against the Russians, that they are deliberately dumping remain unsupported by evidence—or even explanation—and do not deserve to be taken seriously. (By dumping, I mean selling below incremental cost even when it is possible to get more, an action which can only be explained as harassment or an attempt to eliminate a competitor. I have yet to see a single example of this in the oil market. By "dumping" is usually meant selling at a price low enough to annoy competitors, and, of course, there has been plenty of this.)

Against all the evidence there remains yet a widespread opinion that the big companies are so big—and therefore so strong—and have such "financial power" or other "power" that in the German phrase *"Sie werden alles schon machen"*: They will make everything nice and tidy and proper again. It is neither the first nor the last time that these words of "economic power" or "big business" remind us of Talleyrand's remark that God gave man speech so he could hide his thoughts—or, we must add, his lack of thought. And it is quite possible that these companies will be so flattered by this legend of their "power" that they will accept the responsibility for managing the market in their own name, which would be a disastrous mistake for them. The record since Suez is one of their loss of control while a market emerged. It is now the turn of the governments of the producing countries (with some help from consuming countries) who claim the right of "consultation" before any price change and the right to refuse royalties calculated on the basis of prices below posted prices. Thus their percentage of real prices has increased from around 50 to around 60 percent.

In three countries the royalty paid to the government remains a percentage: Venezuela, Algeria, and Libya (where the situation is rather unclear at the moment). Here the royalties have no important influence on the price. In trying to control prices directly, the government of Venezuela has recognized this fact, but the degree of success is naturally hard to gauge. (A commission of coordination will not recognize any price they consider unduly low; the company can sell for less, but then the lower price will be ignored for tax purposes.) The president of British Petroleum (B.P.) has also recently recognized this fact, criticizing the practice of figuring royalties as a percentage because this posed no obstacle to the continued fall of prices. But this practice exists because it is profitable to the countries which follow it. The interests of all producers and of all producing countries, taken as a whole, would be to decree, as in fact is done in the other producing countries, an amount per barrel. This is today around an average of 71 cents per barrel (lower for some heavy crudes: about 61 cents for the 27° crude of Kahfji, 66 cents for the 27° of Safaniya).[11] This royalty, as a floor to price, will stay as long as nobody tries to reduce the payment to the host country. Here is a true mechanism of price control. But can it last for a long time? If the three countries stay outside the arrangement, one can say definitely not. If they fall into line, as seems likely, it is less certain; the answer cannot be categorical, but, with certain reservations, it seems that the answer must remain negative.

This opinion is based on the lack of that mastery of supply which remains the condition *sine qua non*. Lacking this, the contradiction between the general interest and the individual interest does not get resolved. The time of a very quiet and slow competition among a handful of gasoline marketers in a small restrained national market is gone. We now have a crude-oil market, which, even if it includes only a small portion of the total, is enough to do its usual work; fringes of newcomers in gasoline; rivals of almost equal stature in heavy fuel oil; for middle distillates competition is between the two extremes. And for all these products, the competition is on a constantly larger scale because of the growth of the market and perhaps because of its approach to an all-European scale. In consequence the pace of competition has speeded up, and the control of supply can no longer remain implicit in refraining from doing anything to upset prices. And the wide variation among the producing costs of the various countries makes the problem still more difficult.

Everyone agrees with B.P. in wanting a fixed royalty which would act as barrier to price cuts; but, if the same royalty per barrel were applied everywhere, the whole market would be laid open to producers with the lowest costs (especially Kuwait) who would know that henceforth their competitors could no longer sell below the current price for fear of losing money and hence could no longer meet any price cuts.

Besides, the best price for one is not the best for the other; estimates of future receipts and rates of discounting them are not the same. Hence a different schedule of royalties for each producer, matching reasonably well his schedule of costs and market possibilities, does not come of itself. It must be made, and even that does not suffice. It must have the approval of all the others, for *every important producer has the power of veto*. Surely the producing countries can make such an agreement. But this does not mean that it will get done; indeed, the mistaken confidence in royalties as sufficient barriers to price reductions hinders them from taking measures in good time.

As matters stand today, of course, no company would dare to propose to a government that the royalty be cut, that is, that it be treated as a percentage of a diminished market price. But suppose it is a government which needs more money and suggests that its company make a special contract at a special low price, with royalty specially reduced, the whole thing to be secret (which it will be, but which it will not remain). The complexities of crude-oil quality, viscosity, sulfur content, and tanker freights allow a wide choice among methods of hiding the price for some time. Or, what if a government suspects another of doing this, cannot be sure the report is false (supposing it is), and remembers the time-honored rule about one's partner in such an enterprise? Do him quick, before he does you? Such a development need not be probable in this or the next year, but the chance of its happening at least once over a number of years is the sum of all the small chances in any one. One incident or one suspicion is enough for one to fear a weakness and start thinking about getting out.

The wide dispersion of reserves relative to production levels and hence in the present value of a barrel used up today instead of tomorrow; in current and discounted costs; and, therefore, in the market price which would be most profitable to one or another; the uncertainties in forecasting demand and hence the slight chance of resolving the various claims to market shares, including that of the Soviet Union, make it very difficult to see a lasting agreement. There is no logical impossibility, and in any case we will never see a rapid crumpling of the price structure. Too many obstacles to the unrestrained play of competition remain, including especially the regulations imposed by the most important consuming countries; and the half-effective measures taken by the producing countries will at least have the effect of slowing down the process and keeping it from going to the limit. But the direction of prices seems less doubtful, unless there is an international agreement like the one just concluded for coffee (leaving 15 percent of productive capacity outside), or like the agreement on airline passenger fares (which is today facing collapse because of the wide variations in costs among airlines). But the present tendency is actually in the other direction. The producing countries are actively seeking new concessionnaires for the areas reclaimed from the producing companies, which will in time be translated into competition in the sale of crude oil and its products.

Now if prices are not maintained they will, little by little, gravitate toward costs of production. The difficulties of defining crude-oil production costs are well known, and we propose no general method of measuring them. But our object is much more limited—to define that cost which would serve as the floor to price in the Middle East (and in Venezuela) between 1963 and 1975, nothing more. In this much more modest task, we can try an approach to production cost, and at least eliminate some errors, thus promoting the work of those who can go further than we. We are looking for the cost as a price floor even though we would *not* expect the price to go down that far. But it is the spread between actual price and the one which would exist under unlimited competition (i.e., long-run incremental cost of the producing industry) which registers the tension in the market and the force of downward pressure. Therefore it is important to know if the industry incremental cost per ton is in the neighborhood of $2.00, or $5.00, or $7.00 because a pressure proportional to an $8.00 difference ($10.00 less $2.00) is much more important than a pressure proportional to $5.00 ($10.00 less $5.00) or to $3.00.

Let us look first at the cost of a single field or deposit. Fixed costs are often thought to represent most of it; hence the incremental costs which set the floor to price are thought to be exceedingly low, the competitive price falling nearly to zero. And it is true that once producing capacity is in operation, the well dug and equipped, operating costs are very low. *But this fact has no importance* in an industry where capacity must be increased 10–15 percent annually because of growing consumption and natural loss of pressure and capacity. To sell crude oil today at a price which would not cover the cost of replacing capacity when one is actually engaged in digging and equipping new wells is unreasonable, and is not done. (The exception is in the United States, because of a legal and regulatory system peculiar to it, and which exists nowhere else, so we need not discuss it here.) Therefore the relevant incremental cost is not the very low operating cost but the sum of development plus operating cost. The industry really shows unjustified jittery nerves on the subject of costs because of the mistaken idea that the bare operating cost is an important fact in relation to price.

The industry incremental cost can be roughly defined as the cost of development plus extraction of the poorest deposit needed to make supply equal demand.[12] This incremental cost can in theory be quite high compared with the average cost; unfortunately, we have no information from which to estimate it. But given the known relations among depths and production rates of the various deposits, if the average development-production cost is now around $2.00 per ton in the Middle East,[13] the marginal cost can hardly be more than double. In Venezuela, the variety of costs is so great that the average of $7.00 per ton has less meaning. But for the sake of example, not by way of prediction: If the price in Venezuela is aligned on a Middle East price midway between the $4.00 marginal cost and the $10.00 real price early in 1963, that is, at $7.00 per ton, the maximum Venezuela price must be that plus a $2.25 freight advantage, hence $9.25. Hence all Venezuelan production which costs no more than the average plus 32 percent can survive, but only if the royalties are adjusted accordingly. But these estimates are only for illustration and should not of themselves give the appearance of a precision which does not really exist.

The situation will change when the national oil companies, who have already acquired areas for oil search, find producible reserves. Of course, their territories take in the whole gamut, from the big Rumaila field in Iraq, some of which can be put in production soon to other areas which will never be worth anything. One can only be sure that one or two national companies at least will (in addition to N.I.O.C., already a going concern) find some good reserves, without trying to guess which will be the lucky one. The national companies can do their figuring without bothersome complications as to the division of profits between landowner and operator, and without the need to consider certain kinds of risks. No doubt they will begin by following all the irrelevant accounting rules, but common sense will not wait long to break through. Hence their reckoning is useful in showing the true price ceiling. Over the period 1946–61, according to the Chase Manhattan Bank, outlays for production, including all pipelines, terminal tankage, docks, and even most findings costs (only geological-geophysical expenses and lease rentals and bonuses are excluded), were $3,406 million. At the end of 1961, daily capacity was around 6.8 million barrels (average of 5.6 million adjusted for growth during the year and 15 percent capacity not used). In the extreme case where there was no loss of pressure and no loss of the rate of output in any well between 1946 and 1961, the cost of establishing an initial capacity to produce one barrel per day was therefore just over $500. If, at the other extreme, one estimates the annual loss of capacity at 7.5 percent (normal elsewhere but too high in the Middle East), the cost of developing one barrel daily is $341.[14] Using a midway hypothesis, the cost would be $420. If the cost of operation is taken at 10 cents per barrel (50 percent higher than the average in *Étude sur les perspectives*, p. 89), the profit earned by selling a barrel for $1.00 is $0.90, or $328 per year or 78 percent of the investment returned the first year, and earnings of 65 percent per year for the first ten years.[15]

Let us emphasize that we are not trying to calculate "the rate" of profit, either total or average, of any private or public company. Such a calculation seems unnecessary for our particular purpose, and besides it would require predictions impossible for us on the proper rate of discount, degree of risk, etc. But we simply get an idea, however imprecise, of the profits which could be realized in the short run. If profit during the first year was of the order of three-fourths of the investment, in three years it would be regained along with net earnings of 125 percent. Of course, there are deposits much less rich than the average, others more so. But it is hard to imagine any operator forever holding back his activity for years and not starting to exploit his property unless he has firm assurance that others facing the same situation will do the same. It is not easy to imagine that a government will never let its company make sales at such a price, and taking half or more of the profit, at a price which is gradually becoming an open secret. Hence a price as low as $1.00 per barrel (roughly $7.00 to $7.50 per ton), though not imminent, is not unthinkable, fairly soon.

The calculations which purport to show that the profits of any given company or group are no more than some low and hence "reasonable" level on the whole investment (including that outside of production) are not relevant. For one thing, rates of profit on past investments and contracts (including some very costly tanker purchases and charters) are not necessarily a good guide to profits tomorrow, which guide decisions taken today. Moreover, a company which passes up an investment because the profit on the whole operation, including transport and refining, is not good enough hands the market over to producers who would rather sell their crude oil than take it further downstream. Formerly, when those open-market outlets hardly existed, this consideration did not exist either. But today the loss of sales has pushed the companies toward a competition none of them has wanted.

We can sum up our discussion:
1. If the price of crude oil does not change, the price of the whole barrel of refined products will probably decrease mildly. Heavy fuel oil will not change much from its present $13 per ton; a considerable increase seems out of the question.

2. If the producing countries can make a durable agreement which will above all settle the capacities and sales of all of them, the price of heavy fuel can be pushed a little higher than the price of American coal which would be available in northern Europe, if the governments there permit its entry, at about $10 per metric ton, equal to a little over $14 per ton of heavy fuel oil.[16] But the prices of the other refined products can be kept much higher; there is no comparable ceiling.

3. If the producing countries cannot make this agreement, all petroleum prices are going to drop very considerably, but it seems impossible to indicate how much.

4. Royalties are not a primary influence on prices, but they can be quite important as a method of making the agreement effective. If prices fall, the division of profits will be a burning question between oil companies and governments and the occasion for serious and even disagreable argument.

In addition:

5. The economic interest of the Soviet Union as an exporting nation requires that the world price be high, so that they can undercut it a bit. Their political interest is to be the champion of the underdeveloped nations in supporting their claims to higher prices for their raw products while remaining the friend of the other poor nations, non-producers, by furnishing them oil more cheaply. this price policy is therefore consistent.

6. The closing of the American market has no doubt aggravated the overabundance of oil since 1959. But we must not overstate its importance because this market had never been open as a practical matter. If the market were ever opened (not "reopened"), the bargaining between sellers and independent buyers would lead to a fall in price. What happened in Germany, Italy, and Japan, a half-open market, rapidly growing, with some arms' length bargaining, would be repeated in the United States, but on a much larger scale.

The writer has no suggestion for an oil or energy policy. He does venture to suggest that an ostrich policy is not useful. Failure to look at the real influences on price today, because we have been unable to measure them precisely, is a bad policy for anyone.

Notes

This article is a slightly revised translation of an article published in French in the December, 1963, issue of the *Revue de l'Institut Français du Pétrole*, and appears here with permission. It is part of a project of research on the world oil market since 1945, supported by Resources for the Future, Washington, D.C. See my essay,

"The World Oil Outlook," in *Natural Resources and International Development*, ed. Marion Clawson (Baltimore: Johns Hopkins Press, 1964), for a treatment of the theories and methods used here.

I wish to thank the Institut Français du Pétrole, especially Mme Jacqueline Funck and M. Jean Chappelle, for their kind hospitality. It is both a pleasure and a duty to acknowledge the suggestions, criticisms, and discussion of J. Barnea, M. Boudard, G. Brondel, L. Bruni, B. Corradini, J. Curry, R. Deam, S. Friis, C. Grigg, H. Gripaios, J. Hartmann, J. Hartshorn, V. Henny, J. Jorgensen, L. Kaplan, P. Maillet, W. Newby, G. Parisot, F. Parra, D. Ovens, J. Ritchie, W. Stewart, and P. Wack. These persons bear no responsibility for any errors or opinions whatever.

1. The widely quoted "Only fools and affiliates pay posted prices" has been made much more precise: "Posted prices are the ones that fools, some affiliates, certain underdeveloped countries, France and Britain pay [and] are irrelevant for sensible oil consumers ... Japanese, Swedes, some Germans, and Italians" (*Economist* (London), November 9, 1963, p. 578).

2. See the *Rapport général de la Communauté européenne du Charbon et de l'Acier* (February 1, 1962–January 31, 1963) (Luxembourg, 1963), p. 203.

3. We assume A.P.I. 16°, specific gravity 0.9593, 6.6 barrels per metric ton for heavy fuel oil. Hence the prices of $1.89 and $1.98 per barrel equate to $12.50 and $13.10 per metric ton, respectively.

4. The difference in yield is 47.1 less 36.4, or 10.7 percent, hence 4.5 gallons per barrel. The loss of revenue is 8.8 less 4.5, hence 4.3 cents per gallon of the charge, or 4.5 times 4.3, 19.3 cents per barrel.

5. Francisco R. Parra, "Demand Patterns and Crude Gravities" (paper published by OPEC (1963)), p. 16.

6. See *Petroleum Press Service*, September, 1961.

7. The following is based on *Platt's Oilgram, the Journal de la marine marchande*, and *Petroleum Press Service*, January–May, 1963.

8. See E. S. Sellers and L. C. Strang, "The Refining Pattern," in *The Oil Industry Tomorrow* (Institute of Petroleum, 1962); and W. J. Newby and R. J. Deam, "Optimization and Operations Research," *Proceedings of the Institute of Chemical Engineers*, XL (1962), 350–55.

9. See "The World Oil Outlook," *op. cit.*, for the detailed reasons.

10. Only Venezuela seems to have renounced this right, in aiming only at a modest annual increase in production—not too easy to attain. And the Venezuelans are getting impatient.

11. *Petroleum Intelligence Weekly*, May 13, 1963, calculated from Parra, *op. cit.*, p. 19. These two great deposits are really only one and produce the same gravity oil (see *Petroleum Press Service*, May, 1963, p. 170).

12. Finding costs no longer are part of the price floor, as demonstrated in "World Oil Outlook."

13. In this and the following paragraphs, we use the cost figures of the *Étude sur les perspectives*, which seem too high for Venezuela by comparison with the statistics published by the government of that country.

14. Our actual reasoning can be quickly, if a little crudely, summarized: Taking 1956 as the mid-year of the 1946–61 period, because of the swift increase in production, assume all capacity installed in that year, earlier installation balancing later. Then in five years, there is a loss of 32 percent, so that the 6.8 million barrels represent an original installation of just over 10 billion barrels, costing $340.6 a barrel. Incidentally, if we define development cost as equaling that price which would make the present value of the expected cash flow just equal to the investment needed to generate it, then assuming a 2.5 percent decline rate and a 20 percent rate of return, Middle East development cost is 20.3 cents per barrel. But this idea must be much further elaborated before it can be useful.

15. We assume that the annual loss is henceforth 7.5 percent, even if it was only about half of that previously, so that our profit calculations are on the conservative side.

16. To summarize very briefly, and *for a steady flow on a very large scale only*: Contracts have recently been made for delivery on the northeast coast of the United States, at about $7.50 per short ton, by reason of lower f.o.b. prices and lower transport costs by integral trains. Hampton Roads is closer to the mines, and lower freights allow a laid-down cost around $7.00. The distance from Hampton Roads to the northwest coast of Europe is the same as from the eastern Mediterranean, and a coal carrier is nothing but a simpler oil tanker; hence the cost of transport is comparable to that from Sidon to the Havre-Hamburg range. If we assume ships of only medium size, around 40,000 tons dead weight, we cannot assume freights of scale minus 50 but rather minus 45 percent, hence of $2.06 per long ton to Le Havre, $2.26 to Hamburg, or, taking a middle figure, of $2.16 per long ton, $1.90 per short ton. Hence the c.i.f. price of steam coal at the European coast would be about $8.90 per short ton, $9.90 per metric ton.

15   Is the Oil Shortage Real? Oil Companies as OPEC Tax Collectors

The United States currently consumes more energy than any other country. Over the next dozen years, our energy consumption may double. Oil and gas provide three-fourths of our energy. Domestic reserves could supply this projected demand only at excessive costs, and large-scale supply of nuclear energy is more than a decade away. By the end of this decade, we will probably be importing very substantial quantities of our oil.

It is widely believed that this situation will constitute a major foreign policy problem in the coming decade with implications ranging from adverse effects on our balance of payments to a changed political balance in the Middle East. Negotiations between oil companies and oil-producing countries have been front page news almost continuously for the past two years, with the companies recently agreeing to producing-country "participation" in ownership. *The New York Times* has announced editorially that "the squeeze on oil has begun," and the Ford Foundation is financing a large-scale study of world energy problems. Oil companies have spent considerable amounts on advertisements to inform us about the problem.

Given these views, it is rather startling to find a highly respected M.I.T. economist and oil expert stating that there is "absolutely no basis to fear an acute oil scarcity over the next 15 years." Professor Adelman, while acknowledging that the United States is confronted with a local exhaustion of its low cost oil and gas, nevertheless argues in the following article that not only is the world energy crisis "a fiction," but that to the extent that there is a foreign policy problem, it is in considerable part caused by inept policies of the U.S. government.

The multinational oil companies have become, in the words of the board chairman of British Petroleum, the "tax collecting agency" of the producing

Reprinted from *Foreign Policy* 9 (1972): 69–107.

nations. In 1972, the companies operated the greatest monopoly in history and transferred about $15 billion from the consuming countries to their principals. If the arrangement continues, a conservative estimate for 1980 collection is over $55 billion per year. Much of that wealth will be available to disrupt the world monetary system and promote armed conflict. Oil supply is now much more insecure. Monopoly, the power to overcharge, is the power to withhold supply. Among nations, an embargo is an act of war, and the threat of an oil embargo ushered in the Organization of Petroleum Exporting Countries (OPEC) cartel.

The oil companies are now the agents of a foreign power. They will be blamed for impairing the sovereignty of the consuming countries, and quite unjustly. They only did the will of the OPEC nations and of the consuming countries themselves, notably the United States. The consumers' "strange and self-abuse" is the key to how the events of 1970–71 turned a slowly retreating into a rapidly advancing monopoly.

The most important player in the game is the American State Department. This agency is deplorably poorly informed in mineral resource economics, the oil industry, the history of oil crises and the participation therein of the Arabs with whom it is obsessed; in fact, State cannot even give an accurate account of its own recent doings.

Prediction is unavoidable but risky. In 1963 I though that, abstracting from inflation, a price of $1 per barrel at the Persian Gulf was not unlikely fairly soon. In terms of 1963 dollars it did go to 92 cents by early 1970. As predicted, supply remained excessive, and the companies could not control the market. But on the political side, the prediction went all wrong in 1970–71. Although I had warned that the producing countries might threaten a cutoff of supply, and urged insurance against it, I was much mistaken to call it an unlikely event. Nor did I expect the consuming countries, especially the United States, or cooperate so zealously.[1] I may be equally wrong to expect that consuming countries will continue this way for most or all of the 1970s.

The unanimous opinion issuing from companies and governments in the capitalist, communist, and Third World is that the price reversal of 1970 and 1971 resulted from a surge in demand, or change from surplus to scarcity, from a buyers' to a sellers' market. The story has no resemblance to the facts. The 1970 increase in consumption over 1969 was somewhat below the 1960–1970 average in all areas. The increase in 1971 over 1970, in Western Europe and Japan, was about half the decade average. In the first quarter of 1972, Western European consumption was only 1.5 percent above the previous year. By mid-1972, excess producing capacity, a rarity in world oil (i.e., outside North America) was almost universal and had led to drastic government action, especially in Venezuela and Iraq. The industry was "suffering from having provided the facilities for an increase in trade which did not materialize." A drastic unforeseen slowdown in growth and unused capacity would make prices fall, not rise, in any competitive market.

Some powerful force has overridden demand and supply. This force did not enter before the middle of 1970, at the earliest. Up to that time the trend of prices had been downward, and long-term contracts had been at lower prices than short-term, indicating that the industry expected still lower prices in the future, even as far as 10 years ahead.[2]

If demand exceeds supply at current prices, sellers and buyers acting individually make new bargains at higher prices. When supply exceeds demand yet prices are raised, the conclaves, joint actions, and "justifications" are strong evidence of collusion, not scarcity.

More precisely: in a competitive market, a surge in demand or shrinkage in supply raises price because it puts a strain on the productive apparatus. To produce additional output requires higher costs; unless compensated by higher prices, the additional output will not be supplied.

If there were increasing long run scarcity at the Persian Gulf, discoveries falling behind consumption, the reservoirs would be exploited more intensively to offset decline, and to maintain and expand production. More capital and more labor would be required per additional barrel of producing capacity. In fact, between 1960 and 1970 (the last year available), the investment needed per unit of new crude oil capacity fell by over 50 percent, despite a rising general price level. Labor requirements (which are both for construction and operation) have fallen even more drastically. Supply has not only not tightened, it has been getting easier.[3]

The world "energy crisis" or "energy shortage" is a fiction.[4] But belief in the fiction is a fact. It makes people accept higher oil prices as imposed by nature, when they are really fixed by collusion. And sellers of all fuels, whatever their conflicts, can stand in harmony on the platform of high oil prices.

Twenty years ago, the Paley Commission made the classic statement of the problem: "Exhaustion is not waking up to find the cupboard is bare but the need to devote constantly increasing efforts to acquiring each pound of materials from natural resources which are dwindling both in quality and quantity.... The essence of the materials problem is costs."

It is worth assuming arbitrarily that in the future supply will tighten. The worst that can happen is zero new discoveries. Table 15.1 shows Persian

Table 15.1
Persian Gulf production and reserves, zero discoveries model, 1971–1985

1971			
Production		6	BBY
Reserves		367	BB
Production/reserves		1.6	%
Reserves plus 50 percent		550	BB
1971–85			
Average growth per year	8	11	%
1985			
Production	17	25	BBY
Cumulative 1972–85	143	178	BB
Remaining	407	372	BB
Production/reserves	4.0	6.7	%

BB = billion barrels
BBY = billion barrels per year; a billion = one thousand million.
Source: 1971 production and reserves, from *Oil & Gas Journal*, December 31, 1971.

Gulf production and reserves in the zero-discoveries model, recognizing that reserves in fields known in 1971 can be expanded by development and discoveries of new pools in the old fields. The assumption of 50 percent expansion is highly conservative in the light of American experience, considering also that probably most Persian Gulf reserves (like most production) are in fields discovered in the last 20 years.

In 1950, Persian Gulf reserves were estimated at 42 billion barrels, mostly in eight large fields still producing today at ever-higher rates with no peaking out. In 1951–71 inclusive, 47 billion barrels were extracted. At end-1971 reserves were 367 billions, mostly in 26 large fields, including the original eight. On the basis of production, one may estimate that nearly half the reserves are in fields operating in 1950, nearly 2 fourth in fields discovered in 1950–59, between a fourth and a third in 1960–69 discoveries, which have the greatest expansion potential (Reserve data from BP *Statistical Review of the World Oil Industry* and *Oil & Gas Journal*).

Production growth in 1971–85 is estimated first according to a recent BP forecast of 7.7 percent, which takes account of rising U.S. imports, to come mostly from the Persian Gulf. Doubtless also it registers, as does a Shell forecast, the cessation of growth in European imports as North Sea oil and gas takes over.[5] Indeed, Persian Gulf shipments to Europe will probably be lower in 1980 than in 1972—rising and then falling in the interim. But to be on the safe side, we also estimate 1972–85 production by extrapolating the long time growth rate.

The cumulated production 1972–85 is subtracted from expanded end-1971 reserves. The higher the production-reserve ratio, the higher is cost, all else being equal. The zero-discoveries model is drastic to the point of absurdity. Moreover, it sets to zero the reserves of African and Persian Gulf natural gas, which at current prices are worth producing, and which equate to an additional 90 billion barrels oil equivalent. Even so, the 1985 production-reserve percent is much lower than is planned for similar, i.e. high capacity, reservoirs in the North Sea or Alaska, which are usually in the range of 7 to 11 percent.

Depletion of reserves at the Persian Gulf is only about 1.5 percent a year. It is uneconomic to turn over an inventory so slowly. But Persian Gulf operators have not been free to expand output and displace higher cost production from other areas because this would wreck the world price structure. Therefore, it is meaningless to average production-reserve ratios for the whole world, as is too often done. A barrel of reserves found and developed elsewhere in the world is from five to seven times as important in terms of productive capacity as a barrel at the Persian Gulf. In other words, one could displace production from the entire Persian Gulf with reserves from one-fifth to one-seventh as large. And this is perhaps the only constructive aspect of the current drive for self-sufficiency in oil. This zero-discoveries model yields a much higher production-reserves percent, hence a substantial increase in investment requirements and current operating costs per barrel. Today at the Persian Gulf, capital and operating costs are each about 5 cents per barrel; under our extreme assumptions, they are roughly double. The difference between 10 and 20 cents measures the value of discovering new fields: it takes the strain off the old.

No Basis for Fears

The zero-discoveries model only estimates the worst that could happen; it is not a prediction of what will happen. When the procedure was applied in 1965, current and projected costs were higher than they are now, since many new discoveries have freshened the mix, not to speak of improvements in technology.

There is no more basis for fears of acute oil scarcity in the next 15 years than there was 15 years ago—and the fears were strong in 1957. The myth that rising imports (of the United States) will "turn the market around" is only the latest version of the myth that rising imports (of Europe and Japan) would "dry out the surplus in 1957–70."[6]

More generally: supply and demand are registered in incremental cost, which is and long will be a negligible fraction of the current crude oil price of about $1.90 per barrel. Hence *supply and demand are irrelevant to the current and expected price of crude oil.* All that matters is whether the monopoly will flourish or fade.

In Europe and Japan, there was a mild and temporary shortage of refining capacity in early 1970. At the same time, a tanker shortage put rates at the highest level since shortly after the closing of the Suez Canal, and raised product prices.

In May 1970 the trans-Arabian pipeline was blocked by Syria to obtain higher payments for the transit rights, while the Libyan government began to impose production cutbacks on most of the companies operating there, to force them to agree to higher taxes. Although the direct effect of the cutback and closure was small, the effect on tanker rates was spectacular, and product prices and profits shot up.

The companies producing in Libya speedily agreed to a tax increase. The Persian Gulf producing countries then demanded and received the same increase, whereupon Libya demanded a further increase and the Persian Gulf countries followed suit. Finally, agreements were signed at Tehran in February 1971, increasing tax and royalty payments at the Persian Gulf as of June 1971 by about 47 cents per barrel, and rising to about 66 cents in 1975. North African and Nigerian increases were larger. In Venezuela the previous 1966 agreement was disregarded and higher taxes were simply legislated. These taxes are in form income taxes, in fact excise taxes, in cents per barrel. Like any other excise tax they are treated as a cost and become a floor to price. No oil company can commit for less than the sum of tax-plus-cost per barrel.[7]

Government-Company Harmony

The multinational companies producing oil were amenable to these tax increases because as was openly said on the morrow of Tehran, they used the occasion to increase their margins and return on investment in both crude and products. In Great Britain the object was stated: to cover the tax increase "and leave some over," and the February 1971 tax increase was matched by a product price increase perhaps half again as great. The best summary of the results was by a well known financial analyst, Kenneth E. Hill, who called the agreements "truly an unexpected boon for the worldwide industry."

Mr. Hill rightly emphasized product price increases, but arm's length crude prices also increased by more than the tax increases. When the producing countries made fresh demands later in 1971, an American invest-ment advisory service (United Business Services) remarked that tax in-creases were actually favorable to oil company profits. And 1971 was easily the best year for company profits since 1963, although there was a profit slide off later in the year, as competition in products though not yet in crude again reasserted itself.

The price pattern is set for the 1970s. From time to time, either in pursuance or in violation of the Tehran-Tripoli "agreements" the tax is increased, whereupon prices increase as much or more, but then tend to erode as the companies compete very slowly at the crude level and less slowly at the products level. Thus prices increase in steps, yet at any given moment there is usually a buyer's market, i.e., more is available than is demanded at the price, which is under downward pressure.

The companies' margin will therefore wax and wane, but they benefit by the new order. They cannot, even if they would, mediate between pro-ducing and consuming nations. As individual competitors, they are vulner-able to producing-nation threats to hit them one at a time. As a group, they can profit by a higher tax through raising prices in concert, for the higher tax is that clear signal to which they respond without communication. The Secretary General of OPEC, Dr. Nadim Pachachi, said truly that there is no basic conflict between companies and producing nations. The then head of Shell, Sir David Barran, spoke of a "marriage" of companies and producing governments. Most precise of all was Sir Eric Drake, the chairman of BP, who called the companies a "tax collecting agency," for both producing and consuming Country governments. There is, however, a difference in kind between serving a government in its own country to collect revenue from its own citizens, and serving a government to collect revenue from other countries.

Leading Role of the United States

Without active support from the United States, OPEC might never have achieved much. When the first Libyan cutbacks were decreed, in May 1970, the United States could have easily convened the oil companies to work out an insurance scheme whereby any single company forced to shut down would have crude oil supplied by the others at tax-plus-cost from another source. (The stable was possibly locked a year after the horse was stolen.) Had that been done, all companies might have been shut down, and the

Libyan government would have lost all production income. It would have been helpful but not necessary to freeze its deposits abroad. The OPEC nations were unprepared for conflict. Their unity would have been severely tested and probably destroyed. The revenue losses of Libya would have been gains to all other producing nations, and all would have realized the danger of trying to pressure the consuming countries. Any Libyan division or brigade commander could consider how he and friends might gain several billions of dollars a year, and other billions deposited abroad, by issuing the right marching orders.

Failure to oppose does not necessarily imply that the United States favored the result. But there was unambiguous action shortly thereafter. A month after the November agreements with Libya, a special OPEC meeting in Caracas first resolved on "concrete and simultaneous action," but this had not been explained or translated into a threat of cutoff even as late as January 13, nor by January 16, when the companies submitted their proposals for higher and escalating taxes.[8]

Then came the turning point: the United States convened a meeting in Paris of the OECD nations (who account for most oil consumption) on January 20. There is no public record of the meeting, but—as will become clear below—there is no doubt that the American representatives and the oil companies assured the other governments that if they offered no resistance to higher oil prices they could at least count on five years' secure supply at stable or only slightly rising prices.

The OECD meeting could have kept silent, thereby keeping the OPEC nations guessing, and moderating their demands for feat of counteraction. Or they might have told the press they were sure the OPEC nations were too mature and statesmanlike to do anything drastic, because after all the OECD nations had some drastic options open to them too ... but why inflame opinion by talking about those things? Instead an OECD spokesman praised the companies' offer, and declined to estimate its cost to the consuming countries. He stated that the meeting had not discussed "contingency arrangements for coping with an oil shortage." This was an advance capitulation. The OPEC nations now had a signal to go full speed ahead because there would be no resistance.

Before January 20, an open threat by the OPEC nations would not have been credible, in view of the previous failure of even mild attempts at production regulation in 1965 and 1966. But after the capitulation, threats were credible and were made often. (This is clear from a careful reading of the press in January and February 1971.) They culminated in a resolution passed on February 7 by nine OPEC members, including Venezuela but not

Indonesia, providing for an embargo after two weeks if their demands were not met. The Iranian Finance Minister, chief of the producing nations' team, said: "There is no question of negotiations or resuming negotiations. It's just the acceptance of our terms." The companies were resigned to this, but wanted assurances that what they accepted would not be changed for five years.

The United States had been active in the meantime. Our Under Secretary of State arrived in Tehran January 17, publicly stating his government's interest in "stable and predictable" prices, which in context meant higher prices. He told the Shah of Iran the damage that would be done to Europe and Japan if oil supplies were cut off. Perhaps this is why the Shah soon thereafter made the first threat of a cutoff of supply. It is hard to imagine a more effective incitement to extreme action than to hear that this will do one's opponents great damage.

Resistance to the OPEC demands would have shattered the nascent cartel. As late as January 14, the Shah told the press: "If the oil producing countries suffer even the slightest defeat, it would be the death-knell for OPEC, and from then on the countries would no longer have the courage to get together."

When the Tehran agreement was announced, another State Department special press conference hailed it, referring many times to "stability" and "durability." They "expected the previously turbulent international oil situation to calm down following the new agreements." They must really have believed this! Otherwise the would not have claimed credit for Mr. Irwin or for Secretary Rogers, or induced President Nixon's office to announce that he too was pleased. They must have said this in Paris in January and again at an OECD meeting in May. We now live with the consequences.

State Department representative James Akins told a Senate Committee in February 1972: "The approach we made in the Persian Gulf [was] primarily because of the threat to cut off oil production.... We informed the countries that we were disturbed by their threats, and these were withdrawn very shortly after our trip." The public record outlined above shows that the threats of embargo began after the Under Secretary's arrival, culminated in OPEC Resolution XXII.131 on February 7, *and were never withdrawn*.

Scraps of Paper

The oil companies knew better than to take the "agreements" seriously; they had been there before. To be sure, one could cite many a statement by an oil executive about the "valuable assurances of stability," but this was ritual. The London *Economist*, always in close touch with the industry, expected any agreements to last only a few months, given the "persistent bad faith." The best summary was made by *Petroleum Intelligence Weekly*: "If such agreements were worth anything the present crisis wouldn't exist."

This was borne out in August of 1971. Devaluation of the dollar, the occasion for new demands, was of course an incident in the worldwide price inflation to which the Tehran and Tripoli agreements had adjusted by providing for periodic escalation. Moreover, Persian Gulf revenues were mostly not payable in dollars. The new element in the situation was not the increased dollar cost of imports to the producing countries, but the fact that prices in dollars increased, especially in Germany and Japan. This was another windfall gain to the companies, just as in early 1970. Again the producing countries were able to take most of that gain in the consuming countries because the multinational companies were the producers of oil as well as sellers of refined products.

The "oil companies had hailed the agreements as guaranteeing a semblance of stability in oil prices ... they would seek to pass on the impact of any new cost [tax] increases." The new demands, said the chairman of Jersey Standard (Esso, or now Exxon), were a violation of the Tehran agreements, but "the industry will solve these problems just as our differences with them were reconciled earlier this year and before," i.e. higher taxes and higher prices. This was precisely correct both as to substance and as to ritual. The OPEC governments made their demands. The companies made an offer. The governments refused it and broke off the talks. The companies made a better offer, taxes were raised again, and crude oil prices with them.

Even before this deal, the producing nations had already made an additional demand, for so-called "participation." The companies said they were distressed that the agreements "have not led to the long peace ... that they had anticipated." They would resist the demands as a violation of the agreements. Whereupon the governments "announced that they would take part in a 'combined action' if they didn't receive 'satisfaction,'" and the companies agreed to negotiate. In March, the Aramco companies who account for nearly all output in Saudi Arabia conceded participation "in principle."

"Participation," by recently negotiated companies and various Arabian governments, is a misnomer. "Pseudo-participation" would be more apt. "Participation" does not mean that the government actually produces or sells oil, or transfers it downstream for refining and sale. As we will see later, selling oil is what Saudi Arabia wisely aims to avoid. "Participation" is simply an ingenious way of further increasing the tax per barrel without touching either posted prices or nominal tax rates, thus apparently respecting the Tehran agreements. Once the tax increase is decided, everything can be cut to fit. The same oil is still sold or transferred by the same companies. On the terms discussed early in 1972, "participation" would mean about 9 cents more tax per barrel.[9] Those who believe that this assures supply, stable prices and a solution to the balance of payments problem will believe anything.

There has been unparalleled turbulence since the State Department special conference. Venezuela dispensed with the elaborate sophistry of "agreements," and legislated: an additional tax increase in 1971 and again in early 1972 with another expected in early 1973; nationalization of natural gas; the requirement that companies deposit increasing sums of money lest they permit properties to run down before the national takeover in 1984; and the extension of this "reversion" to all facilities rather than only producing facilities. Confronted with declining production because it was cheaper for the companies to lift additional output from the Persian Gulf, Venezuela set minimum production rates, with fines for insufficient output.

In Libya, the government followed the Persian Gulf countries in demanding and getting an increase on the same pretext of monetary adjustment; and also in demanding participation, whether "participation" or the real thing is not yet clear. In December 1971, when Iran seized two islands near the mouth of the Persian Gulf, Libya seized the properties of British Petroleum in "retaliation"; any stick is good enough to beat a dog.

The Algerian government took two-thirds of the output of the French companies, who were "compensated" with what little remained after deducting newly calculated taxes.

In Iraq, the operating Iraq Petroleum Company cut back output sharply during 1972 for the same reason as everywhere else in the Mediterranean (where the main field delivers via pipeline)—costs plus taxes were lower at the Persian Gulf, where capacity was being quickly and cheaply expanded. Iraq demanded that production be restored, and that IPC make a long-term commitment to expand output by 10 percent per year. The IPC counteroffer not being acceptable, Iraq made headlines by seizing the Kirkuk field June 1, then offered forthwith to sell at "reduced and competitive prices," for spot delivery or long-term contracts. This threat was aimed at the most sensitive point of the world oil industry; the permanent potential oversupply which in Iraq (and other countries) had already been made actual. Price-cutting is intolerable in a cartel; to avoid it, a flurry of complex negotiations began. A loan was soon made by other Arab OPEC members.

"Behind the Arab nations' action ... lies an offer by Iraq to sell its newly nationalized oil at a cut rate, which would have driven down the revenues received by the other countries for their oil." This may also explain the gentlemanlike behavior of the expropriated IPC, which did not attempt to blacklist Iraq oil to be sold in non-Communist markets.

Onward and Upward with Taxes and Prices

The genie is out of the bottle. The OPEC nations have had a great success with the threat of embargo and will not put the weapon away. The turbulence will continue as taxes and prices are raised again and again. The producing nations are sure of oil company cooperation and consuming-country nonresistance. This is a necessary condition. There are two purely economic reasons why the situation cannot be stable.

1. The crude oil price can go much higher before it reaches the monopoly equilibrium or point of greatest profit.

The average price in Europe of a barrel of oil products in 1969–70 was about $13 per barrel. It is higher today. If the new tax rates were doubled, say from $1.50 to $3 per barrel at the Persian Gulf, a straight pass-through into product prices would be an increase of only 10–14 percent. It is doubtful that such an increase would have any noticeable effect on oil consumption. Moreover, about half of the European price consists of taxes levied by the various consuming-country governments. The producing nations have long insisted that in justice they *ought* to receive some or most of this amount. Be that as it may, most or all of this tax *can* be transferred from consuming to producing nations, with help from consuming-country governments who dislike unpopularity through higher fuel prices. The Italian government collaborated early in 1971.[10]

The current price of oil, however far above the competitive level, is still much less than alternatives. The producing nations are not a whit displeased by big expensive projects to produce oil or gas from coal or shale or tar sands, which are a constant reminder of what a bargain crude is, even at higher prices. Particularly outside the United States, nuclear power sets a high ceiling, coal a much higher ceiling. The price of British coal has long and well served sellers of fuel oil in Britain, who priced at or slightly below coal-equivalent. Small wonder that the head of Shell appealed in October 1971 of the maintenance of a British coal industry.

There has therefore been much discussion, mostly oral, of the goal of the Persian Gulf nations being the U.S. price; or $5 per barrel, etc. These are attainable goals, and we must therefore expect attempts to reach them.

2. The producing nations cannot fix prices without using the multinational companies. All price-fixing cartels must *either* control output *or* detect and prevent individual price reductions, which would erode the price down toward the competitive level. The OPEC tax system accomplishes this simply and efficiently. Every important OPEC nation publishes its taxes per barrel; they are a public record, impossible to falsify much. Outright suppression would be a confession of cheating. Once the taxes are set by concerted company-government action, the price floor of taxes-plus-cost is safe, and the floor can be jacked up from time to time, as in early 1971, or early 1972, or by "participation."

It is essential for the cartel that the oil companies continue as *crude oil marketers*, paying the excise tax before selling the crude or refining to sell it as products.

Were the producing nations the sellers of crude, paying the companies in cash or oil for their services, the cartel would crumble. The floor to price would then be not the tax-plus-cost, but only bare cost. The producing nations would need to set and obey production quotas. Otherwise, they would inevitably chisel and bring prices down by selling incremental amounts at discount prices. Each seller nation would be forced to chisel to retain markets because it could no longer be assured of the collaboration of all the other sellers. Every cartel has in time been destroyed by one then some members chiselling and cheating; without the instrument of the multinational companies and the cooperation of the consuming countries, OPEC would be an ordinary cartel. And national companies have always been and still are price cutters.[11]

Chiselling will accelerate if national companies go "downstream" into refining and marketing. One can transfer oil to downstream subsidiaries or partners at high f.o.b. prices, but with fictitious low tanker rates or generous delivery credits. The producing nation can put up most of the money or take a minority participation, or lend at less than market interest rates. One can arrange buyback deals, barter deals, and exchanges of crude in one part of the world for availability elsewhere. The world oil cartel in the 1930s was eroded by this kind of piecemeal competition, and so will the new cartel of the 1970s if the individual producing nations become the sellers of oil.

The Saudi Arabian petroleum minister, Sheik Yamani, who designed "participation," warned in 1968 against nationalizing the oil companies, and making them "buyers and brokers" of crude oil. This would, he argued truly, lead to "collapse" of oil prices and benefit only the consuming countries. The experts retained by OPEC also warned in 1971 that "participation" must not interfere with marketing of the oil through the companies.

More recently, in 1971, Sheik Yamani warned that "participation" had to provide the right kind of "marketing operations." In 1972 he added: "We are concerned that prices in world markets do not fall down."

OPEC has come not to expel but to exploit. And if the excess crude oil supply were not permanent, Sheik Yamani would have no cause for the "concern" he rightly feels.

We may therefore conclude: the producing countries can raise prices and revenues further by jacking up the excise tax floor, in concert. Conversely, if and when the consuming countries want to be rid of the cartel, they can take their companies out of crude oil marketing. To avoid taxation, they can decommission the tax collecting agents who are their own creation.

So far, the consuming countries have gone in precisely the opposite direction. As they develop high cost substitutes, and strive to get their respective companies, public or "private," into crude oil production and marketing, they will rivet the tax collection agency more firmly on their necks. It is time to ask why they do this, and whether the policy may change.

One can only guess at the unstated reasons why the United States has put OPEC in the driver's seat. First, American companies have a large producing interest in the world market. In 1971, American companies produced about 6.5 billion barrels outside the United States. For every cent of increase in prices above that in tax, there is an additional $65 million in profit.[12] Second, the higher energy costs will now be imposed on competitors in world markets; and in petrochemicals, higher raw material costs as well. Third, the United States has a large domestic oil producing industry. The less the difference between domestic and world prices, the less the tension between producing and consuming regions.

Fourth, the United States desired to appease the producing nations, buying popularity with someone else's money and trying to mitigate the tension caused by the Arab-Israel strife, which, however, is irrelevant to oil. If the Arab-Israeli dispute were settled tomorrow, the producing nations would not slow down for one minute their drive for ever-higher prices and taxes. The acknowledged leader of the Persian Gulf nations in early 1971 was Iran, which has in one important respect—the Trans-Israel Pipe Line—actually cooperated with Israel more than the United States, which in 1957 and 1968 discouraged the pipeline.[13]

The State Department View

In a recent speech—to the West Texas Oil and Gas Association—the director of the State Department Office of Fuels and Energy, James Akins, professed he could not sleep for worry over the possibility of a "supply crisis" caused by even one Arab nation stopping oil production. Such a "crisis" is a fantasy. Five Arab countries produce an aggregate of *one* MBD; they would never be missed. In 1951, Iran, producing nearly 40 percent of Persian Gulf output, shut down; yet 1951 Persian Gulf output actually rose. No Arab or non-Arab country is nearly that important today. In the winter of 1966–67, Iraq—about 10 percent then as now—shut down, and there was not even a ripple on the stream.

If any proof were needed that an Arab boycott will hurt only the Arabs and soon collapse, the 1967 experience should suffice. The *Wall Street Journal*, for example, said that the former Secretary General of OPEC, Francisco R. Parra, "can't conceive of any political situation arising in the Middle East that would lead to confiscation of investments held by the oil companies. Should another Arab-Israeli war break out, Mr. Parra doesn't expect any repetition of the unsuccessful attempt by the Arab nations to embargo oil shipments to some Western nations. 'I don't believe oil can effectively be used as a political weapon by withholding supplies from market—there just can't be an effective selective embargo,' he asserted."

The Oil Import Task Force report, signed by the Secretary of State and not contested on this point by the minority, explained why partial shutdowns or boycotts could not be sustained, concluding: "Thus to have a problem one must postulate something approaching a total denial to all markets of all or most Arab oil." It might help if State explained why it no longer agrees.

Along with warnings about "the Arabs," the State Department has taken to warnings of oil scarcity. Thus Undersecretary Irwin warned the OECD in May 1972 of a worldwide "shortage" of 20 MBD by 1980, because of rising consumption. Mr. Irwin's speech was widely noted and commented on. Three weeks later, Iraq moved at Kirkuk, confident of eventual success because of the "growing energy requirements of the industrialized countries," and growing U.S. imports.

Mr. Akins had already outdone Mr. Irwin in a speech to the Independent Petroleum Association of America, warning that "by 1976 our position could be nothing short of desperate," and that Persian Gulf reserves would decline after 1980. The basis of these fears is a well-kept secret which the economist cannot penetrate. But the prediction of a Persian Gulf price of $5 by 1980 must be taken seriously. There was not even a perfunctory disclaimer of expressing only personal opinions in the speech or one to the National Coal Association. He is voicing government policy. In another speech, he spoke of the "widespread recognition ... that it is not in the Arabs' interests to allow the companies to continue expansion of production at will, and that the producing countries, most notably Saudi Arabia, must [sic] follow Libya's and Kuwait's leads in imposing production limitations."

It seems odd to have an American official telling "the Arabs" they should restrict output. Kuwait has found the argument persuasive and has limited output. But this is the only clear example. Libyan oil is overpriced, i.e. overtaxed, and better bargains are available elsewhere. In fact, the expulsion of British Petroleum in December was seen as a "windfall" to the industry because of excessive supply. According to Platt's Oilgram News Service: "Companies have been anxious to reduce production in Libya but 'no company had the courage to do it and now Libya is making BP do it 100 percent,' one observer said." No other Arab country has restricted, and "few ... are likely to follow Kuwait's lead," despite the State Department telling them they "must." Saudi Arabia is engaged in a record expansion of capacity. So is Iran, whose Finance Minister directly rejected the argument in March of 1972. For the whole Middle East, 1972 drilling was expected in February to exceed 1971 by a massive 74 percent.

Akins also makes the baffling statement (in the IPAA speech) that "the sellers' market" arrived in June 1967. Yet prices continued to slide for three years more, and Mr. Akins himself notes that neither buyers nor sellers knew the "sellers' market" had come. He never explains it. Almost surely he refers to the Suez Canal closure, which by raising transport costs should somewhat *weaken* the demand for crude oil. But the effect of the Suez closure is negligible either way. Reopening of the Canal would equate to a 9 percent addition to the world tanker fleet, which has been growing at nearly 13 percent per year: loss of the Canal is a loss of eight and one-half months growth. Indeed the presence or absence of the Suez Canal is less than the error of estimate of the tankers available at any given time.[14]

The same State Department source feared a world shortage because "the Arabs" [sic] would find it difficult or impossible to raise the "enormous sums of capital" needed for new production. In 1970 (most recent year available), total production expenditures in the "Middle East," i.e., Persian Gulf *plus* some substantial expenditures in Turkey, Israel, and Syria, *plus* some payments to governments, amounted to $300 million. In 1972, the revenues of the Persian Gulf nations will amount to about $9 billion. (See table 15.2.) The expenditures are less than two weeks' revenues. The Kirkuk field just confiscated in Iraq requires less than $4 million annually to maintain the rate of output—revenues from one day's capacity output.

Table 15.2
Approximate OPEC revenues, 1972

Area	Estimated 1972 output (billion brls)*	Per barrel revenues**	Total revenues ($ billions)
Persian Gulf	6.50	$1.42	$9.2
Libya, Algeria	1.20	2.14	2.6
Nigeria	0.63	1.85	1.2
Venezuela	1.10	1.61	1.8
Indonesia	0.37	1.50	0.5
	9.80	$8.52	$15.3

*Output assumed at same rate as first quarter 1972.
**Petroleum Intelligence Weekly: *Persian Gulf, February 14, 1972; Libya, Algeria, May 15, 1972; Nigeria, May 3, 1971, and July 3, 1972; Venezuela, December 27, 1971; Indonesia, rough guess.*

If the producing nations had to spend $300 million in order to obtain $600 million in revenue, i.e., a 100 percent return, they would spend that money; the alternative would be to receive nothing at all. And the $300 million net revenue would be about 3 percent of the tribute they obtain today by using the multinational companies. In other words, to talk about their "needs" and "plans" is totally irrelevant to how much they can get before they can spend.

Perhaps the OPEC countries (including the non-Arabs who do not exist for State but do produce 45 percent of OPEC oil) may be convinced they should restrict output in concert because oil in the ground will appreciate faster than money in the bank. Perhaps too there will be discussion in the United States: why our government is so poorly informed on oil economics; why it repeats "Arabs-oil ... oil-Arabs" as though slogans proved something logic could not; whether the national interest is well served by sponsoring, supporting, and urging on the cartel; and whether our interests may change when, as is generally expected, our imports are substantially larger.

The Changing American Interest

First, security has been greatly impaired for all importing countries by the cohesion of the OPEC nations which made an embargo feasible.

Second, the balance of payments impact will soon turn unfavorable to us, as it is to all other importers.[15]

The fact will slowly be recognized, that nearly all of the oil deficit could be abolished by getting American companies out of crude oil marketing, to produce on contract for the producing countries, who could then compete the price way down. The companies' profits (and contribution to the balance of payments) would not be much less, and in the long run they might be greater, as the experience in Venezuela proves: the companies producing there are at or over the loss line.

Larger American imports will if anything tend to put the world price down. The process was seen on a small scale after 1966, when quotas on (heavy) residual fuel imports were lifted. Imports increased considerably, and the price *decreased*. Moreover, concern over air pollution was growing rapidly, and alarm was felt over possible loss of markets for residual fuel oil. Hence the Venezuelan government made agreements with Esso and Shell granting them lower taxes on production of low-sulfur fuel oil. This bit of history was too rapidly forgotten.[16]

The declining price of fuel oil in the face of greater demand would be inexplicable in a competitive market, but is to be expected when the price is far above cost. It is exactly what happened in Europe to embarrass coal. The hope of greater profits on increased sales, and the knowledge that large buyers have now an incentive to roam the market and look for every chance of a better deal, means that one must reduce the price before one's rivals tie up the good customers. As American quotas are relaxed, refiners who have a crude deficit will becomes exactly the kind of large-scale buyer whom Sheik Yamani rightly fears.

The prospect of world prices rising because of large-scale American imports has alarmed Europe and Asia, and the United States government has gladly fanned those fears. But they have no basis in theory or experience.

Let the reader excuse our saying again what needs to be said often: larger consumption only raises price in a competitive market, by raising marginal cost. In so awesomely noncompetitive a market, cost is not relevant because price is 10 to 20 times cost. Supply and demand have nothing to do with the world price of oil: only the strength of the cartel matters.

Other Consuming Countries

Consuming governments are staying in the same groove which served them badly between 1957 and 1970, and worse afterward. Prices had risen in the 1950s because the oil companies were able to act in concert without overt collusion: they responded to a signal from the United States. Prices then jumped for a time when the Suez Canal was cut. The reaction was fear of shortage. One heard in 1957 what one hears now—"True, reserves are ample, but in 15 years, say by 1972, they will mostly be gone! We must guard against the shortage, obtain concessions of our own, protect domestic energy industries against future scarcity, etc." Thereby the consuming countries committed themselves to high oil prices.

The consuming countries were all the more ready to fear these imaginary demons because they had invested heavily in coal. The decline in fuel oil prices after 1957 was greeted with disbelief and resentment. Prices of oil assumed in government energy plans and forecasts were always much higher than actual market. In 1962 (and 1964) the EEC energy experts made a long-term forecast of heavy fuel oil at $18 per metric ton, when it was about $13. They were bitterly denounced for so low a forecast. Yet even now in mid-1972, fuel oil in Western Europe is only $14.50, i.e., in 1962 prices $10.75 per ton. Seldom has so costly a mistake been so long and stubbornly maintained. Nationalized industries—and others which could be influenced or pressured—were and still are reserved to coal. Worse yet, the artificial European coal prices became a cost standard for building nuclear power plants; in Great Britain they are wildly uneconomic.

The costly insistence on self-sufficiency was mostly uninformed fear of the multinational oil companies. The more the companies lost control of the market and competed down the price of fuel oil, losing profits thereby, the more resentment at their "ruthless economic warfare." As late as 1972, a British economist still writes of the oil company "design" to drive out coal. Fear of the multinational firms leads consuming countries not only to protect coal but to seek "their own" oil through government-owned or sponsored companies. Thereby the consuming-country government acquires a vested interest in high oil prices. Low oil prices, or the possibility thereof, become not an opportunity but a scandal, to be ignored as far as possible.

The fear of shortage in the 1970s as in the 1950s leads to attempts to obtain oil concessions. It may make sense to run risks in new areas where governments will keep taxes low. There is much oil which is profitable to find and develop at today's prices, even at costs 25 times that in the Persian Gulf. A non-Japanese can hardly object when Japan proposes to spend some $3 billion in the near future to find and develop new oil resources. If spent in new areas it will certainly add to the wealth of the world, and— perhaps—not be a loss to Japan. But there is nothing gained in seeking new concessions in the old areas, or buying into old concessions. Such a policy does not add any resources. The price paid for concession shares will discount the profits, which may not continue long. Perhaps worst of all, in committing itself to take oil from "its" concessions, the consuming country loses all independence in buying, and is worse exploited than it could ever be by the multinational companies.

The French Experience

The policy of seeking "independence" has been carried farthest in France. In 1962, agreements were reached with newly independent Algeria, inaugurating a "new type" of relationship, free from the burden of colonialism, etc. (One hears similar language today in Japan.) In early 1971, M. Fontaine described in Le Monde the dreary succession of broken promises, seizures, spoliation and the like. Yet no more than the French government could he or his newspaper bring itself to discard the policy; there were supposed political advantages, such as lessening Soviet influence in the Western Mediterranean. The logical result was the two-thirds confiscation in 1972 of what they had fondly thought to be "their own" oil.

The head of ERAP, the wholly-state-owned French company (as distinguished from Compagnie Française des Pétroles, only 35 percent state owned), summed up 10 years' experience and loss of the Algerian oil as "une opération blanche." Had the funds been invested at a steady rate and drawn a 7 percent return, private or social (hospitals, schools, highways, etc.), it would have been worth one-third more in 1972. But that is only a small part of the real social cost. There has been substantial French aid to the Algerian economy and French oil prices have been among the highest in Europe. But the French insist on rose-colored glasses. A break-even operation is viewed as economic. High oil prices and aid to Algeria, loading French industry with heavy costs and taxes that reduce its export capability, are viewed as a help to the balance of payments.

Four months after Algeria was written off, Iraq approached France as soon as they seized the Kirkuk field from Iraq Petroleum Company. Their experience had taught them who was an easy mark. In 1961, they had seized the whole IPC concession outside of fields actually producing, but although the expropriated area included the great undeveloped North Rumaila field nobody leased it. Then in 1967, after the Six-Day War, France obtained a large concession in Iraq for ERAP, "ratified with great pomp in Baghdad (and hailed throughout the Middle East) as a great victory over Anglo-American imperialism." The usually sober Le Monde was thrilled. Someone was needed "who would not flinch" when IPC "showed their teeth," someone "capable of braving the anger of the members of IPC."

Because of France, the "Anglo-Americans [lose] any chance of expansion into the hitherto-unexplored parts of the country." They have been out-maneuvered; they cannot block France from "a place in the untouched zones of Iraq without provoking a grave political crisis." This is their just reward because "on the morrow of the last war they would not let France into the game in this region."

Having used North Rumaila as bait to take in the French. Iraq dangled it before others, then decided to develop the field itself, with Russian assistance. There was great annoyance in France, where doubt was expressed that Iraq was capable of developing the field. But in April 1972, shipments began in the presence of Mr. Kosygin, exclaiming "Arab oil to the Arabs!" By early 1971, ERAP had found three fields worth developing, whereupon Iraq demanded higher payments than in the contract. ERAP was willing to give more, but not as much as demanded, and negotiations dragged on. Predictably, the French blamed the deadlock on the machinations of IPC, trying to block their intrusion into what *Le Monde* called "the private hunting preserve of the Anglo-Saxons."

In June 1972, when Iraq seized the Kirkuk field and threatened price cutting, they "preserved French interests in Iraq." Surely, they told newsmen, the French ought to be no more scrupulous in Iraq than the Americans, who had offered to do business with Algeria after the confiscation of French interests there. France, said *Le Monde*, feared a rejection of the Iraq offer "would harm its prestige in the Near East and would be taken as a break with Gaullist policy in the region"; while acceptance would allow France to "serve as a bridge between the West and the left wing regimes of the Arab world, a role whereby she, alone, can hope to counterbalance the growing Soviet influence." (Does the Gaullist policy help in oil matters, or does France accept higher oil costs in order to keep the policy going? One wishes for something intelligible.) A few days later came a Soviet-Iraq agreement on economic cooperation. This was no break in policy; the Baghdad regime had lifted its ban on Communist political activity, and accepted two Communists in the government. But of course, the greater the Soviet influence, the greater the need to counterbalance it, hence the more concessions would be made to the Baghdad regime in oil affairs.

When the strong man of the Iraqi cabinet, Vice Premier Saddam Hussein, visited Paris in June, he had a resounding success. The agreement with France gave CFP (the French partner in IPC) "une position privilégiée," which comes to this: CFP is obliged to lift its full share of Iraq oil for 10 years under the same conditions as before the nationalization: exactly that long-term commitment which it rejected as too expensive when it was a partner in IPC. Small wonder that CFP did not want this "position privilégiée." "The reason is simple—the price is too high ..."

France also acquired the "right" to buy additional crude—which Iraq had just offered to all the world at reduced prices. But France will buy not at reduced but at "commercial prices," i.e., higher than charged any knowledgeable arm's length buyer who has alternatives. Finally, France will extend about $80 million of long term credits to Iraq. This, and future credits and grants, is an unacknowledged addition to the price of the oil.

Thus the French have again been had, most royally, and by their own strenuous effort.

How are we to understand this rigid determination that France have "its own" oil, whereby France is humiliated and cheated?

Two elements of an explanation are worth suggesting, because they are not peculiar to France. One is the romantic political aura surrounding oil, which lets all manner of nonsense sound plausible. "Whatever touches on oil is at once adorned with romance. No other raw material stirs the imagination like this one, nor the taste for flowery language," wrote Edgar Faure in 1938. Another key is to be found in such phrases as "oil-hungry France" or "France assured of oil needs," etc. Similarly, in discussing Japan, Professor Brzezinski speaks repeatedly of "access to raw materials"[17] as being so self-evident and serious a problem that it need not be explained. Yet we cannot point to one example of lack of access. To pay for "access," through higher prices or otherwise, makes no sense, no matter how one views the future:

1. The price of crude oil, set by a world monopoly, is many times what is enough to make it worthwhile to expand output. Therefore, even if price declines and especially if it rises, there will always be more crude oil available than can be sold, as there is now and has always been.

2. Assume the contrary: that oil is becoming increasingly scarce, and that the price will reach $5 or whatever. At this price, the market is cleared, and just as with a monopolized market, anyone who can pay the price gets all he wants.

3. There is real fear, exploited but not created by the U.S. government, that massive American oil and gas imports will somehow preclude buyers from other countries, especially if the producing nations take the advice to limit output. Let us assume they do so. Then lower-cost and more profitable companies will outbid their rivals for the limited supply. Japanese iron and steel companies, for example, are obviously much lower-cost than their American rivals. The dwindling of the American export surplus seems to

show a higher cost level; if so, high oil prices will harm this country more than others.

4. One often-expressed fear is that the American multinational companies will divert supplies to American customers in preference to non-American. But if there is some constraint such that both groups cannot be fully supplied, then the price must rise. To imagine American companies deliberately holding down the price, in order to precipitate a shortage, in order to be able to discriminate, is fantasy. They would not wish to do it, and their masters the producing nations would not allow it.

5. The OPEC nations may wish to deny oil to some particular country. But if some or even most of them do so, the capacity of others will be available, and at most there will be a reshuffling of customers. Yet let us now assume that all OPEC nations unite to boycott one country. They must also prevent diversion of supplies of crude oil and products from other consuming countries to the victim. Yet nobody has suggested why the OPEC nations should join in this porfitless persecution. Moreover, non-OPEC oil is large relative to a single consuming country's needs.

6. Even if all the foregoing is incorrect, and "access" is a real problem, it is useless to try to obtain access through a company owned by the consuming nation, since real power is in the producing nation.

The obsession with a false problem of "access to oil" wastes time and distracts attention from the real problem of security of supply. The old or new multinational companies can do nothing good or bad for security because they have no control of supply, no power to cut off anybody or to protect them from cutoff. Nobody owns oil at the wellhead or underground reserves any more except the governments who have the physical force above ground.

A Look Ahead

Oil supply is threatened by one and only one danger: a concerted shutdown by the OPEC nations. No single nation can do any harm. The rhetorical question "Would you like to see Saudi Arabia supply one-third of the oil?" is only marginally relevant. The fewer the sellers and the larger their market shares, the easier for them to collaborate and act as one. The central question is their union or disunion. If a single large seller breaks away, or a few minor ones, the cartel breaks down in a stampede for the exit. The cartel is only needed, only exists, to thwart the basic condition of massive potential excess capacity—ability to expand output at costs below prices—and prevent it from becoming actual.

Hence lower prices and secure supply are the two sides of the same coin: absence of monopoly, or impotence of disunion.

The monopoly may still have its finest hours before it, and prices should rise well into the decade. The fewer the sellers the better, and there will presently be fewer Persian Gulf states. Most of them have too few men, and stuffing them full of money makes them worth occupying. A decade ago, Iraq claimed Kuwait, and was only stopped by the threat of force: the British presence, now gone. Iraq will be all the more ready to occupy Kuwait if Iran occupies the Kirkuk area, site of the great oil field just expropriated. The local population are not Arabs but Kurds Indo-European in language and Sunnite Moslem in religion, like the Iranians. If, they behaved themselves the Iranian army might be hailed as liberators from the chronic bloody struggle with the Baghdad regime. A new pipeline to the Mediterranean could go through Iran and Turkey.

The important consuming countries show no sign of understanding their plight; in mid-1972 "European nations are believed to be concerned that another stalemate [on "participation"] could impair vitally needed oil supplies.... The companies are under considerable pressure to reach an agreement."[18]

Also, the large consumer countries have export interests which will benefit by the higher oil prices because of oil nations' greater purchasing power. Export industries often have disproportionate political power, even if the real economic benefit to the nation, i.e., higher incomes to labor and capital than from the next best alternatives, are piddling compared to the outfolw on oil.

Europe is rapidly becoming an important oil producer. Some European countries will become small net importers, some will be large net oil sellers. The head of Norsk Hydro oil operations recently noted Norway's "economic interest in high prices." He recognized that the OPEC gains "were forced through by threats of a boycott." Instead of maundering about "political stability," he defined it: "first and foremost a political system under which agreements and terms of licenses are respected even if the circumstances may have changed ... [and under which] everyone ... feels secure that supply will be maintained in all circumstances." It is an indirect but devastating comment on American policy.

The less-developed nations will suffer the most, with no offsets. For example, India today consumes about 150 million barrels per year, and is expected to use about 345 in 1980. The burden of monopoly pricing is direct (paying higher prices for imports) and indirect (being forced to find and produce higher-cost domestic oil). It amounts in total to about $225 million ($1.50 × 150 million) per year, and increasing rapidly. Yet at the 1972 UNCTAD meeting there was no breath of criticism of the oil-producing nations. Solidarity prevailed: things were felt to be going well "on the oil front," and, said *Le Monde*, the same ought to happen on other fronts.

This favorable public attitude also holds in the developed countries. A private monopoly which extracted $1.5 billion per year from consumers would be denounced and probably destroyed; were they American, some executives would be in jail. An intergovernmental monopoly 10 times as big is viewed as a bit of redress by the Third World.

Now one may approve this double standard, or deplore it, or laugh to keep from crying, but it is a truth with consequences: no important resistance seems likely in the near term. In time, attitudes may change.

1. The fictitious "world energy crisis" will gradually fade as it did after 1957, and the slow growth of understanding of oil prices will resume. This influence is minor but not negligible.

2. In 1972, the transfer from consuming to the OPEC nations will be about $15 billion. (See table 15.2.) If the tax doubles (and the price is therefore about $3.35) and if output increases by 8 percent per year, then the 1980 transfer will be over $56 billion per year. This is a very conservative forecast as compared with those of the Departments of State or Commerce as cited earlier.

3. Some of the billions will be spent in ways some consuming countries find irksome or dangerous. The large amounts paid to Libya have already cost the NATO nations additional payments to Malta, for which Mr. Mintoff could not have bargained without Libyan help.

4. Payments to the producing nations will total about $242 billion over the nine years 1972–1980. If these nations spend, say, three-fourths on goods and services from abroad and save 25 percent by buying foreign assets, the additions to their holdings will be about $61 billion. The oil companies see themselves as the decently paid investment managers for this fund; as Schumpeter said, "This is the way the bourgeois mind works, always will work, even in sight of the hangman's rope."

There will be monetary disorders when large holders speculate against a particular currency. Unlike the oil market, where the producing countries must act in concert or accomplish nothing, even a single nation with big enough foreign balances can do substantial damage to the world monetary system, or try to bring down a government it dislikes.

5. Security of supply has been severely impaired by the Paris capitulation and the great success of the threat of embargo. Hints of "concerted action"

since then have been too numerous to list. Even more upsetting than the threats are the assurances. For they imply power to stop the flow.

Security of supply—limited but genuine—can be had by stockpiling, combined with detailed plans for severe rationing, supplemented by high excise taxes, to reduce oil consumption and thereby increase the effective size of the stockpile. The expense will be heavy (but had consuming countries done this years ago, they would have made large savings).

The larger the reserves piled up by the OPEC nations, the greater their power to withhold oil. Hence the higher the price, and the greater the insecurity, the easier for the OPEC nations to make it still more expensive and insecure. The consuming countries can have cheapness and security only by a clean break with the past: get the multinational oil companies out of curde oil marketing; let them remain as producers under contract and as buyers of crude to transport, refine and sell as products. The real owners, the producing nations, must then assume the role of sellers and they should be assisted in competing the price of crude oil down. The Yamani prescription will be as sound then as in 1968, or 1971, or 1972.

It is a simple and elegant maneuver to destroy the cartel by removing an essential part—the multinational company as crude oil marketers fixing the price on a firm excise tax floor. But this would only minimize conflict and confrontation; it is too late to avoid them. The producing countries, like many raw troops, have been welded by success into a real force, and the huge sums they receive and accumulate will be both the incentive and the means to fight, by embargo, monetary disruption, or even local wars. There will be non-negligible damage. to have put the power and the motive into the producers' hands was light-minded folly by the American government.

Moreover, clean breaks with past policy are rare. The honest confession of error is less likely than anger at the cartel's local agents, the multinational companies, and attempts to restrict and penalize them. Yet this misconception is exactly what has led to past mistakes. Bypassing the companies to make direct deals with producing nations can be helpful only when the objective is clearly seen: to mobilize national buying power, encourage domestic oil buyers to avoid established channels, and help compete prices down. More usually such deals sacrifice all buying independence in a vain attempt to get a good "connection," or placate a producing nation, and only raise costs.

The greatest difficulty in following the Yamani formula is the need for the leading consuming countries to act together. For example, the United States tax law might recognize, either by statute or judicial decision, that the "income" taxes paid to OPEC nations were really excise taxes, hence not deductible from U.S. income tax. Higher taxes coupled with the unceasing demands of the OPEC countries might well push one or more of these companies past patience or profit, and they would withdraw to become a contractor or buyer, helping to undermine the cartel.

Yet today other large consuming countries would fall over themselves trying to get one of their countries into the empty slot, and promising anything to the producing nation. Hence it would be literally worse than useless for the United States to take the first steps, without firm assurances from at least France, Germany, Italy, and Japan, that they would not try to replace the American company. These countries are still obsessed with vain notions of getting "access" or "security" through their own companies, and the suggestion that they refrain from taking their "just share," and ending their long-resented "exclusion" from "the game," seems an obvious attempt to help the American companies keep their predominance. It is an old sad story. If one looks for the "real motives," he will never hear what is being said.

The multinational companies will probably survive the crisis. Yet there is a real danger that they will be forced out of crude oil production. This would be a grievous waste of resources and could precipitate a genuine shortage of crude oil.

What happens to oil in the 1970s depends altogether on the consuming countries. If they are as slow to learn as they have been, then the projection of $55 billion annual tribute paid the OPEC nations by 1980 may be surpassed. But they may also learn that transferring those billions is not only dangerous but *unnecessary*. Their energy economics would need to be updated at least to 1952, when the Paley Commission explained that shortage means only cost; they might then see that the "world energy shortage" is a myth, that crude oil continues in oversupply, as the Venezuelans, the Iraqis, and the Saudi Arabs have recognized. And the consuming nations' strategic thinking would need to be updated at least to 1914, when Winston Churchill, who was then a young fox, not an old lion, explained to the House of Commons that access to oil is only a special case of monopoly; the power to withhold is the power to overcharge.[19]

Notes

1. My publications summarized are: "Les Prix Pétroliers à Long Terme," Revue de l'Institut Français du Pétrole, December 1963; (trans.) "Oil Prices in the Long Run," *Journal of Business of the University of Chicago*, April 1964. Price evolution: See Ch. VI, Appendix, of The World Petroleum Market, Resources for the Future, 1972 (hereafter cited as W.P.M). Supply cutoff: *Government Intervention in the Price*

Mechanism, Hearings before the Subcommittee on Antitrust and Monopoly of the Committee on the Judiciary, p. 17. U.S. Senate, 91st Congress. 1st Session, 1969.

2. Growth rates and price trends: W.P.M., Ch. VIII; *BP Statistical Review of the World Petroleum Industry; Petroleum Press Service*, June 1972, p. 222, Quotation from *Presentation to a meeting of financial analysts in Tokyo on Friday, May 12, 1972*, by F. S. McFadzean, Managing Director of Shell.

3. W.P.M., Ch. II and Ch. VII. For later data, see my paper, "Long Run Cost Trends" in John J. Schanz, (ed.), *Balancing Supply and Demand* (1972).

4. The United States "energy crisis" is a confusion of two problems. First, environmental costs are slowing down electric power growth and threatening blackouts. The worse the slowdown, the less the drain on fuel supply. Second, there has been gradual exhaustion of lower-cost oil and gas resources in the Lower 48 States. Natural gas deserves speical mention, for the world has been deeply impressed by American business executives and cabinet members rocketing about the world like unguided missiles in search of gas supplies; particularly coming hat in hand to beg gas of the Soviet Union. One folly has led to another. Prices of American natural gas have been held at a level well below what would clear the market, generating a huge excess demand, all channeled overseas. Import prices have soared and will probably rise further if domestic price-fixing is not abolished. Profits to the overseas producing nations who own the gas will be lush. American companies have tried to arrange deals and obtain a part of the gains; American government officials have helped the stampede. The gas shortage could be abolished by the simple expedient of abandoning price ceilings. Gas might still be imported, but at lower prices, in smaller amounts. The strain on coal and oil resources would actually be less, since higher domestic prices would increase domestic supply of natural gas.

5. Assume that American imports from the Persian Gulf rise at a constant percentage rate from 310 TBD (thousand barrels daily) in 1971 to 10 MBD (million barrels daily) in 1980 and to 15 MBD in 1985. Then cumulative imports are 7.5 billion barrels through 1980 and 23.4 billion through 1985: respectively 2 percent and 6 percent of end-of-1971 Persian Gulf reserves. In the next 15 years, many times more than these amounts will be developed into new reserves, even if there are zero discoveries of new fields. McFadzean, op. cit., Chart 11 on Western Europe.

6. M. A. Adelman, *The Present and Future State of the World Oil Industry* (lectures, Japanese translation) (Petroleum Association of Japan, 1965), pp. 11–33, and W.P.M., Ch, II; also National Petrolem Council U.S. Energy Outlook, Vol. 2 (1971), pp. 41–53.

7. Tax is calculated as follows: output multiplied by posted prices equals fictional "receipts." Production costs are subtracted, and however calculated they are very small. The difference is the fictional "profit," which goes usually 55 percent to the nation. Thus the tax per barrel is completely independent of actual receipts, and only very slightly affected by costs, hence almost completely independent of profits. Therefore it is an almost pure excise tax.

8. Neither the *New York times* nor the *Wall Street Journal*, in their stories on the subject (January 14, 17, 19, 1971) had any reference to any retaliation or concerted action on the proposal.

9. The concession company and host government need to determine four items: (*a*) The government owes the concessionaire a certain sum per year to cover the amortized cost of the equity share. (*b*) The government loses the taxes if formerly received on the share it now "owns." (*c*) the concessionaire owes the government the "price" of the oil which the government owns, and which it now "sells" to the company. (*d*) The concessionaire owes the government its pro-rata share of the year's profits of the operating company. The subject of the negotiation is by what amount ($c + d$) shall exceed ($a + b$). The 9 cent estimate is from *Petroleum Press Service*, April 1972, p. 118.

10. Dr. M. S. Al-Mahdi, chief of the Economic Department of OPEC, in a paper partly summarized in Middle East Economic Survey, July 14, 1972, p. 11, estimates the 1970 Western Europe average consumer price as $13.14, of which 57.3 percent was tax. See also: *Direction des Carburants: Rapport Annuel 1969*. Italian collaboration: *Petroleum Intelligence Weekly*, May 24, 1971.

11. *Petroleum Press Service*, February 1972, pp. 53 and 64, notes that Algeria and Libya have shaved prices to move product.

12. See W.P.M., Ch. VIII, note 32, for the calculation.

13. Wall Steet Journal, February 20, 1957 (the State Department though a pipeline through Iraq would be preferable) and *Platt's Oilgram News Service*, April 22, 1968.

14. G. I. Jenkins, "Company Uncertainty and Decision Making," *Petroleum Review*, June 1972, p. 213.

15. Secretary of Commerce Peterson, in the *New York Times*, June 20, 1972, p. 51, estimates the American balance of payments deficit on oil account as $26 billion a year in 1980 if imports are 4.38 billion barrels. This implies $5.94 per barrel delivered, hence probably about the same $5 per barrel f.o.b. at which State aims.

16. W.P.M., Ch. VII.

17. Zbigniew Brzezinski, *The Fragile Blossom: Crisis and Change in Japan* (1972), pp. 46–47, 71. In justice to Professor Brzezinski, one should note that he slides quickly from "access" to "price" which is the only real problem.

18. A. P. Dispatch in *International Herald Tribune*, August 19–20, 1972.

19. See J. E. Hartshorn, *Oil Companies and Governments* (1967 ed.), pp. 255–260.

16

Politics, Economics, and World Oil

Zen Buddhist monks used to torment novices by asking: "What is the sound of one hand clapping?" That sound has become deafening in recent years: the official predictions that because world oil consumption will increase, oil must grow more scarce and the price must increase. But scarcity is the pressure of *demand* upon *supply*. To omit either element is nonsense. They are united in the true measure of scarcity, long-run marginal cost. The only relevant question is whether, as consumption grows, society must keep putting more or less into the ground to get out another barrel.

Long-run marginal cost is mostly the return on the investment needed to develop additional capacity. Failure to discover new flush reservoirs means ever more intensive development of old fields, hence rising development investment and cost per unit, and rising prices. Anticipated price-cost increases delay development of some deposits, forcing more intensive work on the remaining ones, hence higher costs. Thereby a development cost increase serves as a distant early warning signal of future scarcity, bringing it into the present. Conversely, a stable (or declining) marginal cost means no greater scarcity, and this is the actual case. For the Persian Gulf, or even for the whole world outside North America, real costs have been sharply declining, and even if they were now to reverse course and climb, as is always possible, they would be a negligible fraction of price. The current flood of projections from here to eternity is a pitiful and futile attempt to replace the price-cost thermometer-thermostat, but they are official truth. One projects "needs" and "amounts available" to find a "surplus" or "deficit" regardless of elasticities of demand or supply.[1]

A Royal Dutch Shell executive sums up the world oil market: "The underlying situation of supply and demand remains one of potential sur-

Reprinted from *Papers & Proceedings of the American Economic Association* 64 (2, 1974): 58–67.

plus. Yet the producing countries manage to reap the rewards of a sellers' market by creating a producer's monopoly" (Geoffrey Chandler).

I Monopoly

The multinational oil companies are not junior partners but rather agents of that monopoly, the members of the Organization of Petroleum Exporting Countries (OPEC) (but not OPEC itself). Aside from short-term flights, the price is now around $8 and (probably) close to the long-run profit-maximizing level set by the competition of substitute energy sources, as the Shah of Iran has stated (*New York Times* (*NYT*), Dec. 24, 1973). The official truth stated by Secretary of State Henry Kissinger, that prices have risen because of a surge of demand against inelastic supply (*NYT*, Dec. 12, 1973), is in utter conflict with the fact of enormous supply elasticity at cost of at most one-fortieth of the current price.

The popular slogan "avoid overbidding" suggests that oil prices have been bid up by demand exceeding supply, which is untrue, and also betrays a misunderstanding of what has been happening in 1972–73. Current supply-demand fluctuated, with occasional excess capacity. But the demand for crude for *later* delivery was insatiable because buyers knew prices were going to be raised. Buyers had little down-side risk. If the producing countries delivered at the contract price, buyers would make a speculative gain; if they delivered at the expected higher prices little would be lost. Whereupon the OPEC countries turned around and cited the rising contract prices as a reason for raising their taxes—thereby putting a firm tax floor under the higher prices and validating the expectations. "Reasons" are as plentiful as blackberries; what matters is the power to raise the price of oil close to the cost of (expensive) substitutes.

Monopoly means control of supply, hence power to stop it, hence dependence and insecurity. Food is more essential than fuel, yet nobody is "dependent" on any farmer or on all farmers together, because farmers cannot act together to control and if need be withhold their production. Our "dependence" on imports exists only because of the cartel and (in the short run) the Arab majority bloc. Its history is extremely important: "those who ignore the past are condemned to repeat it," and we have already repeated it once. The key words in that history are *threats* by the producers, and *collaboration* by the consuming nations, especially the United States. The threat of an embargo gave the cartel its first triumph: the Tehran "agreements" of February 1971, whose expected and actual effect was to raise prices at a time of slack demand. The documented record of the

1970–71 events shows that only *after* American-sponsored capitulation to producing country demands in January did anyone dare voice public threats. The American policy maker did not blush to tell a Senate committee that threats had been made *before* the capitulation—and ceased upon his request; See M. A. Adelman (1973). He later explained that the threats had been made privately (James Akins). This evades the issue; threats are made in private so that they may be denied, reinterpreted, or repudiated. And to say that the threats ceased is completely false in the light of the numerous public statements which culminated in a formal OPEC resolution, issued just before the Tehran agreements, threatening "total embargo"—and equally numerous threats since.

The first triumph of blackmail announced more to come—as some were then denounced for saying. Our government "expected the previously turbulent world oil situation to calm down following the new agreement." In fact, the five-year Tehran agreement lasted four months, and after several "revisions" was pronounced "dead" last fall when the Persian Gulf nations unilaterally raised prices. Perhaps they were bored with what an oilman called "the charade of negotiations." (*NYT*, Oct. 19, 1973.) But the American policy maker may be right in claiming that the Tehran agreements "worked well" (Akins)—from his point of view. So also with the proposal for preferential entry into the United States for Saudi Arabian oil—the most insecure source conceivable. The State Department was "enthusiastic" (*Oil and Gas Journal* (*OGJ*), Oct. 9, 1972), for reasons not explained. Nobody can doubt that its "exaggerated talk of an energy crisis greatly strengthened the bargaining power of the Arab states" (Petroleum Press Service (PPS) Nov. 1973).

II Shooting War and Economic War

Middle East politics, specifically the Arab-Israel tension, have had no effect on the price, and a Middle East Settlement will do nothing at all to keep that price from increasing to the monopoly level. The producing nations will take what they can get. The monopoly revenues make peace unlikely. (See below.)

The shooting war and economic war waged by a subgroup of the cartel —the Arab oil producers—were invited by repeated American statements, of which the public record is probably only the tip of the iceberg, and whose complete exploration would richly repay a Congressional inquiry. The Saudis were told they were the last best hope of civilization, we had to have their oil, and would they not please produce it, even though it was not (we said) in their economic interest to do so? No revenues were high enough to induce the Saudi government to agree to big production increases; something extra must be done for them. (*Wall Street Journal* (*WSJ*), Aug. 15, 1973; *OGJ*, Sept. 10, 1973.) This was a self-fulfilling prophecy. For if we believe it and are willing to do something extra for the Saudis, they are glad to demand it.

The buyer is asking to be had who tells a seller, "I know you don't want any more business but please just to do me a favor won't you sell me something?" There are few such buyers because they don't stay in business very long. Not so in government.

Sheik Yamani, the Saudi Arabian petroleum minister, recently asserted that before the recent cutbacks, when Saudi Arabia was producing eight million barrels per day (MBD), "we were producing at a much higher rate than what we should for our economy (*Meet the Press* (*MP*), Dec. 9, 1973). And that was a sacrifice on our part." It amounted to "losing money." Sheik Yamani says, without a smile, that his government has been producing not for its benefit but for sweet charity. He speaks as a man who expects to be believed. But that's no wonder, for the United States Government was saying this publicly before he was.

But if eight MBD is a production rate "much" too high for Saudi Arabia's good, twenty MBD is catastrophically too high, and we will owe them three times as much or more in 1980 than we do now. To keep the oil flowing, we will impose a just peace in the Middle East this year. Next year it will have to be even more just, and the year after that ... and so on.

This official truth about needing to do something for Saudi Arabia, because it is not worth their while to expand output, is all implicit, never set down for analysis. But it appears to rest on two assumptions. (a) "Oil in the ground appreciates faster than money in the bank," abbreviated OGMB. It is often embellished by saying that the dollar has depreciated, and prices on the New York Stock Exchange have gone to pot, ergo, there is no place to invest. In fact that dollar may be an undervalued currency, or payment may be in another, and in any case the annual volume of capital formation in the developed world (not to mention the total stock of existing purchasable assets) is many times the future revenues of even Saudi Arabia. But let that go: OGMB is at best meaningless without specific numbers. The current price of Persian Gulf oil is about $8. If 8 percent is a safe interest rate, then a barrel is worth holding, instead of a corporate bond, for four years for an expected price rise to $11, and for nine years for an expected price of $16. The price is not going to appreciate indefinitely at 8 percent per year: it is not going to $32 in eighteen years, nor to $64 in twenty-seven years. But Saudi Arabian crude reserves are fifty times current output, and can be greatly increased at negligible cost. They are held back in order not to wreck prices. OGMB is an irrelevance in a noncompetitive market.

(b) Saudi Arabia (and others) will limit their oil revenues to what they "need." This means—if it means anything—that they will hold back output short of the monopoly optimum, i.e., the point where it maximizes the present worth of their assets. It is an odd assumption, to say the least, and quite unsupported. If King Faisal acts like a true dynast to serve his successors, family, retainers, friends, etc., the best way to insure this is to maximize present worth.

We are better off with less talk of "need" and a little thought about economics. Saudi Arabia, like the U.S. Steel Corporation or the Texas Railroad Commission in other days, has the usual problem of Mr. Big in a cartel: find the combination of price and quantity which will maximize group profits—or more generally, best serve the economic interests of the producers. They can fix the price and let the price determine quantity; or fix the quantity and let it determine price, but these are only two routes to the same goal. No blandishments will make them expand output; anyone who thinks he can persuade them is merely stroking his ego and reminding us how right was a Scottish professor of moral philosophy who warned against the "overweening conceit" of men "in their own abilities." Repeated assurances of how badly we need them are simply taken as evidence of inelastic demand and signal the monopolist that there is greater profit in even greater restriction.

The drift of American policy was visible in these statements that we owed Saudi Arabia, to whom we sent as ambassador the principal architect and defender of the Tehran "agreements." His earlier statement that "a seller's market arrived in June 1967" disregards three years' price decline but reveals his belief that the Six-Day War was a calamity to be reversed. He "think(s) the OPEC countries should be granted substantial increases," in order to induce alternative energy sources needed "to avoid an energy crisis in the 1980s, or 1990s," a "crisis" again assumed, never explained. Also, "price increases will hurt America's commercial competitors Europe and Japan," and Saudi Arabian revenues would mostly be invested in the United States (*Economist (Ec.)*, Nov. 26, 1973).

Saudi Arabia "planned the Arab strategy for the (1973) Middle East War," both shooting war and economic war (*LeMonde (LM)*, Oct. 9, 1973; *NYT News of the Week in Review (NWR)*, Oct. 14, 1973; *OGJ*, Oct. 15, 1973; *NYT*, Nov. 10, 1973; see also *NYT Mag.*, Nov. 18, 1973). King Faisal and Prince Saud al-Faisal had stated they needed to put pressure on the United States. But "the U.S. can get along without Arab oil until the end of

the decade" (*OGJ*, Sept. 12, 1973). Therefore it was necessary to reduce
total production deeply and deprive others of more oil in order to deprive
the United States of less. A selective embargo was taken seriously by our
principal policy maker but by nobody else (Akins 1973).

III Surrender without a Fight

The cutbacks have been a great political success. We are right back to the
1930s, when European nations looked for a deal with the aggressor in the
hope he would go jump on somebody else, and when German generals
opposed to aggression were discredited by the willingness of the Western
powers to give away other people's lands and lives; so too the moderates
among the Arabs. For, confronted with the cutbacks, the Europeans and
Japanese stood clear of the Americans, however dangerous that was for
them. More important, in my opinion, was their inaction at home: oil stocks
were not spread over time by rationing, i.e., not used as a defensive weapon
to gain time wherein to carry out a plan, but as a means of putting off
the unpopular decisions to curtail demand. Most important was European
eagerness to collaborate with the Arabs rather than each other. "Arabs
don't have to police their own boycotts. Sycophant nations are doing it for
them" (*WSJ*, Nov. 6, 1973). The Common Market countries refused to ship
or pool oil resources, as requested by the Dutch who had been picked out
as a special victim. Apparently the Dutch are getting some covert help—
but only after they threatened to cut off natural gas deliveries to France and
other nearby countries.

Japan had been more pro-Arab than any large country but France, and
had stood aloof from other consuming nations, lest they offend (Petroleum
Intelligence Weekly (*PIW*), May 14, 1973), only to find itself accused of
"odious neutrality" (*NYT*, Oct. 18, 1973). Saudi Arabia was ready to make
new demands "because of their success in recent years in enforcing a
boycott ..." (*WSJ*, Nov. 7, 1973; *NYT*, Nov. 9, 1973).

A cut in British deliveries "... is clearly causing embarrassment to the
government, which ... had received assurances [sic] from Arab countries
..." (Platt's Oilgram (*POPS*), Nov. 20, 1973). The French government is
embarrassed over reduced supplies (*NYT*, Nov. 20, 1973). Such governments are especially reluctant to begin rationing because it would be an
"admission of failure," i.e., groveling did not insure oil supply (*PIW*, Nov.
19, 1973; *LM*, Nov. 23, 1973).

The servility of consuming governments, playing the Abbe Alberoni to
the Arabs' Duc de Vendôme (see Luigi Barzini), has made the original Arab

demands of no importance. A weapon which makes consumer nations shake like jelly cannot be contained by a scrap of paper enumerating Israeli security or Palestinians' rights, etc.—there are far bigger objectives now to be considered. Moreover, Saudi money, to be multiplied many fold, can procure more arms from many sources, freeing the Arabs from whatever control the Soviet Union might exercise. This makes fresh wars likely if not inevitable, especially when the Saudis begin shopping for the nuclear weapons they can well afford. Already there is a semiofficial Egyptian call for nuclear weapons, which would cost only an estimated $1 billion, stimulated by "a high-level Washington visitor" to Cairo (*NYT*, Nov. 24, 1973).

IV   Economic Failure, Political Success

Yet the cutback failed badly to reduce American supply. At its maximum (as of December) it amounted to 4.7 MBD, about 14 percent of all oil moving in international trade. Hence had there been just enough leakage and diversion to put us as well off as oil importers generally, our import loss would have been about 14 percent. Now, for the four weeks ending November 16, our combined imports of crude and products averaged 6.55 MBD. Since the boycott date was October 17, and Persian Gulf—U.S. transit time is about a month, this amount measures the preboycott level of shipments. For the next four weeks, through December 14, the average was 6.10 MBD, indicating a loss of about 450 thousand barrels daily, 7 percent of imports, about 2.4 percent of total supply. The truly vulnerable place was the East Coast's heavy reliance on residual fuel oil, much from Caribbean and Canadian refineries which also ran some Arab crude oil and might therefore be forced to stop all shipments to this country in order not to lose some supply. An Arab resolution of November 26 to cut off the Caribbean and other transshipment centers (*OGJ*, Dec. 10, 1973) shows that by mid-November the Arabs realized their failure and their resolve to damage this country where they could. Yet on November 8 our ambassador to Saudi Arabia had warned that the plight of the East Coast would be "critical" if Arab oil supplies were not increased "in a matter of days" (sic) (*NYT*, Nov. 10, 1973). This was wildly untrue.

The Arabs' 25 percent cutback in their production was scheduled originally to keep increasing 5 percent per month until Israel withdrew to her 1967 boundaries and "the legal rights of the Palestinian people" were restored. But the Arab oil exporters' meeting of December 26 reduced the cutback to 15 percent, ignored the two conditions, and let it be understood that the cutback would be cancelled upon Israeli withdrawal from the west bank of the Suez Canal (*NYT*, Nov. 26, 1973). Furthermore, the "friendly" nations (Britain, France) were guaranteed Arab oil even in excess of the base amount (September 1973), which means that their previous imports of non-Arab oil are completely freed for the not-so-friendly (Japan) or the unfriendly nations (United States, Netherlands).

To what extent this failure of the production cutback to reduce U.S. supply is due to cheating by the Arab producers and to diversion of non-Arab oil is as yet impossible to say.

V   Monopoly Harmful to Consuming Nations

Relief at this failure should not obscure the fact that the oil cartel is very harmful to American interests. (a) In 1974 customers, including us, will be paying out well over $100 billion, and over 1972–80 cumulative the transfer to the producing countries will be several times that. The richer these nations are, the better they can maintain an embargo to make supply yet more insecure—as the Arab production cutbacks remind us. (b) The world monetary system will be harmed by huge amounts of liquid funds ready to move at a moment's notice, not to serve the holders' malice (the usual straw man) but for self-protection. Controls on capital movements to prevent this danger will in themselves be harmful. (c) Restrictions on American imports, because of the expected oil deficit, have already embroiled us with our main trading partners in Europe and Asia, not only because of John Connally's bluster and bullying but also over the substance of our demand to get more than we give (*NYT*, May 10, 1973).

(d) The risk of mineral exploitation in less-developed countries is much greater; concessions and contracts are now worthless. (e) The hope of a rule of law for the world's oceans has gone by the board because of the hugely inflated artificial value of any possibility of oil. (f) A vast arms buildup is just beginning in the Persian Gulf. Producers have billions available and every little patch of barren ground or barren seawater is actually or potentially worth fighting over.

The arms buildup reminds us that although the oil monopoly will cost us dear, there will be gains for exporters and for contractors for construction, investment management, public relations, etc. There will be plums for many in the industrialized nations and crumbs for less-developed countries. Those "working for the petrodollar," paid or enriched by the monopoly, are highly influential. Moreover, each industrialized nation can hope that the burden will be borne by them in proportion to their oil consumption, but that they will get a disproportionate share of export and investment business. M. Pompidou appears to have talked to King Faisal of little else but French exports during their May 1973 meeting (*LM*, May 15, 1973); he is now "shocked" that anyone thinks exports have much to do with his Middle East policy (*LM*, Nov. 19, 1973).

VI   Implications for Policy

Only in the long run can we get the cartel off our backs, and it will not be easy, quick, or cheap. It is necessary but no longer sufficient to stop the oil producing companies from being the vehicle for the price-fixing agreement of the producing governments. (1) Expelling the companies and losing their know-how would be a huge waste of resources, harmful to all. But if they simply produced (and developed and explored) and were paid in money or a modest share of the oil, the producing countries would have to do their own selling and monitor thousands of transactions all over the world. The companies have managed the difficult task of determining output shares because they have sold the bulk of the final product; the producer nations would inherit the task without the means. Nothing in the history of the trade suggests they would succeed; even the tight cartel of the 1930s was eroded, and it never faced an independent refining industry.

A managing director of Royal Dutch Shell has well said that in buying from producing countries the multinational oil companies "have formidable advantages." (See G. A. Wagner and A. Glimmerveen.) Once they become "formidable" buyers of crude oil rather than tax collecting agents, the market will look considerably different from what it does today. The oil companies are a big gun pointing toward the consuming countries, which ought to be pointed the other way. Hence real nationalization is greatly to the advantage of the consuming countries.

The producing countries may yet oblige us, as did Algeria and Iraq, by first expelling the companies and then inviting them back as contractors or by doing their own selling of most of their oil as "participation." This is good for the individual country in the short run and bad for the group in the longer run—the classic cartel dilemma. It is imprudent to assume they will be so helpful, but the chances of this happening look better in late 1973 than I expected a year earlier; see Adelman (1973). Perhaps such prophecies will be realized as those of Thomas R. Stauffer in 1970: "We conclude ... that prices will probably sink below the $1.15 level and that ... non-concessionary oil will drive out concessionary oil." The price-under-mining effect of direct sale by the producing countries' national companies ("non-concessionary oil") remains a key variable if the consuming countries want to make it one.

The American government ought not to force American companies into being contractors, since they would merely be displaced by European or Asian companies. it must be done in unison or not at all.

By the time most consuming nations see their interests a bit more clearly, some will have taken another step: put oil imports under quota, to sell the tickets on sealed competitive bids. Any country which wished to expand or even retain its market in the United States would have to share its gains with the Treasury. This would not reduce the price of oil to the consumer. There would be in effect a tax on imported oil which would keep the domestic price level high also. (In my opinion a high energy price is desirable to reduce pollution and congestion. Those who disagree with this policy judgment may yet prefer to have the money go to the American not the Saudi government.)

If the producing countries succeeded in collusively fixing quota ticket prices, we would be no worse off, but chances of success are small because it would not take much cheating to fill the quota. Detection of cheating would be difficult and might be made impossible by Theodore Moran's suggestion that prices in any given bid be kept permanently secret. There would be no way of knowing whether any country's higher exports were due to its cheating.

The current price level is so much higher than the cost of producing oil, *even in high-cost deposits*—see Adelman (1972)—that trickles, then streams of new supply in the 1970's are a foregone conclusion, and they have been the bane of all cartels. Given supertankers and superports, a barrel of oil anywhere in the world is a barrel everywhere, at a transport cost of a dollar, which is little compared to the producing nation's profit. Only the shortage of men and materials keeps this potential from becoming actual. But even now the producing countries are not deceived about the "world oil shortage." Saudi Arabia, as mentioned earlier, tried for preferential entry into the United States, which only makes sense when more people are trying to enter than there are places to set them. Venezuela keeps proposing worldwide prorationing. Iraq expelled the Iraq Petroleum Corporation from the largest oilfield because they refused to expand output, which under the new regime will have doubled or tripled from 1972 to 1975. When the consuming countries want to get rid of the burden they can; but at present there is no will, hence no way.

This brings us back to the dismal present and decisions to be made soon. The Arabs have failed to cripple us; the Administration is trying to snatch defeat from the jaws of victory to serve some grand design not yet revealed to us. Our greatest immediate danger lies in a super-Tehran agreement for "cooperation" of producing and consuming states, announce by a flourish of trumpets on a TV spectacular, with the same promise made by the same people who brought us the first Tehran that *this time* "the previously turbulent would oil situation" will *really* "quiet down." The ambassador to Saudi Arabia, who in 1972 told the Arabs that it was in their interest to curtail output, told us that for lack of oil our condition would be "desperate" by 1976, (Adelman 1973) and thought the Tehran agreement had worked well, etc., has suggested a world commodity agreement to set oil prices and ensure availability (*NYT*, Apr. 16, 1973). It would be a one-way street, preventing independent action by consumer states to promote price reductions. But if the monopoly holds and the price can be rigged higher, up it will go. A few weeks ago, in proclaiming the Tehran agreements dead, Sheik Yamani supplied a classic formula: "We in Saudi Arabia would have liked to honor and abide by the Tehran agreements, but ..." circumstances had changed (Middle East Economic Survey (*MEES*) Sept. 7, 1973). Sheik Yamani may one day say that he and his colleagues would have *dearly loved* to honor and abide by the Kissinger agreements, but ... circumstances, etc. The supersubtle diplomat is no match for the fellow who grabs what is in his reach, then asks if you want to fight to get it back. But it may not even be necessary. For in waving proudly an "understanding" with Saudi Arabia to let output increase to 20 MBD or whatever, our government will not realize that there is no meaning whatever to an agreement which does not specify both quantity and price. For if Saudi Arabia's interests are better served by producing less, it raises price to where there is less demanded.

As regards supply outside this country, a sound world oil policy for the short run is to do and say nothing. There are some virtues in necessity. Without a world agreement, each producing nation will seek to maximize its own profit. If Saudi Arabia will for years play the statesman and hold back on output expansion, we are no worse off; if they retaliate against any rivals, we have gained enormously. Similarly with the consuming countries: some of them will recover from their panic and will begin inviting producers to make some special deals for disguised low prices, to put the cartel on the slippery slope. This country needs not *ordnung* but disarray in the cartel. But we cannot by statesmanlike action cure the nonexistent world oil shortage.

However, there are some matters where action may help. Sheik Yamani warned in early 1973 that any attempt at consumers' self-defense meant "war," and "their [i.e., our] industries and civilization would collapse" (Platt's Oilgram News Service (*PONS*), Feb. 22, 1973). By November 9, he and his colleagues "are letting the word out that the present cutbacks in oil output are the limit." The reasons mentioned are possible Western responses: food, manufactures (including armaments), and military action (*NYT*, Nov. 10, 1973) They who had talked of "war" and suited the action to the word understand the language. We had better learn it quickly.

There is as yet no weakening in our infatuation with Saudi Arabia, to whom we seem resolved to return bounty for evil done to us. In late November "a very high official in the Nixon Administration who is a policy maker in this area" told a reporter "he feels King Faisal ... at the last minute would prevent any serious economic harm from being done to this country because he is at heart a friend of the United States" (*MP*, Nov. 25, 1973). Meanwhile, King Faisal is "angry with Mr. Sadat" of Egypt for being too cooperative with the Americans (*Ec.*, Nov. 24, 1973). Without doubt the Saudis feel they have every right to be hostile to the United States, and it is not for an American to say they are wrong. But our safety demands that we recognize which way is down.

The Saudi connection, which our government values so highly, is no asset but a heavy liability. The profits of Aramco, whose protection is a perfectly legitimate national objective, will be kept at a level needed to secure incremental investment, and can scarcely amount to a billion dollars annually even if Aramco reaches 20 MBD. If the Saudi investment portfolio reaches $100 billion, a 0.1 percent per year management fee is the most the management company can reasonably expect. This is less than the extraordinary expenditures already forced upon us this year by King Faisal's shooting war, and it is insignificant compared with the losses of national product here and throughout the world, due to the oil embargo: 1 percent of GNP lost is $13 billion per year.

In war one seeks not to be strong everywhere, but only at the strategic points. For the non-Communist world the decisive point is the United States. This country should immediately take steps to separate itself completely from Arab oil sources. Once we are beyond the reach of oil cutoffs, they can no longer pressure us. Then there is no profit in tormenting Europe and Asia, and risking retaliation, as an indirect means of pressuring the United States.

Our overseas imports before the cutback were about six MBD. Future imports will for a time be larger, but will come nowhere near the ten or more MBD freely predicted a short time ago, because of the drive for greater self-sufficiency. The four largest non-Arab oil exporters—Iran, Venezuela, Nigeria, and Indonesia—already produce thirteen MBD, and their production will grow substantially, Iran alone being a good bet for 10 million MBD in a few years, especially if we act. (Our current ambassador to Saudi Arabia insisted in September 1972 that Iran *had been* interested in production increases, but no longer (*OGJ*, Sept. 25, 1973), which was contradicted by previous public evidence (*OGJ*, Aug. 14, 1973, Sept. 4, 1973, Sept. 13, 1973), and also the expansion program decided early in 1973.)

Two routes ought to be examined. One is to bar or penalize imports from countries declaring embargoes against us or pressuring third parties to embargo us (see above). Or the United States could make contracts with any countries desiring preferential entry, in return for which they would guarantee certain minimum amounts. We would of course have to promise —and keep our promise—to pay the very high world prices. But as shown earlier, this price will likely be in the neighborhood of what it would cost us anyway to produce at home from substitute sources. Richard Gardner has embarrassed our government by pointing out that Saudi Arabia has violated their treaty with us providing for mutual most-favored-nation treatment (*NYT*, Dec. 19, 1973). We need only tell the Saudis their embargo on shipments to us is henceforth permanent, their status having been cancelled by their own act.

As George F. Kennan, a respected scholar and ex-diplomat, has well shown, in saving ourselves, we save our friends abroad, by making boycotts against them unrewarding and therefore unlikely.

Notes

I wish to thank Harry J. Colish, Richard L. Gordon, Richard B. Mancke, and Joseph L. Yager for comments on an earlier draft; errors are my own.

1. Elementary economics is ignored in grain as in oil: the Department of Agriculture's Economic Research Service was never consulted on the notorious 1972 wheat sale to Soviet Russia (*NYT*, Oct. 7, 1973).

References

M. A. Adelman, *The World Petroleum Market*, Baltimore, 1972.

———, "Is the Oil Shortage Real? Oil Companies as OPEC Tax Collectors," *Foreign Policy, 9*, Jan. 1973.

J. E. Akins, "This Time the Wolf is Here," *Foreign Affairs, 51*, Apr. 1973.

L. Barzini, *The Italians*, 1964.

G. Chandler, "Some Current Thoughts on the Oil Industry," *Petroleum Rev.*, Presidential address, Institute of Petroleum, 27, Jan. 1973.

G. F. Kennan, "And Thank You Very Much," *New York Times*, Op. Ed., Dec. 2, 1973.

T. R. Stauffer, "Price Formation in the Eastern Hemisphere: Concessionary versus Non-Concessionary Oil," in Zuhayr Mikdashi, et al., *Continuity and Change in the World Oil Industry*, Beirut 1970.

G. A. Wagner and A. Glimmerveen, Presentation to a meeting of financial analysts in The Hague on Oct. 4, 1973.

American Petroleum Institute, *Weekly Statist, Bull. (API)*.

British Petroleum Statistical Review of the World Oil Industry (BP).

Bureau of Mines, monthly releases *(BP)*.

Economist, London *(Ec.)*

LeMonde (LM).

Meet the Press, NBC Television *(MP)*.

Middle East Economic Survey (MEES).

New York Times (NYT).

New York Times, News of the Week in Review (NYT NWR).

Oil and Gas J. (OGJ).

Petroleum Intelligence Weekly (PIW).

Petroleum Press Service *(PPS)*.

Platt's Oilgram News Service *(PONS)*.

Platt's Oilgram Price Service *(POPS)*.

Wall Street Journal (WSJ).

17   The World Oil Cartel: Scarcity, Economics, and Politics

I shall try to maintain two propositions. First, future scarcity cannot possibly explain the current price of oil in the international market. In fact, a group of oil-producing nations have formed a cartel like any other, but not like every other. No cartel is like every other cartel; each is a historical individual. My second thesis is that for the immediate future the elements of strength look more impressive than the elements of weakness and that the cartel will not soon disappear.

On the first proposition, I apply the ideas of economists who in the 1950s and 1960s reconciled an elegant theory and some awkward facts. In theory, mineral resources were limited; costs and prices had to increase over time. The future scarcity threw its shadow far ahead through the discounting mechanisms, and prices rose at approximately the rate of interest. Thus mankind was never in danger of driving blindly off the cliff of apparent plenty into the void of materials running out, but received signals a long way ahead. The awkward fact was that minerals prices did not persistently rise over the long run. The minerals industries were acting at any moment as though their admittedly finite stocks were infinite; and in retrospect they were right to act this way.

The new theory was stated in the 1967 papers by Richard L. Gordon (5) and by the late Orris Herfindahl (6). Their reward has been to be ignored, not only by policymakers but even by fellow economists. Let me restate their thought briefly.

Ali minerals are limited because the earth itself is. Where the limit lies, we shall never know and neither will our descendants, ever. Oil, for example, is only one member of a large class of combustibles which in the fullness of time will include seawater, granite, the wind, and the sun in amounts never contemplated today. However, we ignore these far-off pos-

Reprinted from *Quarterly Review of Economics & Business* 16 (Summer 1976): 7–18.

Table 17.1
Assumptions

---

1. In A.D. 2000, oil reserves disappearing, substitutes and synethetic oils available at $16 per barrel (Source: oil company, 1975 technology). Conventional oil price equates.
2. In A.D. 2000, Persian Gulf average costs $2.50 per barrel, hence economic rent $13.50.
3. Discount rate, real, 10 percent.
4. Economic rent, present value $1.25 (that is, $13.50 × 1.1^{-25}).
5. Persian Gulf 1975 development cost $0.25.

Tentative conclusion

6. Competitive 1975 Persian Gulf price $1.50 (that is, $1.25 + $0.25), price rises approximately 10 percent per year (that is, $1.50 × 1.1^{25} = 16).

---

sibilities and deal only with shale oil, tar sands, coal, and to a minor and dispensable extent, uranium. The only difference between oil and these other combustibles is that oil is cheaper to extract and use. When and as it becomes more expensive, people will give over the search for it and we shall never get to the end of the stock of oil. In that real sense oil is inexhaustible.

Table 17.1 shows the assumptions I would like to test. By A.D. 2000, oil reserves, that is, visible usable stocks, will be rapidly disappearing and all growth in consumption must come from substitutes and synthetic oils, which are available at $16 a barrel, an oil company estimate of what can be done with 1975 technology. The price of conventional oil must therefore also be $16. By the year 2000 the average production cost of Persian Gulf crude oil will be about ten times the present level or about $2.50. Hence there is an economic rent of $13.50 per barrel. (If the cost rises more than we assume, the rent will be less, and also the present value.) If an asset oil-in-the-ground is worth that much, net of production cost, in 25 years, at what price must one sell it today in order to suffer no loss? I am assuming a discount rate (in real terms) of 10 percent. If we consider the last period of price stability, 1957–65, when the GNP deflator was rising at only 1.6 percent per year, a fair approximation to the riskless rate was a median yield of 4.0 percent on US taxable bonds. The median after-tax return on equity for all manufacturing was 10.3 percent.

A discount rate of 10 percent real may be too low. It attaches no particular risk to the possibility of improved technology putting the price down below $16. As we shall see later, this risk is only one special case in a larger class.

The present value (1975) of the 2000 economic rent is about $1.25 a barrel. (Recently President Kingman Brewster of Yale University proposed

Table 17.2
Test (excluding communist areas)

Demand

1. Total energy consumption 1953–73, 4.6 percent per year growth.
2. Total oil consumption 1953–73, 7.0 percent per year growth.
3. Autonomous oil demand growth assumed to decline to 4.6 percent in A.D. 2000, averaging 5.8 percent per year, 1975–2000.
4. Assumed demand elasticity $= -0.3$, long run.
5. Annual consumption increase, with 10 percent annual price increase, 2.8 percent (that is, $1.058 \times 1.1^{-0.3}$).

Consumption

6. Starting level 47.9 million barrels daily, 17.5 billion barrels a year ($= 1973$ level, omits recession).
7. Cumulative consumption 1976–2000: 620 billion barrels (that is, $17.5 \sum_1^{25} (1.028)^{25}$).

Reserves

8. Proved reserves in known reservoirs (recoverable "with reasonable certainty" with existing costs, prices, technology) end-1974: 609 billion barrels.
9. Additions to reserves in known reservoirs: Persian Gulf "worst case": 170 billion barrels.
10. Additions to reserves in known reservoirs: US: 60 billion barrels. (Sources: (1 and 8)).
11. Rest of noncommunist world, assuming Persian Gulf proportion, 70 billion barrels. (That is, $165 \times (170/404)$.)
12. Minimum additions in *known* reservoirs, 300 billion barrels.
13. Expected *discoveries* 1976–2000, 641 billion barrels. (Source: (7) (unexplored deeper offshore may add another 1,250 billion barrels).)

---

a "value-subtracted tax" for the use of nonrenewable resources. The rent in table 17.1 is exactly that.) In summary, if we expect to be running out of oil by the year 2000, under competitive conditions the 1975 Persian Gulf price should be around $1.50.

In table 17.2 we see whether this estimate can be squared with what we know about current oil resources outside the communist areas. First, as to consumption: Over the 20 years before the market convulsions of late 1973, total energy use was growing at about 4.6 percent a year. Oil consumption grew faster, at about 7 percent a year, as oil displaced the other fuels. This was a period of declining fuel prices and a world growth rate that most observers do not expect to see maintained for the rest of this century. (In 1925–68, energy and oil growth were respectively 2.8 and 6.1 percent.)[1] However I assume that the autonomous growth in demand for oil declines steadily from 7 to 4.6 percent a year, averaging 5.8 percent a year. I assume elasticity of demand in the long run as -0.3, which is at the low end of the range of published estimates. Essentially it means that if price increases by a factor of 10, consumption will decrease by 50 percent. Such results are not achieved overnight but require time enough for households and firms to change the apparatus they use for fuel consumption. Let me mention two illustrative facts: (1) Per capita income in Sweden is about as high as in the United States but per capita energy consumption is about half; and (2) The oil industry appears to agree with the president of General Motors who said last summer that automobiles on the road in 1980 would use less gasoline than did automobiles on the road in 1973. That could be wrong. Also, the change in American gasoline consumption may be due less to rising gasoline prices than to a change in consumption patterns, which in turn is largely a response to congestion and pollution. In any case, with 10 percent annual price increases, the combination of an autonomous increase of 5.8 percent and our demand elasticity of -0.3 is consumption growing at 2.8 percent a year.

Cumulative consumption for the rest of the century is about 620 billion barrels.

Turning now to the visible stock of oil: proved reserves in known reservoirs are mostly what can be produced at prices not of 1975 but nearer to $2 a barrel. Proved reserves, the industry ready-shelf inventory, were about 609 billion barrels a year ago. Estimates have been made of what can be produced from known reservoirs by more intensive exploitation. A "worst case" for the Persian Gulf is about 170 billion barrels. For the United States, it has been estimated that about 60 billion barrels are available. Particularly in the United States the additional oil is worth recovering only at high prices—the estimator, Standard Oil of Indiana, says about $12 a barrel, a figure to which of course we should not try to hold them very closely. Assuming the Persian Gulf proportion for the rest of the world, we obtain a minimum addition of about half of proved reserves. So much for known reservoirs. A recent estimate, generally considered conservative, is of 641 billion barrels to be discovered, though deeper offshore areas may add twice that (1; 8 and personal communication; and 7).

To speak of discoveries, of course, refutes the idea of oil as a nonrenewable resource. The economic asset oil reserves are certainly renewable and replaceable by the economic processes of finding and of improved recovery. The question is the cost at the margin of discovery or of better exploitation.

No allowance has been made for natural gas which, outside the United States and the Soviet Union, has not been sought for its own sake but has been found as the accidental result of the search for oil. The reserves known today outside these two countries are in heat value a large fraction of known oil reserves but are not worth exploiting. Given the prices in our scheme, they would be worth exploiting. The technology already exists and is commercial at prices lower than those we contemplate for the year 2000. Gas reserves are also expansible, like oil reserves.

In summary: the assumptions in table 17.1 about the current value of future economic rents because of supposedly limited oil supplies are well within the limits set by our knowledge of oil resources. Indeed, they rattle around inside those limits. The most important implication of this quick review is the way in which a market system operates to take account of scarcities long before they occur and to provide feedback to change the basic data.

The expectation in 1975 of higher prices later will lead to considerable investment in new knowledge: of the earth's crust, of better extraction methods to leave underground less than the current 70 percent in the United States and the over-80 percent elsewhere; and knowledge also of how to make better use of increasingly higher-priced fuels. I have merely done a worst case, using known data. Prices are made by endless iteration and reiteration, as new data enter.

Some would say that a market system cannot possibly handle so large a number of combinations and uncertainties; others, that only a market system is flexible enough to incorporate new data as they appear. Either way, the discounting process is the only way to avoid the impossible task of playing God, as though we really knew what was underground or aboveground.

The test was no forecast. Whether in fact, absent monopoly, the price would rise at all from 1975, I have no idea. In 1938 reserves as then known were being depleted at the rate of 6 percent a year and obviously this could not go on forever. In 1975 reserves are being depleted at the rate of nearly 3 percent a year and just as obviously this cannot go on forever. But whatever scarcity *may* come to pass is fully, perhaps over fully, accounted for in a price which is around $1.50 a barrel. If we bent every assumption, we might double it.

Now for recent price history: Five years ago the Persian Gulf price (at 1975 values) was about $2. It is now about $11.50 and it will undoubtedly be raised again as the industrial countries recover from the current recession. The current price has no possible relation to scarcity, present or future, known or feared. Therefore, having cleared away the unfact, we are free to look at the fact, the control of price by a group of exporting countries, the members of the Organization of Petroleum Exporting Countries. OPEC is not important in itself but the nations composing it constitute the greatest monopoly in history, its tribute now being over $100 billion a year.

The forces acting against the cartel are subsumed in the fact of excess capacity. This is the usual nemesis of cartels, since it puts in motion the sequence of small price reductions by some sellers to gain additional sales volume, then competitive or matching reductions. Each cartel member must avoid acting for his own independent good and must do what is best for the group as a whole. The greater the burden of excess capacity, the greater the temptation to act independently, the greater the fear of others' independent action, and the higher the probability of severe erosion or breakdown. So the fate of the cartel depends essentially on the strength of exogenous factors, demand and uncontrolled supply, versus the strength of an endogenous factor, the cohesion of the group. All too often either one of these factors is treated in isolation as though the other were not there.

By mid-1975, production of the OPEC nations was around 26 million barrels daily and unused capacity was 12 million, or nearly half. Clearly great strain was being exerted. Just as clearly there was great strength, for the price was actually raised at the end of September. Let us therefore look at the principal factors of strength.

One preliminary but important comment: political factors are not likely to damage the cartel any more than they have helped it. It is widely but wrongly believed that the cartel and the level of oil prices are somehow connected with political strife in the Middle East. However, assume a political settlement acceptable to both Israelis and Arabs. There is simply no reason that anyone should lower the price of oil. Non-Arab members of OPEC are of course pretty emphatic on the point. But there is no disagreement from Sheik Yamani, the Saudi petroleum minister, or from the former American ambassador to Saudi Arabia, who has been relieved of his post because he apparently confused himself with the Saudi ambassador to the United States.[2] They both deny that a political settlement would lead to lower prices. We had better believe them.

The royal road to power is money. Therefore, whatever a nation's political aims, these are best achieved by acting as a good revenue maximizer. Back in the 1920s Soviet Russia, the international pariah, felt free to join several cartels and was welcomed in.

We might also recall that the price increase during October–December 1973 was about $4, that is, from $3 to about $7 a barrel. But during the whole period of OPEC's success beginning in late 1970, the increase in the Persian Gulf has been over $10, from $1.25 to $11.50, so that the increase associated with the embargo has been less than half of the total increase, and it will be a still lower percentage as the price rises more.

But although political *objectives* of these sovereign nations have little to do with the cartel objectives, their sovereignty is a great help. These nations are subject to no law that would limit or abridge their monopoly. It is free enterprise at its freest. The larger Persian Gulf producing nations have or soon will have the ability to occupy their neighbors. The mere threat should be enough.

The second great advantage enjoyed by this cartel is in using the multinational oil companies to make the market clear, ensuring that the amount offered at the prevailing price does not exceed the amount demanded. The multinational oil companies, without any collusion, limit output and allocate it among the producing countries. The system is simple and has worked excellently so far. The exporting countries transfer the great bulk of their oil to the companies at the fixed price. Each company produces only what it can sell at that price. Since margins are very thin, around 2 percent of the price, companies cannot make significant price cuts. As nobody makes lower offers to get more outlet, the market clears at prevailing prices.

The market share of each country depends on what its resident companies can sell. What matters is not "nationalization," but that the exporting nations accept those market shares and shun any large-scale independent selling efforts. This has imposed some strains. Since the companies now have a relatively small stake in operating in any particular country, they are more ready to buy crude elsewhere and have done so, in small amounts. Hence governments have engaged in the novel experience of bargaining over prices and even losing sales. Even when the amounts are tiny they react with surprising vehemence. Algeria has not hesitated to make harsh criticisms of Nigeria and Libya for having given small incentives to their resident companies, preventing them from buying Algerian crude oil. The outstanding nonconformist is Iraq, which has shaded prices just enough to keep output at over 90 percent of capacity and has in consequence now upgraded its 1980 plans by 50 percent. Much of its gain has been at the expense of Kuwait, which has found its former resident companies, Gulf and British Petroleum, uninterested in taking all the oil made available. Kuwait shook a stick at the companies—no oil sales contract whatever— and offered a carrot, a 10-cent price reduction, promptly denounced by Iraq in an official diplomatic note: such reductions would "inspire competitive bidding among producers." Competitive bidding is the clear and present danger and its avoidance is worth many times 10 cents. I expect Kuwait to come to some kind of understanding with the companies. Yet the tie that binds companies to any given source of supply is weaker than ever before. Even with no cataclysmic change, when the margin on crude oil becomes thin, even if a government scrupulously maintains it, the company has shifted its emphasis away from *disposal* of profitable crude oil toward the *procurement* of crude oil for its refining-marketing operations to run at a profit.

My own guess is that the situation will be contained for the immediate future because both parties know that the multinational companies are indispensable. Perhaps the governments could themselves limit output and divide markets. They do not want to find out. Haggling over market shares, surveillance, and compensation of losers would be a constant divisive irritant. Confrontation in council, month after month, would strain and I think severely damage the cartel.

Another advantage of the cartel nations is the superabundant liquidity of some of them. Many a price-fixing agreement has been undermined by reluctant price-cutters, who cannot help themselves because they must have additional cash and can only raise it by increasing sales even at lower prices. Most OPEC governments are in excellent financial shape and have therefore tolerated the companies' sales reductions. Even those which have overspent revenues find their credit is very good. There is a backward bending supply function: the higher the price, the greater the cohesion of the cartel, the less put on the market.

We touch here on a very important point, the rate of expansion of capacity of the fringe of the cartel, the nations which must choose between (1) acting as price takers and expanding output as fast as possible or (2) permitting the companies to operate the cutback scheme or understanding. The fringe nations—broadly the non-Arab members plus Iraq—have mostly refrained from pushing output to the maximum and have chosen rather to bear as great a reduction as the core countries—broadly the Persian Gulf Arab states. If the fringe nations were to sell at capacity and expand capacity, the cartel would be much weaker. Each fringe nation knows that what each does makes no difference. If they see others complying they will most likely do the same. Conversely, every flouting of the implied obligation makes it more likely that others will flout. It is a basic instability; a tendency in either direction becomes self-reinforcing, but today the self-reinforcing tendency strengthens the cartel.

Relations between core and fringe are complicated by the fact that no two governments have quite the same rate of time preference. Some of them want higher prices today even if it means lower prices tomorrow, whereas others would maximize the present value of their assets by a somewhat flatter gradient. A long-run equilibrium monopoly price for Saudi Arabia *would be* lower than for Algeria. But that is a conditional statement, not a reference to any actual prices. There is no truth in the United States government's romance of Saudi Arabia trying to keep down the price. In fact, that nation was the leader, raising prices throughout 1974. They not only acquiesced in the price increase of 1975—recent statements by Sheik Yamani clearly foreshadow further price increases when industrial recovery is farther advanced. However, Saudi Arabia like any prudent monopolist advances the price step-by-step, pausing to test the market before raising it again, and just as with other cartels where costs vary greatly among the cartelists, it may be necessary for the lower-cost producers to make side payments to the higher-cost. In the oil nations' cartel, the side payment would take the form of agreeing to a price higher than would optimize the holdings of the lower-cost producer. However, that problem has not yet become serious.

This brings us to an advantage for the cartel which is potential rather than actual, Saudi Arabia as the restrictor of last resort. In the United States, from the end of World War II to the end of the 1960s Texas absorbed all of the production cutbacks and tolerated excess capacity that was often 75 percent of the total. Texas had about two-thirds of east-of-the-Rockies output, whereas Saudi Arabia accounts today for about one-fourth of OPEC production. They cannot yet serve as the backstop of the cartel and let others produce as they wish. Suppose they had tried to do this in the middle of 1975, when OPEC excess capacity was equal to or a bit greater than Saudi capacity. Saudi output would then be zero, quite an intolerable result, but in the near future they will be able to occupy all the coastal states of the Persian Gulf. Then in similar plight they could produce about 6 million barrels daily. With Iran producing more than 6 million barrels daily and with all fringe nations booming ahead to develop additional capacity, thereby promising attrition of even that 6 million barrels, would this be tolerable? I submit that even the Saudis do not know and rightly do not want to find out.

Let me in passing pay proper disrespect to the slogan that Saudi Arabia would rather keep oil in the ground than money in the bank. A barrel sold today sacrifices the present value of a barrel sold in the future. Saudi Arabian reserves can easily be expanded to 50 years' supply. If the price of oil were then not $11.50 but $111.50, its present value would be less than $1. A monopolist, or member of a joint monopoly, restrains output not for the sake of the distant future but to avoid wrecking the price structure today.

Let me turn now from the factors inside the cartel to those outside. The amount of excess capacity with which the cartel must cope depends on the speed with which noncartel production develops.

The noncartel reaction might at first be supposed very simple: these countries would act like simple price takers and expand output as fast and as far as possible, until its marginal cost is equal to the price.

This is the case in countries where the oil industry is nationalized. The Soviet Union, China, and Mexico are expanding like rational if sometimes sluggish capitalists. However, in most private enterprise countries, political forces have not permitted that simple response of output to higher prices. The economy as a whole would, of course, be benefited by any production whose total cost was less than the import price of equivalent energy, but the producing companies would get "too big a share" of that increased national income. Governments would rather prevent windfall gains than get the production response. Whether right or wrong, this policy prevails and its results must be allowed for. In the United States, oil prices are under control, thereby subsidizing consumption, inhibiting production, and promoting imports. Field price regulation of natural gas has done it for years. Expansion of low-sulfur coal, particularly in the Rocky Mountain states, has been prevented largely by those states, both directly and through their congressional delegations. To some extent this is a matter of concern over the environment and to some extent a desire to share in the windfall gain; whatever the reason, the production response is prevented.

In Canada higher prices led actually to large-scale *disinvestment*—the provincial and national governments raised taxes enough to send scores of rigs migrating southward. The result was to decrease Canadian reserves, which in turn set off a further reaction, to restrict exports lest Canada run out of oil; this will diminish reserves still more. In the United Kingdom, the price explosion of 1973 led to a North Sea profits explosion which had two effects. One was a wild bidding up of factor prices. The other was a steep increase in taxation, which recently drew back short of taking all of the economic rents. The slippage in the North Sea has already been considerable, so that expected output in any given year of the near future will be considerably less than attainable, and there is also a considerable reluctance by private investors to explore and develop further.

Norway is a special case; a small country with large potential which it restrains for several reasons; fear of the impact of excessive development on an attractive way of life; the illusion of scarcity and belief that prices must rise far more; distaste for unearned income; fear of foreign business; and so on. In time the fears and hopes will be seen to be unwarranted, the dangers avoidable, and the ceiling lifted, but surely not so far as to equate cost with price.

It would be tedious to extend the list but I draw the general conclusion, which is again that of a backward bending supply curve—past some point, higher price in the world market has led to less, not more, investment in the non-OPEC countries because other objectives have overborne the desire for increased national income.

I come now to the reactions of the consuming countries as such to the price increases of the cartel. There are several reasons that public opinion will tolerate and even defend actions which had they been taken by private parties would have brought swift punishment. There is the Club of Rome syndrome, that we are quickly running out of everything and hence the price increase is actually a good thing enforcing a little more thrift upon us. There is also a feeling of guilt in the face of the poor nations of the world, a wish to make it up to them. Recently, a Swedish minister of state, speaking at the United Nations General Assembly, congratulated OPEC for having broken through the domination of the advanced industrial countries. I do not see what good is done by making the poorest nations still more poor and by giving the Saud family—4,000 adult males—an income of $100 million a day. However, belief is all that matters.

Moreover, the rapidly escalating imports of the OPEC nations from $20 billion in 1972 to $100 billion estimated by Morgan Guaranty for 1976 are building up a powerful vested interest in the consuming countries. Thousands of people have jobs and some are getting rich selling them goods and services. The Office of Munitions Control in the State Department has released the federal registration certificates of 1,033 companies licensed to make or export armaments. It is a fairly good cross-section of American business, including 153 of the *Fortune* largest 500 companies. Academia is included, a wholly owned subsidiary of Cornell University. Overseas sales of munitions in 1974 were $11 billion, of which an increasing proportion is going to the Persian Gulf.

The United States is the most important consuming nation. It is impossible to give any kind of statement of American policy. A mystery or void remains at its center. In 1972, I gave considerable offense by saying that the State Department was actively helping the cartel but I could only speculate as to the reasons. Insiders were baffled too. The hearings of the Church subcommittee have shown that in 1970, when the Libyan demands were ready to blow the door off the hinges, some oil companies were for resisting, some for compliance, and some waffled. The United States government was determined that the Libyans should get what they wanted but the then head of Royal Dutch Shell, writing three years later, could not give any clear account why. American support for the cartel is shown in Secretary Kissinger's statement that the price before December 1973 had been "too low." The nearest he came to explaining "too low" was in saying that "the demand for oil had outrun the inducement to invest." This is at least an intelligible statement. The 1973 investment requirements for Persian Gulf oil production are rather generously put at $200 per daily barrel and the operating expense at 10 cents per barrel. A $3 price meant a return on investment of 529 percent per year. Later the secretary seemed to abandon any economic rationale, alleging that 1974 prices were "political." One would have thought that a price which increases the sellers' net revenues needs no further explanation. Since the end of 1973 there has been preachment and admonition, with occasional warnings that somebody may go too far. In September 1974, Mr. Kissinger made a "tough" speech in New York and Mr. Ford made a "tough" speech in Detroit. The then Federal Energy Administrator John Sawhill was asked what plans there were for getting the world price down. He replied truthfully that there were none. Mr. Kissinger was angry and Mr. Sawhill was fired.

Our policy at its best is import reduction. However, lower imports can affect the cartel only by adding to excess capacity. But in 1974—75 the growth in excess capacity was greater and faster, hence with more shock effect, than anything the United States could accomplish. The cartel took the strain and kept raising prices. "Conservation" generally will not affect the world price unless used as a lever to disrupt the cartel and no such act is now contemplated.

The United States is now negotiating to purchase oil from the Soviet Union, but that country has no current or expected excess capacity. Every barrel they sell to us is subtracted from sales elsewhere. They are a small part of the world market and can sell anything at the world price. The very fact that our government has been spending so much time and effort on this empty show is a good index to our policy: the empty barrel making the most noise. Bluster, self-deceit, fantasies of self-sufficiency—these explain why the producing nations have taken the measure of the United States and fear us not.

The forthcoming conferences on energy and raw materials between consuming and producing nations will hear talk of interdependence. The oil-exporting countries will be told they cannot prosper if their customers are in a depression—though the experience of the last two years shows this is false. If the industrial nations give investment guarantees to the OPEC nations with the largest foreign exchange surpluses, that will be a disguised price increase. It will also strengthen the core at the expense of the fringe. A long-term deal to fix what Mr. Kissinger has called "a just price" seems less likely now, fortunately. A sovereign monopolist cannot be held to any agreement. A private firm or individual is constrained by competition or law, or both. Anyone who welshes on a deal is either abandoned, as people go elsewhere to do business, or else a court orders him to keep his word or have his assets seized, but the cartel has suppressed competition and there is no law against the sovereign.

Summing up, I would say that the strong points are more impressive for the immediate future than the weaknesses and that we must therefore expect to see continued increase in prices. Admittedly, things may change, and swiftly. Even great success does not change the basically fragile nature of a cartel, which is the home of the self-fulfilling prophecy and the self-reinforcing trend. Saudi Arabia may be the restrictor of last resort, but it has swiftly built producing capacity which it cannot possibly use even well into the 1980s. It is a hedge or more accurately a threat that if anyone starts any price war, they will finish it. Cartel-watchers should pay attention to the role of the oil companies as the market-clearing instrument. Eventually some consuming nations may realize that the Iraq government, in the remark quoted earlier, state the cartel's greatest fear, "Competitive bidding among producers." But that is another story.

Notes

The David Kinley Lecture, delivered at the University of Illinois at Urbana-Champaign, 4 December 1975.

1. For 1925–68, (3, Tables 1–6); for 1953–73, (2).

2. (4, p. 63). He "argued that OPEC could do no ill because it was under the thumb of the Saudis and the Saudis believed in lower prices. Sadly, while Mr. Akins spoke, prices still went up."

References

1. Z. R. Beydoun and H. V. Dunnington, *Petroleum Geology and Resources of the Middle East* (Beaconsfield, England: Scientific Press Ltd., 1975).

2. British Petroleum Company, *Statistical Review of the World Oil Industry* (London, 1975).

3. Joel Darmstadter and others, *Energy in the World Economy* (Baltimore: Johns Hopkins Press, for Resources for the Future, 1971).

4. *Economist* (London), 23 August 1975, p. 63.

5. Richard L. Cordon, "A Reinterpretation of the Pure Theory of Exhaustion," Journal of Political Economy, Vol. 75 (June 1967), pp. 274–86.

6. Orris C. Herfindahl, "Depletion and Economic Theory," in Mason Gaffney, ed., *Extractive Industries and Taxation* (Madison: University of Wisconsin Press, 1967).

7. John D. Moody, paper presented at World Petroleum Congress, May 1975.

8. *Oil and Gas Journal* (17 November 1975), p. 26.

18

Constraints on the World Oil Monopoly Price

1 Introduction

An earlier paper (Adelman 1976) urged that the current world oil price had nothing to do with real scarcity, but was set by a monopoly both vulnerable and very strong. The purpose is now to make some limited predictions about future prices.

Non-competitive markets are notoriously hard to analyze, because we have no precise theory of small-group actions. Furthermore, the monopoly's great successes since the 1970 Libyan negotiations have been and still are a learning process.

We identify the leading actors and sketch their options, indicating those we think the most probable. In the following section we see that the consuming nations have the power to damage or possibly even wreck the monopoly, but prefer to cooperate with it. But they may use that power inadvertently, in reacting to balance-of-payment and inflationary difficulties. As described in section 3, this danger becomes an element of risk to be considered by the monopoly, which is a cartel with a safety net: a larger seller who would if need be act as the single supplier of the residual amount demanded at the monopoly price. In the next section it appears that the multi-national oil companies, possibly no longer strictly necessary, are still very useful to the cartel in coordinating price and output. But using them compounds some of the difficulties of coordination. Because of these problems and risks we finally come to the conclusion that the cartel will only slowly and gradually approach profit- or wealth-maximization.

Reprinted from *Resources & Energy* 1 (January 1978): 3–19.

2 Consuming Countries

There was active American help to the cartel in 1970–74,[1] and official policy is a now more openly stated: OPEC is good for us.[2] Otherwise, consuming countries have been passive.

Policy-makers in consuming countries firmly believe, for some never-stated and hence irrefutable reason, that the world oil price will be held below the market-clearing level. It logically follows that there will be a "gap," with more demanded than is offered. Therefore, the danger is not merely a high price, but "not enough oil for our needs." Since the market will not clear, it follows that oil will be distributed by favor and influence. Hence the ever-repeated need for 'access' (Congressional Reference Service 1977, p. 61) and "assurances of supply," which are non-problems if the market clears. Europeans and Japanese fear that the United States has somehow got Saudi Arab output pre-empted, so that other nations will not be able to buy as much as they wish.[3] The nations yearn for self-sufficiency.[4] Hence they fear to renounce nuclear reprocessing.[5]

The gap is like the horizon, always receding as we go toward it. In 1972, the State Department predicted a shortage of 20 MBD by 1986,[6] indeed, their chief energy expert warned that "by 1976, our position could be nothing short of desperate."[7] Their "exaggerated talk of an energy crisis greatly strengthened the bargaining power of the Arab states."[8] Today, the IEA predicts a world oil shortage of 14 MBD—in 1985.[9] The WAES (1977) Report has the same message; it summarizes very well the consensus view. "We can't afford to alert the public to the problem of the cartel because we're too scared, says one Carter official. It's hard to bare our teeth at the Arabs when we're grovelling for their oil."[10] Nobody can explain that "grovelling" is perfectly useless because the producers will charge the price that suits them, at which price there will be all that every purchaser demands, be he loved or hated.

"The gap" is a fiction, but belief in fiction is a fact. It will keep the consuming nations passive and compliant in the future as in the past.

Yet a rational monopolist must consider that consumer-country actions with a low probability of occurrence would have substantial consequences if they did occur.

The United States could auction import entitlements to divert revenues from the cartel to this country's treasury. The Economic Task Force of the then President-elect Carter recommended such a plan.[11] It has not been heard from since. When the plan was explained to Mr. Schlesinger, his reaction was: "It would work. But do we dare let it work?"[12] The answer clearly is No, but the option is there.

I once argued that an excise tax in consuming countries could force the world price down as the producing governments has used it to force the price up (Adelman 1972, pp. 261–262). More recently, Houthakker (1976, pp. 29–36) has suggested an import tariff and made estimates of its effect on cartel production. I now think that a flat levy would not have any such effect, but an ad valorem tariff or tax would, *if* the proportion increased with the cartel price and revenue. In effect, it would be a progressive income tax.

Assume the cartel to be a single monopolist. Since cost is negligible, profit is maximized where marginal revenue becomes zero, at the point on the demand curve where price elasticity is -1.0. In figure 18.1, total profit is the topmost line, a function of quantity produced. Price per unit is the slope of a line from the origin to any point on the profit line. Lower production and rising prices generate higher profits as long as demand stays in the inelastic region. If the demand for oil is now in this region, then as OPEC increases price and forgoes production, profits rise. OPEC would move over time to output level Q_3 where its profits would be maximized.

Suppose the consuming countries introduce a proportional tax equal to a/P. At today's level of output, represented by Q_1, the tax would result in a net after-tax producers' profit of $P_1 a_1$. OPEC would increase after-tax profits by raising its prices and collecting $P_2 a_2$. If the consuming govern-

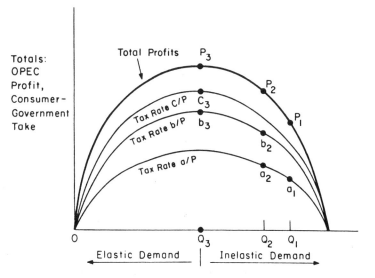

Figure 18.1
How consumer-country taxes could absorb increasing fractions of OPEC revenues

ments responded by raising the tax rate to b/P, the OPEC governments could maximize profits by collecting $P_3 b_3$. But a consumer outlay of P_3 would be the maximum. The producers would have exhausted their price-raising power. Then consumer governments could raise the tax rate to c/P, or higher, approaching as near to 100 percent as they thought prudent—just as OPEC countries do today.

If the consumer countries made the tax rate proportional to the price, then the cartel would be on notice that a higher price would mean lower revenue (see appendix A). Of course, estimates of the demand and revenue curves could be—probably would be—badly wrong. But the principle seems clear: *the consuming governments have the power to pre-empt all the profit of the producing countries.*

No consuming country would today contemplate such a policy. Yet they may inadvertently do, step by step, what they would never dream of doing deliberately. Large sudden changes in oil prices might induce action to check imports, including taxes or tariffs on crude oil products. The moral for the cartel nations: minimize risk by raising the price in small increments, and at times when the world economy is most healthy.

It is doubtful that the OPEC nations have made any rigorous analysis of the problem, but they have long been aware of what the Secretary General of OPEC recently called "competition to get a larger slice of the same cake: the value generated by a barrel of crude oil."[13] As just demonstrated, the more the consuming countries raise their taxes, the less left for producers. Therefore, aside from policy questions, a key variable in any modeling effort must be: taxes and tariffs imposed by consuming countries.

It is frequently suggested that the consuming nations can increase the output of the producers by some kind of political or economic accommodation. But any such favor, once granted and irrevocable, is of no account. The succession of broken Saudi promises in 1971–74[14] was prefigured in the 1973 comment of Sheik Yamani: "We in Saudi Arabia would have liked to honor and abide by the [1971] Tehran Agreement, but ..." Circumstances, he said, had changed.[15]

The record of broken promises is not explicable by Saudi original sin or bad character but by the market structure. An agreement with sovereign monopolists is unenforceable, since there is neither competition nor law to make them keep their work.

3   The Producing Countries as a Cartel

We need make no assumptions about the objectives of the producing governments. Whether political or military power, or consumption, or investment, or anything, the more wealth the better. There is no sacrifice or trade-off for anything else. Hence analysis of economic objectives suffices for non-economic.

To a first approximation, we have thought of the cartel countries as a single perfect monopoly, approaching its target by degrees, as shown in figure 18.1.

In fact there are a dozen countries of whom Saudi Arabia is the biggest producer, and has the greatest unused potential capacity. We should avoid prejudgment of the producing nations as *either* (a) a cartel who need the consent of most or all of the members, and some scheme for sharing output, *or* (b) a dominant firm as residual supplier. Perhaps the truth incorporates both hypotheses.

Table 18.1 sets out the group's problem of actual and potential excess capacity in the face of highly uncertain demand. In 1977−78, there was a severe worldwide glut of crude oil, and "increasingly frenzied predictions of long-term scarcity."[16]

The large discrepancy between the CIA projection for 1985 (column a) and one which seems more likely to me (column d), may be more apparent than real. If their estimates of supply and demand at a constant price are correct, then one must expect—as they do—a considerable price increase in the early 1980s, if not sooner. Now, the real Western European oil product price nearly doubled between 1972 and 1976.[17] To assume that from 1973 to 1985 it will have increased by a factor of 2.5 seems conservative. Assuming long-run product demand elasticity of − 0.3 within the relevant range, the consumption estimate in column d merely makes explicit allowance for the assumptions of columns a−c.

Thus far we have merely drawn the logical consequences of the CIA (and similar) calculations. But we do reject their assumption of large Communist net imports. The Soviet Government is incapable of paying for such imports, and is capable of severely compressing demand and speeding up nuclear and coal. The oil industry has pointed to large not fully developed Soviet fields, and pipelines therefrom.[18] It takes seriously the Soviet program of nearly two million barrels daily of net exports in 1980.[19] China is already committed to 300 thousand barrels daily (TBD) in 1982, to Japan alone.[20] I have arbitrarily assumed that the trend to rising Communist exports is reversed in 1980−85, but the evidence is really non-existent.

Other supply factors compound the uncertainty. The CIA has made no specific allowance for the increase in natural gas production, which will displace oil almost one for one. The increase in North Sea gas from 1976 to 1985 will be about 650 thousand barrels daily oil equivalent (TBDOE).[21]

Table 18.1
Consumption and residual OPEC production, 1973–85 (in millions of barrels daily)

	1973	1976	1980 (a)	1980 (b)	1985 (a)	1985 (b)	1985 (c)	1985 (d)	1985 (e)
World (excl. Communist areas) total consumption	47.6	48.4	55.8	52.6*	70.4	60.3*	68.8	63.0	—
Non-OPEC supply	16.4	17.5	22.0	20.9	21.4	26.4*	27.6	28.5	—
U.S.	10.9	9.7	10.0	9.6	10.5	11.0	11.2	12.0	—
Canada	2.1	1.6	1.5	1.2	1.4	1.0	1.4	1.5	—
W. Europe	0.4	0.9	3.7	3.5	4.5	4.3	4.7	4.5	—
Other	2.2	4.2	6.1	5.6	8.9	9.1	9.4	9.5	—
Communist net exports	0.8	1.1	0.2	1.0*	−4.0	1.0*	1.0	1.0	—
OPEC	31.2	30.9	33.8	31.7	49.0	33.9	41.2	34.5	28.6
Outside southern Persian Gulf	18.2	17.5	21.6	18.6	21.8	20.5	22.6	22.0	22.0
Southern Persian Gulf (excl. Saudi Arabia)	5.4	4.9	6.4	4.7	6.7	4.9	7.0	0–4.0	0.0
Saudi Arabia	7.6	8.5	8.5	8.3	20.5	8.5	11.6	8.5–12.5	6.6

Sources for columns a–e:
(a) CIA, April, 1977 (but assuming all OPEC except Saudi Arabia at capacity).
(b) Anonymous oil company, *Oil & Gas Journal*, October 10, 1977, p. 43. *Assume 1 MBD Communist block exports.
(c) Congressional Research Service (1977, p. 63), mid-point of ranges.
(d) *Consumption:* CIA estimate × (0.76/0.85). CIA estimates "conservation" as reducing consumption by 15 percent. *Alternative:* Assume real 1985 consumer price 2.5 times 1973 price, and demand elasticity −0.3. Then $(2.5)^{-0.3} = 0.76$. *Non-OPEC supply:* Author's estimates.
(e) IEA, "vigorous policies" scenario.

Iranian gas shipments to the Soviet Union will permit 1980 additional Soviet exports of 350 TBDOE, domestic development of an additional 614 TBDOE.[22] World trade in LNG, BP estimates, may reach 3 MBDOE by 1985;[23] it seems prudent to reckon on about 2 MBDOE. Non-Communist natural gas liquid production is forecast as growing faster than consumption; by over 836 TBD (Culbertson 1977, p. 480). Thus, there is a good chance of OPEC demand being lower by nearly 5 million barrels daily. To incorporate it into our forecast would give it a mock precision. But the point of table 18.1 is that there is great uncertainty *as to the net residual demand for OPEC oil.*

Column e embodies a projection I consider improbably low, to test the hypothesis that the cartel will not be disrupted or destroyed even by that large a reduction in net OPEC demand. Assuming that there are only 6.6 MBD demanded from countries which last year produced nearly 14, can Saudi Arabia take the whole burden of excess capacity, letting the others produce as much as they wish?

We need not reach the question. The cartel members are sovereign nations and can suppress competition by force or the threat of force. Iran can limit out-shipments from the Persian Gulf. Saudi Arabia can invade and occupy its neighbors. Distances are short, local populations scanty, the terrain ideal for a quick grab. Today these neighbors account for six million barrels daily of capacity. They can be taken out quickly, if they do not cut back as they are told.

The cartel will not be broken by insufficient net demand. The hypothesis that Saudi Arabia *can be* the restrictor of last resort is very robust. It does not follow that they *will be*, as we now show.

Table 18.2 shows the tension between the interest of the cartel and of its senior member.

The elasticity of demand for total OPEC crude oil (column 5) approximates that for oil products (column 1). If an assumed product demand elasticity is low, a stiff increase in the price of Persian Gulf oil would serve the cartel as a whole. But if Saudi Arabia is really the restrictor of last resort, then their interests may be very different from those of the cartel as a whole. On the CIA projection, a doubling of the world price of oil would double non-Saudi revenues, but increase Saudi revenues by only 32 percent. On every other projection, there would be a substantial decrease.

Nobody should take the actual numbers in columns 5–6 too seriously. But the differences, between 1970 and 1973 on the one side and 1976 and later years on the other, are so gross that they show a basic change in the relations between the largest seller and its partners.

Table 18.2
Elasticity of demand for OPEC oil and for Saudi oil as residual supply

Year	Long-run ED for oil products (1)	P (crude)/ P (products) (2)	World prod./ OPEC prod. (3)	OPEC prod./ Saudi prod. (4)	Elasticity of demand for OPEC oil [(1) × (2) × (3)] (5)	Elasticity of demand for Saudi oil [(1) × (2) × (3) × (4)] (6)
1970	−0.3	0.1	1.5	6.2	−0.04	−0.28
1973	−0.3	0.2	1.5	4.1	−0.09	−0.37
1976	−0.3	0.5	1.6	3.6	−0.24	−0.86
1985 a	−0.3	0.6	1.4	2.4	−0.25	−0.60
1985 b	−0.3	0.6	1.7	4.0	−0.31	−1.24
1985 c	−0.3	0.6	1.7	3.6	−0.31	−1.40
1985 d	−0.3	0.6	1.9	4.1	−0.34	−1.40

Sources for columns 1–4:

(1) Assumed.

(2) Persian Gulf/Western Europe retail; for 1980–85 assumed $18/$30.

(3) See table 18.1

(4) See table 18.2

General note. Price elasticity of non-OPEC supply assumed zero, as rough average of forward- and backward-bending supply functions. See section 4 below.

The Saudis *could* be the residual supplier or restrictor of last resort if they had to, but then they would have little interest in raising the price. Others get the benefit, they bear the cost.

An accommodation is necessary: the others must somehow restrain their output and let Saudi Arabia have a sufficient share of the market to let them benefit from a price increase. The Saudi maneuvre of December 1976 is one way of reaching the result. There have been several such incidents and there will be more, each unpredictable, raising the world price of oil again.

But any such market sharing is difficult to maintain, not only because of the lack of formal machinery (of which more below) but because of the pervasive uncertainty. Suppose that Saudi Arabia is content to be the residual supplier of say 8 million barrels daily, and that world consumption is lower than expected by two MBD, a fluctuation or error of only 3 percent. For Saudi Arabia, the loss is 25 percent. As a random fluctuation, it is bearable. As a permanent loss, it seems intolerably high—not to mention the start of a downward trend. Simple prudence forbids the Saudis to run such risks.

In summary, any model of the OPEC nations as *either* a cartel *or* a dominant-firm monopoly is much too simple. Both models have elements of the truth. Indeed, the knowledge that Saudi Arabia could if need be serve as restrictor of last resort is a strong backstop to the cartel. It strengthens the willingness of the other large producers to restrain output. If they have little fear of the cartel collapsing, they have no reason to invest heavily today to expand output to make the best of an uncontrolled lower price. But the caution advisable for the cartel as a whole is reinforced by the caution which uncertainty forces upon the dominant firm. Therefore, the chances are that there will always be much un-exerted price-raising power in the system.

This caution in raising prices is of course a new departure for Saudi Arabia. Throughout 1974, while repeatedly urging the virtues of lower prices, they were repeatedly the price leaders at the Persian Gulf, the Iranian 'hawks' being glad to follow.[24] Thus they increased their take from $7 per barrel at the beginning of the year[25] (the usual higher number is retroactive adjustment) to $10.12 by the end of the year. Beginning in 1975, they not only talked moderation but practiced it, and the reason is simple economic interest. They also have earned millions of golden opinions in the United States, no bad thing from their point of view, but quite unnecessary to explain their price behavior.

We may now consider whether the cartel is much affected by the optimal rate at which oil below ground should be traded for money above ground.

The writer would be wealthy if he had $1000 for every time he has been told that "oil in the ground appreciates faster than money above ground." This means that the real value of oil is growing faster than the relevant rate of discount. If that were really true, nobody should produce any oil. That would raise the price immediately to where the statement would cease to be true.

In fact, for any operator, the optimal rate of depletion of an oil reservoir depends on expected prices, costs, and discount rates. As was shown in Adelman (1972, pp. 50–52) and Adelman–Jacoby (1979), the average cost per barrel of developing a reservoir is approximated by $C = (I/Q)(a + r)$, where Q = initial peak capacity; I = investment (including present value of future operating outlays); a = the peak depletion rate = Q/R, where R = proved reserves; and r = the discount rate. A decision to accelerate or not accelerate output depends on marginal cost at the intensive margin, which is $MC = (I/Q)(a + r)^2/r$. Thus marginal cost rises approximately as the square of the peak production: reserve ratio. An additional barrel produced today sacrifices a lower-cost barrel tomorrow. Moreover, MC increases even faster where additional wells induce interference and lower output per well, i.e., where (I/Q) is no constant but an increasing function of Q/R. And too high a rate of output may actually lose part of the producible reserves.

Where marginal cost in a given reservoir is just equal to price, the development plan is optimal because the higher cost of faster depletion is just offset by the quicker receipt of revenues. Then one looks for underdeveloped reservoirs where incremental cost is still below price and there is room for expansion.

For a competitive firm, present and future prices and discount rates are external facts. In adapting to those facts, as they perceive them, oil and gas producers have complex asset management problems. They must from time to time decide whether, given costs at the margin, they are better off producing the incremental barrel now or later.

But a little reflection will show that at current or even much higher output rates *Saudi Arabia has no asset management problems*. If the Saudis took their 8.5 MBD "ceiling" seriously, their end-1976 proved reserves would last 35 years, proved-plus-probable reserves nearly 60 years. In addition, there are new deposits, already found, not reflected in reserves; not to mention deposits to be found.

Thus in Saudi Arabia a barrel not produced today does not lower costs, it is simply lost for decades. The present value of those far-off barrels is zero, even with inadequate allowances for risk: technological progress in production or consumption limiting the price increase; political–military action by neighbors or others; erosion of the cartel.[26]

A comparison of oil-in-ground versus money-in-bank (OGMB) is only valid at the margin and at the current margin oil in the ground is worthless to Saudi Arabia compared with money for investment, consumption, armaments, or influence (see appendix B). It would be a losing game to hold back production if the Saudi decision-makers could treat price as a datum outside their control. But the Saudis must and do limit production to maintain the price. For them, the OGMB comparison is superfluous. Its popularity shows how cost functions have been neglected in the literature. It also shows the power of repeated slogans which are plausible because they are not examined, and then seem clear because they are familiar.

At it was put by the Congressional Research Service (1977, p. 62): "Many observers feel the Saudis may agree ['to produce substantially more oil'] if the proper economic and political climate can be created." The Saudis will boost output to the extent that it will boost revenues. They have never done anything else, nor should they be expected to act irrationally.

4   Collusive Machinery, Backward Supply Curves, and Other Problems

The multi-national companies clear the market without anything resembling collusion. Each company sells what it can, and produces only what it can sell. Therefore, the amount offered is only equal to the amount demanded, and there is no pressure on prices. The margins allowed producing companies (15–25 cents) are too narrow to permit them any but trifling price reductions. Hence, no company can offer substantial discounts in order to get additional business. The cartel governments have only one simple implied agreement, that they will sell the great bulk of their output through the companies and not directly.

The great merit of this odd market sharing mechanism is that it avoids the divisive, and probably impossible, task of prorationing. But it works haphazardly, Companies have begun to look from country to country, in search of better deals. Mostly they feel free to shop only for small incremental quantities. Even so, some countries' output has been subject to strong fluctuations. Legend to the contrary notwithstanding, governments are insisting on output maintenance.

If the governments are to keep using the companies, they confront three inter-related problems: company margins; price differentials; and governments' market shares. The relative values of various crude oils keep changing incessantly because product markets and tanker rates change. Without a system of prompt corresponding adjustments in (a) crude oil price differentials there are strong fluctuations in (b) company margins, since (a) is large relative to (b). As companies move from one supplier government to another, there are unforeseen changes in governments' market shares. The OPEC countries have shown themselves very sensitive to crude price differentials which are a negligible percentage of the price of crude.

The 1977 flap over a "two-tier price system" was the latest but not the last squabble over differentials which influence market share. Saudi Arabia did a bold maneuvre in late 1976, in obtaining a price increase, first chiselling mildly from it to increase market share, then joining it, obtaining thus the best of both worlds and great political credit to boot. They will make similar moves in the future, perhaps not always as successfully.

The hope for a "right" price structure to end these disputes over market shares is illusory. The problem can only be solved ad hoc, temporarily. There is a constant tendency toward erosion of prices, which is best remedied by raising the price of crude oil, with everyone starting out at a new higher base line. Weakness in product prices and in open market crude oil prices may be a harbinger of a cartel price increase—the contrary of ordinary competitive conditions. At end-1976, crude was in great surplus, and the price was increased; again in mid-1977.

We stated earlier that a producing government's political objectives could always be subsumed in its economic objectives. But there are significant differences between governments and private firms as oil operators and as cartelists. No private firms could ever have dreamed of organizing so massive a transfer of wealth. We urged in another paper that in these circumstances the supply curves were often backward bending: the higher the price, the less the investment (Adelman 1976). The richer and more liquid are the producing governments, the less likely that one of them will be the reluctant price cutter who knows that secret rebates are dangerous, but must have additional revenues to pay his bills. Governments with large balances can avoid price shading. Contrariwise, the more precarious the finances of the producing governments, the greater the pressure to cut prices, and the danger to the cartel.

This backward bend is at least a partial explanation why, outside the United States, there has been no great surge in drilling since the price explosion, even a mild decline from mid-1976 to mid-1977.[27] The number of offshore drilling rigs, a good index of exploration, has doubled in five years, and the increase has levelled off;[28] a solid but not spectacular advance. Various countries offer examples.

In Venezuela, dwindling exploration in 1965−75 was due in large degree to company awareness of impending nationalization. But new-field exploratory wells (wildcats) drilled in Venezuela in 1973−75 were respectively ten, six and one.[29] In early 1977, not one new field wildcat was drilling.[30] The Orinoco heavy oil belt, with possibly a trillion barrels, remains a geological fact, not an economic asset, awaiting a research-development effort. The surge in revenues has dulled the public awareness of declining capacity. Those in charge know the situation and are trying to turn the ship around: 1978 exploratory expenditures are budgeted at 2.5 times 1976, and may in time increase by a factor of 5.[31]

In Indonesia, the inflow of funds was so great that caution was thrown to the winds and huge commitments made by a largely unsupervised oil company. This forced the government into unilateral contract revisions to obtain cash, which in turn nearly dried up exploration. Efforts are now being made to restore incentives, with perhaps some modest success. In Mexico the price explosion on the morrow of the great Reforma discoveries provided ammunition both for those who would expand output faster and for their opponents. The expansionist party is now on top. "Our task is to develop gas and oil for export as quickly as possible to generate foreign exchange," says Jorge Diaz Serrano, the head of Petroleos Mexicanos.[32] The policy may or may not persist.

The correlation between a producing country's deficit on current account, and its willingness to expand, may not be precise, but it is highly important.

5   Summary and Longer-term Views

One may doubt that any model can capture the subtleties of monopoly power exercised by a group like the OPEC nations. A determinate forecast of prices and production for a given year, or their path over time, with confidence limits, seems beyond our powers. One might suppose that estimates of a perfect monopoly price set the outer bounds, but as Eckbo (1976, pp. 106−110) has pointed out, the uncertainty about an imperfect monopoly inhibits investment, thus leading in time to lower production and a higher price.

However, the price should gravitate slowly *toward* the monopoly level, which is much higher than current. It will probably never get there. Turbulence will continue as the tension between Saudi Arabia and its partners needs to be resolved each time before the price can be raised. The huge trade deficits of the importing nations have strained the world monetary system, led to increasing protectionism and had some part in the recession of 1974–75, and the disappointing stagnation of 1976–77. If our analysis is sound, and the cartel has great unexerted price raising power, better business conditions and a strengthening of the world financial machinery will be a signal to raise prices again. Oil-producer imports will doubtless continue to grow, but so will the value of exports. Therefore, the oft-heard expectation that the oil-exporters' current surpluses will tend to zero by the early 1980s seems without foundation. If the exporters continue to act rationally, their program must be to raise prices and push the world monetary system toward the brink, but (we hope) not too close.

Past the mid-1980s, the picture will change, responding to forces some of which are not visible today.

Appendix A

(1)

$$P = P(Q) \qquad \text{[Demand function]}, \tag{1}$$

$$V = V(P) \qquad \text{[Tax rate]}, \tag{2}$$

$$TR = PQ(1 - V) \quad \text{[Total revenues neglecting costs]}, \tag{3}$$

$$d(TR)/dQ = PQ(-dV/dQ) + (1 - V)(P + Q(dP/dQ)). \tag{4}$$

Setting $d(TR)/dQ = 0$ to maximize TR,

$$PQ(-dV/dQ) + P + Q(dP/dQ) - VP - VQ(dP/dQ) = 0, \tag{5}$$

$$P(-Q[dV/dQ] + 1 - V) = -Q(dP/dQ) + VQ(dP/dQ)$$

$$= Q(dP/dQ)(V - 1), \tag{6}$$

$$P_{max} = Q(dP/dQ)\left[\frac{V - 1}{1 - V - Q(dV/dQ)}\right]. \tag{7}$$

The quantity in brackets must be evaluated, as follows:

$$\left[-1 - \frac{Q(dV/dQ)}{V - 1}\right]^{-1} = \left[-1 - \frac{Q(dV/dP)(dP/dQ)}{V - 1}\right]^{-1}. \tag{8}$$

(2)

If the tax rate $V = 0$, or if $V = $ a constant, then

$$dV/dQ = 0.$$

The quantity in brackets $= -1$, and

$P_{max} = -Q(dP/dQ) > 0,$

(since $dP/dQ < 0$, $P_{max} > 0$).

If V is a positive constant and $1 > V > 0$, then:

The quantity in brackets $= (V - 1)/(1 - V) = -1,$

and

$P_{max} = [-Q(dP/dQ)(V - 1)/(1 - V)] > 0,$

(since $V < 1$, $[(V - 1)/(1 - V)] < 0$], $P_{max} > 0$).

Thus Q_{max} is the same for $V = 0$, or for $V = $ a positive constant, since

$(d(PQ)/dQ) = P + Q(dP/dQ),$

and where the left-hand term is zero for a maximum,

$Q_{max} = -P(dQ/dP) > 0.$

(3)

If V is a positive function of P, and $1 > V > 0$, then the expression in brackets in Eq. (8) is negative because the absolute value of the fraction is non-zero, and it is being subtracted from -1.

Let $V_3 > V_2$, then the value of the right-hand fraction is greater. (At the limit $V \to 1$, the fraction $\to \infty$.) Then the value of the whole denominator is less, the value of the whole expression in brackets is greater, and $P_{max\,3} < P_{max\,2}$.

Appendix B: Present Value of Saudi Arabian Reserves

It is assumed that the price of oil is $13 in year 0 and increases, in real terms, by 10 percent per year for 10 years to its ultimate maximum of $34, where it stays indefinitely. Proved reserves in year 0 are assumed 150 billion barrels.

Ultimate reserves are assumed alternatively at 150 billion barrels (i.e., zero additions in known fields, no discoveries) and at 300 billion.

Discount rates are assumed alternatively at 5 and at 10 percent.

Production Plan I sets a ceiling of 8.5 million barrels daily (3.1 billion barrels per year) until reserves are 20 times production; thereafter production declines at 5 percent per year.

Table 18.3

| Ultimate proved reserves (billion barrels) | Present value ($ billions) | | | |
| | 5 percent discount | | 10 percent discount | |
	Plan I	Plan II	Plan I	Plan II
150	1306	1596	684	1109
300	1705	3292	803	1764

Production Plan II requires only that reserves must always be at least 20 times production. In the year 0, production is, therefore, 150 × 0.05 = 7.5 billion barrels, or 20 million barrels daily. If current proved reserves are also ultimate reserves, production declines indefinitely at 5 percent. If 150 billion barrels more can be added, it is assumed they are added at a rate just enough to permit the 20 MBD rate to the be maintained until the year 21 and after, when it declines at 5 percent per year.

With three alternative assumptions, there are eight possible outcomes, as follows: shown in table 18.3. In no case does the present value of Plan I come close to Plan II. The crucial assumption does not involve any of the three alternatives, but rather that there is an ultimate ceiling to price, assumed here to be 2.6 times the 1977 price.

Plan I looks even worse to the extent that the Plan I ceiling is held below 8.5 MBD, or the ultimate ceiling held below $34, which I consider improbably high

Notes

This paper is part of an ongoing research project at M.I.T., denoted NSF SIA 75–00739. It is an extensive revision of one given at the Workshop on Supply–Demand Analysis at Brookhaven National Laboratory on 1 June 1977. I am indebted to Paul L. Eckbo, James L. Paddock, James L. Smith, and especially to Leslie Cookenboo, Jr., and Martin B. Zimmerman; responsibility for any errors is my own.

1. I once gave great offense by pointing this out; subsequent events and evidence now in the public domain shows how much I understated the case. See "How OPEC came to power," *Forbes*, April 18, 1976. It is commonplace to say of the former State Department energy expert and 1973–75 Ambassador to Saudi Arabia that he acted like the Saudi Ambassador to the U.S.

2. "Huge OPEC oil price rise benefited U.S.," *Washington Post*, July 10, 1977, is an excellent paraphrase of the official view.

3. See the joint statement in *Keidanren Review* no. 43, February, 1977, by Federation of Economic Organizations, Japan Atomic Industrial Forum, and Committee

for Energy Policy Promotion: "However, in view of the actions of the oil producing countries in the Middle East, increasing imports of oil by the U.S.A., and other trends, it is all too uncertain whether Japan will be able to secure such a huge amount of petroleum."

4. See Michel Grenon (1973, passim), and Guy de Carmoy (1977, Introduction, pp. 37, 55, 80, 93, 117) who referred to West Germany's "strong" position and "progress toward energy independence."

5. For example, *Economist*, April 16, 1977; *New York Times*, September 9, 1977.

6. *New York Times*, May 27, 1972.

7. *Oil & Gas Journal*, May 15, 1972.

8. *Petroleum Economist*, November, 1973.

9. *New York Times*, March 17, 1977.

10. *Wall Street Journal*, October 21, 1977.

11. *Oil & Gas Journal*, January 10, 1977.

12. Quoted in *New Republic*, May 21, 1977. Some other aspects of the meeting are not accurately reported, to my recollection. See also *The Washington Post*, July 10, 1977.

13. *Petroleum Intelligence Weekly*, May 16, 1977.

14. There were at least four 1971–73 price changes, each one in violation of an agreement or assurance; and three violations of less formal assurances in 1974. There was also the promised auction in the late summer of 1974; and the October promise not to allow any output reduction; American officials complained that this broken promise "pulled the rug from under them." See *Oil & Gas Journal*, March 17, 1975.

15. *Middle East Economic Survey*, September 7, 1973.

16. *Economist*, August 27, 1977, p. 88.

17. By "real price" we mean the product price versus (a) all other prices, not the product price versus (b) the total retail price index. The difference between (a) and (b) is small but not negligible. In terms of (b), the increase was about two-thirds.

18. *Oil & Gas Journal*, May 2, 1977; May 16, 1977, Newsletter p. 4.

19. *Petroleum Economist*, February, 1977.

20. *Petroleum Economist*, January, 1978.

21. Wood Mackenzie & Co., February 11, 1977.

22. *Petroleum Economist*, May, 1977; *Oil & Gas Journal*, June 6, 1977.

23. BP, LNG—*The Next Ten Years*, 1976. According to a study by the Institute of Gas Technology, LNG supplied in 1976 was 1.8 BCFD. New plants "committed," "probable," and "possible" by 1980 would account for 3.6, 4.4, and 16.0 BCFD,

respectively. If one assigns a probability of 0.75 to the "probable" and 0.25 to the "possible," increased trade by 1980 would amount to 10.9 BCFD, or 1.8 MBDOE. *Oil & Gas Journal,* June 20, 1977 (Shaheen and Vora 1977).

24. *Petroleum Intelligence Weekly,* March 11, June 17, November 25, 1974.

25. *Petroleum Intelligence Weekly,* December 31, 1973.

26. Mancke (1977, pp. 167–168) argues that too high a short-run price would bring in new competing sources of energy, hence lower the price in the long run. On this reasoning, it pays crude-rich Saudi Arabia to be a price moderate. The Mancke thesis, in terms of our argument, is that the higher the current price, the greater the risk of lower future prices. Future revenues should then be discounted heavily relative to current ones.

27. *Oil & Gas Journal,* August 22, 1977.

28. *Oil & Gas Journal,* September 12, 1977.

29. Ministry of Mines and Hydrocarbons, *Petroleo y Otros Datos Estadisticos,* respective years.

30. Id., *Monthly Bulletin,* April, 1977.

31. *Oil & Gas Journal,* September 12, 1977.

32. *Petroleum Intelligence Weekly,* June 6, 1977.

References

Adelman, M. A., 1972, The world petroleum market (Johns Hopkins University Press, Baltimore, MD).

Adelman, M. A., 1976, The world oil cartel: Scarcity, economics and politics, Quarterly Review of Economics and Business 6, no. 2, 7–18.

Adelman. M. A. and Henry D. Jacoby, 1979, Alternative methods of supply forecasting, Advances in the economics of energy and resources, vol. 2, JAI Press.

Carmoy, Guy de, 1977, Energy for Europe (American Enterprise Institute, Washington, DC).

Congressional Reference Service, 1977, Toward project interdependence, 95th Cong., 1st Sess., Committee on Energy and Natural Resources, Publication 95-31 (U.S. Government Printing Office, Washington, DC).

Culbertson, W. L., 1977, NGL faces uncertain future, in: Petroleum 2000, Oil & Gas Journal, Aug.

Eckbo, Paul L., 1976, The future of world oil (Ballinger, Cambridge, MA).

Grenon, Michel, 1973, Ce monde affamé d'énergie (Laffont, Paris).

Houthakker, H. S., 1976, The price of oil (American Enterprise Institute, Washington, DC).

Mancke, Richard B., 1977, Recent world pricing: The Saudi enigma, Energy Policy 5, June, 167–168.

Shaheen, E. I. and M. K. Vora, 1977, Worldwide LNG survey cites existing, planned projects, Oil & Gas Journal, June 20.

WAES, 1977, Workshop on alternative energy strategies, Energy: Global prospects 1985–2000 (McGraw-Hill, New York).

19   The Clumsy Cartel

The recent price explosions in the world oil market result from the tardy recognition of the post-1973 consumption slowdown. Such odd results could not happen in a competitive market, but they are not at all strange in the world of the cartel. An analogy may help explain. A diver in the sea cannot go lower than the sea floor, nor higher than the water's surface. He is nearly weightless, and can float at any depth between these extremes, but the slightest impact or effort sends him up or down. Similarly, in any market, the price cannot drop below incremental cost, since such a drop would choke off supply, nor can it rise above the level that would maximize profit to a monopoly, since the monopoly would gain by putting the price back down. But in a once-competitive market, where the price has been rising toward some unknown monopoly optimum, the price can hold steady or can move drastically up or down in response to very slight impulses. In this range the price may shown no response, or even a perverse response, to changes in demand. Since 1973, price response has been perverse. This was clearly the case in 1974, as the world headed into recession. It is so again in 1979.

During 1973–1978, real incomes in the non-Communist industrialized countries rose 13 percent, but oil use nevertheless was flat at approximately 50 million barrels daily (MBD). Exports actually fell, by about 7 percent, among the nations of the Organization of Petroleum Exporting Countries (OPEC). These nations have, with some strain, carried a large actual excess capacity, and a huge potential excess; Saudi Arabia operates only 15 of its 37 known fields.

Despite the declining demand for its oil, OPEC has raised the price toward the cartel profit-maximizing level. The best approximation to a

---

Reprinted from *The Energy Journal* 1 (no. 1, 1980): 43–53.

world price is the producing government's "take" on Saudi Arabian Light. From $7 a barrel on December 31, 1973, it went to nearly $11 by end-1974, and will have gone to $18 by July 1, 1979. Of course, in real terms, the increase is much less. Nor has it come smoothly. Initially, inflation plus the unforeseen dollar devaluation put the real price down, to a degree that the producers did not intend. This is now being made up.

It was possible for some time to view the stagnation of demand as a temporary phenomenon. As recently as two years ago, the consensus view—taking as the prime example the report by the Central Intelligence Agency (CIA)—was that non-Communist consumption in 1985 would be over 70 MBD and demand on OPEC would be 49 MBD. These are now seen as massive overestimates. The Saudi Arab cutback in expansion plans is a direct result. But the cartel has grown more clumsy these last few years. Formerly, it set the price and left allocation of output to the oil companies. The companies obtained from various countries a mix of crude liftings that matched expected sales of products. Surpluses and deficits were small and soon corrected. Today the main producing countries have begun to set production levels themselves. But levels established by their prior decisions cannot, except by chance, equal consumer demand even in total, still less by types and locations. Discrepancies are large, and take longer to reduce; they trigger speculation, which exaggerates the resulting price movements.

Late last year, the cartel was ponderously working out a higher price level, when the Iranian revolution presented it with both an opportunity and a problem. In nine months, they have still not been able to accomplish a stable higher price level, or a supply-demand balance. Whatever happens, in later years there will be more disturbances, local shortages (and surpluses), speculative runups, political and monetary fallout. That is normal in the new international economic order prevailing in oil since 1970, and expecially since 1973. Those who think it can be cured by consuming less, or producing more elsewhere, have not bothered to look at the market.

Let us look first at oil consumption prospects. The growth in world income will not again approach the 5 percent per year of pre-1973, chiefly because most of the catching up with the United States has been done, in Europe and elsewhere in the developed world. There are other nonrecurring factors, such as slower population growth and labor force transfer out of rural underemployment into productive work. Hence if all went smoothly, we should expect a convergence toward the U.S. long-run rate of increase of around 3 percent. But things will not go smoothly. The disruption of the world monetary-financial system and the instability of currencies were at least aggravated by the enormous OPEC surpluses.

These dwindled in 1975–1978, but big surpluses are coming back with the price increases. Consuming countries may overreact with deflation of income to offset balance-of-payments problems. This is all the more likely because they are plagued with inflation, and the choice has been to cool down the economy and risk a recession to restrain prices. Hence the Organization for Economic Cooperation and Development (OECD), looking at the 3.5 percent gross national product (GNP) increase for the year 1978, expects a decline in the growth rate through 1979.

Had there been no energy price increases, energy use would track income faithfully. Some work done at the M.I.T. World Oil Project suggests that price elasticities are quite high in the very long run but that the adjustment process is very slow. And this theory seems to be confirmed by the fact that energy use, per unit of income, has slowly but persistently decreased.[1]

Among the seven largest OECD members, the median decline has been a bit over 1.5 percent per year. I think energy use would continue declining slowly for years, even with no further increases in price, as the stock of energy-using equipment was gradually replaced. But with fresh crude oil price increases, there are new waves of response. Furthermore, consumer-country governments will discourage consumption, mostly for balance-of-payments reasons, through taxes or automobile performance requirements. In effect, we levy a heavy tax on driving, which consumers accept because it doesn't *look* like a tax. The incidence and results of all these restrictions are quite unpredictable, I think, but not their direction.

All in all, if incomes grow by about 3 percent per year, energy use will probably grow by less than 2 percent. If we are going into a recession, the next five years may be as the last five.

The oil share of energy will probably not decrease much in the next decade. The future of nuclear power is clouded. Coal will displace some oil and gas even more, but only to a limited extent.

II

Worldwide, supply elasticity does not greatly differ from zero. In some countries, higher prices do elicit greater supply: an orthodox foward-sloping supply curve. In other countries, the richer they get, the easier it becomes for them to be good cartelists and restrain output. The more they change, the less they produce: a backward-bending curve. In still other countries, both forward- and backward-bending curves are at work.

First, let us look at the small but rational part of world supply: Communist net exports. They grew from 1 to 1.5 MBD and will probably be higher by the mid-1980s, as the Chinese industry keeps growing and the Soviet Union scrambles to produce or conserve oil to export in exchange for scarce foreign resources. Comparative advantage will matter more than "need." Soviet gas growth will at least offset any oil decrease. But in the world picture, Communist exports will remain very small.

In the non-OPEC non-Communist world, the big new factor is Mexico. The recoverable contents of known fields are enormous and the constraint is how fast they can be developed. By 1985, Mexico probably *could* produce 4.5 MBD and half as much gas equivalent. I do not know what the Mexicans will do. Four years ago their goal was self-sufficiency. Two years ago it was full speed ahead. The current president leaves office in 1982 and cannot bind his successor. If the government of Mexico has enough confidence in its ability to cope with large revenue flows, production will go higher. Comparisons with Iran are not appropriate, because Mexican oil and gas revenues are so much smaller a part of the national product.

The U.S. government has prevented natural gas sales from Mexico to the United States and avowedly fears that too-rapid growth of Mexican imports would "disrupt our carefully nurtured relationships with the Middle East" (*New York Times*, November 30, 1978). These relationships are carefully left unexplained.

Elsewhere, I can discern no big surprises, pleasant or unpleasant. Worldwide, the soaring price has not brought about any surge in drilling. Since contracts were used for bonfires in 1973, risk in many countries is great. If an oil operator loses money, the loss is his; if he makes a good discovery, a dissatisfied landlord rewrites the deal. World Bank financing of oil and gas development in less developed countries (LDCs) may be quite a help to some poor nations. One hopes so. But such financing can be no more than a help; it cannot by itself assure that development will be successful.

In the United States, high prices mean windfall profits. Half the profits would normally go to the government as income tax. But the American public and government prefer to give up their half only if they can deprive the detested oilman of his half. Other nations have their own versions of this rule. Thus the higher price has a political effect which depresses oil exploration and development.

In all countries, oil is thought to have an intrinsic value. The higher the price, the more firmly people are convinced that its real value is even higher than the price. It logically follows that the seller is always conferring a benefit on the buyer. Why do the undeserving foreigner a favor? So the

United States thinks Alaskan oil is too good for the Americans; many in Britain think it too good for the continentals, and so on. The net result: high prices discourage some oil development in the United States, Canada, and elsewhere, again yielding the backward-bending curve. These are price-taker nations, and their actions are an important help to the OPEC nations.

III

We turn now to the OPEC nations, joined in loose but effective federation. I hear there is no cartel because supply and demand, "market forces," explain the current price increase. How true: "As agreed at the last OPEC meeting in Geneva, they have trimmed supply in line with the partial restoration of Iranian production. The object of the cutbacks is to keep the market tight and let the pricing initiative remain with OPEC members" (*Oil & Gas Journal*, May 21, 1979). That sounds like a potent market force. But hear someone in high office at the Department of Energy (DOE): "The planet Earth is producing less oil than the people on it want." Thus, the scarcity is due to nature, which is to say the market is competitive. You can believe that if you like. Sometimes the point is made more explicitly: the OPEC nations are really not accomplishing anything. They "administer" the price, and in a tight market an "administered price" rises more slowly.

I complained many years ago that "administered prices" was a catchy phrase signifying nothing. But the devil sees deeper. As Mephistopheles advised the hopeful student, you most need a *word* when you have no *idea*. The cartel's price administration allegedly slows an upward price movement "when the market is tight." But who is making the market tight?

There is also a revival of the concept that oil in the ground is worth more than money in the bank (OGMB). In Saudi Arabia today, the production ceiling of 8.5 MBD means that a barrel not lifted today is postponed for 50 to 100 years. During the middle 1960s, the last period of price stability, a riskless interest rate was about 3 percent. At the same time, in some of my own work, I observed a necessary return on oil development in the United States, with no political risk, of about 9 percent. In the Middle East and elsewhere, it was 20 percent on private oil development. On Saudi Arabian development, considering the technological, economic, political, and military risks that confront the Saud family (as they did the Pahlavi family), a 10-percent interest rate seems conservative. At that rate, a barrel of oil fetching $12.50 in 1978 would need to fetch $1350 in 50 years to be worth holding in the ground for that length of time. OGMB places no constraint on any independent action. Saudi Arabia must restrain output to maintain the price.

Also, the heads of state have been fuming over the high spot prices which allegedly give unrealistic ideas to the producing nations—the very ones who made the market tight and forced spot prices skyward. This preoccupation with trivia speaks for itself.

Anyway, there is an orthodox view which underlies policy of this and all other consuming countries. The OPEC nations supposedly are willing to produce a certain maximum amount of oil. We are given to believe that if we, the consumers, stay inside that limit, we may expect happiness, "enough oil for our needs," stable or maybe even declining real prices. If we cannot restrain ourselves: disaster. At best, prices will skyrocket. Worse, there could be a dangerous struggle for scarce resources, as nation elbows nation for the dwindling supply. Now, if oil is allocated by price, however "unfairly," there is no energy gap, no struggle, no problem of "access." But for reasons never revealed, the price is *not* expected to allocate oil supplies, even though all logic and experience tell us that it has, and does, and will. Europeans and Japanese are frightened and envious of supposed U.S. "access' and our "special relationships" with producing nations. One would suppose that the experience of the 1973–1974 so-called embargo would have taught people a lesson, when we were the special enemy and yet did better than Britain and France, the special friends, though not as well as "odiously neutral" Japan.

Anyway, the idea that there is some fixed limit of output to which consumers must adapt turns reality on its head. The cartel core nations do not control the net demand upon them. They control supply, and they react to changes in demand by changing production. But the adaptation is not automatic or smooth, and recently the mechanism has been wound too tight for anybody's good, as cartel nations have cut production *too much*— after which they claim the market is pushing up the prices. There are two reasons: the diminishing role of the multinational oil companies, and the unexpected shocks to supply.

IV

Previously the cartel could avoid most of the hard decisions on output— on total, type, and location—by leaving them to the oil companies. But as indicated at the start, the oil companies are ceasing to function as buffers between producer and consumer; they are gradually becoming buyers for their own refining operations. The producing countries are becoming sellers, with the usual problems. For years they have in vain lavished money and computer time and struggled over price differentials which are a very small, almost negligible, fraction of the price. Trouble is, even a small difference in net value of one crude relative to another will tempt buyers to the better offer, and deprive other countries of sales. With supply and demand continuously changing, buyers constantly have an incentive to change suppliers. The amounts involved are typically small, but sellers are alarmed by the prospect of price erosion starting at the fringes. This is normal cartel behavior.

Nigeria, early in 1977, thought it had a deal with Libya and Algeria to hold the line on the quality and location premiums for their light low-sulfur crudes. By mid-1978, the Nigerians had learned—the hard way—that ancient formula of cartel behavior: when you have a friend, tried and true, do him quick before he does you. Nigeria lost nearly a third of its revenues, and was forced to borrow heavily.

The allocation problem was then raised by the loss of production from Iran, briefly 10 percent of world supply, but mostly 3 to 4 percent. Most industries work with more than that much slack. The airlines have had five times as big a problem with the loss of the DC-10, and have handled it without fuss. The loss of oil could quite easily have been made up by expansion in other countries. But Abu Dhabi and Kuwait told us in November there would be no output expansion—we should go use up our stockpiles. (Others have said the same—here is a sensitive point.) Saudi Arabia increased, though not as much as it could. The price was raised in December. But then history began to repeat itself.

In 1974, after the 1973 price hike, the Saudis led the price increases through the pretext of "participation." Again in 1979, after the 1978 price hike, they led the price increases through the pretext of borrowing fourth-quarter output. But they wanted more. Therefore, late in January, with Iran down, Saudi Arabia cut output from 10.5 to 8 MBD overnight, touching off an immediate explosion in spot prices, and soon in contract prices. In February, Saudi Arab output was partly restored, to 9.5 MBD, and in March it was back down to 8.5 MBD. At the end of March came the wrangle in Geneva over who should move over how much. While we shiver over wells drying up, these people repress the surplus.

In mid-April, Iran's output was up to an unexpectedly high 4.7 MBD, prompting Saudi Arabia to promulgate a ceiling of 8.5 MBD for the second quarter. But then Iran apparently receded to about 4 MBD. So spot prices again jumped in early May. By end-June, they had stabilized at record high levels. At the OPEC meeting, Saudi Arabia announced a marker crude price of $18, up 42 percent in six months. Two weeks later, they agreed to allow another 1 MBD indicating that they were content with $18 per barrel—for the time being.

Nobody can tell what to expect in Iran. With 7 MBD of capacity, Iran had been a good enough cartel partner to hold output to 5.5 MBD or even less. We are now told they will produce only 3.5 MBD. I expect that a government with effective control of southern Iran would aim at higher production. Oil revenues have been nearly half of the gross domestic product. The country badly needs imported food, raw materials, industrial goods, and parts, Dangerous urban unemployment is widespread. There are many claimants for assistance and subsistence. Hence the target will, I think, go well above 3.5 MBD. But the expulsion of skilled foreign personnel means that Iran cannot go back to its old production levels.

Hence our best single-valued estimate might be for only 3.5 MBD, in some such fashion as:

(1) Output (MBD)	(2) Probability	(3) (1) × (2)
0	.20	0.0
3.5	.33	1.2
5.0	.47	2.3
—	1.00	3.5

Thus Iranian output will probably be down, perhaps by 1 to 2 MBD, as compared with early 1978. But this drop is partly balanced by developments in neighboring Iraq. Capacity there is now perceived as 4 MBD, 1 MBD higher than a year ago. It is not all deliverable capacity, but soon will be. On balance the long-run impact of the Iranian revolution will be favorable to the cartel, but hardly enough to represent a crucial factor.

We must put aside the ceilings and projections so popular here in Washington, which forecast OPEC capacity and output as if it were an independent variable. *The OPEC nations will install such capacity, and operate such fractions of it, as suits their interests.* With more or less demanded, they will produce more or less, at their price. They can't predict it any better than we.

The economic motive for Saudi output restriction reinforces the political one: the greater their revenues and wealth, the stronger their political clout. Hear the U.S. Embassy in Jiddah: If we would accede to Saudi Arab wishes, "they would give us all the oil we need and at good prices" (*Business Week*, April 9, 1979). Possibly they would—for as long as six months. The Saudis have repeatedly broken agreements—not because they are bad people, but because you cannot compel a sovereign monopolist to keep his word. But the Saudis know the Americans are amenable to this kind of pressure, and will therefore keep pressing.

V

The basic problem is simple; and simple problems are the hardest to solve. The Saudis, their neighbors, and others, are fine-tuning a cartel with coarse instruments. Current consumption is poorly measured by available statistics. Even the production numbers are getting unreliable. Supply has to be kept tight despite panic, hoarding, and spot price gyrations, because the controllers are afraid of losing control. They can handle the large excess *capacity*. They want to avoid the much smaller but more dangerous surplus of actual *supply*, perhaps 2 MBD a year ago, which keeps prices under pressure. That is why we must expect a continuing bumpy ride in the years ahead. When prices are raised, the OPEC nations are willing to make room for Saudi production. As their expenditures approach income and they run toward or into deficit, they become unwilling to do so, and threaten to shove the whole burden onto the Saudis, who resolve the contradiction by raising the price again, to the benefit of themselves and others. Unexpected events like the Iranian revolution are opportunities to be seized, despite these dangers.

In the short run, the cartel is restrained by a desire not to damage world monetary and trading relations. If the price goes to $18, for example, the surplus on current account will be running by late 1979 at $60 billion annually.[2] Nominally that is nearly equal to 1974, a year of recession, but in real terms it is about a third less.

So long as the price remains below the long-run monopoly optimum, this process will go on, with each new incident unpredictable. The richer the producing nations, the more easily they can reduce output, and the less will be their incentive to expand it. So the situation will get better for them, and worse for us.

Where the long-run optimum monopoly price lies I do not know. If the cartel should ever be perceived as anywhere near it, there would be real danger to them. Without much more room to raise prices to consumers, an ad valorem tariff on oil would become a deduction from the cartel's revenues. The petrodollar flow could, at the limit, be wholly diverted to consumer-country governments.[3] But even a small probability makes the crystal ball cloudy for the late 1980s.

Notes

1. I refer to the average energy-income relation, not the "incremental energy-income coefficient," a confused, unhelpful notion. See my "Energy-Income Coefficients, Their Use and Abuse", Working Paper Number MIT-EL 79-024 WP, May 1979.

2. Adapted from Rimmer de Vries, "Implications of the New Oil Situation," *World Financial Markets* (Morgan Guaranty Trust Company), May 1979, table 4, assuming 27 MBD exports.

3. For a formal proof, see "Constraints on the World Monopoly Price," *Resources & Energy* 1 (1979), 5–7, 17–18.

References

Adelman, M. A. "Constraints on the World Monopoly Price." *Resources and Energy* 1 (1979), 5–7, 17–18.

———. "Energy-Income Coefficients: Their Use and Abuse." Working Paper MIT-EL 79-024 WP, May 1979.

de Vries, Rimmer. "Implications of the New Oil Situation." *World Financial Markets*, May 1979.

20   OPEC as a Cartel

I Introduction

The organization OPEC is no more than a convenient forum for the con-
stituent nations. They have formed a loosely cooperating oligopoly—or
cartel, if you prefer two syllables to twelve. But no two cartels are the
same. They are all historical individuals, who change over time, and the
OPEC cartel has changed greatly.

I wrote in 1973, before the embargo:[1]

The monopoly ceiling is set by the competition of more expensive sources of
crude oil, or by consumers' reducing their expenditures on oil products. This
ceiling is very far above even the current price, and hence we must expect the
cartel to keep raising the price throughout the 1970's. But for the longer run, the
crystal ball becomes clouded, because there are factors working both to strengthen
and to weaken the cartel. The net effect is a residual, which is basically unstable.
Small changes can produce large effects. But at least we can try to set out what
forces are worth watching carefully.

The 1970s are past. The ceiling on energy prices, we can now see, is set
by opportunities to invest in greater thermal efficiency more than by new
sources of crude oil. The question is whether the cartel is approaching the
ceiling, whether they can keep raising the price. I will try to set out how
the cartel arrived at its present position, as a place from which we can
attempt to look into the future.

I cannot claim (as many do) to know what motivates the OPEC members, but we can recognize what is to their economic advantage. The reader
must judge for himself whether noneconomic motives are superfluous in
explaining their actions.

Portions of this paper previously appeared in *OPEC Behavior & World Oil Prices*. Griffin and
Teece, eds. (London: Allen & Unwin, 1982), 37−57; and *Annual Review of Energy* 15 (1982):
20−21.

II   A Review of Alternative Theories of OPEC Behavior: OPEC as a Wealth-Maximizing Group

Management, in conventional economics, tries to maximize the present value of an enterprise. Present value consists of all estimated future revenues and costs, discounted down to the present. Estimating and discounting are two kinds of forecasting procedures, which the human race carries out imperfectly. Inside any given firm, even under pure competition, there will be different visions of what is possible or inevitable. One man's prudence is another man's folly.

Uncertainties and clashes of opinion within the individual firm are magnified in a collusive group. Not only are there more possible viewpoints, but also real clashes of interest. Firms have different costs; hence the best price for one is not necessarily the best for another. In mineral production, this is particularly noticeable, because differences in reserve positions represent differences in cost.

So operating a cartel is often a complicated business of reconciling various objectives, patching up compromises, following rules of thumb, and revising bargains once made. Some years ago,[2] I suggested that the best approximation to a model of the OPEC cartel was somewhere between two polar cases. One case was the residual-firm monopolist, or the large seller who lets everybody else maximize profits individually, choosing their own production levels. The large seller then makes up the difference, varying his production to control the price. This is what Texas and Louisiana state prorationing systems did in the United States during 1935–70. The larger the market share of the residual seller, the easier for him to carry the load. At the other extreme, one could think of all the nations getting together to agree to some kind of price and output combination which suited nobody perfectly, but was accepted as the best compromise.

The two models are the horns of the sellers' dilemma. The residual-firm monopoly is easy to operate. One firm tailors its output to set the price, which the rest take as given. But the price, and the aggregate profit to the group, is less than what could be achieved by all sellers cooperating.

The firms or sellers may wobble from one model to the other in trying to escape as many of the rigors of competition as possible. The number of expedients is almost infinite. It is dismaying and amusing to see people brandish a particular cartel model, and proclaim that because this particular model does not describe reality, there is no cartel, and everything is done by the individual actions of the sellers. Of course each seller acts individually in his own individual interest. But his own individual interest is served by as close an approximation to a monopoly as he and his fellow members can manage.

Low Discount Theories

One version of the noncollusive thesis of the OPEC nations can be stated succinctly. The producing governments have much lower discount rates than oil companies, particularly oil companies that knew in the 1960s that in the Middle East and elsewhere there was always a good chance of expropriation. The lower the operator's discount rate, the lower his preferred production rate, since he will be willing to leave oil in the ground longer. Hence, when governments gained control of their own resources in the 1970s, they produced less, raising the price.

We first test this against the historical record. During the 1950s and 1960s, governments grew even more powerful relative to the companies. This can be measured very nicely by the proportion of profits which they took in taxes, which went from 50 percent in 1950 to over 80 percent in 1970. Hence, over this period there should have been a gradual tightening up of production and and increase in prices. In fact, real oil prices fell.

Let us try another test. In 1950–70, there was constant disagreement over production levels. *Countries always wanted more production than companies.* The quarrel was annually publicized in Iran, but the whole period was summed up very well by Mr. Howard Page of Exxon.[3]

The Iranian government was, as every other government, always trying to get more than their agreement called for. If I were in their position, I would do the same, but you have to realize this is like a balloon, push it in one place, it comes out in another. So if we acceded to all these demands we would get it in the neck.

The companies knew what the market would take, and knew they could not produce and sell more without driving prices sharply down. They might "get it in the neck" too, by refusing demands. Iraq was a leader; for example, in June 1972 it kicked out the Iraq Petroleum Company for not producing at high enough rates. Since then, Iraq has increased capacity, from 1.7 MMB/D to about 4 MMB/D.

During 1970–71, the control swung completely to the side of the producing countries. So here at last one might have seen a growing scarcity in the market and rising prices. In fact, prices rose in 1971–73 only by the amount of higher taxes collusively fixed, and there was a growing surplus. When the Arab countries cut production during the so-called embargo of 1973–74, this was a deliberate collusive act, not the gradual every-country-for-itself tightening of production schedules implicit in the low discount theories.

Thus the noncollusive theory of lower discount rates is in conflict with the historical record through 1973–74. We will see later that it does not perform any better for more recent years. But it is time now to ask whether the major assumption is justified: that lower discount rates will bring about lower production levels.[4] Let me ask a simple question: why does not every owner of a mineral reserve deplete it all in the first year? The reason is obviously that if he pushes the rate of depletion too high, he will be confronted by swiftly rising marginal costs, to the point where faster depletion will lose money. Therefore, every mineral operator from the beginning of time has been forced to solve this problem of the optimum depletion rate by trading off the higher present value of faster depletion against the higher cost. If the depletion rate is below optimal, the incremental money in the bank from additional output is worth more than the incremental mineral in the ground. At rates above optimal, the additional money in the bank is worth less than the additional mineral in the ground, and output should be cut back.

Yet public opinion and policy has been ruled by an empty dogma that "oil in the ground is worth more than money in the bank." Such an un-qualified statement does not even rise to the dignity of error. It is gibberish.

Suppose now that oil depletion in some lease is optimal. Under competition, the operator cannot affect prices and costs, he takes them as given. He may expect increased prices or anything else,[5] but he has made what he thinks is the best possible adjustment to them. Now introduce one change—a lowering of the discount rate. On the one hand, it encourages a lower rate of production because the present value of a barrel left in the ground is now higher. On the other hand, it raises the present value of the cash flow of any project. The operator must revise his previous tradeoff. But there is absolutely no reason to suppose that the new optimal depletion rate must go up *or* down. Thus, depending on the magnitude of the discount rate, a lower discount rate can bring about higher production, and over other ranges a lower discount rate results in lower production.

In figure 20.1 the horizontal axis represents the depletion rate, while the vertical axis represents the investment and the present value of gross revenues. Both are given as a percentage of the maximum value, that is, proved reserves times price (net of operating costs). The assumed cost function has a fixed component: the operator must pay 5 percent of the maximum value of the deposit (price × reserves) just to get started. The other restriction is that if he were to deplete the deposit at a rate of 50

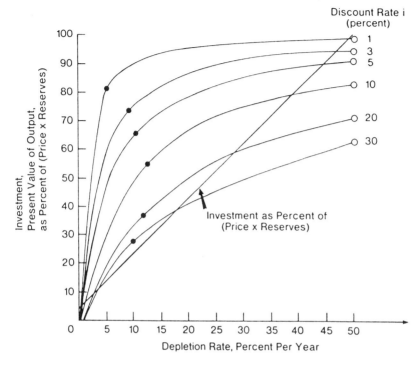

Figure 20.1
Relation of discount rate, investment, and optimal depletion. Solid circles: optimal for given discount rate.

percent per year, he would need to invest that same ultimate value.[6] So the limits of the possible outcome lie between zero and 50 percent annual depletion. The tradeoff between getting more present value by accelerating output, and paying more for that present value, can be "eyeballed" by recalling that for maximum present value the slope of the investment line must equal the slope of the present value curve. At a 1 percent discount rate, the optimum depletion rate is slightly over 6 percent per year. As one gets into the world of commercial reality, discounting at 5 percent, the optimal depletion goes to 12.4 percent. It varies little thereafter, but drops slightly on reaching 20 percent discount. And above 31 percent discount, there is a shutdown.

The discount rate applicable to any expected return from an investment depends on the risk, which is an objective fact. It has nothing to do with any individual's subjective time preference or risk preference. An individual will prefer one risk-return package to another, but this has nothing to do with the risk, the return, or the market value of the package. An individual who prizes safety of capital before all else buys short-term Treasury Bills. In theory and practice they track the inflation rate to yield approximately a zero real return. A more venturesome person will choose a diversified portfolio of seasoned common stocks and accept the risk in order to realize a real return, a little over 6 percent.[7] An oil property, large or small, is undiversified and (except under circumstances too special to detain us) inherently more risky than the common-stock portfolio. Hence our remark that discount rates below the neighborhood of 6 percent, real, are not relevant.

Although our example shows depletion rates rising with discount rates, it is only a special case, the result of our assumptions about the relation of prices to costs. In general, a changed discount rate can work either way. *But as risk becomes greater, and pushes up the discount rate sharply, depletion rates must fall, even to zero,* because fresh investment ceases. If that is happening in many places, then of course prices will rise.

But we need to consider risk, over and above normal commercial risk, to allow for the probability of an irreversible expropriation. A little algebra (see appendix A) will show that the risky rate is somewhat greater than the sum of the normal commercial rate plus that probability. In 1970, when I wrote my book on world oil, I used a 20 percent after-tax rate, which company personnel told me they were using. (A few years later they were using 40 percent in some places.) If a "normal" commercial discount rate was 9 percent, this was an implicit prediction of a 50–50 chance of expropriation in 7.2 years. But perhaps 9 percent was too high because of the absence of geological risk in many countries. Accordingly, if a normal commercial rate was 6 percent, then in the middle and late 1960s the time to a 50–50 chance of expropriation was about 5.4 years. With hindsight, one concludes neither estimate can be called unreasonable.

Again our best example is in Iraq. Because of unfriendly relations between company and government, and the 1962 expropriation of the whole concession outside the fields actually being operated, Iraq had in effect told the companies that they must reckon with a very high rate of discount. Accordingly, they invested very little in that country, and capacity stagnated. This led, in turn, to expropriation, as already noted.

What would be a reasonable discount rate for a government, above the normal commercial rate in oil? The owners of the oil, whether a party, a junta, a family, a dynasty, etc., must know that they can be overthrown at any time by violence, their usual form of political argument. Suppose you think that your family or party has, say, three chances in four of still being in power in 1991. Then the chance of being overthrown during this year are just under 3 percent, and if 6 percent is a commercial rate, your discount rate should be 9.1 percent. Of course, reasonable persons will disagree on chances of survival, just as they do in private business. But the notion that Third World governments discount oil revenues at abnormally *low* discount rates is in conflict with the facts.[8]

The distinction between the *fact* of risk and the varying *attitudes* to it helps us dispose of another legend: that the Saudis or Kuwaitis or others are naturally reluctant to trade their solid black gold for "depreciating paper," or depreciating dollars. First, as to denominating the price in dollars, this is a nonissue. They can be paid in any currency they choose, or if paid in dollars it takes a computer a fraction of one microsecond to convert into any other currency.

Saudi Arabia has apparently emphasized security, and bought low-risk low-yield assets. Kuwait has bought real estate and equities. Both of them, and other OPEC nations, have also invested heavily in real assets at home, many ultra-risky. But their preferences are not relevant to the risk and return on any given asset, only on their choice among assets.

With this in mind, we can trade off current against future receipts from oil reserves. Let us suppose that higher prices are expected. (In truth, those higher prices are not determined independently; they are the result of monopoly restriction. But we can overlook that.) The supposed Saudi Arab target is 8.5 MMB/D, and proved-plus-probable reserves total 175 billion barrels. The country is hardly explored, and an allowance of another 75 billion barrels is highly conservative. Hence a production rate of 8.5 MMB/D means that a barrel not now produced would not be produced for eighty years. This is much too simple a calculation, of course, but the errors work on both sides, and can be disregarded.

A discount rate around 9 percent is conservative for the Saud family is no more immortal than the Pahlavi family. If one discounts at a rate of half of that, which is so "conservative" as to be reckless, then a dollar to be received in eighty years is worth only 3¢ today. I do not know the price eighty years from now, but will take the highest prediction I have heard, which is $90; that would give us a present value of $2.70.

III OPEC Pricing: Economic versus Political Factors

In one respect, a group of governments should conform more closely to a cartel model than a group of private companies. A group of price-fixing companies may be restrained not only by anti-trust laws but by the disapproval of their fellow citizens, and the power of a government to make life unpleasant for them. But nobody dares oppose a sovereign state, and the OPEC nations have become accustomed to the anxiously deferential tone of all the consuming countries. Hence they fit the model well.

But companies exist only to make money; governments do not, but then neither do private owners. Governments and stockholders want money for many purposes, some of which they do not know themselves. But the more money they have the better, whatever they want to buy, whether it be investment, consumption, influence, armaments, or anything else. Getting should not be confused with spending, just as the risks on various assets should not be confused with various attitudes to risk. There is no conflict or tradeoff between more wealth and other purposes.

In 1973, the Arab "embargo" against the United States and the Netherlands was a political failure, at least for a time, and had to be called off without any of its objectives being accomplished. The impact upon the target United States was less than upon the "favored" and "friendly" British and French. But it was a stunning economic success, in raising the basic price from about $2 per barrel in early October to $7 on January 1, 1974.

Some have argued that the Arabs knew this was going to happen, and that they "really wanted" the extra money and did not care about political goals. That is unwarranted and unnecessary. Their political goals were helped by their enrichment, while their economic goals were in no way lessened by the hope of political gains. King Faisal was like the Spanish conquistador explaining why he came to the New World: "to serve God, and get rich." No conflict there.

Let us note just one possible exception to the rule that the more wealth, the better. Where oil revenues are a very large part of a nation's income a government may slow down—or speed up—oil production because of its effects on the whole economy. This is certainly a possible difference between companies and governments, but it must be investigated, in any given case, to see how important it is in practice.

Revenue Target Theories

Instead of any such questions, we are ruled by a set of dogmas to the effect that some at least of the OPEC governments set production according to their "revenue needs." Any production in excess of what they "need" to sell is against their interests and done only as a favor to us. The higher the price, the less governments need to produce to satisfy those fixed needs. The less they produce the higher the price will be. We have a backward bending supply curve. I will indicate later a different sense in which back-ward bending curves really do apply. But with some exceptions, revenue needs explain only short-run phenomena.

Saudi Arabia has for years been telling us that for the sake of the world economy they produce more than they want to produce. Thus they are making a "sacrifice." They say so without a smile. No wonder: American officials had been telling them this for some time. Back in 1973 their revenue needs were $4 billion. For 1981, their projected expenditures state their needs at $88 billion per year. Allowing for higher prices, the increase in their needs has been by a factor of ten in seven years. So much for needs which—common sense ought to tell us—are what people think they can get.

Twist and turn as we will, there is no way of explaining the Saudi output level by needs or by the desire to conserve oil for future use. But there is a simple and straightforward explanation: if they produced more, they would wreck prices. So instead of installing 20 MMB/D capacity, as they once planned, they hesitate over going to 14 MMB/D. They operate fifteen fields out of a known fifty, and instead of drilling 177 oil wells (1973) they are down to 55 (1979).

IV   OPEC Pricing: An Historical Interpretation

From our long investigation of what the cartel is not, let us look at the cartel as it really is, an association of countries with similar but not identical interests. For twenty-one years their horizons have expanded as they started small and succeeded on an ever grander scale. The whole decade 1960–70 was spent just increasing their share of a price that was slowly dropping. By 1968, they felt confident enough to issue a set of resolutions which should have been carefully read. The bottom line: they would not be bound by any contract or agreement. Invoke the magic phrase of "changing circumstances," and all commitments are dissolved. In 1970 and 1971, they learned to their delight that when they tackled the bigger and more rewarding task of raising the price level itself, there would be no resistance from the consuming country governments. The five-year agreement of January–February, 1971, of which our State Department was so proud, lasted about five months, and by late 1973, before the war broke out, it was simply torn up. As one oilman put it: perhaps the OPEC nations had "grown tired of the charade of negotiations."

At this point, and almost inadvertently, the cartel raised prices from $2 to a little over $7 a barrel (as of January 1, 1974), by a three-stage process:

(1) restrict output, leading to (2) swift increase in spot prices, followed by (3) a catch-up increase in official or contract prices.

In January 1974, the first system was resumed, with greater success. From the $7 on January 1 the amount per barrel due the producing governments was raised to about $10.50 by November of that year. Contrary to official legend, the public record shows that the Saudis were the price leader throughout this period. The Iranian hawks talked big, but were price followers. The Saudis did talk in favor of lower prices, before, during, and after they raised prices. Along the way, they promised in July to have an auction in August, which would bring down prices; then they cancelled the auction. An October promise: they would not permit output to be reduced, and thereby would put pressure on prices. By March 1975, American officials were complaining that the Saudis had "pulled the rug out from under them" by permitting output to be reduced.

But in 1975–77, the first price-raising method did not work well. Prices were raised from time to time, but not by much, and soon the world inflation cancelled the increases. The deterioration of the dollar after 1977 made things worse for them. They felt inhibited in raising prices for a time because the enormous surpluses which they were accumulating were a danger to the world monetary banking system, since all the surpluses came from consuming countries, but were only invested in a few. But the current account surplus went effectively to zero in a matter of four years. It should not have happened. Remember the official truth: the OPEC nations' expenditures were limited by their need, so they would keep saving the surpluses. In fact, the Saudis even had a budget deficit in 1978.

The other obstacle was in the machinery of price increases. Up to this point, the OPEC nations had used the producing companies as their collectors when the revenues were in the form of a tax. Although the concessionaires had been reduced to the status of producing contractors and customers, they could still be used to match production with market demand. There was no collusion among companies, since they had no market power. But each producing company would lift only what it though it could sell, and their total purchases equalled their total estimated sales.

This was an odd haphazard way to set market shares, but it was effective. The producing nations did not get into the difficult divisive task of trying to carve up the market. Instead they left it to a mechanism which was outside their control and which they did not need to control. The companies all bought at prices fixed by the cartel, and then sold as much as they could at those prices, plus the cost of transport, refining, and marketing.

But this system allowed small amounts of competition to seep into the marketplace. The trouble was that the relative values of crude oils were (and are) constantly changing, moving around because of constant changes in relative demands for the various petroleum products. But since the crude oil prices were rigidly set out in advance, crudes yielding higher fractions of some products became unexpectedly good buys, while other crudes became bad buys. Thus, fixed prices meant fluctuating market shares. The more the oil companies are cut loose to become buyers, the more of this we will see. Here and there some countries who were slow to reduce premiums and differentials suffered sharp losses in sales. Since there was a chronic surplus, as is usual in a cartel, some governments were seriously embarrassed. The best example is Nigeria, which in 1976–77 thought it had an arrangement with its neighbors and fellow producers of light sweet crudes, Algeria and Libya. By the spring of 1978 they realized that their fellow Africans were undercutting them by shading prices, and Nigeria was in serious financial straits, having overspent its declining income.

Millions of dollars and many hours of computer time were spent in the attempt to arrive at a "right" set of differentials, all in vain. The failure was, I think, generally acknowledged by 1978. Now attention began to be directed at direct production control, which would keep market shares, if not completely stable, at least predictable. Of course, all these tensions could have been avoided if the Saudis had really been producing more than they needed. They would have let everybody else sell all they wanted and would themselves have only made up the difference. They did nothing of the sort. But the Saudis as senior partners led the way in direct production control by establishing the system of fixing light and heavy crude proportions. This, it was hoped, would stabilize the differentials and keep them from being the subject of too much competition. But the 65–35 requirement was as everyone knew only a step in the right direction. Despite it, the oil glut worsened.[9] Then the Iranian revolution burst on the scene.

The Iranian revolution is generally considered as the cause for the price jump of 1979–80, from about $12 to about $32 per barrel. But this cannot possibly be true. Over the period October 1978–March 1979, the loss of Iran output was perhaps 2.5 million barrels daily. Unused capacity outside Iran was more than three times as great.[10]

In late 1978, there was a noticeable increase in spot prices, but this was regarded in December as anticipating an OPEC price increase.[11] After a relapse, prices again rose in January, to not quite $20. Then on January 20, 1979—a day to remember—Saudi Arabia cut production from 10.4 to 8.0

MMB/D. The cut was only partly restored, to 9.5 MMB/D, on February 1, and by mid-February the price had jumped to over $31.

"It's one thing for the Saudis to use the 8.5 million allowable in normal times to create a nice tight supply situation," said an oilman, "it's another to use it to create a world crisis." In aiming at the "nice tight" market, they achieved the crisis.

The Saudi cut in production had a double impact. It reduced supply, but, more important, it made demand surge. The intense *uncertainty* of supply pushed every prospective buyer into panic. The value of a product is the loss suffered by not having it. (The economist's old friend consumer surplus is Dr. Jekyll turned Mr. Hyde.) The penalty for running dry is so great that, to ward it off, oil will be pursued at even the most extravagant price. For this reason, and not any actual shortage of oil, the spot price went through what was then considered the roof. The producing governments started to raise their contract or official list prices, either by charging premiums, or simply by finding reasons to withdraw from the contract market and sell at spot themselves.

No end of abuse has been heaped upon the spot market, and time and expense lavished on trying to keep companies out of it or to get into it. No public figure had the good sense to point out that spot prices merely register current excess demand, and that the cuts in output and the complete uncertainty of next month's output had precipitated the excess demand.

At the end of March, the spot price had declined from $31 to around $24. Indeed, a glut threatened. The Gulf nations met to determine what to do next. Sheik Yamani chastised the Iraqis for producing too much oil (half a million barrels daily) and trying to cover it up, causing the glut. Prices kept declining—until it was realized in mid-April that Saudi Arabia had again cut production. Again, prices soared because of the loss of supply and the renewed uncertainty and panic.[12]

We may oversimplify a little to say that by the middle of 1979 the spot market had gone about as high as it was to go. From early 1979 to mid-1980, government selling prices caught up with spot prices, first by a rich variety of devices and subterfuges, then by raising of official list prices. Saudi Arabia "led the regiment from behind," keeping its own official price usually $2 or so below the price for equivalent crudes sold by others.[13] Yamani reassured all, toward the end of June, that "Saudi Arabia would never allow [OPEC] prices to rise to $20 a barrel."[14] From consumer countries there were repeated hallelujah choruses of congratulations on Saudi statesmanship and forbearance. But in January 1981, when the Saudi official price was $32, Yamani called the price explosion "another corrective move," that is, deliberate and intentional, as it truly was.

In October 1979, the glut again threatened, and by summer 1980 it was in full force. The OPEC nations made a "gentlemen's agreement" to cut production by 10 percent, that is, by approximately 2.7 MMB/D. Whether this was greater or less than the existing glut we will never know, for the Iran–Iraq war broke out before we could find out. The war may have been a blessing in disguise (to consumers) because the gentlemen's agreement was cancelled, and there was increased production almost everywhere.

The loss of Iraq output, and of the remains of Iran's, did not much disturb the market, because of higher inventories and because the Saudis had raised the price about as high as they wanted it. They kept it from rising further by keeping output around 10 MMB/D. The big worry for all remains how to cut back to accommodate Iran and Iraq when and if they return to the market. It all sounds very familiar to the student of collusive price fixing:[15]

The Gulf producers are carefully monitoring limited resumption of oil exports by Iraq and Iran ...

A market crunch between OPEC members themselves as soon as Iraq and Iran resume substantial exports is their preoccupation. Iran especially ... won't find it easy to persuade others to move over and make room in the market. Saudi Arabia carried the burden of a previous market shift in 1975, when it reduced production from 8.5 to 7 mbd. But Yamani has indicated that Saudi Arabia is not ready to repeat anything along these lines ...

It is time to sum up the new cartel method of raising prices before turning to the question of the ultimate ceiling. Members control production by each government, stating in advance the amount each will be producing in the next month. This, they hope, avoids the danger of supply fluctuations, and unexpected embarrassing losses of market share. In fact, it drastically destabilizes the market.

Short-Run Stabilization Problems

The trouble is, nobody can fine-tune a market with such coarse instruments. We should contrast it with the system of production control that existed in the pleasant city of Austin, Texas. The Texas Railroad Commission controlled output to prevent it from exceeding market demand at the current price.[16] From time to time the price would be increased, and the Commission would validate that increase by not letting excess supply drive the price down. This was done very efficiently and smoothly, as acknowledged even by those who pointed out that the whole system was after all nothing but a domestic cartel. The Commission had the companies' demand forecasts for the next month, and they also had excellent inventory data, with a lag of only about a week or two. When stocks appeared to be accumulating, production would be cut back. If inventories appeared to be falling below the amount needed to support current production, production allowables would be increased. Everybody knew that stability was the Commission's object, and therefore nobody worried about small changes up or down.

There is a painful contrast between production management by the Texas Railroad Commission and by the OPEC core nations, where production figures are about a month behind. Consumption data even for the OECD nations are six months out of date. Inventory information is about seven months out of date, even for the International Energy Agency, which gets reports from about three dozen companies, and extrapolates for the rest. There is enough noise in the data for short-term movements to be quite misleading. Nobody knows the inventories in the hands of consumers (see table 20.1). And outside of the IEA nations, there is mostly statistical darkness.

Accordingly, the decisions of the Saudis and their colleagues are made in ignorance. This in itself might not be so bad if they were equally willing to overshoot or undershoot, and to compensate promptly for error. But that is not the case. Their choice is a biased choice. They will not risk a glut, and they are willing to risk a shortage. Everybody in the trade knows this, and is slow to sell with the appearance of a glut, quick to buy with the fear of a shortage. So even the fear of shortage produces a shortage, and sends up the spot price, as refiners and consumers scramble for every available barrel: not because they want it, but because they fear to be caught without it.

This system of brinkmanship by the OPEC core magnifies any real shortages that might come about, and makes supply very insecure everywhere. Events like the Iranian revolution, which should produce at most a ripple, have produced a series of convulsions and may do so again. But for the OPEC nations, their response to the Iranian revolution has been a tremendous success, even greater than in 1973–74. At that time, the so-called embargo raised the price from about $2 to $7 a barrel. The recent increase, from $12 to $32, was in real terms much greater than the 1973–74 hike. It can happen again almost any time, because the only defense against short-term fluctuations is a large inventory. Private inventories have accumulated and will probably stay at a permanently higher level than before 1979. But the consuming nations have been slow to stockpile. Partly, it is misinformed stinginess, but partly also the slogan of 'cooperation not confrontation' with the OPEC nations.

Table 20.1
Approximate non-communist consumption (in MMB/D)

		1973	1980	January–June 1981
1	Non-communist production:			
	a crude oil	45.9	45.2	43.0
	b natural gas liquids	2.6	3.4	3.2
		48.5	48.6	46.2
2	*plus* communist exports	0.8	1.1	0.9
3	*less* OPEC consumption	1.6	2.8	2.9
4	*less* stock additions	0.4	0.3	0.4
5	*equals* non-communist consumption	47.3	46.6	43.8
	Supplied by:			
6	OPEC exports	29.8	24.6	21.6
7	Non-OPEC sources	17.9	22.3	22.6

Sources (by line):

1a *Oil and Gas Journal* (OPEC: 31.0, 26.8, 24.0).

 b *Oil and Gas Journal*, mid-year Gas Processing Issue. Entry for 1973 for OPEC (0.252) and other non-US (.648) estimated. Entry for 1981 assumed in proportion to change in crude oil output (OPEC: 0.252, 0.591, 0.529).

2 1973, 1980: *BP Statistical Review*; and allowing 0.5 MMB/D as Soviet exports to Cuba, Vietnam, and North Korea. I am indebted to Anthony F. G. Scanlon for this information. 1981: assumed 20 percent less.

3 1973: *International Petroleum Annual*; 1980: Chase Manhattan Bank, *The Petroleum Situation*, Jan.–Feb. 1981; 1981: assumed same rate of increase as 1973–80.

4 EIA, International Energy Indicators, Oct.–Nov. 1981.

6 OPEC production, see lines 1a and 1b *less* line 3.

7 Line 5 plus line 4 less line 6.

V Long-Run Pricing Policy

Now in mid-1981, it is time to ask: how high can the price go ultimately? The market response to price increase is so slow and uncertain that it will be hard to tell even in retrospect when the monopoly maximum has been reached. It may have happened already. My own belief, before 1978, was that the OPEC nations would (and should in their own interest) be much more cautious about raising the price toward the ultimate ceiling, and not risk inflicting fresh damage on the world economic system, and possibly arousing defensive reactions from the consuming nations. I overestimated their caution.

Synthetics as a constraint? The long-run objectives of the OPEC nations are well stated in the February 1980 report of the Committee of Ministers headed by Sheik Yamani: keep raising the real price of oil to the region of the cost of synthetic fuels, but not so fast as to severely restrict economic growth in the OECD nations. This is a sensible policy for a group monopoly, which would not wish to raise the price so high and lose so many sales as to diminish net revenues. I would have only the reservation that massive synthetic production is so far off in the future that it is no binding constraint today.

Lower Consumption—the Binding Constraint

Something stronger has intervened. In the non-communist world, and omitting the OPEC countries where oil is not a normal commodity but a handout, oil consumption for the first half of 1981 is hardly above 1972.[17] Nothing like this has ever happened before. In 1930–33, the American GNP fell by a third, and other countries fared almost as badly. But world oil use decreased by only 5 percent, and by 1935 it had set a new high record. In the 1970s there has been a nine-year stagnation, despite the fact that aggregate national product last year in the industrialized world was about 26 percent above 1972, and will probably be about the same this year. What we need to explain is a fall of 21 percent in the amount of oil used per unit of income. Total energy per unit of income has declined almost as much, with a small degree of substitution away from oil.

To take a gross simplification: under conditions existing before 1973, a 1 percent higher price meant about .75 percent lower energy consumption —eventually. But the reaction was and is very slow because it is an investment process, replacing the whole energy-using stock of capital. In a stationary economy, the half-life of this process appears to be roughly about 9 years. We can check this against the fact that the average service life of corporate capital assets is about 20 years. Were the replacement process linear, it would be one-fourth completed in 5 years, half finished in 10 years, and completed in 20 years. It seems not unreasonable that the more promising changes are made first, and approximate an exponential decline: so far as I can discern, the process is one-fourth over in 3.8 years, half over in 9.2 years, three-fourths over in 19 years, and never ceases altogether.

An allowance for economic growth shortens the half-life to about seven years. Of course, the apparent precision is misleading, but I think that the change in energy consumption from 1973 to 1978 is consistent with, although it is not sufficient to prove, elasticity around 0.75 and a seven-year half-life.[18] The response for oil is somewhat greater than the response for energy in general, because there has been some small substitution of other fuels for oil. Most of the decrease in oil use, adjusted for national product, is to be explained by that original price jump in 1973–74. Indeed, in Western Europe the real price of oil in local currencies was actually lower in 1978 than it was in 1974. Yet consumption per unit of income kept creeping down year after year. The important point is that in 1981 the effects of the first price increase have been only a little more than half-way felt, and the second price increase is just beginning to be felt. Its impact will probably be greater.

Demand elasticity is not a constant but, rather, depends on the price. The higher the price of any product, the greater the reward of substituting away from it. Consider every place where one might save one, two, three, etc., barrels of oil per year by spending $100. When oil (1981 dollars) was about $2.50 a barrel, a barrel was not worth saving to earn 2.5 percent per year. When the price was $12 a barrel, a 12 percent real return before taxes was perhaps acceptable. At $36 a barrel, the rate of return is handsome and the only question is how soon the investment will be made. Now imagine an array of such opportunities in millions of homes and workshops all over the world, and we can see a strong reason for expecting elasticity of demand for energy in general, and oil in particular, to be higher now than it was in 1973. The effect will be felt from now into the next century. How drastically it will affect consumption I will not try to say.

With the energy use per unit of product declining, and that for oil declining a little faster, we need an estimate of economic growth in order to make any kind of forecast for the consumption of energy and oil. Aside from forced official optimism, I doubt that anybody looks forward to any better performance in the 1980s than the 2.5 percent per year since 1973. I would not try to guess how much of the down deflection in world economic growth is due to the direct and indirect effects of the oil price shocks. But some of it is undoubtedly due to the investment process, just mentioned, aimed at saving oil or energy. The investment is a lesser evil. It is not utilized to increase output; it is a subtraction from economic growth. With economic growth abnormally slow, and the continuing decline in energy and oil consumption per unit of product, total energy consumption will grow very slowly if at all, while oil consumption is going to drift downward.

For the first time in 120 years, oil is no longer a growth industry; it is probably a declining industry. Meanwhile, the supply of non-OPEC oil is slowly inching upward. It would be greater today if there had not been such counterproductive policies in the large consuming-producing countries, notably the United States, Canada, Australia, the UK and Norway. In every one of these countries, price controls and taxes have been overused, and the attempt to acquire all the rents has gone past the point of diminishing returns. Rising prices have aggravated the mistake. The higher the price, the greater the incentive to squeeze the goose too hard. Still, it has only diminished not reversed the normal supply response to higher prices.

The net result of stagnant consumption and non-OPEC increases in production is a decline of OPEC exports. In 1973, OPEC exports reached 30 million barrels daily. As recently as June 1978, IEA spoke the official truth: that the demand for OPEC exports would reach 45 ($\pm$3) MMB/D in 1985. The problem was somehow to maneuver and induce and cajole and persuade them to produce 'enough for our needs'. In fact, production has been limited by consumption. The amount of OPEC oil demanded in 1981 is under 22 MMB/D—less than half of that predicted for 1985 by IEA and others.[19]

Nobody should extrapolate from short run changes, but plainly OPEC exports in the 1980s are going to be lower than in the 1970s. This does not mean that the cartel has made a mistake. Profits are far higher at the higher prices and lower sales. There is still room for further price increases, in my opinion, but anyone who takes the contrary view can muster some strong evidence.

Future Oil Prices: a Personal View

To calculate actual elasticities of demand and of noncartel supply is worth doing, but the results seem too weak and inaccurate for direct application. The cartel will never hear the clang of a market bell: you have raised prices too high, start a retreat! The pressure upon them is rather the pressure upon their cohesion, when excess capacity becomes burdensome. Hence we must reconsider the two-model theory suggested earlier.

As the "fringe" of OPEC producers outside the Persian Gulf run up their expenditures to equal and surpass their receipts, they will demand that the Saudis and others in the Gulf "core" go along with them on higher prices. Their nuisance value is considerable, because their aggregate excess capacity is roughly 1 MMB/D. But the fringe can only pressure the core within limits, because if they force the core to carry all the excess capacity, then in effect the fringe will get the benefit of the higher prices, while the core will bear the burden. Or, what amounts to the same thing, they will greatly increase the elasticity of demand for oil from the core, especially Saudi Arabia. To alleviate this conflict, the report of the OPEC long-term strategy committee proposed side payments to governments reducing output: a sound strategy not easily carried out.

Both sides know that a price higher than optimal in the long run is much more profitable in the short run, because of the slow demand reaction mentioned earlier. As appendix B shows, plausible reaction times and discount rates bring discounted elasticity to about half that of un-discounted. Finally, and perhaps most important, so long as the OPEC nations maintain the current system of production control, the system is unstable in the upward direction, and a price hike is almost guaranteed at any time unless the core nations take active roles toward preventing it. For these reasons, I would expect still higher (real) prices in the 1980s, despite weak demand.

The Saudis are rightly worried about these developments. Sheik Yamani has been explaining the concept of demand elasticity, and Saudi actions speak louder than words. Their 1979 output cutbacks drove the price up to $32 from $12. Their output maintenance in 1980–81 has kept the price from going still higher. For the time being, at least, they have stopped telling us that they would dearly love to produce half or less of what they are now producing:[20]

> The problem now for the Kingdom is that ... the world might simply require much less oil from Saudi Arabia by the middle of the decade than the level of oil production necessary (sic) to sustain the huge industrial enterprises the country has planned ... The rapid fall in oil production could also spell political trouble for the Saudi government ... "Any sustained cutback in government expenditure and largesse could translate into political problems," said one high ranking Western diplomat.

Nobody can predict how much the Saudis would be willing to reduce their output; nobody in OPEC wants to find out. But if the current budget is around $88 billion, then there may be trouble if real prices decline below the current $32 and output drops below 7.5 MMB/D.

The great worry of the OPEC nations is a break in their solidarity. I mentioned earlier than I held little credence for the usual backward bending curve, whereby nations who prefer not to produce their oil cut back production, which raises prices, giving them even more embarrassing money, which forces them to cut production still more, etc. But I have suggested another form of the backward bending curve. The higher the price, the better the financial condition of the sellers, and the less pressure on them to cheat and undersell each other in order to pay their bills.

Whatever the reason, a backward bending supply curve is unstable, both up *and* down. Once the price begins to slip, the OPEC nations will be under great pressure to produce more in order to acquire more revenue, and the more they produce, the further the price falls. Certainly, this has been the experience with a group like CIPEC, a pitiful shadow of OPEC, which the copper producing nations have tried to operate.

If OPEC is in serious trouble trying to coordinate their aims, they would sustain great damage if the consuming countries imposed a quota auction or a sliding scale *ad valorem* import tariff.[21] A higher price would mean a higher tariff, and even lower sales. A country reducing its price gets in effect a matching grant from the US government, with which to undersell its rivals.

Changing Role of Oil Companies

The multinational oil companies have become buyers; they are no longer sales agents of the producing countries. This process has been ongoing since 1973, and is far from complete, but was greatly speeded up in 1979–80. Most crude oil is today being sold directly by the OPEC national oil companies to a variety of multinationals, brokers, traders, independent refiners, and governments, who use some and sell some. Oil is being traded and sold around as never before. Heating oil futures are being routinely traded. We have the beginnings of a wide decentralized oil market.

Previously a few companies were tied to particular concessions, from which they lifted the oil and sold it to third parties, or used it in their own refineries. There were only a few prices to watch. Producing profits were high enough to make it cheaper to produce oil than to buy it. Today, the companies take almost nothing for sale to others. They have either been expelled from production or earn modest profits. All are now net buyers, and they actively look from supplier to supplier to obtain even a slightly better deal. During the current surplus oil companies are postponing deliveries, and inventing technical problems at the refinery in order to cancel orders or in the field to cut back production. There are reports of a 'price revolt among contract customers ... actual bargaining is underway in a number of cases.'[22] "Actual bargaining" over contract prices had never been reported. In June, the Kuwait Oil Minister accused Gulf Oil and BP of "haggling." Tradesmen, not gentlemen!—the minister was rightly shocked. Buyers free to roam the market and take advantage of better offers are destabilizers of any collusive price. They have the potential to become, what they are not yet, so many loose cannons on the deck.

U.S. price controls are gone, and American production is now integrated into the world market, where it amounts to more than a fifth of the total. American producers have long been accustomed to respond quickly to price signals, and force a response on their rivals. There is constant comparison of prices now, and a few cents too many mean a lost sale. Sellers know not on whom to align, and find themselves reducing prices to maintain output because they cannot see their rivals, and hence cannot exchange reassurances that they will not cut prices.

The OPEC nations made a serious mistake in getting rid of the oil companies as their producing and selling agents. But the change seems irreversible. All in all, quite a spectacular situation could materialize, with the world price falling dramatically, though the chances of it happening are remote. The collapse of Iran has changed the market greatly. It is doubtful whether they can arrive at more than 3.5 MMB/D capacity, only half of what it used to be, because of their reckless behavior in neglecting the wells and driving out both Iranian and foreign skilled personnel. The Iranian disaster and the Iran–Iraq War have been a piece of great good fortune for Iran's neighbors. In future, they will contrive more such good luck. Saudi Arabia has the slight military edge to occupy neighbors, including even Kuwait if the Iraqis do not get there first. The war has shown that even a low level of air and patrol-boat power, ineffectually applied, can keep loading ports out of operation. The important point to remember is: a million barrels of your neighbor's production suppressed, which you in turn supply, is worth at current prices over $11 billion per year. It is an investment you cannot refuse. Given the Saudis, alone or with one other enforcer, the supply from cartel core should hold together.

I hope we manage to avoid such false questions as to whether "the market will be loose," or "the market will be tight," etc. The market will be both: loose, because of excess capacity which has existed since 1908 (the first great Persian find): tight, because when slack threatens the cartel managers haul in so quickly as to create a strain, perhaps a painful one. This happened twice in 1978–79, and might have occurred again in September 1980 had it not been for the unexpected outbreak of war, and the cancellation of the "gentlemen's agreement." We live in a market controlled by the cartel, and the worst thing we can do is to ignore that simple fact.

If the real price of oil goes up again, the U.S. domestic industry will benefit. But it will make complete decontrol, that is, repeal of the so-called windfall profits tax, more difficult. On the other hand, if the price goes down, I think domestic oil and gas production will be protected by tariffs or quotas. The world in general may be heading into a great divorce between internal energy markets and world markets. There will of course be squabbles over who has access to the lower cost international crude, so circumstances may be in some respects back to where they were ten years ago.

Appendix

A   Discount Rates: Risk of Sudden Loss

There is a probability p that an owner will, within any given year, suffer a sudden complete and irrevocable loss of his producing property. A private owner would fear expropriation, a dynast would fear revolution.

   The probability of survival is then $(1 - p)$, and chance of survival from now through the year t is $(1 - p)^t$, because to survive year t one must also survive every previous year.

   Let i be the rate of discount covering normal commercial risk, and let r be the risky rate covering sudden loss in addition to normal risk. Then the present value of \$X to be received in year t is:

$$PV(\$X)_t = \$X(1 - p)^t/(1 + i)^t = \$X(1 + r)^t \tag{1}$$

$$r = (i + p)/(1 - p), \quad p = (r - i)/(1 + r) \tag{2}$$

If $(1 - p)^T = 0.5$, i.e. a 50-50 chance of loss in year T:

$$T = -.693/\ln(1 - p) \tag{3}$$

   Example: let the normal risky rate be 12%. If in 1990 we believe there is a 50-50 chance of sudden complete loss by the year 2010, then $p = .034$, and $r = 16.0\%$.

B   Discount Rates and Demand Elasticity

The usual timeless definition of price elasticity, where Q_a and P_a are the changed price and output, and P_b and Q_b are the original price and output, is:

$$Q_a/Q_b = (P_a/P_b)^E \tag{1}$$

   Assume now that the price change is immediate, but the demand reaction takes effect over time, declining exponentially:

$$Q_t = Q_b e^{-ct} + Q_a(1 - e^{-ct}) \tag{2}$$

If c is zero, $Q_t = Q_b$.

If c is very large, $Q_t \to Q_a$, and there is no lag.

   Let i be the appropriate discount rate. Then the present value of production in the year t is:

$$PV(P_aQ_t) = P_aQ_te^{-it}$$

$$= P_aQ_be^{-(c+i)t} + P_aQ_ae^{-it} - P_aQ_ae^{-(c+i)t} \qquad (3)$$

$$\int_0^\infty PV(P_aQ_t)dt = \int_0^\infty P_aQ_te^{-it}dt = P_a(Q_b/(c+i)$$

$$+ Q_a/i - Q_a/(c+i)) \qquad (4)$$

With the original price, the present value of the stream would be:

$$\int_0^\infty P_bQ_be^{-it}dt = P_bQ_b/i \qquad (5)$$

Now compare the present value of two options: price change or no price change. With timeless elasticity, $Q_a/Q_b = (P_a/P_b)^E$, or $(P_aQ_a/P_bQ_b) = (P_a/P_b)^{E+1}$. But with present-value-weighted elasticity, called E', we have:

$$(P_a/P_b)^{E'+1} = P_a[(Q_b/(c+i) + Q_a/i - Q_a/(c+i)]/(P_bQ_b/i)$$

$$= P_a/P_b[i/(c+i) + (Q_a/Q_b)(1 - (i/(c+i)))]$$

$$= P_aP_b[i/(c+i) + (P_aP_b)^E(1 - i(c+i))]$$

Dividing both sides by (P_a/P_b), we have:

$$(P_a/P_b)E' = i/(c+i) + (P_a/P_b)^E(1 - (i/(c+i))) \qquad (6)$$

(As c becomes very large, the fraction approaches zero, and the two sides reduce to: $E' = E$.)

Example: assume a 50% price increase, or $(P_a/P_b) = 1.5$; also that timeless $E = -1.0$, $c = .10$ (i.e. half-life seven years), $i = .10$. Then:

$$(P_a/P_b)^{E'} = .5 + (.67)(.5) = .83, \text{ and } E' = -0.45$$

A lower discount rate, e.g. .075, would raise E' to -0.50.

Notes

Research underlying this chapter has been supported by the National Science Foundation under Grant No. DAR 78-19044 and by the MIT Center for Energy Policy Research. I have benefited much from a long collaboration with Henry D. Jacoby and James L. Paddock, and from the comments of Richard L. Gordon, James M. Griffin, David Teece, and Philip K. Verleger, Jr. However, all views expressed commit only the writer, who is solely responsible for any errors.

1. Adelman (1973), p. 1256.

2. Adelman (1978).

3. Church Committee Hearings, Part VII, p. 228.

4. The following is adapted from Richard L. Gordon, who first demonstrated that the effect of interest rates on output rates is indeterminate.

5. Reasons are set forth in Chapter 1 for future price expectations.

6. This is very low cost oil in an improbably prolific deposit. More realistic assumptions would make the cost line steeper and allow much less variation among optimal depletion rates.

7. The most up-to-date and I believe most widely accepted estimates are by Ibbetson and Sinquefield (1979), esp. p. 23. It is only a minor criticism to note that their use of the Consumer Price Index overstates the inflation rate and understates the real return.

8. David Teece has pointed out that if foreign assets are in the name of the government, they are also subject to seizure. Hence it pays to keep more foreign assets in accounts which one's successors cannot claim. It does not affect the optimal revenue total.

9. This paragraph is based on *Petroleum Economist* (1978), June, p. 230; ibid., August, p. 328; and particularly December, p. 499.

10. *Petroleum Intelligence Weekly*, January 29, 1979, p. 9. A sufficient reason for not using the CIA capacity numbers is their vagueness of definition.

11. *Petroleum Economist, op. cit.*

12. *Petroleum Intelligence Weekly*, April 9 and April 16, 1979.

13. This narrative is based on several sources. The weekly prices are from a book by Philip K. Verleger, Jr. The output changes are from *Petroleum Intelligence Weekly*, as are most of the reports of meetings and speeches; the rest from the *New York Times* and *Wall Street Journal*.

14. *New York Times*, June 22, 1979.

15. *Petroleum Intelligence Weekly*, November 24, 1980 and December 15, 1980.

16. Lovejoy and Homan (1967) and MacDonald (1971).

17. The estimate is more than usually imprecise because of our ignorance of stock changes. The second half of 1981 will probably be even more enigmatic, but consumption will be less.

18. In 1978, US energy consumption per unit of GNP was .9158 times the 1973 level. At a rough estimate, the increase in real price to final users was 40 percent. If the long run elasticity was about $-.75$, the ultimate reduction in energy per unit would be by 22 percent, to .7770 of the 1973 level. Substituting these values into the equation in appendix B:

$$.9158 = e^{-5c} + .78 - .78e^{-5c}$$

$$c = .0948, \text{ half-life} = h = 7.3$$

An estimate may also be drawn from the results of the ISTUM model (Sant et al., 1980, pp. 27–37). In 1978, energy use was down 10 percent from 1973 in its sample of users, and it would pay 5 percent or more, real, to reduce it by 32 percent altogether. One can calculate:

$.90 = e^{-5c} + .68 - .68e^{-5c}$

$c = .0725, \quad h = 9.56$

But the estimated .68 as ultimate consumption seems too low because the 5 percent return seems too low. It yields an implicit long run elasticity of -1.15—not impossible, of course, but on the high side.

19. In the summer of 1981, OPEC exports dropped below 20, but I believe this to be a temporary low because of massive de-stocking.

20. *New York Times*, March 23, 1981.

21. On the auction, see *Oil & Gas Journal*, January 10, 1977; on the tariff, see Adelman (1978).

22. *Petroleum Intelligence Weekly*, June 8, 1981.

21

Oil-Producing Countries' Discount Rates

1 Introduction

The great bulk of world oil resources and reserves are owned by a few small less-developed countries (LDCs). To make the best use of assets, they must choose between near-term and farther-off costs and benefits. This requires a set of appropriate discount rates.

The rates may be implicit, never stated as such. If a party is willing to give up a dollar today for two dollars expected in 14 years, he may not realize that he is using a five percent discount rate, any more than the party unwilling to wait even four years is aware that he is using more than 20 percent. Both parties are like the man who talked prose for 40 years without knowing it was prose. Their actions may reveal their preferences more accurately than could their words.

We are particularly interested in two areas of choice.

(1) *The optimal rate of reserve depletion*, which determines the timing and scale of investment. The owners must decide at what point the present value of an additional barrel left in the ground exceeds the price (for a competitor) or the marginal revenue (for a monopoly).

(The unqualified statement that "oil in the ground is worth more than money in the bank" logically implies that the optimal depletion rate is zero. It has been a very influential dogma.)

Today the government-owner usually makes the investment–production decisions directly. However, some still negotiate with private companies (usually foreign) to find and develop oil. They need to know both their own and the companies' discount rates in order to make the deal best for themselves. Blitzer, Lessard and Paddock (1984) have pointed out that both parties benefit by assigning risks to the side better able to bear them.

Reprinted from *Resources & Energy* 8 (December 1986): 309–329.

There seems to be limited but increasing recognition of this principle (McPherson and Palmer 1984). We aim at some rough measure of the risk discrepancy.

(2) *Elasticity of demand.* Since some oil producers are organized in a cartel, they must consider demand in order to choose the optimal price-output combination. Consumption reacts to price with a considerable lag. The decision to raise prices must incorporate two assumptions: at what rate the sales loss from higher prices comes about, reducing income in later years, and at what rate to discount that lower income. Similarly with a proposed lower price.

To speak of "the rate" of discount is of course to oversimplify. To every risk class there corresponds a discount rate. An oil company invests among other things in trucks, which can be moved freely and easily resold; in drilling equipment, which is moved from well to well at considerable expense and can only be resold in a narrow market at highly variable prices; and in exploration wells in remote areas, which are literally sunk costs. The three risk classes require three discount rates. However, this paper is not concerned with the family of rates within the firm, but rather with the difference between two groups of firms, private versus public.

We first summarize the estimates of discount rates applicable to private parties in developed countries with diversified capital markets. We next indicate the factors which would tend to make the producing nations' discount rates higher or lower than the private rate. We arrive at LDC discount rates which are much *higher* than those of private firms in developed economies. We consider some of the possible objections to our findings, and conclude with some very limited conclusions about the effect on depletion rates and oil prices.

2   Private Oil and Gas Producers' Discount Rates

Tables 21.1 a, b present some recent estimates of the discount rates, or cost of capital, of private firms producing crude oil and natural gas in the United States and Canada. Because the industry is so international, these rates apply to any large private firm in the industrial world.

There is some variation, as is to be expected. In my view, the Baldwin–Mason–Ruback estimate is too high because it is based on only one year. It is statistically robust because it is based on a large enough sample to represent 1979 conditions, but the year 1979 is not a good sample of the recent past.

Table 21.1a
Estimates of discount rates (real) for crude oil and natural gas companies (in percent per year)

Estimator	Time period	Riskless rate	Asset risk factor β	Real cost of capital on: Equity	Real cost of capital on: Assets
Terry and Hill	1953	n.a.	n.a.	n.a.	8
Eggleston	1964	n.a.	n.a.	n.a.	9
Pogue	1974–1978	n.a.	1.070	13.1	11.2
Baldwin, Mason and Ruback	1978–1979	2.0	1.234	n.a.	12.9
Paddock	1960–1982	2.0	n.a.	12.0	10.2
	1970–1982	2.0	n.a.	11.8	10.0
Data Metrics	1972	0.5	1.12	11.9	9.6
	1982	0.5	1.02	13.3	9.3
Herold, inc.	1980s	n.a.	n.a.	n.a.	10–20
McPherson and Palmer	1980s	n.a.	n.a.	n.a.	15–20
Arthur Andersen & Co.	1980s	n.a.	n.a.	n.a.	10

Sources: Terry and Hill, and Eggleston, in: Adelman (1972), Pogue, in: U.S. Federal Energy Regulatory Commission, Williams Pipe Line Co., Docket Nos. OR79-1, et al., Verified Statement. Exhibit GAP-2. Baldwin, Mason and Ruback, "Cost of Capital for the Cold Lake Project," unpublished paper in MIT Center for Energy Policy Research—Sloan School of Management Workshop, Energy Project Evaluation, April 21–23, 1983. Paddock, unpublished paper, 1984. Paddock also estimates long-term realized rather than expected returns, which reflect the significant losses to fixed-interest debt holders as average market yields rose: 8.3 and 8.0 percent, respectively. Data Metrics (G. Campbell Watkins), The Oil and Gas Investment Climate: Changes Over a Decade (Canadian Energy Research Institute, Study No. 20, June 1984, ch. 3; capital costs computed). Herold, Inc., periodical appraisals. McPherson and Palmer, in: McPherson and Palmer (1984). Arthur Andersen & Co., Oil and Gas Reserve Disclosures (Survey of 300 Public Companies 1980–1983, published 1984).

Table 21.1b
Calculation of cost of capital from Watkins study

	1972	1982
Asset β	1.12	1.02
Equity β	1.4	1.48
Real c.o.c.	11.9	13.3

Cost of equity 1972 $= RF1972 + \beta 1972\,(M1972 - RF1972)$
$\qquad 11.9 = 0.5 \quad + 1.4 \quad (M1972 - 0.5)$
$\qquad\qquad M1972 = 8.643$

Cost of equity 1982 $= RF1982 + \beta 1982\,(M1982 - RF1982)$
$\qquad 13.3 = 0.5 \quad + 1.48 \quad (M1982 - 0.5)$
$\qquad\qquad M1982 = 9.149$

Cost of asset capital 1972 $= 0.5 + 1.12\,(8.64 - 0.5) = 9.617$
Cost of asset capital 1982 $= 0.5 + 1.02\,(9.15 - 0.5) = 9.392$

A very brief review of elementary finance theory is necessary to see how we will go from the private discount rate to the rate at which a government should discount its oil and gas revenues.

The usual formulation is: $D = RF + \beta(RM - RF)$, where D is the expected discount rate, RF the expected risk-free rate, and RM the expected return on a diversified portfolio of assets. Historical series are entered for RF and RM as the best approximations. β is the measure of covariance between the market rate RM and the return on the particular asset in question, estimated by least-squares regression. As just seen, any two estimates of D will vary, depending upon the observations composing RM and RF.

The premium over the risk-free rate is a return for risk, conceived as the undiversifiable variability of the gains from operating the venture to which the investors' funds are committed. The variability is unknown because the future is unknown, but is expected to be much like the past. The chances of gaining or losing by holding and operating the asset an additional year are measured by the fluctuations in the past.

Past fluctuations are measured by the standard deviation of past gains and losses. But the risk measure β reflects not the variability of the asset itself, but the variability which that asset contributes to the "market portfolio," the whole portfolio of assets owned by or available to investors. The distinction between variance and covariance will be of particular importance.

If there is perfect covariance between the given asset's income and the market portfolio's income, the asset neither adds to nor subtracts from the risk of holding the portfolio, β is unity, and the risk premium for the asset is that for the market generally.

If the asset's earnings fluctuate with the gains of the whole portfolio, but more widely, then it adds something to risk; if less widely, it diminishes risk. Or if the asset's earnings fluctuate out of harmony with the rest of the market portfolio, then it tends to stabilize the portfolio's earnings, and diminish risk. In such instances, β is less than unity.

The asset might seem very risky in isolation, if we knew only its variance. But its interaction with the market portfolio might be such as to make its incremental risk very low, and the discount rate should reflect this. Conceivably, the asset's earnings might even fluctuate inversely to the portfolio's. The asset might be worth taking on as a diversifier even when there were expected losses not gains. Because of the covariance, the discount rate on the asset in question might be zero, or even negative.

The β on a corporation is measured in two stages. First, the gains to holding a share of corporate stock are measured against the market portfolio, and an equity β computed. This is adjusted or unlevered (usually simply multiplied) by the ratio of equity to total equity-plus-debt of the firm in question, to derive an asset β.

The reason for this adjustment is that the equity β incorporates not only the business risk in holding the asset, but also the financial risk of leveraging. When there are obligations such as debts or leases, part of the stream of net revenues is pre-committed. The residual, revenues minus pre-fixed contractual payments, is the more volatile stream determining risk and return to the shareholder. (This assumes that the debt is riskless to the creditor, which may not be quite true. See table 21.1, note explaining the Paddock estimates.)

The stock market does not include all other assets an owner might hold, or his other sources of income, although those others may be highly correlated with the stock market. The use of a stock market β may overstate variability to some degree, though there is no reason in theory why it must (Stambaugh (1982) concludes it does not).

The usual assumption is that any individual investor can diversify against the market portfolio. Hence the differences in risk between any two assets or projects depend only on the characteristics of the two assets. We will soon be compelled to depart from this assumption.

3 Preliminary Observations about Nation-Owners

There has long been controversy over the use of private discount rates to determine the "social discount rate" which is to govern the investment decisions of public bodies. But we do not address this question. We seek only to know at what rate to discount the flow of revenues from petroleum-producing assets, in order to calculate a present value of the flow. Then it is comparable with any other flow, from an existing or proposed asset (compare Lind 1982).

The risk premium does not depend on the time preference of the discounter.[1] Risk, unlike beauty, is not in the eye of the beholder; like the mountain, it is simply there. The greater the risk, the lower the present value of a given flow.

Owners' needs, and attitudes to risk, govern their choices of assets. "If you can't stand the heat, get out of the kitchen." If the assets held are too risky for a given owner's taste or needs, they should be exchanged for lower-yield lower-risk holdings. A nation-state may be more or less risk-averse than a private firm or household. But a given bundle of assets comprising an oil company presents the same risk to one or the other—*unless* their portfolios are radically different (of which more below).

One reads, even in professional papers, the OPEC nations discount at a low rate "... because the opportunity cost of money for the host country is relatively low" (Deacon and Mead 1985, p. 491). This can only mean that the host country invests only in low risk–low return securities. But this is an irrelevant comparison, however popular. The host country's investment in petroleum is investment in a high-risk activity, as table 21.1a shows.

Cartel Nations are Rational

A common misconception is that the OPEC nations are arm-waving wild men, nuts, incapable of making rational policy. At worst this is mere prejudice; at best it is simply gratuitous and unfounded.

Internal OPEC documents rarely get into the public press, but those which do are revealing: for example, the 1980 report of the OPEC long-term strategy committee (summarized in Petroleum Intelligence Weekly 1980), or a paper submitted by Iran to an OPEC committee meeting (Petroleum Intelligence Weekly 1983). One may disagree with what is said, but the arguments are respectable and certainly the tone is calm.

Kaddafi, Khomeini, and others less flamboyant, are bloody-minded, full of hate, see the United States as the Great Satan, etc. But whatever their goals, the more revenues the better to advance them. Some, for a time, may overlook this. The "moderate" Bani-Sadr (who had an economics degree) allowed much of the Iranian oil industry to be ruined, possibly because he really believed it was not "needed." His more ferocious successors have acted much more rationally. Their minds were concentrated by the Iraqi attack, and the need for money to buy arms. Hence they settled claims with the United States, and moved swiftly to carry out their agreement. "This curious blend of Holy War against the Great Satan and business-as-usual with his bankers is typical of the paradox that is Khomeini's Iran" (Smith 1984).

Of course, wishful illusions may influence risk perception. Especially around 1980, there was supposed to be less risk in oil or gas because prices would not fluctuate, only rise onward and upward, forever and ever. Political bodies are learning the lesson a little more slowly and painfully than private. Our purpose is to ascertain the reality toward which they are trending.

4 Forces Tending to Lower Government-Owners' Discount Rates

Governments, especially OPEC governments, should in some respects discount at a lower rate than U.S. companies. There is nearly always much less geological risk than in the United States, and sometimes hardly any. Deposits are typically larger and not exhausted as soon, hence there need be less probing of the unknown. There has never been much true exploration in Saudi Arabia, for example, because, although it always pays to find cheaper oil, it cannot be much cheaper. Of 50 known oil fields, only 15 are currently operated (American Association of Petroleum Geologists Bulletin 1981, 1982, 1983;[2] Oil & Gas Journal 1984[3]).

There is no risk of unfavorable government action to reduce profits, since the nation-owner is sovereign.

However, these two risk reductions are relatively small because geological and political variations are largely uncorrelated with general market changes. Hence they serve as diversifiers, and add relatively little to the riskiness of the hypothetical portfolio. Accordingly, their absence does not much diminish risk.

A more complex issue is that of fluctuations in revenues. Let us defer discussion of one component of revenues, i.e., sales volume, and consider first the net revenue per unit sold: price less unit cost.

Unit cost in the OPEC nations is usually only a minor or even negligible fraction of U.S. cost (Adelman 1986a, b). Since unit net revenue is a residual, the lower the cost, the less the fluctuations.[4]

In normal times, of the sort we have not seen since 1973, and are not likely to see again soon, price fluctuations would be correlated positively with the general market. Hence the lower net revenue fluctuations for a lower-cost producer would be a net risk reduction, possibly an important one.

However, there are two modifications. (1) One is the cartel itself. Far from bringing stability—the usual dogma—it has greatly increased price fluctuations and risk. (2) The price movements have been mostly contracyclical, because oil is so large an industry that large price increases hurt world economic growth, and price decreases help. This was true after 1973, and again after 1978. The brisk recovery in North America and the slower one in Europe and Asia since 1982 have coincided with major price decreases. The collapse in early 1986 has seemed favorable to economic growth.

Since higher oil prices and much higher profits have coincided with lower profits elsewhere, fluctuating oil prices have been a diversifier for private owners.

But for the cartel nations, price fluctuations have not been exogenous events, but rather the result of their own actions. Hence it would be fallacious to argue that the offsets to oil price increases, acting as a diversifier, have been beneficial to these nations.

However, the chances of another price explosion seem to be less than previously, and even if one again happened, there seems to be much less room for a profitable increase. Hence the contra-cyclical nature of oil profits may have disappeared, or at least lessened, and the lower costs of the producing countries may now be an appreciable stabilizer.

Or, what points to the same conclusion derived from option theory, the less the expected future variability, the less the value of the option held by a high-cost producer, who hopes for a windfall gain some day. But a low-cost producer remains indifferent.

I would conclude, without trying to quantify the proposition, that the forces tending to reduce the exporting nations' discount rates are non-negligible, but minor.

5   Forces Tending to Raise Exporter Nations' Discount Rates

Amplified Output Fluctuations

Cartel oil has been the oil of last resort because its price is never lower and often higher than non-cartel oil. Cartelists produce only what they can sell, without undermining the price. Since late 1985, they have of course been striving with all their might to make non-cartel producers share that responsibility for supporting the price. But so far (June 1986) they have not succeeded. Non-cartel producers have felt free to shade or reduce prices in order to maintain sales volume. They sell all they can produce, and take whatever price they can get. Nor can we doubt that if non-cartel producers agree with the cartel on production sharing, they will be quick to repudiate responsibility as soon as members or non-members cheat.

Accordingly, non-OPEC oil production has fluctuated very little this past decade. The United States was stable, other areas grew quite steadily. The cartel nations (OPEC plus Mexico after 1981) have absorbed all the fluctuations in oil output.

The cartel's gradual secular loss of markets due to the long-run effect of higher prices in curbing demand and stimulating supply is uncorrelated risk.

But the variability of cartel sales has been largely an amplified version of changes in oil and energy consumption in response to general business conditions. It is correlated risk and non-diversifiable. On this count, cartel nations' oil income is much more risky than oil income generally.

The National "Portfolio"

We turn now to a more pervasive difference between public and private owners. The basic assumption of the capital asset pricing model, as pointed out earlier, is that a given asset is only a minor part of a broad portfolio. Or what comes to the same thing, the income from a given asset must be small in relation to all other sources of income.

Industrial Countries   In the United States in 1982, oil and gas production net revenues were only 2.25 percent of the GNP; in Britain they were expected to peak at about five percent in 1984–1985.[5]

The national or social discount rate on oil–gas properties owned or taxed by a large industrial country can therefore be no more than the 10–11 percent shown in table 21.1. It can hardly be much less, because the income flow from the stock market portfolio is already so widely diversified that it closely approaches the maximum possible for any income flow. The social or national discount rate on petroleum extraction cannot possibly be as low as the five percent used as the standard in British nationalized industries (HMSO 1978; Rees 1979).

In smaller industrial countries, like Norway and the Netherlands, there is less diversification through the national income. There is, however, a perverse kind of diversification, even a contra-cyclical effect, which has become a cliché, the "Dutch disease." Oil or gas exports lead to an overvalued currency, which in turn reduces non-hydrocarbon exports. (This has been widely discussed. For a good brief account, see The Economist 1982.)

LDC Owners   Once we get beyond the oil producers of the developed world, we confront a difference in degree so great it becomes one in kind.

All the OPEC producers, and to an important degree Mexico, are in the position of the individual or corporate person whose oil holdings are most of its holdings, and oil income most of its income.[6]

Some of the oil producing nations have built up substantial holdings of foreign assets, but with the exception of Kuwait and Brunei, the income derived from them is only a small proportion of oil income. For example, in mid-1984, Saudi Arabia had about $100–120 billion of foreign assets

(Wall Street Journal 1984a; Financial Times 1984).[7] We take the lower estimate to allow for non-earning assets like Iraqi "debts." For comparability, we should impute to this amount the current 11 percent (real) rate of return on assets of corresponding risk, not the much lower rates on lower-risk securities, hence an annual yield of $9.6–$13.2 billion. When the kingdom produced 8.5 million barrels daily (mbd) for sale at $34, total oil income was $104 billion (assuming production costs at 50 cents per barrel), and the oil percent was no less than 104/(104 + 13.2) or 89 percent. Since then, oil income has dropped precipitately, but so have foreign income-earning assets, which today are apparently no more than $55 billion (Wall Street Journal 1986).[8] The financial embarassemnt of the kingdom is shown by its failure to calculate and publish an annual budget for 1986.

The 1982 oil percent of GNP among the Persian Gulf producers lay between 65 (Saudi Arabia) and 70 (Kuwait), except in Iran, where in 1981 it was 40. For the largest non-Persian Gulf producers it is less: Algeria 32, Indonesia 16, Nigeria 26, Libya 40, Venezuela 18 (USCIA 1983).

But national income figures understate oil-dependence, because a large fraction of the non-oil industries and occupations are really oil-dependent. Either they are direct oil-service industries, or else they represent the spending of oil-derived incomes. With no oil income, they lose their reason for existence.

In a developed economy, the receivers of oil income have skills or property which can be switched from oil to non-oil activities, although the amount of non-oil income will presumably be less than the amount of previous oil-derived income.

But this is not true of the oil-producing LDCs. Even industries which look independent, e.g., which are exporters or import-substitutes, may be subsidized—a use of resources, not a source of income. Saudi Arabia exports wheat, but this is an expensive hobby, not farming income, since the government buys in from local farmers at seven times the world price (Wall Street Journal 1984b).

The new refineries and petrochemical plants, now beginning large-scale exporting, are more than a hobby, less than a source of income. Worldwide, these industries are overbuilt and shrinking. Nobody who is free to choose is building refineries. Some are being sold at prices only a small fraction of construction costs.

The oil exporters' capital and operating costs are higher than their competitors'. Their crude oil costs, for a refining or petrochemical operation, are no lower. The true opportunity costs of crude oil is its market value, since the alternative to processing the crude is selling it. This is strictly true for a competitive firm or an observant cartelist, who stays inside his production quota. For a cheating cartelist, this is not true. But given enough cheating the cartel disappears, and the statement is again true.

Whether the oil-based industries will in time be regarded as at least a means of education, or as merely "cathedrals in the desert," does not concern us here. They are small or negligible income-earners, hence non-diversifiers for oil production.

Indeed, the situation is even more extreme, in that oil development damages pre-existing industries more severely than in the developed countries. Nigeria is probably the outstanding example of oil revenues making a country even more oil dependent. Agricultural output has declined, and the towns have attracted a large parasitic population (no less so for being very poor) for whom the governments must provide food and other imported necessities at subsidized low prices. In a less extreme form, the same affliction holds of the other exporters (World Bank 1981, Amuzegar 1982). Even when oil exports are a relatively small percentage of national income, they may be a very high percentage of imports. Mexico has become a well-known example.

As the then Secretary-General of OPEC warned (Attiga 1981): "[The] gains of oil-induced growth tend to increase rather than decrease the dependence ... on the quantity and price of crude oil exports."

A private person with a high but uncertain income from his one holding, who dislikes the high risk, could sell part of the holding, and buy other assets, to lower his total risk. But to sell part of their oil holdings is precisely what the exporting nations cannot do. It is politically impossible; indeed, utterly repugnant. After all, they only recently nationalized their respective oil industries. And even if they were willing to sell they would find few takers, who would offer insultingly low prices, because of the risk of later expropriation.

Hence each oil exporting nation is locked into its holding of the one asset which accounts for most of its income, or most of its foreign exchange earnings. They would quickly perish without the oil-derived purchasing power to buy foreign food, manufactured products, and services. Here is perhaps the most important single difference between private and public holdings.

Measuring Additional Risk for Cartel Nations   The increased risk in holding one asset is well illustrated by Pogue (1980). He took the fluctuations of the whole stock market as unity. His sample of 18 industries taken as a group had an equity β of 1.03, not much greater than the market as a whole. Then,

Chapter 21

allowing for leverage, he arrived at an asset β of only 0.81 for the whole group.

But if we assume that a holder held stock in only one industry, and was not free to diversify his portfolio, then the relevant variable is not the security's *covariance* with the market, but only the *variance* of the single industry. Every individual industry had a much larger standard deviation that did the whole market; on the average, it was 2.3 times as large (Pogue, Exhibit GAP 2).

The investor confined to one security, who cannot diversify even into individual holdings within the industry, is running an even greater risk.

Cartel Nations as Leveraged Corporations

We remarked earlier that to arrive at the β for total assets, we must remove the effect of leveraging. But the oil-producing nations are leveraged. They are like private companies with high levels of debt or high rentals, i.e., with large prior claims on their gross income. The governments tend, even more than private persons, to anticipate and overspend future income, saddle themselves with debts or other commitments. The greater the oil income, the more they leverage it.

The financial history of the OPEC nations is revealing. Even in the 1950s, when oil revenues were trifling by today's standards, governments strongly complained that it was difficult to live with fluctuating incomes. The tension became intolerable in 1959, when some of the multinational oil companies responded to lower market prices by reducing the revenues per barrel. A direct result was the 1960 Baghdad meeting which launched OPEC. As the preamble put it: "any fluctuation in the price of petroleum necessarily affects the implementation of the Members' programmes" (OPEC 1984). Of course, one could deal with fluctuations by saving a large fraction of one's current income and accumulate financial assets to use as a stabilizer. Neither then nor now did it seem like an available option.

Much higher revenues have not only increased oil dependence, but have also led to much greater commitments to spend oil revenues, and even anticipate them. In 1974, the current account surplus of the OPEC nations was $69 billion, several times any previous peak. By 1978, the surplus was gone; Saudi Arabia ran both a budget and foreign-exchange deficit. The reason for this massive turnabout was a surge in imports of goods and services, and in spending outside the respective countries (IMF 1982, 1986).

The discomfiture of the governments was strongly voiced in 1978. The then OPEC Secretary-General warned that if OPEC exports stagnated there would be "political and economic disasters" in the OPEC nations because of revenue cutbacks and disappointed expectations (Jaidah 1978). There was nothing new or startling in this warning: it was generally accepted as true, leading to the correct expectation of a price increase coming in 1979, slack market or not.

The opportunity was taken in 1979–1981, when despite the absence of any shortage—as is generally recognized today—prices were driven up to more than double, in real terms, by restricting output and panicking the market. The 1980 current account surplus was "only" $111 billion because imports chased up so fast. The surplus gave way to a deficit in two years, and the OPEC nations remain in deficit Saudi Arabia is in deficit on both budget and current account (IMF 1986; SAMA 1984).

Thus the OPEC and some non-OPEC exporters have managed to put themselves into the position of a highly leveraged corporation. If we adjust the risk premium without any allowance for un-leveraging—because the holder is in fact leveraged—the risk premium becomes 8 × 2.3, or 18.4 percent, and the total required return or cost of capital is then 20.4 percent. Some of these governments have made the analogy exact by going deeply into debt, but this is only the most extreme example.

Leveraging of Mineral Income in the XVI Century   There is a historical precedent. King Philip II of Spain used the proceeds of a huge mining business (silver from Mexico and Peru) to take over a good sized business in ocean shipping and wholesale groceries (the annexation of Portugal). In seeking power and glory, King Philip spent the combined proceeds—and more. His chief problem was a fluctuating revenue stream, the irregularity of his large income. "The crucial service (which the Genoese bankers) performed for the king of Spain was to provide him with a *regular* income, by converting the fiscal revenues and American silver, which were both *irregular* sources of finance" (Braudel 1979, p. 165—emphasis in original). The other side of the coin was that in 90 years, there were six major financial crises in Genoa; "all had Spanish origins" (Braudel 1979, p. 162). Philip II was the wealthiest monarch in Christendom, and went broke the most often. Accordingly, he paid increasingly high interest rates, because his creditors realized, sometimes a bit late, that the risk had been transferred to them (Elliott 1963; Braudel 1966).

Problems of Adaptation to Lower Revenues   Nobody knows how much of these governments' outlays are irreducible. (For a careful examination, though now outdated, see Moran (1978). The corresponding numbers would be much higher today.)

Cutting the incomes and subsidies of various groups may threaten social unrest or revolution. We referred earlier to the grotesque subsidy to Saudi Arab wheat farming. It has proved impossible to eliminate, and extremely difficult even to reduce.

If some of the payments are untouchable, like a corporation's rental and interest payments, this concentrates the fluctuations on the remainder of the revenues, which fluctuate more than does the total. This vulnerability to fluctuations should make a rational owner put a high discount rate on future incomes.

Political Instability

There is an additional source of risk, resulting from the inherent instability of most of these governments. Domestic opposition has no outlet but conspiracy and violence; they are also threatened by their neighbors.

Suppose we have been able to calculate, according to the capital asset pricing model, a risk adjusted rate of discount, call it i. It is not hard to show (Adelman 1982, pp. 59–60) that if there is a probability p that the owner of a mineral deposit will, within any given year, suffer a sudden complete and irrevocable loss of his property, the true discount rate r, adjusted for that risk, is

$$r = (i + p)/(1 - p). \tag{1}$$

Suppose we believe there is a 50–50 chance of a ruling party or faction or junta or family being overthrown from inside or outside within 20 years. This in any given year, there is a 3.4 percent chance of overthrow. If the discount rate, for ordinary business risk, is 20 percent, then the risk-adjusted rate is: $r = (0.20 + 0.034)/(1 - 0.034) = 24.2$ percent.[9]

When calculating oil development costs in the 1960s, I assumed a nine percent cost of capital in the United States, and 20 percent for firms operating in the OPEC nations (Adelman 1972, ch. 2). It did not occur to me that this discount rate (which, I was informed, was about what oil companies were using) was an implicit forecast of an even chance of expropriation within 7.2 years. That is

$$p = (r - i)/(1 + r) = (0.20 - 0.09)/1.2 = 0.092, \quad \text{and}$$

$$(1 - 0.092)^{7.2} = 0.5.$$

If we take the year of forecast as 1966, that was not a bad guess.

Summary

If governments were subject only to the risks facing a producer of oil and gas in the United States, they should properly discount future income streams at about ten percent, i.e., two percent riskless and eight percent risk permium. (The capital market would furnish no equity funds at a lower rate.) If we conservatively assume that they have no control over at least one-fourth of their incomes, then they should add about two percent to the risk premium, and discount at about 12 percent. If we recognize that they cannot diversify income to any significant degree, the required rate goes sharply higher, probably above 20 percent. Recognizing the probability of a "short sharp shock" to the current regime requires another substantial boost. The total varies among nations, of course, but for the current regime in Saudi Arabia it must exceed 20 percent. For Kuwait it is lower, since true non-oil income, derived from foreign investment, is higher in relation to oil income. For all others, it must be higher.

Some Objections Considered

The range of discount rates suggested here, from 8–11 percent in the United States to two–three times that much in the OPEC countries, will probably arouse some disagreement.

The "r Percent rule"

One reason is the widely held belief in the "Hotelling paradigm or r percent rule" (Miller and Upton 1985), according to which minerals prices, less extraction costs, must inevitably rise at the relevant rate of interest. It would follow logically that future receipts (and, with some adjustment, future prices) should be discounted at a near-riskless rate. Certainly price appreciation at any risky rate is not of this world. Fifty years at ten percent per year is an increase by a factor of 117; 100 years, by a factor of nearly 14,000.

The attempts to measure the Hotelling effect have assumed riskless discount rates, without however trying to justify them or discuss the actual risks of mineral operations, including petroleum (Heal and Barrow 1981, U.K. Treasury bills; Smith 1981, prime commercial loans, high grade municipals, one-year corporate bonds, 30-year corporate bonds, and stock exchange call loans; Devarajan and Fisher 1981, no reference to appropriate discount rates; Marshalla and Nesbitt 1986, a range of 2–6 percent).

In this paper, I will merely state without trying to justify a position. The failure of econometric verification of the price-increase paradigm is due neither to inadequate data nor inadequate econometricians. The Hotelling principle is correct: the discounted net return from extracting a mineral unit from a given deposit in any year must equal that in any other year, which in turn equals any return from a holding with equal risk. This is no truism; it is a basic insight into mineral economics. But the Hotelling principle does not require the paradigm of net prices rising *at all*, at any rate. Mineral scarcity is the uncertain fluctuating result of conflicting forces: diminishing returns versus increasing knowledge. Prices therefore rise and fall. Discount rates for the minerals industries, which incorporate price risk, should be— and are—in the normal commercial range.

Optimal Depletion Rates

One can cite some respected names in support of the proposition that the higher the interest rate, or the greater the risk, the higher the optimal depletion rate and the faster the exhaustion of a mineral deposit; and vice versa (Dasgupta and Heal 1979; ICF 1979; Kay and Mirrlees 1975; Nordhaus 1973; Pindyck 1978; Posner 1972[10] and Solow 1974). As the ICF (1979) authors state (p. II-5): "If extractors become less fearful that their fields will be expropriated, it is no longer rational to pump as vigorously, much as if there were an unanticipated reduction in the interest rate."

But this idea is mistaken. A changed discount rate can raise *or* lower the optimal depletion rate (Gordon 1966; Adelman 1982). It is true that ceteris paribus a higher interest rate makes it less attractive to keep an asset in the ground, and favors increased extraction. It is also true that investment per unit of output rises with the rate of output, and with cumulative output, since one factor, the deposit, is fixed. But the higher interest rate makes the increasing investment per unit more expensive. The first effect promotes investment and output, the second depresses it.

Clearly, the relation between the discount rate and the optimal depletion rate is complex and depends on current and expected costs and prices. Let us take an extreme but realistic case, where cost—investment requirements per unit of capacity—is very low. Here the first effect tends to overbear the second. Hence the high discount rates of the LDC exporting nations should on the whole induce higher depletion rates—assuming they act as competitors. But this effect has been dominated, of course, by the need to restrict output to maintain prices. We now turn to this aspect.

7 Exploitation of a Monopoly Position

We have shown elsewhere that if the reaction of consumption to a higher price takes time, and the consumption reduction declines exponentially, then the relation between timeless elasticity E and present-value-weighted elasticity E' is as follows:

$$(P_a/P_b)^{E'} = (i/(c + i)) + (P_a/P_b)^E \times (1 - (i/(c + i))), \qquad (2)$$

where P_a and P_b are prices before and after the change, i is the discount rate, and c is the exponential decay rate of the consumption effect. Table 21.2 gives some illustrative cases.

Table 21.2
Timeless elasticity and present-value-weighted elasticity

Definitions
Q_b = quantity before price change
Q_a = quantity after price change
P_b = price before change
P_a = price after change
E = timeless elasticity of demand
E' = present-value-weighted elasticity of demand
i = risk-adjusted discount (interest) rate
h = half-life of effect of price change on quantity change
c = annual rate of exponential decay of effect of price change
e = exponential

Relations
$e^{-ch} = 0.5$, hence $-ch = -0.693$, $c = 0.693/h$
$(P_a/P_b)^{E'} = (1/(c + i)) = (P_a/P_b)^E * (1 - (i/(c + i)))$

Assumptions

$P_a/P_b =$	1.01		
E =	-1.0		
h =	3	5	7
hence c =	0.231	0.139	0.099

Values assumed	E'	Values assumed	E'
$c = 0.231$ $i = 0.10$	-0.697	$c = 0.231$ $i = 0.25$	-0.479
$c = 0.139$ $i = 0.10$	-0.580	$c = 0.139$ $i = 0.25$	-0.327
$c = 0.099$ $i = 0.1$	-0.496	$c = 0.099$ $i = 0.25$	-0.322

Assume that demand elasticity for a product is unity. If the effect were felt immediately, or if the discount rate were zero, it would not pay a monopolist to raise the price. But if the delay has a half-life of, e.g., seven years, then with a ten percent discount rate the effective elasticity is only about -0.5, and with a 25 percent discount rate, elasticity is only -0.32. A one percent price increase would increase the discounted present value of revenues by 0.68 percent; a one percent decrease would lower revenues in the same proportion.

This, in my opinion, is the most important effect of higher discount rates and shorter time horizons: a cartel gravitates toward a policy of "take the money and run."

8 Exporter Country Attitudes

It may be objected that even if high discount rates are correct in theory, and oil-exporting governments should in their own interest use them, yet they believe low discount rates are "right," and act accordingly.

This argument is often confused with another one: that revenues from oil sold today bring not wealth but "illth" to the nation: conspicuous waste, social disruption, etc. This argument assumes as a fact that more income is bad. If so, one should keep the oil in the ground whether it is worth much or little. The nation deliberately chooses a second-best. The best would be to produce the oil and invest the proceeds for the benefit of this and future generations. But one assumes it will not be well invested. Better therefore to keep it in the ground, where it has at least *some* value. Perhaps the policy will improve in the future.[11]

On its premises, the argument is sound. The risk, which governs the present value of the flow of revenues, is not relevant. Of course, one man's "waste and corruption" is another man's delight. Moreover, an income corruptly gained, then reinvested abroad in productive assets, is a net gain to the economy, however unjustly distributed. Public or private investment in a money-losing enterprise which requires subsidized imports to keep functioning, is a running sore on the body politic, however fair, just, and reasonable is the division of the burden.

Returning to discount rates: certainly oil-exporting governments (and others) have long insisted that they consider far-off gains very close to present gains, and would therefore prefer to keep oil in the ground than put money in their purse.

But an unsupported statement by an interested party is not good evidence. These governments want consumers to believe that they are producing more than economic interest would indicate, or making a "sacrifice" for the sake of the world economy. Thus we owe them political or other favors to insure "access" to oil. Certainly the belief that our statesmen must and do assure "access" has been a foundation-dogma for U.S. policy-makers for well over a decade (Kissinger, Foreword, in Ebinger 1982, a volume dedicated to the proposition that "access" is a major problem).

No good reason has ever been given for assuming the dogma that exporting nations produce more oil and more revenues than they wish. Moreover, the surge of imports noted above, which twice turned massive OPEC surpluses into deficits, would be sufficient proof that these governments want more revenues, not less to spend. Furthermore, during the repeated oil gluts since 1973, there have been repeated opportunities for Saudi Arabia and others with small populations to let others have the market, and keep their oil in the ground, as they say they yearn to do. Of course, they have done no such foolish thing, but rather maneuvered and fought for the largest possible market share compatible with maintaining the price. Better to watch what they do than what they say.

But perhaps producers, including exporting governments, may simply be mistaken, impressed by fashionable Club-of-Rome hysteria, or more sober papers in various journals, or endless repetition by statesmen in the consuming countries, or just blindly following an un-examined rule.

This argument is not to be lightly dismissed. But it can only be tested, if at all, by an appeal to history. The difficulty is that an expected rise in price acts like a lower discount rate. Before 1982, the oil industry expected that prices were inexorably headed upward (Oil & Gas Journal 1982,[12] 1984). In this sense, the industry acted for a time as if their discount rates were considerably lower than market rates. The oil exporting nations acted just like private parties, but they were much more vulnerable to price decreases —another way of saying their risks were greater.

9   Conclusion

Non-industrial oil exporting countries, as rational income-receivers and wealth-holders, should discount future oil revenues at rates much higher than private oil producers, in no case below 20 percent per year, and mostly above 25 percent.

We drew attention to the Blitzer–Lessard–Paddock (1984) paper suggesting that the discrepancy in price risk between oil companies and governments made it profitable for both sides to put the risk on the oil companies, and compensate them for taking it. If our argument is sound, the potential gains are indeed great.

The short horizons of the cartel nations favor large quick price boosts. But they also force some cartelists into breaking away and playing the reluctant price cutter in order to obtain immediate cash benefits, however short-sighted they know their actions to be. A report of a recent OPEC meeting stated: 'Partly, many experts say, the problem is OPEC's seeming inability to do without instant gratification ... "Two barrels is something I hold, it's real," a source close to delegates said, "One barrel, for a higher price, is a promise. So I hang on to what I have"' (Tagliabue 1986).

Notes

The research for this paper has been supported by the National Science Foundation, grant no. SES-8412971, and by the Center for Energy Policy Research of the M.I.T. Energy Laboratory. I am obliged to Paul C. Carpenter, Diderik Lund, Michael C. Lynch, James L. Paddock, and Jeffrey C. Stewart for comments on an earlier draft. But any opinions, findings, conclusions or recommendations expressed herein are those of the author, and do not necessarily reflect the views of the NSF or any other person or group.

1. Strictly speaking, the riskless rate summarizes the pure rate of time preference of the various individuals in the same way as a market price sums up their tastes.

2. "World Energy Developments," issue: Vol. 65, no. 10 (October 1981) pages 2135 and 2142. Data not available in later years. However, ten discoveries (excluding pools found adjacent to previous discoveries) were reported in that and subsequent issues. Their economic feasibility is not reported. See Vol. 66, no. 11 (November 1982) pages 2012–2013, and Vol. 67, no. 10 (October 1983) page 1699.

3. Specific field production is no longer published.

4. The variability of net profit margins is much reduced in the United States by the so-called windfall profits tax, which is really an excise tax on the difference between the market price and a base price. Thus the government takes most of a price increase and bears most of a price decrease. The tax was an important earnings stabilizer until the price collapse of 1985–1986.

5. According to the *Survey of Current Business*, July 1983, pp. 68–69, 1982 gross national product in current dollars was $3.073 billion. Gross product in all mining was $116 billion. Oil and gas extraction accounted for 60 percent of net mining income (without capital consumption adjustment). Accordingly, we may estimate oil and gas extraction gross income at $69.6 billion. This is roughly corroborated by the Bureau of the Census, *Annual Survey of Oil and Gas 1982*, Table 5 ("net company interest statistics"). Total lease revenues from oil and gas sales were $103 billion. Subtracting $46 billion of capitalized expenditures, we have roughly $56 billion that might be called gross income to the factors. Since the *Annual Survey* is

no longer published, it is not possible to update the comparison. For the U.K., see *The Economist*, June 9, 1984, p. 67.

6. Diderik Lund has pointed out that with large-scale oil or gas production, the composition of the national portfolio changes. One might expect that the in-ground asset is exchanged for various above-ground assets. Thus the portfolio changes, the risk-weighted interest rate becomes endogenous. and an analytical solution of the sequential optimum depletion rate much more complex. I believe Lund is correct. If the presence of oil wealth makes the nation-owner more not less oil-dependent, the risk-adjusted rate is even higher than our simplified analysis would indicate.

7. The *Wall Street Journal* quoting from Saudi Arabian Monetary Agency (SAMA) gives the $120 billion estimate; the *Financial Times* estimates $110 billion Saudi foreign assets.

8. Estimate from V. Zanoyan, Director Middle East Economic Service.

9. As in large matters, so in small, "Observers who knew [Iran] before the revolution say there is probably more [corruption] now. Before the revolution, those holding top jobs skimmed 2–3% off contracts. Now, since people frequently get sacked for political reasons, they have to make their money faster; so they take 10% or more" (*The Economist* 1984b).

10. Note, however, the argument at pp. 429–430 and 439 n., which gets close to the idea of cost increasing with the rate of output.

11. Michael C. Lynch has suggested that if E is called the percentage of income "not wasted," then the asset value is $V(t) = E \times P(n) \times (1 + i)^n$, where $V(t)$ is the asset value at the present time, $P(n)$ is the price received n years ago, and i the interest rate at which one might have invested it. But he points out that there is a hidden assumption, namely that the government will henceforth spend the money "wisely". Otherwise, the income from the reinvested asset will itself be "wasted" at the same rate. Then one faces the original problem: produce and sell the oil, or keep it.

12. 2–3 percent upward, real.

References

Adelman, M. A., 1972, The world petroleum market, 53–54.

Adelman, M. A., 1982, OPEC as a cartel, in: James M. Griffin and David J. Teece, eds., Oil prices and the future of OPEC (Allen & Unwin, London) 39–61.

Adelman, M. A., 1986a, Scarcity and world oil prices, Review of Economics and Statistics 68, no. 3.

Adelman, M. A., 1986b, The competitive floor to world oil prices, The Energy Journal 7, no. 4.

Adelman, M. A., John C. Houghton, Gordon M. Kaufman and Martin B. Zimmerman, 1983, Energy resources in an uncertain future (Ballinger, Cambridge, MA).

American Association of Petroleum Geologists Bulletin, 1981, Vol. 65, no. 10, 2135, 2142.

American Association of Petroleum Geologists Bulletin, 1982, Vol. 66, no. 11, 2012–2013.

American Association of Petroleum Geologists Bulletin, 1983, Vol. 67, no. 10, 1669.

Amuzegar, Jahangir, 1982, Oil wealth: A very mixed blessing, Foreign Affairs 60, no. 4.

Attiga, Ali A., 1981, Economic development of oil producing countries, OPEC Bulletin 11, no. 11.

Blitzer, Charles R., Donald M. Lessard and James L. Paddock, 1984, Risk-bearing and the choice of contract forms for oil exploration and development, The Energy Journal 5, no. 1, 1–28.

Boskin, Michael J., Marc S. Robinson, Terrance O'Reilly and Praveen Kumar, 1985, New estimates of the value of federal mineral rights and land, American Economic Review 75, no. 4, 923–936.

Braudel, Fernand, 1966, The Mediterranean and the Mediterranean World in the era of Philip II, Revised edition, 697, 960–962.

Braudel, Fernand, 1984, The perspective of the world: Civilization and capitalism, 15–18th centuries (Original French edition: 1979) (Harper & Row, New York) 165.

Brealey, Richard and Stewart C. Myers, 1984, Principles of corporate finance (McGraw-Hill, New York) 2nd ed., Part III.

Dasgupta, P. S. and G. M. Heal, 1979, Economic theory and exhaustible resources (Cambridge University Press, Cambridge).

Deacon, Robert T. and Walter J. Mead, 1985, The oil and gas industry, in: William A. Vogely, ed., Economics of the mineral industries (American Institute of Mining, Metallurgical and Petroleum Engineers, New York).

Devarajan, Shantayanan and Anthony C. Fisher, 1981, Hotelling's economics of exhaustible resources: Fifty years later, Journal of Economic Literature 19, 65–73.

Ebinger, Charles K. et al., 1982, Energy and natinal security in the 1980s (Ballinger, Cambridge, MA).

Elliott, J. H., 1963, Imperial Spain (Martin's Press, New York) chs. 5, 8.

Financial Times, 1984, August 1, p. 10.

Gordon, Richard L., 1966, Conservation and the theory of exhaustible resources, Canadian Journal of Economics & Political Science 32, no. 3, 319–326.

Heal, Geoffrey, 1975, Economic aspects of natural resource depletion, in: Pearce and Rose (1975) 118–139.

Heal, Geoffrey and Michael Barrow, 1981, The relationship between interest rates and metal price movements, Review of Economic Studies 47, 161–181.

Her Majesty's Stationery Office (HMSO), 1978, The nationalised industries, Cmd. 7131 (HMSO, London).

ICF Inc., 1979, Imperfect competition in the international energy market: A computerized Nash–Cournot model (Department of Energy Office of Policy and Evaluation), May.

International Monetary Fund (IMF), 1982, International Financial Statistics (IMF, Washington, DC).

International Monetary Fund (IMF), 1984, World economic outlook (IMF, Washington, DC) 189, 195.

International Monetary Fund (IMF), 1986, International Financial Statistics (IMF, Washington, DC).

Jaidah, Ali, 1978, Article in: Petroleum Intelligence Weekly, Sept. 25.

Kay, J. A. and James A. Mirrlees, 1975, The desirability of natural resource depletion, in: Pearce and Rose (1975).

Lind, R. C., ed., 1982, Discounting for time and risk in energy policy (Resources for the Future, Washington, DC).

McPherson, Charles P. and Keith Palmer, 1984, New approaches to profit sharing in developing countries, Oil & Gas Journal, June 25, 119–128.

Marshalla, Robert A. and Dale M. Nesbitt, 1986, Future world oil prices and production levels: An economic analysis, The Energy Journal 7, no. 1, 1–22.

Miller, Merton H. and Charles W. Upton, 1985, A test of the Hotelling valuation principle, Journal of Political Economy 93, no. 1, 1–25.

Moran, Theodore H., 1978, Oil prices and the future of OPEC (Resources for the Future, Washington, DC).

Morse, Edward L., 1986, After the fall: The politics of oil, Foreign Affairs 64, no. 4, 792–811.

Nordhaus, William D., 1973, The allocation of energy resources, Brookings papers on Economic Activity 3.

Oil & Gas Journal, 1982, Annual drilling issue, Sept. 27.

Oil & Gas Journal, 1983, Supplement, World wide oil, Dec. 26, 106.

Oil & Gas Journal, 1984, July 16, 32.

OPEC, 1984, OPEC official resolutions and press releases 1960–1983 (Pergamon Press, Exeter), 1.

Pearce, D. W. and James Rose, eds., 1975, The economics of natural resource depletion (Macmillan, London).

Petroleum Economist, 1966 (formerly Petroleum Press Service) Sept., 326.

Petroleum Intelligence Weekly, 1980, Special supplement, May 12.

Petroleum Intelligence Weekly, 1983, May 21.

Pindyck, Robert S., 1978, Gains to producers from the cartelization of exhaustible resources, Review of Economics and Statistics 60, no. 2, 238–251, esp. 242.

Posner, Michael V., 1972, The rate of depletion of gas fields, Economic Journal 52, Special issue, 429–441.

Rees, Ray, 1979, The pricing policies of the nationalised industries, The Three Banks Review, June.

Saudi Arabian Monetary Agency (SAMA), 1984, Annual report.

Smith, Terence, 1984, Iran: Five years of fanaticism, New York Times Magazine, Feb. 12, 32.

Smith, V. Kerry, 1981, The empirical relevance of Hotelling's model for natural resources, Resources and Energy 3, 105–117.

Solow, Robert M., 1974, The economics of resources or the resources of economics, American Economic Review 64, 1–14.

Stambaugh, Robert F., 1982, On the exclusion of assets from tests of the two parameter model: A sensitivity analysis, Journal of Financial Economics 10, 237–268.

Survey of Current Business, 1983, July, 68–69.

Tagliabue, J., 1986, Behind the OPEC deadlock, New York times, Aug. 4, D1.

The Economist, 1982, Troubled little rich boys, in: Holland survey, Jan. 30 (London).

The Economist, 1984a, June 9, 67 (London).

The Economist, 1984b, Aug, 25, 28 (London).

U.S. Central Intelligence Agency (USCIA), 1983, Handbook of economic statistics, 23.

U.S. Department of Commerce—Bureau of the Census (USDC–BC), 1984, Annual survey of oil and gas 1982 (Washington, DC).

U.S. Department of Commerce—Bureau of Economic Analysis (USDC–BEA), 1983, July, 68–69.

Wall Street Journal, 1984a, July 24, 38.

Wall Street Journal, 1984b, Saudi wheat farms tap subsidies, aquifers, May 29, 34

Wall Street Journal, 1986, Saudi wealth said to fade amid drop in world oil prices, April 7, 3.

World Bank, World development report 1981 (World Bank, Washington, DC).

III

Public Policy toward International Oil

22 Security of Eastern Hemisphere Fuel Supply

Security of fuel supply for Europe, Japan, and the rest of the non-Communist Eastern Hemisphere (hereafter called "the Area") can be had, not only without additional cost, but at a large net saving. Indeed, the 1967 crisis will be a blessing if it forces a hard look at some facts that governments have not been able to recognize or act upon because of domestic political pressures and fixed positions.

I

What is the security problem? There have been two sudden reductions of supply ten years apart, and there can be more at any time on short notice. In one way, these crises are like fires or accidents—we want assurance against being struck without warning. But assurance of fuel supply actually reduces the chances of "fire." For if the Area is secure, the threat to deprive it of fuel is empty, and the attempt is unlikely.

Supply was reduced by the Suez Canal closure, and the cost of being unprepared will not finally be paid for some years. But by 1969–70, the Canal will be only a minor instrument and its closure a minor nuisance, since large tankers will in any case be carrying most of the load, and west-of-Suez productive capacity will be much increased. It was largely a happy accident. Contrary to the fable which will be agreed upon as future history, no statesman's foresight provided those tankers. On the contrary, they were built by Japanese (and Swedes) and bought by shipowners and oil companies for the sake of profit and in the teeth of accusations of unfair competition and unpatriotic conduct. The shipbuilding capacity is in

Originally MIT Department of Economics *Working Paper No. 6*, December 1967. Translated versions appeared in French, Italian, and Japanese periodicals. Condensed in *Petroleum Press Service* (January 1968).

place, however, and the 1967 shutdown will keep it going harder and longer.

Our concern now must be with production. The worst possible case is a shutdown by the concerted action of all or nearly all producing countries. No single producing country matters. Even in 1951–54, Iraq, Kuwait, and Saudi Arabia moved quickly to fill the 35 percent gap left by the Iranian shutdown. In the winter of 1966–67, when the Syrians stopped the flow from Kirkuk in Iraq to the Mediterranean, there was not a ripple in the slightly changed flow pattern. Yet the loss of Iranian output was 660,000 barrels daily, that of northern Iraq nearly 900,000.[1] It is a measure of the growth and maturation of the industry in the fifteen years' interval.

Loss of two of the Big Five of the Eastern Hemisphere (Iran, Iraq, Saudi Arabia, Kuwait, Libya) would be at least a minor nuisance; three might be serious, at least for a year to eighteen months. Within that time, the lost capacity could, if need be, be replaced by the rest of the oil-producing nations. But as it became apparent that the producing country was risking a permanent loss of its chief or only source of revenue, either the government would allow production to resume, or else it would be overthrown by those who wanted the revenue.

Hence the extreme of the security problem is clear enough: *be prepared for a total cessation for a limited period.*

II

Diversified supply of oil, and domestic coal production, have been the favored means to security, but diversification has been the accidental result of oil companies seeking oil. Policy had nothing to do with it. The widespread impression that the 1957 Suez crisis led to exploration in North and West Africa is not true; Nigeria had been explored for years, and its first major field had already been brought in.[2] Libya acreage had been taken up in 1955; and in Algeria two major fields (Hassi Messaoud and Edjele) had been found after decades of search and some minor finds dating back to 1918 in what was then French North Africa.[3] Diversification has been rather a disappointment, though not altogether useless. Of course it has helped to establish substantial new oil-producing countries since 1957, for the more such countries, the harder to plan and enforce a total shutdown. But anything which makes cooperation likely, or nonconformity difficult, makes diversification less effective. The opening of great new areas in North Africa threatened to be no help and has been of limited help, since these areas joined in the temporary embargo, such as it was. The quarrel of one nation in the Middle East-North African area has a good chance of being the quarrel of all. The Libyan oil workers' union headquarters in Cairo delayed resumption elsewhere. Only the Nigerian shutdown could be called an unlucky accident, unrelated to the Middle East crisis. Venezuela, Iran, and Indonesia, unaffected by the embargo, are all old-timers in oil. Any search for diversification due to the 1956–57 crisis, which would not otherwise have come about, has been a waste.

But while a new petroleum area may add to security once it has large-scale production, there is no advance assurance that any particular exploration effort in a new area, or even several taken together, will be anything but a dead loss. The odds are always against finding anything, and they are very long against finding anything worth finding. Hence the feverish discussion of crash exploration programs in new areas "to diversify supply sources" is foolish. If money is spent in new untried areas, it will probably be lost. On the other hand, if the exploration is in areas now producing, there may (possibly) be a commercial profit, but there can be no gain in security. And even the improbable combination of large new discoveries in new areas will not give any security until many years are past and the need may have passed. Oll exploration for security is precisely like a man trying to provide for his old age by going to the race track to wager his hard earned pay.

Another kind of diversification is altogether worthless: for a consuming country to import from more than one of the existing producing countries. Any sacrifice or higher cost incurred this way is a deadweight loss because it does not in the least diminish the threat of a concerted shutdown.

A nationally owned company (wholly or partly) like BP in Great Britain, or CFP or ERAP in France, or ENI in Italy cannot provide security of supply any more than a privately owned company. Indeed, it is a more tempting target. But public or private ownership is simply irrelevant to the chances of a concerted shutdown. Nor does a private company owned by nationals of a given country make that country any more secure than if the company were owned by foreigners.

Unfortunately, in every security crisis a cry goes up to "diversify" within or without the established areas by subsidizing local companies to explore. Suppliers and contractors will be kept busy, and some private concerns will take long risks with public money. Some may become rich. Nobody else will gain.

But this is not quite the story—indeed it may be the lesser half. For there is a perfectly sincere belief, particularly in Continental Europe, that oil is somehow special. Oil is not a vulgar commodity like the others, but must be the stuff of high strategy and national policy. One must not be "at the mercy of the companies"—whatever that means—especially since they are huge companies, huge international companies, huge "Anglo-Saxon" companies. To many Continental Europeans, this is the security problem. Their politeness in rarely saying this publicly has not served them well, nor anybody else. For if the fear were voiced and freely discussed, it would be seen to be groundless. "The companies" can only cut off or threaten or exploit a given country if they can act together as a unit. But even the loose cartel of the 1930s has been dead nearly thirty years; like John Brown's body, it is moldering in the grave, but the myth goes marching on. Like other delusions, it harms those who believe it.

Perhaps forty years ago or more the handful of Anglo-American companies who were then the international industry could have been used as the tool of British and American policy. Hence there may have been sense in laws like the French act of 1928. But to imagine the companies as tools of Anglo-American policy today is far-fetched. The producing countries would not permit it, and they have the physical force on the spot. Indeed, the Anglo-Americans were singled out during the brief 1967 boycott. Fear of "dependence on the oil companies" is just another distressing example of prejudice against big business and against foreigners. Xenophobia is not only wrong but, like most prejudices, expensive.

III

Domestic coal production obviously gives *permanent* assurance of a *part* of the fuel supply, which is badly out of joint with the need of temporary assurance of *all* or nearly all its fuel supply. What is the price of this limited security? We can make some approximate calculations for Western Europe.

The cheapest grade of coal in the European Coal and Steel Community is priced about $16 per metric ton at the mine.[4] Subsidies come to over $5, so the total cost to the economy can be no less than $21.[5] A metric ton of fuel oil has nearly 1.5 times the heat value of a metric ton of coal, and hence would be no more or less expensive than if it cost $31.[6]

Since 1958, heavy fuel oil has been freely available at the Channel ports at about $12 per metric ton, varying perhaps by 10 percent up or down. Past mid-1966, up to the outbreak of war, it was steady around $10.50.[7] The loss to the E.E.C. Countries' economy is $20–$21 per metric ton of oil equivalent (t.o.e.). British costs seem much lower, in the neighborhood of $14.75 per metric ton. Taken together, the weighted average cost is $18.30 per ton, $27/t.o.e. and average loss to O.E.C.D. Europe is about $16.35/t.o.e.[8]

So bruising is this simple fact to so many commercial, political, and intellectual egotisms that many ingenious explanations are offered and eagerly accepted why oil prices are "abnormally" and "temporarily" [sic] low. By confusion over "marginal cost," the "depressed" prices are seriously ascribed to a surplus of refining capacity, which in fact was so chronically short of demand that it doubled in the six years 1960–66. But truth, like cheerfulness, will break through. The experts of the European Communities, who in 1962 had projected a long-term value for heavy fuel oil of $18 per metric ton, revised it in early 1966—showing a commendable independence of spirit—to $12.50, thus wiping out most of the wishful reckoning.[9]

To be sure, the coal cost is an aggregate or average. Some mines cost much less than others to operate, and indeed the refusal of governments to let the whole range of cost be calculated and published, their insistence on average costing and on prices to cover average costs, deserves more attention than it has received. But retrenchment is too little too late. Lord Robens of the British National Coal Board is sufficient authority. His cheapest pits, he avers, can produce at 3 pence per therm (35 cents per million btu) or $14.50 per metric t.o.e. If we only give him more time and much more money he can some day produce much more coal at this rock-bottom figure.[10] Unfortunately, it is many years since oil was this high at the Channel ports.

In 1966 coal production in the O.E.C.D. countries of Europe was about 212 million t.o.e., excluding coking coal.[11] Their total replacement by oil would have saved $3.5 (£1.25) billion per year. That was the deadweight loss to Western Europe.

The figure may seem too bad to be true. As a near-term projection, it is an underestimate. First, coal costs are increasing every year. Second, heavy oil costs less in Southern Europe ($1 per tone less in Italy). Third, if coal were phased out to be replaced by oil, the price of oil would almost certainly *decrease*. For the Middle East reserves are so vast that additional capacity can be created to produce several times the current output and at a cost so low that it would be vastly profitable to do so.[12] Freedom by European buyers to buy in the cheapest market would send oil company salesmen rushing to every electricity company as the first step in expanding sales, and the resulting competition would send prices down. The lessons of recent experience are plain: in those countries where trade in fuel is freest, and sales most buoyant, prices are lowest.

Fourth and perhaps in the long run most important: the price of coal is being used as a reference price or standard by which to judge new energy sources, such as nuclear power. In Britain, the Dungeness B power station will produce electric power according to the original estimates, at $15.60 (£5.6) per metric t.o.e.[13] It is painful to see the near-euphoria which this produces among British observers who simply pay no attention to oil because it is excluded by hypothesis—it is some kind of odd stuff which, as everyone knows, sells at a temporarily abnormally low price. Late in 1966 the estimated Dungeness B cost was further increased.[14] Even looking beyond to the next generation of reactors, and assuming the best, Sir William Penney estimates that *if* the later A.G.R. stations perform as hoped for, generating costs will by the mid-1970s equate to fossil fuel at 2.25 d/therm (25.3 cents/mbtu), heavy fuel oil at $10.90, which is not even as good as what is available right now and takes no account of advancing technology in fossil fuel use (which Sir William, like all observers, considers as very impressive in the recent past).[15] But with fictitious coal prices as a standard, huge amounts of scarce capital may be wasted on uneconomic nuclear power stations to match the near quarter of a billion dollars (£89 million) which the National Coal Board pours annually down holes in the ground.[16] The E.E.C. is even more wasteful because their coal is even more expensive.

Of course one cannot tolerate the abrupt dismissal of close to a million mine employees. Once this is understood, the whole problem of fuel cheapness and security is bathed in light: *European coal production is no longer an industry, it is only a means of social insurance.* Awkward and wasteful, it can be abolished to the immense gain of the miners themselves before anyone else. To see why, we should first reckon the costs of an adequate security program by stockpiling crude oil.

IV

The cheapest and best place to store crude oil is at the ocean terminals where it arrives. These are imposing enough today, but not compared with the terminals for supertankers of 300,000 tons, the first of which is going up at Bantry Bay in Ireland, others in Japan. Storage and oil to fill it should be provided at government expense, but for the sake of economy, private enterprise should manage the facilities and commingle oil freely with theirs. For additional capacity is a valuable right to an oil company. The reason in brief is that larger tankers are much cheaper than small ones, but require much more storage capacity ashore. The interval between tanker arrivals increases in strict proportion to the increased size of the ships. But the amount of inventory needed increases somewhat more than proportionately. In effect, many small tankers are a spreading of risk, and fewer large tankers a concentration. Therefore, if an oil company managing a given amount of oil in storage were permitted to draw upon the government stock within a range of, say, 10 percent, provided only that replacement was made within a short period, it might be worth their while to bid for the right to manage the inventory.

In any case, the operating storage cost would be very low, but the capital outlay on the facilities and of the oil to fill them would be heavy, and the annual expense would essentially be the interest on the capital employed. The writer's calculations of storage cost, made some years ago, seem to have been taken seriously by other observers,[17] but the new conditions have made them obsolete. Today storage facilities can be provided at a big ocean terminal for about $1.25 per barrel.[18] Oil can be purchased f.o.b. the Persian Gulf today by big credit-worthy buyers for less than $1.25 (the coincidence of the two figures is purely accidental, of course) and shipped, emphasizing the cheaper summer seasons, at 43 cents per barrel to Rotterdam and 37 cents to Marseille or Northern Italy. (Under the usual method of rate quotation, this would be INTAscale less 65 percent through Suez, less 67.5 around the Cape.) An average delivered cost to Europe would then be about $1.65, North and South taken together. There should be no undignified hassle over this price. The oil companies are selling for less to some buyers and realizing less from crude devoted to their refining-marketing operations. The value of a barrel of products sold in Europe, less marketing and refining costs (which must include a market rate of return on the capital employed), does not return them as much as $1.25 today.[19]

Thus the capital outlay needed to store a barrel is about $1.25 + $1.65 = $2.90. The notional interest rate should not be mere interest cost to the government, but rather the return that the funds would fetch in private industry. Or, what comes to the same thing, the burden should be reckoned as the amount that would be needed to pay he holders of debt securities and equity securities to advance the money to a private low-risk enterprise—including also that part of the profit enjoyed by government as tax receiver. By this standard, the 4.5 percent used to reckon atomic power projects in the United States, or coal in the United Kingdom, is nonsensical, and even the 7.5 percent used in the United Kingdom is too low. We will use 10 percent discount, and an allowance for the limited life of the facilities (25 years) would raise the effective annual capital charge to nearly 11 percent. Then the annual capital cost of storing a barrel of oil is 30 cents, and adding 5 cents for operating costs, the total is 35 cents. In other words, if we had to keep in stock a whole year's supply, the cost would be 35 cents per barrel; six months would cost half.

How many months' supply do we need? the French Minister of Industry in November 1966, estimated six months' because the economies of the producing nations could not support a longer shutdown.[20] If M. Marcellin meant that none of the supplying countries could hold out any longer, he was surely wrong; but if he meant that not all of them could hold out even that long and that the chain was as strong as the weakest link, he was right. The producing nations involved in the 1967 crisis never were able to close ranks even at the start, and their embargo began crumbling almost as soon as it began. Hence six months seems much longer than necessary, but it will serve as the upper end of the range. Six months' special storage costing 18 cents per barrel plus the normal commercial stock of about 45 days, plus at least one month by stretching the stock through rationing, gives Europe nearly nine months.

The government of South Africa has had to make similar calculations, but their danger is of course much greater since they could conceivably find both producing countries and consuming countries lined up against them, and as a relatively small market, they could not count on the producing nations being subject to unbearable pressure because of lost revenues. There are no official estimates, but the *Rand Daily Mail* of Johannesburg has reported that the government was providing eighteen months' supply,[21] and I believe the report has not been denied.

Although six months' inventory atop the normal two seems adequate, we can backstop it very cheaply with two years' supply for the electric power industry. Dual-firing is cheap to install when going from coal to oil, but not the reverse. Henceforth all new power stations should be oil, but as a security measure they should either be made double-firing from the outset (as are coastal stations in the United States and Scandinavia) or at least required to provide the stoker space needed in case of a later conversion to dual-firing. Coal production can then make a last contribution to the welfare of Europe. The coal itself is costless, for it will in any case be produced as the industry is phased out. The problem is only the cheapest and least unsightly place to store it, taking due account of where it will be eventually used. The electric power industry of O.E.C.D. Europe used 153 million metric t.o.e. in 1964, or 240 million short tons of coal.[22] In the United States, ground storage is provided, and profitably, for private companies at 15 cents per short ton during he peak December–July period, with a movement in and out; so 20 cents per short ton per year of dead storage seems more than adequate.[23] Two years' supply under 1964 conditions would mean a full year's supply in 1974 since the industry has been approximately doubling every decade and would cost $96 million.

Thus Europe could be assured of from one to two years' electricity supply and well over nine months' supply of oil (for some, though not all, of the heavy fuel oil could be diverted to non-electricity consumption, and to a significant extent the slack would be transmitted to the lighter fuels) at an annual cost under 1965 conditions of about $872 (£312) million. (This is 17.5 cents per barrel multiplied by 4.4 billion barrels of oil-equivalent of total oil and coal energy used excluding coking coal and adding the $96 million for coal storage.) Since the annual cost of supporting a superfluous coal industry was in 1964 $3.5 (£1.25) billion, the substitution of adequate security for inadequate security actually saves Europe $2.6 billion (£9.30 million) per year.

If, as now seems more likely, only three months' special supply need be stored, the cost would be $484 (£176) million and annual savings over $3 (£1.07) billion.

V

Once we turn from where we should be going to how to get there, the academic researcher's knowledge runs into sharply diminishing returns. But three problems are worth a quick glance: the time period, the coal miners, and the balance of payments.

Even if storage for security were accepted tomorrow as a policy or objective, it would take at least a year to perfect actual programs, to find likely sites, etc. Indeed, the size of the stockpile would have to be carefully reckoned. The estimates made in this paper have taken no account, for example, of European natural gas as part of the energy supply. Yet within a short time it will not be negligible. It might also be worth a last effort to inquire into American coal, which would be only slightly more expensive to buy (and much cheaper to store) if the high United States railroad freight rate, discriminatory against export sales, were lowered. Chances of success do not look too good. The writer had occasion to warn, on the basis of data ending in 1963, that if the discrimination did not cease, steam coal exports to Western Europe would dwindle.[24] They have in fact dropped by over 30 percent in three years, at a time when total E.E.C. fuel consumption is up 11 percent.[25] But the official optimism about a big market for United States steam coal at only slightly less than current prices remains unshaken and based on the same comfortable illusion that oil prices are temporarily abnormally low.

If it takes two to three years before plans are drawn up and storage built, no time is lost because it will take that long for prices to come back to mid-1967 levels. At the time of writing (beginning October 1967) there is no sign of an early reopening of the Suez Canal. Mr. George Brown was apparently unsuccessful in trying to get Norwegian support for his proposal to have clearing work done at the expense of the maritime nations, but with all receipts going to the United Arab Republic and taking no notice of the problem of the navigation of Israeli ships in the canal.[26]

Probably the canal will some day be reopened under circumstances not foreseeable today. But its importance will be much less, and even the absolute volume of shipments may never regain the mid-1967 level. There has already been much silting, and a decrease in maximum permissible draft from 38 to 34 feet means that the largest ship acceptable drops from about 60,000 to about 34,000 deadweight tons, which in view of the distribution of ship sizes is drastic indeed. Hence a new equilibrium must wait on the addition of enough large tankers (175,000 tons and upward) to round the Cape at total costs somewhat lower than the old canal transit by smaller ships.

The time needed to perfect plans and build facilities could also be used for the redeployment of mine labor. By the end of 1967, Western European underground and surface workers taken together will number about 900,000,[27] and their average wage is around $2500 (£893) per year. Hence, even to pay them all their current wages for their lifetime would cost about $2.2 billion (£785 million) a year, leaving a clear economic gain, which would increase rapidly over time. In practice, coal employees age fifty-five and over would probably be retired forthwith on full salary, while younger men could be released with either current wages guaranteed for a time ahead, or a lump-sum payment, so that either way they were sure of not losing out. Generosity should be the order of the day. Society benefits from changing these men from pensioners to productive workers and should therefore stand the costs of changing them. Of course I assume here a certain value judgment: that we own certain duties to our fellow citizens as individuals or as families, but that we owe nothing to a corporate personality known as "the coal industry," and nothing more than thanks to those who, like Lord Robens, have tried their considerable and commendable best to do the impossible. Others will feel insulted at the proposal to put away "their" coal industry, but there is no arguing about tastes.

This brings us to the balance of payments. Getting rid of coal means a large addition to the import content of fuel. Furthermore, four months' supply, say, when Area fuel needs are about 14 million barrels daily, means

1.7 billion barrels of storage, costing, if my estimates are correct, nearly $5 (£1.79) billion. Import content of both oil supply and storage varies widely among nations. Only one general remark is in order.

The balance of payments can be considered as a short-term liquidity *constraint*, like the cash management of a private firm. Expenditures profitable to a business enterprise must either be postponed or else covered by special financing arrangements if the necessary funds are not otherwise available. But to refrain from profitable expenditures permanently because cash is not available immediately is the kind of ultra-conservatism which assures the death of the enterprise.

For a nation, the balance of payments may be regarded as not a temporary liquidity constraint but as a permanent policy objective: autarchy. It is an expensive luxury for rich countries, but not ruinous. However, given fixed exchange rates, it means permanent incurable foreign-exchange deficits. For if an economy is to accept expensive food, cement, energy, or what not for the sake of saving foreign exchange, the level of domestic costs is so high that exports cannot find markets. The plight of underdeveloped countries, undone by their passion for import substitution, ought to serve as a warning to those more fortunate.

There is no dilemma of cheap *versus* secure fuel for Europe, nor for Japan, Australia, and other Asiatic nations. The only way to ensure cheap and secure fuel is to stockpile oil and get rid of coal. The measurable economic gain is huge, but the non-economic gain is not to be despised: the end of a filthy scar on the landscape.

Notes

1. In 1950 Iran output was 663 thousand b/d of a total Middle East output of 1760, or 37.6 percent. See annual reviews, recently entitled "World Wide Oil," in the *Oil and Gas Journal*, and recently *Oil and Gas International*.

2. See the *Oil and Gas Journal*, December 26, 1966, p. 122, giving discovery dates of Nigerian fields, each one of which represented an effort of at least a few years, perhaps of many.

3. *Oil and Gas Journal*, December 31, 1956, p. 154, on the beginnings of Libyan exploration, and on Morocco, Algeria, and Gabon. There is also mention of an encouraging oil show in Nigeria, other than the discovery recorded in n. 2.

4. European Coal and Steel Community, 1967, *Annual Report*, Statistical Appendix, Table 13. Taxes are excluded; they range from 1 percent in Belgium to 11 percent in France. An average of prices weighted by total output in the various producing basins is $16.10.

5. E.C.S.C., *Nouvelles Réflexions sur les Perspectives Energétiques, de la Communauté +
Européenne* (1966), p. 21. These are largely supplementary labor costs. A weighted
average (1966 *Annual Report*, Statistical Appendix, Table 2) is $5.11. Hence total
average cost per ton is $16.10 + $5.11 = $21.21.

6. Conversion factors can only be approximate. Those used here are from *Petroleum
Press Service*, giving fuel oil 18.3 and bituminous coal from 10.2 to 14.6 thousand
btu/lb., we calculate with a middle value of 12.35. Then 18.30/12.35 = 1.48, and
$21.21 × 1.48 = $31.40.

7. There is a variety of sources, the periodic reports being in *Platt's Oilgram Price
Service* (New York) and *Europa Ol-Telegramm* (Hamburg). During the first half of
1967 it was around $10.70 for barge lots; cargoes were about 25 cents cheaper.
Hence $31.40 less $10.50 is $20.90. Moreover, the operating cost is somewhat less
in burning oil than coal.

8. According to the National Board for Prices & Incomes, *Report No. 12: Coal Prices*
(Cmd. 2919, 1966), total estimated colliery expenditure 1966−67 was £810 million plus £10 million for fixed asset replacement. Total debt was £960 million
(p. 2); an interest charge of 7.5 percent is applied, rather than the official one of 4.8
percent, which means £72/73 million. Although interest is a fixed cost, it must
be used as a proxy for the capital cost of maintaining a given rate of output. (The
Prices & Income Board notes that electricity earns 6.75 percent, gas higher than 6
percent, and "industry generally" 12 to 14 percent. Surely the last figure is a closer
approximation to the true drain on the British economy. However, we use the 7.5
percent of the United Kingdom Atomic Energy Authority as a conservative estimate of capital cost.) Total cost is then £893 million, which comes to £5.27 or
$14.75/ton for 170 million tons. E.E.C. plus U.K. production totals 380 million
tons, averaging $17.30 per ton, or $27.05 per ton of oil equivalent. Subtracting
$10.70 gives $16.35. We take no account of the very small production in other
countries.

   This estimate seems consistent with that of Turvey and Nobay, in the *Economic
Journal*, vol. 75 (December 1965), p. 792, of coal sold "to industry" in 1964 at £5.8
($16.25) per ton, since a delivery charge is presumably included. (Sources and
methods are not explained.) Brechling and Surrey, "An International Comparison
of Production Techniques: The Coal-Fired Electricity Generating Industry,"
National Institute Economic Review, May 1966, p. 33, gives the 1963 average price
of coal delivered to generating plants as 42 pence (49 cents) per million btu, a
much better measure of price. assuming 29 million btu per long ton (12,400
btu/pound and 2240 pound tons), the price per ton would be £5.02 ($14.05). This
again seems consistent, since coal delivered to electric generating plants would be
expected to be cheaper than the average for all coal at the mine. According to the
Central Electricity Generating Board, *Annual Report and Accounts 1966−67*, pp. 4
and 13, the cost in 1966 exceeded 46.9 pence.

9. Compare *Nouvelles Réflexions* (1966), p. 27, with the *Etude sur les Perspectives
Energétiques à Long Terme de la Communauté Européenne* (1962), Ch. 9, Sec. 4. The
Etude was reviewed in the *Economic Journal*, vol. 74 (1964), by E. F. Schumacher,
identified only as living in London. He criticized projection thirteen years ahead,

to 1975: "These figures are not worth the paper they are written on. They are a case of spurious verisimilitude bordering on mendacity."

An article in the London *Times* (April 11, 1963), had predicted thirty-seven years ahead, to A.D. 2000: a steeply rising real cost or even physical shortage of fuel. The writer was economic adviser to the National Coal Board, E. F. Schumacher.

10. Address to Coal Industry Society, March 6, 1967.

11. U.S. Bureau of Mines, *International Coal Trade*, May 1967, p. 17 gives 398 million tons, or 269 million t.o.e. Coking coal consumption in 1964 was estimated by O.E.C.D., *Energy Policy* (1966), p. 32, at 65 million t.o.e., or 96 m.t.c.e., and it has not changed appreciably since. Imports in 1966 were just under 25 million metric tons, and if we assume that half was for coking coal, then European production of coking coal (8 percent or less) was about (96 less 12) 84 m.t.c.e. or 57 m.t.o.e. Hence European coal produced for other than coke was in 1966 about 314 m.t.c.e. or 212 m.t.o.e. Reckoning at $16.35 per m.t.o.e., this comes to $3.47 billion.

12. M. A. Adelman, "Oil Production Costs in Four Areas," *1966 Proceedings of the Council on Economics*, A.I.M.E. (American Institute of Mining, Metallurgical and Petroleum Engineers); conveniently summarized in *Petroleum Press Service*, May 1966. Hereafter cited as O.P.C.F.A.

13. Tentative estimates are presented in detail in my letter to *The Economist*, July 17, 1965, p. 272. Revised estimates based on C.E.G.B. data were presented to the Tokyo meeting of the World Power Congress in October 1966.

14. Testimony presented to the Select Committee on Science and Technology in March 1967 by Mr. Brown; the calculations are as of September 1966.

15. Sir William Penney, *Nuclear Power* (the Citrine Lecture 1967), pp. 8–9.

16. During 1960–65, N.C.B. expenditures were £532 ($1490) million, £89 ($242) million annually; specific colliery expenditure was £462 ($1295) million, £77 ($216) million annually. But even noncolliery expenditures are for coal products. Hence the total is coal investment, and totally wasteful.

17. "The World Oil Outlook," in *National Resources and Economic Development*, ed., Marion Clawson (John Hopkins Press for Resources for the Future, 1964), pp. 121–23. Cited in *P.E.P., A Fuel Policy for Britain* (1965?), p. 183.

18. Compare the $1.27/barrel at Kharg Island in Iran (OPCFA). Construction costs at Bantry would be lower, land costs higher. The first Japanese central terminal system will include storage facilities for three million tons (22.2 million barrels). The cost of the entire project, including sea berths, docks, pumps, etc., is estimated at $32.2 (£11.5) million, or $1.45 (£0.518) per barrel. *Zosen* August 1967, p. 18. Clearly a doubling or more of storage alone would cost only a fraction of the average cost of the whole operation. Hence our investment figure may be much too high.

19. The detailed evidence is in a study now in preparation, well informed persons in the trade will not (privately) contradict the statement.

20. République Française, Assemblée Nationale, 2e Séance du novembre 1966, p. 4321.

21. *Rand Daily Mail* (Johannesburg), August 24, 1966, p. 1.

22. In 1965 (later figures not available) O.E.C.D. Europe consumed 918.4 m.t.c.e. non-coking coal plus oil. Bureau of Mines, *International Coal Trade*, February 1967, p. 15. Conversion of the total to oil is on the basis of equivalence of coal to crude oil, not fuel oil, but using the same source and method as in note 12, the proportion is a barrel of oil of $34°$ gravity equal to 0.207 metric tons of coal, hence 4.44 billion barrels.

23. Interstate Commerce Commission Tariff 1355-A, Bessemer & Lake Erie R. R. that the operation is profitable is shown by the later expansion of the original facilities, and by another railroad setting up a similar installation. Another terminal was announced early in 1967, with initial capacity of 1.2 million and ultimate capacity of 4.5 million short tons, costing $5.75 (£2.05) million. *N.C.P.C. Newsletter*, February 2, 1967, p. 4. Hence the capacity cost per ton lies between $2.85 (£1.02) and $1.28 (£0.46) but much nearer the smaller figure. At 11 percent capital charge, the cost would be about 14 cents (1 shilling) per short ton per year, which is consistent with the other estimates. Capital and operating costs would be lower for dead storage, but these are at best first approximations.

24. M. A. Adelman, "American Coal in Western Europe," *Journal of Industrial Economics*, vol. 14, 1966.

25. For exports of steam coal, see *International Coal Trade*, July 1967, p. 6. For total Community consumption see *Annual Reports*: 1964, p. 60, 1967, p. 65.

26. *Journal de la Marine Marchande*, 31 August 1967, p. 1931.

27. According to the *Colliery Guardian* (London), January 20, 1967, U.K. coal manpower fell from 510,556 end-1963 to 446,788 end-1965 and 413, 667 end-1966. The annual decline rate over the three years was thus 7 percent, in 1966, 7.5 percent. The *Report* of the National Board for Prices and Income, *op. cit.*, expects an increasing loss rate (p. 6), and the end-1966 employment noted above is lower than their estimate. Hence to subtract 7 additional percent for an end-1967 estimate of 385,000 seems conservative.

The attentive reader will have noticed that British labor requirements per ton are much higher than E.C.S.C., yet prices are much lower. This anomaly might repay further study.

According to the *Annual Reports* of the European Coal and Steel Community, the 1963–66 decline (as of end-September) averaged 5.6 percent per year, but was down 11 percent in 1965–66 alone (1967, tab. 42). From the first half of 1966 to that of 1967, the decline in underground workers was 13.5 percent. (*International Coal Trade*, August 1967, p. 9.) Projecting the September 1966 figure forward by fifteen months at that rate comes to 525 thousand. Added to the British total, this is 910 thousand for all Western Europe.

The highest-paid workers in the E.C.S.C. coal mines receive respectively $2640, $2900, $2800, in Germany, Belgium, and France, respectively. E.C.S.C. 1967 *Annual Report*, tab. 53.

23

The Energy Problem

My great teacher, Joseph Schumpeter, once said that rational thought was only a special case of proper business management. He went a bit too far there, as he often did to shock his audience. But a series on "business problem of the 1970s" is a good focus for analyzing the energy problems of the next decade.

We can give short shrift to "the energy crisis." There are plenty of fossils fuels and no limit to potential electrical capacity. It is all a matter of money. Anybody asking whether "supplies will be adequate" to meet our "needs" or "requirements" should go back to square one and start asking the relevant questions: how much will customers demand, at a given price at a given time; how much will it pay business to bring forth, at a given place at a given time; at what point do the lines cross, to clear the market?

Our trouble is that a lot of lines are not crossing. There is no crisis but a collection of problems, engendered partly by bad luck and partly by bad management. They will not soon disappear. Business and consumers must look forward to a disturbed period of rising prices, shifting and unexpected relationships among energy sources, uncertain supply, and political storms.

Energy is supplied, and responds to effective demand, through a network of markets which are today functioning badly, for three broad reasons. First are the errors, lags, and frictions inevitable in a changing, improving economy.

Second is the long overdue phasing-in of external social costs of energy production and use—damage to the environment—into the accounts of the companies which compose the energy industries. As a people, we talk a good game of free enterprise. In practice, in some areas, we have long followed Karl Marx's slogan, "to each according to his needs." We have

Reprinted from *Business Problems of the Seventies* (New York: New York University Press, 1973), 123–140.

socialized the streets and highways, the air and the water, letting anyone have his fill at no cost. Then we wonder at congestion and pollution.

The costs of non-pollution can in theory and will in time be incorporated into the supply prices of energy. They will be borne by the ultimate consumers to the extent that a cleaner environment is desired, which can only be worked out as a political consensus, regional in some respects, national in others. In retrospect, these will look like fairly simple calculations and later generations will wonder why we were so slow and awkward in working them out. As Thomas Jefferson said in his old age, his own generation was very much like succeeding generations—but without their experience, and a day of experience was worth a year of theory. But the process of "internalizing" these costs is appallingly slow. Not only are we truly ignorant of much basic data but there is also a general climate of mistrust, a great deal of nostalgia for a partly non-existent past, and finally the lack of any machinery to bring together information and policy into a forum for efficient analysis and decision. The law courts have taken the strain which they were not designed to do.

The third reason for market failure and probably the most important is the distortion of the mechanism by public policy or private monopoly, thereby generating shortages and surpluses which are not only damaging but lead to further interference and loss.

These three types of market failures can be discussed by reviewing the most important energy markets.

Electric Power

(1) For 20 years after World War II, generating costs were substantially reduced by building larger and better plants. The process petered out in 1965, for reasons not entirely clear. Actual new capacity fell somewhat short of expected, and many of the new plants have been unreliable. Unexpected shutdowns have sometimes made far-off waves. Nuclear power came on slowly because it took longer to de-bug than expected. The inflation of 1965 and afterward bore especially severely on construction costs including both nuclear and fossil fuel construction. Finally, there was probably also a once-and-for-all shift to new electrical appliances in many households.

(2) Environmental costs have been imposed not only in the form of more severe, hence more costly standards, but in opposition to any new generating plant and most of all to new nuclear plants, because of fear of thermal pollution, and accidents on site and in waste disposal. The social

machinery for handling these types of opposition is defective. The Atomic Energy Commission licenses nuclear generating plants. State and local agencies license fossil fuel plants. Any plant can be challenged in the courts under the National Environmental Policy Act. The required environmental impact statements have been numerous, bulky, often unread, and also ineffective. Where a court for very good reasons feels itself uninformed, the only safe action and perhaps the only proper one is to prevent any possible irreparable harm and stop the project.

Much of the opposition has really been not to environmental impact but to the feeling that we somehow "don't need anymore electricity." This has been confused with the belief, which may be perfectly justifiable, that we would be better off with zero population growth. Yet 80 percent of the growth in electric power use is accounted for rising income levels and only 20 percent by rising population. The promising new technologies, some of them absurdly simple, and some highly complex, ranging from cooling ponds where fish thrive to dry cooling towers, must be discussed amidst the din of adversary shouting and the uncertainty as to whether new plants will be permitted at all in any given place.

(3) The last reason for the electrical power shortage has been in the fact that electrical power prices have been set to cover historical costs. During inflation, power is therefore artificially cheap. It is sold at prices which cannot be maintained in the long run. Business and consumers have been subsidized and misled into making ever more electricity-intensive investments.

Electricity demand is generally considered unresponsive to price. In fact our meager knowledge of this relation is an embarrassment. But so far as we can tell, residential-commercial demand has about a unit elasticity, and industrial demand is around 2, i.e., a 1 percent decrease in the price will give about a 2 percent increase in the amount demanded. These are long run responses. Let us suppose the demand for electricity as a whole has an elasticity of about 1.5, long run. Since 1958, the general price level has risen by 47 percent, while the price of electricity has remained approximately constant. If we suppose that because of built-in lags the elasticity of the response to date has been around unity, then a decrease in the real price of 32 percent (1.0/1.47) would generate a consumption increase of roughly 32 percent; it we assume longer lags and a response elasticity of only 0.75, the amount demanded will increase about 24 percent. Thus, the artificially low prices explain much of the unexpectedly fast growth of electricity demand in the late 1960s, just when supply ceased to expand at the previous rate.

Coal

At about the same time that the long-term productivity increases in coal mining seemed to be petering out temporarily or permanently, the Health Mine and Safety Act of 1969 made production more expensive. Whether the average increase in price was nearer to 50 cents per ton or $1.50 per ton will in time become more clear. For new large mines I suspect the true figure is closer to the lower one. But this is minor indeed compared to the environmental restrictions which have very sharply limited the use of coal. So far there is no way of low cost low-sulfur burning. Desulfurizing of stack gases has been extensively studied and has so far been quite a disappointment both as to operating efficiency and as to cost. Whether standards need be as high as they have recently been set is a question that needs to be studied rather more than it has been. Opinion certainly varies from one side of the Atlantic to the other. But it seems doubtful that standards will be greatly relaxed in the near future. And if one suspects as I do that standards have been set somewhat more severely in the recent past than they will eventually be set, I have difficulty in deciding whether the greater misfortune would be in keeping them as they are or in a backlash which would sacrifice the substantial progress made so far.

Underground mining of coal is "damn dirty, damn dull, and damn dangerous." It is also damaging to the environment by reason of acid drainage and dumps. Strip mining of coal can be very damaging on steep hillsides which are the rule in the East, but in the high plains of the Rocky Mountains there are huge deposits of low-sulfur coal which can be cheaply strip-mined and where the terrain can be restored at a cost per ton which seems quite low in relation to the production cost. But the development of these deposits is blocked today by local opposition. I admit to sympathy for people, particularly the Indian tribe which has refused proffered leases. who put their money where their mouth is. They prefer the way of life they have known, having few neighbors within sight. They resent and fear the invasion of their states by a horde of foreigners from outlandish places like Illinois or Pennsylvania who will turn the place upside down. I suspect the final result will be reached by the usual political process. In words of one syllable: there are more of us than there are of them. But for the time being coal cannot take the strain from natural gas and oil. Nobody can predict when if ever the large amounts of coal in the ground will become a useful stock of "reserves."

Natural Gas

Natural gas is an outstanding example of the three tendencies we note.
(1) First, the natural and the unforeseen. There has been a failure of discovery that goes back about 15–20 years. To some extent the rapidly rising price level of the 1950s expressed this growing scarcity. Curiously enough however there appeared to be an equilibrium of supply and demand from about 1957 to 1966. Ceiling prices fixed by the Federal Power Commission did no more than ratify prices reached in the market. The reason was basically that reserves in the field were sold in great lots to meet the expected demand in the near and distant future. A reserve of gas was like a durable product and the demand for gas reserves was subject to the familiar accelerator phenomenon, which can also be a decelerator. Suppose for example that the demand for gas by consumers has been growing at 5 percent per year, and that old commitments have been expiring at the rate of about 2 percent per year. Hence total demand has been growing by 7 percent. In order to keep a proper or normal ratio of reserves to consumption, which we will assume at 20 to 1, reserves must be expanded at the rate of 1.4 times the current *increase* in consumption, i.e., 20 × 7 percent equals 140 percent. Suppose that demand increases this year by only 3 percent instead of the usual 5. This is so minor a perturbation that we might easily overlook it. Yet the total increase is now 5 percent per year instead of 7, the required stock of new reserves is now 100 percent rather than 140 percent, a decline of nearly one third. And this lower demand for new reserves for a time masked the underlying situation of growing scarcity.

But starting in 1965, this retardation ended along with several developments which all fell the wrong way. Inflation increased costs and stimulated demand. There was a growing exhaustion of low-cost deposits.
(2) The growing severity of environmental requirements also increased the demand for gas at any given price, because it was a clean-burning fuel.
(3) Had the market been allowed to work, the price of gas would have increased very considerably. But the rigid ceilings now curtailed the development of new gas reserves while gas as demanded by consumers from pipelines soared. The result was a huge excess of demand over supply. Nobody could have predicted the changing ratio of reserves demanded to new gas consumed, or the impact of the inflation. The mistake was in not letting the market for natural gas adjust to changes, which is the chief social purpose of setting up a market system in the first place. True, for years some tried to persuade themselves and the rest of us that natural gas

production was really not a competitive market, but fortunately that argument has been so discredited as no longer to need discussion.

The effects of the "regulation-induced shortage" as my colleague Paul MacAvoy well names it, may endure to the end of the century. All the excess demand has been channeled into offshore sources, chiefly liquid natural gas to be imported starting in the late 1970s. The prices are extravagantly high and still rising, and these prices are the direct result of the artificially low prices set by regulation. Moreover, the high-priced gas is not offered to consumers at that price. It is rolled in with much cheaper gas. Thus gas consumers, both residential and business, are confronted—for the time being—with little change in price. They are deceived into still large purchases of, and commitments to, natural gas. One could not design a better system to maximize the excess demand and instability.

The gas industry has roamed the world to flush out available supplies—for example, diverting Algerian gas from Europe, where it would normally go at lower transport cost. Thereby we have alarmed other large consuming nations with fears of a nonexistent world shortage. In fact, outside the United States natural gas supplies are even more overabundant than crude oil supplies, which we will discuss later. The advisability of letting prices rise in order to stimulate supply is now generally recognized. I am not an optimist on the response. As I mentioned earlier, new discoveries have been declining for many years. It is wrong to extrapolate without some theory, but a simple theory, sampling of prospects without replacement, would seem to indicate that barring some breakthrough there will simply be less and less found in the years to come, at higher costs.

The main response to higher prices must therefore be on the side of demand. At present somewhat more than half of all natural gas is consumed by industry, mostly in or near the principal gas-producing areas. In 1970, industrial gas used in the producing areas was about equal to all residential consumption. Higher prices would direct the gas away from industry to residential users, and permit a doubling of their consumption, with no imported gas.

The current pattern of gas consumption was created by the historic accident that natural gas was produced in areas with relatively low population density, far from the great urban centers to which it had to be transported at relatively high cost. Hence the price at the wellhead had to be very low relative to coal and oil to clear the market under competitive conditions. Therefore it displaced those fuels. Given the relatively high prices which would clear the market today the old pattern is no longer appropriate.

But there seems to be an inbred reluctance to discuss the role of price as controlling demand to ration the supply. It is a little bit like the attitude toward discussions of sex in public a generation or two ago. It was felt that somehow nice people didn't talk about such things. Similarly one looks in vain for any discussion in all the welter of congressional and public debate about "the energy crisis" and how to conserve the precious stuff, for an acknowledgment that whatever is or is not discovered, higher prices will take gas out from under boilers in the Southwest and send it to Chicago and New York. If this were done soon, liquid natural gas projects would be cancelled, and a gross extravagance avoided. It would be best that a few survive, as a constant warning of past folly and a reminder of what not to do.

Domestic Crude Oil

(1) As with natural gas, starting somewhat earlier, going somewhat more gradually, discoveries have diminished very much over the years. During 1945–50, about 4/5 of the new reserves created were from newly discovered fields, the rest by more extensive development of old fields. By the middle 1960s, the process had been reversed. It would be only a mild exaggeration to say that the domestic oil industry devotes itself to creating *new reserves* out of *old fields*.

Reserves are not discovered. They are the ready shelf inventory, created by drilling wells and installing production capacity. There is a very large cushion of oil in fields already known which can and in time will be developed, at markedly increased cost.

(2) The environmental impact on the oil industry has been largely in the complete stoppage of refinery building. Because of opposition to permitting refinery construction, and because of uncertainty about product specifications, particularly lead, refining capacity is now substantially short of demand and the discrepancy increases every day. As we will see shortly, this is not the only reason for the shortage.

(3) But the market in crude oil and refined products is an outstanding example of antisocial distortion of market mechanisms. For years state output restrictions had kept prices artificially high and promoted the creation of much excess capacity. (For drawing attention to this fact I was once denounced by name by the then Democratic Governor of Texas, Mr. John B. Connally). These high prices were reinforced by tax inducements and also by quota limitations on imports.

Over the last three years the situation has changed quite drastically, but our thinking and policy have not changed with it. Excess capacity dried up partly because of improved regulation, partly because of the growing real scarcity, and partly because import controls which had formerly been a prop to prices now turned into the contrary. From about the spring of 1970 onward, the threat of greater imports was used as a price control device, a warning that if any sellers or buyers tried to raise prices the valve would be considerably opened. In the meantime, since the static prices discouraged expansion of capacity, the growth in consumption was satisfied by growing imports. Thus it is a gross oversimplification to say that domestic oil can no longer be expanded. It all depends on the price. When and as the price rises, as it will probably do in the not too distant future, domestic oil-producing capacity can be maintained or even increased. The United States could even supply all of its oil consumption from domestic sources if it were ready to pay.

But particularly since August 1971 we have had ceilings on both crude oil and refined products at a time of generally rising costs and prices both in this country and abroad. The result has been to remove any remaining possibility of expanding refinery capacity, and has therefore precipitated what is at this time a painful shortage of products, especially gasoline and light heating oil. European refineries have had little or no excess capacity with which to take the strain, and even the small shipments to the United States have made Western European prices soar. The maintenance of price ceilings has generated an excess demand which is perhaps less dramatic than that in natural gas but more widespread and perhaps more damaging. Refiners with insufficient supply have tended to cut down or cut off deliveries to unaffiliated distributors who have been disproportionately important in keeping the markets competitive.

International Crude Oil Supply

Everything said up to now can be summarized in the statement that domestic energy resources have not expanded as rapidly as has demand, and that a solution could be found in letting prices increase to equate them. But we have so far neglected the most important single source of additional energy supplies, imports from the Caribbean and above all, in the future, from the Persian Gulf. Here the situation is totally unlike the United States. Instead of increasing scarcity, which means only one thing, the need to put more and more money into the ground to take out less and less oil and gas, supply is becoming even cheaper. But the cartel of the principal producing nations has been able to raise prices to a level ten to twenty times production costs at the Persian Gulf and greater increases are on the way.

In the United States, we must talk about supply and demand. Abroad, this is irrelevant. Larger imports into the United States have scared Europe and Asia, and our government has not scrupled to play on those fears with threats of taking the oil away from them. Theory and experience both prove that this is only the latest version of "rising demand will dry out the surplus" which has been popular since 1945, since when the real price of oil is down over 50 percent. There has rarely been any surplus of producing capacity, but there has always been and remains a great potential surplus, as there must be when prices are over ten times cost and rising. All that matters is: can the cartel hold together, or fall apart? This is a mighty tough question, but I would rather consider without answering it than make irrelevant distracting talk of supply and demand, like the drunk who lost his wallet on one side of the street and crossed to look for it under the street light on the other side.

The cartel can endure as long as potential competition is not translated into actual. Will the consuming nations take thought and reason together to get rid of the cartel by inducing competition? Possibly they will, since the cartel is injurious to them.

World monopoly means insecure foreign supply. Monopoly is control of supply, hence power to stop it. The cartel was launched in early 1971 at Tehran after the United States intervened to guarantee its success. That story has been fully documented (in my article in *Foreign Policy*, December 1972).

After American intervention, not before, there were public threats of boycotts and then a formal OPEC resolution threatening a total embargo. Since then there have been repeated threats of embargo. Sometimes they are in the form of "assurances": of course supply would not be cut off because the producing nations felt such a deep "moral responsibility." Last February Sheik Yamani, the petroleum minister of Saudi Arabia, warned that any attempt at self-defense by the consuming nations meant "war" and "their industries and civilization would collapse."

A State Department spokesman, on the morrow of Tehran in February 1971, looked upon his work and found it good. "The previously turbulent would oil situation would now quiet down." He did not blush to say to a Senate Committee a year later that the threats had been withdrawn on his request. This is how the situation has quieted down and how the threats have been withdrawn.

Insecurity arises from monopoly, it arises from nothing else. Only the union of the producing nations gives them any strength. They are united on the desire for more money, not united on any political issue. Specifically, a settlement of the Arab-Israel dispute is devoutly to be wished but it will do nothing at all for the supply and availability of oil. Iran, the principal architect of the cartel, has in one important respect been more friendly to Israel than has the United States—they have encouraged the Trans-Israel Pipe Line where our government discouraged it. They did this to save money and get a transport by-pass.

If the Arabs ever attempted to cut off the United States for political reasons, the non-Arab members of OPEC would simply divert shipments from non-American customers to American. Not for love and not for fun (though they would enjoy spiting the Arabs) but for money. Whereupon the Arabs would ship more to Europe and Asia and the net result would be simply a big confusing costly annoying switch of customers and no harm otherwise. If this is common sense, it is also the lesson of experience. In 1967 a boycott of the United States and also of Great Britain and Germany, whose dependence on imported oil was greater than the United States will ever be, failed miserably. In 1968 the then Secretary General of OPEC summed it up very nicely: you can't have a partial boycott or "selective embargo." The same question was raised by the 1970 report of the Oil Import Task Force. They were unanimous and neither the State Department nor anybody else dissented in concluding that to have a security problem you had to have a denial of all Arab oil to all customers.

If the Arabs were to allow production to rise as fast as demanded, and *then* were to cut off supply abruptly to all customers, they would precipitate a crisis. With stockpiles and rationing, this could easily be handled; otherwise, improvisation and haste would make great waste. But nobody doubts that would be done, which is why the Arabs will no more try it in the future than in the past. Colonel Kaddafi, to judge by some recent and oddly plaintive utterances, appears now to understand this.

The injection of political irrelevancies only distracts us from the one problem: the collective monopoly of the OPEC nations. You will hear again and again in the years to come how our foreign policy will be affected thus and so because of our oil needs. This is all a blank irrelevance and shows once again how national policy may be governed by myth, conjecture and slogan.

A boycott by all producers to extort more revenue is a real and serious danger. Any attempted partial boycott would disrupt the cartel, hence it would be very favorable to this and other consuming nations. The obsession with Arab oil (60 percent of OPEC output) only ignores the nature of a monopoly.

The cartel is very harmful to American interests even aside from the constant danger of interrupted supply. By 1980 (assuming output increases 8 percent per year, and prices rise at a uniform rate to $5 per barrel at the Persian Gulf) we will be sending out something like 26 billion dollars a year. All consumers, including us, will be shelling out something like 80 or more billion dollars a year. Over 1972–1980 cumulative, the transfer will be around 360 billion dollars. This is not only a useless burden. The richer these nations, the greater their power to hold out in a boycott and the more they can raise prices and make us yet more insecure. Conversely, the more we are able to check the price rise or even reduce prices the more safe we are and the greater the future savings. Lower prices are thrice blessed: they save us money in the short run, still more money in the long run, and bring more security in the interim.

The world monetary system will be endangered because of a huge amount of funds ready to slosh around the world and there will need to be controls on capital transfers which will do everybody harm. An additional injury: because of the expected big oil deficit, the United States has already started to restrict imports. This will provoke retaliation by our trading partners and will harm our most export-capable industries.

It will also harm U.S. interests by giving juveniles like Colonel Kaddafi of Libya billions of dollars for acting out their fantasies. Last June he made the front page by claiming that he would settle American race relations, drive the British from Northern Ireland, destroy Israel, chastise the Filipinos, convert the world to Islam, and a few other trifles. He has left his mark in Malta and Chad. The Sudan government has accused him of complicity in the murder of the three diplomats. He is paymaster to Amin of Uganda, who kicked out the Asians and claims to commune with God— who is apparently alive and well and living in Libya. Just four years ago Libya was a nice, safe, conservative pro-Western monarchy, like Saudi Arabia today, which is perhaps the super-Libya of the future.

All this adds up to a formidable problem in foreign economic policy. I have suggested that the oil companies, although continuing to produce, should be prevented from being tax collectors. But the United States cannot do it alone. Our blundering has so scared and embittered the Europeans and Asians that they will not follow us in any proposal for joint action. We have sold them on the legend that having "our" companies operate in the oil concessions guarantees us access and reasonable treatment. The Europeans and Asians are pitifully eager to get "their" companies into the act in the vain hope of getting "access." In fact, the only ones with control of supply are the governments. "Power grows out of a barrel of a gun."

But we can do something immediately, to benefit us, to serve as an example to them, and as a basis for joint planning. Aside from Canadian oil, all other imports should be permitted only by the use of sealed competitive bids. We could offer short and long term quotas, up to say 3 years. In so doing, we put it to each producing country: if you want to sell here and profit enormously, you must give up some of the gains to the Treasury of the United States If you don't, someone else will. A system of sealed competitive bids would make the United States a magnet for oil all over the world, including some non-OPEC oil. It would bring in revenue to cover the cost of stockpiling and indeed provide a good return on the investment. It would also begin to strain the unity of the cartel by giving the maximum opportunity to compete which means the maximum chance to double cross for fear of being double crossed.

Not all exporting countries should be treated alike. Non-OPEC members should be given favored treatment. So should Indonesia, which refused to sign the 1971 boycott threat. Nigeria was not then an OPEC member. It only seems fair to presume them innocent until proved guilty of waging economic war.

Among the OPEC members none have made so many threats to security of supply as has Saudi Arabia, and therefore they should be in a special disfavored class.

There are other details to be worked out, such as independent distributors who might have a set aside. All quotas are rigid and can lead to spot shortages, but since there must in any event be a stockpiling system for national security, this can probably provide the necessary amount of stretch.

The President's Energy Message of April 1973

This is essentially an interim statement. It pays no heed to international oil. Obviously there is as yet no decision on the previous policy of collaborating with the cartel, and feeding some members of it Caesar's meat upon which their egos have grown so great. The removal of import restrictions is a temporary expedient. At present, prices of domestic and world oil are approximately equal, and the domestic industry can sell all it produces. But the future price of world oil is unstable and unpredictable. Yet until we have some idea of the price, we cannot tell how much will be available from domestic sources. (In my opinion, even a knowledge of the price would not let us calculate that number, simply for lack of the basic cost data.)

The recommendation that new interstate natural gas contracts be free of regulation is not important since the number of new contracts is too small a part of total sales to matter, and will do nothing to redirect the large amount of gas being wasted as boiler fuel, and which could speedily cure the shortage in the consuming areas.

The proposals for energy conservation can be of some use as disseminating information on how to cut down on fuel bills. But energy conservation for its own sake regardless of price is the talk of the madman in *Dr. Strangelove*, obsessed with his "precious bodily fluids." To name a price, or propose a tax, is to find out how seriously people want a thing.

Perhaps the Congressional forum will help clarify the issues. Here the Petroleum Reserves and Import Policy bill, introduced by Senator Henry M. Jackson, is one of the most welcome developments in years. Some provisions are not clear, and some I would not favor. But it has great merits. It focuses on imports and security as the chief problems. And it faces the security problem by calling for stockpiling, for importing more from relatively secure sources, and for aiming at "competitive energy industries and markets, both domestic and international." We need competition, not as some good in-itself, but because it destroys economic power dangerous to all the world, and means lower prices and security of supply.

Early hearings on the Jackson bill could do much to clarify the issues.

Nuclear Power and Other Nonfossil Sources

Light water reactors are now a well-established form of power generation, and will doubtless provide the bulk of all new installations in a few years. It is urgently necessary, as indicated earlier, that the certification power be centralized and the process greatly speeded up.

We are now being bombarded with a great many proposals for unconventional power sources. I think we should be clear on what they can and cannot offer us. Looking the world over, there is no sign of increasing scarcity of fuel supplies. If we take the few necessary steps to break up the world oil cartel, we can import much larger amounts and gradually phase out the restrictions and security measures, though there should be the utmost caution in doing so until we are sure that the cartel is well and truly dead, which in the nature of things is risky to assume for years to come.

But by the time the cartel is indeed dead, say the early 1980s, the fossil fuels situation may have changed much to our disadvantage. We do not know what future discoveries will be, nor at what costs they can be exploited. Hence it makes good sense to take out insurance by investing in new energy technologies. This kind of investment must largely be from public sources, since we would wish the new technology to be available to all and this would make it a relatively poor risk or proposition for the business concern that would bear all the expense but perhaps not get much of the profit.

I suggest that the golden rule for government support should be: research yes, commercial development no.

The search for new knowledge is relatively inexpensive. Most ideas will turn out to be worthless, and all we can reasonably hope is that one or two will pay.

As good examples of what to do and what not to do, let me first suggest the two bonus programs carried out by the Atomic Energy Commission to encourage the finding of new uranium ore deposits. In each case, new uranium ore came out from behind the woodwork so fast that the program was fairly soon suspended. I would view it as a success, not as two failures, because it confirmed what we are most nervous about, rightly or wrongly, which is the supply of the ore. If we look at the steady price of uranium ore on long-term contracts, it is clear that this is not an inhibiting factor. Furthermore, the supply becomes much greater as one goes up the cost ladder. Yet the price of uranium ore is only part of the price of uranium fuel, which in turn is only a minor portion of the total cost of nuclear electric power.

But the commitment to a program of commercial development of breeder reactors seems like exactly what not to do. The best we can hope for is that by 1985 we will have a breeder technology that will be inferior to light water reactors of that date, which will have behind them operating experience of 15 to 20 years. All the breeder does for us is to stretch out the supply of the plentiful factor. This really makes no sense. Research on better breeder reactors does make sense, as does research on atomic fusion, which is today science rather than technology.

Concluding Remarks

It is clear from what I have said that most or all of the problems we face, and the unpleasantnesses to which we must look forward, are the result of ill-advised public policy. Energy is a special case of the general question: how shall we best use the flexible and powerful instrument known as a competitive market? It is neither ordained of God nor contrived by the devil, only a useful human invention. Use of markets is of course the antithesis of laissez-faire, which would permit private monopoly. The market is only the best means of registering the constraints of nature and knowledge—supply—and the scheme of relative preferences—demand. These are of course in perpetual change. But external costs and collective preferences require government action to set up the data so that the market can register them. The problem is not whether government should or should not stand aside, but rather how government is best to operate. The failures to use the market mechanism have been no less marked than the derangement of it. I see no promise of any early general improvement. Yet it may not be too much to hope that some costly lessons have been learned these past ten years, and that the necessary good sense will be applied to solving the complex mass of problems that are today misnamed in the gross as "the energy crisis."

24   Oil Import Quota Auctions

The United States, acting alone, can disrupt the cartel of the oil-producing governments and bring down the price it pays for imported crude oil.

This would be a drastic policy change. From early 1970 to the end of 1973, our government helped and encouraged the cartel. After the price exploded to about $7.00 per barrel, the Administration began making faces, wagging fingers, striking attitudes, and warning in heavy tones that someone might go too far. The late Kind Faisal is said to have been a dour man, but surely we succeeded in making him laugh. In September 1974 our policy was summed up perfectly: while Secretary Kissinger made a "tough" speech in New York and President Ford made a "tough" speech in Detroit, Federal Energy Administrator John Sawhill was asked what plans there were for getting the world price down. He replied there were none. Mr. Kissinger was angry and Mr. Sawhill was fired. By November 1974 the price was up to $10.50 per barrel and is now $11.50. It will be raised again when economic conditions improve.

A monopoly of sovereign states is unrestrained by competition or by any law. They cannot be held to any contract. Shouting or cooing at them deserves and gets only their contempt. An agreement would tie our hands, not theirs.

What we should do is put a limit on U.S. oil imports and sell import entitlements (or quota tickets) at public auction by sealed bids. This would at least contain the cartel and would probably do it heavy damage. The cartel has maintained a remarkable discipline by using the oil companies to limit output, share markets, and let everyone check on everyone else. We can prevent this use of the oil companies without even slightly hampering either their operations or the continuing flow of oil.

The auction system should not be used to reduce oil consumption, or even to reduce imports. For by reducing imports we would lessen supply

Reprinted from *Challenge* 18 (no. 6, 1976): 17–22.

and eventually raise prices. In this case, the temptation would be strong to allocate or ration the limited imports, thus increasing the burden by trying to hide it. Indeed the main benefit of quota tickets is a lower import cost of oil, although limiting imports can also provide security for investment in the production of domestic fossil fuels and nuclear power.

How to Limit Imports without a Shortage

The scheme would have to start small in order to establish an efficient routine quickly. Imports should be set at a level equal to what importers would demand at existing prices, with a mandate that the level of imports permitted should not create scarcity in the United States. The control lever would be a careful watch on inventories.

At the end of June 1975, stocks of crude oil and products totaled 1,071 million barrels and covered 69 days' consumption and 198 days' imports. Only a minor fraction of stocks are actually available to cover fluctuations in demand, but that fraction provides us with plenty of room to correct mistakes.

For example, suppose that the Federal Energy Administration (FEA) estimates that demand for imports next month will equal imports a year ago plus an expected 4 percent growth factor, Suppose they have under-estimated badly, that demand for imports is really up 10 percent. Then the error would be 6 percent of imports, about 0.3 million barrels a day or 10 million barrels in a month. Stocks would be drawn down by 1 percent. The next month the FEA could raise the import allocation to bring the stocks back up.

The state of Texas (with a little help from Louisiana) used this system for many years. Its task was much more demanding, since it had to control nearly two-thirds of the output east of California, and mistakes therefore had a much bigger impact. Even those who (like myself) questioned the policy, never doubted that it was efficiently carried out.

Frequent auctions—say, once a month—would prevent accumulated surpluses or deficits. They would also help to avoid the disruption of oil trade logistics, and would counter cartel power.

Protection of Domestic Fossil Fuels and Nuclear Power

Current high oil prices are a strong incentive to expand domestic energy sources, but he incentive is diluted by uncertainty over cartel behavior. We are getting the worst of both worlds—high prices *and* lagging investment.

Let us say that a proposed project can just about return a satisfactory profit at today's prices, allowing for the usual risks. But then, if the investors know there is a nonnegligible chance that the cartel will deliberately cut prices to destroy competition, the investment will not be made.

A tariff, on the other hand, would raise prices and damage the economy, but it would not protect us. The big Persian Gulf producer countries have such low costs that they can absorb any tariff. Worse yet, they could by prearrangement step up imports into the United States, despite the tariff, to undermine domestic prices. Even if a tariff were effective we would not be able to determine how much additional domestic output would be forthcoming at any given price. Therefore we would incur heavy costs without even knowing what we were getting in return.

By contrast, a limit on imports, set at a level where it will not affect the import price, is standing notice that there is an unlimited market for domestic energy sources *if* the price can be met. For example, if domestic oil production ceases to decline and starts to grow, excess inventories will accumulate. Then imports must be cut. It is always imports which must move over to accommodate the domestic industry.

In effect, we would be giving an unlimited guaranteed market to domestic energy industries. They could not be undersold by any special price cuts. Of course, if there were a worldwide price reduction, some backstop measure, such as setting an upper limit to imports, might have to be taken. That might force the domestic price above the world price—but it would win us security. Still, as we shall proceed to show, even the higher domestic price could be offset by higher government revenues.

Weakening the Cartel

If for any reason the cartel broke up today it would reconstitute itself tomorrow. The most strenuous, violent efforts would be made to put it together again. Instead of talking about "destroying" the cartel, we should take measures to contain or damage it. If we need a metaphor, it should be severe erosion, not collapse.

A cartel's weak point is excess capacity. The classic breakdown sequence is: (1) incremental sales at less than the collusive price, with incremental revenues for the cheaters; (2) matching of price cuts, with the bigger cartelists, reluctant to cut, losing market shares to the smaller; (3) accusations, confrontations, and then (4) renewed agreements among the cartelists, but with mutual suspicion and readiness to retaliate. The cycle may be repeated many times before cheating through flagrant price cuts begins to accelerate, and dumping today looks better than bigger losses tomorrow. Then comes a stampede to the exit.

The Administration's program to reduce consumption in the United States cannot even annoy the cartel. At heavy cost, reduced oil consumption can increase excess capacity only slightly, with no effect. Since the end of 1973, cartel excess capacity has rapidly built up to about 10 million barrels daily, a third of production. In the spring, it was about 12 million barrels a day. Yet over this very period the price has not only failed to decline but has actually risen from about $7.00 or $8.00 to $11.50. Excess capacity by itself will not bring down the price or curb the cartel. An additional 2 or 3 million barrels a day is a normal mild fluctuation. But a large excess is a lever if we have the will to use it.

The cartel has been able to solve the classic problem of limiting production and dividing markets. The producing countries transfer the great bulk of their oil at their fixed price through integrated oil companies which refrain from collusion. (Company collusion has been an influential myth hiding the real source of market power, government collusion.) Each company sells all it can and produces only what it can sell. The companies cannot compete by offering lower prices, because their margins are too narrow, roughly 2 to 3 percent of crude oil prices. The market share of each exporting government depends on what its resident companies can sell. It is a somewhat haphazard system, but it works, so long as the governments accept these market shares and do not sell large amounts directly. Hence, despite "participation" and "nationalization," they continue to sell through the companies. But we can remove the companies from the crude oil marketing process, leaving them in place to produce, transport, refine, and sell products. It would force governments to compete with each other in the American market.

Phase 1: Getting Started

The first object should be to let the oil trade make the quota auction system a matter of routine. Our motto should be: Start small. The number of tickets issued would be approximately equal to the amount desired, at current prices. Therefore the tickets would have no scarcity value—but only a small convenience or insurance value—since importers and exporters would have to possess tickets to stay in business. Hence there would be enough demand for tickets, and enough oil supply, to meet consumer demand. On each transaction, the importer and supplier would decide who was to bid for how many tickets. They could offer only a few cents per barrel.

Tickets should be sold monthly. I suggest that half of them be valid for the month after the auction, the other half assorted among validity periods of three, six, and twelve months. Proportions could be changed later, after public hearings, to suit the convenience of refiners and distributors. Quota tickets should be freely transferable, like stock certificates, recording the name of each transferee and also informing the selling agent, the U.S. Treasury, to prevent counterfeiting. An active resale market in tickets should be encouraged, perhaps by maintaining a public computer file of all wishing to buy or sell tickets.

In any given month, the oil trade could use not only the tickets covering that month's demand, but also the stock of tickets valid for future use. This would permit flexibility in planning, and commitments for months or even years ahead, as long as the system was expected to last. Nobody would ever need to slow down operations for lack of tickets. The value of tickets would also be kept very low during the phase-in period. The producing governments would ignore the auction system, since there would be nothing they could or needed to do about it. Oil would be lifted and sold as before.

Phase 2: The Exporting Governments Are Forced into the Act

Once the quota auction system was running smoothly, we would have created a market where the cartelist governments could cheat to gain incremental revenues by selling behind each other's backs, each knowing that others might be selling it out.

The secrecy would be achieved by letting *anybody* bid, with no requirement except a certified check for the deposit. Then cartel governments could use front men. A lawyer or broker deposits a check for several score million dollars, without revealing his sponsor. But the identity of nominal bidders could be kept secret for at least a short time to prevent bugging, tapping, or kidnapping.

There is a second barrier to knowing the real bidders: since tickets could be transferred, a given shipload of oil arriving here could be covered by tickets issued to various people at various times. A third barrier: transshipment terminals are fed by sources all over the world. Oil would be arriving in the United States from the Bahamas, Japan, Rotterdam, France, etc. The cost of diversion, reloading, and even mixing would be very small relative to the price. A fourth secrecy barrier, crude or product exchanges, exists because there would already be a substantial and growing open market. For example, a broker acting for Iraq buys tickets, sells Iraq oil for delivery in

Europe and Asia, displacing other oil which the broker ships to the United States, shipment covered by the tickets. Iraq gets the incremental production and revenues. The United States gets the rebates. Some exporting nation somewhere loses U.S. sales and wants to recoup. Because of the transshipment and swapping, higher U.S. sales by some governments would not necessarily indicate cheating. Countries making higher U.S. sales could always explain it—and usually correctly—by better quality, lower sulfur premiums, lower freight costs, better business conditions, and so on.

Cheating would be practical immediately, and it would be very tempting to any nation wanting incremental sales. We assume no cartel nation would try it, at first, while tickets were dirt cheap. But once the value of a ticket exceeded a few cents per barrel, oil companies could no longer afford it. They would be out of the act except as front men. Governments would now have to bid, not only to get additional sales but to keep what they already had.

All barrels imported into the United States would be incremental barrels, up for grabs every month. No exporting country could count on any sales in the American market, through the inside track of its resident companies or through other long-term buyers who had a large U.S. market. The exporting nations would have to keep on buying tickets to compete on equal terms with excess oil from all over the world coming here to find a home.

OPEC capacity is now 38 million barrels daily, and growing. Sales to countries other than the United States account for about 22 million. Thus, taking the rest of the world as safely divided up, there remain about 16 million barrels daily of OPEC capacity and 2 or more million barrels daily of non-OPEC capacity available to supply the American market. But our imports are less than one-third of the 18 million barrels daily. Excess capacity vis-à-vis the United States is proportionately much larger than excess capacity vis-à-vis the whole world.

Frequent auctions would be a convenience to the trade but a torment to the cartel. They would want as little price bargaining as possible, with very few price and sales decisions taken at any given time. When every seller knows what everyone else is charging, he can easily conform. He knows also that everyone is watching him. With monthly auctions there is no time even to start tracing who has bid what. Considering the need to compete for every barrel, it is hard to imagine how the cartel nations could keep from bidding up the price of a ticket month after month.

The revenues from the auctions could be refunded to consumers generally, or used to subsidize low-income consumers, or public transport, or energy research and development. But we should not count the chickens before they hatch.

Spreading Damage to the Cartel

The cartel would of course try to prevent the spread of competition. But containment would be difficult, costly, and probably impossible. For one thing, other large consuming nations would be watching with keen interest. However timid and obsequious they had been up to now, our example would be hard to ignore.

Producer countries who lost their market share in the United States in any given month would need to recoup their losses the next month, not only in this country but elsewhere. For example, if Venezuela was bid out of the American market, it would lose nearly 40 percent of its revenues and would be forced to sell in Europe. In these days of a huge tanker surplus and very low transport costs, pressure at one place becomes pressure everywhere. Some exporting governments would already have overspent their revenues and more would need money in the future. They would all want Saudi Arabia to act as the industry statesman and cut back production to make room for them. Were there no great excess capacity, Saudi Arabia would accede. It would reason: "the capacity of the would-be chiselers is limited; let them use it fully. Better for us to lose part of the market than to retaliate and risk breaking prices." But for the near future, excess capacity would be so great that if those who wanted to chisel expanded to their limit, Saudi Arabia could be forced down to levels it could not tolerate. (In mid-1975, if Saudi Arabia had shut down completely, capacity would have exceeded demand.) At some point it would have to retaliate and risk disrupting the cartel.

In any case, it would be in our interest to have the lesser producers expand at the expense of Saudi Arabia. The more the Saudis lost their market share, the less concentrated, and hence the weaker, the cartel would be. The biggest producing nation is our chief enemy *ex officio*, because it is the chief cartelist.

A government which wanted more American sales would need to negotiate with American refiners and distributors, who could offer them a market—if the government provided tickets, or money to buy them. Oil companies large and small would move from being the agents for exporting governments to being their customers. They would shop around for better deals. As customers, oil companies would be working for us, not for the exporting governments.

To make use of the companies as customers, the U.S. government should sell tickets but should not buy, sell, or allocate oil. A U.S. government buying monopoly, mediating between customers needing an infinite variety of oils and suppliers seeking to know their customers' needs, would be engaged in "shuttle diplomacy" to the thousandth degree. Even if it did not break down in confusion, it would be counter-productive. Secrecy would be lost, since the supplier would have to identify himself to his customer, the government. The cartel would need to make only one decision, to fix the price to the one customer. Cartel governments would not be under pressure to decide individually every month how much to bid. We would lose the benefit of their not knowing who was not to be trusted. The more customers they had, the harder it would be to control the better deals some of those customers might be getting.

Reaction of Cartel Governments

The cartel nations would probably meet quickly to stop the hemorrhage of revenues to the United States and to other nations following our example. They would surely pledge not to pay rebates, but that would change nothing.

There is no way of finding out the cheaters, who along with non-OPEC nations would have the inside track. To divide the American market among cartel members would be another empty gesture.

The only thing they could do would be to set up a joint selling agency, with exclusive rights to sell all cartel oil. The sooner they did this, the worse matters would be for them and the better they would be for us. The company buffer would be gone. The governments would have the constant divisive job of haggling over market shares. Confrontation in council, month after month, is what they now avoid. We should force it on them. Acrimony and suspicion would be cumulative, increased by frequent meetings and arguments over sharing the burden of excess capacity, which would in turn aggravate the usual difference of opinion about the best price to charge. The OPEC meeting of September 1975, with its still-unresolved haggling over small quality and freight premiums, is a mild sample of what we can bring about.

The cartel might buy up all tickets to destroy them. This would be a boycott as ineffective as the "embargo" of 1973–74, when the United States did as well as the "friends" of the Arabs. The production cutback was real. A selective boycott is as impossible now as it was then. If it were tried, prices of tickets would shoot up, benefiting us at their expense. If no tickets were presented for one or two weeks, the FEA could order special auctions, extend the expiration dates of all outstanding tickets or increase their value, or at worst briefly suspend the import limitation. Since the United States accounts for only 12 percent of cartel production, even a very low rate of defection would suffice. Furthermore, as governments boycotting the United States tried to recoup their losses in sales, there would be great downward pressure on prices everywhere else in the world.

Is There a Case for Doing Nothing?

Many people in Washington were confident, in early 1974, that the price would soon come down without our doing anything about it. It has since risen by half. Spontaneous reduction looks even less likely now than it did then. In my opinion, the dominant cartel members have increased long-run earnings by raising the price. But even if they preferred a lower price they would find it necessary to raise the price as a bribe to the smaller producers, who want to get more money immediately. In return, the smaller countries restrain output instead of shading prices.

Time is not necessarily on the side of the consumer nations. Excess capacity can be gradually worked off. Some expansion plans have already been sharply cut back in the smaller countries. Smaller and militarily weaker producers will be afraid to expand capacity. Thanks to American armaments and training, Saudi Arabia and Iran will soon be able to occupy some oil-rich neighbors and stop production. The mere threat may suffice. The fewer the members, the stronger the cartel and the worse for its customers.

This Administration's obsession with expanding Saudi Arabian capacity is the worst possible strategy. The higher its market share, the less room there is for others, the stronger the cartel. An auction quota scheme would provide unlimited sales for small countries, at the expense of the larger ones.

What if the Scheme Fails?

If the scheme fails, we lose nothing and gain some respect from the cartel. Showing them that we understand our plight and are looking for ways to oppose them should make them at least a little more cautious.

"Dialogue" with the oil exporters, as a group, has been taking place for years. It goes like this: *They*: "This is it." *We*: "Yes, boss."

An auction quota scheme would be an invitation to genuine dialogue with each individual exporting country. Then we would say: "If you want to sell oil in the States at your rivals' expense, see us next month."

25

Coping with Supply Insecurity

Introduction and Summary

Since the end of World War II, there have been six world oil supply disruptions, in 1951, 1956, 1967, 1973, 1979, and 1980—one year in six, and the frequency seems to be increasing. This danger will continue, for there are many sources of disruption. Although the probability of any one type in any one year is low, the chances of escaping them all for several years are also low.

An oil glut does not prevent disruption. Indeed the OPEC attempt to evade the 1978 glut was the direct cause of the 1979 shortage.

Some disruptions have had only negligible price effects, some have been devastating. Supply *crises* are a demand phenomenon. Our problem is not a slightly lower output but a surge of demand for hoarding, prompted by uncertainty and self-fulfilling fear. Therefore, it is useless and pernicious for governments or the IEA to calculate a supply "short-fall" and try to redirect supplies.

Public stockpiles can mitigate a crisis, and very likely prevent it altogether, if we let prices govern the rate of use. We should renounce price controls and allocations, domestic or international. The cost of stockpiling should be covered by a permanent security tariff, convertible into a disruption tariff.

All this would seem to be in tune with the philosophy of the current administration, but I fear that harmony is more apparent than real.

A Backward Glance

In 1948, there began a set of escalating restrictions on crude oil imports into the United States, first by congressional committee, then by the Texas

Reprinted from *The Energy Journal* 3 (April 1982): 1–17.

Railroad Commission, then by a "voluntary" program, and finally by mandatory controls in 1959. Foreign oil supply was deemed "insecure" but just why, and to what extent, was never seriously analyzed until 1970.[1]

In 1967, after the Middle East war, I wrote a paper defining the problem as a temporary disruption. I recommended large-scale stockpiling of oil (and also coal in coastal power stations), and I opposed subsidies to domestic production, or "diversification" among sources that might fail at the same time for the same reason. The paper was published in French, Italian, and Japanese, but I could not get it published in English, though the *Petroleum Economist* (then *Petroleum Press Service*) carried an excellent summary.

In the summer of 1973, as I had the previous year in Japan, I made a tour of eight European countries to ask various persons in government and industry what was being done to assure security of oil supply. Shortly after I finished a draft report, it was overtaken by events: the war and the "embargo." Accordingly, I put the draft away. Small loss, because all it said was: "Nothing will come of nothing." Nothing was being done for security in Europe and Japan because it was hoped that somehow nothing would happen. There was much discourse about political accommodation with oil producers, of "cooperation, dialogue, and interdependence." We continue to hear it.

I Nature of the Problem

We address not the long-run problem of the average price paid to oil-exporting nations and the average amount they will produce, but rather sudden unforeseen fluctuations in supply which produce amplified fluctuations in price. The need to distinguish these issues is hidden by the fruitless controversy over whether we face a "glut" or a "shortage." Whatever happens we will face temporary disruptions, for various reasons.

Embargoes, Cutbacks, Political Strife

Another "embargo" like that of 1973–74, though less likely today, is possible. An embargo is inherently inefficient because in order to hurt one or two buyers, one must hit everybody by a general production cutback. The target nation cannot be cut off, because of swapping customers and supplies, diversion of shipments, and trans-shipments. In 1973–74, the United States was hurt less than Britain and France. The world oil market, like the world ocean, is one great pool.

The oil companies deserve high marks for doing efficiently in 1973–74 what would otherwise have been done sloppily, slowly, and at higher cost. But if oil becomes more scarce in any one nation, the price there rises swiftly relative to other places. Anyone with an available cargo can make large amounts of money by shipping it there. This thwarted the oil embargo of Italy in 1935, and the Arab embargo of the United States and the Netherlands in 1973.

It is curious how the nations refuse to accept the fact of a single market and remain obsessed with particular suppliers—the biggest or second biggest one, etc.—and the supposed need for its good will.

An embargo is a deliberate act with intent to injure. The 1973 embargo was a violation of treaties of commerce, navigation, and friendship with the United States. The violation might not be covered up next time, as it was then. It would risk deliberate retaliation.

A more important danger than a deliberate production cutback is the fact that nearly all major exporters are undemocratic and unstable. The Outs can displace the Ins only by conspiracy and violence. Iran should have, but did not, teach us the lesson: avoid close friendship with the Ins.

These countries are also mostly unruly and lawless toward each other. (Saudi Arabia has been no exception.) And, unfortunately, internal strife makes external aggression more likely. True, the Iraqis, when they attacked Iran, recalled that they first taught those "insolent Persians" a lesson around A.D. 650, and it was high time to teach them another. These 1,300-year-old hatreds may be good for another 1,300 years. But surely the weakness of Iran after the revolution invited the attack.

The Danger of Disappointment and Oil Glut

Oil oversupply, and glutted markets, are also a source of instability. In 1978, markets were glutted and prices weak. The OPEC Secretary General warned that if OPEC exports stagnated there would be "political and economic disasters" in the OPEC nations because of revenue cutbacks and disappointed expectations.[2] Supply cutbacks to force prices up were therefore likely, and arrived soon after, as we will see.

In 1981, OPEC exports were down by roughly a third from the 1978 level. The "political and economic disasters" have been prevented, so far, by prices which in real terms are well over twice those of 1978. But expectations rise as rapidly as revenues. The price explosion of 1979 crystallized immediately into higher spending programs in the exporting nations. Even the very mild price decreases of 1980–81 have led to serious

internal strains within these governments. Claimants for funds have struggled to shift the burden of cutbacks onto others. The inability to cut
expenditures has paralyzed some of these countries' will to face market
conditions and reduce prices, and they have lost heavily in sales and
revenues. The spending of oil revenues generates a perceived need for
even higher revenues. "[The] gains of oil-induced growth tend to increase
rather than decrease the dependence ... on the quantity and price of crude
oil exports."[3]

Thus market glut is a political destabilizer. Higher prices are a temporary
pacifier. But it is no longer clear that oil prices can be profitably raised. The
point of unit elasticity, or decreasing marginal revenues, may or may not
yet have been reached. It is certainly closer than in 1978. The odds are
today against any price increase for the next year or two. Continuing
inflation will therefore erode real prices and revenues. It is a sad paradox:
weak prices make for political strife, loss of supply, and hence irregularly
spurting prices.

The Danger of Iran and Iraq Back on the Market

Cartel agreement on output cutbacks is difficult and divisive. It has been
avoidable because the collapse of Iran and its war with Iraq has been a piece
of great good luck for the cartel. If Iran and Iraq return to the market in
large volumes, similar good luck will be contrived. The Persian Gulf war
has shown how even small air and naval forces, however, ineffectually
used, can suppress oil loading for export, though not oil production. The
Persian Gulf states will use force or the threat of force to contain excess
supply.

A million barrels daily of output gained, or its loss prevented, is at
current prices worth over $12 billion per year. The necessary hardware
and personnel cost only a small fraction of the annual gain. That is an
investment some can't refuse. But military actions are easier to start than to
stop.

The Clumsy Cartel

As important as any shock is the market mechanism to which it happens.
Between 1973–74 and 1979, the cartel fixed prices and let output adjust.
Since late 1978, it has been trying to manage output to raise or maintain
prices. That policy was recently reaffirmed.[4] Unfortunately, nobody can
fine tune with coarse instruments. Years ago, the Texas Railroad Commis-

sion regulated output using accurate timely information on production, consumption, and inventories. Worldwide, these data are imprecise, and are months or years delayed. The cartel is forced to act in ignorance. Except when improbably lucky, they must overshoot or undershoot. But while they fear a glut, they will allow us to bear a shortage, and every buyer and seller knows it can happen anytime. Officials of the European Economic Community, after a swing around the Persian Gulf in June 1979, said that the Gulf nations are trying to maintain a small chronic shortage.[5] One of them accurately called it "brinkmanship," which some thought in terribly bad taste.[6]

The Iranian revolution did not produce the crisis. Consumption practically equalled production in the last quarter of 1978. In the first quarter of 1979, worldwide inventory drawdown was 5.5 million barrels daily, but this was a normal seasonal movement. A year earlier, amid glut, the drawdown was 5.1 mbd. (In the United States, crude stocks began to rise in late January, and by early March they actually exceeded the year-end level.) Moreover, some of the 1979 product inventory drawdown was apparent not real: a transfer into distributors' and consumers' stocks. After March 1979, production always exceeded consumption, yet prices continued to rise. Furthermore, there was at all times excess capacity of over 4 mbd.[7] There had been some spot price increases in the fall, based largely on the expectation of official price increases later, but nothing resembling panic until the deliberate Saudi cut on January 20, 1979, from over 10 mbd to 8 mbd. An apprehensive oilman had summed up the problem perfectly: it was one thing for the Saudis to cut back to maintain "a nice tight supply situation." But it was something else for them to "create a world crisis."[8] Prices exploded in February. When markets stabilized again, at higher prices, Saudi Arabia again cut output, in April–June, and prices spurted again. In June 1979, Sheikh Yamani said his government would not permit the price to go as high as $20.[9] But in January 1981, he called the price explosion of 1979–80 "another corrective action" like 1973–74, which indicates deliberate policy, not accident. Any time they try to overcome a glut and create "a nice tight supply situation," a crisis may be close.

The Soviet Union is not an independent source of danger to oil supply. It would of course like to be a spoiler and deny us oil by exploiting local conflicts, making little ones into big ones.

Unfortunately, there is a powerful legend or stereotype of the energy-famished bear stretching his greedy paw toward the Persian Gulf because he cannot "satisfy his needs" with domestic supply. But "needs" should be spelled "nonsense." All the USSR can get out of occupying the Persian Gulf is cheaper energy. This is not its worth the cost, still less the risk of war. It is deplorable to see our Secretary of Defense repeat the legend that the Soviet Union is about to become an oil importer, particularly when his own Defense Intelligence Agency has concluded—and few will dispute today—that the Soviet Union will continue as a net hydrocarbon exporter throughout the 1980s.

II Supply Crises Are a Demand Phenomenon

In every supply disruption, we can see in retrospect that the difference between the amount supplied and the amount consumed was very small. Inventories were more than adequate to cover it. But the amount *demanded* in the market place was much greater than what was to be *consumed*. The excess of demand is registered in the changes in the spot price.

Recently Exxon Corporation had the courage to estimate worldwide inventories, including those past the primary distributors, at roughly 6 months' or 180 days' supply. Suppose that each holder tries to increase his stocks by a modest 10 percent within a 60-day period. Over that period, then, the amount demanded will be 30 percent larger.

Reason for Panic

The reason for the surge in demand and the desire to hoard is so familiar that we tend to overlook it. The value of any product is measured by the damage inflicted by not having it. (It is our old friend consumer surplus, Dr. Jekyll, suddenly becoming Mr. Hyde.) Refiners or distributors or consumers fearing physical dearth—actually running dry—will hold back all they can, and demand more than they intend to use. This additional demand is much greater than any expected or perceived shortfall.

Planning for supply disruptions is geared to loss of output, and tries to adjust to a smaller total physical flow by rearranging physical flows. Unfortunately, it is largely irrelevant to the real problem—the desire to maintain and increase inventories.

Spot Prices and "Mainstream" Prices

Most oil moves under contract or at prices based on contract. Since nobody can accurately predict sales, one usually has a small excess or deficit, absorbed in inventory changes. The spot market is the place where companies bring those temporary excess supplies and excess demands too large for inventory absorption. These excess amounts usually cancel, but not every day or every week. Consequently, there are usually small ups and downs in spot prices. Prices elsewhere do not respond immediately to changes in the spot markets. In normal times it is to everyone's interest that "mainstream markets" remain sluggish.

But useful habits are sometimes harmful. Once a shortage begins, spot prices move up, but not prices in mainstream markets, nor consumer prices, so there is no restraint on demand. Anyone holding an inventory, and seeing spot prices move up radically, has good reason to expect that mainstream prices will soon be higher. Thus the hope of gain is added to the fear of loss through dearth. Everyone hangs on all the harder to oil, to build or retain stocks.

Spot Prices, Government Selling Prices, and Restriction

In 1979 the exporting nations soon began to cancel contracts or to reduce deliveries in order to sell into the higher-priced spot markets.

Only the presence of excess demand makes this diversion profitable, and also permits sellers to impose and enforce all kinds of restraints, like promising to use the oil only in their own country and not transship; or to use it only in their own refinery and not sell it to anyone, and so on. Private buyers are willing, and governments are downright eager, to be seen accepting constraints. It shows their power to keep their own nationals supplied at the expense of others. They are doing something, not just standing there.

Thus excess demand not only raises the market-clearing price, but also serves to Balkanize the market and thus make it inefficient. Buyers find their customary suppliers suddenly disappearing or unable to supply them, and this feeds panic. The flexibility of the system is lost. Those who have agreed to restriction on destination or use explain that much as they would love to help, they cannot ship to others because they have given their word not to.

The United States in 1979 as World Paradigm

In this respect, the paradigm is the United States under allocation in 1979. Every time that any segment of the market was guaranteed its "needs," they would take all they consumed and more, thus making the shortage worse for everybody else. When farmers were given their "needs" of diesel oil, it soon was necessary to guarantee truckers their "needs" also. Governors of the various states received gasoline set-asides that reduced the supply available to everybody else. I will not rehearse the all-too-familiar story of how the attempt to allocate products, area by area, month by month, generated worse shortages. But the United States in 1979 is the model for the international market, given excess demand overall and even transient full supply to some. The excess demand is funneled into the spot market, driving prices there ever higher and making buyers bid even more frenziedly.

The almost unquestioned major premise among governments that in an emergency there has got to be a "fair allocation at reasonable prices" is possibly the greatest single aggravating force in making disruptions worse then they need to be.

The Persian Gulf War of 1980: A Non-Crisis

Let us consider the latest history lesson, the outbreak of the Persian Gulf war in late 1980. The loss of supply was greater than the loss from the Iranian revolution. But spot prices rose only briefly and then came down. The reasons are not in doubt. First, the OPEC nations cancelled their "gentlemen's agreement" for a 10-percent production cut, between 2.5 and 3 mbd. Second, inventories in the hands of private parties and governments were considerably higher than two years earlier. Finally, spot prices had lost their sting, because there was less reason to expect high contract prices and consumer prices. Many perceived that Saudi Arabia, having engineered a rise from $12 to $32 (now $34), thought it was enough. The higher spot price of October 1980 was perceived as being a temporary upward fluctuation, and did not lead to a grab for inventories and a continued bidding up.

III   Coping with Insecurity

The situation is alleviated to some degree by the developments in world markets. Non-Communist consumption in 1981 was actually below its 1973 level. In that year, OPEC exports accounted for about two-thirds of non-Communist consumption, and in 1981 for less than 45 percent. I expect the export decline to continue, as oil consumption stagnates or declines and non-OPEC production creeps up. Yet, this tendency to lower OPEC exports was well under way in 1979, and it did not spare us a worse convulsion than in 1973. There is no prospect that supply out of the unstable areas will cease to be of great importance to the consuming countries, and therefore no prospect of eliminating insecurity.

The Non-Solutions

"Energy independence" was always a delusion. Even if by some miracle U.S. imports went to zero, a reduction in worldwide output would be a reduction in supply everywhere. A shock to the world economy is an immediate shock to us. The same delusive hope of insulating one's nation from the world makes the Europeans and Japanese envious of our mythical "special relationship" with Saudi Arabia, as they were of our "special relationship" with Iran. It leads them into shabby deals and maneuvers that have done them no good.

We will continue to hear arguments for some kind of agreement with the oil-exporting countries, whereby they promise us "reasonably assured supplies" in return for higher prices, "access" to technology, etc., etc. The OPEC long-term strategy committee endorsed such as agreement and will continue to emphasize it. During the 1980 presidential campaign, it was advocated by Mr. Kennedy on the left, Mr. Connally on the right, and Mr. Carter somewhere in between. Doubtless it will be high on the agenda of any "global negotiations." We must at all costs avoid any such agreement. It is impossible to keep the oil exporters, who are sovereign monopolists, to their word. Anyone who doubts this should look at the long dreary list of broken promises since 1971. The latest was mentioned earlier: the Saudis' 1979 assurance of a price below $20.

Private Stockpiling

The only defense or mitigation of a supply crisis lies in stockpiling. I think it is unreasonable to expect private stockpiling to do the job. Preventing excess demand and upward-spiraling prices is a public good. A speculator tries to buy cheap to make a profit by selling dear in the future. The private sector is helpful to the extent that speculators buy during period of slack, in the hope of making a killing during shortages. We should put no obstacle in the way of those who wish to do so. Some of course speculate the other way, i.e., they cut back inventories to gamble that the government will seize others' stocks to turn over to them at "fair and reasonable prices." The law that expired in 1981 expressly forbade the accumulation of inventories in excess of one's own "needs." It was a good example to avoid.

Nevertheless, although private inventory accumulation should not be discouraged, it should not be relied on, because the risks are too great to attract speculators. Consider a hypothetical investor who might have bought Saudi Arab Light oil for speculation in June 1974, when the new order emerged pretty clearly. He would have lost, in real terms, over the next four years. Had he held on another year, he would have had 2.5 times, real, his original investment (reckoning a constant inflation rate of 10 percent per year). This would be a five-year real return of 20 percent per year. But had he held the barrel another two years, to mid-1981, the seven-year real return would have been down to 7 percent per year. Thus the investment would be a highly risky one, and correct timing would make all the difference.

Let us give the standard Capital Asset Pricing Model its due. The wide year-to-year fluctuations would be essentially independent of fluctuations in all other assets except gold and other such mirrors for panic. Thus to an investor with a diversified portfolio, the investment in oil might seem non-risky, once its diversification effect was allowed for. On past performance, oil speculation might look like a good bet, but experience does not confirm the theory.

Since late 1980, once it appeared that the Iran–Iraq war was not going to precipitate another crisis, the oil industry has been liquidating inventory. The usual, and doubtless valid, explanation is current high interest rates, roughly 6 to 10 percent, real. But then the net expected return on oil stocks, including the diversification effect, must be lower. Oil appears not worth holding for speculation, only for normal business needs, though the "normal" will probably be higher than in the past, and the growing flexibility of refining facilities is a growing stock of services with a similar effect.

There are a number of places in the world that conveniently bring together nearness to tidewater and a permissive tax or regulatory authority. Storing oil in large amounts in these pleasant climates would be a natural way of speculation, but this has not been done so far.

I argued earlier that wherever the ultimate ceiling to crude oil prices might be, we are obviously much closer than we were in 1974 or even 1978. Hence the future will probably not see so great an increase as the past. The experience of the last seven years is an upward-biased predictor. It is more than possible that the maximum has even been reached or exceeded. But even if one takes seriously some confident predictions that the real price of oil will be $100 per barrel at the end of the century, which I do not believe, this amounts after all to only 6 percent per year, a return that seems insufficient to attract private investment.

IV   The Strategic Petroleum Reserve

A public stockpile is our only means of defense. The Strategic Petroleum Reserve (SPR) was established by law at the end of 1975. For three years there was bad luck, bad management, and little accumulation. In late 1978, the Carter administration made an agreement with Saudi Arabia, whereby it promised to stop buying for the SPR in return for a promise that the Saudis would maintain a high rate of output. The Saudis broke their promise within two months, but we kept to ours for over two years, until Congress overrode President Carter and required that the fill be resumed. (Some would now like to deny the existence of this agreement, but they cannot explain away the public record. And if a congressional committee were to question the former President and his cabinet, there would be no doubt.) This was the latest proof of why we must avoid the "cooperation-dialogue-interdependence" trap.

The neglect of the SPR, and the irredeemable waste of time during which we should have been filling it, has arisen partly from lack of understanding, partly from misplaced economy, and partly from the strong opposition of the exporting countries, who have often denounced it. Their opposition to stockpiles, like their abhorrence of taxes and tariffs on oil, shows that they have a much better understanding of oil markets than we give them credit for.

Their most usual complaint is that a stockpile would permit us to bring down the price of crude oil. In a competitive market, this would be impossible. Accumulation of a stockpile would raise demand and price temporarily; its decumulation would lower the price, again temporarily. But in a non-competitive market, small causes can have large effects. A temporary surplus, as we have repeatedly seen, is a grave embarrassment to the OPEC nations. When a price is set far above the competitive level, a temporary break could be permanent.

A large enough stockpile could therefore, in theory, disrupt the cartel and bring the price crashing down. In my opinion, a stockpile should not be used for this purpose, whatever the temptation.

Decision Rules for the SPR

The purpose of the stockpile is to quell panic and, if necessary, buy the time needed to react. I maintained earlier that supply disruptions were damaging primarily because of sudden increases in demand for hoarding. Trying to estimate the shortfall is nearly useless. The only reliable measure of market imbalance is the spot price.

The government should be the oil seller of last resort, just as a central bank is a lender of last resort. We ought to adopt Victorian financial wisdom for handling panics: lend freely and without limit, but charge all the traffic will bear. This is diametrically opposed to the current regime.

The IEA rule, for example, is that (some kind of) measures should be taken when the "shortfall" reaches 7 percent. During the last crisis, it never went that high, and nothing was done. Yet the price nearly tripled.

To trigger sales by some shortfall estimate is wrong because we will have only a very inaccurate idea of the shortfall until a long time afterward. Moreover, if the analysis of this paper is correct, the amount of the shortfall has little or nothing to do with the market disturbance. If traders fear a crisis, and demand large amounts for hoarding, a crisis is sure. Our problem is to avoid this demand surge. (In technical language, we are not concerned with the steepness of the shortrun demand curve when supply decreases; we are concerned with a large rightward shift in the short-run demand curve.)

The rate and timing of stockpile sales cannot be predetermined; it depends on how great the demand is for hoarding.

The rule that prices should be "reasonable" or somehow less than the traffic will bear, is bad policy. It discourages private stock building and encourages "short selling," i.e., lessening of inventories during normal or glut periods in the expectation that the government will ration or allocate oil at less than market prices during shortages.

Public reserve stocks should be used for prevention, not for cure. We should not try to guess at a shortfall, nor try to redirect oil shipments according to indefinable criteria that are sure to provoke disagreement and backbiting. All this amid an unseemly scramble for valuable pieces of paper—entitlements to buy at less than market prices. But if we can avoid or diminish the demand surge for hoarding, the spot market should not rise fast or far. As we have seen, in past crises, the actual deficit has been small, or nonexistent, and has not lasted long. Had there been no hoarding demand surge, prices would not have risen much, and there would not have been public panic that insisted on rationing and/or price control, thereby making things much worse than they needed to be.

Our suggested rule could hardly be more simple. The SPR "window" should be open for sale at all times, to sell any amount of crude oil. The buyer would pay the highest price being charged anywhere in the world on the day of purchase or on the day of delivery, whichever was higher, *plus* the cost of a year's storage.

For anyone fearing dearth, the price is a bargain. Nobody else would want to buy. Anyone tempted to buy for speculation must consider that the spot price incorporates expected increases as perceived in the marketplace. Therefore he had better have some pretty good reasons for pitting his own judgment against the market, and paying top dollar for the privilege of doing so. With no demand for hoarding, we would have quiet spot markets and a repeat of the 1980 non-crisis, unless the loss of supply were to far exceed anything known up to now.

In the United States, inventories actually rose by 62 million barrels in the last quarter of 1978. In the first quarter of 1979, they declined by 132 million barrels, which was less than the decline a year earlier, and only 10 percent of total private inventories. Normal commercial stocks can easily accommodate such a change. If nobody had feared dearth, there would have been no problem.

We may now consider how big a stockpile we need. One approach is to figure the macro-effects of given supply disruptions. Such calculations are difficult, and involve many unprovable assumptions. My suggestion would be that we take the worst foreseeable case: a complete loss of supply from the Persian Gulf, which today is about one-third of non-Communist, non-OPEC consumption. This is a worse case than, say, the blockage of the Straits of Hormuz, since much of the oil produced in the Persian Gulf can be shipped overland by pipelines. It is from six to seven times as great as the losses suffered in 1973 and 1979.

Suppose that prices are left unimpeded to work out the distribution among nations. Then the total loss of one-third of the total supply would be approximately the same everywhere. That happens to be the share of oil imports today in the United States, so it is a handy assumption that we lose all imports.

The National Petroleum Council recently estimated that various measures for fuel conservation and extra output would provide between 2.3 and 2.8 million barrels daily. It would be more prudent to assume only 1.5 million, which would bring the drawdown of the SPR, assuming no private drawdowns, to about 4 mbd. A six-month stockpile would then be 750 million barrels, and indeed most responsible estimates have been in the range between 500 million and 1 billion. The SPR would last longer than six months. First, private inventories can be drawn down substantially. Second, consumption would be restricted further by the higher prices, although it is hard to say how much.

Deliberate embargoes would become impossible with a substantial SPR, since this country would be in a position to take all sorts of counteraction, which the embargoing nations would be anxious not to see. The fear and anxiety of the wheels grinding to a stop in consuming countries, massive unemployment and immobilizing of the labor force, and so on, would no longer put the pistol to this nation's head.

It is difficult to conceive of an emergency lasting longer than six months. The worst case would obviously be one or more Persian Gulf countries starting a "little war" that would escalate into a larger one. Such an eventuality is of course the reason for the current attempt to build up a rapid deployment force.

Good use of the SPR would prevent panic and buy time. To use it properly, we urgently need air, naval, and ground forces available at the Persian Gulf within hours and days rather than months and years. It would shield the Soviet Union from the temptation to try an adventure. Unfortunately, the United States is in the same difficult position as the leading member of a cartel. What the leader does, makes a big difference. A minor participant can expect others to cover for him, because failure to do so would only make matters worse for them. The leading member cannot hope for any such consideration. What he does, or fails to do, is decisive, and he must assume his responsibilities.

The governments of the various consuming countries are doing very little to help the United States defend the Persian Gulf, even though their economies would be injured even more by a supply crisis than would ours. They know that the United States cannot afford, in its own interest, to neglect the responsibility of protecting and controlling the Persian Gulf area. It is an unhealthy condition.

V   Managing a Price-oriented Policy

The SPR today is less than a third of what it should be, the fill rate appears to be decreasing, and it is not clear what the Congress and the Chief Executive have in mind for it. Yet it remains our only hope for avoiding the panic, and mitigating the upward wild spiral in prices, which will follow when the next supply disruption comes, as come it will.

In what follows, I simply assume that the will and good sense are there to keep filling it rapidly, and pass the problems raised in quick review.

As I indicated earlier, supply disruptions are serious because of the surge in demand, which should be met by building an SPR and depleting it at current spot prices. Those prices will be lower than if we were trying to manage or allocate supply. But this in turn requires some measures meant to affect prices, although they are not to be directly fixed.

Paying for the Strategic Petroleum Reserve

If we agree that oil imports are insecure, and that an SPR would make us tolerably secure, it follows that every barrel imported carries with it the cost of maintaining the reserve. That cost should be recognized and made explicit. At current levels of imports, I would reckon it roughly at $3 per barrel.[10] But the precise amount is unimportant; the principle is, imported oil costs the economy more. It is self-deception to pretend otherwise, and bad social policy to subsidize imports by covering part of the true cost out of the Treasury.

A tariff on oil imports would also provide much-needed revenue in the near future, when the deficits threaten to surpass anything previously known. (With imports in the neighborhood of 5.5 million barrels daily, and a landed cost of about $35, annual revenues would be $7 billion.)

If the domestic price of oil were to rise by the amount of the tariff, which is likely but not certain, Windfall Profits Tax receipts would also increase. We refrain from making any estimates, for the problem is swallowed up in a bigger one—what to do after the crisis happens and spot prices rise.

There should be no attempt to allocate supplies, either inside the United States or internationally. During a disruption, the principal need is to move relatively small amounts of crude around the world as quickly as possible to where they are needed most. This is best left to private enterprise bent on making money out of the redirection.

With the huge exception of the SPR, therefore, my suggestion is to rely on private markets to get the crude oil and products moving, and to make the best of the limited supply.

Private windfall gains are, in general, best captured through the income tax. The misnamed Windfall Profits Tax is really an excise tax, and much can be said against it as a permanent measure, but during a disruption it will capture immediately a large part of the disruption gains. The speed is worth the inefficiency. In addition, we need a disruption tariff, over and above the permanent security tariff mentioned earlier. We can combine the two needs by a single tariff *ad valorem*, with a sliding scale; for example, at a $34 price, it would be 10 percent, while at a $50 price it would be 20 percent, or $10.

Some of the tax will fall not on consumers but on the producing nations, who have long understood that the higher the excise taxes levied on oil products in the consuming countries, the less is left for them. An *ad valorem* tariff could raise the consumer price toward or even past the point of unit elasticity, where further increases would actually reduce sales. The exporting nations would be forced to reduce prices, as a lesser evil. Their understanding would be helped because the *ad valorem* tariff is in effect a matching grant: anyone selling at a lower price pays a lower tax. Anyone trying to raise prices will be doubly penalized. At the limit, importing countries could divert all oil revenues into their own economies.[11]

With large revenues coming into the Treasury, the problem will be to get them back into the economy, and quickly. Rough justice is the best we can hope for. The most obvious channel is by an immediate reduction in Social Security deductions. Income tax refunds and rebates are unfortunately slow. Some people will get too much. Our concern ought to be not with those who do not get "enough," but with that fraction who cannot bear it. To those at the poverty level, sharply higher oil prices are a burden because of reduced total real income. They need additional dollars, not special allocations.

Conclusions

Supply disruptions are likely. If we store oil, and let prices distribute the oil, we can prevent disruption from becoming a crisis. We should influence prices by tariffs, partly because we can pass some of the burden back to the exporting nations. If they treat this as confrontation, so be it; but it is unlikely. Recall that after minatory language about how we "must not" stockpile, when we resumed it in October 1980, the exporting nations actually increased output.

The theme of this annual meeting is "Energy in the Reagan Era." The Reagan administration appears to have no policy for coping with the supply disruptions. Talk of "the market" only delays use of market mechanisms.

When the next crisis suddenly comes and prices rise, huge amounts of money will be transferred from the pockets of consumers to private parties and to governments. If we remain unprepared, there will be resentment, turmoil, and hurried schemes for rationing, allocation, and price control. We have twice suffered these convulsions, which is twice too many.

Notes

Presidential address, Third Annual Meeting, International Association of Energy Economists, Houston, Texas, November 13, 1981. The research underlying this paper has been supported in part by the National Science Foundation under Grant No. DAR 78-19044, and by the Center for Energy Policy Research at the Massachusetts Institute of Technology. The author is indebted to the comments and suggestions of Henry D. Jacoby, James L. Paddock, Thomas L. Neff, and Martin B. Zimmerman. They are not responsible for errors, however.

1. Task Force on Oil Import Control. *The Oil Import Question* (1970).

2. Ali Jaidah, quoted in *Petroleum Intelligence Weekly* (September 25, 1978). OPEC

production that year was 31.5 mbd (including natural gas liquids); consumption was estimated at 2.4 mbd.

3. Ali A. Attiga (Secretary-General of OPEC), "Economic Development of Oil Producing Countries," *OPEC Bulletin* 11 (November 1981): 11. The whole article deserves careful reading.

4. *The Wall Street Journal,* 2 November 1981: 2.

5. *Oil and Gas Journal* (9 July 1979): 35.

6. Ibid.; and see also the July 16 (p. NL2) and July 23 (p. NL4) issues.

7. Inventories: See DOE, *International Energy Indicators.* Capacity: *Petroleum Intelligence Weekly.* The CIA capacity measure is not used because it is not fully explained, and is in conflict with actual production data, as well as other evidence.

8. *Petroleum Intelligence Weekly* (15 January 1979): 1.

9. *New York times,* 22 June 1979.

10. Reckoning the value of the oil and the cost of storage, a barrel would cost about $40, a stockpile of 750 million barrels some $30 billion. The discount rate would be about 20 percent, nominal not real because we cannot be sure that the value of the oil will rise with the general inflation rate. Dividing $6 billion annual cost by about 2 billion annual imports (5.5 million barrels daily) gives the cost per barrel.

11. For proof of these propositions, see my "Constraints on the World Oil Monopoly Prices," *Resources and Energy* (1978).

26

International Oil Agreements

Introduction: Agreement Is on the Current Agenda

The 1980 report of the Brandt Commission, calling for "a global agreement ... between oil producing and consuming countries" to assure adequate production at reasonable prices, states the gist of innumerable reports, articles, speeches, and resolutions, urging cooperation, dialogue, and interdependence.

The OPEC nations have always professed to desire such an agreement. At the climax of their stubborn, often bitter maneuvering for their respective market shares, "Sheik Yamani revived the call for an international dialogue between oil producers and consumers."[1] Four months later, when their latest agreement seemed to be holding, the OPEC ministers reiterated their interest.[2]

OPEC support for the idea is natural. The triumphs of 1973–1974 and of 1979–1980 have, like other great conquests, proved somewhat difficult to maintain—though price collapse seems unlikely. Efforts at international agreement would abort any attempts by consuming countries to resist or reverse the control of the market held by the OPEC nations. Moreover, it might also offer some protection against customers' prying and probing for weak spots as they try to do a little better than others.

Important people in the consuming countries think similarly. The 1980 Venice summit of the OECD nations called for such an agreement. During the presidential campaign it was favored by candidates left and right of the incumbent, Jimmy Carter, who also desired it. (The Reagan administration has not commented, to my knowledge.) More recently, former Chancellor Schmidt of West Germany has said, "When the heads of government of the industrial world talk to each other at top level, they should envisage

Reprinted from *The Energy Journal* 5 (July 1984): 1–9.

follow-up talks at top level with the major oil-producing countries too.... I therefore regard it as legitimate to stabilise longer-term price expectations with a bundle of measures: price-and-quantity agreements between oil-producing and oil-consuming countries.....'"[3] The Group of 30, a high-level body of international economic and monetary experts and government officials who have been meeting over the past three years, believes it had "some success in moderating the run-up in oil prices ... it helped to persuade OPEC to hold its marker price to $34 a barrel" instead of $40.[4]

As a *New York Times* article noted, "the West may see political advantages ... in helping to keep OPEC alive. Stable prices would bolster Saudi Arabia and other Gulf states, all relatively firm friends of the West ... It would also improve North-South relations. In return, the West might get what it has sought in vain up to now—a long term agreement with the major producers for reasonable price increases in return for guaranteed supplies and an end to disruptive oil shocks.'"[5] American strategists, the *Times* noted on another occasion, see a "silver lining in the stable, pro-Western Gulf that high oil prices have helped to create."[6]

High oil prices and revenues certainly have made the Gulf what it is. American strategists' belief that the Gulf is "stable" and "pro-Western" is itself an important fact.

An important sign of the times is the new Oxford University Institute for Energy Studies, funded by the Organization of Arab Petroleum Exporting Countries, the Arab Banking Corporation, and the Arab Petroleum Investment Corporation—but also by the U.K. Department of Energy, the Swedish Energy Research Commission, the Institut Francais du Pétrole, the (Japanese) Institute of Energy Economics, and the European Economic Community.[7] No doubt they will be heard from on such agreements.

Finally, the continuing problem of oil supply security is perceived—rightly or wrongly—as needing some kind of agreement among consuming nations. Such an agreement has proved difficult to obtain, even on paper. In wrestling with the problem it is only a step to thinking of global or bilateral negotiations. The OPEC nations, reasonably enough, strongly dislike security stocks, which most consuming nations now have partially built. "To resolve this apparent conflict of interest is only one of the matters waiting to be sorted out by negotiation between the governments of the exporting and importing countries."[8]

The retiring head of the International Energy Agency (IEA) thinks the present calm market provides an opportunity for "mutual confidence-building" between producers and consumers.[9] Indeed, like the man who spoke prose for 40 years without realizing it, many have implicitly expressed the need for an agreement and a belief in its feasibility. Some maintain (a) that a political price must be paid for oil; or (b) that the producing nations will produce more oil, in return for political or other nonmonetary benefits, than they would produce without them; or (c) that these nations now produce or have produced more than suits their economic interests, or can be induced to produce more—all these assume that if the consuming nations, chiefly the United States, would engage themselves to do something, the producing nations would do something corresponding to provide a cheaper or more reliable flow of oil. Somehow, each side is to bind itself *to do something it would not otherwise do*, for the sake of the other.

A Thesis

An effective producer-consumer agreement is impossible even in theory, hence injurious in practice. This proposition will first be set forth as a theory, then tested against an agreement or succession of agreements that has existed for more than ten years: the "special relationship" of the United States with Saudi Arabia, so much envied in Europe and Japan.

Conditions for an Agreement

The are at least three conditions for an agreement, none of which is now found in international oil.

First, *each party must know what it must do*: in this case, how much to produce and sell, how much to buy, and at what price. An agreement must name a schedule of prices for crudes by quality and location, and specify the production of each type.

Recent experience has underlined that at any given price of crude oil, we do not know how much will be demanded or how much supplied. Conversely at any given volume offered, prices will diverge noticeably up and down, from what is quoted.

Even in the unlikely event of an overall supply-demand balance, there would still be many surpluses and shortages of particular crude oils. Sales of any given crude oil are highly sensitive to even small price differentials. Since 1973, the OPEC nations have struggled without success to square the circle: reconcile preset price differentials with present market shares. Since 1980 their disputes have become open and bitter. Nor have the IEA nations ever settled the problem of the prices at which oil supplies are to be shared during emergencies.

This is a basic dilemma. At almost every moment, there will be shortages or surpluses to be allocated. An agreement providing for constantly changing allocation of supply sources and of markets, which requires a knowledge of the schedules of amounts demanded and forthcoming of every type of crude oil, is impossible. But without price, volume, and allocation, an agreement is, as the lawyers say, void for vagueness.

The second condition for an agreement is that *each party must be able to withdraw its offer if its terms are not met.* If the consuming countries acted as a unit, they might withhold the food, manufactured products, technology, and services without which the oil-exporting nations would quickly perish. Then there might be room for a bargain on the basis of complementary needs: "they need our goods and services, we need their oil." But the consumer countries have never considered such a withholding strategy. (Nor should they, in my opinion.) If one nation does not supply food, manufactures, and so on, others will. The Persian Gulf nations also need our protection against each other and against the Soviet Union. We cannot withdraw this protection because it would risk the loss of oil supply. In short, we have nothing to offer the oil-exporting nations that they will not have from us anyway. As reasonable folk, they will give us nothing for it.

Third, and perhaps most important, *an agreement needs to be enforceable.* In ordinary commercial life, the enforcement is by competition or law, or both. If anyone persistently fails to deliver or to pay up, the word gets around, customers or suppliers go elsewhere, and in time he is out of business. Or a court can seize his assets or even send him to jail. But competition has been abolished by the monopoly with whom we are to make an agreement, and there is no enforcement of law against a sovereign state. It has been suggested that the OPEC nations have been disciplined by the loss of sales since the second price explosion. But current revenues are greater than those realized on the higher sales volume in 1978. The price increase was no mistake, though the timing might have been better.

Like the industrial countries, then, the oil-exporting nations have nothing to offer, because they can give no binding assurance of anything. They are like minors who cannot be sued, hence are not credit-worthy. To get nothing, we need give them nothing. If we do as they wish, they will still do what they like. We cannot buy their good will, nor buy off their ill will, because they will not stay bought.

The U.S.-Saudi Special Relationship, 1971–1973

The Tehran agreements of February 1971 were between the Persian Gulf nations and the then concession companies, but the U.S. government was a participant in fact, and even claimed credit, asserting that the previously turbulent oil market would now quiet down. The five-year agreement lasted about five months, however. After several unilateral revisions, it was finally discarded in September 1973. Sheikh Yamani made a classic summary: "We in Saudi Arabia would have liked to honor and abide by the Tehran agreements, but ..." Perhaps, as someone said at the time, he was simply bored by the charade of negotiations. A month later there was war and now a quasi-agreement. If a consuming country did what pleased a subset of oil producers, the Arab countries, there would be a reward; if not, a punishment.

Three groups were identified. Britain and France were "friendly, preferred" countries. Japanese policy was considered "odious neutrality." (The current Japanese prime minister, Mr. Nakasone, was then minister of international trade and industry, and he must have been pained by this judgment, in view of his efforts to promote good relations.) The United States had its brand-new special relationship, i.e., as the special enemy. It was to suffer a boycott—which was, incidentally, a clear violation of the treaty of commerce, navigation, and friendship between Saudi Arabia and the United States.

In even a moderately efficient market, there can be no partial embargo against one or a few customers. The world oil market, like the world ocean, is one great pool. By diversion or evasion or swaps, oil should flow toward those places where total oil supply is scarcest and the price highest. Therefore, these three groups should in theory have suffered the same degree of scarcity. What actually happened is still an open question. There are several imprecise ways of measuring the shortage or shortfall. Apparently, the Japanese did best, the favored French and British did worst, and the United States was somewhere in the middle. I believe this result is most likely due to noise in the system and in the statistics, but perhaps the British and French suffered because they allowed themselves to be taken for granted.

Former Secretary Kissinger has written that in 1973 he had no idea of what he now knows: that an embargo against one country does not work. (His chief oil policymaker had publicly warned of a devastating Arab embargo of the United States, leaving others unharmed.) One wonders how much better the United States and other governments would do today.

The Relationship in 1974–1975

In early 1974 the relationship was renewed. The United States publicly avowed that past prices had been too low, but that current prices were too high. The Saudis repeatedly agreed that prices should be rolled back. And they repeatedly raised prices. The public record is clear. The Iranian hawks talked big, but they were price followers. Iran had a contract requiring their concessionnaires to match the payments per barrel made elsewhere in the Gulf. This clause was repeatedly invoked because of Saudi increases. Twice Mr. Kissinger flew to Riyadh and announced that he and his friend the king had agreed that prices should be lowered. Each time, Saudi Government take per barrel, the price floor, was soon raised. From $7 per barrel on January 1, it was increased to $10.50 by November.

In July 1974, the Saudis promised an auction to bring down prices. In August, they canceled the auction. In October, they promised that they would not let output be reduced and thus would bring downward pressure on prices. In March 1975, American officials complained that Saudi permission to lower output had "pulled the rug from under" the United States.

The Relationship in 1976–1980

Jimmy Carter had considerable correspondence with the Saudis even before his inauguration. It will probably never be made public, which is a pity, since it might reveal something about the unstated major premises or assumptions that underlay the policy of the Carter administration. He sent as a special unofficial representative a former U.S. ambassador who, it was unkindly but not unjustly said, had confused himself with the Saudi Ambassador to the United States, and who stayed in presidential favor at least through the happening atop Camp David in July 1979.

Saudi sources were quoted in 1980 as saying there had been an agreement, very early in the Carter administration, whereby the Saudis "became" the price moderates (which they had supposedly been all along). In early 1977, administration officials were briefing the press to explain that high OPEC oil prices really benefited this country.

In late 1978, with the old regime in Iran crumbling and its oil output threatened, he Saudis made a new agreement with the Carter administration. They would stabilize the oil price (then $12.50) by producing more. In return, the United States would stop building its Strategic Petroleum Reserve. The Carter administration was pleased with the arrangement; at the end of November 1978 it urged that imports of oil from Mexico not increase too fast lest they jeopardize "carefully nurtured relationships in the Middle East," i.e., with Saudi Arabia.

The Saudis did increase output, through mid-January. The price rose irregularly, since supply still seemed uncertain. Then it soared spectacularly when the Saudis cut daily output from 10.5 million to 8.0 million barrels, on January 20, 1979.

The U.S. secretary of commerce, who chanced to be in Riyadh at the time, had asked Prince Fahd (then the effective ruler) not to cut production and had been assured that it would not be cut. But cut it was. There was an immediate price jump at the auction in nearby Abu Dhabi. During late January and February, prices rose by more than in the five previous months. In February output was partly restored, to 9.5 million barrels.

At the end of March, an oil glut was again feared. The Persian Gulf producers met to discuss production restraint. The Saudis upbraided Iraq for producing too much; in April they cut output again, to 8.5 million barrels daily. The lower production held for three months, during which time the spot price rose to a new peak.

Throughout this period, contract prices were rising irregulary, but in June 1979, Sheikh Yamani reassured the Toyko summit that "Saudi Arabia would never [sic] allow prices to rise to $20 per barrel." (In January 1981, when the price was $32 per barrel, the minister described the 1979–1980 price explosion as "another corrective move," i.e., a deliberate and intentional step, as it was.)

In July 1979, spot prices stabilized when the Saudis raised output back to 9.5 million barrels a day.

The net result of Saudi actions, taken in concert with their neighbors between October 1978 and October 1981, was to increase the price of oil from $12.50 to $34. At any moment they could have put the price down, or prevented it from going up, by raising output to capacity, announcing that they would maintain that output as long as needed. More important than the greater supply would have been the end of uncertainty and of panic buying to hoard.

This panic buying was the only reason for the spot price increases. Consumption never exceeded production by more than the usual winter deficit, and commercial stocks were ample enough to take care of commercial fluctuations. Beyond the sufficient production there was plenty of unused capacity, but no assurance of using it.

But the United States kept its word. Acquisitions for the Strategic Petroleum Reserve stopped in March 1979, the same month as the Persian Gulf conference on output reduction.

Shortly after, the Saudis were annoyed because the U.S. Department of Justice wished to obtain some documents from the Aramco companies in connection with an investigation of the international oil industry. These Aramco documents were in the United States, and the Justice Department had the legal power to obtain them. But when Saudi Arabia objected, the demand for documents was withdrawn. (I believe the Justice Department's decision, in December 1983, to end the investigation, was correct. But of course my opinion must always be somewhat shadowed by the possibility that additional documents might have changed it.)

The Saudis had taken the measure of President Carter. There were no further purchases for the Strategic Petroleum Reserve, even when, in late 1979, one could no longer plead a "tight" oil market as an excuse. In February 1980 the Secretary of Energy flew to Riyadh to beg the royal assent to resume purchases. Permission was not granted. Twice in a year, the Saudis could veto the enforcement of U.S. law in the United States. At this point, Congress began to take a hand, and gradually purchases were resumed.

Conclusion: Experience

Those who ignore the past are condemned to repeat it. The United States proved in the 1970s what the French had already proved in Algeria in the 1960s—that an international oil agreement, or a variety known as a special relationship, will bring nothing but economic loss and humiliation to the consuming nation. Yet it continues to be widely favored.

We can explain this to some extent. A trip to Arabia, to Africa, to a summit to discuss energy, or to the UN to lecture the producing nations on their duty to the world economy—these are all ego trips. The statesman believes he is gaining "access" to oil, or moderating the price rise and preventing long-run shortage, or helping moderates against radicals, or improving North-South relations, or something. In July 1979, President Carter "could scarcely conceal his pleasure at the news from Riyadh: his 'friend' King Fahd had just agreed to push Saudi oil production toward [sic] 10 million barrels a day."[10] Mr. Carter was not unique in being willing to pay for the pleasure of self-delusion.

The public is naturally reluctant to see that its leaders are merely blowing smoke. We all have a strong desire to believe we have some voice in determining the sauce with which we are to be eaten.

The danger of sudden interruptions of oil supply will continue, because of the probability of war, revolution, and clumsy cartel management. Indeed, the glut may again be the proximate cause of the shortage, as it was in 1978–1979. Then the cartel took in the slack so fast as to create an intolerable strain. Now and in the future, a severe winter, together with upturn in world economic activity, a mild restocking, *and* a reluctance to increase output, could easily give us another price explosion.

Furthermore, even the mild price decline, which aggravated—though it did not cause—the financial difficulties of many exporting nations, has made Western banks and governments anxious or downright fearful about further price declines. This too contributes to the yearning for agreements to shore up the current price level, while assuring no more explosions. Thus the desire for security and a lack of understanding of the oil market will keep international agreements on the agenda, even if they make no sense.

Two Conclusions: Policy

1. If the futility and irrelevance of international oil commitments were recognized, making foreign policy would be simpler. Our governments would cease to complicate life by worrying about the effects of this or that action on oil supply and price. Whether or not we do as the oil exporters wish, they will do whatever they please. Whatever importing nations do or fail to do, the exporting nations will produce that amount of oil, and sell it at that price, which best suits their group interest—to the extent that they can perceive that interest and stick together to serve it.

2. Relations between producing and importing countries are more stable when there is mutual respect. A lowering of the importers' anxiety level over exporters' attitudes, a quest for real security of supply, would help.

Notes

This paper was presented at the Sixth Annual International Conference of the International Association of Energy Economists/British Institute of Energy Economics, at Churchill College, Cambridge, United Kingdom, April 9–11, 1984.

1. *Wall Street Journal*, February 11, 1983.

2. *Wall Street Journal*, June 9, 1983.

3. *The Economist*, February 26, 1983, pp. 22, 29.

4. Leonard Silk, "What to Do About OPEC Now," *New York Times*, March 18, 1983.

5. Paul Lewis, "Nothing Comes Cheap, Not Even Low Oil Prices," *New York Times*, January 30, 1983.

6. "West Fears Too Much of a Good Thing," *New York Times*, March 6, 1983.

7. *Petroleum Economist*, November 1983, p. 434. Only objections by Iran kept OPEC from funding the institute two years ago.

8. *Petroleum Economist*, December 1983, p. 451.

9. *Petroleum Intelligence Weekly*, February 27, 1984, p. 6.

10. Edwin M. Yoder, Jr., "Don't Blame Big Oil," *Washington Post*, December 14, 1983.

27   Oil Fallacies

The twentieth century has been so rich in disasters that the oil price explosions since 1970 belong nowhere near the top of the list. But they do belong on it. The less-developed countries (LDCs) have suffered most, through direct income losses and devastated forests, while every industrial country has experienced a sharp drop in economic growth. Productivity stagnated, largely because of the abysmal performance of most economies in the periods of 1973–75 and 1978–82. The decline in private savings has been even larger in other industrial countries than in the United States and, according to economist Barry Bosworth, "can be traced to the lower rates of income growth that have prevailed since the first oil shock of 1973."

Oil is so significant in the international economy that forecasts of economic growth are routinely qualified with the caveat: "provided there is no oil shock." Throughout the 1970s and 1980s, investment in conservation measures, made in order to achieve lower energy consumption, inevitably diverted investment from other uses. Sluggish growth in productivity created sluggish growth in living standards, and the social fabric has come under increasing strain. Income distribution is again a political issue. The recent war of all against all over the U.S. budget is an indication of this strain.[1]

Member governments of the Organization of Petroleum Exporting Countries (OPEC) have used their enormous oil revenues largely for unproductive government expenditures, especially armaments and subsidies, which soon led to inflation. Thus, as economist Alan Gelb has pointed out, it is even "possible to make the case that [OPEC] oil exporters ended the period worse off than they would have been ... with constant real oil prices."

The petrodollar flood of the 1970s twice afforded Iraq the military capability to seek more petrodollars, first from the nearby oil fields in Iran in

Reprinted from *Foreign Policy* (Spring 1991): 2–16.

1980, then from those in Kuwait in August 1990. The Iran venture failed, despite an estimated million dead, 2 million wounded, and more than 2 million refugees on both sides. The venture in Kuwait is still uncertain at this writing. But if the Iraqis are able to rebuild their military machine, a brisk revenue stream from higher oil prices will again generate the wherewithal for even bigger Iraqi ventures, possibly leading to control of all Persian Gulf oil. To adjudicate Iraqi financial and territorial claims, as former National Security Adviser Zbigniew Brzezinski has suggested, is to neglect the forest for one small tree.

To understand how and why oil price explosions occur, a review of basic oil economics—and some historical perspective—is essential. The price of any product or service equates the amount supplied with the amount demanded. To be sure, if government fixes a price below the market-clearing level, demand will exceed supply, as with natural gas in the 1960s and 1970s and with the mile-long gasoline lines in 1973 and 1979, both of which were caused by decisions of the U.S. government.

Minerals are essentially inexhaustible. Oil, gas, coal, and copper, for example, will never be depleted. Investment in exploration and development creates an in-ground inventory of proved reserves, constantly used and replaced. If replacement cost—the investment required to find and develop new deposits—drifts so high that nobody will pay a price sufficient to justify additional investment, the inventory will not be replenished. the industry will disappear no matter how much remains in the ground—an amount unknown, probably unknowable, and ultimately unimportant.

"Finite limited resources," therefore, is an empty slogan. Only cost and price matter. They are determined by a tug-of-war between diminishing returns and increasing knowledge. Historically, knowledge has won and almost all mineral prices have decreased, though this need not always be true. If costs rise, they will inflict higher prices, which will choke off demand.

For nearly a century, the world price of oil has been far above the cost of finding and developing new reserves. The multinational oil companies —the original reserve owners—slowly lost control of the market after World War II. From 1947 to 1970, the inflation-adjusted price of oil declined by about 80 percent. Twenty years ago the OPEC nations took over, reversing that trend. As sovereign states, these new oil reserve owners have been free to push prices to the ceiling—the maximum profit, as they perceive it. Yet their perceptions have clearly differed from those of the private owners of oil reserves.

Clumsy OPEC

The OPEC nations are dependent on the most unstable part of a single industry. They face unusual military and internal political risks. In theory, they should pursue short-term gains and neglect long-term consequences, and that is precisely what they have done: raise prices too high, and quickly overspend revenues. The OPEC current account (exports minus imports of goods and services) went from a huge surplus in 1974 to nearly zero in 1978. The surplus of 1980, which was even bigger than that of 1974, went negative in only two years. The new surplus of 1990–91 will also vanish.

The practical problem for OPEC is that prices cannot be fine-tuned with the coarse instruments available. In principle, OPEC should, in setting oil prices, calculate the most profitable price-output combination. Yet in practice, OPEC lacks the basic knowledge to do so. It is even harder for OPEC to allocate the burden of restricting output. When the OPEC governments displaced the multinational companies in the early 1970s, they lost agents who were skilled in mediating among the various oil-exporting nations as well as in slowing down competitive forces.

Without precise timely data on consumption, inventories, even production, the OPEC cartel is flying blind, with several hands grabbing at the controls. Because the OPEC governments overspend their actual incomes and are chronically short of cash, they overreact. Any deal eventually unravels and is replaced by another.

The highly volatile price of oil has not been created by "the market," but rather by unchecked monopoly power, the desire for quick payoff, quarrels over burden sharing, and imprecise control. A grade of oil known as Arab Light, for example, in 1990 dollars, was approximately $3.75 per barrel in 1970, $23 in 1978, $54 in 1980, and $16 in 1986. At the end of June 1990, oil at nearly $13 per barrel was, in fact, overpriced. Excess inventories precluded the normal autumn sales upturn. All OPEC members with excess capacity had overproduced. Kuwait was more candid about this than other overproducing nations, or perhaps only more nervous. In March 1989, Saudi Arabia signed a nonaggression pact with Iraq, without the consent of the Gulf Cooperation Council. But when Kuwait privately asked Iraq for such a pact soon afterward, it was brusquely refused. Kuwait felt threatened and was perhaps even more eager to sell. This glut was the real cause of the recent price upheaval. It concentrated the minds of the OPEC nations on the objective of reducing output. The Iraqi invasion of Kuwait was one result.

On July 12, 1990, Saudi Arabia announced it would cut output, having first obtained assurances that the other OPEC countries (including Kuwait) would do likewise. On July 17, Iraq became the agreements' enforcer and threatened the overproducers. Both times, prices surged. News of the Iraqi deployment along the Kuwaiti border the following week again sent prices sharply upward. And an OPEC agreement to cut output, announced July 27, raised the target price further yet.

The Iraqi threat underscored the pressure for higher prices from Iran, Iraq, and Saudi Arabia. The Saudi government threatened that its "protection would not be extended to Kuwait in the face of Iraqi anger." Press accounts repeatedly mentioned the cooperation of the three countries. One oil expert spoke of Iraq's threatening posture as "the most important development for the oil industry since the 1979 Iranian revolution," while another described a "Saddam factor" to explain OPEC behavior. To the Indonesian oil minister it was "a whole new ballgame," for which he thanked Saudi Arabia and Iraq.

The July 27 agreement was equally significant, as oil analyst John Lichtblau summed up at the time: "It's a sea change. Higher prices were always within OPEC's grasp if they adhered to discipline. This time discipline is guaranteed by a principal player which carries a loaded gun." Kuwait had submitted—a point forgotten today. There was still fear of a renewed price drop later because of bloated inventories and stagnant consumption, but that remained to be seen. As a beneficiary of this increase. Saudi Arabia conveniently ignored the Iraqi threat.

But then the enforcer, like many before him, decided there was more profit as a hijacker. On August 2 Iraq seized Kuwait and the Saudis' hired gun was pointed right at them. On August 6 the United Nations Security Council ordered a blockade of Iraq and of occupied Kuwait. By August 24, the price of oil had hit nearly $30 a barrel.

However, the blockade alone does not explain the August price jump. It required also the deliberate inaction of the OPEC producers, since there was enough excess capacity within OPEC to replace the lost output. But those OPEC nations with excess capacity refused to act. Instead of quieting panic by announcing an output increase, they were silent. They carefully dithered, allegedly to seek OPEC unanimity that they could not get and did not need. Their real concern was to insure higher prices. The delay made buyers more fearful, and drove them to overbid more.

By mid-August, Indonesia, Iran, Libya, and Nigeria had increased production—but not Saudi Arabia, the United Arab Emirates, or Venezuela, which feared that more production would weaken OPEC. Not until August

19 did Saudi Arabia publicly pledge higher output. A few days later, Venezuela ended its three weeks of indecision, announcing an increase. But even then, the markets were still not fully convinced that either promised increase would actually be forthcoming. Fears and hopes kept the price like a feather, lifting on every breeze of rumor.

Since output was greater than consumption during June, the market was weak. Output increased in July, yet the price still rose. Although there was probably a shortfall in August, at most the accumulated deficit between August and October was hardly more than 100 million barrels, as compared with world inventories around 4.5 billion. Yet the price soared. The paradox of production exceeding consumption while prices rise has baffled and angered many.

The price jump results from the sudden injection of additional "precautionary demand." Since lack of fuel can shut down a refiner or user, oil becomes a bargain if it is even a little chapter than shutdown loss. Customers over-order for fear of uncertain supply. Then, as prices rise, there is another big increase of "speculative demand" in anticipation of yet higher prices. This becomes, for a time, a self-fulfilling prediction; given uncertain supply, additional demand drives up the price even as production exceeds consumption.

This is the third time the OPEC nations have followed a ratchet model. This process—artificially inflating oil prices and then sustaining them at high levels—occurs in three stages: First, an actual or likely production cut drives up the spot price, generating panic buying and hoarding. Next, as panic subsides, governments raise the official contract or target prices. These new higher prices must then meet the test of the market, leading to the third stage, in which demand falls off and cartel members cut back output to hold up the price—maintaining the pose of being swept along by irresistible market forces.

Some argue that price hikes and income transfers from buyers to sellers have not seriously affected the economy because it is only a small fraction of world gross national product. By such logic, nothing much happened in 1973 and 1979. In fact, disruption of trade and financial flows has already injured the world economy, especially those nations teetering on the brink of recession and those particularly vulnerable in the Third World and Eastern Europe.

It is useful to look past the current emergency and assume that, one way or another, Iraq and Kuwait will resume their roles in the world market. Then, the first question is, What price level will the OPEC nations try to hold? A cash-rich position relieves the pressure on OPEC members to sell more at discount prices. Hence they are able to keep the price high for at least a while.

In June 1990, most OPEC nations' oil revenues were being used to pay interest, reward friends, buy off enemies, or share among the family. But since June, these countries have all gained heavily. Saudi Arabia's oil revenues, for example, have increased from an annual rate of approximately $24 billion in June to around $85 billion after August, with an inadequate percentage of the gain being spent to support the multinational force defending the Saudis and arrayed against Iraq.

The cartel nations will probably not try to hold the price level above $30 per barrel, assuming they have not forgotten an important lesson from the recent past: In 1983, for example, only three years after the last price peak, the real value of OPEC revenues was actually less than in 1978, just before the price increases.

Consumption is set to fall, just as in the two previous crises. First, the worldwide recession will reduce demand. Second, as panic subsides, oil will pour into the market, much of it from "downstream" inventories of distributors and consumers. Finally, some additional conservation will occur along with a renewed flight from insecure supply. As in 1974 and 1979, the OPEC nations will cut output to hold or raise the price.

The public record shows that in 1974, as demand shrank drastically, the Saudis led the way both in cutting oil output and in raising the excise tax (and price). The "hawkish" Shah of Iran merely followed the Saudis' lead. Saudi Arabia was again the prime mover in 1979, cutting output in January and in April to drive up the price. Soft words and hard actions served them well. In time, in early 1975 and early 1981, the real price began to erode. It will again.

During the past two oil crises the world oil shortage was a fiction. But belief in that fiction endures. As General William Tecumseh Sherman once said: "When people believe a delusion they believe it harder than a real fact."

In 1977 and 1978, the International Energy Agency projected a "shortfall" of a maximum of 12 million barrels daily by 1985; in 1977 then U.S. Secretary of Energy James Schlesinger warned of "a major economic and political crisis in the mid-1980s as the world's oil wells start to run dry and a physical scramble for energy develops," and President Jimmy Carter warned that worldwide reserves might be gone by the end of the 1980s.

Worldwide reserves in 1977 were 645 billion barrels. Through 1990, about 320 billion barrels were produced. But reserves now stand at just less than a trillion barrels. In 1981 the International Energy Workshop (IEW), which compiles price forecasts year by year, projected oil prices of just more than $70 per barrel by 1990, in today's dollars, and $92 per barrel by 2000. In every year after 1981, as the actual price per barrel went down, so did the forecasts' starting position. But from that position, the price would always rise. The great shortage is like the horizon, always receding as one moves toward it.

The IEW's forecasts were and are based on two assumptions: First, non-OPEC and small OPEC producers would eventually deplete their reserves. Second, the big OPEC producers would exhaust their excess capacity. Both assumptions were wrong, even when oil was $15 per barrel, let alone $30.

The United States (excluding Alaska) is the extreme example of the very old oil province. In 1930, its "remaining recoverable reserves" were just more than 13 billion barrels. In the next 59 years, the "lower 48" produced not 13 but approximately 130 billion barrels and had nearly 20 billion left. Yet there were very few significant discoveries. The "dividend" of 140 billion barrels was chiefly the continued expansion of old fields, most modest, some amazing. the Kern River field in California, discovered in 1899, had produced 331 million barrels by 1942, and had 54 million "remaining reserves." But in the next 47 years, it produced 922 million barrels, and had slightly more than 694 "remaining reserves" at the end of 1989. Oil production in the United States is probably declining today not because of depleted resources, but because of rising cost.

The rest of the non-OPEC world has still not drilled as many wells as had the United States by 1930. Non-OPEC countries can expect larger expansion of old oil fields, and also larger discoveries. Although production has continued to rise since 1980 throughout ten years of declining prices, there have been high barriers to increased production. Development and start-up costs are not a significant barrier since at "low" mid-1990 prices, most oil supplies are cheap to develop. The two big obstacles to non-OPEC expansion have been, first, over-taxation; and second, capital starvation and/or corruption in national oil companies, which usually engage in large-scale kickbacks, payoffs, and featherbedding.

Yet recently, common sense has been leaking into the system, indication that these barriers are slowly being overcome. To attract oil company investment, taxes in many producing countries have not only been lowered, but have been more rationally related to cost and profit. Countries that once threw investors out now want them back. For the first time in 20 years, oil companies find themselves "spoiled for choice." Even after the price crash of 1987, non-OPEC reserves have kept rising; more reserves today mean more production tomorrow.

But increased non-OPEC production is not the only factor to disturb the cartel's domination over oil prices. Natural gas is a sleeping giant beginning to stir. Even in the United States, gas reserves added in 1988 were the second highest ever and the Canadian supply is also rising. Production today is clearly limited by demand, not by supply. Outside North America, the gas era is just beginning. Border prices in Europe fell by nearly 50 percent from 1985 to 1989. Once a "boutique fuel," gas has become a bulk fuel used by both households and industry worldwide. And since contract prices for gas are now largely independent of oil, in many uses natural gas consumption will gradually displace oil.

Yet even if all this depresses oil demand, OPEC states will continue to expand their oil capacity. Today, despite excess capacity—which is the only reason prices were dropping until July 1990—nearly all OPEC nations are expanding production. Although many projects announced will be aborted, OPEC will still be able to produce more than its members can sell. Indeed, they have no choice but to do so. Without excess capacity, a cartel member lacks bargaining power over production quotas. A member that threatens continued overproduction to undermine prices has leverage in OPEC negotiations. That is how Iraq gained a larger quota in 1989. Each member believes it must protect itself by building excess capacity. Therefore, OPEC capacity will always exceed the demand for OPEC oil.

The cartel is not about to vanish. The rewards are too great. Once the members settle their present differences, they will cut production, raise the price, and the old cycle will continue: cheating, threats and promises, meetings, agreements, higher prices, and so on. Lack of cash, however, is a chronic danger, because the OPEC nations (Kuwait aside) find it difficult or impossible to hold onto their money.

The Iraqi aggression against Iran in 1980 did relatively little damage to oil markets, but it did postpone expansion that would otherwise have taken place. the lasting effect on the market of the aggression of 1990 is still unknown. Yet if Saddam Hussein remains in power, perhaps after having left Kuwait, higher prices will give him many more petrodollars with which to buy many more weapons. Unless steps are taken to limit his military power over the long run, that alone ensures more oil shocks. If he disappears, lesser threats will surface.

The proportion of oil imported by the United States is of only minor importance, yet it has become the focus of debate during the present crisis. Japan and Germany import practically all of their oil, but are not perceptibly worse off economically than the United States. The world oil market, like the world ocean, is one great pool. The price is the same at every border. Who exports the oil Americans consume is irrelevant. Slightly higher production in this country, which is all the United States can hope for, will not affect price or security because it is a negligible fraction of the world market.

Those who want the United States to produce its way out of the "problem," and those who want Americans to conserve their way out, are both the victims of an illusion. There is no shortage or gap, only a high price. At the higher price, some additional investment in production and conservation will be profitable, but at best it will be a minor offset. Subsidizing otherwise unprofitable investment, through tax breaks for example, to replace imported oil will only aggravate the economic loss. Congress should cast a cold and penny-pinching eye on any direct or indirect subsidy, as it will only lessen the pool of funds for productive investment.

Two important tasks, however, cannot be left to private hands. One is research; the other is the Strategic Petroleum Reserve (SPR), which should be enlarged for use in the next crisis. More important, it should be readied for use. In 1990, unlike 1973 and 1979, the consuming nations had, and missed, their chance to avoid the price explosion. The three big holders of strategic reserves—the United States, Germany, and Japan—waited for a "real physical shortage," which will never happen.

Price explosions are rooted in individuals' fears of shortage. Their fright is rational, but can be prevented. The SPR needs to be a seller of last resort, to assure buyers a constant ready supply. Prevention of precautionary and speculative overbuying will prevent panic and prevent or moderate price increases in oil markets, just as the Federal Reserve System prevents panic in money markets. Had the SPR been used early on in the Gulf crisis, there would have been little panic demand. There might have been a mild and reversible price rise, but no explosion.

In 1970–71, the U.S. State Department helped Libya and the Persian Gulf nations obtain the Tehran and Tripoli agreements that launched OPEC conquests. The department expected the previously turbulent international oil situation to calm down following the agreements.

Then and now, the U.S. government attached great importance to good relations with Persian Gulf producer states, particularly to its "special relationship" with Saudi Arabia. This fantasy should not have survived the so-called embargo against the United States in 1973–74, when Arab producers halted oil shipments to the United States; yet the oil supply in the United States diminished less, if anything, than in Great Britain and France.

A selective embargo cannot work because there is only one world oil market. If supply is curtailed more in one country, higher prices pull in more oil until prices equate.

What hurt in 1973 was not any empty embargo against America, but the Arab producers' production cutback—"radical" Iraq excluded—that raised prices everywhere. The cutback's alleged purpose was to obtain Palestinian rights. But the cutback was dropped in December 1973, after only two months, when higher prices were assured. These governments' devotion to the Palestinian cause was loud, but not deep.

The United States learned nothing from the oil shocks of the 1970s but kept seeking good will and "influence" among the producing nations. But the influence of the United States over OPEC has been, in the words of historian Henry Adams, "the influence of the whale over its captors—the charm of a huge, helpless, and profitable victim." By January 1974 the oil market was flooded and only repeated output cuts held the price up. Yet for five months between mid-October and mid-March, then Secretary of State Henry Kissinger spent scarce time and political capital urging Arab producers to end the meaningless "embargo." During 1974, he flew twice to Riyadh to announce that he and his friend King Faisal had agreed that prices should be lower. Yet each time, the price was soon raised. As a result, then American Ambassador to Saudi Arabia James Akins, who had originally sounded the false alarm of "embargo," was dismissed.

In 1976, fearing higher oil prices, President-elect Carter's economic task force approved a proposal whereby the United States could use OPEC excess capacity as a lever for damaging or destroying the cartel. But the Carter administration, which believed huge price rises benefited the United States, preferred "groveling for Arab oil," to use their own language. One doesn't see much with one's belly to the ground. The Carter administration boasted of "unprecedented closeness in the Middle East," and argued that Mexican exports should not be allowed to disrupt "carefully nurtured relationships in the Middle East." The nature of those relationships was quietly left unexplained.

The Bush administration tried to establish closer ties with Saudi Arabia and Iraq. A week before the Iraqi invasion, U.S. Ambassador to Iraq April Glaspie told Saddam Hussein that the United States sympathized with his "need" for funds to keep a million under arms in a country of 18 million; that the United states welcomed a higher oil price, perhaps over $25; and that it had no opinion on Iraq's border dispute with Kuwait.

The verdict of experience is that cooperation with these nations will not keep prices down, or even affect their actions. But a minimum objective is attainable and important: Do nothing to help the cartel.

The "Dialogue" Fraud

There have been many proposals by eminent persons for "cooperation" and "dialogue" between producer and consumer governments to stabilize the price at fair, just, and reasonable levels. We will hear many more. But the producer governments, as sovereign monopolists, cannot be held to any agreement because they are subject neither to competition nor to law. The history of Saudi promises on oil supply since 1970 is a dreary tale of violations, the attempted embargo of 1973 being just one example.

During 1974, there were repeated Saudi promises that they would help get oil prices down. But as demand fell, their repeated cuts in output kept prices up. They were the leaders in repeatedly raising the excise tax—the floor for oil prices—from $7 per barrel on January 1 to nearly $11 at year-end. Iran required its resident companies to match the payments per barrel made elsewhere in the Gulf. This clause was repeatedly triggered by Saudi increases.

In May 1974, the Saudis promised an oil auction to get prices down; in September they canceled it. In October, they promised that output would not be reduced. By March 1975 U.S. government sources were complaining that Saudi output cuts had "pulled the rug from under U.S. strategy."

In late 1978 the Saudis promised to stabilize the price by maintaining output, and in late January 1979 they repeated the promise in Riyadh to visiting U.S. officials. But on January 20, they cut output, panicking the market and making the price surge upward. In April they cut again, with the same result. Not until July did they again increase output. In June 1979, they promised that they would "never" allow the price to exceed $20 per barrel; eventually they officially made it $34.

If consuming countries cannot believe promises, they must disregard threats. Whatever the outcome of the current Gulf war, a violent anti-American reaction among both the peoples of the Middle East and some or all of their governments is likely. But this will not affect oil supply. To the extent that they can control supply, the producer nations will offer the amount of oil that profits them most. Their good will or ill will has been and is irrelevant.

For oil supply and price, what counts is whether or not Saddam Hussein's regime survives with its arms intact. If the regime survives, without a large U.S. presence—counter-pressure from neighbors is negligible, and arms limitation meaningless without force to back it—the whole region, and a far more effective oil monopoly, is his. Higher revenues will buy more arms, which will lead to more conquest and hence higher oil revenues. As he occupies one neighbor after another, he will absorb their wealth and gain territory for launching further attacks.

The petrodollar flood has made the Iraqi empire. When Iraq claimed Kuwait in 1961, the British frowned them down. In 1990, Iraq swallowed Kuwait in one day, and only American armies kept Iraq out of Saudi Arabia.

Monopoly oil prices and revenues have kept the Middle East, and the world, in growing turmoil since 1970. Enforcement of the cartel price set off the 1990 crisis. But, as in 1971, the knee-jerk reaction of the American foreign policy establishment was to suppress competition. The State Department expressed sympathy for Saddam Hussein's "needs" in the summer of 1990; even after the invasion some actually proposed offering concessions to Iraq regarding oil pricing and production. (Kuwait made the concessions; much good it did them.) This is even less excusable today, after two decades of appeasing the monopolists.

Note

1. The economic analysis in this section is in part drawn from the following sources: Ernst R. Berndt and David O. Wood. "Energy Price Shocks and Productivity Growth: A Survey," in Richard L. Gordon et al., eds., *Energy: Markets and Regulation* (Cambridge: MIT Press, 1987); Stanley Fischer, "Symposium on the Slowdown in Productivity Growth," *Journal of Economic Perspectives* 2. no. 4 (Fall 1988): 3–58; Alan Gelb and Associates, *Oil Windfalls: Blessing or Curse?* (Washington: Oxford University Press for the World Bank, 1988); John R. Moroney, "Energy, Capital, and Technological Change in the United States," Working Paper 88-34, Texas A&M University, November 1988.

Index